OREGON ARCHAEOLOGY

Oregon Archaeology

C. MELVIN AIKENS

THOMAS J. CONNOLLY

& DENNIS L. JENKINS

Oregon State University Press Corvallis

The authors and the Oregon State University Press gratefully acknowledge the generous financial support of the Bureau of Land Management to the production of this volume.

∞This paper meets the requirements of ANSI/NISO Z39.48-1992 (Permanence of Paper).

Library of Congress Cataloging-in-Publication Data

Aikens, C. Melvin.
  Oregon archaeology / C. Melvin Aikens, Thomas J. Connolly, Dennis L. Jenkins.
    p. cm.
  Includes bibliographical references and index.
  ISBN 978-0-87071-606-5 (alk. paper) – ISBN 978-0-87071-645-4 (ebook)
    1. Indians of North America – Oregon – Antiquities. 2. Prehistoric peoples – Oregon – Antiquities. 3. Excavations (Archaeology) – Oregon. 4. Antiquities, Prehistoric – Oregon. 5. Oregon – Antiquities. I. Connolly, Thomas J. II. Jenkins, Dennis L.
  III. Title.
  E78.O6A643 2011
  979.5'01–dc23

                    2011019521

Oregon State University Press
121 The Valley Library
Corvallis OR 97331-4501
541-737-3166 • fax 541-737-3170
www.osupress.oregonstate.edu

Contents

Preface and Acknowledgments

Oregon has a deep and varied history, and archaeological research has revealed a great deal more about it since the last general survey, *Archaeology of Oregon*, (first published in 1984) was revised in 1993. The book originated as a public outreach project of the Oregon State Office, USDA Bureau of Land Management, fostered by Dr. Y.T. (Jack) Witherspoon. We thank Dr. Witherspoon for his crucial impetus, and also Dr. Richard C. Hanes, who supported the 1993 book's publication and sustained distribution over many years and has facilitated generous BLM financial support for the production of important new illustrations in the present volume.

That earlier volume took an essentially encyclopedic approach, providing descriptions of the most important sites that were then known and studied. This volume presents more of a historical narrative as revealed by evidence from critical sites. Our objective is to offer an updated review that systematically attends to the major cultural patterns and historical trends so far discerned in the human story of Old Oregon and provides substantial evidence in support of the narrative. As a practical matter, though, it is not possible to give equal attention to all the available research contributions in a book of reasonable size, or to discuss particular issues or areas of research as fully as can be done in more narrowly focused scholarly offerings. To help alleviate this problem, we have supplied citations throughout the text to many studies that will provide the inquiring reader with data and interpretation beyond what we are able to present here. Another divergence from the 1993 volume, which focused entirely on Native American culture history, is the inclusion here of selected studies in contact-historic period archaeology to illustrate some aspects of the first encounters between Native Americans and newcomers of European and Asian heritage.

It will be seen from the bibliography that the number of contributors to this synthesis is large indeed, and we thank our many colleagues represented there, whose research and ideas make up the substance of this book. We are particularly pleased to thank five initially anonymous OSU Press reviewers of the working manuscript, who—at our request—were ultimately willing to reveal their names (Brian O'Neill, Dennis Griffin, Mark Tveskov, Loren Davis, and Guy Tasa) so that we could acknowledge them for their insightful, valuable, and sometimes stern counsel. Their comments influenced the ultimate framing of this presentation and challenged us explicitly with the problems inherent in trying to compose a unified book about an area (Oregon) that is highly differentiated geographically and culturally, and poses quite different research issues in different regions. As will be seen, because of these factors we could not apply a uniform set of organizational conventions to all the regional chapters, though we have sought to keep the individual narratives on generally parallel tracks and to cover the key issues for each region. The fact that the book's chapters were composed by three different authors further limited stylistic uniformity, although we all read, critiqued, and contributed to one another's texts, and we collectively take responsibility for the book's overall coverage. The reviewers also directed our attention to the matter of how to properly compose a book suitable for a broad and diverse readership. Museum professionals speak of "streakers," "strollers," and "studiers" among the people who pass through their institutions, and are at pains to accommodate the interest level of all three kinds of visitors. We have written this book with general readers, college students, and our professional colleagues all in mind, and hope we have achieved a reasonable balance. We are of course responsible for the interpretations we have adopted, though we think they are generally congruent with prevailing opinion among our colleagues.

Special appreciation for photographs and other images used in this volume is extended to Kenneth M. Ames (Portland State University); R. Lee Lyman (University of Missouri); Rick Minor, Bob Musil, Allen B. Cox, and Kevin C. McCornack (Heritage Research Associates, Eugene); R. Scott Byram (Byram Archaeological Consulting and University of California Archaeological Research Facility); Dennis Gray (Cascade Research); Jeff LaLande (LaLande Archaeology & History Services); Mark Tveskov (Southern Oregon University Laboratory of Anthropology); William Andrefsky (Washington State University); Brian O'Neill, Patrick O'Grady, Pamela Endzweig, and Chris White (University of Oregon Museum of Natural & Cultural History); illustrators Eric Carlson and Lance Peterson; photographers Brian Lanker and Jack Liu; and mapmaker Lawrence Andreas (Allen Cartographic). Co-author Thomas Connolly crafted many illustrations throughout the book.

We would also like to acknowledge the ongoing financial support that has been indispensible to all the research drawn on in this book, which has come from many agencies, including the USDI Bureau of Land Management, USDA Forest Service, U.S. Fish and Wildlife Service, U.S. Army Corps of Engineers, Oregon Department of Transportation, and U.S. National Science Foundation. We laud the cadre of archaeologists in all these agencies, and in the Oregon State Historic Preservation Office, for their support of ongoing research into Oregon archaeology, and for their daily stewardship of Oregon's ancient historical record that is preserved in archaeological sites all across the state.

We feel a special debt to current and past Native American tribal leaders and liaisons who have helped us personally (and the archaeological profession as a whole) gain important insights into their cultural values, views of their own history, and views of archaeology. There are many more we could name, including tribal students and crew members, but we are grateful for input over many years from Gordon Bettles, Perry Chocktoot, and Gerald Skelton (the Klamath Tribes); Minerva Soucie, Charisse Soucie, and Diane Teeman (the Burns Paiute Tribe); Catherine Dickson and Jeff Van Pelt (Confederated Tribes of the Umatilla Indian Reservation); Sally Bird (Confederated Tribes of the Warm Springs); Robert Kentta (Confederated Tribes of Siletz); Eirik Thorsgard, Don Day, David Lewis, June Olson, and Khanie Schultz (Confederated Tribes of Grand Ronde); Don Ivy and Nicole Norris (Coquille Indian Tribe); Tooter Ansures, Sue Shaffer, Jessie Plueard, and Steve Rondeau (Cow Creek Band of Umpqua Indians); and Howard Crombie and Arrow Coyote (Coos, Lower Umpqua, Siuslaw, Tribes).

Finally, we are grateful for the combination of advocacy and forbearance with which we have been treated by our editor, Mary Braun, of the Oregon State University Press, throughout the gestation of this book. Thank you, Mary.

C. Melvin Aikens, Thomas J. Connolly, Dennis L. Jenkins,
University of Oregon Museum of Natural and Cultural History.

Chapter One
Archaeology, Ethnology, Ecology, and Human History on the Millennial Scale

Oregon's archaeological history begins with the traces of its earliest currently known human occupants, which are dated to about 14,500 years ago at the Paisley Caves near Summer Lake, in the desert country east of the Cascades. This chapter introduces some of the main research approaches that have helped reveal the archaeological stories to follow, and concludes with some background notes on the Old World antecedents of the first Americans.

As is well known, the human kind spread throughout the world long before the development of writing and documentary history. Texts pertaining to the American continents began to appear somewhat before 2,000 years ago in temple inscriptions of Mexico and Central America, and for the lands farther north only about 500 years ago in the handwritten navigational logs, diaries, and business records of European mariners. Mentions of Oregon itself are found in the notations of mariners, traders, trappers, missionaries, settlers, miners, and soldiers who began arriving about 300 years ago to seek their fortunes in the region. Fortunately, however, many connections to the human past reach back vastly farther than written histories. First of all, it is no mere platitude that the past lives on in the present. The great body of knowledge shared today within the human family was gained through experience and accumulated over countless generations, as the elder members of every household passed on what they knew to the younger ones by both example and direct instruction. Traditional knowledge and belief, much of it truly ancient, is embedded and carried forward in living stories, songs, art, dances, and the learned skills and productions of artisans and specialists of every kind. In our modern world, many traditional products and values are carefully preserved in museum collections of tools, clothing, and art objects that were made and used long ago by various peoples, while many oral traditions passed down through the generations have been captured and made immutable in written texts. It is often said that learning about the past is a key to better understanding the present; the converse is also true: the present offers innumerable clues to human life and activity in the past.

Archaeological research itself begins from the fact that many of the artifacts, houses, and other cultural features that people created long ago still exist, buried in the earth or surviving in the open. In such sites are found the actual bones of animals and residues of plants that people ate as food, and manufactures of myriad kinds, made by humans out of available natural materials. From ancient objects, complete or fragmentary, we can learn much about human history that may have dropped out of our shared body of knowledge over time, for certainly not everything in the busy lives of people is remembered and passed down in descriptive detail. Even within the period of early written history in North America, the lives of ordinary people like farmers, herders, road builders, merchants, miners, loggers, and soldiers tend to be little described in the written texts of their times or fully preserved in oral tradition. These people too had stories that can be illuminated by the objects and structures they left behind.

Ethnology and Archaeological Interpretation

An archaeologist in training learns to identify and interpret artifacts, structures, and other specimens from the past by studying the knowledge and experience of people who made and used such items in times still remembered. In Oregon as elsewhere, much about traditional technology, language, and customs has been recorded in recent historical times from the testimony of Native people who still practiced or remembered the traditional way of life. Such records are deemed *ethnohistory* if they stem from the incidental inquiries and observations of early visitors such as traders, trappers, or settlers. If they stem from interviews and observations among traditional Native groups conducted by later scholars (anthropologists, historians, linguists, and others) they are called *ethnography*, while comparative studies based on such information are termed *ethnology*. In all cases the key point is to learn about a people's traditional way of life through their own testimony and/or direct observation of their actions. Native scholars have also published their own memoirs and studies, a trend that began in the later nineteenth century and is growing rapidly today.

Ancient flaked-stone arrow points, knives, scrapers, and drills, or more perishable objects such as antler digging-stick handles, sheep-horn wrenches, willow fish traps, and plant-fiber nets and sandals, all can be identified because similar objects were still being used by indigenous peoples within living memory. On the other hand, some discovered objects have no obvious recent counterparts. Newly invented technologies replace older forms, while many artifacts may have served multiple functions. Such cases challenge the archaeologist's imagination and demand new modes of study and interpretation, for example the experimental replication and use of unfamiliar objects, or the chemical analysis of residues found on them.

The traditional harvesting, hunting, manufacturing, social, and ceremonial *behaviors* or *activities* of indigenous peoples, still retained in living memory or early written records, or inferred from the contexts within which artifacts and natural materials are found, also guide archaeological study of the past. In pursuing life on their home landscapes, aboriginal Oregonians gathered a wide variety of plant foods, medicines, and raw materials for household manufactures; hunted and fished for many kinds of animals; and gathered together for social activities, religious observances, trade, the negotiation and celebration of marriages, the naming of offspring, and other purposes. Particular sets of artifacts buried in archaeological sites may bespeak such activities.

We also learn from the *places* where artifacts or cultural features indicate human visitation. The localities where particular natural resources were to be found at particular seasons determined the locations and times of many human activities. Spring root crops bloomed in the uplands, fish spawned in lakes and rivers, marmots came out of hibernation among upland rim rocks and ledges, seeds ripened in grassy flats, migrating birds rested and fed at lakes and marshes, deer were driven down from the high mountains by early winter snow, and so on. Various old camps now preserved as archaeological sites can be studied to reconstruct the annual cycle of a people's specific movements and economic activities at times deep in the past. Of course, peoples' social behaviors may change over time, and the archaeologists' powers of observation and imagination are continuously challenged to find and understand any such changes.

A rich ethnohistoric, ethnographic, and linguistic literature holds a wealth of information about traditional Oregon Native American social organization, languages, beliefs, customs, society, subsistence, and material culture, including art and architecture. In aboriginal times Oregon was home

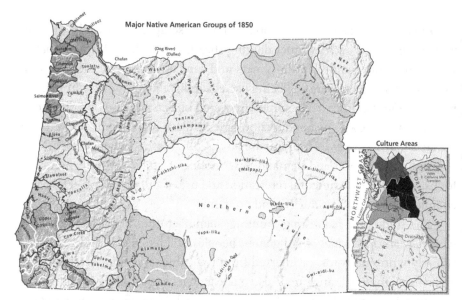

Fig. 1.1. Geographical distribution of major Oregon Native groups in 1850 (*Atlas of Oregon* 2001:11).

to dozens of separate bands and tribes, who spoke an impressive variety of languages (fig. 1.1). For Oregon and the Northwest as a whole, the journals of early trappers and traders to be found in Hudson's Bay Company archives are extremely important for the early contact period information they contain. Rich syntheses based on such materials have been published by Anastasio (1972) and Stern (1993, 1996), and in the same vein are many ethnographic accounts put down on paper by anthropologists and linguists who lived and worked closely with Native people during the nineteenth and twentieth centuries (e.g., Barrett 1910; Gatschet 1890; Hunn and Selam 1990; Jacobs 1945; Kelly 1932; Ray 1939; Spier 1930; Stern 1966; and Whiting 1950).

Regional volumes of the *Handbook of North American Indians* offer voluminous compendia of scholarly records and discussions. Walker (1998) treats the Plateau, Suttles (1990) the Northwest Coast, and d'Azevedo (1986) the Great Basin. The California handbook (Heizer 1978) also contains much that is relevant to Oregon. These volumes additionally provide archaeological and environmental syntheses that reach far beyond Oregon's borders, placing it in broader context. For western Oregon a voluminous archive of early government documents relating to Indian affairs has been gathered by the Southwest Oregon Research Project (SWORP) at the University of Oregon and is available for study in the university library (Lewis 2001). Many more sources are identified in appropriate places throughout this book.

Of course, while an ethnological perspective is crucial to the basic interpretation of old archaeological sites, it is essential to recognize as well that human lifeways tend to change over time. Local populations may grow because climate change improves food resources, or perhaps because additional people move in to share an area's bounty. Or populations may dwindle because fewer people can be supported when a warming or cooling climate leads to reduced availability of the local plants and animals they depend on for food. Changing population densities also affect how people organize their seasonal and daily activities and movements. Thus, interpretations based on ethnographic analogies must not be casually or simplistically applied; they must be supported by multifaceted archaeological evidence.

Environment and Archaeological Interpretation

Discussions throughout this book address the ways in which human communities are integral parts of the ecosystems in which they live. Local geography has a major effect on the kinds of human activity carried out at any given site, and archaeological research must therefore pay close attention to environmental patterns and their changes over time. The earth's climate has fluctuated throughout geological history, and in complex ways. Climatologists recognize both short-term and long-term cycles of change, which may exist independently of one another, being driven by different forces. Variations in the energy output of the sun, irregularities in the earth's orbit, and the complex circulation of the oceans and atmosphere all influence climate, and typically on different time scales. Powerful or unusually sustained volcanic eruptions can cast great amounts of fine ash and dust into the upper air, reflecting some of the sun's heat back into space, and can thus affect temperature and climate on the ground for long periods. Due to a multiplicity of such forces the earth has undergone repeated long-term cycles of cooling and warming, as well as many briefer and less extreme climatic fluctuations. Large or long-persistent fluctuations can affect the distribution and abundance of plants and animals on which people depend for their livelihoods. It is easy to recognize in many archaeological localities that extreme environmental events in the past would have affected any people present during the time of change, as discussed further below.

Archaeological method includes a broad array of scientific approaches to fieldwork and laboratory analysis, and here we briefly introduce a few of the methods most widely applied in Oregon research. Readers wanting to know more can find a wealth of additional information in Maschner and Chippendale's massive (2005) *Handbook of Archaeological Methods*, compiled by experts in many forms of analysis.

Artifact Typology and Site Stratigraphy. Classifying specimens and determining their relative age is the most basic form of archaeological research, equivalent to the study of fossilized bones in the field of paleontology. The artifact types, food bones, and plant materials from human occupation sites tell us much about what people were doing there, and as such specimens change over time they bespeak changes in the lifeways and cultural contacts of the people who made and gathered them. Especially important are sites where recognizable strata or layers of earth, shell, or other materials built up over time, and where artifacts and biotic remains can be found in those same layers. In the early days of archaeology before scientific methods such as radiocarbon dating were developed, the careful study of site stratigraphy was the only reliable way to define the sequence of cultural change within a region, and it remains a crucial method today.

Geomorphology. Oregon's landscapes have been continuously shaped and reshaped on both grand and local scales by tectonic uplifting, volcanic eruptions, lava flows, and the erosion and re-deposition of silts, sands, and gravels by wind, rain, floods, rivers, and ocean currents. Though the rate of sea level rise has slowed during about the last 5,000 years, sea level has risen continuously along most of the Oregon coast since the end of the Ice Age, flooding many early sites that people undoubtedly created along the Pacific shore before that time. This circumstance, combined with plate tectonic effects such as earthquakes, tsunamis, and the rapid buildup of deep sediments at the mouths of coastal rivers, as well as ocean winds that created huge sand dunes over extensive areas, makes the Oregon Coast a particularly challenging region in which to find evidence of early human occupation. Inland, colossal late Pleistocene Missoula Floods roared down the Columbia drainage scores of times over a period of several thousand years and each time backed water, floating ice, and suspended sediments far up the Snake River, Willamette Valley, and other tributaries. During the same period Oregon's Northern Great Basin held dozens of lakes, some vast, that all together covered thousands of square miles. With the onset of middle Holocene warmth and aridity, however, many small lakes dried up completely while larger ones became shallow and marshy, and perhaps seasonally dry. Long dunes of silt and sand were piled up along the edges of dry or seasonally dry lakebeds by prevailing winds that blew across their dusty surfaces. In the moister Willamette Valley and southwestern mountains, annual floods draining off the surrounding high terrain have repeatedly scoured interior valley floors in some places and built up deep sediments in others.

As may be readily imagined, all these geomorphic processes have affected the archaeological record in various places and pose challenges to the development of a full account of Oregon's prehistoric cultures. The problem is surely most extensive and acute along the Pacific Coast, where research cited in the coastal chapter pays close attention to regional geomorphology in order to identify spots where archaeological records might survive. Much is also being learned about impacts wrought on human communities by periodic earthquakes and tsunamis, the gradual infilling of bays, and other geological changes in the natural environment. In the Willamette Valley, geomorphic studies of the Long Tom River drainage west of Eugene, and Mill Creek near Salem, have shown how people related to their changing landscapes over long periods. Similar research has also contributed significantly to our understanding of human adaptation as climates fluctuated through wet and dry cycles in the Fort Rock Valley of Oregon's Northern Great Basin.

In many cases, geomorphic forces led to the accumulation of sediments in which artifacts became embedded, and thus helped build up valuable stratigraphic records at some archaeological sites. Conversely, sites on very stable geomorphic surfaces may have accumulated archaeological traces over thousands of years, but because there was no accompanying sedimentary deposition all their specimens are found together on the same old surface in *palimpsests*. In other situations sediments may accumulate, but if they are fine and easily moved by wind, as is common in the dunes and sandy flats of Oregon's Great Basin and Plateau regions, periodic *wind deflation* has dropped artifacts of varying age onto the same underlying resistant surfaces, also creating palimpsest deposits. Such palimpsest sites are of interest in that they document repeated occupation of certain areas over thousands of years, but they do not permit the accurate dating or recognition of specific archaeological assemblages from different periods.

Radiocarbon Dating. Radiocarbon dating, in use since 1950, is central to modern archaeology (Taylor and Aitken 1997). It relies on the fact that all living organisms absorb carbon from atmospheric CO^2 as a result of their life processes. The unstable ^{14}C molecule, or *isotope* contained in CO^2 loses electrons over time at a rate known as its *half-life*, which has been measured scientifically. This decay process goes on continuously, even within living organisms. But living organisms are always taking in fresh ^{14}C, so the amount they contain remains at the same level as exists in the atmosphere during their lifetimes. When a plant or animal dies, however, it no longer takes in fresh ^{14}C, and thereafter normal radioactive decay steadily reduces the amount contained in the dead organism's remains. The ratio of stable carbon isotopes (mostly ^{12}C) to unstable carbon isotopes (^{14}C) in an organic archaeological specimen can be measured in the laboratory, and the number of years since the death of the plant or animal specimen can be calculated from this ratio.

Radiocarbon dating is therefore simply a measure of the carbon present in a sample of organic material. There is an important variable in accurate ^{14}C dating of ancient specimens, however, because solar and climatic cycles cause the amount of CO_2 (and hence ^{14}C) in the Earth's atmosphere to rise and fall slightly over long periods of time, and these fluctuations affect the accuracy of radiocarbon dates. The problem was recognized in the early days of radiocarbon dating research, but decades of experimental work were needed

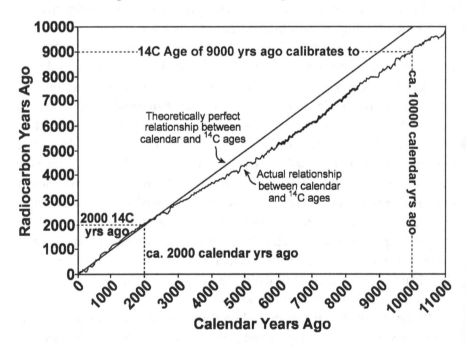

Fig. 1.2. Radiocarbon calibration curve; the straight line shows what a perfect relationship between radiocarbon and calendar years would look like; the serrated line shows how actual ^{14}C ages of annual tree-ring growth segments diverge from their true calendar year ages over time.

to develop correction protocols that could precisely convert laboratory measurements of ^{14}C into true calendar year time scales. Decades of research focused on running thousands of laboratory ^{14}C measurements on the wood of annual growth rings cut from trees such as North American bristlecone pines and European oaks. These trees can live for thousands of years, which allows the exact age of their individual growth-rings to be determined simply by counting back from the year in which the tree was cut. Through measuring the ^{14}C content of many samples of exactly known calendar age, a long-term correction curve has been plotted that allows the accurate conversion of laboratory-measured radiocarbon ages ("^{14}C years") into actual calendar years before the present (cal. years BP). This *tree-ring calibration* method is now well developed, and computerized protocols quickly translate laboratory radiocarbon measurements into calendar dates (fig. 1.2).

It is important to note that earlier editions of *Archaeology of Oregon* (Aikens 1984, 1993), the present book's predecessor, along with most other general texts written before about A.D. 2000, report dates based on laboratory measurements that were not subjected to the corrections described here. All of the ^{14}C dates cited in the present book that were originally determined by older methods have been re-calibrated using the online Cologne Radiocarbon Calibration and Paleoclimate Research Package (CalPal). The dates have also been rounded and described as "about" such and such an age, in acknowledgement of other (lesser) precision limitations inherent in radiocarbon dating. Calibrated dates are identified by the suffix "cal. BP", or alternatively by the expression "calendar years ago." Approximate archaeological dates not rigorously fixed by direct ^{14}C determinations are expressed as "years ago." Thus, a ^{14}C date given in this book for a particular site or event may differ somewhat from one given in a source published earlier. For some years to come, readers of old and new archaeological texts will have to pay attention to the differences between older and more recently established radiocarbon time scales.

Obsidian Chemical Analysis and Hydration Dating. Obsidian, a volcanic glass unusually widespread in Oregon, is an excellent material for making a variety of tools and its detailed study has proven highly informative and useful in archaeological research. Obsidian is formed when volcanic magma of rhyolitic composition is pushed to the surface and cools rapidly. Each obsidian flow has a distinctive "signature" that consists of its own particular combination of chemical elements and their varying abundances. Through laboratory analysis, the geochemical signatures of obsidian artifacts found in archaeological sites can be compared to those of individual obsidian flows, and in that way the sources of raw tool stone used by site occupants can be specifically identified. This type of analysis has proven extremely valuable for mapping ancient people's movements and trading activities.

Obsidian has another property that allows it to be used also as a dating tool. Like all glasses, it very slowly takes in trace amounts of water at the molecular level through its surfaces that are exposed to the atmosphere. Under a microscope, a cross-section slide cut from an artifact will show a *hydration layer* holding water molecules that have accumulated since the time when that artifact was freshly flaked out of a piece of obsidian. Hydration rim thickness can be measured in microns, and where hydrated obsidian artifacts are found closely associated with a sufficient set of radiocarbon dates, it is possible to use those ^{14}C dates to calculate a *hydration rate* for that kind of obsidian. Thereafter one can determine the age of other artifacts of the same obsidian found in similar circumstances by their hydration thicknesses alone. Obsidian analysis plays an important role in Oregon archaeology, as will be seen throughout this book.

Floral, Faunal, and Taphonomic Analysis. The pollen spread by grasses, shrubs, flowering plants, and trees is a main source of information about past environments. Pollen, so named after the Latin word for "dust," is microscopically small and floats in the air. It can be carried from a few feet to hundreds of miles, depending on the anatomy of the pollen grain and circumstances of atmospheric circulation. Pollen eventually settles to earth, and when it falls into lakes, bogs, wet meadows, or other places where continuous saturation by water inhibits microbial agents of decay, it may be preserved for thousands or even millions of years. In Oregon, long cores drawn from sediments that slowly accumulated in places like Wildhorse Lake, Fish Lake, and Diamond Pond on Steens Mountain (Chapter 2) may preserve continuous pollen records for thousands of years (Mehringer 1986, Wigand 1987). Pollen grains are extremely varied and distinctive in form, so many types are identifiable under a microscope. The grains can be extracted from sediment cores, identified, and counted. The rise and fall in the pollen counts of different species over time can be graphed to create a long-term picture of local changes in temperature and moisture over thousands of years. Such information reveals the environmental conditions people lived under at various times in the past, and in Oregon it has been very important to our understanding of the different cultural and ecological adaptations found in the archaeological record.

Animal bones and plant remains, which are often preserved in archaeological sites, can be analyzed to learn the nature of a local environment and the use that people made of it while living there. Residents used plant and animal products both as food and as raw material for making artifacts and structures, so the specimens found can directly portray people's adaptation to their natural surroundings. Where a site was occupied over a long period, changes in climate and human activity may be recorded in its stratigraphic record. For studies of this kind to be successful it is crucial to identify the site's biotic remains accurately and to establish reliably whether they are present due to human activities or those of other sometime residents such as coyotes or wood rats. It is also essential to know whether or not the specimens have remained where they were originally deposited, undisturbed and unmixed by erosion, rodent burrowing, or other forces. Thus archaeologists must analyze in detail the depositional context of specimens found in a site, and any patterns of breakage, predator gnawing, or other such factors observed on them, in order to arrive at reliable conclusions. This kind of contextual analysis, called *taphonomy* (the study of death assemblages), has been important to studies throughout Oregon.

Archaeological Places and Culture Areas in Oregon

The archaeology of place—that is, of the natural settings of individual sites and special localities—looms large in the following chapters. Each archaeological site was a chosen place in which certain human activities occurred, and one among a much larger set of places where people conducted the many and varied activities of their lives throughout the changing seasons of the year and over the span of many years. People were strongly connected to their traditional territories by a deep knowledge of their places, seasons, and products, which had been taught to them by their elders and was continuously renewed by ongoing experience. Such knowledge greatly advantaged families who were long established in an area and tended to keep them there over generations.

In Oregon as throughout Native America, learned patterns of subsistence, technology, and community organization tended to spread throughout the natural environments to which they were particularly well suited (Kroeber 1939). In western North America the largest cultural and natural areas were the Northwest Coast, running from the Gulf of Alaska to about

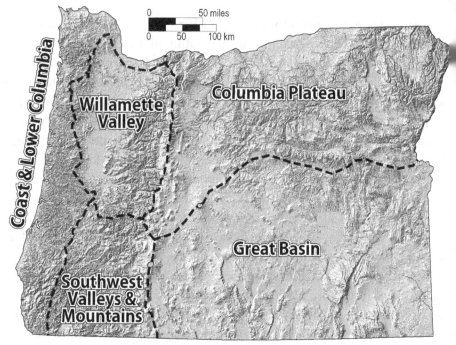

Fig. 1.3. Archaeological areas of Oregon.

Cape Mendocino in northern California; the Interior Plateau, extending from the Cascades to the Rockies and south from the Canadian Sub-Arctic to the Columbia River drainage; the Great Basin, lying between the Sierra-Cascades and Rockies and stretching from east-central Oregon southward to the Colorado River; and California, as defined mainly by the modern state's political borders west of the Sierra-Cascades.

It is a striking fact that four of the five major cultural and natural areas of western North America—excepting only the agricultural Southwest—touch each other within modern Oregon's political boundaries (fig. 1.3). East of the Cascades, northern Oregon natives participated in the Plateau culture area, while those living in central and southeastern Oregon were part of the Great Basin culture area. People of the Columbia River estuary and Oregon Coast participated in the Northwest Coast culture pattern. Oregon's Willamette Valley and southwestern mountains and valleys, like each another in many ways, both share cultural and environmental similarities with California on the south and the Plateau on the north.

We begin our archaeological narrative with the Northern Great Basin region (ch. 2) because it is the most-studied part of Oregon and contains the oldest occupation sites currently known. The account then proceeds through the Plateau (ch. 3), the Lower Columbia and Coast (ch. 4), the Willamette Valley (ch. 5), and the Southwestern Mountains and Valleys (ch. 6). The book's final chapter (ch. 7) discusses cultural diversity and interaction within aboriginal Oregon as a whole, and concludes with an epilogue on the cultural resource laws and institutions that support archaeological research throughout the state. A brief archaeological perspective on the First Americans' arrival in the New World, which pertains equally to all cultural areas of Oregon, closes this introductory chapter.

The Coming of the First Americans

It is well established by fossil evidence that the human lineage first appeared in Africa, with clearly ancestral hominids traced back to about 5 million years ago. People like ourselves, *Homo sapiens*, emerged from earlier *Homo erectus* in Africa about 150,000 years ago, and over time replaced their predecessors throughout Eurasia. For a long time *Homo sapiens* people were limited to the tropical and temperate regions of the Old World, but with developing knowledge and technology they were able to move farther and farther north despite increasingly longer and colder high-latitude winters.

The initial pioneers of arctic climes were temperate zone hunter-gatherers who were already technologically quite sophisticated, and whose warmseason forays showed them that the northern regions were wonderfully rich in game of all kinds. Well-equipped and hardy people could live there year round and prosper despite the extremely rigorous polar winters, and groups over a broad front began developing the ability to do so during the latest glacial stage of Pleistocene times. Deep ice sheets then overspread much of Europe, but in the south of Europe and all across the vast unglaciated plains of the Eurasian north lived huge mammoths and mastodons, herds of caribou and bison numbering in the thousands, and numerous bands of musk ox, among other large animals. There was also an abundance of smaller hares, foxes, martens, and other land animals that were important to the human populations for their warm furs as well as their meat. Each summer clouds of migratory birds flew up from the equatorial south to raise families in the endless tundra wetlands. Freshwater fishes were abundant all year in the great rivers that flowed north out of the continental interior, while anadromous salmon swam up those same rivers in the millions to spawn during the arctic summer, and seals, sea lions, dolphins, and even whales came near shore along the edges of the Arctic Ocean.

Archaeological evidence from Europe and northern Eurasia shows that between about 45,000 and 35,000 years ago Upper Paleolithic people of modern *Homo sapiens* type adapted themselves to the cold ice-age environment by learning to cut and sew animal skins for warm protective clothing, to make portable skin tents for the warmer seasons, and to dig and cover snug, semi-underground earth lodges that kept them from the extreme winter cold. In regions where caves were common, as in much of Europe, they too were used for shelter. The archaeological record from this time on gives evidence of sophisticated hunting, fishing, and trapping technologies that people employed to amass food stores which were readily preserved in the freezing winter climate and gave human communities the ability to live in the high northern latitudes the year around.

Dated to the same time that people were settling into northern continental Eurasia is artifactual evidence of flourishing human activity on both the main Japanese islands and small islands well offshore. This demonstrates beyond doubt that far-eastern coastal peoples of the late Pleistocene had watercraft sturdy and dependable enough to brave the open ocean and thus had the crucial equipment to flourish throughout the extensive North Pacific coastal environment of rivers, inlets, bays, and offshore islands that such technology opened up to them (Erlandson 2002; Ikawa-Smith 2004). The North Pacific is a zone which, like the continental arctic, is extremely rich in a great variety of abundant food resources, and in fact much archaeological evidence throughout Japan, the Russian Far East, Korea, and northern China shows the presence of late Pleistocene and early Holocene peoples who made a very good living from the woodland and waterside habitats of the region (Aikens, Zhushchikhovskaya, and Rhee 2009).

These originally disparate continental and coastal streams of cultural development interfaced and flowed together in the North Pacific region, and fostered a sizeable late Pleistocene/early Holocene human population in far northeast Asia. It was a growing population with all the knowledge and equipment needed to cross the Beringian zone between Russia and Alaska and move into the American continents. In due course these people did cross, by both coastal and interior routes, and opened up a whole new world to the human species (Barton et al. 2004; Madsen 2004; Ubelaker 2006).

As the extreme arctic climate began to moderate with an onset of global warming after about 18,000 years ago, people were able to establish themselves farther and farther north, and in greater numbers. The earliest bands might have reached the high arctic Bering Sea Land Bridge between Siberia and Alaska and crossed over before rising seas already being fed by glacial melt water flooded it, or they may have crossed a subsequently open Bering Strait on winter-frozen ice, or by boat in the warm season. Once on the American side, some groups passed southward out of Alaska through the interior mountains and plains as the receding late glacial ice permitted, while littoral hunter-fisher-gatherers boated and lived their way down the Pacific coast under the same conditions. By at least 14,500 cal. BP people were unmistakably present in Oregon (Chapter 2), while human bones directly dated to about 11,600 cal. BP on the Santa Barbara Channel Islands of Southern California and to 11,200 cal. BP on islands of southeast Alaska show people early established in offshore settings that could only have been reached by watercraft (Dixon et al. 1997; Erlandson et al. 1996).

The late Pleistocene population that hived off these First American pioneers lived on in northeast Asia to become the indigenous peoples who remain today the American Indians' closest genetic, cultural, linguistic, and spiritual relatives. The sophisticated and specialized stone, bone, and antler tools, tailored skin clothing, weather-tight housing, skin boats, and other cultural elements that first made human life possible in the far north have remained part of the indigenous cultural inventory up to modern times in both northern Eurasia and far North America. Both in the interior and along the coast this nexus has remained a zone of cultural intercourse throughout Holocene times, and it is obvious in myriad ways that Asian and American North Pacific and arctic peoples still keep a close living kinship (Aikens and Zhushchikhovskaya 2010).

In Alaska the Dry Creek, Moose Creek, Walker Road, Broken Mammoth, and Swan Point sites, all near Fairbanks, have been shown by a number of ^{14}C dates to fall between about 14,000 and 13,000 cal. BP (Goebel 2004, Holmes 1998, Holmes et al. 2001). A number of sites farther south have yielded dates as old as these, and a few have produced earlier dates, though it is often suspected that individual radiocarbon samples may have been contaminated, or stratigraphic disturbances may have created misleading associations between the artifacts found and the organics used in ^{14}C dating. Such disputed sites include Fort Rock Cave, Oregon, with a date of about 16,000 cal. BP; Wilson Butte Cave, Idaho, with dates around 18,000 cal. BP; Meadowcroft

Rockshelter, Pennsylvania, with dates between about 16,000 and 23,500 cal. BP; Cactus Hill, Pennsylvania, with three dates that fall around 20,000 cal. BP; and Monte Verde, Chile, with dates of about 15,000 cal. BP (Barton et al. 2004). Some of these sites may be truly ancient, but there is currently no overwhelming consensus on their age by specialists familiar with the evidence. However, at the Paisley Caves in Oregon, feces directly ^{14}C dated to 14,500 cal. BP have been shown to contain human DNA of Native American type, and bone and antler artifacts independently ^{14}C dated to about the same time were found in direct association (Jenkins 2007). Much more information on the Paisley Caves will be found in Chapter 2.

The earliest human skeletal remains currently known in Oregon's vicinity are those of southern Idaho's Buhl Woman, dated about 13,000 cal. BP. Slightly later are those of southeastern Washington's Kennewick Man, dated ca. 9400 cal. BP, and western Nevada's Spirit Cave Man, dated about 10,650 cal. BP (Barton et al. 2004). These three individuals share certain features of skull morphology that link them to slightly later human skeletons from various parts of North America and Northeast Asia, including Japan (Nelson et al. 2006). Studies of mitochondrial DNA from modern populations confirm a close genetic linkage between Native American peoples as a whole and Asians living today across a broad zone from Siberia to northern China (Schurr 2004).

The earliest widespread and typologically well-defined archaeological culture in North America is the Clovis complex, distributed north/south from Alaska to Costa Rica and east/west from Nova Scotia to California. In Oregon, Clovis fluted points have not been directly dated but many are known as surface finds at the Dietz site and in the Catlow Valley east of the Cascades, with others found also in northern and western parts of the state. A large number of ^{14}C determinations from sites located mainly in the Plains and Southwest have been interpreted as placing the Clovis archaeological horizon between about 13,000 and 12,000 cal. BP (Haynes 1992), while a more rigorous subsequent evaluation calls into question many dates and suggests that Clovis may have spread throughout the North American continent in as little as 400 years, between about 13,200 and 12,800 cal. BP (Waters and Stafford 2007).

In the interior West—desert country today—sagebrush and grassland were already widespread during the late Pleistocene, but high elevations where trees now grow were then covered with low arctic tundra vegetation. Coniferous trees now seen on the highest Great Basin mountaintops then lay much farther down slope, in places spreading out into valleys that are filled with sagebrush today. Lake Bonneville in Utah, Lake Lahontan in Nevada, and a number of smaller lakes in Oregon were at their greatest extent during the last glacial maximum of about 24,000–20,000 cal. BP, but were shrinking rapidly by about 18,000 cal. BP. Farther west, mountain glaciers continued to exist much later in the Cascades, while the Pacific shoreline in some places lay more than a mile seaward of where it is today. Rapid sea level rise thereafter submerged ancient coastlines and vigorously eroded coastal margins.

The basic climatic and vegetational patterns of today's Holocene period were largely in place by about 12,000 to 11,000 cal. BP. In Oregon's Northern Great Basin, the Paisley 5 Mile Point Caves, Fort Rock Cave, the Connley Caves, and the Dietz site, among others, had already seen their first occupations during the time of transition between Pleistocene and Holocene climatic conditions (Chapter 2). All of Oregon's regions have yielded artifact types that belong to the late Pleistocene/early Holocene period, though the independent dating evidence is not everywhere as strong as that established for some Great Basin sites. These threads will be picked up in the regional chapters that follow.

Precisely when the first people arrived in the Americas is a controversial topic. There is much evidence to be considered, and a great deal of argument and counter-argument about the strengths and ambiguities of the various sets of evidence that have been obtained by research. There is still no consensus among experts about exactly how and when the first people arrived in the western hemisphere (Meltzer 2009), but a very substantial array of evidence from northern Eurasia and the Americas leaves no realistic doubt of a broader conclusion: that the first Americans arrived in their new homeland near the end of the Pleistocene period, when animal species which subsequently went extinct—including horse, camel, giant bison, mammoth, and mastodon—still roamed northern Eurasia and the American continents. As will be seen in Chapter 2, Oregon's Paisley Caves are strongly in contention as one of the most rigorously and convincingly documented places of very early human occupation in the New World.

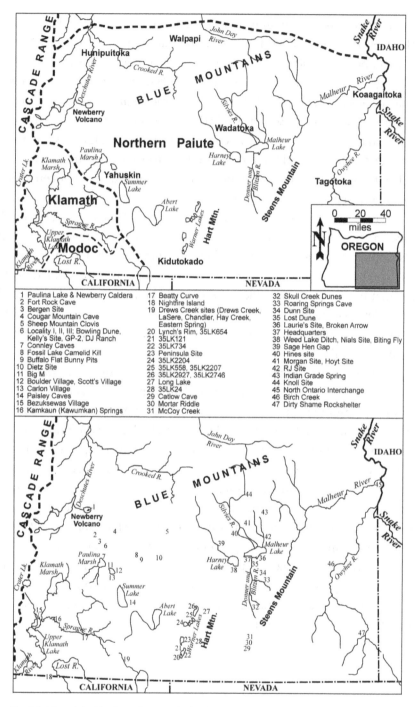

1 Paulina Lake & Newberry Caldera
2 Fort Rock Cave
3 Bergen Site
4 Cougar Mountain Cave
5 Sheep Mountain Clovis
6 Locality I, II, III; Bowling Dune,
   Kelly's Site, GP-2, DJ Ranch
7 Connley Caves
8 Fossil Lake Camelid Kill
9 Buffalo Flat Bunny Pits
10 Dietz Site
11 Big M
12 Boulder Village, Scott's Village
13 Carlon Village
14 Paisley Caves
15 Bezuksewas Village
16 Kamkaun (Kawumkan) Springs

17 Beatty Curve
18 Nightfire Island
19 Drews Creek sites (Drews Creek,
   LaSere, Chandler, Hay Creek,
   Eastern Spring)
20 Lynch's Rim, 35LK654
21 35LK121
22 35LK734
23 Peninsula Site
24 35LK2204
25 35LK558, 35LK2207
26 35LK2927, 35LK2746
27 Long Lake
28 35LK24
29 Catlow Cave
30 Mortar Riddle
31 McCoy Creek

32 Skull Creek Dunes
33 Roaring Springs Cave
34 Dunn Site
35 Lost Dune
36 Laurie's Site, Broken Arrow
37 Headquarters
38 Weed Lake Ditch, Nials Site, Biting Fly
39 Sage Hen Gap
40 Hines site
41 Morgan Site, Hoyt Site
42 RJ Site
43 Indian Grade Spring
44 Knoll Site
45 North Ontario Interchange
46 Birch Creek
47 Dirty Shame Rockshelter

Fig. 2.1. Map of the Northern Great Basin showing Native group locations (*top*) and site locations (*bottom*).

Chapter 2
Northern Great Basin

The study of Oregon prehistory was pioneered by archaeological research in the Northern Great Basin. Beginning in the mid-1930s, work by Luther S. Cressman of the University of Oregon and an interdisciplinary team of scientists including paleontologists, geologists, paleoclimatologists, and others, demonstrated the high antiquity of a desert culture now known not only from evidence in Oregon but throughout the intermontane regions of Idaho, California, Nevada, and Utah (Cressman, Williams, and Krieger 1940; Cressman et al. 1942). Cressman's interdisciplinary approach is commonplace today, but was innovative in the 1930s. The evidence his team amassed gave substance to Cressman's hypothesis of Ice Age human occupance in the Northern Great Basin, an idea that was advanced for its time, ran contrary to prevailing opinion, and was unpopular with prominent North American archaeologists. This early archaeological foundation, together with the large body of evidence since built upon it (Aikens and Jenkins 1994a; Bedwell 1973; Jenkins, Connolly, and Aikens 2004a), and the fact that some of the oldest sites known in the state are found here, make the Northern Great Basin a fitting place to begin the narrative of Oregon's past (fig. 2.1).

Environment and Climate

The elements of the natural landscape most critical to hunter-gatherer land-use strategies are topography, water, flora, and fauna. The four are closely related, with variations in topography—geology, elevation, degree of slope, direction of exposure, stream courses, springs, marshes, and lakes—controlling effective moisture and the distribution of plants and animals in any given locality. In general, areas that are topographically diverse, with lowlands, uplands, wetlands, and dry lands, are also biotically diverse. They offer greater possibilities for access to the variety of food and material resources necessary for survival than do more uniform landscapes. The ethnographic sketches of the Paiute, Klamath, and Modoc which follow in this chapter depict seasonal rounds that reflect the importance of environmental variation to hunting and gathering people.

Strictly speaking, the hydrologic Great Basin is characterized by a series of closed, internally draining basins such as Oregon's Fort Rock, Chewaucan, and Harney basins. Culturally, and with respect to geology and biotic attributes, the Northern Great Basin can be considered, as it is here, to include the Klamath Basin to the west (part of the Klamath River system which drains to the Pacific) and the Owyhee Plateau to the east (part of the Snake/Columbia River system, also draining to the Pacific).

The natural setting to which Oregon's Great Basin peoples were adapted was a rich one—extreme and demanding, yet generous to those who knew it well. The region is high desert with basin floor elevations ranging between 3,500 and 4,500 feet. Topographic relief is considerable throughout Oregon's Great Basin region, with differences of up to 5,000 feet between mountain peak and valley floor. In the north, the High Lava Plains region is an extensive tableland given relief by scattered volcanic buttes, cinder cones, lava flows, and broad flat valleys filled with deep alluvium covered in places by a thick mantle of volcanic ash. To the south it merges with the Basin and Range physiographic region, which is characterized by long north-south fault-block plateaus and mountain ranges separated by broad open valleys (fig. 2.2). This province extends south well beyond the boundaries of Oregon, across Nevada and Arizona into northern Mexico. To the east-southeast is the Owyhee Upland, a rough, uneven plateau that is ancient and much eroded, being deeply incised by the canyons of the Owyhee and Malheur rivers and their tributaries. This unique high desert landscape is dotted with springs, marshes, and shallow lakes connected by meandering streams. Some of these ultimately flow to the Pacific while others flow into shallow lake basins from which they evaporate in the hot summer sun.

Temperature fluctuations over all this area are extreme. Freezing, snowy winters and hot, dry summers are the rule. A large diurnal–nocturnal variance in temperatures is usual, especially in summer, when the temperature of a given place might range above 100°F during the day, and drop to 50°F at night. Water availability is greatly affected by altitude; cool highlands receive the most precipitation and retain it the longest, while water naturally collects in the lowlands, although evaporation is rapid. Aridity is the general

Fig. 2.2. Northern Great Basin environments: *above*, Diamond Swamp at the foot of Steens Mountain, view east; *right*, basin and range topography, Summer Lake Basin, view west.

condition in the lowlands, but many valleys and basins nevertheless contain lakes and marshes fed by runoff. These fluctuate greatly from year to year, and even from season to season as the degree of precipitation and evaporation vary. They are most persistent where upland moisture catchments are large, and more ephemeral where catchments are small. Springs may be found in virtually any locality, their occurrence determined by circumstances of geomorphology, bedding, and faulting.

Native Peoples

Three groups of native peoples occupied the Northern Great Basin, all of whom practiced the ancestral lifeway well into the nineteenth century and are clearly heirs to extremely ancient cultural traditions. These peoples made most of their tools in quite similar forms, gathered mostly the same kinds of plants, and hunted mostly the same kinds of animals, but each had distinctive settlement–subsistence patterns that reflect important environmental variations in the abundance and distribution of critical resources. The lifeways of these groups, as recorded in the nineteenth century, provide a guide to understanding the ancient cultures attested by archaeological evidence, and historic and prehistoric tend to merge in detailing some of the more timeless aspects of these high desert cultures. We begin with the Northern Paiute, who occupied the largest and driest eastern portion of Oregon's Northern Great Basin at the time of historic contact with Euroamericans.

Northern Paiute. The Northern Paiute speak a Numic language, affiliated with the Uto-Aztecan sub-phylum of the Aztec-Tanoan language phylum. Linguistic relatives of the Northern Paiute are found throughout the arid west of North America, from Oregon deep into Mexico. The Northern Paiute generally occupied the High Lava Plains, Basin and Range, and Owyhee Uplands physiographic regions of central and southeast Oregon. They were semi-nomadic, making their living by hunting, gathering, and fishing. While individual bands generally occupied home tracts or districts (*tibiwa*), the boundaries of these districts often overlapped considerably with those of their neighbors and group composition was generally quite fluid, allowing people to move freely to available food sources (Fowler and Liljeblad 2006). Band names typically reflected prominent or locally distinctive food resources. For instance, the *Wadatika* or Harney Valley (Burns) Paiutes were named after wada, a small black seed growing in abundance on flood plains around Malheur and Harney lakes. Throughout most of the year the Paiute lived in small loosely organized family groups led by a recognized headman.

The annual round of the Harney Valley Paiutes was broadly typical of many Great Basin groups (fig. 2.3). March was the spring month when the groundhog first appeared. People were at this time still living in their winter encampments near Malheur Lake and the modern town of Burns, eating stored foods and such game as could be obtained. April was the month when the first green shoots appeared through the snow; by late April or early May, the Indian potato month had begun. This brought the first major economic and social event of the new year, the spring trek to root camp. The root camp of the Harney Valley people was actually not a single locality but a vast area in the seemingly barren (to the eyes of the uninformed) hills around Stinkingwater Pass, on the northeastern rim of the Great Basin. There, "Indian potatoes"—bitterroot, biscuitroot, yampa, wild onion and other

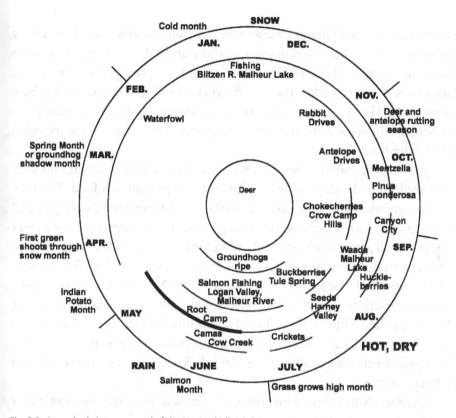

Fig. 2.3. Annual subsistence round of the Harney Valley Paiute.

species—grew in inexhaustible quantity. People congregated in large groups, some coming hundreds of miles or more to participate in the harvest. Some remained in the root camp as long as a month or so, building up stores for the following winter and enjoying the company of friends and relatives from miles around. The gathering was intertribal, with non-Paiute groups from the Columbia Plateau region across the mountains also participating (Couture et al. 1986; Reitz 1995). Archaeological evidence from Stinkingwater Pass suggests that this pattern probably dates back at least 4,000 years (Aikens and Jenkins 1994b; Jenkins and Connolly 1990; Pettigrew 1979).

While the root camp was still in full swing, groups of men moved on to the headwaters of the Malheur River. A tributary of the Snake, this river carried spawning Chinook salmon. Women joined in the fishing as they concluded their work at the root camp, and the task of catching and drying salmon for winter stores continued for several weeks. The time by now was late May–early June, the salmon month. Vast fields of blue camas lilies bloomed between Malheur Lake and the surrounding foothills. Their starchy white bulbs were harvested in great quantity and baked in large earth ovens for winter stores. Marmots were also "ripe" during this period, and special trips were made to collect them in the rocky foothills. People moving back toward the Harney Valley from root and salmon camps in the mountains conducted these harvests, and stored the proceeds in caches to be retrieved in the fall for winter use.

July was the month when the grass grew high. Crickets thrived, and were collected to be dried, pounded, and stored as a protein-rich food. The relatively rainy and cool spring gave way to the hot, dry summer. During July and early August, people dispersed in small groups, roving where they could hunt elk and small game, catch fish, and gather the first currants and huckleberries of the season. In late August and September, the seeds and berries of many plants were ready for harvest. The *Wadatika*, or "Wada-eaters," congregated in large groups to collect wada seeds (*Sueda depressa*), around the shore of Malheur Lake. Other plants collected at this time included goosefoot, Indian ricegrass, Great Basin wild rye, mule's ear, and other desert plants. At suitable locations buckberries, huckleberries, and chokecherries were harvested, and elk were hunted.

October–November, the rutting season, was the time for deer hunts and antelope and rabbit drives. Seeds of shooting star and ponderosa pine were collected. Winter encampments were established at traditional places near water and not too far from previously established food caches. The cold winter months of the year, from December through April, were spent in winter encampments. People ranged out as weather permitted for fishing, waterfowling, and hunting, but the stores of dried food built up during the preceding months constituted the primary food resource at this season, and it was not uncommon for people to experience some hunger before spring arrived.

The day-to-day tasks and annual cycle exemplified by the Harney Valley Paiute year are well represented in the archaeological sites of the Northern Great Basin. Gathering activities are attested by digging sticks, carrying baskets, and milling stones. Hunting is represented by the atlatl and dart, the bow and arrow, stone projectile points, stone knives and scrapers and bone scraps. Recent DNA and blood protein analysis of human feces found in dry caves of the region adds new and exciting evidence of long-past meals. Extensive travel is indicated by rich finds of sagebrush-bark and bulrush sandals, obsidian artifacts of tool stone from distant volcanoes, and shell beads from as far away as southern California and even northern Mexico (Jenkins and Erlandson 1996; Jenkins et al. 2004). Among the thousands of known sites are winter villages and special-activity camps of various kinds. Although the match between prehistoric lifeways and that of the historic Paiute people is neither complete nor exact, the evidence leaves no doubt of their basic similarity.

In the nineteenth century, the western edge of the generally arid Paiute country interfaced with that of the Klamath-Modoc along the eastern edge of the cooler, moister highlands that ramp down from the Cascades to meet the open sagebrush desert of the Basin-and-Range province. The boundary zone was then the strip comprising the Fort Rock, Summer Lake, Chewaucan, Warner, and Surprise Valley basins, all of which receive substantial runoff from the highlands farther west. Isabel Kelly (1932) was told by Surprise Valley Paiute people that their ancestors had driven previous Klamath inhabitants out of eastern Oregon and claimed the land for themselves.

Modoc. The Modoc and their cousins the Klamath spoke dialects of an isolate of the Penutian language phylum which was common on the Columbia Plateau and in regions bordering the Pacific from Alaska to California. This linguistic connection, combined with obvious cultural similarities such as pithouse villages, increased settlement stability, an emphasis on wealth and social position, and a focus on fishing and root collection, has led many authors to discuss the Modoc and Klamath as a southern extension of the Plateau cultural sphere (Stern 1998b; Walker 1998). Research conducted over the last 25 years suggests that they and other Penutian-speaking groups had a long history in the Great Basin however, at one time living around desert wetlands throughout southern Oregon and northwestern Nevada; the historic Klamath and Modoc thus serve as a reliable model for much of the Northern Great Basin archaeological record.

In the historic period, the Modoc occupied the southwestern corner of the Basin and Range on what is now the Oregon-California border. Centered in the Lost River area, their territory was somewhat more reliably watered than much of the Paiute territory farther to the east, but generally drier than that of the Klamath to the north and west. There were three recognized historic Modoc bands, but personnel were free to move to other band areas as they saw fit (Ray 1963:201–211). Modoc settlements were located near important hunting grounds, productive fishing stations, and rich root grounds. The Modoc located winter pithouse villages on the southern shores of Lower

Klamath Lake, at Tule Lake, Clear Lake, Willow Creek, and Lost River. The greater productivity of gathering food in such locations promoted a somewhat greater degree of sedentism than the Northern Paiute generally experienced. The resultant wealth, supplemented by booty taken in raids against traditional enemies and through the sale of slaves to Northwest Coastal tribes at The Dalles, was important to the social status of Modoc leaders.

Permanent Modoc winter villages typically comprised three to seven lodges. As spring approached, the Modoc moved out of their winter villages and began annual rounds of sucker fishing, root collecting, and hunting, establishing temporary camps, hamlets, and villages throughout the spring, summer and early fall at harvest sites. The best village locations were in areas where the women could collect roots while the men fished and hunted nearby (Kroeber 1925:318; Masten 1985:328; Powers 1877:252; Ray 1963:201–211).

The Modoc began harvesting epos (*Perideridia oregona*) and biscuitroot at the end of the spring sucker runs. Epos, a root called 'Yampah' by Northern Paiutes (Fowler and Rhode (2006:342), played a large role in the Modoc economy (Ray 1963:198). Primary house locations at springtime villages were near streams where trout and suckers were available within easy walking distance of root-digging grounds. A move was necessary during June and July, when camas (*Camassia* spp.) bloomed in wet meadows bordering coniferous forests at elevations between 4,000 and 7,000 feet.

Goose Lake was a favorite area for waterfowl hunting by the Modoc (Ray 1963:182, 189, 210). By late July the Modoc began hunting deer and pronghorn antelope in lowland locations (Ray 1963:184–188). Late July through September, women collected a variety of seeds and berries. Both the Modoc and the Klamath collected seeds with a snowshoe-shaped seed beater constructed of closely woven juniper withes. The Modoc generally placed more emphasis on small seed collection than the Klamath, however, and were also more likely to use conical baskets like those typically found throughout the Great Basin. Nuts and berries were favorites of both the Modoc and Klamath (Barrett 1910:243; Gatschet 1890; Ray 1963:199–200, 218; Stern 1966:5, 14).

The second major run of suckers occurred during late August and early September. After this run subsided the men traveled to higher elevations to hunt deer, elk, mountain sheep, and bear. The women accompanied them to collect huckleberries and other high elevation berries. As October arrived, the groups returned to their winter villages to repair their houses, bring in winter supplies, and, among other things, begin hunting deer in earnest. Goose Lake was a favorite area for the Modoc to hunt antelope and deer. In December, the winter trout run commenced (Barrett 1910:243; Ray 1963:182–183, 210; Stern 1966:13–14; Voegelin 1942:58). Throughout the cold winter months the Modoc occupied warm, semi-subterranean, earth-covered lodges, participated in social events, and waited eagerly for the first fresh foods (greens and fish) of spring.

Klamath. As mentioned above, the Klamath and Modoc languages are associated with the Penutian language stock (Aoki 1963; Stern 1966). The Klamath and Modoc dialects were mutually intelligible, though the two tribes considered themselves quite separate peoples distinguished by geographic designations (Kroeber 1925:319). Though distinct socially, the Klamath and Modoc generally lived in peace and commonly joined together for military ventures against their traditional enemies, the Northern Paiute, Achumawi (Pit River), and Shasta, with whom they often disputed territorial boundaries and resource rights (Ray 1963:xii, 134–135, 139). Klamath-Modoc relationships included trading, festivities, and marriage. These relationships served to strengthen social networks important to maintaining up-to-date information on the availability and productivity of plant and animal resources throughout the region.

The Klamath lived in the richest environmental settings along the western periphery of the Northern Great Basin. Here, in the marshes, along the rivers, and around the lakes at the eastern base of the Cascades, they lived in larger and more sedentary groups than either the Paiutes or Modoc. Correspondingly, they led a more socially structured existence within traditional village catchment areas. Wealth and social status were more important and formalized among the Klamath. The larger Klamath community consisted of six "tribelets," geographically distinct clusters of villages. Most were concentrated around Klamath Lake, and up the Williamson River to Klamath Marsh, while several villages collectively identified as the upland Klamath resided in the Sprague River Valley.

Like the Modoc, the Klamath followed a two-village settlement system centered on permanent winter and temporary spring/summer villages. Klamath spring and summer settlements were generally located near prime fishing locations and large wocas (water-lily) patches. Their winter settlements were located in sheltered spots near springs on the shores of lakes and marshes and at particularly good fishing and foraging spots along the Williamson and Sprague Rivers. These villages typically ranged from a few to a hundred or more semi-subterranean earth lodges. Houses ranged from small two-family dwelling units to the very large multi-family houses of influential families. Fishing and summer villages were semi-permanent in nature, being re-occupied year after year.

As soon as the snows ended, the Klamath partially dismantled their winter houses to let them dry out during the summer and moved to their early spring (March–April) fishing camps. The aged and infirm, who could not travel, moved into smaller huts and were tended by children. Provisions were periodically taken to them by young adults traveling in dugout canoes. The Klamath generally tried to situate their fishing camps close to their winter villages, in order to minimize the cost of transporting dried fish back for winter provision. The fishing season lasted approximately a month. The women processed the fish and harvested biscuitroot, epos, and camas as available (Ray 1963:180–196; Spier 1930). Later in the summer they collected water lily, or wocas (*Nuphar plysepalum*), seeds in vast quantities from shallow lakes and marshes using dugout canoes, while the men fished for trout and suckers, hunted small game, and caught birds attracted to decoys in nets. After the late summer fish runs the Klamath traveled to higher elevations where the men hunted deer, elk, mountain sheep, and bear, while the women gathered huckleberries and other high elevation berries. As October arrived, people returned to their winter villages to rebuild and refurbish their winter houses. Fishing continued throughout the winter, providing fresh food to supplement dried stores that had been put up throughout the rest of the year. Winter was the season for ceremonies, feasting, storytelling, and other social events.

Time and Environmental Change

The first Oregonians arrived near the end of the Pleistocene, when the world's climate was in transition from the cold of the glacial age to the warmth of the current era, the Holocene. Glaciers in the Cascades, Steens, and Blue mountains dwindled and disappeared. Modern Malheur, Harney, Summer, Abert, Goose, and the Warner Valley lakes are all shrunken remnants of what were huge bodies of water during the Pleistocene. Many pluvial lakes, as these Ice Age water bodies are called, have vanished completely, leaving only broad, gently sloping plains surrounded by prominent shorelines carved bathtub-ring fashion into the flanks of surrounding hills (fig. 2.4). In some parts of eastern Oregon, beach lines occur as much as 350 feet above the basin floors; the pluvial lakes that made these beaches were not only of vast extent, but were deep and cold. Consequently, they were not as productive of food resources, nor as attractive to human occupation, as the shallow, warm water lakes and marshes that replaced them during the Holocene.

Animals that went extinct in this region at the end of the glacial age included peccaries, giant ground sloth, giant bison, camel, horse, mastodon, and mammoth. Some of these, such as the giant ground sloth, have never been found in association with cultural remains. Important species that survived to the present include antelope, deer, elk, mountain sheep, bear, cottontail rabbit, jackrabbits, and many other small mammals. Predators include cougar, bobcat, badger, and coyote. The grizzly bear and gray wolf were present until the twentieth century. A multitude of local and migratory birds and fish added important variety to the Native diet. Plant species of late glacial times were essentially those seen today in the region, but boreal trees such as whitebark pine, spruce, and fir were more abundant. Timberlines stood lower, and alpine species were more broadly distributed. The sagebrush-grassland communities of lower elevations were richer in grass cover and more diverse than they are today.

The long-term relationship between environmental change and human occupation patterns within Oregon's Northern Great Basin was examined by the interdisciplinary Steens Mountain project (Aikens, Grayson, and Mehringer 1982; Beck 1984; Jones 1984; Wilde 1985). Pollen cores extracted from Wildhorse Lake at the top of Steens Mountain, from Fish Lake at intermediate elevation, and from Diamond Pond on the valley floor not far from Malheur

Fig. 2.4.
Pleistocene
shorelines in
Catlow Valley.

Lake, along with the geoarchaeological evidence of Skull Creek Dunes in the southern Catlow Valley, yielded a detailed paleoenvironmental record that effectively spanned all of Holocene time in the Steens-Catlow region (Mehringer 1985; Mehringer and Wigand 1986, 1990; Wigand 1987). Subsequent research in the Fort Rock basin has broadened and refined this regional record.

Accumulated evidence shows that by about 12,000 years ago in the Northern Great Basin, cold-tolerant trees were colonizing high terrain previously covered only by arctic tundra vegetation. Sagebrush, juniper, and other species followed these trees upslope as temperatures continued to rise. From about 7,800 to 5,600 years ago the climate was generally arid, occasionally broken by short, sharp shifts to somewhat greater moisture (Mehringer and Cannon 1994; Jenkins, Droz, and Connolly 2004). The overall trend toward drought continued, however, and many Great Basin lakes dried up completely. Signs of this period of aridity survive in the form of extensive dune fields along the easterly edges of today's Great Basin lakes and playas, which were formed as prevailing winds carried fine sediments off dried lakebeds exposed by evaporation. Rebirth of the lakes was well under way by 5,600 years ago, related to global cooling that also brought glacial advances in the Cascades and elsewhere. This cooler, moister climate regime has continued, punctuated by significant short-term fluctuations between wet and dry, to the present time. The most recent fluctuation of this type occurred during a four-year period of above-average precipitation during the early 1980s, when throughout eastern Oregon—and the Great Basin as a whole—shallow lakes and marshes were reborn on long-dry playas in some local basins, and in others deepened and expanded significantly before shrinking back to previous conditions after the middle of the decade.

Cultural Chronology and Time Markers

Culturally the passage of time is reflected in technological advances in toolmaking, distinctive material types used to make tools, stylistic changes, and artwork applied to utilitarian and ceremonial objects. The earliest well-dated stone projectile points made by Oregon's Great Basin people were large stemmed, bipointed, and leaf-shaped bifaces belonging to the Western Stemmed point complex (fig. 2.5), used variously as tips for heavy thrusting spears, atlatl dart points, and knives. The most ancient of these (fig. 2.6) were found in the bottom of Paisley 5 Mile Point Cave 5, where they are dated to

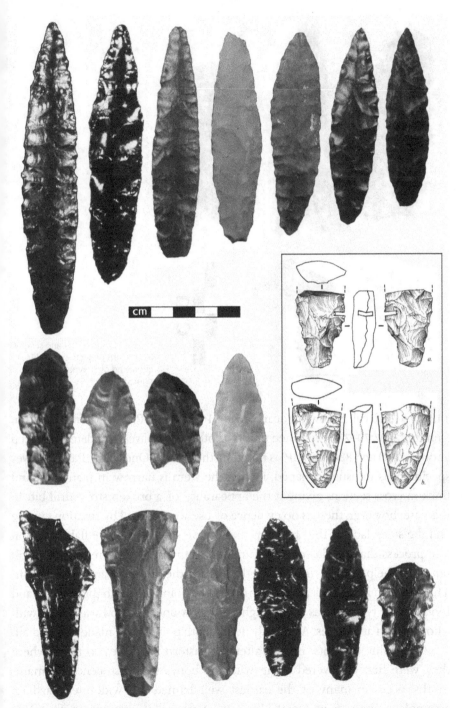

Fig. 2.5. Lanceolate and Western Stemmed points from Cougar Mt. Cave and Paisley 5 Mile Point Caves (illustrated in box).

Fig. 2.6. Clovis points and scrapers. Note sharp projections used for engraving or incising on bottom right scraper.

14,500–13,000 cal. BP by radiocarbon and 16,500 cal. BP by obsidian hydration (Jenkins 2007:70–77). Stemmed points at other sites have been dated between about 13,000 and 8200 cal. BP, as noted further below. One of the Paisley Caves specimens is unusually shaped, in that the stem is narrow in plan view and thick in cross-section, giving it the appearance of a broken stone drill bit. In this case, however, there is no evidence of use-wear caused by rotation cutting and the steep face of the "bit" appears to have several pressure flake scars on it, a process that would serve no functional purpose if it were indeed a drill but might help to more firmly seat the stem in the socket of a point foreshaft. The other is a more typical Western Stemmed point similar to the Haskett and Lind Coulee types. It has a thoroughly edge-ground base and was found with a horse tooth and bones. As already noted, both points were made of obsidian.

Clovis fluted points, named after the eastern New Mexico town where they were first discovered along with the bones of Pleistocene age mammoths, occur in many of the earliest well-defined and widespread artifact assemblages known in North America. Such points have been found as isolates throughout most of Oregon, but they have only been found in concentrations at a few localities, the best known being the Dietz site near Alkali Lake (Willig, Aikens, and Fagan 1988). Fluted point assemblages have also been recently found at the Sage Hen Gap and Sheep Mountain sites west of Burns in Harney County (O'Grady et al. 2009). Such points have not been radiocarbon dated in Oregon, but dates from the Lehner, Murray Springs, and other sites in New Mexico and Arizona show that Clovis fluted points there were in use between 13,200 and 12,800 cal. BP (Waters and Stafford 2007). These rigorously vetted dates are employed in this book to define the Clovis time horizon, but it must be noted that dates from sites elsewhere in North America suggest—somewhat less reliably—a considerably longer Clovis time range (Haynes and Huckell 2007; Taylor et al. 1996). Nearer to Oregon, Clovis points from the East Wenatchee site in Washington were found to overlie and thus postdate Glacier Peak volcanic ash dated to approximately 13,250 cal. BP (Mehringer 1988; Mehringer and Foit 1990).

A radiocarbon date from Connley Cave 4B in Oregon places a Western Stemmed point there at around 13,100 cal. BP, and a date from Smith Creek Cave in Nevada places Western Stemmed Points there around 13,000 cal. BP, making the oldest dated examples of this type in and near Oregon about as early as Clovis is dated in the Southwestern United States. There are also dates on Western Stemmed points at Cooper's Ferry, Idaho, of about 13,400 cal. BP, while many other dates show that Western Stemmed continues long after the disappearance of the Clovis complex (Beck and Jones 2010; Davis and Schweger 2004; Pendleton 1979; Warren and Crabtree 1986:184). Known predominantly from sites dated between about 12,800 and 8200 cal. BP, the Windust type, which also belongs to the Western Stemmed complex, has been found widely distributed throughout eastern Oregon. The Western Stemmed complex includes a number of similar but individually named projectile point types, including the Lake Mojave, Silver Lake, Haskett, Cougar Mountain, Lind Coulee, and Sadmat types, all variants of a wide-spread technological tradition emphasizing long stems and weakly developed shoulders (Musil 2004; Figure 2.5a). Some long, narrow, leaf-shaped points appear to be at least comparably early and possibly even earlier at some sites.

A dramatic shift to projectile points that are generally notched on the sides, corners, or bases begins about 7500 cal. BP. These points are smaller, used to tip light javelins or darts that were hurled with the aid of an atlatl, or spear-thrower. The Cascade point appeared before the Northern Side-notched type, though the Northern Side-notched and un-notched Cascade types often occur together (fig. 2.7). Both types are common throughout the Northwest, but reach their southerly limits approximately at the latitude of the Oregon-Nevada border. Corner-notched points of the Elko, Gatecliff, and Pinto series occupy portions of the same time span. They co-occur in Oregon with the Northern Side-notched and Cascade types after about 7500 cal. BP, but continue far to the south as well, being common throughout the deserts of Nevada and Utah, and extending into southern California. In Oregon, the Elko series is predominant after about 4500 cal. BP, and is frequently found

Fig. 2.7. Projectile point types of the Northern Great Basin. Top, (left to right) Foliate and Northern Side-notched; middle, Elko, Gatecliff Split-stem; bottom, Rosegate, Gunther, and Desert Side-notched.

with Gatecliff and Humboldt series points until about 1500 cal. BP (fig. 2.7).

Small points made for the bow and arrow mark the last 2,000 years of pre-historic time (fig. 2.7). The Rose Spring, Eastgate, and Desert Side-notched types are widespread throughout the western deserts. The Rose Spring and Eastgate types, most common in eastern Oregon, are closely related in both age and technology, so that an inclusive category termed the Rosegate series has been proposed (Thomas 1981). The relatively less common Desert Side-notched type was probably made after about 1000 cal. BP in some parts of the Great Basin, but in Oregon it appears only in very late (<500 years ago) or historic (post-contact) contexts (fig. 2.7).

While other projectile points were also made, the types named here are the best defined, most readily recognizable, and best dated. Since the time spans over which they were made have been established, these types afford the archaeologist a means of roughly dating human occupation at any location where they occur. In cases where organic matter datable by the radiocarbon method is absent and obsidian hydration dating has not been conducted, they often provide the only evidence for assessing the age of prehistoric remains. For this reason, projectile points are particularly valuable as archaeological evidence, and that is why "arrowheads" (projectile points) found on the sur-face should be left where they are found—once they are removed, the age of a site may be impossible to determine.

Time and Culture History

As previously noted, the Northern Great Basin is Oregon's best-known ar-chaeological region because it has been the focus of several long-term re-search projects. Luther Cressman—the "father of Oregon archaeology" (fig. 2.8)—focused most of the efforts of his long career there, establishing an interdisciplinary research program that would continue as the University of Oregon archaeological field school. Through this program he demonstrated the extreme time depth of human occupations in the arid American West and discovered the famous sagebrush bark sandals found at Fort Rock Cave, and other sites. In the 1960s he directed the research of his student Stephen Bedwell, who defined the "Western Pluvial Lakes Tradition" of the late Pleistocene and early Holocene and uncovered, in an excavation outside the mouth of Fort Rock Cave, charcoal that may represent the oldest radiocarbon dated hearth in North America, some 15,800 years old.

The University of Oregon's Northern Great Basin archaeological field school continued in Cressman's tradition during the 1970s with the Dirty Shame Rockshelter and Steens Mountain projects under the direction of C. Melvin Aikens (Aikens, Cole, and Stuckenrath 1977; Aikens, Grayson, and Mehringer 1982; Beck 1984, Jones 1984, Wilde 1985). This work was followed in the early 1980s by the Chewaucan Marsh-Abert Lake Project, pursued by Richard M. Pettigrew (1985) and Albert C. Oetting (1989). The unusually wet mid-1980s brought tremendous flooding to the Harney Basin as the ancient lakes filled. Waves cut away at shorelines and islands of Malheur and Harney lakes, exposing hundreds of sites, thousands of artifacts, and many human burials. The resulting frenzy of illegal artifact collection and site vandalism touched off a series of law enforcement investigations, subsequent archaeological surveys, human burial recoveries, and human osteology studies that continued well into the 1990s (Oetting 1990a, 1990b, 1991, 1992; Hemphill and Larson 1999).

The University of Oregon Northern Great Basin field school was reinvigorated by Aikens and Dennis L. Jenkins in 1989 with the establishment of the Fort Rock Basin Prehistory Project (1989–1999), which has expanded into the more inclusive Northern Great Basin Prehistory Project (1999–present). The broad impact of these research programs lies in the fact that their more than 75 years of fieldwork provide a greater body of accumulated data for the Northern Great Basin than for any other region of Oregon. The archaeology of this region is divided below into named time periods to help the reader track cultural changes and social patterns across time. Period boundaries generally reflect important climatic shifts that influenced the biotic landscape,

Fig. 2.8. Luther S. Cressman, the "father of Oregon Archaeology," at Fort Rock Cave, 1966.

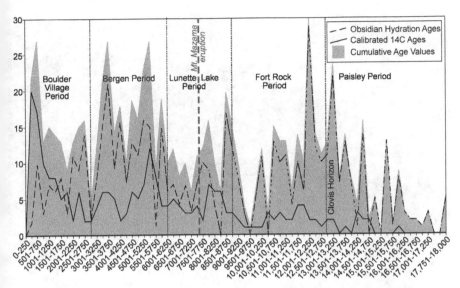

Fig. 2.9. Stacked frequency graph (calibrated radiocarbon ages over obsidian hydration ages) shows chronology of cultural events in the Fort Rock and Summer Lake Basins. Numbers show calendar years before present.

and thus the ways in which people interacted with their environment. Each phase defined in the figure is named after the site that best exhibits the defining cultural characteristics and chronology of its time period (fig. 2.9).

Paisley Period (>15,700 to 12,900 Years Ago)

The Paisley Period is named after the Paisley 5 Mile Point Caves (35LK3400) near Summer Lake, where Cressman (1942) reported finding Pleistocene animal bones associated with stone tools, and where the University of Oregon field school later recovered ancient human DNA in dried feces directly dated to about 14,500 cal. BP. The beginning age assigned to the period here is tentative; it reflects a small but growing body of radiocarbon and obsidian hydration dates obtained from Fort Rock Cave, the Connley Caves, and the Paisley Caves. The Paisley Period incorporates pre-Clovis time and what may have been a local "Clovis intrusion" into the area some 13,000 or so years ago. It ends at roughly 12,900 cal. BP with the onset of the short-lived (about 1,300 years) but intense late Pleistocene cold surge known as the Younger Dryas climatic event. Elsewhere in North America, this time marks the end of Clovis and the beginning of Folsom and similarly dated late fluted point assemblages (Meltzer 2009:284).

Fig. 2.10. Paisley 5 Mile Point Caves, view northeast.

The Paisley Caves are located on the highest shoreline of pluvial Lake Chewaucan in the Summer Lake basin (fig. 2.10). Digging the site between 1938 and 1940, Cressman and his students discovered in Cave 3 a U-shaped living floor—cleared of stones and outlined with boulders—well below a Mount Mazama volcanic ash layer that we now know to be about 7,600 years old. Bones of late Pleistocene camel, bison, horse, and waterfowl had apparently been tossed aside from this living floor, piling up around it, particularly near the rear wall of the cave. A small assemblage of obsidian artifacts—none of them chronologically diagnostic—was recovered from the living floor and surrounding area. The bone discard pattern and charring of some of the specimens suggested to Cressman that these animal bones represented food remains left by the cave occupants (Cressman et al. 1942:93, 1966:41,1986:121; Cressman and Williams 1940). Other archaeologists (Heizer and Baumhoff 1970:5; Krieger 1944; Jennings 1986) later questioned his interpretation, however, on the grounds that Cressman did not provide adequate documentation to show that the artifacts and the remains of extinct animals were truly associated. It was not until recently that new excavations, artifacts, and ancient DNA analysis provided incontrovertible proof of the contemporaneity of humans and Pleistocene animals at this now famous early site (Gilbert et al. 2008; Jenkins 2007; Rasmussen et al. 2009).

Recent Excavations at the Paisley 5 Mile Point Caves (35LK3400)

The University of Oregon's Northern Great Basin archaeological field school conducted new excavations at the Paisley Caves between 2002 and 2010. Bones of now-extinct Pleistocene camel and horse, as well as animals that have lived on from Pleistocene times into the present, were recovered from caves 2, 3, and 5. In caves 2 and 5 both artifacts and the bones of extinct animals occurred in sufficient numbers to strongly demonstrate their direct stratigraphic association. Camel, horse, bison, mountain sheep, fish, and waterfowl bones were found in Cave 5 together with stone and bone tools, tiny sewing threads (.04 millimeters in diameter) made of grass, fibrous plants, animal sinew, and hair (fig. 2.11). Even more convincing evidence consisted of dried human feces (fig. 2.12) found near a large ash feature and in a small pit containing camel, horse, mountain sheep, waterfowl, and fish bones. This "Bone Pit" was covered by a stone slab, and a second stone slab stood on end above the southern rim of the pit. The dried feces (or *coprolite*) it contained, conclusively identified as human by DNA analysis, was radiocarbon dated twice to a mean age of 14,500 cal. BP. Specimens from inside and slightly above the pit, including a mountain sheep jaw, camelid mandibles and foot bones, horse hooves and bones, and the bones of duck, rabbit, and pika, were dated between 16,190 cal. BP and 13,030 cal. BP (fig. 2.13). Modified bones in and around the ash feature nearby include a broad, thick piece of bear bone with prominent "saw-like" teeth (fig. 2.14) that was dated at 14,230 cal. BP, a narrower spatula-shaped bone, and a possible awl fragment, both of the latter

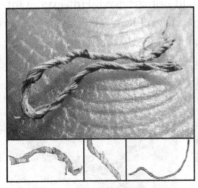

Left, Fig. 2.11. Twisted grass and sinew threads for sewing (thickness .04 mm) from Paisley Cave 5.
Right, Fig. 2.12. Human coprolite from the "Bone Pit" at Paisley Cave 5, dated to 14,280 cal. BP.

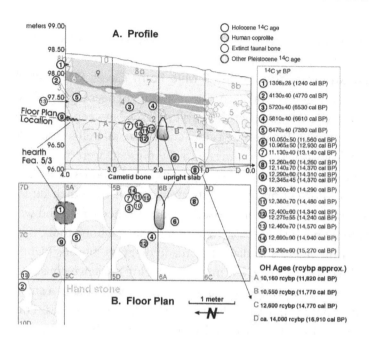

A. Profile

○ Holocene ¹⁴C age
○ Human coprolite
○ Extinct faunal bone
○ Other Pleistocene ¹⁴C age

¹⁴C yr BP
① 1308±26 (1240 cal BP)
② 4130±40 (4770 cal BP)
③ 5720±40 (6530 cal BP)
④ 5810±40 (6610 cal BP)
⑤ 6470±40 (7380 cal BP)
⑥ 10,050±50 (11,560 cal BP) 10,965±50 (12,930 cal BP)
⑦ 11,130±40 (13,140 cal BP)
⑧ 12,260±60 (14,260 cal BP) 12,140±70 (14,370 cal BP)
⑨ 12,290±60 (14,310 cal BP) 12,345±45 (14,370 cal BP)
⑩ 12,300±40 (14,290 cal BP)
⑪ 12,380±70 (14,480 cal BP)
⑫ 12,400±60 (14,340 cal BP) 12,275±55 (14,240 cal BP)
⑬ 12,460±70 (14,570 cal BP)
⑭ 12,690±90 (14,940 cal BP)
⑮ 13,260±60 (15,270 cal BP)

OH Ages (rcybp approx.)
A 10,160 rcybp (11,820 cal BP)
B 10,550 rcybp (11,770 cal BP)
C 12,600 rcybp (14,770 cal BP)
D ca. 14,000 rcybp (16,910 cal BP)

B. Floor Plan

Fig. 2.13. Stratigraphic profile (*above*) and Floor plan (*below*) of North Block excavations in Paisley Cave 5 at the end of 2003 field season.

having rounded edges that were either ground or use-worn. Obsidian and chert flakes were recovered with these items. One in particular has a highly polished surface, indicating it had been flaked off of a heavily used cutting or scraping tool while it was being resharpened in that location.

A wooden artifact made of willow—a possible dart foreshaft butt or plug—was found in a nearby excavation along with a broad bone spatula. This wooden tool, dated at 11,540 cal. BP, is from the later Fort Rock period, while the broad rib-shaped bone found slightly below it could not be directly dated because the bone protein (collagen) had not survived. However, a human coprolite recovered from the 5 centimeter level immediately below the broad modified bone was dated to 14,420 cal. BP, exactly the same age as that obtained from a large mammal bone fragment recovered nearby.

The bases of three stemmed points have been recovered from deep in the Paisley Cave 5 deposits, the two most complete of which have already been described and illustrated in the section "Cultural Chronology and Time Markers" above. One of these, which was recovered in the North Block about 2 meters south of the

Fig. 2.14. Modified bear bone dated to 14,280 cal. BP at Paisley Cave 5.

Bone Pit and from the same stratum and has been repeatedly dated at about 14,500 cal. BP, has a stem that is narrow in plan view and thick in cross-section. Applying the "fast" (2.75 microns per 1000 years) and "slow" (2.25 microns per 1000 years) obsidian hydration rates developed for the South Block and North Block areas of Cave 5 to this specimen suggests it was made sometime between 13,500 and 16,500 years ago and is thus older than points of the Clovis type. The other point, recovered from Unit 5/16 adjacent to the South Block, is a more typical Western Stemmed point base similar in shape to those of the Haskett and Lind Coulee types. It has a thoroughly edge-ground base and was found with a horse tooth and several horse bones. It was found *in situ* in a compact mud lens in the basal LU1b ("Gray Sand") stratum in which the oldest cultural remains were found in this portion of the cave. Radiocarbon dating of sagebrush twigs recovered from the nearest excavation unit wall 5 centimeters above, at, and below the elevation of this specimen firmly brackets it between dates of 12,960, 13,410, and 13,720 cal. BP, respectively.

While one could wish there were more artifacts from the deepest and oldest archaeological deposits, it is abundantly clear that occupations at the Paisley Caves were always very brief, leaving behind only thin scatters of stone, bone, and fecal matter, of which little survived the depredations of illegal artifact mining to be recovered by archaeologists. Further compelling evidence, however, comes in the form of ancient human DNA in fecal remains.

Human coprolites, tested for mitochondrial DNA, protein residues, plant pollen, and phytoliths, show that the site occupants were Native Americans with very close genetic ties to Siberian/Asian populations (Jenkins 2007; Gilbert et al. 2008). One of three coprolites dating from this period shows that one individual who camped at the site had eaten a variety of plants including grass seed, and may have consumed a tea. Another coprolite contained a very high quantity of lomatium pollen, showing that the person who left it had probably eaten a springtime meal of roots. This shows that people at a very early time were already making regular use of the same plant foods that continued to be important in the diets of later Native Americans. The third coprolite gave chemical evidence of the meat of bison, fox, and sage grouse. Horse bones were found near one of the early stemmed points found at the Paisley Caves, and protein residue analysis conducted on a polished hand stone found near the Cave 5 "Bone Pit" showed that it had been used to process horse tissues, possibly by pounding or grinding dried flesh or crushing bone to extract its marrow.

In sum, the Paisley Caves site is extremely important because it is the first place in the New World that incontrovertible human traces—including human DNA in dried feces on the one hand, and obvious stone and bone artifacts on the other—have been directly dated in excess of 14,000 years ago. These remains demonstrate that people were living in the central Oregon desert centuries earlier than has been conclusively documented by human traces anywhere else in the New World.

Fossil Lake Camelid Kill Site (35LK524). Potentially of the Paisley Period is the Camelid Kill Site, excavated by Rick Minor, Lee Spencer, and Don Dumond in 1977 at Fossil Lake in the northeastern end of the Fort Rock basin (Minor and Spencer (1977). They recovered fragments of a lanceolate projectile point among camelid bones that were found eroding from a mound of ancient lakebed sediment. The camelid remains—probably the extinct Pleistocene species *Camelops hesternus*—were found in three bone concentrations on the surface. With two of the bone concentrations, separated by a distance of about 50 feet, were fragments of a projectile point that clearly fitted together and a biface/projectile point base that was not part of the first point. The bones were mapped in place, removed, and the underlying sediments excavated. Though more bones and an obsidian flake were found just below the surface, the association of the flaked stone artifacts with the faunal remains could not be clearly established because of the near-surface context (Minor and Spencer 1977). Radiocarbon dating of bone collagen returned an age for the camelid of approximately 12,000–11,500 cal. BP; confirmation of this age by additional testing is necessary, however, to address whether the dates are spuriously young due to the bone's absorption of younger carbon from local groundwater.

Dietz Site (35LK1529). Clovis occupation, which belongs to the later part of the Paisley Period, is particularly well attested at the Dietz site, located in the Alkali Basin immediately east of the Fort Rock area near Wagontire in central Oregon. Now watered only by ephemeral streams, the Alkali Basin held a large deep-water pluvial lake in later Pleistocene times. The Dietz archaeological site is an extensive scatter of flaked stone artifacts and lithic debris found at the base of a low ridge on the edge of a small dry lake or "playa" near the northernmost end of Pluvial Lake Alkali. This shallow basin apparently fluctuated in depth, sometimes drying to a wet meadow maintained by ephemeral surface water, seeps and springs, and eventually dried completely as the lake continued to recede with the end of the Pleistocene.

The artifacts lay exposed on the surface. Extensive excavations, both manual and with a backhoe, failed to find any appreciable buried deposits (fig. 2.15).

Investigated by Judith A. Willig (1988, 1989), John L. Fagan (1988), and the University of Oregon field school between 1983 and 1985, and subsequently by the University of Nevada-Reno Sundance Archaeological Research Fund in 1996 and 1997 (Pinson 1999, 2004), the Dietz site produced a large assemblage of fluted points and otherwise diagnostic Clovis-era artifacts, representing a period closely dated in Arizona-New Mexico sites to about 13,200–12,800 cal. BP, as noted above. The Dietz site is currently one of only three recorded Clovis-era sites in Oregon where multiple artifacts have been recovered, though Clovis fluted points are reported widely as isolated surface finds. No radiocarbon dating was possible at the Dietz site, but the artifacts suggest that its Clovis occupations were contemporaneous with late Pleistocene fauna, as has been established elsewhere in North America. However, only one camelid bone of an extinct Pleistocene species was recovered from the Dietz site and that bone—which came from shallow surface deposits—has not been reliably proven to be associated with the human occupations.

Five areas of the Dietz site were Clovis concentrations, with fluted points, flute flakes, and biface projectile point blanks broken during fluting attempts. Specimens included 61 complete and fragmentary fluted points, 25 blanks, and 25 fluting flakes that are identifiable with the Clovis lithic tradition (fig. 2.16). Much of the obsidian tool stone came from Horse Mountain, less than a mile away, and some was from as yet unidentified sources farther afield.

Fig. 2.15. Surface stripping by University of Oregon field school crew at the Dietz Clovis site.

Fig. 2.16.
Dietz site Clovis points.

As described by Fagan (1988:397), "The Clovis tool kit used at the Dietz site included large and small fluted points; biface blanks, knives or preforms; end scrapers; side scrapers; flute flakes; multiple-tip gravers; single tip gravers, some of which were made from broken points; percussion-produced blade-like flakes and flake tools; possible wedges; hammerstones; and abrasive stones. In addition, based on the debitage, it is suspected that batons of wood, antler, bone, or ivory were used for percussion flaking."

Also found at two areas within the larger Dietz site, but not within the Clovis artifact concentrations, were 31 large stemmed and shouldered points assignable to the Western Stemmed tradition. Grinding stones were found near some of these latter specimens. The Clovis and Western Stemmed assemblages from the Dietz site are both substantial, but quite different in their attributes. Fagan (1988) believed that two different groups of people are represented, the Clovis folk having a recognizably different lithic technology and being more narrowly focused on a hunting lifeway than were the Western Stemmed folk. Willig (1988) stressed the idea of cultural continuity between Clovis and Western Stemmed, believing that the Clovis people represented at the Dietz site were well along the way to developing a broad-spectrum hunting-gathering "paleo-archaic" adaptation that became the basis of subsequent Western Stemmed and Great Basin desert culture. Dating evidence developed since the publication of these authors' research, and especially the new evidence from the Paisley Caves, now shows that stemmed projectile points appeared in the region before Clovis time, rather than after it, as Fagan, Willig and many other Great Basin prehistorians had believed (Willig, Aikens, and Fagan 1988).

In the present book both Western Stemmed and Clovis cultural patterns are recognized as belonging to the Paisley Period. Current thinking among North American archaeologists emphasizes the fact that local technological traditions and subsistence strategies varied across differing ecological settings

(Cannon and Meltzer 2004; Meltzer 2009). Where large game animals were bountiful, it is thought, people may have developed more specialized hunting traditions (mammoth hunting, for example), but in many (if not most) situations they probably consumed a broad range of food types—including plants, fish, birds, insects, reptiles, and mammals of all sizes—in the proportions in which they were encountered (for an alternative point of view see Haynes 2002, 2009). Based on what we know of broader associations, the Western Stemmed people attested at the Dietz site may have been more broad-spectrum and opportunistic in their subsistence strategies, and the Clovis folk relatively more focused on following and hunting large game.

Sage Hen Gap (35HA3548). Sage Hen Gap is a fluted point (Clovis) site not many miles north of the Dietz site, found by Bureau of Land Management (BLM) archaeologists in the 1980s. Field investigations were conducted in 2007 by the University of Oregon field school under the direction of Patrick O'Grady, working closely with BLM archeologist Scott Thomas (O'Grady et al. 2009). The site appears to have been a good ambush location for hunting large game as they funneled down from higher terrain through narrow, steep wash bottoms cut into a high ridge. Archaeologists have so far recovered seven fluted points, a Western Stemmed point, 13 fluting flakes, three gravers, seven nodules exhibiting controlled-overshot flakes (a distinctive Clovis flaking method), 10 bifaces with overshot flake scars, 12 overshot flakes, and more than a thousand obsidian flakes (Rondeau 2007a, 2007b). Importantly, there are very few artifacts on the site that are clearly younger than Clovis.

Sheep Mountain Clovis Site (35HA3667). The Sheep Mountain site is located in and around a small meadow that once held a shallow pond on a low ridge saddle some miles north of Wagontire Mountain and the Dietz site. Geoarchaeological investigations undertaken by Patrick O'Grady, William Lyons, and the University of Oregon field school revealed buried deposits to a depth of about 130 centimeters. To date, two Clovis points and a much larger number of Western Stemmed points have been recovered from the surface. Stemmed points have been recovered from the upper 80 centimeters of the site while artifacts of probable Clovis age, none diagnostic, have been found in the "Yellow Sand" stratum underlying the darker gray brown upper strata.

Catlow Cave. Cressman (1940) reported finding extinct Pleistocene horse bones near the top of lakeshore gravels at Catlow Cave, located in the southern end of the Catlow Valley in central Oregon some 90 miles south of Burns. He suggested that this site may have been occupied as early as the Paisley Caves farther west, which he was also investigating at the time. Alex Krieger (1944) later reported, however, that he himself, as one of Cressman's crew members, had seen what he believed was a modern horse bone tumble down from near the modern surface. Though Cressman published a response to Krieger's criticism, stating once again that he had demonstrated the Pleistocene age of the horse bone, the age and cultural association of this specimen remains in question. Regrettably, the horse specimen is no longer to be found in the site collection, so the issue cannot be resolved by radiocarbon dating the bone of contention. Cressman also found human bones in the Pleistocene gravels, but in the pre-radiocarbon dating era there was no way for him to prove that the scattered bones were as old as the gravels. They may have simply been buried or mixed in with the gravels by humans or animals digging in the cave at a later date. A planned reinvestigation of the cave in the late 1970s that was intended to resolve this issue was foiled by the thorough mining and destruction of the remaining deposits by artifact collectors shortly before field work was scheduled to begin (Wilde 1985). This sorry event took place in defiance of signs and barriers erected at the mouth of the cave by the Bureau of Land Management to safeguard its archaeological evidence. The human bones themselves, never directly radiocarbon dated, were repatriated and reburied under the Native American Graves Protection and Repatriation Act of 1990.

Though Cressman's claimed evidence for Pleistocene human occupation at Catlow Cave is not verifiable, both this site and Roaring Springs Cave, near the north end of Catlow Valley, remain famous for their large assemblages of later-period perishable artifacts, and more will be said below about their rich contribution to the archaeology of those later periods.

Ecological, Technological, and Social Patterns of the Paisley Period. Recent studies of coprolites from the Paisley Caves show that the First Oregonians, indeed the First Americans, had strong genetic ties to Siberian and Asian populations. Their adaptation to Northern Great Basin environments during the Paisley Period (>15,700–12,900 cal. BP) took place within the context of dramatic climatic and ecological changes occurring at the end of the last glacial age, when many of the plants and animals important to the later Native cultures of the region were already available for consumption by these early inhabitants.

People were certainly present at Paisley Caves by about 14,500 cal. BP—possibly earlier—and already well adapted to the high desert environment. Pleistocene camelids, horses, ancient bison, and American lions were still extant in the Paisley region (Jenkins 2007). Faunal, botanical, DNA, FTIR (Fourier Transform Infra Red), and protein residue studies of the Paisley Caves human coprolites indicate that people there ate bison, camelids, horse, canids (dogs, fox, coyote, and wolf), deer, mountain sheep, pronghorn (antelope), perhaps peccaries (small pigs), and sage grouse. Various plants are also attested, including "desert parsley" (*Apiacaea* sp.), goosefoot (*Chenopodiacea* sp.), grasses, sunflower, cactus, and rose hips. People undoubtedly consumed other currently unidentified plants and animals for food, tea, and medicine. The Paisley Period diet, as seen from the caves, was well-rounded, and suggests that by 14,500 cal. BP the people of the Northern Great Basin were adapted to a rich mosaic of ecological settings that included forests, marshes, lakes, and rivers, as well as dry, rocky uplands and open desert terrains. This indicates that Paisley Period folk practiced basically the same kind of broad-spectrum dietary regime that was typical of later periods in the same region, though they surely also pursued large game energetically when and where it was reasonably available, as suggested by scattered Clovis artifacts and sites from the later Paisley Period. Finally, it is clear that—as was the case in later times—Paisley Period people routinely covered long distances in their quests. This is proved beyond question by the regularity with which dulled and broken stone tools made of non-local obsidians are found discarded in Paisley Period camps far from the place of their volcanic origin.

Stone tool assemblages of the Paisley Period variously include lanceolate, Clovis fluted, and Western Stemmed projectile points, along with biface blanks, knives, gravers, scrapers, used flakes, cores, and occasional handstones for grinding, pounding, abrading, and polishing. Lanceolate, leaf-shaped, and Western Stemmed points continued to be used into the following Fort Rock Period, as discussed below. Typically, all of these point types occur as surface finds in a variety of ecological settings across Oregon. In the Northern Great Basin they seem to be most commonly associated with ancient water sources. Cressman (1940) reported on possible cultural associations (Clovis?) involving bone foreshafts and the recovery of a fluted point in marsh deposits containing Pleistocene fossils at Lower Klamath Lake. Similarly, though apparently in a much better-defined context, Beaton (1991) reported a radiocarbon date of 13,500 cal. BP on a hearth encountered in a shelter at Tule Lake. The unusually large Dietz site collection from a small sub-basin at the northern edge of Pluvial Lake Alkali (Fagan 1988, Willig 1988) also shows that there were certain favorable locations where people stayed longer and more intense activity resulted in dense concentrations of artifacts. It is also likely that particularly favorable localities of this sort were visited more frequently than others.

Another distinctive artifact type of the Paisley Period is the beveled solid bone rod, generally found in or attributed to Clovis assemblages, which may have served as part of a composite foreshaft used in hafting a stone point, or as a point itself (Boldurian and Cotter 1999:95–100; Cressman et al. 1942:100). In Oregon, these have been found in the vicinity of fluted points and the bones of megafauna on the floor of shallow lakes at the Narrows site at Lower Klamath Lake and at Silver Lake (Wingard 2001:584; Howe 1968:60; Cressman 1940), though all are surface or collector finds and none have been recovered *in situ* from datable contexts.

It is important to ponder the reasons why it has taken archaeologists so long to recognize the existence of the earliest Paisley Period assemblages. One key is surely the fact that such assemblages are few and scattered in the first place, simply because they represent the first stage of human entry into the Northern Great Basin. A second key factor evident from recent Paisley Caves research is that in its high-mobility broad-spectrum ecological adaptation, the Paisley Period assemblage is generally indistinguishable from that of the following Fort Rock Period cultures, which are often found at the bottoms of the region's stratified caves. Simply put, Paisley Period traces, when present in such sites, have been hard to single out. The Clovis complexes, on the other hand, which also fall within the Paisley Period, have been readily recognized by their specialized lithic technology and typically separate locations. Obviously, Clovis sites in the open were dominated by activities different from those carried out by groups that camped in cave settings. The most likely interpretation is that Clovis bands, which typically emphasized hunting over other kinds of harvesting, entered the region during the Paisley Period and persisted briefly, while the broader-spectrum lifeway of the Paisley Cave dwellers persisted far longer, on into the Fort Rock and subsequent periods. Singling out and dating the early Paisley Period occupation in the cave sites where it occurs has therefore required new technologies such as DNA and protein residue extraction, high-precision AMS radiocarbon dating of individual artifacts and specimens, and obsidian hydration to tease out the evidence of its early existence from the highly similar traces that define the subsequent Fort Rock Period in many Northern Great Basin sites.

Fort Rock Period (12,900 to 9000 Years Ago)

The gradual post-glacial warming trend that characterized the Paisley Period was abruptly reversed about 12,900 years ago by a pulse of cooler conditions known as the Younger Dryas, which we use to mark the beginning of the Fort Rock Period. This period is named for the famous Fort Rock Cave in Central Oregon, about 50 miles south of Bend, where the world's oldest shoes—actually sandals made of cords twined from sagebrush bark—were recovered. The period from about 12,900 to 9,000 years ago was one of continued slow drying during which localized shallow-water lakes and marshes with fringing grasslands replaced the previously vast and deep pluvial lakes of the Pleistocene era. In the early deposits of Fort Rock Cave, the Connley Caves, and the Cougar Mountain Caves, located at different points around the edges of the Fort Rock basin, rich cultural assemblages suggest that the main economic focus of early Holocene Northern Great Basin occupants was on resources found in and around shallow-water wetland settings (Bedwell 1973).

Comparing early Holocene assemblages of the Fort Rock basin to those of similar age farther south in the western Great Basin, Bedwell (1973) found strong similarities in projectile point styles, the consistent presence of large scrapers made of fine-grained volcanic materials such as basalt, andesite, and rhyolite, and the location of sites along the shores of ancient lakes and marshes. He drew strong attention to this culture's evident cultural focus on wetlands resources, particularly waterfowl, by naming it the Western Pluvial Lakes Tradition. The horizon markers of the WPLT, here locally identified as the Fort Rock Period, are Western Stemmed points, lanceolate and large foliate projectile points, crescents, large scrapers, and gravers (fig. 2.17). Other tools included choppers, cobblestone tools for battering, polishing, and abrading, manos, and the occasional ground stone slab used for processing small seeds and dried meat.

Important sites of the Fort Rock Period include many with buried cultural deposits. The caves located near marshes in the Fort Rock and Summer Lake basins are important examples of sites occupied during the late fall and winter, while excavations at the Paulina Lake, Buffalo Flat Bunny Pits, Tucker site, and various Harney Basin sites like Catlow and Roaring Springs caves farther east, offer a comprehensive picture of spring, summer, and early fall seasonal movements across a broad range of ecological settings.

Fort Rock Cave (35LK1). Fort Rock Cave is located approximately 1.5 miles west of Fort Rock State Park in a low volcanic ridge that was wave-cut by pluvial Lake Fort Rock during a late Pleistocene high stand. Facing south-west into the prevailing winds, the cave is roughly 20 meters front to back by 10 meters wide (fig. 2.18). A University of Oregon crew digging there in 1938 under Cressman's direction found cultural deposits that averaged about 1.3 meters in depth (Cressman, Williams, and Krieger 1940:56–60; Bedwell 1973). Volcanic ash from the eruption of Mt. Mazama some 7,600 years ago was en-countered not far below a dense surface layer of cow and horse manure. Below the volcanic ash was a cultural deposit containing Fort Rock-style sagebrush bark sandals (fig. 2.19), later radiocarbon dated between about 10,500 and 9300 cal. BP (Connolly and Barker 2004, 2008). About a hundred complete and frag-mentary specimens were removed by Cressman. After his excavations artifact collectors relentlessly mined the cave, removing an undetermined number of additional sandals and no doubt other materials. In fact, the cave deposits were subsequently so thoroughly churned that scientific excavations by Bedwell and Cressman in 1966 found little undisturbed deposit left in the cave (Bedwell 1973:14; Bedwell and Cressman 1971:6).

Fig. 2.17. Fort Rock Period points from Connley Caves and crescent (*right*) from Alvord Desert.

Fig. 2.18. Fort Rock Cave, 1966.   Fig. 2.19 Fort Rock type sagebrush bark sandals.

Returning to the site in 1967, a University of Oregon field crew pushed aside several large boulders that lay outside the cave mouth to clear a space for further excavation. Below one of these they recovered charcoal fragments and stone artifacts at the top of Pleistocene lake gravels. Charcoal from this find produced a calibrated age of about 15,800 calendar years ago. Considering the extreme age of this date it is somewhat surprising that no Pleistocene faunal remains such as camelids, horses, or pika were found, but the excavation was very small and only a small quantity of unidentifiable large mammal bone fragments were present (Bedwell 1970). The artifact and faunal assemblage associated with the charcoal amounts to only a few items—two Western Stemmed projectile point fragments, a mano, a scraper, and a few stone flakes. The assemblage is very similar in composition to later tool kits of the Western Pluvial Lakes Tradition, and consequently, most specialists have expressed doubt about the validity of this date and its association with artifacts generally thought to be from a much later period. With the recent recognition of the well-documented Paisley Period occupation at the not too distant Paisley Caves, however, it is important to entertain the possibility that the earliest Fort Rock Cave occupation corresponds to that period, as the radiocarbon date suggests.

Connley Caves (35LK50). The Connley Caves (fig. 2.20), located near Paulina Marsh some 10 miles south of Fort Rock, provided much of the data from which Bedwell (1973) developed his concept of the Western Pluvial Lakes Tradition; it was there that large quantities of waterfowl bone were found in deposits dated between 13,000 and 9000 cal. BP. The Connley Caves site is composed of eight wave-cut rockshelters eroded by Pleistocene Lake Fort Rock at the height of the last glacial period into a south-facing cliff of crumbly welded volcanic tuff. Interestingly this tuff, originally molten rock, incorporated gravel- to boulder-sized chunks of rhyolite and fine-grained basalt that were extracted and used much later by the site's inhabitants for making projectile points, scrapers, and the occasional bifacial knife (see those in fig. 2.17).

Excavation of a 2x2-meter test pit inside Cave No. 4 reached a maximum depth of roughly 3.4 meters and was still encountering artifacts when the excavation was terminated due to its extreme depth and dangerous conditions. Later excavations employed a backhoe to remove earth that had been disturbed by artifact collectors above lenses of Mount Mazama volcanic ash in Caves 4 and 5, and this was followed by additional manual excavations in each cave. Corner-notched and "eared" Elko series projectile points were recovered from below the Mazama ash lens in these units along with Western Stemmed and foliate projectile points. However, the co-occurrence of Elko points with Western Stemmed points was not duplicated at the Connley Caves during later University of Oregon excavations. Nor were these types found together at the surrounding Paisley Caves, Paulina Lake Campground, Buffalo Flat Bunny Pits, or Tucker sites, all of which date to the same general period. Consequently, it seems most likely that the co-occurrence of Elko (younger) and Western Stemmed (older) points reported at the Connley Caves by Bedwell was caused by undetected stratigraphic mixing. Other evidence suggests that he was correct, however, in reporting that large basalt scrapers, lanceolate, and foliate projectile points were increasingly abundant in deeper levels throughout the site.

Three cultural components have been identified by subsequent re-analysis of the pre-Mazama deposits excavated by Bedwell's crew. The earliest—based on radiocarbon and obsidian hydration dating—correlates with the Paisley Period, dating between about 15,800 and 13,110 cal. BP. The second belongs to the Fort Rock Period and the third to the earliest portion of the following Lunette Lake Period between 8500 and 8000 cal. BP. Chronologically diagnostic artifacts and radiocarbon dates verify that the site continued to be sporadically occupied into the historic period (Jenkins, Connolly, and Aikens 2004).

More recent excavations were conducted by Jenkins and the University of Oregon field school at the Connley Caves between 1999 and 2001 (Beck et al. 2004; Jenkins 2002). Excavation of a large pit in front of Cave 5 reached bedrock at a depth of nearly 4.6 meters (fig. 2.21), and sagebrush charcoal produced a radiocarbon age of 10,940 cal. BP from deposits well above bedrock. However, a number of thick obsidian hydration measurements on artifacts in and below the Fort Rock Period component identified from this excavation suggest that even older occupations occurred at the site, perhaps consistent in age (15,800 cal. BP) with the earliest assemblage from Fort Rock Cave that was mentioned

Left, Fig. 2.20. University of Oregon field school excavations at Connley Cave 6 (2000).
Right, Fig. 2.21. University of Oregon field school excavations at Connley Cave 5 (2001).

above as possibly representing the early Paisley Period there. The Fort Rock Period deposits at the Connley Caves produced foliate, Western Stemmed, and lanceolate projectile points, some of which were complete. They also documented the presence of bison and large numbers of basalt scrapers. Bedwell (1970:191) suggested in a footnote that the scraper types seen in the early Western Pluvial Lakes Tradition (Fort Rock Period) assemblages might indicate both processing of large mammal hides and more intensive winter occupation of the caves.

The distinctions between the Fort Rock Period component and the rather thin record of an overlying Lunette Lake Period component are quite obvious and suggest that the site was primarily used as a longer term base camp for big game hunting during the Fort Rock occupations, but as a shorter term hunting/collecting camp during the later Lunette Lake occupations. Only point fragments and small amounts of flaking debris were recovered from these later deposits, suggesting that visitors were by then not generally making points and other tools at the Connley Caves but simply replacing items used up or broken there with spares brought along on short-term forays from base camps elsewhere.

The Connley Caves are ideally situated for wintertime occupations, which seem to have dominated during the Fort Rock period. They provide excellent access to natural resources concentrated in both the marsh below (waterfowl, fish, lagomorphs, cattail, and bulrush), and the wooded Connley Hills surrounding the caves (bison, elk, deer, grouse). Paulina Marsh now harbors both resident and seasonally migratory waterfowl populations, and is productive habitat for jackrabbits and cottontails the year around. Additionally, mule deer and elk come down out of the higher elevations along the northern, western, and southern edges of the Fort Rock basin to winter in both the Connley Hills and around Paulina Marsh. Data from the caves suggest that these same geographically determined patterns were prevalent in ancient times as well.

Grayson (1979:446) interprets the faunal data from the Connley Caves, particularly the undifferentiated sex and age patterns seen in sage grouse populations, as best fitting an occupation of the site from late fall to springtime. Connolly (1995:16) notes that jackrabbits and cottontails became less common at the site over the long 13,000–9000 cal. BP duration of the Fort Rock period, possibly reflecting the fact that these animals generally do not migrate long distances and are susceptible to local depletion of numbers when intensively exploited by local human populations.

Cougar Mountain Cave (35LK55). Cougar Mountain Cave, not far away from the Fort Rock and Connley caves, was dug to bedrock in 1958 by John Cowles, an avid artifact collector. In his report Cowles says that he kept track of artifact proveniences by one-foot levels (Cowles 1960), but subsequent efforts by Layton (1972) to work with his uncatalogued collection were hampered by a lack of precisely recorded information on artifact associations, as well as a lack of radiocarbon dates. Nevertheless, despite dating ambiguities the site is important because it was filled to a depth of six and a half feet with exceptionally rich cultural deposits containing artifacts highly comparable to those of the Fort Rock and Connley caves.

Cowles reported that exclusively lanceolate, foliate, and Western Stemmed points, along with one crescent, came from the lowest two feet of deposits (see previous fig. 2.5). The site is the location for which the Cougar Mountain point—a variety of the Western Stemmed type—is named. Bison bones (which are dated only before about 8900 cal. BP at the Connley Caves) occurred in the lower two feet of deposits at Cougar Mountain Cave, where deer and mountain sheep bones were also common. Other artifacts included well-made ovate knives, scrapers, abraders and manos, stone drills, pipes, bone awls, bone atlatl spurs, bone needles, pressure flakers, bone beads, shell beads, basketry, twine, sandals, matting, leather, and wooden artifacts. Sagebrush bark sandals were fairly common and frequently muddy, which may indicate wintertime occupations. One sandal made of tule was later radiocarbon dated to 9530 cal. BP (Connolly and Barker 2004). This rich assemblage is identified by the current authors with the Fort Rock period and possibly to some degree also with the Paisley period. Other artifacts, including smoking pipes, pressure flakers, and bone beads, are of types commonly found considerably later in other Fort Rock basin sites, and were probably mixed inadvertently with earlier specimens during Cowles' excavations. The bison, deer, and mountain sheep bones common in its early levels suggest that Cougar Mountain Cave was a winter base camp, probably occupied at that season for the same ecological reasons as were the Fort Rock and Connley Caves, as discussed above.

Paisley 5 Mile Point Caves (35LK3400). Fort Rock Period archaeology is well represented at the Paisley Caves. Most notably, the radiocarbon dating of finely spun grass threads found at the Paisley Caves indicates that sewing with tiny threads was done there by at least 12,500 cal. BP, which falls within the Fort Rock Period. Needles were reportedly found at both the Paisley Caves and Cougar Mountain Cave by artifact collectors, though unfortunately in both cases the specimens are unprovenienced and undated (Cowles 1960:27). Needles and needle blanks have been recovered in controlled contexts from late glacial and early Holocene deposits at the Tule Lake Rockshelter (Erlandson, personal communication), the Marmes Rockshelter (Hicks 2004:237) and Lind Coulee sites (Irwin and Moody 1978:93–106) in Washington, the Buhl Burial in Idaho (Green et al. 1998:450; Yohe and Woods 2002:21), and the Bonneville Estates Rockshelter in Nevada (David Rhode, personal communication).

Paulina Lake (35DS34). Investigations at the Paulina Lake site, some 25 miles northwest of Fort Rock in the Newberry Volcano National Monument, identified three early Holocene cultural components ranging between 11,000 and 7600 cal. BP, all buried under Mt. Mazama tephra. This site lies on the boundary between Oregon's Great Basin and Columbia Plateau cultural regions, and is important to the archaeological narratives of both areas (see also ch. 3). Fort Rock Period occupation is recognized in both Component 1, dated to about 11,000 cal. BP, and Component 2, dated from roughly 10,500 to 8500 cal. BP (Connolly and Jenkins 1999).

A storage pit identified with Paulina Lake Component 1 was roughly one meter in diameter and 45 centimeters deep. Grass pollen and starch granules suggest that this pit was probably grass-lined; other pollens included mock orange (*Philadelphus*) and willowweed (*Onagraceae*) (Connolly and Jenkins 1999:103). Associated artifacts include Windust and foliate points, bifaces, expedient flake tools, and an end scraper.

Paulina Component 2 comprised the majority of cultural deposits from the site. Excavations clearly defined the circumference of a small elongated wickiup or tepee-like structure with a well-defined hearth near the center. Nearby semi-circular spaces cleared of stone suggest the presence of additional houses, but architectural elements were not preserved. The extant structure was roughly five meters long and four meters wide. It was surrounded by stout posts up to 20 centimeters in diameter but does not appear to have had an excavated floor. Radiocarbon determinations on three of the posts indicate the structure was built ca. 9500 cal. BP. Macrobotanical and pollen analysis of the hearth identified chokecherry (*Prunus* cf. *emarginata*), bulrush (*Scirpus* sp.), sedge (*Cyperaceae*), an unidentified nutlet, possible edible tissue, hazelnut (*Corylus*), salmonberry or blackberry (*Rubus*), lomatium (*Apiaceae*), and a variety of herbs, in addition to various woods used for fuel. Besides the usual projectile points (Windust and foliate types, many with edge-ground stems) and bifaces, the assemblage is distinguished by a rich array of cobble-stone tools, including ground, battered, scratched, and pecked abraders, hammerstones, mauls, girdled stones, a plummet stone, handstones, and grinding slabs. Protein residues of rabbit, bison, bear, deer, and possibly mountain sheep were detected on chipped stone tools (Williams and Fagan 1999).

Component 2 at Paulina Lake clearly represents a summer base camp, at which a broad range of plants and animals were processed. The surrounding environment appears to have been biotically rich and plant life was diverse. The artifact assemblage is likewise rich and diverse, the two sets of factors suggesting that people stayed at the site for a good portion of the summer and conducted many different kinds of activities while there. Though the site is located in a caldera that in later periods was visited primarily to quarry obsidian for trade, during the Fort Rock Period quarrying was chiefly a secondary activity, for the purpose of replacing chipped stone tools broken or worn down during a long summer season of hunting, gathering, and food processing. Most of the abundant discarded tools here were made of nonlocal obsidian that originated at sources to the south, primarily in the Fort Rock basin. Notably, the summer residential use of Newberry Caldera during the Fort Rock Period is contemporary with and complementary to the apparent late fall-through-winter residential use of caves in the adjacent Fort Rock basin. Together these sites suggest a relatively stable resident population in the Paulina-Fort Rock area, in marked contrast to the more highly mobile and broadly dispersed foragers typical of the early Holocene.

Buffalo Flat Bunny Pits (35LK1180, 35LK1881, 35LK2076, 35LK2095). Four sites on Buffalo Flat, near the east end of the Fort Rock basin (Oetting

1993, 1994a), yielded cultural remains ranging in age from ca. 11,500 to 8900 cal. BP, placing them within the Fort Rock Period. Two sites (35LK1881 and 35LK2076) produced pit features filled with datable charcoal and thousands of rabbit bones. These hearths or ovens ranged in size from small (two feet in diameter) to very large (8 by 10 feet across). Radiocarbon dates associated with the cooking pits produced ages from about 11,500 to 8900 cal. BP. Sparse stone tool assemblages included Western Stemmed projectile points, bifaces, cores, utilized flakes, mano and metate fragments, and grooved abraders. More than 14,000 bones and fragments were recovered from one site, 10,000 from inside a single large pit and the remaining 4,000 from surrounding deposits. At least 98% of the identifiable bones are jackrabbit. Unlike cottontails, jackrabbits do not burrow, and are highly susceptible to being driven into long nets by large groups of communal drivers. Rabbit drives were a favored technique of the Paiute, Shoshone, and other groups who occupied the Great Basin at the time of historic contact, and the Buffalo Flat sites indicate a very early start date for the mass processing and cooking necessarily associated with such large scale, organized drives (Oetting 1993:673).

Ethnographic accounts detail the importance of rabbit drives in both the economic and social life of ethnographic period Great Basin Shoshoneans (Steward 1938; Fowler 1992:77–78). Beyond providing meat for immediate consumption, rabbits caught in large nets provided fur strips for the production of warm rabbit-skin blankets, which were needed as both clothing and bedding during the cold winters. The drives drew large crowds of hunters and their families from long distances, providing an opportunity for a generally week-long festival or *fandango* during which people danced, arranged marriages, gambled, traded, and exchanged information vital to their survival. The evidence from Buffalo Flat suggests that such gatherings have been an important social and economic institution in the Northern Great Basin for some 11,000 years.

East of the Fort Rock basin is the large structural depression that is the Harney/Malheur Basin, where Malheur, Mud, and Harney lakes form an interconnected system of marsh and open water that is flanked by the Wagontire Mountains to the west, the Blue Mountains to the north, and Steens Mountain to the east. The higher elevations capture precipitation that is fed into the lakes via Silver Creek and the Silvies River from the north and the Blitzen River from the south. Throughout the era of human occupation the resulting wetlands have comprised the biotically richest locality—and most attractive year-round human habitat—to be found in the region, while the flanking highlands have offered additional warm season hunting and collecting opportunities.

Large stemmed lanceolate and Windust type points, markers of the Fort Rock Period, are known from many locations around the Harney-Malheur basin, on both modern playa surfaces and at higher elevation on a ridge quite distant from the lake (Fagan and Sage 1974). A lithic complex that included a point of Lind Coulee type, leaf-shaped points, a flaked stone crescent, and lithic flakes, has been identified from eroded contexts near an old beach line and radio-carbon dated to 9650 cal. BP (Gehr 1980). Later excavations of the Weed Lake Ditch (35HA341), Nials (35HA2828), and Biting Fly (35HA1260) sites (Wriston 2003; Branigan 2000; Bonstead 2000) by the University of Nevada-Reno (UNR) field school recovered Western Stemmed projectile points (Haskett type), stemmed point fragments, crescents, a bone bead preform, bifaces, unifaces, utilized flakes, and cores. Lithic flakes and bone were fairly common. Bone assemblages from some of these sites clearly indicate a lake-marsh orienta-tion with wetland-adapted birds, such as grebes, coots, geese, ducks, and rails, dominating the cultural faunal assemblage, as in certain contemporary sites of the Fort Rock basin to the west. Not surprisingly, rabbits, and at some sites fish, are the next most common, followed by canids (dog, coyote, wolf) and artiodactyls (deer, antelope, mountain sheep). There is no evidence of ground stone to indicate that plants were processed at these sites.

Dirty Shame Rockshelter (35ML65). Dirty Shame Rockshelter, located on Antelope Creek several miles above its confluence with the Owyhee River (a tributary of the Columbia/Snake river system) in Oregon's extreme southeast corner, was visited repeatedly from 10,700 cal. BP into the late Holocene (fig. 2.22). Occupation began during the Fort Rock Period, represented by compo-nents labeled Zone VI and Zone V (Aikens, Cole, and Stuckenrath 1977). No constructed cultural features such as storage pits, stone-lined hearths, or houses were found there, but a clear living floor was encountered at the bottom of the excavation. Here in Zone VI, at a depth of about 16 feet (fig. 2.23), excavators found a rich archaeological deposit composed of 10 sandals and sandal frag-ments, matting, net fragments, cordage, a cut stick, a large percussion flake and many small pressure flakes, a lanceolate projectile point, mussel shell, and a flat rock that may have served as an anvil. A radiocarbon date of 10,710 cal. BP dates this "floor" to the Fort Rock Period, when the site was apparently a summer-fall base camp from which many kinds of activities were conducted. Fort Rock and Spiral Weft sagebrush bark sandals from the site have been radiocarbon dated between 9890 and 8600 cal. BP (Connolly and Barker 2004).

Left, Fig. 2.22. Dirty Shame Rockshelter under excavation
Right, Fig. 2.23. Dirty Shame Rockshelter excavation showing Fort Rock Period deposits below, later wickiup floor and burned wall stubs of the much later Boulder Village Period above.

Ecological, Technological, and Social Patterns of the Fort Rock Period. Sites of the Fort Rock Period are much more common than those of the preceding Paisley Period. The human population of the Northern Great Basin was undoubtedly much greater by Fort Rock times. The similarity of the artifacts associated with these two periods, however, as well as the sheer volume of cultural material produced during the Fort Rock Period, may also be masking earlier and not particularly distinctive Paisley Period assemblages at some sites.

Though populations were growing, people continued to be thinly dispersed across the landscape for much of the year. Subsistence involved acquiring a broad range of food items. Large game that was available included deer, mountain sheep, antelope, and bison; however, horses, camels, and other Pleistocene game were no longer available by the beginning of the Fort Rock Period. People followed seasonal rounds that took them to many varied locations, sometimes covering long distances, as shown by the common occurrence at archaeological sites of obsidian artifacts made of stone from distant sources. Winters appear to have been spent in caves and rockshelters at various locations near lowland lakes and marshes, where foraging for fresh food—migratory game animals, waterfowl, terrestrial fowl, rabbits, plants, and possibly fish—was reasonably profitable throughout the winter and early spring. While fish and waterfowl are common elements at such sites (Bedwell 1973; Bonstead 2000; Wriston 2003), there currently is no evidence of specialized fishing or fowling equipment. Crescents, though thought by some to be transverse-mounted points for hunting waterfowl, often exhibit damage and use wear that is more consistent with cutting and scraping activities (Beck and Jones 2009). They may have been used to process marsh plants such as tule, cattail, and willow, as well as animal resources. Nets could have been used in the mass harvesting of not only rabbits, as at the Buffalo Flat Bunny Pits, but also of fish and waterfowl, of course, and are known from similarly early contexts elsewhere in the Great Basin (Aikens and Madsen 1986). Cordage useful in net production has been dated as early as 12,300 cal. BP, along with rope (12,000 cal. BP) and threads (12,500 cal. BP). Clearly, the use of nets could have been an important hunting technique during the Fort Rock Period.

Some portion of people's summers was spent at higher elevations, hunting large game and collecting nuts, berries, chokecherries, roots, and seeds. While there is evidence for a small-volume storage or cache pit at the Paulina Lake site, there is no evidence to suggest large-volume storage that might indicate people were processing large quantities of extra food for winter consumption. Large-volume storage was perhaps unnecessary at this time in a landscape of abundance occupied by relatively few people. The intensive processing of rabbits in large ovens at the Fort Rock basin's Buffalo Flat Bunny Pits may attest to communal rabbit drives similar to those enjoyed by the historic Northern Paiutes, where much of the meat was immediately consumed by those involved in the hunts, while the skins were prepared and kept for later fashioning into warm robes and blankets for the cold season.

Stone tool assemblages of the Fort Rock Period are substantially larger in total number and variety of artifact types than is common in known Paisley Period assemblages. They typically include Western Stemmed point types such as Haskett, Cougar Mountain, Silver Lake, Lake Mojave, Parman, and Windust, as well as lanceolate, leaf-shaped (foliate), and Black Rock Desert concave base. Bifacially chipped stone artifacts include cores, blanks, knives, crescents, and drills. Perhaps the most notable element of these assemblages is the large number of unifacially chipped stone tools, including large, thick scrapers made of basalt (notable in contrast to obsidian-dominated tool kits in later sites), gravers with sharp little nubs, and edge-modified flakes. These tools are thought to be the multifunctional "Swiss Army Knives" of the period and offer strong evidence of the high degree of mobility involved in the characteristic lifestyle of the time. Ground stone includes the occasional hand stone (mano) and grinding slab, generally made from locally available materials. In larger assemblages, such as those at Paulina Lake, there are tabular abrading stones exhibiting deep scratches and grooves which probably result from bone, stone, and wooden toolmaking and maintenance. At least one heavily used dart shaft straightener, made of soft volcanic scoria and used to sand branch nubs off wooden shafts, was recovered from the Paisley Caves. Other artifacts from there included the butt of a willow dart or foreshaft, a wooden peg, braided sagebrush rope and cordage, and a sewing needle and threads.

The sewing gear is of particular interest to our understanding of these earliest Americans, as the ability to sew warm, close-fitting clothing was absolutely necessary to the colonization of the New World from Asia via the high and bitterly cold arctic latitudes (Turner 2002:147). It is not surprising that sewing remained an important activity for the newly arrived colonists, whose new, early postglacial American environment was still much colder than it would be later, and so it is that tiny sewing needles have been recovered not only from the Paisley Caves in Oregon but also from late Pleistocene sites in California, Washington, Idaho, and Nevada (Hicks 2004:238; Green et al. 1998:438–439; Hockett, personal communication). It is remarkable that in Paisley Cave 5, fragments of sewing threads as small as modern threads—.04 millimeters in diameter—survived some 12,500 years! The tiny bone needles and threads made of sinew, processed grass, and other fibrous plants are found along with numbers of leather scraps, suggesting that containers, form-fitting clothes, and shelters were still being made of hide in those times.

Perishable artifacts that are more definitive of the new environment and which have been recovered from caves throughout the region during the Fort Rock Period include the famous Fort Rock sagebrush bark sandals, rope, and cordage. Fort Rock-style sandals made of shredded sagebrush bark appeared by about 10,500 cal. BP and continued to approximately 9300 cal. BP, when the style was abruptly (possibly within ≤100 years) replaced by Multiple Warp and Spiral Weft sandals. Discussing this shift, Connolly and Barker (2004:250) conclude that "the technological and stylistic changes noted in basketry for this dynamic period compels us to consider the possibility that an important population change—and not simply cultural adaptation due to changing climatic factors—may have occurred in the Northern Great Basin some 9,000 years ago." Remarkably, in spite of the abundance of twined basketry from later times, little basketry is known to be contemporary with the sandals and cordage of the Fort Rock Period.

Lunette Lake Period (9,000 to 6,000 Years Ago)

The Lunette Lake Period begins well before the Mt. Mazama eruption of about 7,600 BP and concludes some 1,600 years after it. Named for a small ephemeral lake fronting the Locality III site in the south-central Fort Rock basin, this is a period of generally increasing temperature and aridity, although the climactic eruption of Mt. Mazama in the middle of the Lunette Lake Period apparently coincided with a brief localized rise in the water level of lakes and marshes that suggests an interval of cooler climate. Sediments accumulated more slowly in the Paisley Caves at about the same time, perhaps indicating some increase in local precipitation and corresponding vegetation there. Drought conditions apparently returned within a few centuries of the Mt. Mazama eruption and

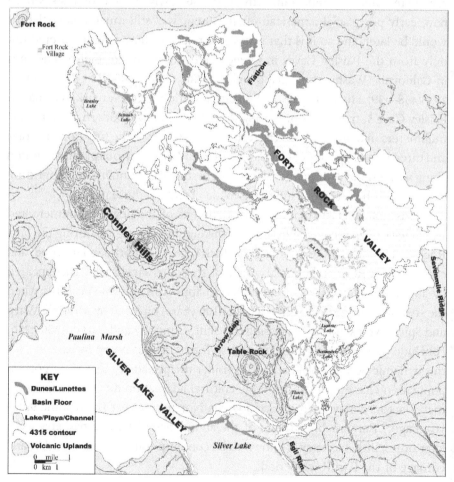

Fig. 2.24. Fort Rock channel and marsh system.

continued until about 6,000 years ago. While people probably never abandoned the area completely, they do appear to have been relatively few in number during this time, and generally quite mobile, seldom staying long at any one site.

Archaeological sites spanning much of the Lunette Lake period are somewhat difficult to find, although not truly rare; they are predominantly hunting and foraging camps of brief occupation. Important sites include Locality III, small campsites along the Silver Lake-Fort Rock channel system, the Connley and Paisley Caves, and Paulina Lake. In far southeastern Oregon, Skull Creek Dunes, Catlow and Roaring Springs Caves in the Catlow Valley, and Dirty Shame Rockshelter in the Owyhee Uplands also saw occupation at this time.

Locality III (35LK3035) and Small Campsites of the Silver Lake-Fort Rock Channel System. At various times during the Lunette Lake Period, water draining from foothills to the west and south overflowed Paulina Marsh and Silver Lake at the southern end of the Fort Rock basin and coursed around the south end of the Connley Hills, then north through an extensive channel system that extended all the way to paleo Lake Beasley near the modern village of Fort Rock in the northwest corner of the basin (fig. 2.24). On these occasions higher-elevation runoff flooded many blown-out playas and ponds along the way—including Lunette Lake—and turned the desert into fertile marsh and grassland (Jenkins, Droz, and Connolly 2004).

Locality III (35LK3035) is a large site located on the north shore of the now-dry bed of Lunette Lake, named for a high curving dune formed of sediment blown up from the lakebed during alternating wet and dry spells (fig. 2.25). This dune contains the leavings of people who camped there repeatedly

Fig. 2.25. East Locus excavations at Locality III.

as silt and sand slowly accumulated. Initially investigated by Peter Mehringer and William Cannon (1994) and later by the UO field school (Jenkins 2000; Jenkins, Droz, and Connolly 2004), Locality III is composed of three dense scatters of chipped stone tools, flaking debris, broken ground stone artifacts, and small bone fragments that were once contained in the dune but dropped onto an underlying hardpan surface as wind eroded the sand. It is an excellent example of the short-term occupation sites typical of the Silver Lake-Fort Rock Channel environmental setting, where advantageous localities were visited again and again over thousands of years. Stratigraphic profiles tell a story of alternating wet and dry lake phases, each marked by varying quantities of silt and sand (Mehringer and Cannon 1994; Droz 1997).

Locality III has been dated by 19 radiocarbon assays ranging from 11,890 to 3580 cal. BP, but the focus of interest here is the Lunette Lake Period hearths, which are dated between 8600 and 6300 cal. BP (fig. 2.26). They are small and shallow and generally surrounded by very thin scatters of stone flakes, the occasional tool (variously foliate points, bifaces, scrapers and utilized flakes, ground stone slabs and hand stones), bones of young rabbit and waterfowl, and egg shells (Jenkins 2000; O'Grady 2004; Singer 2004). Occupations could not have been for more than a few days at a time, since stone tools must be constantly resharpened with use and the amount of obsidian debris around the hearths—a direct indicator of occupation length or activity intensity—is unusually small. During the Lunette Lake Period, Locality III was repeatedly occupied during the spring and summer, as can be inferred from the remains of young rabbits caught from the grasslands surrounding the channel system and waterfowl eggs collected from the lakeshores. People may have been moving

Fig. 2.26. Lunette Lake Period hearth at Locality III, dated to 8580 cal. BP.

every few days from one lake or pond to another along the Silver Lake-Fort Rock channel system, hunting rabbits, harvesting waterfowl and their eggs, and collecting seeds and roots. Though fish must have been present, there is no evidence of fishing equipment or storage features to indicate they were caught or collected in appreciable numbers during the Lunette Lake Period.

In addition to Locality III there are many small campsites located in the dunes along the Silver Lake-Fort Rock channel system in the Fort Rock Valley. Other nearby sites containing small hearths dating from the Lunette Lake period include Locality I, Locality II, Bowling Dune (35LK2992), Bergen (35LK3175), Kelly's Site, GP-2 (35LK2778), and DJ Ranch (35LK2758). In every case, small quantities of chipped and ground stone tools, stone flakes, and bone indicate that Lunette Lake Period occupations—as at Locality III—were generally very brief, perhaps lasting only a day or two at a time. Projectile points typical of the period tend to be leaf-shaped foliates, with occasional large side-notched points showing up just after the 7600 cal. BP eruption of Mt. Mazama. As already emphasized, while sites in the dunes and marshes were frequently occupied, each stay was of only a few days duration. Rabbit and waterfowl bones are the most common faunal remains, although bones of fish and large mammals (including mountain sheep, deer, and pronghorn) indicate that these were also taken when available. Ground stone is present but generally only in small quantities. Seeds, pollen, and starch granules recovered from soil samples indicate that grass and various weed seeds such as *Chenopodium* and wada, and edible root crops such as camas and biscuit root, were collected and processed at the sites (Prouty 1994, 2004).

Despite previous speculations to the contrary (Bedwell 1973), there is no evidence that the eruption of Mt. Mazama–which took place during the Lunette Lake Period–disrupted human settlement in the Fort Rock basin for any appreciable length of time (Jenkins 2000:101; Mehringer and Cannon 1994:323), although human use of areas to the north and west, as at the Paulina Lake site, was significantly altered in places where ash deposits were very deep. Plants, animals, and people of the Fort Rock basin seem to have adapted quickly to the new layer of ash, which was soon blown up into dunes and sand sheets that surrounded the periodically dry floors of small lakes and ponds throughout the region. The fact that post-Mazama hearths dating from about 7500 to 6200 cal. BP are commonly found buried in silt and sand blown from the floors of nearby playas shows that people who may have fled the terrifying eruptions returned soon after they ceased.

Paisley (35LK3400) and Connley Caves (35LK50). The cave sites of the greater region also saw only very brief visits during the Lunette Lake Period. Small hearths surrounded by very scanty quantities of obsidian flakes and small mammal bones were encountered in each of the Paisley Caves. Located just below the Mazama ash, the sagebrush charcoal of their fires has consistently dated between 8400 and 8500 cal. BP. A small fragment of tule basket recovered in Paisley Cave 2 and dated to 8480 cal. BP provides evidence for the use of that technology during this period.

At the Connley Caves, the "Transitional Phase" identified by Bedwell (1973) corresponds to the Lunette Lake Period as identified here. He dated it between 8630 and 7990 cal. BP, based on three samples of charcoal from just below the Mazama ash. Citing changes in the use of fuel wood from pine to juniper and a general reduction in the quantity of cultural debris, he reported this as a period of increased temperatures and decreased populations. Jenkins, Connolly, and Aikens (2004) subsequently noted that projectile points in the Lunette Lake component at the Connley Caves were predominantly foliate types that were almost always broken, indicating they had been brought to the site complete, discarded when they were damaged, and replaced with new points that had been made at previously visited obsidian sources and carried along. They see this stone tool pattern as evidence for brief site occupations related to hunting of local game. High mobility appears in many cases to have been an adaptation to lowered precipitation and reduced plant diversity throughout large portions of the region both before and after the Mt. Mazama ashfall.

Paulina Lake (35DS34). At Paulina Lake, in the caldera of Newberry Volcano north of the Fort Rock basin and directly downwind of the Mt. Mazama eruption, volcanic ash fell far more heavily than it did in the Fort Rock basin, and covered much of the landscape to a depth of three to four feet. In the Newberry caldera the Lunette Lake Period is marked by a lack of the houses and stable occupation for which the preceding Fort Rock Period site at Paulina is most famous (Connolly 1999). Instead, a reduction in the diversity of artifact types, and an increase in projectile points and preforms, is evidence that during the Lunette Lake Period the Paulina Lake area was occupied for briefer periods of time than previously. People carried out a smaller range of tasks, mainly hunting around the lakes and replenishing their stocks of projectile points and bifacial preforms from the local obsidian flows. In that setting, the deep and highly permeable Mazama ashfall had the effect of sequestering ground water far enough below the surface to reduce plant productivity and thereby game density, and forced subsequent populations to lead more mobile lives, moving frequently and staying only briefly in any given locality.

Ecological, Technological, and Social Patterns of the Lunette Lake Period. The transition from the Fort Rock to the Lunette Lake Period at roughly 9000 cal. BP in the Northern Great Basin was comparable in many ways to a transition from the Windust to the Cascade Phase that occurred on the Columbia Plateau at the same time (Ames 1988). Cultural assemblages of the Fort Rock Period were often rich in both density and diversity of artifact types—the most notable specimens technologically being the Fort Rock sagebrush bark sandals—so much so that Cressman (1986:122) referred to this period as "the climax of cultural development in the Fort Rock basin." If that was the case, the following Lunette Lake Period was the antithesis to "cultural development." Projectile points continued to be predominantly leaf-shaped, and were commonly found in sites containing only small game such as rabbits and waterfowl. The large well-formed scrapers and tiny gravers commonly encountered in earlier assemblages are for the most part gone from Lunette Lake assemblages, replaced only by the occasional utilized flake. Ground stone tools are common, though not overly abundant, and are not generally well shaped, perhaps indicating they were used briefly and left behind. Hearths are small, shallow, simple affairs scooped from the ground and prone to rapid burial by blowing dust. Perishable artifacts such as those seen earlier in the caves are not to be found in the open sites that comprise the main record of this period.

The Lunette Lake Period was a relatively dry time when many of the larger Northern Great Basin lakes disappeared, only occasionally refilling during brief wet intervals. Sites were temporary hunting and foraging camps found primarily on the margins of permanent lakes, such as the Paulina Lake site, and near intermittent/seasonal lakes and ponds, like the Locality III site. No houses or storage pits are known from this period. Population mobility was high; the human response to generally dry conditions and reduced biological diversity was to focus briefly on locally productive resources, then move on. People moved from camp to camp, hunting rabbits and waterfowl in the lowland grasslands and marshes, and collecting waterfowl eggs, camas, and small seeds in season. In forested zones at higher elevations they hunted deer and elk, moving camps frequently to maintain adequate levels of economic yield. This highly mobile adaptation to both decreased moisture and decreased biotic productivity was successful, though it undoubtedly slowed growth in human populations; less mobile or vigorous members of a group (infants, the sick, and the elderly) would have been under intense pressure to keep up, and mortality rates must have been high among those elements (Jenkins, Connolly, and Aikens 2004b:8).

New technological concepts and artifact styles appeared during this time of high mobility and increased interregional interaction. While foliate projectile points continue throughout the period, Northern Side-notched projectile points were added just after the climactic eruption of Mt. Mazama at about 7600 cal. BP. Fort Rock-style sandals disappear, and are replaced by Multiple Warp and Spiral Weft sandals. Decorated twined basketry is added to the inventory of perishable artifacts. Extreme mobility—sometimes over long distances, as people moved out of biologically impoverished areas and into more productive zones—probably stimulated both cultural interactions and population shifts.

Bergen Period (6,000 to 3,000 Years Ago)

Beginning roughly 6,000 years ago, the Bergen Period is named after the largest known middle Holocene village site in the Fort Rock basin. This period was one of moderate temperatures and increased precipitation. Water levels began to rise in lakes, marshes, and ponds throughout the Northern Great Basin and adjacent Klamath Basin about 6200 cal. BP (Aikens and Jenkins 1994b; Sampson 1985). The pollen record from Diamond Pond, at the base of Steens Mountain in far east-central Oregon, indicates increasing precipitation as measured by more sagebrush and grass pollen, while at the same time reduced pollen levels from plants that grow on salty playa sediments show that previously exposed lakebeds were under water. Additionally, the low level of juniper pollen suggests suppression of this cold-intolerant tree by somewhat colder winters (Wigand 1987). This cooler, wetter climate dramatically increased the biotic productivity of lowland lakes and marshes, and no doubt helped set the stage for the development of stable settlements. The hallmark of the Bergen Period was the construction of houses and large storage pits on the fringes of marshes throughout the region.

Bergen Site (35LK3175). University of Oregon excavations at this site, near the western edge of the Fort Rock basin, began in 1998 and continued through 2000. Initially, auger holes as deep as 10 feet were spaced at 150-foot intervals along the crest of a great dune that curved around the eastern and northern edges of an old lakebed designated Paleo Lake Beasley, verifying the continuous distribution of cultural materials along the length of the dune for a distance of at least 4000 feet. While projectile point types indicated occupations extending back into the early Holocene, the vast majority of the site occupation occurred during the latter half of the middle Holocene (6000 to 3000 cal. BP), when Elko and Northern Side-notched points were most common. Investigations indicate there were at least two periods of unusually intense occupation. The first dated between 6200 and 5100 cal. BP, and the second between 4200 and 3700 cal. BP (Jenkins, Droz, and Connolly 2004).

Excavation of one complete house and partial excavation of a second revealed multiple occupation floors within depressions roughly one foot deep and thirteen feet in diameter (fig. 2.27). These depressions were surrounded by postholes up to six inches in diameter. The lack of evidence for interior support posts suggests these were wickiup structures similar to the substantial Paiute winter houses known ethnographically from the region, which had walls framed with light poles that could be bent inward and lashed at the top to form a domed or angled roof with a smoke hole at the center (fig. 2.28).Charcoal recovered from soil flotation samples indicate the superstructures were made of willow, as was typical of ethnographic Northern Paiute examples. The exteriors were probably covered with bulrush or grass bundles, or twined mats.

Fig. 2.27. Main house block excavation at the Bergen site.

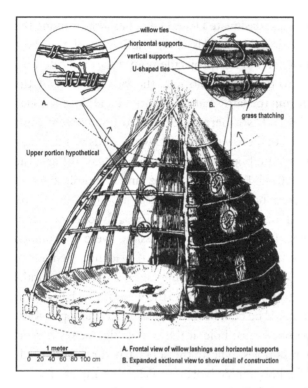

Fig. 2.28. Reconstruction drawing of pole-and-thatch wickiup from Dirty Shame Rockshelter.

Activity areas within the structure included places for food preparation, cooking, sleeping, storage, and stone tool working (Helzer 2001, 2004).

Bulrush, goosefoot, wada, and saltbush seeds along with tiny tui chub bones (fig. 2.29 a–d), were recovered in large quantities from the house floors, along with waterfowl bones (Helzer 2004; O'Grady 2004). Central fireplaces indicate winter occupations, as do the presence of late season seeds, bones of mature migratory waterfowl but few or no egg shells, and deer, elk, mountain sheep, and pronghorn bones. Artifact assemblages included Western Stemmed (1%), foliate (1%), Northern Side-notched (35%), Elko (44%), Gatecliff (8%), and Humboldt (4%) projectile points. There were also bifaces, cores of obsidian from the nearby Cougar Mountain source, scrapers, unifaces, drills, and net weights of stone, along with bone fish gorges/hooks, elk antler billets, large bone awls, bone flaking tools, and ground stone metates, manos, hopper mortars, and pestles. Beads of shell, stone, and bone were also well represented. Abalone (*Haliotis*) shell pendants from Pacific waters, and *Olivella dama* shell beads from the Gulf of California indicate long distance trade extending to southern California and northern Mexico (Largaespada 2006; Bottman 2006; Jenkins et al. 2004).

The Bergen site is located within the normal overwintering grounds of an enormous regional mule deer herd that continues to populate the area today. Pronghorn are known to accompany the deer in large numbers as heavy winter storms drive both from higher elevations surrounding the Fort Rock basin. Elk and mountain sheep bones in marsh-side occupations, including the Bergen site, show that these animals, too, occupied the low, timbered slopes surrounding the marshes, probably coming out to feed in their fringing grasslands as winter storms eased. Everything points to the inhabitants' intentional placement of their site where it would give them ready access to marsh resources (fish, bulrush, and waterfowl) and migratory large game during the winter, when other fresh foods were often difficult for hunter-gatherers to come by and the animals were most susceptible to predation.

Big M (35LK2737). The Big M site is a small village or hamlet located east of Thorn Lake, near the southern end of the Silver Lake-Fort Rock channel system. It lies at the foot of a large tilted fault block that divides the Fort Rock and Summer Lake basins and is not far from Silver Lake itself. In this geographical position, Big M occupants had immediate access to the plants, animals, and other natural resources of both the wet lowlands and the drier

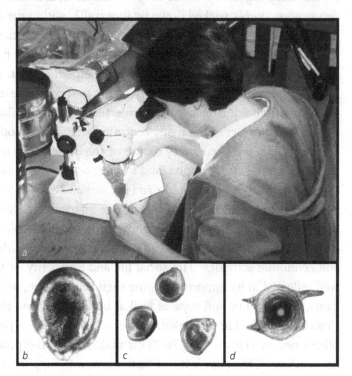

Fig. 2.29. Paleobotanical analysis. a, Marge Helzer picking seeds, charcoal, bone, and lithics from Bergen site soil flotation samples; b, chenopod seed; c, wada seeds; d, Tui chub (minnow) vertebra.

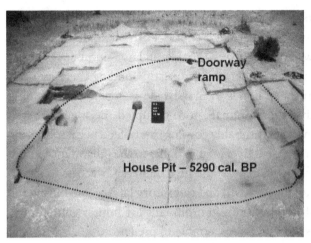

Doorway
ramp

House Pit – 5290 cal. BP

Fig. 2.30. Large house pit floor at the Big M site.

highlands, all within an easy day's walk. Situated next to a small pond near the edge of a marsh, this site was occupied most commonly between about 5600 and 3700 cal. BP. The three structures investigated there include the largest pithouse known in the Fort Rock basin, roughly 20 feet by 17 feet across and 1.5 feet deep (fig. 2.30). While the two smaller houses had very shallow floor depressions simply packed down by foot traffic within the confined space of the walls, the large one was clearly excavated into the ancient lake bar underlying the site. It contained an interior hearth and a cache pit filled with tools and debris, including a basalt tubular stone pipe fragment, an atlatl weight, a highly polished rectangular bone spoon bit, two complete manos, a complete pestle, a Humboldt Concave base projectile point, and utilized flakes.

Clear indicators of the many centuries over which people came to Big M, and the stable, semi-sedentary nature of the occupations lived out there, are the site's houses, storage pits, and numerous Northern Side-notched, Elko, Gatecliff Split-stem, Humboldt, and occasional Western Stemmed projectile points. There are also atlatl weights, large bifaces, an elk antler wedge, bone awls, polished bone tools of all kinds, drills, fishing hooks and net weights, and copious quantities of ground stone that represent various technological and economic activities. The social life and prosperity of the community is well reflected in its imported marine shell beads, bone, tooth, and shell pendants, bone spoons and toys, as well as bone, stone, and clay smoking pipes (Jenkins 1994a). The remarkable diversity of artifact types at this site and others nearby (Howe 1960:51–75) is undoubtedly the product of extended occupations. This high level of sedentism was supported by the intensive processing of a great diversity of fish, rabbits, waterfowl, artiodactyls, small seeds, and roots that were available in the immediate vicinity (Dean 1994; Greenspan 1994). As people moved off in spring for a round of collecting and pursuing a wider range of resources from the surrounding territory, food and generally non-portable items (things not needed for the immediately planned tasks, such as bulrush matting, bags, nets, and grinding stones) were stored in pits or hidden somewhere nearby (Jenkins 2004). A way of life much like that of the ethnographically known Harney Valley Paiutes or the nearby Klamath is suggested (Couture et al. 1986; Spier 1930).

DJ Ranch (35LK2758). DJ Ranch was another stable and long-occupied community with multiple houses, located some miles north of Big M up the same channel system and about a half mile north of the Locality III site. It was situated on the northeast side of a small blowout pond that would only have filled with water when nearby Lunette Lake overflowed. Interestingly, it is here at this shallow pond—not at the deeper lake nearby—that the strongest evidence for fishing in the Silver Lake-Fort Rock channel system marshes was found (fig. 2.31; c,d). University of Oregon field school investigations detailed five episodes of occupation at DJ Ranch (Moessner 2004), spanning most of the Bergen period, and dated to about 5600, 4600, 3700, 2980, and post-2980 cal. BP. The cultural assemblages, which varied significantly in size and content through time, included house floors, cache pits, hearths, post holes, and charcoal-stained soils. Utilitarian artifacts included Northern Side-notched, Elko Corner-notched, Gatecliff Split Stemmed, Western Stemmed, and foliate projectile points, atlatl weights, large bifacial knives, utilized flakes, bone flakers, bone awls, bone fish gorges, stone net weights, a large bone net shuttle, a fancy ground stone maul, abraders, metates, manos, mortars, and pestles. Specimens relating to social activity and long-distance connections included pieces of precious steatite, bone and shell beads that included rare *Olivella* Grooved Rectangle beads from the Channel Islands in southern California (Jenkins and Erlandson 1996), bone gaming pieces, and stone pipes.

While the intensity and length of occupations at DJ Ranch fluctuated through time, peaking around 3700 cal. BP, the site was clearly a favorite winter home over many generations. Bones collected there provide abundant evidence of the hunting of elk, deer, pronghorn, mountain sheep, rabbits, and waterfowl, as well as fishing forays throughout the marshes surrounding the site. Considering the presence of mountain sheep and evidence of them being hunted on nearby mountains, it is clear that the drier, rocky uplands surrounding the basin were also visited regularly (Singer 2004; O'Grady 2004; Paul-Mann 1994). The recovery of charred plant remains indicates the presence of juniper, which today can be found as isolated trees very sparsely scattered throughout the dunes but may have been more common there under slightly warmer and moister regimes in the past. Edible seeds and other plant parts available near the site included those of various grasses, rabbitbrush, knotweed, chenopodium, wada, bulrush, sedge, and camas. Plants brought to the site from drier upland settings included biscuitroot, chokecherry, and fruity tissues (Moessner 2004; Prouty 2004).

Winter house occupations at DJ Ranch had ceased by about 2980 cal. BP. The site continued to be used as a seasonal camp in later times, but houses, storage pits, beads, and fishing equipment are by then conspicuously absent. A prominent stratigraphic change seen in the site deposits at this time suggests a major shift in the local ecology. Post-2980 cal. BP site assemblages most commonly include very low quantities of projectile points, net weights, ground stone fragments, lithic debitage, and bone. This dramatic reduction in cultural materials is an indication that later site occupations were short-term visits.

Bowling Dune (35LK2992). Named for a cache of six large and finely shaped stone balls found there (fig. 2.32), the Bowling Dune site is located

Fig. 2.31. Artifacts from Big M and DJ Ranch sites: bone spoons; net shuttle, awls, and atlatl weight; fish gorges (hooks); and notched tabular net weights.

Fig. 2.32. Stone balls from the
Bowling Dune site.

roughly a mile and a half northwest of DJ Ranch, on a low north-south
trending dune adjacent to a blowout pond. Several living surfaces or processing floors and hearth features were encountered at the site, but it is most
important as a cache location where people made large-volume storage pits.
Bowling Dune is quite isolated from other sites in the area, presumably to
hide the caches from people who might raid them while the owners were
absent. Hiding food and equipment was a common practice of the ethnographic period Klamath, Modoc, and Northern Paiutes in this region, and
would have been just as necessary during the middle Holocene when many
visitors from outside the area regularly visited the Fort Rock basin (Jenkins
2004; Kelly 1932; Ray 1963; Sobel and Bettles 2000).

Cache pits are common in Bergen Period sites throughout the Northern
Great Basin, being found at Locality III, Big M, DJ Ranch, Bowling Dune,
the Bergen site, Dirty Shame Rockshelter (Hanes 1988), and the Dunn site
(Musil 1995). Bowling Dune differs only in that caching appears to have been
its main purpose. Five pits were encountered there, three of which appear
by their arrangement to have been constructed at the same time. Cache pits
of the region are commonly 3.5 to 8.5 feet in diameter and roughly two feet
deep, but at Bowling Dune the largest was ten feet long, seven feet wide,
two feet deep, and capable of holding 140 cubic feet of food and equipment
(fig. 2.33b). Thousands of tui chub bones were recovered from one of the
pits (Jenkins 2004:137; fig. 2.33c). Other indications of food storage included
elevated quantities of grass and cattail pollen, and charred chenopodium,
knotweed, camas, and lomatium tissues, indicating transport to this lowland

Fig. 2.33. Cache pits at the Bowling Dune site.

site from the surrounding uplands. The six finely made, size-graded stone balls for which the site is named were obviously a set of high-value items that were well hidden when the owners left them behind. Radiocarbon dating indicates the Bowling Dune pits were constructed between roughly 5000 and 5500 cal. BP. Projectile points found in and around them included foliates, Northern Side-notched, Elko series, and Gatecliff Split-stem. Occasional Western Stemmed specimens found there no doubt derive from earlier visits to the area (Jenkins 2004). Bone tools and shell beads, while present, were not common, and the Bowling Dune site appears to have been used predominantly as an isolated cache location.

Nightfire Island (4SK4). In the basin of Lower Klamath Lake near the westernmost edge of the Great Basin cultural zone, the Nightfire Island site is located in historic Modoc territory, which straddles the Oregon-California border. An extensive series of radiocarbon dates, 27 in all, demonstrates continuous occupation of the site throughout the last ca. 7,000 years, spanning both the Bergen Period and the subsequent Boulder Village period (which will be treated in later pages). The many dates show that people returned to the spot consistently over millennia, although occasional gaps of a few hundred years suggest intervals of non-use when lake waters may have been too high or too low (Sampson 1985).

The history of occupation at Nightfire Island reflects changing uses of the locality by its human visitors. Lower Klamath Lake, shown by high shorelines and diatomaceous clays to have once been considerably larger and deeper, had shrunk to approximately its historic size by shortly after 7,600 years ago, as shown by the fact that the basal clay layer at the site, deposited in a swampy shoreline, contained a lens of volcanic ash from the Mount Mazama eruption. Occupation began sometime after the Mount Mazama eruption, initially as a seasonal waterfowl hunting station, and eventually as a more permanent settlement. Because the site was located on a low rise within the marshes fringing Lower Klamath Lake, it was sensitive to minor fluctuations in water level, and the nature (and permanence) of occupations throughout the millennia mirror these fluctuations. The earlier part of the site's occupation is ascribable in the main to the Bergen Period, between about 6,000 and 3,000 years ago.

During the site's history, considerable efforts were made to raise the level of the main occupation area by the intermittent deposition of basaltic rubble fill. Rubble deposits first appear by about 7,000 years ago, probably as an attempt to stabilize the swampy shoreline, but tons of basalt rubble were added between about 5,500 and 5,000 years ago, when the site was first used as a residential center. Houses were built on this artificial platform, but were abandoned as the rubble platform sank into the underlying muck, or water levels continued to rise, or both. The best preserved house from this time had a central hearth radiocarbon dated at ca. 4,700 years ago, within a shallowly excavated floor about 3.5 meters in diameter. A pole framework, probably covered with matting, was set back from the excavated floor to provide an interior perimeter bench. Over later millennia, use of the site fluctuated between a sustained settlement and a temporary camp, in response to changing marsh conditions.

Between about 4400 and 2000 cal. BP, overlapping the transition from the Bergen to the Boulder Village periods, substantial pithouses were built on this elevated site, as indicated by clay-lined floors and post holes. During the period of house construction, the platform continued to be augmented with stone rubble. The site at this time probably functioned as a winter village and year-around base of operations. Two cemetery areas with the remains of 45 individuals, some partially cremated in an apparent foreshadowing of historic Modoc custom, came into use toward the end of this period. Arrow points found among human remains suggest that deaths due to violent raids occurred late in the site's history (Boulder Village Period). Only lightly built structures seem to have been made during the final period of occupation, and apparently the site served once again as primarily a warm season fishing/hunting/gathering camp until it passed out of use about 1,000 years ago.

The bones of coots, grebes, scaups, mallards, mergansers, and geese were varyingly common throughout the accumulated deposits. Marked fluctuations in the ratio between ducks that feed by diving in deep water, and those that dabble in shallow marshy settings, suggest a complex history of changes in the local environment. Common mammals included elk, deer, antelope, mountain sheep, jackrabbit, cottontail, mink, otter, coyote, and dog. Bison occurred during the middle period of occupation. Fish bones were found in some abundance, virtually all of the identified sample being tui chubs of the minnow family. Fish bones were best represented in the later part of the occupation, though some traces go back to early times. A broad range of additional bird and mammalian species was represented by limited numbers of recovered specimens. Other than the bison, the faunal remains are of animals that can be found even today in the immediate or near vicinity of Nightfire Island.

The artifact assemblage from Nightfire Island was extensive. Plant food processing is attested by numerous ground stone mortars and pestles, flat milling slabs and handstones, and hopper mortar bases. Hunting technology included an older complex of atlatl dart points identified as Northern Side-notched, Humboldt, Pinto, Elko, and Gold Hill types; and a younger complex of small arrow points belonging to the Rose Spring, Gunther, and Siskiyou or Desert Side-notched types. Fishing technology included grooved stones that were probably sinkers or net weights, and bone prongs for fish spears. Numerous cores and abundant flakes of obsidian, along with pebble hammerstones, give evidence of a well-developed stoneworking industry. Stone mauls, antler wedges, stone drills, and serrated cutting tools, along with such products as handles and beveled bone points, attest the making of wood, bone, and antler artifacts. Eyed needles and bone awls, along with stone flake scrapers and knives, tell of hides being worked and sewn.

Analysis of some 300 projectile points by X-ray fluorescence shows that the Nightfire Island people used obsidian from sources 20 to 35 miles south in the Medicine Lake Highlands, 35 to 85 miles northeast in the region of Sycan Marsh and Tucker Hill, 110 to 120 miles east-northeast in the Warner Mountains and at Quartz Mountain (Hughes 1985). Some 80% of the Northern Side-notched points, generally the earliest type in the sample,

were of southern obsidian from the Medicine Lake Highlands. The somewhat younger Elko points also included many specimens of Medicine Lake
Highland obsidian, but 37% were made of stone from more distant sources to
the north and east. The youngest specimens, arrow points of the Gunther series, showed a return to the pattern of the Northern Side-notched specimens,
with 81% made of southern obsidian from the Medicine Lake sources. This
evidence of shifting obsidian procurement clearly indicates greater contact by
Nightfire Islanders with areas to the north and east during the middle period,
prior to the time the bow and arrow were introduced. This pattern was fairly
well duplicated at the Drews Valley sites near Lakeview, Oregon. It is likely
that changing climate and ecological landscapes led to settlement shifts, resulting in changing proximity between "cultural centers" and critical obsidian
sources (Connolly and Jenkins 1997).

   During the final centuries of occupation (which carried over into the
Boulder Village Period), when Nightfire Islanders were once again depending heavily on Medicine Lake Highland obsidian, they also became
notably involved in the exchange of seashells and finely crafted stone pipes
from the west and south. This development presages the extensive trading
network maintained by the Modoc and Klamath in early historic times,
when it reached as far west as the Pacific coast, and as far north as the
great summer rendezvous at The Dalles of the Columbia River. More is
said about Nightfire Island's broader relationships in Chapter 6.

   **Drews Valley—the Drews Creek (35LK2109) and La Sere (35LK2101)
sites.** Drews Valley, west of Lakeview, is a broad meadow and shrub-steppe
setting located on the western periphery of the Northern Great Basin at
the Klamath Basin/Goose Lake Basin hydrologic divide. At an elevation
of 5,000 feet, this valley supports rich root grounds, marshy springs, a
meandering stream, and cool groves of aspens, and was a favorite spring
and summer village location of the Modoc. Oregon Highway 140 passes
along the lower slopes of the valley at the transition between well drained,
rocky, sagebrush covered slopes—where root crops such as epos, lomatiums, and onions were collected—and the lower, marshier meadows surrounding willow-lined Drews Creek with a multitude of smaller seeps and
springs where camas and seed-bearing forbs and grasses were abundant.
The hills surrounding Drews Valley are covered with juniper, mountain
mahogany, and pine. Creek mouths are choked with picturesque aspen
groves, an ideal setting for summer villages. Survey, test excavations, and

large-scale investigations conducted between 1986 and 1993 as part of a major highway improvement project, produced a wealth of information about this previously little studied region. The Drews Creek and La Sere sites, located on gentle slopes at the valley edge, provided the earliest evidence for the collection and processing of important root crops.

The Drews Creek site (35LK2109) is a very large complex located at the north end of Drews Valley (Jenkins and Norris 2000a). Its many diverse components include temporary campsites, hearths, root baking ovens, a large storage pit, obsidian cobble quarrying and chipping stations, and even a historic logging camp (fig. 2.34). Projectile points include Windust, foliate, Northern Side-notched, Humboldt Concave Base, Gatecliff Split-stem, Elko, and Rose Spring, indicating that this idyllic spot was repeatedly occupied throughout perhaps the last 13,000 years (fig. 2.35), while a composite charcoal sample dated at about 4000 cal. BP matches the preponderance of middle Holocene or Bergen Period (6000–3000 cal. BP) projectile points at the site. Cobble cores, early- to middle-stage biface fragments, and many thousands of obsidian flakes attest to the quarrying of local Drews Creek/Butcher Flat obsidian nodules found in the stream bed. The few faunal remains recovered indicate an early emphasis on small game (squirrels, rabbits, and marmots) with increasing evidence of large game hunting (deer and mountain sheep) through time. A metate, a ground stone paddle, and a pumice abrader attest to the preparation of food (seeds, roots and possibly nuts) and production or maintenance of wooden tools such as digging sticks, atlatls, and dart shafts.

The La Sere site (35LK2101) is located on a broad and gentle southeast-facing slope in sagebrush-steppe just below the juniper timber line, and well above the moist bottomlands a few miles to the west (Jenkins and

Fig. 2.34. Root oven (*left*) and root cache pit (*right*) at the Drews Creek site.

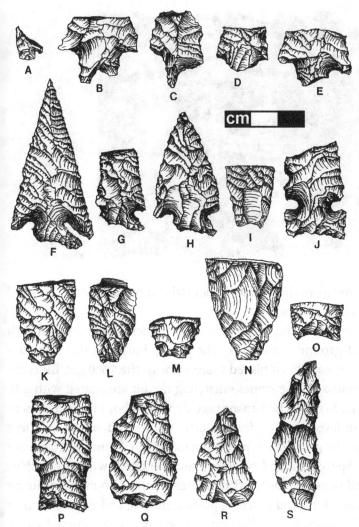

Fig. 2.35. Projectile points and bifaces from the Drews Creek site.

Norris 2000b). Located in a low mound of dark sandy loam deposited long ago by water, and now surrounded by rocky root grounds abounding in lomatiums of different kinds, the site location is something of an anomaly, as it is not located particularly close to any modern water source. Still, the density of tools suggests that La Sere was a favorite campsite perhaps because the island of deep sandy soil within the rocky root grounds made this a good place to set up temporary housekeeping while the women collected roots in the spring and seeds and small mammals (squirrels, gophers, voles, and marmots) in the summer. The men could easily have

Fig. 2.36.
Excavations at the
La Sere site.

hunted large game from this site, and materials for building structures and firewood were close at hand.

A human burial was encountered in a stone-encircled pit capped with a low mound of ground stone slabs. The person buried in this elaborate feature appears to have been placed there prior to the 7600 cal. BP eruption of Mt. Mazama, as the stones encircling the pit are coated with ash. Excavations at La Sere reached an average depth of about three feet, penetrating the thin layer of Mt. Mazama ash at a mean depth of two feet (fig. 2.36). Projectile points were predominantly Elko, Humboldt Concave Base, Gatecliff Split-stem, and Northern Side-notched, with a few older foliate and Windust points included at greater depths. Ground stone items were common and included mortars, pestles, manos, and metates. Other artifacts related to plant food collection and preparation are curved scrapers, which match the description of tools used by the Northern Paiute (Couture et al. 1986) to scrape dirt and skins from roots (fig. 2.37), and large basalt flake and core tools. The use-damaged edges of these items suggest that they were woodworking implements, perhaps employed in the production and resharpening of digging sticks. Radiocarbon dates range from 4485 to 2050 cal. BP, although stratigraphic associations and projectile point types indicate the site was occasionally occupied during pre-Mazama times as well. The evidence indicates that La Sere is one of the earliest documented spring root collection camps in the Northern Great Basin/Klamath Basin area (Jenkins 2000).

A major shift in emphasis toward increased harvesting of root crops may have contributed to the appearance of the two-village (winter and spring/summer) settlement pattern that was prevalent in the region at the time of Euroamerican contact. It appears from the evidence at the Drews Creek and La Sere sites that this transition occurred during the Bergen Period between about 4500 and 3700 cal. BP. Citing evidence collected from these sites and many more in the Fort Rock basin 100 miles to the north, Jenkins and Connolly (2000:376; Jenkins 2000) postulate that the shift to a two-village pattern may have been, in part, a product of increased productivity in root crops related to warmer, wetter springs,

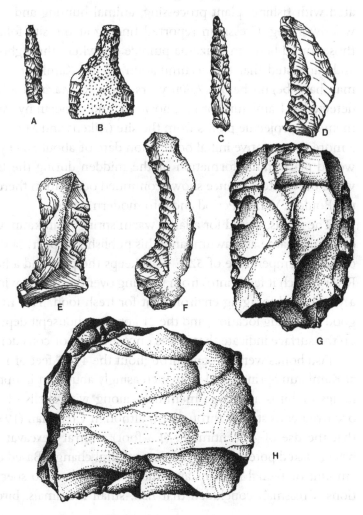

Fig. 2.37. La Sere site examples of artifacts commonly found in root ground sites.

and in part due to gradually increasing human populations. Those who harvested, dried, and stored more of the available spring root crops for use the following winter would have had an advantage over those who continued to count heavily on harvests of late summer and fall resources such as small seeds, small mammals, and large game, which occasionally would not materialize. This scenario is not proven but is a good example of the kinds of testable hypotheses that archaeologists work with to advance our knowledge of the past.

Kamkaun (Kawumkan) Springs (35KL9). Excavations by Cressman (1956) at Kawumkan Springs Midden, on the lower Sprague River in the heart of Klamath territory, recovered stone, bone, and antler tools associated with fishing, plant processing, animal hunting and processing, and woodworking. Cressman reported finding at the site foliate points like those found beneath Mazama pumice elsewhere throughout the region, and suggested that the accumulation of the Kamkaun Springs midden may have begun before 7,600 years ago. No Mazama ash stratum was detected at Kamkaun Springs, however, and obsidian hydration measurements on projectile points from the site (Aikens and Minor 1978) suggest a more conservative initial occupation date of about 5000 years ago. This would place initial formation of the midden during the Bergen Period, while other site evidence shows continued occupation thereafter through the Boulder Village Period and into modern times.

The site is named for a large warm spring (Kamkaun; Cressman rendered the name as Kawumkan in his published report) said to maintain a constant temperature of 52°F. This keeps the pool and adjacent Sprague River (which it feeds into) from freezing over during the winter, providing a year-round foraging environment for fresh food. This made the spot a good wintering location, and the 21 apparent housepit depressions visible on the surface indicate that it was once a village of considerable size.

Fish bones were present throughout the 4 to 5 feet of midden deposit at Kamkaun Springs, and were increasingly abundant in upper levels. The bones of birds and large mammals, along with shells of river mussels, occurred consistently throughout, although Cressman (1956:467) admits that the use of 40-centimeter (1.3 foot) arbitrary excavation levels may have masked potentially significant cultural change. Based on the relative amount of faunal remains and inferences made as to specific tool functions, Cressman concluded that fish, small mammals, birds, freshwater mussels, seeds, and roots were the most important food resources, virtually describing the subsistence patterns of the historic Klamath.

Malheur Lake. High lake levels during the mid-1980s, combined with the erosion that followed as lake waters receded, exposed many human burial sites and artifacts on shorelines and islands of Malheur Lake, in central Oregon south of Burns. A great wealth of archaeological information was being lost as artifact seekers swept into the area and illegally carried away the prehistoric evidence for their personal collections or for sale. Consequently, throughout the 1980s and 1990s the Malheur National Wildlife Refuge conducted archaeological investigations (Raymond 1994), and contracted with various archaeologists to conduct important reconnaissance surveys and test excavations (Aikens and Greenspan 1988; Dugas 1996; Dugas and Bullock 1994; Dugas et al. 1995; Elston and Dugas 1993; Musil 2002; Oetting 1990, 1991). These investigations disclosed a large number of sites with projectile points, large biface "wealth" blades, manos, metates, pestles, mortars, choppers, notched stone net weights, and other specimens lying exposed on the surface. Housepit depressions were also observed, as well as human skeletons that were documented and reburied in place.

Projectile points collected around Malheur Lake for archaeological study ranged from Western Stemmed specimens of the earliest period to Desert Side-notched points of the latest period, showing that people were present in the area throughout Holocene times. The types found in greatest numbers, however, place the start of major occupation at around 6000–3000 BP during the Bergen Period, with a plateau in human activity reached after about 2000 cal. BP, during the later Boulder Village Period (Oetting 1999).

Archaeological surveys identified many later sites around Harney and Malheur lakes, along the Blitzen River that feeds Malheur Lake, and elsewhere in the region. The artifacts found included arrow and dart points for hunting, and milling stones for seed grinding. Bones from excavated sites show that prehistoric people hunted land animals as small as rabbits and as large as bison. They also caught waterfowl and fishes. In all, the accumulated data show that a winter-sedentary/summer-mobile way of life like that of the historic *Wadatika* (Wada-eaters) residents existed in the region over at least the last 4,500 years (O'Grady 2006).

The rich archaeological resources of the Harney Basin have been known since the 1930s, when construction work at the Malheur National

Wildlife Refuge Headquarters encountered artifacts and human burials (Campbell n.d.). The Headquarters Site (35HA403) has been the focus of intermittent site testing since the late 1970s (Aikens and Greenspan 1988; Dugas and Bullock 1994; Musil 2002; Newman et al. 1974). The results of these archaeological projects indicate that the site area is extensive and has been occupied periodically over the last 9,000 years (Musil 2002). Current evidence suggests, however, that it was during the Bergen Period when more intensive, long-term occupations began at the Headquarters Site. An apparent house floor associated with Northern Side-notched and Elko series projectile points was radiocarbon dated at about 5430 cal. BP. Fish, waterfowl, and mammals of various sizes, along with a broad array of marsh plants, were being harvested to support this new level of sedentism. Tools recovered throughout the site strata, but particularly those dated after about 5,500 years ago, included mortars, pestles, manos, and metates, all strong evidence of the importance of storable and possibly imported plant foods to the economy. It may have been at about this time that the local people instituted the ethnographically known pattern of bringing into lakeside settlements, as winter stores, root crops they had gathered and cached the previous spring in the adjacent uplands.

Dunn Site (35HA1261). South of Malheur Lake and several miles east of Blitzen Marsh, on the northeastern edge of Diamond Swamp, is the remnant of a prehistoric village named the Dunn Site, after local residents (Musil 1990, 1992). Excavations at the Dunn Site revealed a semi-subterranean house roughly 13 feet in diameter that exhibited a central fire hearth, a shallow storage pit dug into the floor, and traces of postholes around the edges. Charcoal from the floor gave a late Bergen Period radiocarbon age of 3490 cal. BP. A much earlier occupation of the spot is suggested by one Western Stemmed projectile point found beneath the house floor. A later occupation is poorly attested above a layer of cinders, which fell on the site from an eruption at nearby Diamond Craters sometime after 3440 cal. BP. These earlier and later finds, though not otherwise particularly informative, do indicate that the site was intermittently attractive to people over a long period of time.

Artifacts from the housepit included Elko Eared projectile points; flaked stone bifaces, drills, and scrapers; and fragments of manos, metates, and pestles. Beads and polished fragments of bone were also found, as well as shell disk beads. The fill of the storage pit contained charcoal of pine and sagebrush, grass stems, juniper seeds, and fish bone fragments, as well as lithic flakes. The hearth fill contained similar materials, and further included eight seeds of the goosefoot family and one mustard seed; both species were of dietary importance to Native peoples (Stenholm 1990).

Over 5,000 bone specimens, most highly fragmented and some charred, were recovered from the Dunn Site excavations. The remains of artiodactyls (possibly including deer, elk, antelope, sheep, and bison) were most common, followed by bones of leporids (jackrabbits and cottontails), small rodents, fish (tui chubs, suckers), and muskrats. Overall, the assemblage suggests a generalized hunting pattern, making use of both aquatic and terrestrial habitats in the site vicinity. Notably, however, the most numerous specimens also represent the largest kinds of animals, indicating that first-rank importance was assigned to big game hunting. In this respect the Dunn Site differs from other marshland sites of the area, where fish and smaller animals were relatively better attested (Greenspan 1990). It is quite possible this is evidence of late fall through winter occupations at a site uniquely situated to take advantage not only of waterfowl but also migratory large game, as was the Bergen site in the Fort Rock basin.

Catlow and Roaring Springs Caves. South of Malheur Lake is Catlow Valley, where Catlow and Roaring Springs caves yielded large and important inventories of perishable artifacts (basketry, cordage, and other organic materials). Excavated in 1937 and 1938, the caves are of central importance to the history of scientific archaeological investigation in Oregon (Cressman, Williams, and Krieger 1940; Cressman et al. 1942; Wilde 1985). Both are located west of Steens Mountain, about 30 miles apart along the eastern edge of the Catlow Valley. Catlow Cave, in the south, stands on the highest beach line of Pluvial Lake Catlow, which occupied the valley during Pleistocene times. Roaring Springs Cave, named for the rushing flow of nearby artesian springs, is similarly situated but farther north. Both command broad views of the ancient lakebed, now a sagebrush and grassland landscape broken here and there by patches of marsh and small, shallow ephemeral lakes or ponds.

These two sites seem to have been most heavily occupied during the Bergen Period and are introduced into the discussion here for that reason, but they were in fact visited throughout Holocene times. Their chronology has never been directly established or precisely subdivided, both because the radiocarbon dating method did not exist when they were excavated

during the 1930s, and because the field records made during the excavations do not adequately define stratigraphic layers and the positions of individual artifacts within them. Since the advent of ^{14}C dating in the 1950s,
however, many individual artifact types known from the Catlow Valley
caves have been found and dated at other Great Basin sites. So we know
that sandals of the Fort Rock type from Catlow Cave, now well dated regionally, fall between about 10,200 and 9200 cal. BP (Connolly and Barker
2004), and show that Catlow Cave saw early occupation during the Fort
Rock period. Multiple Warp and Spiral Weft sandals, found in both Catlow
and Roaring Springs caves, are also dated elsewhere and show that both
sites were occupied during subsequent Lunette Lake, Bergen, and Boulder
Village periods. Some of their other specimens are comparable to textiles
that extend into late prehistoric and historic times as well, including traces
of Northern Paiute or Shoshone coiled basketry ^{14}C dated throughout the
last 2,500 years (Connolly 2006), and a few sherds of Northern Paiute /
Shoshone pottery found on the surface at Catlow Cave.

Wilde's (1985) reclassification of the projectile points from these two
Catlow Valley caves adds an additional line of evidence. Both sites contain
the same point types in very similar percentages. A few Western Stemmed
points, which regionally date to about 14,000–8000 cal. BP, show that
people visited the Catlow Valley caves during the Fort Rock Period. Later
Northern Side-notched, Elko Eared, Humboldt Concave Base A, Gatecliff
Split stem, and Elko Corner-notched points are numerous in the caves and
imply continuing occupation between about 9000 and 1500 cal. BP, spanning the subsequent Lunette Lake and Bergen periods. Small Rosegate
and Desert Side-notched arrowpoint types occupy about the last 1500 and
500 years respectively, and place the latest occupation of the caves in the
Boulder Village Period.

Locally available game food resources changed over the time Catlow
Cave was occupied, as documented by the faunal assemblage. The bones
of water birds, including pintail, teal, lesser scaup, goose, coot, and avocet
were largely limited to the deepest level of the cave deposit. Conversely,
the bones of land mammals, including mountain sheep, bison, and rodents, were predominantly from the higher levels. This pattern indicates
the local availability of wetland habitat for aquatic animals earlier in the
history of the site, and its diminution as time went on. Other game species attested in the faunal assemblage were mule deer, marmot, pika,

jackrabbit, and sagehen. Predators, including coyote, fox, lynx, and owl were also represented. Except for the pika, a creature of cooler, moister habitats, all these animals are to be found in the Catlow Valley today. The absence of pronghorn antelope from the faunal collections is surprising, in view of its present abundance in the region. Although it is not possible to characterize the caves' contents systematically in terms of period-by-period continuities and changes, the sites nevertheless have a special value. Their large assemblages of perishable artifacts, as described in the following quotation, are noteworthy because they bring to light aspects of daily life not generally revealed in the lithics-only collections typically found in most archaeological sites:

> The rich haul of artifacts from the sheltered, dry sites of the Northern Great Basin, especially Catlow and Roaring Springs caves, provides one of the clearest reflections yet available of the ancient . . . lifeway. Items of clothing included sagebrush bark sandals and rabbitskin robes. Footwear must have been very important to a people who were obliged to travel far and often, and it is the most abundantly attested form of personal clothing. For gathering, fetching, and carrying there were a variety of twined baskets, soft bags, and nets. Digging sticks of mountain mahogany for taking roots and shoots, and manos and metates for breaking and grinding seeds, were well represented. Atlatls and darts, bows and arrows, and stone projectile points to arm them, all occur in the collections, as do numerous cutting and scraping tools of chipped stone. The hunt provided not only food, but also furs, sinews, and bones used in making clothing, in the hafting of stone tools, in the fashioning of bow strings, and in the making of awls and other manufacturing tools. Flaked stone drills and abrading tools of rough scoriatic basalt further attest the manufacture of wooden objects such as atlatls, bows and associated gear.
>
> Neither was the assemblage unrelievedly utilitarian. Many of the baskets from Roaring Springs Cave had been ornamented in geometric patterns by inlaying fibers of different colors; many of the dart shafts and arrow shafts had been painted with rings of red and blue; . . . a piece of cane had been cut and perforated as a musical flute; and a perforated Olivella shell from the Pacific coast had

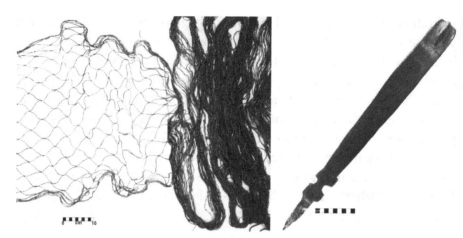

Left, Fig. 2.38. Net from Chewaucan Cave; *right*, Fig. 2.39. Atlatl from Roaring Springs Cave.

perhaps been strung as a bead. The collection illustrated, in short, not only the day-to-day tasks of the desert lifeway, but also some of its pleasures. (Aikens 1982:147)

A net and an atlatl, examples of the normally perishable early artifact types that were preserved in the dryness of Roaring Springs Cave, are shown in figs. 2.38 and 2.39.

Skull Creek Dunes (35HA412). Between Catlow Cave at the south end of the valley and Roaring Springs Cave at the north are the Skull Creek Dunes (fig. 2.40). A large sand sheet formed here during middle Holocene times on the margin of drying pluvial Lake Catlow. Excavations showed that a soil formed after the drying of the lake, and that dune sand blown off the exposed lakebed to the west had just begun to accumulate over this soil when the first known human occupants arrived on the scene. Their encampment left an abundance of obsidian flakes, along with charcoal, bone fragments, and artifacts that included milling stone fragments, hammerstones, and cutting/scraping tools. The earliest projectile point, of the early Holocene Western Stemmed type, was found on lakebed sediments at the bottom of the dune. Mid-Holocene types were much more common, including Elko Eared, Elko Corner-notched, Elko Side-notched, and Humboldt Concave Base A types. Volcanic ash from the eruption of Mount Mazama fell during the time people making these types were frequenting the site, as shown by specimens below, within, and slightly above the 7600 cal. BP Mazama ash layer (Wilde 1985;

Mehringer and Wigand 1986). These findings show people of both the Fort Rock and Lunette Lake periods making use of a dune and slough environment around the point where Skull Creek spilled out of the Steens Mountain foothills onto the valley floor.

Sand continued to accumulate at the Skull Creek dunes, burying this occupation to a depth of more than 10 feet before the dunes stabilized during a period of weathering that formed a distinct soil horizon. A few fragments of Northern Side-notched points and flaked bifaces were found on the weathered soil surface. A foot or so higher, in sands accumulated above this soil, was found a hard-packed living floor on which four fire hearths lay scattered. Charcoal from one of these hearths gave closely congruent ^{14}C dates of ca. 3570 and 3390 cal. BP, which place this occupation near the end of the mid-Holocene Bergen Period. Gatecliff Split stem points were found associated with the living floor, as were hammerstones and milling stone fragments. Sand continued to accumulate, burying this occupation as it had the two previous ones, until a weathering episode again stabilized the dune beneath a strongly developed red soil that caps the Skull Creek sand sheet today. Within this uppermost soil was found a fire hearth that contained charcoal, obsidian flakes, bone fragments, and carbonized animal fat. Biotic remains from the hearth included wada seeds, mountain sheep bone, and remains of small mammals, birds, and fish. Two ^{14}C dates on the hearth were about 1860 and 1725 cal. BP. The accumulated dating and cultural evidence shows that occupation of

Fig. 2.40. Skull Creek Dunes site, Catlow Valley, view east.

the Skull Creek Dunes was centered on the mid-Holocene Lunette Lake and Bergen periods, though the earliest human traces are of the Fort Rock Period and the latest represent the final Boulder Village Period.

Catlow Cave, Roaring Springs Cave, and Skull Creek Dunes are prominent representatives of a hunting-gathering lifeway practiced in the Catlow Valley over millennia. The rich cultural inventories of the caves suggest they served as fall and winter bases for small groups which at other times of year ranged out to harvest the resources of the surrounding region. In ethnohistoric times some Northern Paiute groups wintered in the valley, and one of the remembered settlements was at Roaring Springs (Blyth 1938). The shelter and proximity to wetlands resources afforded by Catlow and Roaring Springs caves clearly would have made them attractive for wintertime use. The Skull Creek Dunes were more likely the scene of seasonal camps occupied when people came to obtain fish from Skull Creek, wada seeds from the margin of the old lakebed, and perhaps the seeds of Indian ricegrass, which flourishes today in the sandy soils. All of the sites, being near water, would also have been favorable localities for stalking large game, and catching or trapping birds and small mammals.

Owyhee River and Uplands. Near Oregon's east-central border is the Birch Creek site (35ML181), located in the lower third of the Owyhee River canyon. A hamlet composed of at least three housepits and associated outdoor features was investigated on a terrace next to the Owyhee River between 1998 and 2008 by the Washington State University archaeological field school (Andrefsky et al. 1999; Andrefsky and Presler 2000; Cole 2001; Andrefsky et al. 2003; Centola 2004). Floors in House 1 were radiocarbon dated to 5130, 4450, and 2500 cal. BP, and a single floor in House 2 was dated to 4450 cal. BP. The dates clearly show the site was a popular residential location during the Bergen Period. Below the houses was a discontinuous lens of Mazama ash, beneath which were found artifacts and domesticated dog remains dated to 7670 cal. BP (Andrefsky, personal communication), giving evidence of earlier Lunette Lake Period visitation as well. Projectile points include Elko, Humboldt, Northern Side-Notched, and Gatecliff series. Turkey Tail points, commonly found in western Idaho sites of the middle Holocene, were present in low numbers (fig. 2.41). Analysis of lithic materials and technology indicates production of obsidian projectile points from sources located predominantly to the north and east as far as the Timber Butte and Owyhee sources in Idaho.

The river was an important provider of food resources to occupants of the Birch Creek site. Mussels and fish supplied large portions of their diet,

Fig. 2.41. Turkey Tail points
from the Birch Creek site,
Owyhee River.

with big horn sheep, deer, bison, coyote, rabbits, marmots, and squirrels adding protein, fat, and industrial materials such as hides, horn, antler, and bone to the economy. Shell and bone beads, incised bone art, bone tools, hopper mortars, and pestles add diversity to the assemblages, suggesting extended seasonal occupations of the site. Technological analysis of points and knives showed a higher percentage of both complete and reworked specimens to be made of non-local obsidian rather than local cherts, reflecting the tendency to resharpen rather than discard bifaces when the occupants were more than a two-day round-trip distance from their home base (Andrefsky 2008).

It is interesting to note that Dirty Shame Rockshelter, in the Owyhee Uplands west of the river on Antelope Creek, has numerous dates for occupation between about 10,800 and 400 cal. BP but yields no dated record at all of human presence between about 6700 and 2900 cal. BP, a time range that includes the entire relatively drier Bergen Period (Aikens, Cole, and Stuckenrath 1977). The thin soils and high evapotranspiration potential of this mostly treeless basalt plateau make it inherently quite dry and this, along with the temperature / moisture fluctuations of the middle Holocene climate, apparently thinned local plant and animal resources to the point that year-round human populations in distant and more productive lowlands simply did not find it economically sound to send expeditions so far for seasonal harvesting. It was only with the generally moister climatic regime and larger populations of post-Bergen Period late Holocene times that people returned to hunting and collecting in the vicinity of Dirty Shame Rockshelter.

Ecological, Technological, and Social Patterns of the Bergen Period. The Bergen period, between 6,000 and 3,000 years ago, was an interval of fluctuating cool-wet and warm-wet climate that in some but not all topographic settings fostered highly productive ecological conditions.

Most notably, at the beginning of the Bergen Period people began to occupy houses and build large cache pits in a number of marsh-side locations, leaving clear evidence of increased residential sedentism. By 5600 cal. BP houses and large storage pits were common in site locations in the Fort Rock and Harney basins that offered easy access to abundant lowland subsistence resources, including fish (tui chubs), seeds, rabbits, and ducks. Upland roots had been used as early as 10,000 cal. BP (Connolly and Jenkins 1999:102), but between 4500 and 3500 cal. BP they came to constitute perhaps as large a part of the Native diet as did grassland and marsh resources. Large game animals were hunted in both uplands and lowlands, and bones found in Bergen Period sites indicate that whole carcasses were often brought back to house sites, hamlets, and villages.

There is an obvious correlation between the construction of houses and the presence of storage pits during this period, developments that were also accompanied by increased numbers and types of artifacts in site assemblages. It must be noted, however, that increasing sedentism offered both risks and rewards. When food was abundant and movement unrestricted, a strategy of high mobility tended to be preferred by hunter-gatherers, as it offered maximum flexibility to move where resources were most abundant and dangers were avoidable. Sedentism could enhance prosperity, but required the calculated risk of committing to a place where the resource base might change over time, or become depleted by overuse. The adoption of long-term food storage fostered some degree of residential permanence, as food harvested at times of abundance was best kept close at hand for later consumption. Such food stores could become another risk associated with sedentism, a risk presented by less prudent neighbors who were experiencing hunger and desperation. On the other hand, extended periods of occupation at house sites provided people with more time for a greater variety of economic, industrial, maintenance, and social activities to occur in one place, enriching their daily lives. Intensive fishing and small seed collection and processing correlates well with the appearance of large-volume storage pits after about 6000 cal. BP (Jenkins 2004).

It is important to note that local population increases do not have to be the direct result of local increases in birth and survival rates (Jenkins 1994b). People undoubtedly moved routinely between sub-basins within the Northern Great Basin in response to changing food resource availability related to changing climatic conditions. There is good archaeological evidence that populations converged on particular locations for extended periods of time to harvest resources that appeared in exceptional abundance. Widely scattered populations in upland territories surrounding places like the Fort Rock, Warner, and Klamath basins, the Klamath and Sycan marshes, and the Deschutes River and Harney Basins, may have periodically gravitated to one or another of these key locations as they were driven from their homes by excessively deep snow, floodwater, or drought. Once residential population levels in these places increased beyond a certain point, however, changes in local settlement, subsistence, and organizational patterns would have been necessary to accommodate them (Jenkins 2000).

Placing a greater dietary emphasis on storable seeds and roots or rapidly repopulating minnows, rabbits, and squirrels, and more effectively intercepting migratory waterfowl, deer, antelope, and elk in overwintering locations, provided obvious ways of increasing economic productivity to cope with increased population densities. People began storing large volumes of seasonally abundant resources like minnows, chenopod, amaranth, wada, and bulrush seeds. They also established houses near the overwintering sites of gregarious birds and artiodactyls, to gain access to important fresh foods for their winter diet. Not all desirable site locations were equally well suited to take advantage of these resources, however, and people responded to such realities by trading, exchanging gifts, and gambling, to effectively redistribute "patchy" resources among communities. The expansion in the types and quantities of artistically embellished artifacts—beads, carved and ground bone tools, pipes, mauls, and stone balls for instance—provide strong evidence of both resource redistribution and increasing social interaction during the Bergen period.

At Nightfire Island in the Lower Klamath Basin, occupants who had built an artificial island for their village abandoned their more permanent pithouses around the end of the Bergen Period about 3100 cal. BP and began to occupy light, above-ground structures. Sampson (1985:511–513) suggests that the post-3100 cal. BP period in the Lower Klamath Basin was characterized by reduced marshes and increased residential mobility. In the Fort Rock and Chewaucan basins, people moved away from their traditional winter hamlets and villages in the marshes about 3,000 years ago and took up winter residence in villages nearer the bases of surrounding hills. While drought may have initially had something to do with the moves in these two basins, it seems most likely that increasing regional dependence on upland root crops after 3500 cal. BP was the main reason for the shift in winter village locations.

In the Harney Basin, what are probably house constructions appear about 5500 cal. BP at the Dunn Site, suggesting that more intensive sedentary occupations around the lakes and marshes of the basin probably occurred simultaneously with similar cultural developments in the Fort Rock basin. However, repeated flooding, erosion, and sand dune development appear to have either eliminated or deeply buried much of the early and middle Holocene archaeological record in the Harney Basin. Consequently, most of the archaeology of these earlier times is so far represented only by projectile points, ground stone, debitage, and a few cultural features. Much work needs to be done to more fully understand cultural history and development in this area, which in time will no doubt yield the kind of more nuanced picture now available for the Fort Rock Basin.

Along the Owyhee River, hamlets and possibly villages of pithouses began to appear in locations where mussels, fish, and terrestrial resources could all be gathered from riverine settings (Andrefsky 2008; Andrefsky et al. 1999; Andrefsky and Presler 2000; Cole 2001; Andrefsky et al. 2003; Centola 2004). The majority of their bifacial stone tools were made of lithic material available within two days walk of the site. Artifacts made of more exotic materials, including obsidian and cherts from Nevada and Idaho, tend to be found in an often completely reduced or "exhausted" condition, the result of repeated resharpening of tools until they were all used up. Occupation intensifies during the Bergen Period along the Malheur and Snake Rivers as well (Green 1982; Jenkins and Connolly 2001, 2010; Jenkins, Connolly, and Baxter 2010). Although no pithouse hamlets or villages are as yet recorded in the Malheur drainage, very little archaeological research has been conducted along the course of this river. Pithouses and villages are known from the confluence of the Owyhee and Snake rivers (Green 1982). An elaborate burial complex with grave goods including large numbers of obsidian "Turkey Tail," Northern Side Notched, and foliate points, along with triangular obsidian bifaces, *Olivella* shell beads from the Pacific coast, and accompanying dog burials, has been encountered in isolated cemetery sites along the Snake River between the Weiser and Owyhee river mouths. While Pavesic (1979, 1985, 1992) has termed this the "Western Idaho Burial Complex," its practitioners undoubtedly included Native Oregonians as well. The location of these cemeteries near the mouths of salmon-bearing tributaries reaching far into the interior of Idaho and Oregon, and down into northern Nevada's Owyhee country, certainly suggests that—like the increasingly settled residents of the Fort

Rock basin—the practitioners of this burial ritual may have been participants in long distance trade networks extending from California, the Columbia Plateau, and the Northwest Coast to the farthest reaches of the northern Great Basin.

Boulder Village Period (3,000 Years Ago to Historic Contact)

Beginning roughly 3,000 years ago, the Boulder Village Period is named for a large aggregation of boulder-outlined house structures in the southeastern Fort Rock basin that is Oregon's largest known residential site seasonally occupied for the specific purpose of collecting and storing root crops. The late Holocene was a time of oscillating weather patterns, with extended periods of increased precipitation followed by periods of reduced precipitation and drought. Water levels rose and fell multiple times in lakes, marshes, and ponds throughout the Northern Great Basin and adjacent Klamath Basin (Mehringer 1986; Sampson 1985; Wigand 1987). While an intense and extended drought has been documented around 2950 cal. BP, the period between 3000 and 2000 cal. BP was generally a time of good environmental conditions, as evidenced by high water in Diamond Pond. After that time, climate fluctuated at roughly 500-year intervals between wet and dry cycles. Drier conditions prevailed between 2,000 and 1,500 years ago; moister conditions returned between 1,500 and 900 years ago; drier conditions followed between 900 and 400 years ago; and the last 400 years appear to have been a time of moderately moist conditions. Throughout the Boulder Village Period human populations remained comparatively high, but apparently fluctuated in density with the changing climate, and during this time people consolidated their use of the more reliably watered areas, particularly the Klamath Basin, and to a lesser degree the Fort Rock, Summer Lake, Warner Valley, and Harney basins.

This shifting pattern is evident in the numerous village settlements of the Chewaucan and Warner Valleys (Oetting 1989; Pettigrew 1980a, 1985; Eiselt 1997), and is reflected in ethnographic sources which suggest that the Klamath and Modoc formerly occupied areas far to the east of their historic distribution (Allison 1994; Fowler and Liljeblad 1986:464; Kelly 1932:72). It is also apparent in the archaeological record of Drews Valley, located within the uplands that separate the Goose Lake and Klamath basins. Obsidian source locations charted for sets of chronologically diagnostic projectile points recovered from a dozen different Drews Valley sites show that for Elko and earlier periods, tool stone sources were mainly located to the northeast, in Oregon's Fort Rock and Chewaucan basins. Most of the remaining exotic obsidian is from other Great Basin sources, primarily from the Goose Lake Basin to the southeast. During the last ca. 1,300 years, however, tool stone has been derived mainly from the Modoc Plateau to the southwest, while sources in the easterly basins are rarely attested (Connolly and Jenkins 1997). These population shifts were motivated in part by changing environmental conditions, but may have also been driven by social factors such as ethnic conflict and changing spheres of economic opportunity.

Boulder Village (35LK2846). Boulder Village is a large site measuring about 1500 feet long north to south by 400 feet east to west, located in the southern uplands of the Fort Rock basin east of Silver Lake. It is situated on the northeast-facing slope of a prominent ridge that overlooks a small nearby perennial lake at about 5,300 feet elevation (Jenkins and Brashear 1994). These uplands are dotted with small ephemeral lake depressions surrounded by upthrust basalt ridges topped with juniper and mountain mahogany. Broad expanses of sagebrush-covered rocky surfaces give rise to rich root grounds containing biscuitroot (*Lomatium* spp.), sego lily (*Calochortus* sp.), yampah (*Perideridia* spp.), onion (*Allium* spp.), and bitterroot (*Lewisia* sp.), from which local and visiting human populations extracted vital fresh food in early spring which they also dried for winter stores. The Boulder Village site includes at least 122 boulder-ringed houses and 48 large cache pits (fig. 2.42). Wild rye (*Elymus cinereus*) and currants are additional edible plants that grow among the massive boulder fields along the ridge. The timber and rye grass endemic to the area provided basic building and thatching materials for house construction.

Documented structures range from a possible storage roughly three feet in diameter to the largest house, which measured 17 feet by 12 feet across. Floors ranged from surface level to 6.5 feet deep. Vandalism by artifact looters has been so extensive at Boulder Village that few foundations appear untouched, and none of the deeper structures has been spared. The University of Oregon field school's excavation of 17 room foundations and cache pits showed that many were closely adjacent and had interlocking walls, suggesting that family groups generally built multiple smaller structures in a block rather than seeking to construct, maintain, and try to heat larger single houses, which would have also required larger roof-support timbers (Jenkins and Brashear 1994). Such room clustering was a typical Klamath-Modoc pattern in spring-summer villages, though the ethnographies do not report stone-encircled houses. The clustered structures were undoubtedly used for a variety of activities, including sleeping, food preparation, eating, and storage, and probably also as menstrual and birthing huts.

Late period arrow points predominate and include Rose Spring, Eastgate, Desert Side-Notched, and Cottonwood Triangular types but earlier dart points (Western Stemmed, foliate, Large Side-Notched, and Elko types) provide evidence for intermittent use of the site in earlier times. Glass trade beads, military buttons, and an iron knife blade show that occupations continued into the historic period. The construction of one house has been precisely dated to A.D. 1855 by the tree-ring dating of associated juniper stumps that were obviously cut with a steel hatchet. Radiocarbon dating indicates the majority of larger and deeper structures were occupied multiple times between 1500 and 200 cal. BP. Peak periods of site occupation occurred between 1500 and 900 cal. BP, 600 and 500 cal. BP, and from about 200 cal. BP until the region's Native Americans were removed to reservations in the 1860s.

Boulder Village was primarily a springtime root collection site. Most structures contained little bone, though projectile points were generally common. The lack of bone suggests that little hunting would have been conducted from the site (though deer, elk, and pronghorn would surely have been available nearby), and it is possible that the weaponry reflects instead a concern for defense from attack by marauders. Certainly, some of the houses were located in difficult-to-reach locations—in large boulder fields which may have served as buffers against attack.

Recovery of tui chub bone and charred seeds of lowland plants such as *chenopodium*, wada, and saltbush definitely indicates that a variety of foods were brought to upland Boulder Village from the Fort Rock lowlands immediately to the west. The short-term work-camp nature of the prehistoric residential occupations at Boulder Village is attested by the general absence there of personal ornamentation (beads and pendants) and the fact that other artifacts (ground stone hopper mortars, pestles, metates, and manos) are generally unshaped, expedient, and minimally worn. When found in undisturbed contexts, such artifacts appear to have generally been stored between wall stones, awaiting their next spring use. While the site is substantial, it shows clear signs of being mainly a task-specific seasonal workplace for the processing of spring root crops. The most likely winter home base of Boulder Village's springtime occupants is Carlon Village (35LK2736), a large lowland

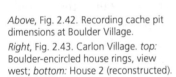

Above, Fig. 2.42. Recording cache pit dimensions at Boulder Village.

Right, Fig. 2.43. Carlon Village. *top:* Boulder-encircled house rings, view west; *bottom:* House 2 (reconstructed).

residential site described below, located 1,000 feet lower in elevation and several miles south and west near Silver Lake, a place of rich marsh resources. At the same time, patterns of exotic obsidian use at outlying habitation sites, like Scott's Village (35LK2844; Jenkins and Brashear 1994:464) in the Boulder Village Uplands, differ from those found at Boulder Village proper as well as those of lowland Carlon Village, and are a strong indication that visitors also commonly came to these rich root grounds from more distant basins to the east and south (O'Grady 1999).

Carlon Village (35LK2736). Carlon Village was a large and stable settlement covering a low peninsula that protrudes into Silver Lake from its southeast shore. Silver Lake is fed by runoff from the low hills west and south of the Fort Rock basin, most of which passes first into Paulina Marsh in the southwest corner of the basin. In wet periods, water flows down a short but well-incised streambed from Paulina Marsh into Silver Lake, and from there on down the Silver Lake-Fort Rock channel system described above in accounts of the preceding Lunette Lake and Bergen periods. Silver Lake is only about 12 feet deep when full to overflowing, and in modern times is often more marsh or grassy playa than lake. When water was high during the early and mid-1980s, however, the lake wrapped around three sides of the peninsula on which Carlon Village sits, suggesting that consideration of its defensibility may have factored into the choice of that site location. Artifacts spanning the entire period of human occupation in the region—including Windust and other Western Stemmed points, foliates, Northern Side-notched, Elko, Humboldt, Gatecliff Split-stem, Rose Spring, Eastgate, Cottonwood Triangular, and Desert Side-notched types—have been recovered from the village site and periodically exposed floor of Silver Lake by archaeologists and generations of artifact collectors. The array demonstrates regular use of the site area over millennia before the peninsula was occupied as a long-term settlement (Howe 1968; Jenkins 1994a; Wingard 2001).

The village component is centered on eight large boulder-encircled houses scattered along the top and ends of the hill (fig. 2.43). Large basalt boulders set on edge, some weighing more than a ton, form waist- to shoulder-high walls encircling living areas that range from 15 to 25 feet in diameter. The larger boulders were secured by wedge-shaped boulder chocks at their bases. Analysis of charcoal recovered from the houses suggests that slender pine timbers were brought from mountain ridges a mile or more from the site to form the house superstructures. The timbers were apparently leaned tepee-like over the stone circles and covered with mats or bundles of insulating grass. The boulder foundations, some of which were first built more than 2,300 years ago, have stood there ever since as testimony to the importance of the site and its builders, though it was tragically pillaged and damaged by artifact hunters in the 1960s and 1970s.

Systematic study of the site was undertaken by the University of Oregon field school in 1997 (Wingard 2001). Some excavation was conducted at each of the eight houses, and House 2—the structure left most intact by collectors—was reconstructed (fig. 2.44b). A suite of 19 radiocarbon dates on charcoal samples recovered from Carlon Village house floors (seven on edible species such as chokecherry, rose, and onions), chronicles near-continuous occupation from about 2350 to 300 cal. BP, while the recovery of glass beads indicates that occupation continued into the historic period. Dating of additional house or living floors found on terraces below the large boulder-ringed houses produced dates of 1970, 1850, and 1650 cal. BP.

Faunal and floral remains indicate that Carlon Village occupants relied heavily on a combination of lowland marsh and upland resources. For example, flotation analysis of soil samples from the living floors yielded traces of mountain mahogany, juniper, greasewood, rabbitbrush, chokecherry, service-berry, and sagebrush, along with charred wood of ponderosa pine. Also re-covered were many small, charred seeds, the identifiable specimens including rush, bulrush, saltsage, pigweed, goosefoot, chenopod, *Sueda* (wada), grass, sedge, knotweed, and juniper (Stenholm 1994: Table 3; Wingard 2001:123). Biscuitroot, chokecherry, rose hips, and serviceberries are important upland food resources that were also identified among charred remains in the soil within the houses.

Geochemical analysis of hundreds of obsidian projectile points from Carlon Village, Boulder Village, and many smaller habitation sites near them shows that the obsidian sources represented among this set correspond closely, suggesting that these various habitation and harvest locations were probably all used by the same community of people. Much greater obsidian source diversity is seen among other small temporary sites elsewhere in the general area, however, suggesting that many of those may have been occu-pied by visitors to the basin who journeyed there from more distant parts to participate in the root harvest.

While very few ornaments and decorated (personalized) tools were found at nearby Boulder Village, they were relatively common at Carlon Village. This fact, along with the architectural opulence of Carlon Village and the presence of wealth items in its boulder-encircled houses, also suggests an elevated social status for the people who built and occupied them. Carlon Village was no doubt the primary social and economic center of its period for the Fort Rock basin (Wingard 2001), and large villages played similar roles in other basins at the same time, as shown below.

Lake Abert. A series of sites near Lake Abert, about 25 miles north of Lakeview, attest to the widespread occurrence of considerable populations centered on large villages during the Boulder Village Period. The local bi-otic setting of the Chewaucan basin is a rich one; west and south of Lake Abert, the extensive upper and lower Chewaucan marshes were fed by the Chewaucan River, which flows out of the high Klamath country east of Gearhart Mountain. The impressively numerous and substantial sites near Lake Abert were discovered during extensive pedestrian surveys of the lake shore zone, conducted in advance of a highway improvement project, that led to the recording of more than 300 new archaeological sites with a cul-ture history spanning the last 13,000 years (Pettigrew 1980a, 1985; Oetting 1988, 1989, 1990). Most importantly, these investigations revealed a previously

Fig. 2.44. Stone ring house at Lake Abert (U.S. Highway 395 in background).

unsuspected pattern of village and hamlet sites distributed around Lake Abert and the Upper and Lower Chewaucan marshes. More than 580 depressions and 73 rock-walled structures representing houses (fig. 2.44), storage, and communal structures were recorded, along with 92 petroglyph boulders and several pictograph (rock painting) panels as well (Pettigrew 1980).

Test excavations in some depressions showed earthen embankments around house perimeters, and floors with central firehearths. These features define substantial pithouses closely similar to structures made by the ethnographic (and prehistoric) Klamath. The observed site pattern is of small aggregations of pithouses in close proximity to marsh, lake, river, or spring, which are surrounded by a broader, more diffuse array of small, short-term activity sites marked by lithic flake scatters and ground stone manos, metates, mortars, and pestles.

A remarkable series of normally perishable artifacts made for the catching, gathering, and processing of local animal and plant resources was preserved in the extreme dryness of nearby Chewaucan Cave, examples of which are shown in figures 2.45 and 2.46. They represent a cache dating to ca. 400 years ago, a time when some of the nearby sites were occupied. No historic artifacts were found at the investigated Lake Abert sites, but their latest radiocarbon determinations (130 and 165 cal. BP) may reach into the nineteenth century.

Today Lake Abert is an aquatic desert, supporting only tiny brine shrimp, fairy shrimp, water fleas, and algae. The abundant archaeological evidence

Left, Fig. 2.45. Large tule fiber bag from Chewaucan Cave.
Right, Fig. 2.46. Large twined basketry tray from Chewaucan Cave.

suggests the lake was more productive in the past, but by late prehistoric times a low water level had concentrated toxic alkaline minerals, the richer lake biota had vanished, and people abandoned the area (Pettigrew 1985). In this connection it is intriguing to note that with severe desiccation and shrinkage of the lake in the late summer of 1992, aquatic vegetation and water birds not previously common at Lake Abert quickly appeared around newly exposed freshwater springs in the shoreline zone that had previously been drowned by the briny lake waters (William J. Cannon, personal communication). This suggests that under certain conditions a productive biota may have attracted people even when lake levels were extremely low.

Apart from the lake's potential productivity, the higher ridges in the Chewaucan Basin, such as Abert Rim and the Coglan Buttes, are rich in roots and other resources that would have been productive at all times (lomatiums, sego lilies, bitter root, berries, chokecherries), and all of them occur in relatively close proximity to village and hamlet locations. Lowland marshes were also rich in wapato, camas, and bulrush. Indeed, the name Chewaucan derives from the Klamath word for the highly prized wapato, or arrowhead plant (*Sagittaria* sp.) which was abundant in the area. When traversing the marsh in 1843, John C. Frémont observed: "Large patches of ground had been torn up by the squaws in digging for roots, as if a farmer had been preparing the land for grain" (Stewart 1999: 105).

An analysis of rock art locations shows that most of the petroglyphs and pictographs of the Abert-Chewaucan locality are concentrated in habitation areas, contrary to common speculation that such images reflect secretive shamanistic practices or the conjuring of "hunting magic" at remote camps. Though certainly having spiritual meaning, rock art occurs here generally in a "living room" or community context, rather than an individual or secretive one (Ricks 1996).

Warner Valley. Warner Valley, east and south beyond the high Abert Rim escarpment that rises precipitously above Abert Lake, was another major theater of prehistoric human activity. Although artifact surface finds indicate human presence in the Warner Valley from late Pleistocene times onward, most of the currently available evidence relates to the late Holocene Boulder Village Period. Well-watered by runoff from the high Warner Mountains to the west, the valley is filled with a chain of lakes and wetlands. In wet years an extensive series of potholes and sloughs forms among the sand dunes toward its northern end. East of the valley rises the abrupt vertical fault scarp of Poker Jim Ridge, beyond which extends Hart Mountain, a tableland some 3,000 feet above the valley floor.

Archaeological reconnaissance has shown that deep, rich village deposits, marsh-edge processing sites, dune-field camps, and rock art displays are found on the floor of Warner Valley. In the adjacent uplands on both sides, rock rings on high overlooks appear to represent both house circles and hunting blinds. Grinding stones and pithouse depressions near small seasonal lakes mark plant-gathering areas, and lithic scatters and isolated artifacts suggest hunting activities. Rock art is also common, as discussed further below. Regrettably, heavy pillaging of archaeological sites by private collectors has damaged or destroyed much of Warner Valley's prehistoric record.

Margaret Weide [née Lyneis] (1968) pioneered the study of aboriginal settlement and cultural history in the Warner Valley and created a settlement model that is still a main point of reference today. Based on archaeological survey and typological analysis of surface collections, Weide defined three broad periods of occupation in the Warner Valley and adjacent uplands: the period before about 3,500 years ago is attested by Cascade foliates, Large Side-notched, and Humboldt Concave-base points; that from about 3,500 to 1,500 years ago is attested by Elko Eared and Elko Corner-notched points; and that after about 1,500 years ago is attested by Rose Spring, Eastgate, and Desert Side-notched points.

The evidence for occupation before 3,500 years ago is found mostly in the uplands, where sites are identified by lithic scatters at local springs, on open flats, and around the edges of shallow collapse lakes or vernal pools that held water in spring and early summer. After about 3,500 years ago, substantial winter village sites appeared on the valley floor at Crump Lake and near the mouths of Deep Creek and Honey Creek, and the great bulk of the known evidence from Warner Valley thus falls in the Boulder Village Period. A second valley floor pattern of the same period was one of many dispersed camps in the dune and slough topography that was widespread in Warner Valley.

Grinding stones, hand stones, mortars and pestles, and projectile points were all found at valley floor sites, but ground stone items were rare in the uplands, where projectile points and flake scrapers of various kinds were the dominant artifacts. Weide noted the primary upland/lowland contrast as being that stone tools used in food grinding were mainly found on the valley floors, while projectile points and flake scrapers indicative of hunting were best represented in the uplands, though also well attested at the lower elevations. The dune-and-slough topography of the valley floor was interpreted as the scene of primarily summertime temporary camps where food grinding, butchering, and hide working were prominent activities (Weide 1968: 221–246).

A generalized model based on Weide's original work and expanded by subsequent researchers (Weide 1974; Couture et al. 1986, Fowler, Hattori, and Creger 1989; Cannon et al. 1990) is depicted graphically in figure 2.47.

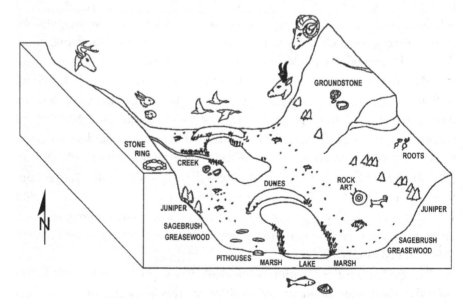

Fig. 2.47. Generalized model of subsistence and settlement in the Warner Valley.

This model proposes that populations which wintered in the lowland areas surrounding Warner Lake were using a tethered subsistence strategy with the lowland lake basin as the primary focus of subsistence activity. Much of the period between April and August was spent in the uplands, however, harvesting and processing plant materials such as bitterroot (*Lomatium spp.*), wild onion (*Allium spp.*), sego lily (*Calochortus macrocarpus*), camas (*Camassia quamash*), wild carrot (*Perideridia spp.*), ponderosa pine (*Pinus ponderosa*), chokecherry (*Prunus virginiana*), wild currant (*Ribes aureum* and *Ribes cerum*), and huckleberry (*Vaccinium membranaceum*). While they were in the uplands, people also hunted and procured lithic materials for tool making.

The University of Nevada, Reno archaeological field school conducted paleoenvironmental studies, survey, and excavations in Warner Valley during the late 1980s and well into the 1990s. Their work explored and developed the general land-use models presented by Weide, Cannon, and others. It resulted in the accumulation of 29 radiocarbon dates—all in the Boulder Village Period—establishing chronological controls for cultural patterns in the Warner Valley for the last 2,800 years of human occupation. Young (2000) conducted extensive fieldwork related to prehistoric landscape morphology and ecological changes spanning the last 4,000 years. Investigating the relationships between archaeological site types and landforms, he determined that while there was significant environmental change over time there was little change in general subsistence strategies. People remained focused on marsh resources throughout the Holocene, though at different locations as varying resource patches were available.

Eiselt (1997, 1998) studied housepits at the Peninsula Site (35LK2579), a large pithouse village on the valley floor, where radiocarbon dates of 610, 450, 450, and 270 cal. BP place much of the occupation late in the Boulder Village Period, a dating supported by the recovery of Desert Side-notched, Cottonwood Triangular, Rose Spring, and Eastgate points in the houses. Faunal and botanical analysis clearly indicates the importance of marsh, lake and lakeshore resources to the inhabitants. Fish (tui chubs and suckers), freshwater clams, waterfowl bones, and carbonized grass and sedge fragments provide direct evidence of the use of local marsh resources. Substantial quantities of artiodactyl bones suggest that hunting of deer and mountain sheep from this site was also an important economic activity.

Charred juniper logs, bulrush matting, and grass bundles provided exquisite details of house constructions in shallow pits generally ranging in depth from about one foot to only a few inches. In diameter they range around 14 feet with one slightly elongated structure being roughly 12x17 feet. Juniper logs leaned inward to form pitched roofs, two layers of bulrush matting were then lashed to the logs in alternating fashion (one horizontal and one vertical). Grass bundles were placed over those and the entire superstructure apparently covered with a thin layer of sun-baked mud. Structural form, basketry, projectile points (Desert Side Notched, Cottonwood Triangular, Rose Spring, Eastgate, and Elko), ground stone tools, and subsistence data all suggest the site occupants may have included both ancestral Northern Paiute and Klamath peoples.

The majority of archaeological surveys and excavations in the Warner Valley have been conducted in the lowlands, in sand dunes, and around lake and marsh shorelines. Tipps (1998) compared artifact assemblages in the foothills and higher elevations with those located in and around the wetlands. Working predominantly from survey data, Tipps (1998:27–28) provided brief artifact summaries for 22 untested sites in the sand dunes. Collections from these sites included Western Stemmed, Concave based, Cascade foliates, Northern Side Notched, Elko, Rose Spring, Eastgate, Desert Side Notched, and Cottonwood Triangular projectile points, indicating that the dune sites had been occupied throughout the entire cultural history of the region. Bifaces, ground stone, and net sinkers are common in these sites. They were clearly places where people conducted a broad range of foraging activities. Cultural features were not generally found at these sites. However, active erosion related to high lake stands of the 1980s had exposed charcoal, mussel shell, and cache pit features in three dune sites along the shores of Campbell and Flagstaff lakes.

Excavations at site 35LK558 resulted in the identification of two hearths and a charcoal-rich stratum. Radiocarbon dating of one of the hearths produced an age of 2880 cal. BP, a date consistent with the recovery of two Elko points from the site surface. Other surface artifacts included an awl, biface, a large bird bone, and ground stone. Similarly, excavations at 35LK2204 explored a charcoal concentration which was ^{14}C dated to 2070 cal. BP, and a twined-textile lined cache pit in this site produced a radiocarbon date of 420 cal. BP. Surface collections recovered 20 Rose Spring and 8 Elko points, which fit very well with these dates, although older medium sized side-notched, Pinto, and Concave Base points were also found, suggesting that the surface assemblages are composite or "palimpsest" collections that include artifacts of earlier time periods unassociated with the radiocarbon-dated features. Finally, excavations at 35LK2207 investigated a shell and charcoal feature eroding from the dune. It produced two ^{14}C dates of 2010 and 1510 cal. BP on shell and charcoal, respectively. No identifiable projectile points were recovered from this site.

Excavations at lake and marsh edge sites 35LK24, 35LK121, 35LK734, and the previously discussed 35LK2579 (Peninsula Site) revealed that these sites probably represent winter villages with multiple housepits at each. Radiocarbon dates cluster within the last 1,000 years, though older occupations are suggested, too, by the recovery of early and middle Holocene projectile points. Rock art is common and considered an artifact form generally indicative of "agglomeration sites," or locations where human populations were clustered on the landscape by good foraging opportunities such as fishing, mussel collecting, seed or root collecting, and hunting (Ricks 1996). Faunal collections vary substantially among these sites, as they do in the Fort Rock basin. Some sites have substantial quantities of fish, mussel, waterfowl, or artiodactyls (deer, pronghorn, mountain sheep), while others have little. Most, if not all, contain the ubiquitous jackrabbit remains. Winter villages were located at lower elevations in spots around the wetlands where fresh food—such as cattail roots, rhizomes, and seeds—was nearly always available in some form.

Assemblages from 22 sites located by surveys in the surrounding foothills include projectile points representative of the entire Holocene, as is typical of sites in sand dune and other lowland settings generally. Rockshelters with associated rock art were present at two sites. Test excavations at various sites produced only two radiocarbon dates, both from rockshelter excavations. Site 35LK2927, which included two rockshelters, three stone rings, and a panel of rock art, produced a date of 620 cal. BP. Site 35LK2746 included six rockshelters and a rock art panel; four of the shelters were tested and a hearth in one of these was dated at 420 cal. BP. These two sites produced very diverse artifact assemblages including projectile points, bifaces, drills, cores, utilized flakes, scrapers, lithic debitage, bone, a little shell, worked and painted wood and bone artifacts, a shell pendant, and shell beads. Glass beads, as well as bones of horse, possibly domesticated sheep, and dogs, suggest that site 35LK2927 contains a significant historic contact period component. Rabbit bone is the most common faunal element. There are no net sinkers and fish bone is rare.

Upland sites tend to exhibit rock cairns, rings and walls, which appear to represent vision quest rock piles, storage facilities, house foundations, and possible fortifications. Though two sites in this setting were tested—the Lynch's Rim Site (35LK690) and 35LK654—no radiocarbon dates are available for upland sites. The largest stone ring site is at Lynch's Rim, which has more than 15 stone enclosures and multiple walls scattered over an area roughly 250 meters long by 170 meters wide. Projectile points from all time periods are present at these sites, as is also true of lowland and mid-elevation sites, but it is clear that these are predominantly late period occupations similar in many ways to stone ring sites in the Fort Rock and Chewaucan basins. Their locations in upland settings suggest that these may well be root-ground habitation sites. Artifact assemblages include projectile points, bifaces, a few drills, scrapers, utilized flakes, ground stone, ocher, and some shell and bone.

Warner Valley Rock Art. Rock art is widespread in the Great Basin generally, and the Warner Valley, which is better studied in this respect than other Oregon parts of the Northern Great Basin, offers a good glimpse of its range and character. Petroglyph figures are abundant, pecked or incised into the desert varnish that naturally forms on rock outcrops and boulders due to long-term weathering. Pictograph figures, drawn with natural pigments on suitable rock surfaces, are present but much less frequent in the existing record, perhaps because of their susceptibility to weathering (Cressman 1937; Loring and Loring 1983; Cannon and Ricks 1986, Ricks 1995).

Site 35LK514 at Long Lake, on the Hart Mountain upland east of Warner Valley, is an especially important rock art locality. A distinctive and powerful early style composed of deeply carved concentric circles, straight and curved parallel lines, and dots, all tightly integrated into large compositions, is unique to this site (fig. 2.48). An extensive panel of these elements barely showed above ground along the base of an outcrop against which earth had accumulated. Excavation revealed that some three feet down a layer of Mt. Mazama volcanic ash several inches thick was banked against the rock. The petroglyph panel extended below this ash layer, continuing a few inches more into underlying clay, demonstrating that the panel significantly predated the 7,600-year-old Mt. Mazama eruption. The style distinctive to this site is termed Long Lake Carved Abstract, and resembles in a generic way many other deeply carved and heavily weathered compositions seen at sites in California, Oregon, and Washington that are thought to be very old (Cannon and Ricks 1986; Ricks 1995; Heizer and Baumhoff 1962).

Other petroglyphs around Long Lake and elsewhere in the Warner Valley represent Great Basin styles typical of more recent millennia, with many rock

Fig. 2.48. Long Lake
Carved Abstract
rock art panel
(Cannon and Ricks
1996).

art panels showing evidence that they were added to by generations of artists. Some elements were pecked out or incised so long ago that they are now easy to miss; they have weathered to completely match the desert varnish on the stones on which they were made, so that only their texture reveals them. Conversely, other elements on the same panel may appear very fresh and hardly weathered. Often, images with greater and lesser degrees of repatination may exist next to each other, or be superimposed over one another.

Four main rock art styles are represented. The heavily weathered Long Lake Carved Abstract style is clearly ancient, dating before 7,600 years ago. Petroglyphs composed of mostly parallel lines, grids, meanders, circles, and dots, moderately to heavily weathered, belong to Great Basin Curvilinear Abstract and Great Basin Rectilinear Abstract styles that are widely known in Oregon, Nevada, California, and Utah (fig. 2.49). These styles are believed to be contemporary with one another, dating between about 3000 and 500 years ago, but the ages must be recognized as quite speculative (Heizer and Baumhoff 1962). The geologically demonstrated great age of the Long Lake Carved Abstract panel seen at Long Lake makes it seem likely that the subsequent styles could be even older than previously thought. The generally least weathered elements at Long Lake, as elsewhere in the desert west, correspond to the Great Basin Representational style, which includes figures of humans, sheep, deer, and lizards. Some even show people riding horses, demonstrating

Fig. 2.49. Petroglyphs of Great Basin Curvilinear, Rectilinear, and Representational styles from Long Lake, Oregon (Cressman 1937: figs. 26, 27).

that petroglyphs in the representational style were made into historical times (fig. 2.49).

In a statistical analysis, Mary Ricks (1996) studied thousands of rock art elements at 117 sites in the Warner Valley region, considering their location, elevation, landform associations, and relationship to plant communities. Quantitative comparisons demonstrate that there is no significant correlation of particular design styles with particular types of sites, except that painted pictographs are correlated with rockshelters, where they have been protected from weathering. Ricks found that the richest accumulations of rock art, both in density and variety of elements, are found at large group aggregation sites, which include both upland root group locations and lower elevation marsh-land settings. In contrast to widespread speculation that aboriginal rock art was fundamentally associated with secretive rituals, "hunting magic," or indi-vidual spirit questing in remote settings, Ricks found that Warner Valley rock art is most commonly associated with public settings and population centers, and she suggests it was most likely created during public ritual activities that were carried out at large seasonal gatherings.

Drews Valley: Chandler, Eastern Spring, and Hay Creek Sites. Archaeological evidence from Drews Valley, some miles south and west of the Lake Abert-Warner Valley area, represents traditional Modoc territory. The archaeological findings are consistent with Modoc ethnographic accounts, which describe upland valleys with rich root grounds, fish-bearing streams, and wooded hills in which deer, bear, and elk could be hunted as good places for spring and summer villages. Research west of the Lakeview/Goose Lake area provides good examples of three site types produced by this settlement pattern.

The Chandler site (35LK2104) is a small hamlet composed of three large stone house rings located on a low rocky ridge that protrudes into the meadowlands of Drews Valley (fig. 2.50a). At least eight associated boulder mortars attest to the importance of root crops to the inhabitants (fig. 2.50b). Surrounded by excellent moist camas grounds to the west, and by better-drained low elevation root grounds (biscuitroot and epos) to the east, the site is perfectly situated for ready access to multiple spring and summer food resources. The house rings are located on private property some distance from the OR Highway 140 right-of-way and could not be tested for subsurface deposits during Oregon Department of Transportation (ODOT)-sponsored research at the site (Connolly and Jenkins 1997; Norris and Jenkins 2000a), but an artifact assemblage recovered from the site surface around the house rings showed that projectile points of Elko types predominated there, suggesting an occupation perhaps several thousand years old. Shovel tests and a 1x1 meter test unit excavated in a lithic scatter that fell within the highway right-of-way at the east end of the site yielded both small Rose Spring arrowpoints and large side-notched dart points, core tools, bifaces, scrapers, utilized flakes, charcoal, and bone. A radiocarbon date of 1950 cal. BP was obtained from the unit.

The Hay Creek site (35LK2102) is located on the banks of a spring draining west to Drews Creek (Jenkins and Norris 2000c). Excavations in the highway right-of-way exposed a shallow housepit depression approximately 22 feet long by 15 feet wide that was dug some 2.5 feet deep into crumbly bedrock (fig. 2.51a). Two house floors were identified, the upper one radiocarbon dated to 930 cal. BP. Rose Spring, Gunther, and Elko points predominated,

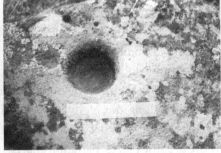

Fig. 2.50. Drews Valley sites: *a*, House ring 1 at the Chandler site; *b*, Drews Valley boulder mortar.

Fig. 2.51. Hay Creek site: *a*, house pit cut in soft bedrock; *b*, root baking oven.

with a few large, side-notched dart points probably of earlier age suggesting that the site was a good place to camp long before the structure was built. Storage pits and ovens were found excavated into the soft bedrock around the house. Stone lined hearths produced radiocarbon dates of 520, 590, 2720, and 2910 cal. BP (fig. 2.51b). Macrobotanical remains, pollen, and an abundance of ground stone attest the importance of root crops (lomatiums and camas), small seeds (*Chenopodium*), and fruits (*Rosaceae*) in the diets of the site occupants. Mortars, pestles, metates, and manos provide strong evidence for root and seed-based food preparation at the site. The pits indicate storage of processed foods for later consumption, perhaps temporary storage in preparation for later movement of supplies from this higher elevation to lowland winter villages. Mule deer bone was most commonly identified with the site's earlier occupations (2700–2900 cal. BP), while mountain sheep remains were found in the later components (500–1000 cal. BP). The archaeological evidence clearly indicates that the economic emphasis at this site was on root collection, though hunting was naturally conducted at the same time.

The Eastern Spring site (35LK2103) is probably an extension of the Hay Creek site complex, since the two are separated by only a short distance (Norris and Jenkins 2000b). The hillside is covered with many flat to slightly depressed clearings several meters in diameter, some of which are certainly housepits. As at the Chandler site, however, they lay outside the highway corridor investigation area and were not excavated. At least eight bedrock mortars, some with pestles in them, were found on the hillside around the little flats. Backhoe trenching along the highway revealed a near-continuous mass of rock-lined ovens, hearths and occupation floors that reached a depth of one meter and more in some places. Flotation analysis of soil samples recovered in and around these features yielded pine, juniper, and sagebrush fuel wood charcoal, as well as charred camas and lomatium bulbs and chokecherry pits. Root-baking ovens and cooking hearths of different kinds had obviously been built, cleaned out, and reused many times at this location. Radiocarbon dates of 1300, 1340, 1415, and 1660 cal. BP were obtained from these and other features. Projectile points included Rose Spring, Eastgate, Gunther, Elko and leaf shaped types. Artifacts included numerous projectile points, mortars, pestles, metates, and manos, many biface fragments, cores of obsidian and basalt, hammerstones, and an interesting curved biface highly suggestive of root scrapers described by Paiute informants in the Harney Basin (Couture et al. 1986).

The Eastern Spring, Hay Creek, and Chandler sites represent various components of early spring and summer foraging camps, hamlets, and root processing locations. Ray (1963:210) notes that Drews Valley was an important Modoc spring and summer village location in which families moved from place to place as they collected different kinds of roots and around which men hunted deer, antelope, and bear. This settlement pattern clearly originated in the preceding Bergen Period—as seen at the Drews Creek and La Sere sites—but the pattern of regularly building house structures in upland settings like Drews Valley and the nearby Gerber Reservoir area (Silvermoon 1994) intensified dramatically during the Boulder Village Period, probably in response to increasing human populations (Jenkins and Connolly 2000). Obsidian studies indicate that during the middle Holocene Bergen Period non-local obsidians came predominantly from sources in the Summer Lake-Chewaucan-Lake Abert and Warner Valley areas, suggesting regular influxes of visitors from these places or trade contacts with populations in those areas. During the last ca. 1,300 years there is a definite shift to traditional Modoc sources, including the local Drews Creek/Butcher Flat source and others to the south-southwest in the Medicine Lakes Highlands (Connolly and Jenkins 1997). The historic Modoc settlement-subsistence pattern seems well established by this point in time.

Harney Basin. In east-central Oregon, Harney Basin archaeology is also dominated by sites of the Boulder Village Period (Fagan 1974; Aikens and Greenspan 1988; Oetting 1990). Relatively large and stable human populations lived around the extensive Harney and Malheur marshes in later prehistoric times (fig. 2.52). Hundreds of their sites were eroded and exposed by wave action during the extreme flooding events that occurred in the mid-1980s. Scatters of artifacts, broken stone, charcoal, food bone, and human remains lay on muddy beaches, making it possible for archaeologists to record sites in considerable detail without excavation. At the same time, artifact collectors

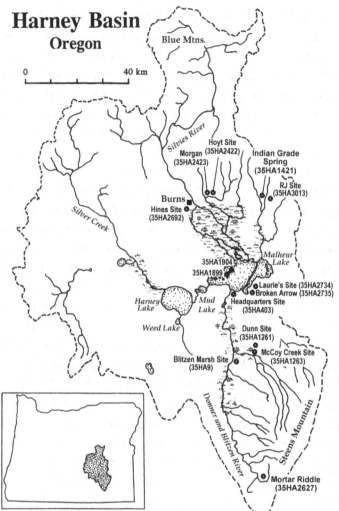

Fig. 2.52. Harney Basin archaeological sites.

swept in to illegally gather artifacts and collect human remains. Working together in exemplary fashion, the Burns Paiute Tribe and the U.S. Fish and Wildlife Service executed a well-thought-out plan to forestall such activity as much as possible by protecting human remains in place, where feasible, and by removing, studying, and reburying other remains as necessary (Hemphill 1999, Simms and Raymond 1999).

Analysis of 50 burials and hundreds of isolated human bones scattered by wave action along the beaches revealed patterns of bone health, damage, and disease which suggested that entire families tended to travel long distances together to their hunting and gathering grounds. Interestingly, this was a pattern quite different from that of contemporary populations in the Stillwater Marsh far to the south near Fallon, Nevada (Hemphill 1999). Also different was the discovery of very large and fancy obsidian "wealth blades," similar to those found among the Klamath and their northern California neighbors. These beautifully crafted bifacial blades are too large and delicate to have been used practically as knives. They are clearly ceremonial in nature, perhaps family heirlooms as well as wealth items. If so, they suggest a greater degree of social stratification than we normally attribute to Great Basin egalitarian societies, and serve as a clear reminder that the ancient past cannot always be adequately interpreted based solely on the oral and ethnohistoric record of modern groups.

Mortar Riddle (35HA2627). The Mortar Riddle site (35HA2627) is located on the Riddle Brothers Ranch Historic District near the Blitzen River (Mueller 2007). This location places the site on the western flank of Steens Mountain at an elevation of about 5,000 feet, with Catlow Valley immediately to the south and west, and the Harney-Malheur Basin to the north and west. Ten radiocarbon dates show intensive occupation of the Mortar Riddle site over the last 1,800 years, putting it firmly within the Boulder Village Period. As indicated by the site name, more than 75 hopper mortar bases, as well as pestles, metates, and manos made of locally available and conveniently shaped rock slabs, show that plant processing was a very important activity there. Soil flotation samples and pollen / phytolith analysis indicate the mortars were used to process roots and seeds. While protein residue analysis provided no direct evidence of bonemeal processing on mortars, the taphonomy of the bones recovered at the site indicates they were commonly broken—presumably on metates and mortars—to facilitate marrow and fat extraction. Hunting of large animals including deer, pronghorn, mountain sheep, and elk was well represented, as was the taking of small animals including squirrels, marmots, and porcupine. The large projectile point assemblage, also reflecting the importance of hunting, includes roughly 500 stone arrow and dart points of Rosegate, Elko, Gatecliff, Humboldt, and foliate types (Epstein 2007). Ready access from the Mortar Riddle site to diverse ecological settings apparently supported relatively sedentary occupations. The presence of apparent house floors, site furniture stones, shell and bone beads, formed bone tools, and gaming pieces all show that the site was an important residential center occupied throughout much of the year.

McCoy Creek (35HA1263). Situated between Malheur Lake and the northwestern base of Steens Mountain, the McCoy Creek Site at the narrows between Diamond Swamp and Diamond Valley was a sedentary community of the Boulder Village Period (Musil 1991, 1992). Excavations in a deep, rich cultural deposit revealed a complex of two firehearths, two storage pits, clusters of flaked and ground stone tools, and thin patches of clay remaining from two consecutive and overlapping house floors. A radiocarbon determination of 1850 cal. BP comes from beneath this complex, and features associated with the house floors produced five additional radiocarbon ages ranging between 1350 and 950 cal. BP.

Another nearby house was discovered at a slightly higher level within the site. Its floor was shallow and roughly circular, 12 feet in diameter, defined by dark-stained earth and some small-diameter burnt posts at places around its edges. Near the center of the floor was a large firehearth, and shallow pits had been dug toward the walls on either side. Charred poles and fragments of grass thatch lay on the floor, along with scattered flaked and ground stone artifacts, suggesting that the structure burned while in use. This dwelling closely resembles the typical winter house of the ethnographic Wadatika Northern Paiute, who occupied the same area; a ^{14}C date of 540 cal. BP on charcoal from the floor places it in very late prehistoric times. Excavations turned up traces of an earlier floor beneath this structure, and trench profiles elsewhere in the site indicated two additional house structures. It is therefore evident that McCoy Creek was occupied from time to time over a considerable period.

The artifact assemblage from McCoy Creek was large and diverse, including flaked stone projectile points, preforms, drills, scrapers, and cores, as well as ground stone manos, metates, hopper mortars, and pestles. A ground stone pipe bowl, bone beads, and a single bead of *dentalium* shell were also found. Projectile points were numerous, with 140 classifiable specimens. Elko and Gatecliff points were associated with the earlier occupations, while Desert Side-notched, Cottonwood Triangular, and small pin-stem corner-notched points like those common along the Columbia River were associated with the later house.

An unusually rich and varied vertebrate faunal assemblage from McCoy Creek included nearly 47,000 bone specimens, of which 18,000 were analyzed in detail (Greenspan 1991). Bones from the early, pre-residential occupation were relatively few, but those associated with the earlier and later house occupations show that the people of McCoy Creek made use of all the major habitats in their vicinity—marsh, lake, stream, and upland. Aquatic animals included mink, muskrat, ducks, grebes, coot, fishes, and spotted frog; terrestrial animals included artiodactyls, canids, bobcat, rabbit, hare, marmot, a variety of small rodents, sage grouse, various perching birds, and some reptiles. Numerous eggshell fragments indicate that people were at the site in late spring and early summer, but evidence suggesting other seasons of occupation is not definitive.

It is notable that fish and fur-bearing mammals are most strongly represented in the occupation dated between about 1500 and 1000 cal. BP, while large game animals were best-represented in the occupation dated around 500 cal. BP. This corresponds strikingly with paleoclimatic evidence from nearby Diamond Pond, which shows that the earlier period was one of generally greater effective moisture in the area, while the later time was one of marked drought.

Flotation analysis of soil samples from hearths and storage pits in the McCoy Creek house structures produced a diverse botanical assemblage (Stenholm 1991). Charred sagebrush, willow/poplar wood, and bunchgrass were common, with seeds of goosefoot and other species also well represented. The fire hearth dated to 1230 cal. BP yielded 12 plant taxa; the bulk of the material was charcoal of sagebrush, with willow/poplar and grass also represented. Nearly 100 charred seeds were mostly of goosefoot and various grasses, but knotweed, dogbane, and possibly fleabane were present in trace amounts. The chenopod seeds were popped open by parching, and the enclosing glumes of the grass seeds had been removed by threshing. All these seeds ripen in late summer, and could have been collected in the site vicinity. The plant assemblage contains plants useful as fuel (big sage), construction material (willow, poplar, and mock orange), flooring and structural material (bunchgrasses), cordage (dogbane), and edible seeds and fruits of goosefoot, juniper, bunchgrass, and knotweed (Stenholm 1991:142).

Lost Dune (35HA792). The Lost Dune Site, located not far north of Diamond Swamp, produced several hundred fragments of Paiute/Shoshone pottery and Desert Side-notched projectile points from a surface blowout in a sand dune field (Thomas, Loring, and Goheen 1983). The site is unusual for several reasons. First, it is one of the few sites in Oregon that contains many sherds of Shoshonean pottery, which is rare in southeast Oregon and found only very late in time. As a rule, both Desert Side-notched points and pottery are considerably less prevalent in Oregon than they are at sites to the east (Idaho and Utah) and south (Nevada and California), where they have been dated from around 1,000 years ago to the historic period. The specimens that are found in Oregon invariably date within the last 500 years. Second, clear evidence for bison hunting around Malheur Lake suggests a possible late period incursion of bison-hunting Shoshoneans from the Snake River Plain into the Harney Basin about 400 cal. BP (Lyons and Mehringer 1998). Third, extensive geochemical analysis of obsidian, chert, sandstone and ceramic artifacts from the Lost Dune Site indicate that tool stone and clay identified there came from sources along the Idaho border and Owyhee and Malheur Rivers, while some of the site's distinctive white chert artifacts originated in the Tosawihi quarry, located in 'White Knife' Shoshone country near Battle Mountain, Nevada (Lyons 2001). In short, the analysis strongly suggested that the Lost Dune occupants were probably visitors who had come to the Harney Basin from the east and south, regions occupied by Northern Paiutes and Shoshones.

Laurie's Site (35HA3074) and Broken Arrow (35HA3075). These sites are located near each other on the southeast shore of Malheur Lake, across an embayment from the Headquarters Site. They are habitation sites incorporating housepits or wickiup floors, where the UO field school excavated dense concentrations of artifacts, botanical, and faunal remains during the summers of 2001 and 2002 (O'Grady 2006). Laurie's Site contains at least eight housepit depressions, while the Broken Arrow Site produced evidence of at least one shallow wickiup floor and possible evidence of others.

Radiocarbon dates indicate occupation at Laurie's Site from ca. 1850 to 1450 cal. BP., and at the Broken Arrow site from about 2000 to 1750 cal. BP. Botanical remains recovered from soil flotation samples include an abundance of locally available marsh and lakeshore seeds such as chenopodium, amaranth, bulrush, cattail, and wada. Laurie's site samples also include mountain mahogany (known to have been used in making wooden digging sticks, bows, and atlatls), willow, and more juniper than was found at Broken Arrow, providing support for the interpretation that the deeper depressions at Laurie's Site were excavated housepits incorporating more substantial roof supports. Faunal remains from both sites include predominantly small to medium-sized mammals (muskrats, beavers, rabbits, hares), waterfowl, and some fish. Larger mammals such as deer and pronghorn occur in moderate proportions as well. Both sites contain equally rich and diverse tool assemblages including Rose Spring, Eastgate, Elko, Humboldt, and foliate points, ground stone tools, many bifaces, drills, scrapers, utilized flakes, cores, a stone ball, a pipe fragment, stone, shell, and bone beads, a pendant, bone awls, and pressure flakers.

While similar sites and assemblages in the Fort Rock basin have been interpreted as winter village or hamlet sites (Jenkins 2000, 2004; Jenkins, Droz, and Connolly 2004), O'Grady (2006) questions whether Laurie's and Broken Arrow were winter sites because of their exposed position, lack of spring or stream water, and generally small quantities of fish—one of the few fresh foods available in the winter. The general lack of immature (unfused) long bones suggests that Laurie's site may have been occupied during the late summer and fall while a perceptible increase in the unfused bone of immature animals at Broken Arrow suggests that site may have been more commonly occupied during the spring and summer.

Indian Grade Spring (35HA1421). Archaeological surveys in the mountains and lowlands around the Harney basin (Oetting 1987; O'Grady 2006; Pettigrew 1979) have documented many small lithic scatters, often with milling stone fragments. One special locality is Stinkingwater Mountain northeast of Malheur Lake, where shallow rocky soils extending over many miles provide optimum habitat for a variety of plants with edible roots. In ethnographic times this was an important root ground for the Wadatika and other Northern Paiute groups as well as for Sahaptin-speaking people from the southern Columbia Plateau. Modern Paiutes from Burns, Warm Springs, and other places still go there to dig sego lily, bitterroot, yampa, wild onion, and biscuitroot (Couture et al. 1986).

Excavations at Indian Grade Spring, on the western slope of Stinkingwater Mountain, recovered artifacts that indicate generalized hunting-gathering and toolmaking activities: projectile points, bifaces, scrapers, drills, knives, spokeshaves, cores, choppers, manos, and metates (Jenkins and Connolly 1990). Charcoal from several small fire hearths and a rock-filled roasting pit gave ^{14}C dates spanning the last 3,000 years, indicating repeated visitations throughout the Boulder Village Period. Little evidence was found that was specifically definitive of root harvesting—just a few charred root bulbs in hearths. However, large quantities of tough basalt stone tools suggest woodworking and the possible production of digging sticks made of local mountain mahogany (Kiigemagi 1989). Beyond these indications, the best clue that Indian Grade Spring may have been a root camp comes simply from its location in a prime root-digging area.

RJ Site (35HA3013). The RJ site is located in the Stinkingwater Mountain root grounds about five miles from Indian Grade Spring. Excavations conducted by the University of Oregon field school recovered Desert Side Notched, Cottonwood Triangular, Rose Spring, Malheur Stemmed, Elko Eared and Corner Notched, Humboldt, and Northern Side Notched projectile points, along with bifaces, basalt choppers, cores, and large flake tools, a drill, and a small amount of ground stone. This tool assemblage is very similar to that recovered from Indian Grade Spring (Jenkins and Connolly 1990; O'Grady 2006), and radiocarbon dates of 3080, 1480, and 900 cal. BP indicate continuing Boulder Village Period visitations throughout the same time that Indian Grade Spring was in regular use. Small stone rings less than three feet in diameter on bedrock could be related to root drying or temporary shelters.

Knoll Site (35HA2530). The Knoll site is similar to the Indian Grade Spring and RJ sites, although it is located north-northwest of them in the Silvies Valley. Whiting (1950:19) reported that the Harney Valley Paiutes picked currants and other berries in the late summer/early fall in this area, and pursued opportunistic hunting and fishing on the way to deer and elk hunting grounds in the Canyon City/John Day area. The recovery of currant or gooseberry remains at the Knoll site, along with ground stone, projectile points, hearths, and lithic debitage, is consistent with the ethnographic record and suggests repeated late summer/early fall visits there. UO field school excavations recovered Elko, Northern Side Notched, and Humboldt projectile points, all of which suggest middle Holocene occupation; this interpretation is supported by obsidian hydration dating of artifacts predominantly made of the locally available Whitewater Ridge obsidian. Radiocarbon dates of 1710, 900, and 460 cal. BP indicate that the site was repeatedly used during the late Holocene as well. Demonstrably later artifacts were few, but the illegal excavations evident at the site may have removed most of the more recent deposits (O'Grady 2006). Human activity at the site clearly began during the Bergen Period and continued through the Boulder Village Period.

Morgan (35HA2423) and Hoyt (35HA2422). These sites, located on low sandy ridges cut through by U.S. Highway 20 northeast of Burns, are situated near lowland grasslands and marshes. Both are relatively small temporary campsites from which hunting and gathering activities were based, but there are some important differences between them. The Morgan site is composed of two distinct activity areas marked by relatively dense cultural remains. The West Locus contained a dense concentration of artifacts including a small group of ground stone fragments, bifaces, hammerstones, edge-modified flakes, cores, and Eastgate and Elko projectile points. Recovered botanical remains included sagebrush charcoal and a fragment of charred root (possibly camas), indicating along with the ground stone that plant processing was an important activity there. A hearth dated to 950 cal. BP places this component of the site within the Boulder Village Period.

There were two components in the East locus of the Morgan site which show that its occupation began during the Bergen Period and continued through the Boulder Village Period. Charcoal from two hearths in the younger upper deposits was dated to 760 and 1170 cal. BP, and associated artifacts included Eastgate, Rose Spring, Cottonwood Triangular, and Elko points. These, along with used flakes, bifaces, a drill, cores, ground stone, and hammerstones suggest temporal and functional parallels with the West locus. Lower in the deposits, Northern Side-notched and Elko points were predominant, and obsidian hydration dating suggests these older deposits may be 4,000 or more years old. Associated botanical remains included sagebrush and juniper charcoal, a trace of an unidentified seed, possible Widgeon grass, and processed edible tissue that may be camas. Faunal remains from both loci indicate the hunting of rabbits, squirrels, voles, some deer or antelope, and birds. The presence of immature rabbit bone (from Pygmy rabbits, Black-tailed, and possibly White-tailed Jackrabbits) and eggshells suggests occupations in the early spring and summer.

The nearby Hoyt site was bisected by the construction of U.S. Highway 20. Preservation of site deposits was best north of the highway and it was here that excavation took place (O'Grady 2006). Projectile points included types known in both the Great Basin and Columbia Plateau, including Rose Spring, Eastgate, and small contracting stem points, Elko Corner-Notched, Elko Eared, Humboldt, and Northern Side-Notched. This assemblage suggests that site occupations began perhaps 4,000–5,000 years ago and spanned the period of technological transition from the atlatl and dart to the bow and arrow. Radiocarbon dating of sagebrush charcoal from a hearth with an associated large metate indicates occupation around 1830 cal. BP. The evidence thus attests a long period of site use that began in the Bergen Period and continued throughout the Boulder Village Period. Dispersed sagebrush charcoal found at greater depth nearby produced a date of 280 cal. BP, which is inconsistent with the rest of the evidence and probably unassociated with the site occupation.

Metates, manos, a pestle, abraders with deep grooves and scratches, scrapers, used flakes, an atlatl weight, drills, bifaces, hammerstones, cores, and bone tools all attest to a broad range of camp maintenance and food foraging and preparation activities. Stone tool production was clearly an important activity at the site, perhaps due to an increased focus on the hunting of both large and small game. Faunal remains were primarily rodents, rabbits, artiodactyls (deer, pronghorn antelope, mountain sheep), and canids (coyote, dog, wolf). Fish and waterfowl were also recovered at this site, apparently indicating some exploitation of Silvies River sloughs nearby. The presence of eggshell indicates some use of the site during the spring. Plant remains—recovered in extremely small quantities—include sagebrush charcoal, grass seeds, unidentified charred seeds, possible biscuit root, and possible processed edible tissues which commonly include fruits, berries, nuts, and roots. Hunting appears to have been somewhat more important than gathering plant materials, perhaps due to the location of the site at the interface between the upland foothills to the north and the broad expanse of grasslands to the south and east.

Hines (35HA2692). The Hines site is located on U.S. Highway 20 in the town of Hines, just south of Burns. The site is strategically located near a seep on the piedmont slope below Burns Butte, providing access to both the productive marshes to the east and the wooded uplands to the west. Projectile points include predominantly Rose Spring, Eastgate, and straight or pinstemmed arrow points, placing the site occupation primarily in the Boulder Village Period. Ephemeral older occupations—probably 5,000–2,000 years ago—are indicated by stratified deeper deposits at the south end of the site and the recovery of three Elko Eared and one Northern Side Notched projectile points. Radiocarbon dating of charcoal obtained from a hearth located in the upper strata of the site and associated with a large metate, indicates occupation around 1060 cal. BP, a date that fits comfortably with the 10 arrow points found scattered around it. The large number of projectile point and biface fragments, representing all stages of lithic reduction from cores to finished tools, suggests they were being produced at the site. The proximity of local obsidian that occurs naturally in the gravels washed off the slopes of nearby Burns Butte was an additional lure of the site location. Accompanying the arrowpoints and bifaces were obsidian and basalt cores, utilized flakes, drills, an abrader, a bone tool, a stone bead, a large complete metate, metate and mano fragments, and a polished bone tool or decorative item.

Stone tool production and food preparation were clearly important activities at the Hines site. Faunal remains included rodents (kangaroo rat, wood rat, muskrat), rabbits and hares, badger, raccoon, beaver, mule deer, elk, and canids (coyote, dog, or wolf). Fish, waterfowl, muskrat, raccoon, and beaver indicate the exploitation of marshlands and sloughs nearby. The presence of egg shell and unfused small mammal bones indicates use of the site at least during spring and early summer. Plant remains include charred camas bulb, sagebrush, serviceberry, rose, pine, and juniper charcoal, charred *chenopodium* and grass seed, and processed edible tissues. While the site produced an unusual quantity of charred edible plant remains, their random distribution throughout site deposits raises some question as to what portion was cultural and what may have been contributed by natural burning. However, considering the faunal, floral, and stone tool assemblages together, there is no doubt that generalized foraging in the marsh to the east and along the ridge to the west were the primary economic activities pursued from this site. There was no clear evidence for structures, although the distribution of point-plotted artifacts clearly indicates the presence of one or more areas of intense activity near the hearth (O'Grady 2006).

Dirty Shame Rockshelter Wickiups (35ML65). After a long period of apparent abandonment during the Lunette Lake and Bergen periods, regular use of the Dirty Shame Rockshelter site resumed after about 2850 cal. BP and effectively spanned the entire Boulder Village Period. The activities that took place at Dirty Shame Rockshelter before and after its long occupational hiatus during the middle Holocene Bergen Period were very similar, but not identical. Stone drills, gravers, uniface scrapers, and used flakes were more common in the later deposits, suggesting that more woodworking, bone-working, and hide-working chores were carried out there than had been the case earlier. Most importantly, well preserved remains of several small conical or domed house structures, framed with willow poles and thatched with native rye grass, were present in the later levels. These were constructed in the same well-engineered way as those of the historic Northern Paiute, suggesting that the people who came to Dirty Shame Rockshelter occupied them for extended periods, as did the historically known people who made such houses in later times. Willig (1982) studied the best-preserved structure in detail from field records and collected specimens, and prepared the architectural reconstruction drawing seen in figure 2.28 (on page 82).

The plant and animal remains from both the earlier and later periods of occupation at Dirty Shame Rockshelter indicate that people came there for the late summer–early fall harvest, while the houses and other evidence of substantial domestic activity suggest the site may have served as a winter encampment. The Owyhee uplands are cold and snowy in the winter, but the setting of Dirty Shame Rockshelter, in a deep canyon out of the wind, with a broad southern exposure to catch the winter sun and a high cliff to store the sun's absorbed warmth, makes this a plausible interpretation (Aikens, Cole, and Stuckenrath 1977).

North Ontario Interchange (35ML1328 and 35ML1379). The North Ontario Interchange sites are located at the confluence of the Snake and Malheur rivers near the intersection of Interstate 84 and Oregon Highway 201 on the Oregon-Idaho border (fig. 2.53). Fine sandy-silt deposits gradually built up as the spring melt waters of the colliding rivers rose gently out of their banks to flood the lowest river terrace. Natives of the region, knowing this pattern, occupied these sites after the waters receded to intercept and catch spawning Chinook salmon, and to collect fresh water mussels from gravel bars along the river channels. Clusters of fire-cracked rock and mussel shells were surrounded by Chinook salmon bones, obsidian Elko points and

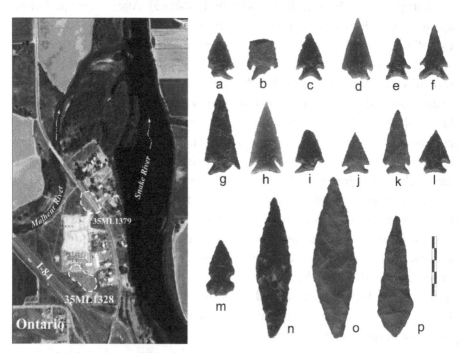

Left, Fig. 2.53. North Ontario Interchange salmon fishing sites at the confluence of the Malheur and Snake rivers; *right*, Fig. 2.54. Projectile points and knives of the North Ontario Interchange sites.

bifaces, basalt unifaces, small quantities of ground stone (including a boulder hopper mortar), hammer stones, shell and bone beads, and lithic chipping debris. The complete lack of arrow points, general lack of large side notched points, foliate, and Western Stemmed points, and nearly exclusive recovery of Elko points, is consistent with a series of radiocarbon dates spanning the period from ca. 3100 to 2600 cal. BP (fig. 2.54).

Obsidian hydration studies, and a single outlier radiocarbon date of 1530 cal. BP, indicated that ephemeral site visits occurred before and after the concentrated period of use, which centered on the early Boulder Village Period. Obsidian studies—both sourcing and hydration—involved 259 artifacts and flakes. Most of the obsidian proved to have been collected from large dispersed sources such as Gregory Creek and Coyote Wells to the west and southwest, although easterly obsidian sources in Idaho (e.g., Timber Butte) and even some as far south as Nevada are also represented, particularly in the earlier periods of occupation (Jenkins et al. 2010).

Ecological, Technological, and Social Patterns of the Boulder Village Period. Marsh, lake, and riverine resources were very important to Northern Great Basin populations throughout the Boulder Village period, as they were for the Northern Paiute (Fowler and Liljeblad 1986), Klamath (Spier 1930), and Modoc (Ray 1963) of the Historic period. Winter pithouse village sites, in many cases featuring stone house rings, were generally built on low prominences located along marsh edges near the base of adjoining foothills (Cressman 1956; Wingard 2001; Eiselt 1998; Oetting 1989; Pettigrew 1985). This winter village pattern reflected the agglomeration of local populations and increasing dependence on especially reliable and seasonally abundant resources, particularly fish where available, and storable upland root crops. Fort Rock and Chewaucan basin populations situated their late fall/winter sites in settings which allowed easy access to both marshes and upland root grounds.

The Carlon Village site, located on a low ridge at Silver Lake, is the best-known and most fully documented example of this late Holocene settlement pattern (Wingard 2001). This impressive site, with eight large stone ring domestic structures (several exceeding 25 feet in diameter) made of huge boulders, was built about 2350 cal. BP. The extraordinary effort expended by the builders of Carlon Village is hugely important; here people were placing their mark on the landscape, even leveraging heavy boulders up on other boulders and decorating them with petroglyphs and pictographs, as if to advertise to

Fig. 2.55.
Petroglyphs and
pictographs
on culturally
emplaced boulder
at Silver Lake.

others their permanence and strength (fig. 2.55). Such architecture, along with extremely rich and complex artifact and faunal assemblages, shows that Carlon Village was a long-term occupation site of special importance. Social stratification within the community is indicated by the presence of large substantial stone ring houses segregated at the top of the ridge, while much more modest houses with shallow earthen floors were located near the base of the ridge.

Obsidian source use patterns suggest that residents of Carlon Village also seasonally occupied the nearby higher elevation Boulder Village site for the spring root harvest (Jenkins and Brashear 1994; Wingard 2001:137). Paired in the typical two-village settlement pattern common historically for Klamath, Modoc, and Northern Paiutes, the Carlon and Boulder Village sites provide new insight into the time depth of these historic subsistence-settlement patterns.

In the Harney Basin, where landforms and ecology varied, houses and hamlets were often placed on slightly elevated spots within the lakes and marshes, as well as around their edges (Oetting 1990, 1999; Carter and Dugas 1994; Musil 1995). Studies of many burials and hundreds of isolated human bones scattered by wave action along lake beaches revealed patterns of bone health, damage, and disease which suggested that entire families tended to travel long distances together to hunting and root grounds. This was a pattern quite different from that of contemporary Paiute populations in the Stillwater Marsh far to the south near Fallon, Nevada (Hemphill 1999), but corresponds well with ethnographic accounts offered by local Burns Paiute tribal members (Couture et al. 1986).

Klamath Basin settlement-subsistence patterns appear to have remained fairly stable over the last 3,000 years. Individual settlements such as Nightfire Island may have changed function and, occasionally location, in response to rising and falling water levels in the Lower Klamath Lake basin. However, in general the more sedentary Klamath-Modoc settlement pattern involving winter villages and spring fishing camps and villages appears to have been well established early in the Bergen Period and to have continued into the Boulder Village Period. There were perhaps some moderate changes in the Goose Lake basin, the most notable being a shift in obsidian procurement from previously used local sources to more distant modern Modoc sources about 1,500 years ago (Connolly and Jenkins 1997).

In sum, Boulder Village Period human populations of the late Holocene in the Northern Great Basin appear to have been relatively large and much more concentrated than in previous times. It is likely that at least some of the motivation to form larger centralized communities, in contrast to the earlier pattern of more widely dispersed family groups, came from heightened consideration of security needs. The location of even some seasonal camps in hard-to-reach settings suggests that safety from surprise attack may have been a concern in that period, as it was in historic times (Spier 1930; Ray 1963; Oetting 1989; Bettinger 1999:330).

Ethnographic sources show that conflict, raiding, and trading were all endemic over a broad area by later prehistoric times (Kelly 1932; Spier 1930), and indeed often related to one another. Raiding for goods and slaves became one element of interaction among neighboring groups of the Boulder Village Period, as clearly seen at Nightfire Island (Sampson 1985). Trade in shells and obsidian also intensified in the Klamath and Columbia River basins during this period. The emergence of a slave trade managed by partners on the Columbia River and counterparts among ancestral Modoc, Klamath, and other peoples of southwest Oregon—as well as adjacent California—seems to have taken place largely in the Boulder Village Period (Sampson 1985; Schulting 1995).

Historic Archaeology

Historic archaeological sites have been widely recorded throughout Oregon's Northern Great Basin in recent decades, though relatively few have been thoroughly investigated. Common types include Native American sites of the contact period, railroad logging grades and camps, lumber milling sites, homesteads and mining sites, and localities associated with nineteenth-century military operations and the early Indian Reservation period. A few illustrative examples are presented here.

Bezuksewas (35KL778). Bezuksewas is the site of a historic Klamath village stretching along the Williamson River downstream from the modern town of Chiloquin (Cheatham et al. 1995; Spier 1930). A small portion of the old village bordering U.S. Highway 97, investigated by the University of Oregon Museum of Natural and Cultural History, produced evidence of habitation spanning at least the last 4,500 years and continuing into the twentieth century. This long-term annual and episodic occupation was supported by intensive fishing, freshwater mussel collecting, and plant collection. Large-volume storage of dried foods—primarily fish, wocas, and camas—helped the Klamath ancestors get through the snowy mountain winters.

The old site was re-occupied by a Klamath family following the formation of the Klamath Reservation in 1864. Artifacts of this period recovered by excavation included metal, glass, ceramics, leather, beads, buttons (including many from U.S. military uniforms), bullets and cartridges, bone, shell, children's toys, and an 1892 U.S. dime, all disposed of in the family dump.

The pre-contact population depended primarily on a diet of fish and vegetal resources, supplemented by freshwater mussels. After the Klamath Reservation was formed, domestic animals and crops–cows, pigs, beans, and Italian plums–supplemented the traditional diet. Fish (suckers, chubs, and salmonids) continued to be important, as did wild plants (knotweed, wild plum, and camas), but other introduced foods also appear, such as lard, baking powder, and canned goods. In pre-contact times, the hunting of large mammals (elk and deer) was apparently limited to opportunistic kills, but hunting increased with the introduction of guns.

Chronologically diagnostic artifacts indicate the farmstead was occupied until about 1910. This was about the time when Klamath Reservation land was officially parceled out to individuals under the Dawes Allotment Act in an effort to encourage tribal members to establish farming households in a manner consistent with colonial America's European heritage. The allottee was granted title to the property in 1910, but died the following year. Following his death, a series of short-term land tenures and subsequent inheritances began, but actual occupation of the property appears to have largely ceased (Cheatham et al. 1995).

Beatty Curve (35KL95). The Beatty Curve site is located about a mile east of the town of Beatty on Highway 140 between Klamath Falls and Lakeview. The highway bisects the site, dividing its gently sloping marsh-edge portion, which contains a deep prehistoric deposit spanning some 8,000 or more years, from its upslope portion, where the historic occupation was focused. Much like Bezuksewas, the best-represented historic occupation at Beatty Curve spans the time from the formation of the Klamath Reservation to ca. 1915, but some artifacts, including brass beads and a Dutch East Indies coin with an 1839 date stamp, suggest contacts during the earlier fur trade era. This research is not yet fully published, but an initial view of it is available in Connolly (2011).

A main focus of excavations in 2007–2009 was on an 8x12 foot cabin probably built by the agency for a chiefly family. This may have been Chief Mosenkasket (later known as Moses Brown), a signer of the Klamath Treaty representing the upper Sprague River Klamath people, or, more likely, James Barkley, a leader favored by the agency. The cabin floor appears to have rested at least partially on bedrock on the upslope side, where some of the wood flooring was preserved. The surviving flooring sections were built exclusively with cut nails, but wire nails were common in the deposits, and it is likely that wire nails were used subsequent to the initial construction for structural repairs or modifications continuing into the twentieth century.

Excavations recovered an abundance of food remains, and along with them personal items such as children's shoes and marbles, hair combs and buttons, shaving razors and firearms—a range suggesting the presence of men, women, and children. Domestic items and hardware were also recovered. Thousands of bones—of both wild game and domestic animals—were found, but relatively few saw-cut bones reflecting butchered meat from a commercial source. Although domesticated animals were commonly eaten, the bone assemblage reflects traditional Native butchery practices and very limited access to commercially processed meats. Very limited use of commercial food products is also evident in the near total absence of cans and condiment bottles.

Surrounding the cabin were various features of ash, charcoal, and burned earth. Although varying amounts of bone and historic debris were associated, these were not clearly food processing or trash burning features. They may be the remains of smudge fires set to enhance the drying of fish or other game; although evidence of associated drying racks was not found, this area produced relatively higher concentrations of fish bone than other parts of the site. Fish remains identified from the site were primarily large suckers, with chubs, salmon and trout also represented. The Klamath people living at this site around the turn of the twentieth century were clearly transitioning from traditional lifeways to a cash economy and a more "Americanized" lifestyle, but were still strongly committed to Native lifestyles. The site is regarded still as an important traditional fishing place.

During the later nineteenth and early twentieth century the rising importance of logging fueled the availability of cheap milled lumber in Bend, LaPine, and Lakeview. Structures of milled lumber were being built all along the northern and western edges of Oregon's Northern Great Basin region at places like Fort Rock, Imperial Valley, Brothers, Hampton, Stauffer, Hamilton, and Blitzen. Settlement booms during unusually wet years between 1900 and 1920 were fostered by land speculators who told glowing stories of cheap desert land waiting to be claimed by far-sighted and enterprising adventurers. Thousands of hapless settlers were attracted to the high desert by promising schemes about irrigation projects soon to bring life-giving water to miles of dry, open country, and were shown maps indicating the railroad would soon reach the farthest towns to provide cheap transportation of their crops to markets in Portland and Seattle. Most of those settling on such isolated desert plots only lasted a few months or years. Beaten by the isolation and unrewarded hard work, they sold out for a few cents on the dollar. Though most of their tiny clapboard cabins have been pulled down for scrap lumber or moved to ranches nearby, some are still to be found slowly collapsing into the timeless dust and sagebrush (see Howe 1968:53 for examples).

Little archaeological excavation has been done at any of these historic sites. A number of log "homestead" cabins, built around the turn of the twentieth century, have been excavated around Sunriver, in the Great Basin / Columbia Plateau boundary zone between Fort Rock and Bend. These studies have typically produced little information. One-room cabins made of lodgepole pine were quickly built to "prove up" on a land claim, but seldom served as primary residences; many were subsequently moved and saw secondary service as auxiliary ranch buildings. The modern community of Fort Rock is one of the few early settlements of this kind in the Northern Great Basin that managed to survive. Unstudied remnants of early households built by the first settlers are still to be seen peeping out of encroaching sand in its vicinity, and a number of old wooden buildings in good condition have been rescued from the surrounding countryside and brought together in an historical display near the modern Fort Rock State Park (Parks 1989).

Summary

The Northern Great Basin, encompassing the entire southeastern quarter of Oregon south of the Blue Mountains and east of the Cascades, has the longest firmly established archaeological record in the Western United States. Dried human feces (*coprolites*) containing ancient human DNA have been recovered from the Paisley Caves and directly dated by the AMS radiocarbon method, establishing that people of Siberian descent were present in the region by at least 14,500 years ago. They were broad-range foragers similar in many aspects to those who followed them. They hunted large game whenever they were available but also consumed small fish and animals, many kinds of plants, and even insects. Sometimes they traveled long distances to reach favorable hunting and collecting areas. People were then sparsely distributed throughout this vast region, but periodic gatherings near unusually productive resources, particularly those found in marshes and adjacent grasslands, helped groups keep in touch with others, who could provide mates for maturing adults and had knowledge to share about the land and resources that all relied on. It was a hard existence but there were undoubtedly also many good times.

By 12,000 years ago, human populations had risen substantially. Artifacts of this time—Western Stemmed, foliate and lanceolate projectile points and large domed scrapers in particular—are fairly common in most basins and it is clear from radiocarbon dating of firepits in the caves of the region that such sites, particularly those near marshes, were regularly visited. At Fort Rock Cave, people replaced their footwear (the famous Fort Rock sagebrush bark sandals) and left their worn-out sandals behind. They spent some of their springs and summers at higher, cooler locations like Paulina Lake hunting large game and gathering the bounty of the land. At other seasons, they gathered in places like Buffalo Flat to catch and process large numbers of rabbits. They ended the year and began the new one in sites such as the Connley and Cougar Mountain caves, located in the juniper forest belts that fringed lowland marshes and grasslands. These sheltered sites were conveniently located in the overwintering grounds of large game (bison, deer, elk, pronghorn, and mountain sheep) and in some cases waterfowl. While these early people spent much of their year in and around marshes, it was probably no more characteristic of them than of those who followed.

Sometime around 9,000 years ago people began to shift their seasonal occupations away from the caves of the region, probably in response to a warming climate and changing ecology. They were still visiting the marshes, at least during the spring and summer, but perhaps no longer stayed around to winter in the caves because of declining local resources. Whatever the cause, people clearly were present in the Northern Great Basin, occupying open sites briefly to take advantage of seasonal resources, but not spending much time in the caves. In some places, notably around Paulina Lake, the deposition of a thick mantle of Mount Mazama volcanic ash about 7,600 years ago changed the local ecology dramatically and Native Americans had to permanently change the way they used the area.

Regardless of the challenges, population continued slowly rising in the region, reaching a critical mass about 6,000 years ago. At about that time the first winter houses were constructed in the Fort Rock basin marshes, signaling a major shift in social and economic endeavors. The appearance of large cache pits indicates that local populations surrendered a degree of their freedom and mobility to begin processing large quantities of storable food and materials that would get them through the cold winters. Hamlets (family settlements of 2 to 3 houses) sprang up around shallow marshes, lakes, and ponds. Fishing, hunting waterfowl, rabbits, and migratory large game, and gathering many kinds of small seeds provided the bounty to support these settlements. Fishing equipment, art, games, smoking pipes, shell beads traded up from California, and decorated utilitarian items such as mauls, manos, mortars, and pestles all attest to the increased social interaction that accompanied increasing sedentism. As populations increased, stable villages developed in especially good locations.

By about 3,000 years ago villages were being relocated to available prominences at the edges of marshes and nearer the base of mountains and foothills, signaling the ever-increasing importance of edible root crops that were available only in the stony mantle of upland settings. Moving nearer the hills reduced the cost of transporting root crops back to the winter village, and may also be an indication of concern for the safety of the occupants and their vital winter food stores. The construction of houses and stone walls in defensible positions, particularly in rich upland root-ground settings like Boulder Village, suggests that social tensions were increasing along with growing regional populations. Becoming more dependent on a good annual harvest of edible roots to accommodate increasing populations could be economically chancy, and may have occasionally led local groups into risky behaviors such as raiding their neighbors. Increasing evidence of violence about 2,000 years ago also corresponds closely in time with the introduction of the bow and arrow, which allows shooting from cover and is thus a better combat weapon than the earlier atlatl and dart. Trading, which appears to have also increased during the late prehistoric period, was a less risky form of acquiring necessary food and luxury items when it worked.

Into this ever-changing situation walked and rode the first small groups of Euroamericans near the beginning of the nineteenth century. The first to arrive were trapper-traders. Quickly passing through in search of lucrative beaver streams and knowledge about the lay of the land and its inhabitants, they left little behind and made little difference in the lives of Northern Great Basin inhabitants. However, within a few decades they were followed by sporadic military explorations such as John C. Frémont's 1843-44 traverse from The Dalles of the Columbia to Pyramid Lake in northwestern Nevada (Stewart 1999). Sometimes violent encounters taught harsh lessons to Northern Paiutes, Klamath, and Modoc, who learned to avoid contacts whenever possible. Fortunately, great distances and rough terrain slowed the settlement of the Northern Great Basin by early miners drawn to the California gold fields, and settlers coming from the lush Willamette Valley. Ultimately though, calamity struck the Native inhabitants in the mid-nineteenth century as waves of gold-seekers headed to California, the Rogue River country, and the Silver City, Idaho and John Day-Canyon City gold fields. Settlers soon followed as markets for cattle, sheep, horses, and lumber in these rapidly expanding population centers opened the eyes of both adventurous western Oregonians and distant eastern capitalists to the grazing, timber, and mineral wealth that was free for the taking east of the Cascades.

A series of wars, dislocations, and treaties in the 1850s, '60s, and '70s forced most local Native populations onto Federal reservations and brought some perilously close to extinction. Towns such as Burns, Bend, Lakeview, Silver Lake, and Klamath Falls were hastily established and thriving by 1900. Convinced by self-interested entrepreneurs that the coming of the railroad was imminent and that cheap transportation to distant markets would increase the value of land in central Oregon, settlers poured into the region. However, the brutally hot, dry, and cold conditions to which Native Americans had successfully adapted for so many thousands of years soon crushed many fanciful dreams and sent most of the beaten dreamers into the region's emerging towns, where they could find paying jobs in lumber mills, irrigation companies, and other business enterprises. Those who stayed in the countryside—largely farmers, stockmen, miners, loggers, and foresters of both Native American and other origins—were and are a tough lot, content to live with the land and wrestle it for a living.

Chapter 3
Columbia Plateau

The Interior Plateau of western North America is a great trough about 200 miles wide and 600 miles long, flanked on the west by the Oregon-Washington Cascades and British Columbia Coast Mountains, and on the east by the Northern Rockies. Its northern part is the Canadian Plateau, a broad zone of low, forested mountains and long, glacially scoured valleys with lakes and meadows. South of the international boundary is the Columbia Plateau, a vast and dramatically eroded lava plain cut by the Columbia River and its tributaries and bounded on the south by the Blue Mountains. Oregon's part of this huge region, south of the big river and reaching into the highest drainages of its tributary streams, is the subject of this chapter.

The Cultural Context

A key ecological factor giving the northern and southern Interior Plateau sub-areas similar cultural histories is that each has a great salmon river, the Fraser in the north and the Columbia in the south, which joins it to the Pacific Ocean and the Northwest Coast cultural area. The greatest aboriginal fisheries of North America existed along these two big rivers. Similarly, both the northern and southern parts of the Interior Plateau contain extensive steppe / grassland and mountainous zones that supported substantial populations of bison, elk, deer, sheep, and other game, along with abundant edible roots, including lomatium, camas, bitterroot, and others. This chapter is specifically about the cultural history of Oregon's Columbia Plateau, but that history reflects certain ecological patterns, developmental trends, and culture-historical threads that are common to the Interior Plateau as a whole.

The Columbia Plateau is composed of layer upon layer of volcanic rock, extruded periodically during the Miocene (25 to 5 million years ago) as hot, highly fluid "flood basalts" that overspread vast areas, emanating most prominently from a main source region around the conjunction of modern Oregon, Washington, and Idaho. The Columbia and its tributaries have incised deep channels that expose these layers to view and define the regional topography as a deeply dissected upland plateau. Along most of Oregon's northern border the Columbia River flows in a broad canyon two to three hundred feet deep. Much human activity, in the past as now, gravitated to the river-washed terraces or benches eroded along the waterside. These gave ready access to an abundance of fish, both the salmon and eels that run up from the sea each spring and summer, and the suckers, sturgeons, and other freshwater species that remain present throughout the year.

The Dalles area, about 170 river miles up the Columbia from the Pacific Ocean, lay at the head of tidewater before Bonneville Dam was built downstream. The modern town of the same name is just a few miles east of the stupendous Columbia Gorge, which was cut over eons by the ancient river even as the volcanic Cascades were rising.

South of the Columbia above The Dalles is the Deschutes-Umatilla Plateau, a nearly flat landscape that slopes gradually upward from about 300 feet above sea level along the river to 2000–3000 feet along its edge some 50 miles inland. The Blue Mountains beyond divide Oregon's Plateau and Northern Great Basin provinces. East of the great northward bend of the Columbia in Oregon's upper right-hand corner are the high Wallowa Mountains, a distinctive extension of the Blue Mountain geological province. The Wallowas are bounded on the east by Hells Canyon, a spectacular mile-deep gorge of the Snake River that marks the Oregon-Idaho border. In this part of Oregon, elevations range from 300 to over 8000 feet and landforms include rugged glaciated mountains, dissected basalt plateaus, deep canyons, and alluvial basins. Much of the area is wooded, but extensive upland meadows are also common.

Across Oregon's section of the Columbia Plateau an altitudinal range of several thousand feet supports diverse floras and faunas that fed the native people, while ancient volcanic activity has emplaced local flows of obsidian that were important to them as tool stone. From west to east the Deschutes, John Day, and Umatilla rivers drain into the Columbia, while farther east the Grande Ronde, Powder, Malheur, and Owyhee Rivers feed the Snake River, itself a tributary of the Columbia. These many streams bring annual runs of Pacific salmon into every corner of Oregon's Plateau and well into its flanking Blue Mountains and Cascades foothills. The entire area has hot summers and cold, snowy winters, though temperature and moisture vary locally with altitude. The highly varied natural landscape of Oregon's Plateau section strongly shaped the patterns of economic adaptation and cultural interaction that its various bands and tribes developed over millennia, as will be seen throughout the following account.

In the ethnohistoric era of the nineteenth century, the Wasco, Wishram, Sahaptin, Molala, Umatilla, Cayuse, and Nez Perce peoples of the area all organized their lives around a summer fishing camp on the Columbia or a major tributary and a winter village in a sheltered area away from the river, with comings and going between the two locations over the course of an annual round. Although a single well-placed site might be able to serve both summer fishing and winter village functions, such situations were rare. People's summertime movements were directed to various dispersed resource areas where task groups could accumulate and prepare for storage the food and other supplies that would see their community through the winter season.

Community division of labor was prominent, with a summertime split between those who would catch and prepare fish at the riverside and those who would hunt game and collect plant foods in the hinterlands. Within these groups a further division of labor by sex and age also prevailed, with women and elders caring for the young children, harvesting plant foods, butchering fish and game, and making household items, while men and older boys fished, hunted, made stone tools, and did other chores. The archaeological record shows that this general pattern of life persisted throughout aboriginal history in the Plateau even as other social factors changed, with human groups at first sparsely scattered and much on the move, then gradually becoming larger and relatively more settled, and the trajectory of population growth and sociocultural complexity rising markedly toward the end of aboriginal times.

The Natural Environment

Plants and animals tend to increase or decrease in abundance as climate becomes warmer or cooler, wetter or dryer. Human communities are similarly affected, depending as they do on the flora and fauna of their environment for food and many other necessities. Thus in studying human history it is also important to study changing conditions in the natural environments that people must cope with over time. A brief account of environmental patterns over the period of human occupation and cultural development in the Plateau will thus set the stage for archaeological discussions to follow.

During the last glacial maximum of about 24,000 to 20,000 years ago, the upper tributaries of the Columbia River, which heads in the Northern Rocky Mountains, were covered by vast snowfields and glaciers, while lesser elevations harbored primarily low tundra vegetation. Severe glacial conditions prevailed all across the top of Eurasia and North America, and on present evidence it is unlikely that any humans entered the high arctic at that time and crossed into the New World over the Bering Land Bridge then exposed between Asia and Alaska.

By about 14,500 cal. BP however, people were present in Oregon, and after 11,000 cal. BP populations grew as postglacial warming continued to raise summer temperatures. Pollen evidence suggests that conditions warmer and drier than those of the present day peaked in the lowlands between about 8500 and 7500 cal. BP, after which the trend was reversed, with increased effective moisture and probably cooler temperatures shown by evidence of descending timberlines. About 6000 cal. BP a rebirth of mountain glaciers indicates a further increase in effective moisture, and pollen evidence shows forest moving downslope into previously drier steppe/grasslands (Chatters 1998).

During the mid-Holocene interval (about 5000–3000 cal. BP) the climate remained wet but cooled further, which brought trees still lower into former steppes and grasslands. It is probable that during this period a later spring freshet and colder river waters created optimal conditions for Plateau salmon populations. A swing back toward warmer temperatures between about 3000 and 2000 cal. BP caused woodlands to move back upslope to some extent, and established the relative balance of forest and grassland that we see in the region today. By this time Native American people were numerous and their societies had taken on most of the essential characteristics seen in the cultures of contact-historic times.

The Missoula Floods Shaped the Human Landscape

In the Plateau as elsewhere, people most likely entered for the first time during the warming that followed the Last Glacial Maximum. During the period of maximum cold and for some thousands of years thereafter, the high Rocky Mountains were laden with glacial ice. This crept down mountain valleys, the ice molecules flowing over one another like slow-moving water under the deep ice's colossal weight. When the moving Purcell Trench lobe of the Cordilleran ice sheet dammed Clark's Fork, a westward-flowing tributary of the Columbia

River, it formed an ice dam that backed up glacial Lake Missoula to form a body of water some 200 miles long and up to 2000 feet deep (about the volume of modern Lake Ontario), drowning the area where Missoula, Montana exists today. Over and over between about 18,500 and 15,000 years ago, when Lake Missoula waters rose to a certain depth they caused the ice dam to become incipiently buoyant. Water leaking under the glacier then eroded tunnels that grew exponentially in diameter until they collapsed, causing a catastrophic breach of the ice dam, which had slowly grown to perhaps three quarters of a mile across, and suddenly releasing up to 500 cubic miles of water in a period of two days or so. Over intervals of 30 to 70 years, the ever-flowing glacier would refill the gash and re-form the ice dam; the glacial lake would refill, eventually becoming deep enough to force a new cycle of erosive tunneling and breach. Geological evidence shows that there were at least 40 and perhaps more than 60 such events, known as the Missoula Floods (also the Spokane or Bretz Floods; Waitt 1985; Waitt and Thorson 1983).

These colossal floods (estimated to exceed 10 times the combined flows of all the earth's rivers today) eroded the vast Channeled Scablands of northeastern Washington. It is calculated that the peak discharge from glacial Lake Missoula was as much as 25 or even 30 million cubic meters per second. A hydraulic dam above Umatilla at the half-mile wide Wallula Gap backed up water to a depth of 1000 feet. At The Dalles, flood-deposited gravel bars can be clearly seen high up the canyon walls, and the high-water marks of different flood episodes are visible as much as 30 miles to the south on the gently up-tilted Deschutes-Umatilla Plateau. These floods also left boulders of Rocky Mountain granite on the high terraces of the middle and lower Columbia River, where they were rafted in chunks of ice that still carried bits of the glacier's bed load. Some flood episodes carried such glacial "erratics" as far as Eugene in western Oregon, when hydraulic damming caused by a narrow passage in the Columbia valley below Portland backed water and ice up the Willamette Valley for more than 100 miles. Geological evidence shows that perhaps dozens of these floods came after the approximately 17,000 cal. BP eruption of Mt. St. Helens S-tephra, but Glacier Peak Layer B tephra on the great terrace of the Columbia below Chelan Falls is dated to about 14,500 cal. BP, showing that the huge ice-age floods had ceased by then (Benito and O'Connor 2003; Waitt 1985, 1994; Waitt and Thorson 1983).

Oregon's pioneering archaeologist Luther S. Cressman was of the opinion that an angularly broken piece of basalt he picked out of Missoula Flood gravels near the mouth of the John Day River was a knife with a zigzag sharpened edge (Cressman et al. 1960:65). He reports that highly respected archaeologists Frank H. H. Roberts, Emil Haury, and John Corbett agreed that it was an artifact, but that lithic technology specialist J. Desmond Clark expressed doubts. The authors of this book, along with two other archaeologists and a geologist who re-examined the specimen together at the University of Oregon Museum of Natural and Cultural History, all side with Clark. In the opinion of these observers, considering both its physical attributes and the geologic situation in which it was found, the specimen is clearly not an artifact, but a naturally broken piece of river gravel.

Cressman also mentions in his 1960 report that Sam Sargent, a staff geologist at The Dalles Dam, told him of broken animal bones and several stone artifacts recovered during mechanical excavations for the navigation locks at The Dalles, reportedly from sands buried beneath cemented Missoula Flood gravels. The lithics, which are also curated at the UO MNCH, were examined at the same time as the John Day River specimen. They are undoubtedly artifacts: small nondescript flakes and a drill-shaped form, all of a reddish chert. But Cressman's report does not say that Sargent personally saw the situation in which they were reportedly found, nor does there exist any written description, map, or photograph to portray their geological context. There is simply no verifiable evidence for ascribing these artifacts a pre-Missoula age. The specimens themselves are of types and a material which was common in the later periods at The Dalles, suggesting that is their most likely age. There is therefore no currently known evidence, from The Dalles or elsewhere, that convincingly documents a direct association between Missoula Flood deposits and human traces of any kind.

It is abundantly clear, however, that the Missoula Floods played a huge role in shaping the landscape upon which people made their living throughout all human existence in the region. This was true not only in the Plateau, but in the Willamette Valley—where backwater flooding contributed to its deep silts, flat floor and pervasive seasonal flooding—and along the lower Columbia River as well.

Pioneer Populations (14,500 to 7,600 Years Ago)

There are traces of human presence in Oregon's Northern Great Basin (ch. 2) by about 14,500 cal. BP, but the earliest artifacts of defined age currently known in its Plateau region are Clovis fluted projectile points, a distinctive type that is not directly dated locally, but has been most precisely ^{14}C dated in the Southwest between about 13,200 and 12,800 cal. BP (Waters and Stafford 2007). Clovis points have been recovered as surface finds on higher elevations away from the Columbia River near The Dalles, Blalock, and Umatilla in Oregon, while near Wenatchee, Washington a large assemblage of Clovis points and other artifacts was excavated at a site not far from the river (Gramly 1993; Mehringer 1988; Mehringer and Foit 1990). Clovis points are also widely known elsewhere in Oregon, most notably at the Dietz site in the Northern Great Basin, but also in Oregon's western valleys and coastal region. These early traces clearly represent small, dispersed groups of people who ranged widely and rapidly, hunting and gathering over a great variety of landscapes (Haynes 2002).

The Dalles. The river-oriented cultural pattern so characteristic of the Plateau is most richly represented along a relatively short stretch of the Columbia River upstream from the modern town of The Dalles, a few miles east of the Cascades. The earliest archaeological record here dates to about 11,000 cal. BP, roughly three millennia after the last of the catastrophic Missoula Floods. At the time of early Euroamerican contact, in the nineteenth century, The Dalles vicinity (including Celilo Falls) was the most prosperous aboriginal fishing and trading area on the Columbia Plateau, and one of the most important fishing centers in all of North America. Celilo Falls marks the upper end of the most densely occupied zone; six or seven miles downriver is the Long Narrows, a tight chute of deep and dangerously fast water named by Lewis and Clark on their 1805 visit (Moulton 2003); and major occupation continued around and below the Big Eddy downstream from the narrows (fig. 3.2).

The Long Narrows and Celilo Falls concentrated upward-running salmon in the millions, and the rocky shores along this reach of the Columbia offered places from which crowds of fishermen with nets and spears could take them in quantity. In addition to the salmon there were similarly migratory lamprey eels, along with many freshwater fishes. Harbor seals also came up the Columbia from the Pacific, while huge freshwater sturgeon that can grow to 14 feet in length and weigh as much as 2,500 pounds still thrive today in deep waters. The setting was brought to perfection by nearly constant summer-fall winds drawn through the high Cascades via the Columbia River Gorge, which afforded optimal conditions for people to dry and preserve the fatty, protein-rich fish provided by the bountiful river.

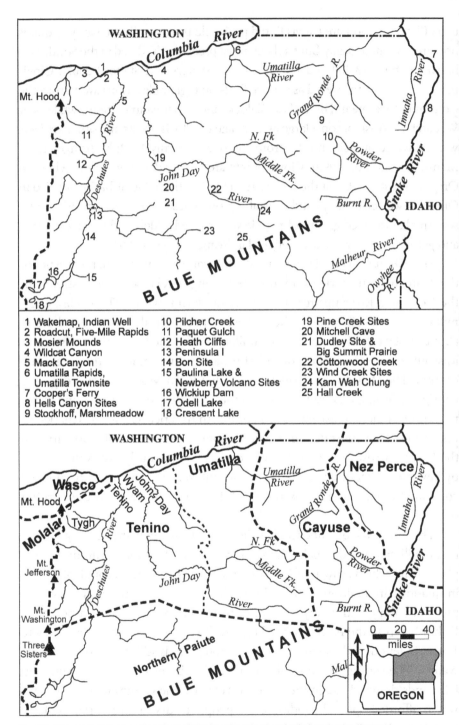

1 Wakemap, Indian Well
2 Roadcut, Five-Mile Rapids
3 Mosier Mounds
4 Wildcat Canyon
5 Mack Canyon
6 Umatilla Rapids,
   Umatilla Townsite
7 Cooper's Ferry
8 Hells Canyon Sites
9 Stockhoff, Marshmeadow
10 Pilcher Creek
11 Paquet Gulch
12 Heath Cliffs
13 Peninsula I
14 Bon Site
15 Paulina Lake &
   Newberry Volcano Sites
16 Wickiup Dam
17 Odell Lake
18 Crescent Lake
19 Pine Creek Sites
20 Mitchell Cave
21 Dudley Site &
   Big Summit Prairie
22 Cottonwood Creek
23 Wind Creek Sites
24 Kam Wah Chung
25 Hall Creek

Fig. 3.1. Columbia Plateau archaeological site locations (*top*) and tribal territories (*bottom*).

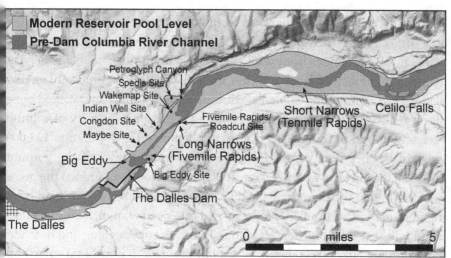

Fig. 3.2. Sites along the Long Narrows of the Columbia River at The Dalles, before and after construction of The Dalles Dam.

Little archaeological study had been carried out in the area when construction work began in the early 1950s on The Dalles Dam, which would deeply flood the river valley, drowning Celilo Falls and the Long Narrows, and backing water as far upstream as the John Day River confluence. Because the dam project supplied very little funding for rescue archaeology, most of the accumulated cultural record of more than eleven millennia was lost under what came to be called Lake Celilo. The Long Narrows disappeared and the roar of Celilo Falls went silent under rising water only a few hours after the floodgates of The Dalles Dam were closed on the morning of March 10, 1957. Limited surveys and several excavations had been conducted, but a compilation from scattered and incomplete records enumerates 83 sites along the flooded stretch, most of them effectively unstudied, that included large villages, cemeteries, burial islands, camps, and extensive rock art panels displaying hundreds of images (Wilke et al. 1983: Table 1, fig. 8). The destruction of the area that was such a central place in the economic and religious life of the Columbia River Indians was a tragic loss that is still felt with deep sadness among Oregon Native peoples.

Roadcut Site. Near the head of the Long Narrows on the Oregon side, the Fivemile Rapids (35WS4) and Roadcut (35WS8) sites mark the downstream and upstream ends of an extensive shoreline zone that offered exceptional fishing opportunities. Excavations into the side of a deep road cut (originally made during the construction of U.S. Highway 30) sampled a deep deposit that yielded the best known record of early occupation in The Dalles area (fig. 3.3). The early period is ^{14}C dated there between about 11,300 and 8800 cal. BP. Specimens from water-laid sediments at the base of the deposit included a number of large and thin stone flakes, some retouched lamellar blades 35 to 58 mm long, some flaked stone scrapers, and a few worked bone pieces (Cressman et al. 1960). Most striking is the great quantity of salmon vertebrae found in immediately overlying deposits (fig. 3.4). Some 125,000 individual bones were counted, said to represent roughly half the amount observed during excavation. A later study that rigorously examined the question of whether the bones actually indicate human fishing, or may have been merely a natural accumulation of spawned-out, dead salmon, leaves no effective doubt that the bone deposit resulted from people catching and butchering salmon (Butler 1993). Bones of rabbit, beaver, otter, muskrat, marmot, badger, fox, and large raptorial birds including condors were also recovered.

Early period projectile points included large stemmed and leaf-shaped forms assignable to the subsequently defined Windust type (Leonhardy and Rice 1970, 1980; Hicks 2004), now known from early sites throughout the Plateau (fig. 3.5). Also part of the cultural inventory were heavy choppers made of pebbles or large flaked bifaces, ovate biface knives, stone graving tools or burins, pebble net sinkers or bolas stones girdled by incised grooves, edge-ground cobbles, flakers and awls made from antler tines, splitting wedges and cylinders made from antler beams, antler atlatl spurs, bone harpoon prongs (weapons for sea mammal hunting), and elk incisor teeth that

Left, Fig 3.3. Roadcut Site excavation.
Right, Fig. 3.4. Salmon vertebrae from the Roadcut Site.

Fig. 3.5. Projectile points, bifaces, and other artifacts of the Plateau early Holocene: Philippi Phase, Wildcat Canyon.

were notched at their tops for suspension. Many worked pieces of deer and elk antler debris from toolmaking were also found. Across the Columbia on the Washington side, the lowest levels of a site called Indian Well (45KL42) yielded some similar items, including cobble choppers, small and large crude lamellar blades, large ovate blades, and well-made leaf-shaped points (Butler 1957). River fishing, land and river hunting of both large and small animals, food processing, and tool manufacture are all indicated by various elements of these assemblages. Fishing was done with both nets and spears, and the principal hunting weapon was the atlatl and dart, which was widely used throughout the Plateau during this era.

Wildcat Canyon. Another cultural assemblage of similar age was discovered upriver at the Wildcat Canyon site (35GM9) on the south bank of the Columbia, just above its confluence with the John Day River (Cole 1967, 1968; Dumond and Minor 1983). The John Day, which drains the Blue Mountains south of the Columbia, flows into the main stem about 25 miles above The Dalles. The site lay at the base of high basalt cliffs on a streamside terrace now flooded by dammed river waters, where traces of occupation were found over an area several hundred feet across. It is a location from which people could have staged both riverine fishing and processing on the one hand, and upland foraging for plants and animals on the other. The earliest cultural remains at Wildcat Canyon are of the Philippi Phase, 10,100–8400 cal. BP, which is cognate with the Early period at The Dalles and the Windust Phase known from Marmes Rockshelter on the lower Snake River of southeastern Washington. Large leaf-shaped, lanceolate, and stemmed points of Windust type indicate hunting, while large knives and scrapers suggest butchering and hide processing. Occasional milling stones and manos indicate the grinding of vegetal foods. A few living surfaces have been discovered, but no clearly defined structures. Relatively sparse remains suggest that Wildcat Canyon hosted only periodic visits throughout the early periods of Plateau occupation, though this was to change markedly after about 3000 cal. BP.

Pilcher Creek and Cooper's Ferry. Occupations of the same period south and east of the big river show that groups with a similar culture foraged widely throughout the mountainous interior. Some of these were surely the same people who fished for salmon along the Columbia, seeking other kinds of resources in the uplands at different seasons. In the Blue Mountains near modern-day LaGrande, the Pilcher Creek (35UN147) site suggests that people were in the uplands as early as they were along the Columbia main stem. Although the site could not be ^{14}C dated, large stemmed and shouldered Windust points and other artifacts found there are comparable to Early Period specimens at the Roadcut site. A diverse assemblage of projectile points, bifacial knives, scrapers, drills, cores, flakes, hammer stones, and edge-ground cobbles, among other things, represents the toolkit of a people who were hunting, collecting, and processing both game animals and plant foods, as well as making and repairing the equipment they relied on in performing these tasks. Perishable bone and plant remains were not found at Pilcher Creek, but the highland setting suggests the pursuit of animals such as elk, deer, and smaller species, and the harvesting of roots, berries, and other plant foods endemic to the locality (Brauner 1985). Comparable Windust points, along with other evidence, are convincingly ^{14}C dated to about 13,000 cal. BP at Cooper's Ferry (10IH73) on the lower Snake River not far from Pilcher Creek in western Idaho's Hells Canyon (Davis and Schweger 2004: 695–700, fig. 5). The Hells Canyon evidence confirms an early date for regional occupation and suggests a probable age for the Pilcher Creek finds as well.

Paulina Lake. West of the Blue Mountains the Paulina Lake site (35DS34), in the Deschutes River headwaters south of Bend, provides abundant further details of life in the uplands during this same period (Connolly 1999). Situated

Fig. 3.6. Paulina Lake Site main excavation block.

in the high caldera of Newberry Volcano at about 6,300 feet elevation, the site is very near the boundary between Oregon's Columbia Plateau and Northern Great Basin cultural regions and is important to the archaeology of both areas (see also ch. 2). In early Holocene times an open Ponderosa pine forest existed in the Newberry Caldera, with ample sunlight to support a diverse understory of berries, shrubs, herbs, and grasses, and the game animals both small and large that feed on them. The earliest archaeological feature found at Paulina Lake was a pit about three feet in diameter and 1.5 feet deep, which contained charcoal that was dated to about 11,000 cal. BP. Pollen found in the pit fill was of fireweed and mock orange. Starch granules and phytoliths from grasses suggest that the pit may also have been used to store grass seeds, or perhaps had been lined with grass.

A large block excavation (figs. 3.6, 3.7) revealed the outlines of a well-defined house floor about 12 feet wide and 15 feet long that had a fire hearth at its center. Its edges were marked by a cleared area and some still-embedded support posts preserved by charring. Portions of other wall posts, charred by a fire that evidently destroyed the structure, lay horizontally on the floor surface. These posts, up to four inches in diameter, were identified as lodgepole pine. Radiocarbon dates on three of them, and from the central hearth, show that the house was built about 9500 cal. BP, making it one of the earliest constructed dwellings yet found in North America (fig. 3.8).

The house's central hearth consisted of a fire pit dug about a foot into the contemporary surface, and surrounded by a shallow hearth area almost three feet in diameter. Botanical remains preserved in the hearth revealed the greatest taxonomic diversity of any archaeological sample taken from the

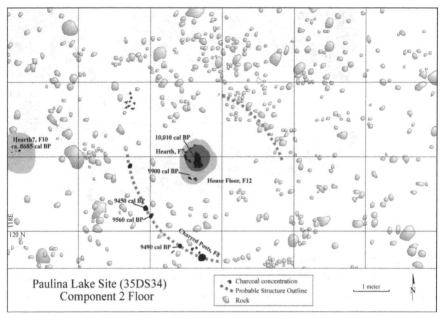

Fig. 3.7. Plan of early house in the Paulina Lake site main excavation.

Fig. 3.8. Reconstruction drawing of early house at Paulina Lake (courtesy Bean Comrada).

caldera, and revealed many plants of economic significance. Both lodgepole and ponderosa pine were used for fuel. Water flotation analysis yielded macrobotanical evidence for sagebrush, which is of interest because ethnographically sagebrush wood was used as fuel and its bark to make rope, matting, and clothing. There were also chokecherry pits, as well as bulrush and other sedges, which could yield seeds for food and fibers used in matting and basketry. Grasses, processed hardwood bark, and a nutlet fragment and fruity tissues were not identifiable to genus or species. Pollen analysis added evidence for *Apiaceae* (a family that includes many important root foods), hazelnut, salmonberries or blackberries, and other grasses and herbs. Finally, analysis of blood residues on stone artifacts showed that rabbits were probably prepared for cooking near the hearth, while bear, mountain sheep, deer, elk, and bison were butchered outside the house (Williams and Fagan 1999).

These and other archaeological features and dates define stable residential camps that were visited repeatedly between about 11,000 and 7600 cal. BP by family or multi-family groups of highly mobile foragers. The limited density of the evidence does not suggest the Paulina Lake site was occupied every year, but when people did come they probably stayed for some weeks or even several months as they harvested the area's multiple resources. Environmental factors strongly imply that occupation was limited to the summer/fall half of the year, because in the early postglacial period—even more than now—deep snow and freezing temperatures in the high caldera would have surely prevented occupation during the winter months.

While harvesting in the caldera, Paulina Lake visitors used the locally abundant obsidian to refurbish their weaponry and tools with new points and cutting edges, abandoning the worn and damaged points, knives, and other lithic artifacts they had arrived with. The discarded specimens show the various directions from which people came on different occasions, as they were made of tool stone from many different places. Geochemical studies identified obsidian from sources all around the compass over a radius of nearly 200 miles, but most of the material came from an area 50 to 70 miles to the south, notably Silver Lake/Sycan Marsh in the Fort Rock Basin and Spodue Mountain beyond (fig. 3.9).

The high mobility of Newberry's aboriginal visitors is further shown by the fact that projectile points and other artifacts of the same types as seen there are widely found across the southern Plateau and adjacent northern Great Basin (fig. 10). In these early times the human population was surely sparse, so that mating networks and other indispensable intercommunity contacts necessarily spanned great distances (Ames 1988). Individual groups probably spent much of their time quite isolated from others, and occasions for larger community gatherings must have been greatly prized.

Wickiup Dam, Odell Lake, and Crescent Lake. Comparable trends can be seen on the flanks of the eastern Cascades, in the uppermost reaches of the Deschutes drainage west of Newberry Volcano. At the Wikiup Dam, Odell Lake (35KL231), and other sites, leaf-shaped and shouldered points, corner-notched points, and other early flaked stone specimens have been found under Mt. Mazama volcanic ash (Cressman 1948; Jaehnig 1993). These are at least 7,600 years old, as shown by the ash layer, and some types may be older. Recent excavations at the nearby Crescent Lake site (35KL749) yielded a ^{14}C date of about 8000 cal. BP for the earliest occupation traces there, found beneath Mt. Mazama volcanic ash (Mulligan 1997). Over 70 projectile points of flaked stone were identified, including lanceolate and stemmed fragments, as well as large side-notched and corner-notched dart points of the Transitional

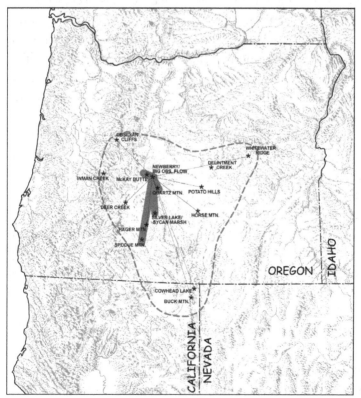

Fig. 3.9. Sources of obsidian recovered at the Paulina Lake Site.

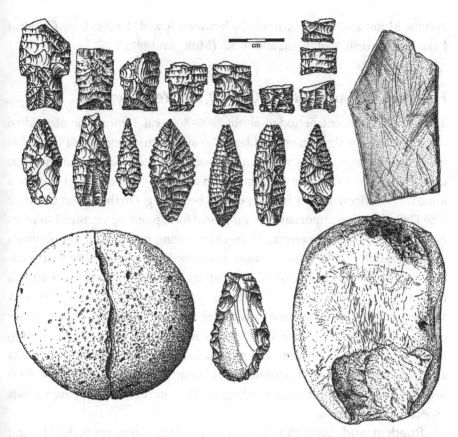

Fig. 3.10. Pre-Mazama artifacts from the Paulina Lake site; projectile points, abrading stone, mano, scraper, and stone hammer.

Period. Small corner-notched and basal-notched arrowpoint types of relatively late prehistoric times were found there as well. Meat and hide processing tools included several biface knives, almost 60 scrapers of various types, and miscellaneous flake tools. A drill and a number of scraper-gravers represent bone or wood working tools, while hammer stones, cores, bifacial performs, and over 20,000 flakes indicate lithic manufacturing. Clearly a set of hunting, gathering, and manufacturing activities centered on local resources is attested. No houses have been found, suggesting that the many specimens there accumulated from recurring brief visits over several millennia rather than longer-term stable occupations. Confirming that these Crescent Lake foragers ranged very widely, obsidian tool stone found at the site came from a large number of different sources: Obsidian Cliffs, McKay Butte, Newberry Volcano, Quartz Mountain, Cougar Mountain, Silver Lake / Sycan Marsh, and

Spodue Mountain, which variously lie between 30 and 70 miles from Crescent Lake to the north, east, west, and south (Mulligan 1997).

Foragers in Transition (7,600 to 3,000 Years Ago)

The middle Holocene period of about 7600–3000 cal. BP was one of gradual but cumulatively significant population growth throughout the Plateau, as many archaeological sites attest. Air-deposited volcanic ash from the 7600 cal. BP eruption of Mount Mazama, seen in many archaeological sites, is a good time-horizon marker for the period's beginning. On the Columbia River The Dalles grew in importance as a regional focal point—an expression of its extraordinary fishing potential. It drew increasing numbers of people from the hinterlands for the salmon season, as attested by the many sites that occur close by the river. Evidence of salmon fishing also appears on the Columbia's main Oregon tributaries, the Deschutes, John Day, and Umatilla rivers. A socioeconomic transformation was under way in the Plateau, from earlier patterns of high mobility and broad-spectrum foraging toward more central-ized community arrangements that included year-around focal settlements and extensive logistical provisions for obtaining, processing, and storing re-sources. Sites known throughout Oregon's Plateau region illuminate various aspects of the process.

Roadcut and Congdon Sites. The Roadcut, Congdon (45KL41), and other sites reveal much about life and work at The Dalles during this long interval. The Roadcut site demonstrates continuity of occupation from the preceding period, but chemically rich groundwater that cemented its deposits greatly limited archaeological specimen recovery. Across the Long Narrows on the Washington side of the river, however, the Congdon site has yielded a detailed inventory of archaeological remains that span the same period. Based on known ages of various artifact types, the earliest Congdon occupa-tion probably dated between about 8,000 and 3,000 years ago.

A complex of hunting equipment widely used during the Transitional Period includes atlatl weights and flaked stone points used with the atlatl and dart: large triangular side-notched points, leaf-shaped bipoints, and triangular points either corner-notched or basally-notched (figs. 3.11, 3.12). Bone gorges attest fishing with lines. Game and plant processing tools include flaked stone knives or scrapers, cobble choppers, hammer stones, pebble scrapers, flat grinding slabs, shallow-basin mortars, deep bowl mortars, and long conical pestles. Manufacturing tools include shaft smoothers, abrading stones, side and end scrapers, T-shaped drills, girdled mauls, and slate whetstones.

The Congdon site, now beneath the waters of Lake Celilo, was a large, low mound 175–200 feet in diameter and over eight feet deep. It was a huge accumulation of habitation debris that included ash lenses, charcoal, and other occupation remains. Private collectors took from it an estimated 20,000 artifacts during the late 1940s and early 1950s, when destruction of the area's sites under reservoir waters soon to be backed up by the new Dalles Dam was an impending threat. Some of these specimens were later deposited at the Washington State Museum in Seattle, and others in the Cashmere Museum near Wenatchee. They now comprise the main artifactual basis for our historical understanding of the people who lived at The Dalles in early times. Two other nearby sites, called "Maybe" and "Other" by the collectors, were smaller than Congdon but add to the evidence for much human activity in the area. The three sites together extended for nearly a mile along the river (Wilke et al. 1983: fig. 8).

Given its position directly on the Long Narrows, there is no doubt that people came to the Congdon locality for the salmon fishing and trading

Left, Fig. 3.11. Projectile points of the Plateau middle Holocene: Canyon Phase, Wildcat Canyon.

Above, Fig. 3.12. Projectile points of the Plateau late Holocene: Wildcat and Quinton phases, Wildcat Canyon, Upper John Day Region.

season, while the great volume of accumulated camp debris shows that their aggregate numbers were large. Excavations revealed no definite house remains, indicating that Congdon was mainly a temporary camp that drew people during the spring–fall fishing season. Most of these visitors undoubtedly came from homes that lay various distances inland on either side of the Columbia. The Dalles' permanent residents must have wintered in a number of the smaller sites that are known to exist in areas set back from the shore and therefore less exposed to the strong, cold winds so characteristic of the area. The Congdon site served also as a cemetery, especially in later times, and hundreds of human burials known from this and other sites suggest that many people made the area their year-round home base.

As time passed the Plateau population grew substantially. This is reflected by site numbers both along the big river and in the uplands to the south. Salmon fishing, long important on the Columbia, was established during the Transitional Period on its tributaries as well. Most interior sites continue from early times to reflect a broad-spectrum economics of hunting-gathering, but salmon and other fishing was added in particular places. Northeast Oregon provides good examples of both interior hunting-gathering and riverine fishing sites.

Stockhoff and Marshmeadow. The Stockhoff and Marshmeadow sites are located within several miles of one another on an upland spur between the Grande Ronde and Baker valleys (McPherson et al. 1981; Womack 1977). Stockhoff (35UN52) is a quarry-workshop as well as a hunting-gathering camp, spread over a large area where fine-grained basalt tool stone is abundant. In addition to great quantities of flaked stone debris, the site has yielded artifacts broken at various stages of manufacture, from cores and initial roughouts to finished items. Edge-ground cobbles found there also give evidence of plant processing. Stockhoff shows traces of visitation over a long period of time, but saw its greatest use between about 8,900 and 4,500 years ago. This is shown by specimens found both below and above volcanic ash from the Mount Mazama eruption, and by leaf-shaped and side-notched projectile points of the Columbia Plateau Cascade phase.

Marshmeadow (35UN95) was a highland camp used for both hunting and gathering, mainly during the period between about 7,600 and 4,500 years ago. Its projectile points are triangular side- and corner-notched forms reminiscent of the Humboldt, Elko and Northern Side-notched types of the Northern Great Basin, and the bones of mountain sheep, pronghorn, and bison show that hunting was a major activity there. Milling stones and pestles indicate vegetal food processing was also important, and dates after about 3700 cal. BP have been obtained on charred bulbs of the camas lily, which local meadows still support in abundance. Flaked stone artifacts give much evidence of tool manufacturing and repair, and tool use-wear studies indicate the importance of butchering and hide processing at the site.

Hells Canyon. River fishing early in this period is attested not far to the east of Stockhoff and Marshmeadow at Kirkwood Bar (10IH699), Deep Gully (10IH1892), and Bernard Rockshelter (10IH483), all within a few miles of one another on the Snake River where it marks the Oregon-Idaho border (Reid and Chatters 1997). These sites show the early importance of fishing by wide-ranging foragers, who were drawn to productive localities even in an extremely mountainous and isolated area. At the bottom of mile-deep Hells Canyon, about 100 river miles up the Snake from its Columbia River confluence, the sites were repeatedly occupied between about 8000 and 6400 cal. BP, as shown by a number of ^{14}C dates. The sites contained fire hearths, artifacts, and bones, but no house features. They were obviously seasonal camps, most likely visited during the late-summer fish runs. All contained an abundance of fish bone, as well as lesser but important amounts of bone from terrestrial mammals. Species included Chinook salmon, sucker, squawfish, minnow, river mussel, deer, bighorn sheep, marmot, badger, dog, grouse, and wood rat. Fishing was clearly the main attraction at all three sites, while the far less abundant mammals were apparently taken opportunistically.

Most interestingly, the artifacts from these sites included no specialized fishing gear such as net weights, harpoon barbs, hooks, or gorges, but instead many leaf-shaped and side-notched projectile points, biface knives, end scrapers, edge ground cobbles, and cobble hammers, choppers, cleavers, and picks. People employed effectively the same kinds of tools at these sites as they used in the adjacent highlands for terrestrial hunting and gathering. A likely explanation for the abundant fish at these sites, in the complete absence of specialized fishing gear, is suggested by contemporary wildlife survey data. These show that in dry years fish become stranded in pools during late-summer low flows in Hells Canyon, where they could have been simply caught by hand, perhaps clubbed or scooped out of the water with carrying baskets.

In addition to these economic elements, indicators were found of a distinctive Western Idaho Archaic Burial Complex (Pavesic 1979, 1985, 1992) centered farther east around Weiser, Idaho. In its fullest form the complex includes cemeteries with flexed, semi-flexed, and cremation burials, along with caches of large bifaces, distinctive side-notched "Turkey tail" points, red ocher, hematite crystals, and beads of Pacific Coast Olivella shell. This considerable degree of middle Holocene burial ceremonialism seems to reflect a growing social complexity in the Oregon/Idaho borderlands that is attested also at Marmes rockshelter farther down the Snake River, and westward down the Columbia River as well.

High Cascades Crescent Lake Transect. Interior upland occupations are also well represented west of the Blue Mountains. An extensive study of archaeological site distributions conducted in the High Cascades shows that a few key environmental factors determined human choice of occupation sites in this upland region throughout aboriginal times (Snyder 1987). Highly detailed Willamette National Forest soil resource inventory maps were used to study the distribution of 189 archaeological sites identified by cultural resource management surveys along an east-west transect oriented to Crescent Lake. Individual land types were identified by factors of soil, vegetation cover, water, exposure, and topography; archaeological site types included lithic scatters, rockshelters, possible housepits, rock cairns, and pictographs. Statistical analysis of site distributions with reference to environmental features showed that a very few types of location contained virtually all the human occupation sites. Projectile point types of known age showed that people had visited these sites throughout the past 8,000 years, and that site occupation patterns were unchanged during that time.

The research showed people drawn throughout time to open lakes and meadows in the geologically recent eastern Cascades, and to areas of rugged, rocky topography in the older western Cascades. Both kinds of environmental settings are stable over long periods because they are based on the underlying bedrock geology, and both are critical to humans because they provide crucially important openings in the otherwise dense forest canopy. Because such openings let sunlight reach the ground they foster an abundance of berries, roots, edible plants, and grasses, all of which in turn attract both game animals and omnivorous human foragers. Archaeological sites were found almost exclusively in such openings, reflecting their special utility to human occupants.

Bon Site. The Bon site (35DS608) near Bend, mainly occupied between about 6000 and 4000 cal. BP, shows early signs of short-term occupation by highly mobile human foragers, followed later by evidence of more residentially anchored logistic collecting (Connolly and Byram 2001). That the earliest visits to the Bon site were quite intermittent is indicated by obsidian dates associated with rather sparse remains, suggesting only brief stopovers. But around 4500 cal. BP the site functioned for some time as an important residential base with a well-defined domestic work area and associated disposal zones. A lack of architectural traces suggests that any structures must have been lightly built, but the discarded artifacts distributed around the perimeter of a central work area clearly demonstrate activities characteristic of a stable base camp. Ground stone tools were common, and starch grain and pollen analyses from some of them show they were used to process grass seeds and probably roots. Dart points of mainly Northern Side-notched type indicate hunting, while an abundance of broken point bases shows that hunters regularly returned home to replace broken projectile heads with new ones. Debitage analysis and geochemical sourcing shows that obsidian procured from nearby Newberry crater was used extensively in tool manufacture and repair. Blood residue found on stone tools indicates the taking of small and large animals, game birds, and fish, the most likely species including mountain sheep, deer, elk, squirrel, porcupine, beaver, ruffed grouse, sage grouse, quail, and minnows or suckers. After this interval of centrally based logistical provisioning, the Bon site reverted to a pattern of occasional use as a hunting/butchering station around 3000, 1000, and 500 cal. BP.

Johnson Site. Farther down the Deschutes drainage near Warm Springs, the Johnson site (35JE51B) has 11 radiocarbon dates falling between about 8000 and 3000 cal. BP. They were associated with many concentrations of cobbles, flaked stone tools, charcoal, and bone, as well as occupation surfaces and storage pits (Pettigrew and Hodges 1995). Best preserved was an early pithouse about 12 feet wide and 15 feet long that had been dug a foot or so into the ground and contained a central hearth pit (fig. 3.13). Charred grass and elongate wood pieces found near the walls were evidently the remains of a fire that had destroyed the superstructure. Stone grinding slabs were found on the floor along with many flaked stone artifacts and fragments of animal bone. Five ^{14}C dates between 6800 and 5700 cal. BP from different places within the housepit suggest the structure may have been rebuilt and re-occupied several times during that interval. Additional traces dated down to about 3000 cal. BP suggest that up to 15 more houses may have been built at the Johnson site in later times, when it apparently comprised a small community rather than an isolated encampment. The Johnson site is of epochal significance in providing the earliest evidence yet known for the construction of substantial

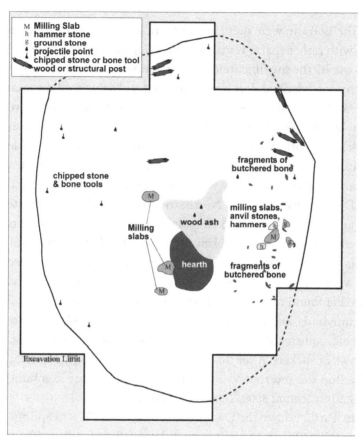

Fig. 3.13. Johnson Site pithouse.

semi-subterranean pithouse communities in the southern Columbia Plateau, and ties the region into a florescent pattern of growing sedentism during late Holocene times that has been defined for the Plateau as a whole (Ames et al. 1998; Chatters and Pokotylo 1998).

Heath Cliffs. The Heath Cliffs site (35JE319), also near Warm Springs, similarly seems to have functioned first as an early foraging base from which the whole spectrum of resources in its vicinity was harvested, then later as a central place within a more anchored pattern of logistical collection and storage of resources (Connolly and Jenkins 1996). Though it yielded initial traces of occupation that obsidian hydration dates place as far back as 9,600 years ago, ^{14}C dates indicate more activity between about 6300 and 3800 cal. BP, when Heath Cliffs seems to have been a seasonally occupied base camp. Substantial quantities of deer and mountain sheep bone show the importance of hunting activities staged from the site, while the collecting of serviceberry, grasses, weedy seed-bearing plants, biscuitroot, and possibly sunflowers and cattails is attested by preserved plant and pollen remains. Associated artifacts included projectile points, bifaces, drills, metates, manos, hopper mortars, pestles, and other items that testify to a variety of hunting, collecting, processing, and manufacturing tasks. Cobble concentrations and carbon-stained patches of soil were also common, probably representing various food-processing and other activities. The later appearance of a roughly circular pithouse about 15 feet across suggests the site ultimately became a more stable residential base as people shifted to a new, logistically organized pattern of resource collection and storage.

Lava Island Rockshelter and Peninsula 1. As previously noted for Hells Canyon in northeast Oregon, early interior river fishing is also documented on the western edge of the Plateau. At Lava Island Rockshelter (35DS86) on the Deschutes River near Bend, fish bone and mussel shell gives evidence for fishing, while deer bone attests land hunting as well (Minor and Toepel 1984a). Radiocarbon dates between about 2,000 and 150 years ago, along with small notched points, indicate late period occupation, while lanceolate points or tool blanks of Newberry obsidian suggest a time range that might reach back more than 7,000 years. At the Peninsula 1 rock shelter (35JE53), also on the Deschutes near Bend, a bone fishhook, a harpoon fragment, and traces of mussel shell, among other specimens, show that people came there for fishing and shellfish gathering. Peninsula 1 was similarly visited over a long period, as indicated by radiocarbon dates of about 4600 and 3200 cal. BP, and by dart and arrow points of types made between about 5,000 years ago and late prehistoric times (Stuemke 1989).

John Day Narrows. Nearer the Plateau's master stream, the same trends can be seen at the John Day Narrows, only a few miles above the river's debouchment into the Columbia. In the ethnographic period this area was part of the Tenino range, as a prime fishing locality and a staging area for hunting and gathering forays into the interior uplands (Wilde et al. 1983; Schalk 1987). Archaeological surveys have identified a series of sites along both sides of the river that appear to have been spring/summer residential bases, field camps, and activity locations. The Morris site (35GM91), on a terrace just below the Narrows, yielded hearths and living floors, but substantial house structures were not detected. Much fish bone, many pestles and fragments of grinding stones, traces of edible roots, and a fragment of charred cake probably made of biscuitroot revealed the broad economic purposes of the site. A ^{14}C date of about 5700 cal. BP was obtained for earlier occupation at the Morris site, and a date of 3300 cal. BP came from the root cake just mentioned. Clearly this was an important summertime provisioning location for a long time, perhaps analogous to the Bon site and others previously mentioned, and likely part of the warm-season range of contemporary people who wintered at the Wildcat Canyon site on the Columbia, just a few miles away.

Cottonwood Creek. Higher up the John Day's southeasterly course into the mountainous interior a similar pattern seems to have persisted, where a few key locations were bases for residentially anchored logistic collecting within a broader region that served mainly as a procurement zone. A pertinent example is the Cottonwood Creek site (35GR1507), located on a minor tributary that flows out of the Blue Mountain uplands to join the John Day River just west of Dayville (Endzweig 2001). A quite dense cultural component there is dated between about 6,600 and 5,000 years ago. Obsidian hydration readings and multiple peaks in debitage frequencies indicate repeated visits to the site. A charcoal lens dated about 5000 cal. BP was found within a larger depression that may have been the floor of a housepit, though excavations had to be terminated before the possibility could be adequately investigated. Large game hunting, hide processing, and stone tool manufacture were attested by side-notched and corner-notched dart points, biface and uniface fragments, cores, utilized flakes, and bone awls or flakers. Four metates, five handstones, and two edge-ground cobbles indicate the processing of seed and root plants, though red ocher stains on many of the specimens—along with the finding of small pieces of loose red and yellow ocher in the site sediments—suggest they were also used in processing pigment for paint.

Cottonwood Creek yielded some 2,600 pieces of animal bone and over 200 pieces of freshwater mussel shell. Most of the bone was too fragmented for full identification, but about 700 items could be assigned to genus, species, or animal size classes. Based on this sample it is evident that deer or deer-sized animals were the most important game processed at the site, followed by jackrabbits and cottontails. One sucker bone was identified, and a number of freshwater mussel fragments. The faunal remains, together with the hunting and plant processing tools already mentioned, complete the picture of a site that people returned to again and again for the purpose of hunting and harvesting plant foods in the surrounding country.

Away from its low-lying canyons, much of the extensive Blue Mountains region appears to have served throughout prehistoric times as a seasonally visited upland resource procurement zone where people regularly came to collect, hunt, and obtain obsidian tool stone, but generally established no winter villages. Highly mobile foragers are known in the region from thin traces dated to early times, and such visitation continued thereafter, but sites always remained small, scattered, and only ephemerally occupied. They continued to be short-stay forager camps, except that, extending into an era of much higher regional populations, they were more often visited in later times and made increasingly visible by traces accumulated over thousands of years. The higher elevation Blue Mountains sites are in this way comparable to the higher-elevation sites of the Cascades, where winter conditions were in neither case conducive to year-round residence. People came into the Blue Mountains from all directions, as shown by damaged and discarded obsidian artifacts at various sites that have been traced to tool stone source areas in the vicinity of Whitewater Ridge to the east, the Malheur basin south of the mountains, and even sources far to the west, in Newberry Caldera, the northern Fort Rock Basin, and the Cascades. It is important to note, however, that while activity patterns remained stable and simple over time within this high-elevation Blue Mountains hinterland, the people who visited there seasonally were also, especially in later times, participants in a broader world of greater social complexity beyond. Wind Creek and Hall Creek clearly exhibit persistent short-term visitation sites of the kind just described.

Wind Creek. Inventory surveys in the Blue Mountains south of Cottonwood Creek show that these forested uplands along the southern edge of the Plateau were used as seasonal resource localities over a long period of time, beginning before about 7300 cal. BP and continuing into the ethnographic period (Armitage 1995). The evidence comes from over 1,000 recorded site locations in the Ochoco National Forest that yielded various stone tools, including many projectile points of types that fall across this time range. Four such sites excavated along Wind Creek (35GR147, 35GR148, 35GR159, 35GR162) produced ^{14}C dates that showed repeated occupations between about 4500 and 900 cal. BP. Ground stone tools used for plant processing, as well as flaking debris from stone tool manufacture, show that both kinds of activities were characteristic throughout the area examined. Projectile points, including both large leaf-shaped and notched points of types used with the atlatl and dart, and smaller triangular notched points used with the bow and arrow, show the importance of hunting as well. Highly fragmented pieces of charred bone from the excavations were from both small and large animals, but the species could not be determined.

Hall Creek. Other research some miles farther east adds to this picture. In a forested area at the headwaters of Silvies Creek and the south fork of the John Day River between Burns and Seneca, excavations at the Hall Creek site (35GR420) revealed projectile points and much evidence of flaking debris from locally available obsidian cobbles. The earliest of these lay buried beneath volcanic ash from the 7600 cal. BP eruption of Mount Mazama. Evidence for stone toolmaking increased above the level of the volcanic ash, and persisted thereafter into historical times. Test excavations at eight other sites in the vicinity, and surface studies at five more, made it clear that the locality had been occasionally visited for toolmaking and incidental hunting-gathering activities for thousands of years. The broken base of a Windust point found at one of the sites shows that someone passed that way as early as 11,600 to 10,000 years ago, but most of the projectile point types signaled mid-Holocene and later occupation. Chokecherry Cave (35GR500), a small rock shelter, was apparently used on different occasions for caching or short-term refuge. As in the neighboring Wind Creek vicinity, no evidence for constructed houses or shelters appeared at any of the sites (Draper and Reid 1989).

Newberry Volcano, Obsidian Toolstone, and Long Distance Trade. A fundamental aspect of the long, slow growth of societal complexity in Oregon's Plateau region, which ultimately came to a focus on the Columbia, is exemplified by the history of long distance trade in Newberry Volcano obsidian. Human occupation of the Newberry caldera had flourished during Pioneer Period times, when life there focused on summertime hunting and gathering in a rich, early postglacial environment, and Newberry obsidian traveled widely in the baggage of the visitors who passed that way. Things became very different after the Mt. Mazama eruption of about 7600 cal. BP had deposited a thick blanket of volcanic ash in the caldera and adjacent high Cascades, followed by local eruptions from vents within Newberry Caldera itself, greatly reducing local biotic productivity. No stable occupation comparable to that of pre-Mazama times occurs in Newberry Caldera after the great ashfall, but evidence does exist to show that small task groups still came to the obsidian sources periodically to quarry tool stone. Around Paulina Lake, the Ashflow Boundary (35DS486), Game Hut Obsidian Quarry (35DS485), Saddle Workshop (35DS220), and East Lake Boat Ramp (35DS219) sites consist almost entirely of flake concentrations that were left behind when raw chunks of obsidian were worked down into

BRITISH COLUMBIA

WASHINGTON

OREGON

Newberry
Volcano

Fig. 3.14. Obsidian of Newberry
Volcano geochemical type identified
from sourced assemblages in
Oregon, Washington, and British
Columbia. Dots show occurrences
outside the 10% contour.

bifacially flaked tool "preforms" for transport out of the caldera. Caches of such preforms, ranging in quantity from several dozen to more than 2,000 artifacts, have been found at various places downstream in the Deschutes region (Scott et al. 1986:15; Swift 1990). These caches were part of a long-lived trading system, as shown by the fact that artifacts made of Newberry Volcano obsidian have been chemically identified at archaeological sites dating from Transitional times into the contact-historic Plateau Period. That the trade system was far-reaching is shown by the fact that artifacts made of Newberry Obsidian have been found all the way up the Deschutes drainage to The Dalles of the Columbia, and far beyond into the Northwest Coast cultural zone of British Columbia's lower Fraser River (fig. 3.14).

In sum, the preceding account shows that over a long period between about 7,600 and 3,000 years ago, Oregon natives of the Columbia main stem and Plateau regions to its south transitioned from a lifeway as foragers more or less continuously on the move to one as more residentially stable logistic collectors who sent out work parties from established home bases to harvest and return with needed subsistence and other materials. Increasing site and artifact numbers show that human groups were gradually becoming more numerous during this same interval, especially in certain favored locations. Over time, substantial winter houses of durable pole and brush construction increasingly marked community home bases. These trends are seen over a broad region in the preceding accounts of the Marshmeadow, Kirkwood Bar, Cottonwood Creek, Bon, Johnson, and Heath Cliffs sites, among others. They set the stage for a major florescence of population and sociocultural complexity during the last 3,000 years of the aboriginal period, when a peak of cultural development was reached along the Columbia River, centering on The Dalles region.

Permanent Settlements and Complex Societies: the Plateau Period (3,000 to 200 Years Ago)

The Dalles of the Columbia flourished increasingly as a fishing and trading center after about 3,000 years ago, reaching its peak during the nineteenth-century contact-historic period. The enormously productive stretch of river that ran down from Celilo Falls to the foot of the Long Narrows became the epicenter of a very populous region. The now-drowned shelving rocks that flanked the river in this area (called *Les Dalles,* or "paving stones," by French *voyageurs*) offered both fishing access and camping grounds for seasonal visitors who came and went in their thousands during the summer salmon runs. The Congdon and other sites previously described continued to be occupied during this period, and new ones were established. It was an era of increasing social complexity and artistic elaboration throughout the Plateau, and other centers were growing in and beyond Oregon at the same time. At various places in the Plateau, including Oregon, the appearance of defensive settlements indicates growing intergroup competition and social stress, in which the bow and arrow, which swept North America between about 3,000 and 1,000 years ago, played an important part. More generally, this period established the "Plateau Pattern," representing a prosperous and socially elaborated fishing/hunting/gathering/trading society that is well described in written nineteenth century ethnohistoric accounts.

The Long Narrows. When Lewis and Clark came down the Columbia in 1805, The Dalles area was home to a multi-ethnic community dominated by the Wishram and Wasco tribes, who respectively controlled the Washington and Oregon sides of the Long Narrows. Both tribes spoke Kiksht, a language that links them with the Chinookan homeland downstream along the lower Columbia and adjacent Pacific Coast. The Chinookans were of the Northwest Coast culture, which they brought upriver to The Dalles only a few generations before Euroamericans arrived there. The Wishram and Wasco moved in among the long-established Tenino, Celilo, Tygh Valley, John Day, and related groups who continued their traditional way of life there and in the country all around. All of the long-established groups spoke local dialects of the Sahaptin language, which was ancient in the area and dominated much of northern Oregon and Eastern Washington.

Trading activity, already well-attested at The Dalles for some thousands of years, reached a high point in the early nineteenth-century contact-historic period, boosted by the appearance of Euroamerican trading goods and Spanish horses. A social class system of Northwest Coast type then prevailed, in which a few wealthy aristocratic lineages enforced their ownership of the best fishing sites and largely controlled the flow of trade. Lower on the social scale was a "middle class" of people such as the families of war chiefs and shamans, followed by poor commoners. At the bottom of the scale were slaves owned by the rich, who were typically captives from other tribes. The Euroamerican seamen, explorers, and overland traders who began to appear in the region in the early 1800s found a well-established system of commerce they could fit right into. Disastrously, however, these outsiders also carried smallpox, malaria, and other previously unknown diseases that spread rapidly through Native communities with catastrophic effects (Boyd 1998, Chatters 2004, Schulting 1995, Spier and Sapir 1930).

Wakemap, Congdon, and Indian Well. Lewis and Clark landed at Wishram, which in 1805 was a thriving settlement of the latest period of aboriginal occupation. It is very near a series of older predecessors—the Congdon, Indian Well, and other nearby sites on the Washington bank of the Columbia, and the Roadcut site just opposite on the Oregon side—but most of the archaeological evidence from its vicinity pertains to more recent times. The archaeological site of Wakemap [wok'um'up] Mound (45KL26), adjacent to the historic Wishram village on the Washington side of the river at the head of the Long Narrows, was a huge midden of accumulated occupation debris up to 20 feet deep that covered an area about 270 by 350 feet across. This mound was the ancient precursor of Wishram, a Native town still occupied today, which was a substantial community of 21 large wooden houses when Lewis and Clark stopped there in 1805 (Moulton 2003). Captain Clark noted the great abandoned mound immediately adjacent to Wishram in his journal for October 24, 1805, saying it had "some remains of houses" and "every appearance of being artificial." Available ^{14}C evidence suggests a date of about 1000 cal. BP for the mound's earliest occupation, which is congruent with the small triangular notched arrow points, stone sculptures, and carved bone artifacts found there. Ancient Wakemap and historic Wishram, side by side, mark an important culture-historical juncture. Wishram is home to a Chinookan community whose linguistic relatives bordered the Columbia downriver to the Pacific Ocean, while evidence from Wakemap represents a preceding settlement of long-established Sahaptin people, who with the Chinookan Wasco and Wishram continue to live in and around The Dalles today.

Strong (1959a, 1959b) characterizes the entire Long Narrows area as one big site, with artifacts, camp debris, and cemeteries everywhere. His impression is well supported by the comprehensive inventory map of Wilke et al. (1983: fig. 8), which shows many occupied areas on both sides of the Columbia. Only a very limited amount of systematic archaeological research was carried out on these sites before most were flooded by reservoir waters. Butler (2007), who was there, reports that an inordinate amount of private looting and vandalism occurred, some of which produced collections that eventually found their way into public museums and research repositories, albeit as undated, incomplete, and mixed assemblages. Most of the recovered specimens are like those dated to the 3000–200 cal. BP era at properly documented sites, however, their sheer abundance showing that the Plateau Period was indeed an era of substantial population and cultural florescence at The Dalles. In addition to settlement debris, domestic artifacts, and cemeteries, there were also many locations where rock art imagery of this period was richly displayed, especially in Spedis Valley and Petroglyph Canyon, now beneath Horsethief Lake northeast of Wakemap Mound.

Rock Art of The Dalles Area. The rich array of rock art seen at The Dalles belongs to a distinctive "Plateau Complex" that is known in southern British Columbia, Idaho, and western Montana, and southward from this reach across Washington into the upper drainages of north-central Oregon's John Day and Deschutes rivers. Plateau rock art originated in the deep past and

Left, Fig. 3.15. Water Spirit and Spedis Owl petroglyphs from The Dalles.
Right, Fig. 3.16. Rock art motifs from various Plateau sites.

reached a climactic stage during the Plateau Period. Keyser (1992) identifies four main local styles for Oregon's part of the Plateau, of which the Central Columbia Plateau style is the most widespread and best represented at The Dalles. It includes both pictographs and petroglyphs, and embodies the most widely distributed elements of the general Plateau repertoire. Common elements are abstract rectilinear and curvilinear designs, rayed arcs, rayed circles, humans with rayed heads or rayed arc headdresses, "thunderbirds" with outstretched wings, deer, and mountain sheep. Paired human figures suggesting twins occur in some sites. Mountain sheep are sometimes shown along with hunters using bows and arrows (figs 3.15, 3.16). McClure (1984) reports that both heavily weathered sheep-hunting scenes and the atlatl and dart were depicted at Petroglyph Canyon (now under water behind The Dalles Dam), both circumstances suggesting great age. Horses with riders, surely historic portrayals, are known from a few sites as well. These observations indicate a long duration for the widespread Central Columbia rock art style, as the atlatl has been ^{14}C dated to around 10,000 cal. BP in western U.S. sites and was largely replaced by the bow and arrow by 2,000 years ago, while horses first appeared in Oregon during the early 1700s.

Rock paintings in the Yakima Polychrome style, which also occurs at The Dalles, are often quite large and form impressive panels of red and white motifs that include rayed arcs, rayed arcs over human faces, and concentric rayed circles. Less common, but extremely distinctive, are human and animal figures with their skeletons prominently depicted. Similar motifs shown on datable artifacts from archaeological deposits suggest that the Yakima Polychrome style dates between about 1200 and 300 cal. BP (Keyser 1992; McClure 1984).

The Long Narrows style is primarily represented at more than 40 rock art sites around The Dalles, but rare examples are found further afield. It is a highly conventionalized style that emphasizes human and animal figures with very distinctive attributes, such as grinning mask faces, exposed ribs, wavy lines, rayed arcs, filled triangles, zigzags, and parallel or reticulated lines. Many images are clearly mythical beings, some of whose attributes and actions are described in traditional stories of the Wishram and other Plateau peoples. Best known among these are Tsagaglalal, a bear-like image, the Spedis Owl, and a distinctive "water monster" with large eyes and wavy lines depending from its lower face. Related stories tell of a child-eating female ogre with big eyes and ears and an ugly face who had an owl for a husband, and of "good" water monsters that lived in the river and rescued people from drowning. A variety of other beings are also mentioned. Often such beings combine both human and animal attributes, which is in keeping with widely shared Native American traditional stories about a past time when people and animals were not separate, as now, but could alternate between forms and intermarry with one another (Keyser 1992; Ray 1939; Spier and Sapir 1930; Teit 1928).

Tsagaglalal, "she who watches" in the Wishram language, is a large and dramatic image pecked into and painted on a basalt ledge at the Long Narrows of the Columbia, not far from the village of Wishram and overlooking a traditional cemetery area (fig. 3.17). One Wishram tale describes her as an ancient chief who the trickster god Coyote turned to stone so that she would stay and watch over the people there in a coming time of great change. Another story tells of a Wishram medicine man who painted the figure on a dark night without moon or stars, when he could not see what he was making. In the morning he was found there in a trance, and it seemed that a spirit had used him to paint the figure. Since that time Tsagaglalal has watched over the Wishram, and generations of people have gone to her for help.

The Tsagaglalal petroglyph, a face or mask with large round eyes and small ears high on the head, shares artistic details with rock art and other representations found along the Columbia from The Dalles down to the river mouth and north along the Pacific coast as far as Alaska. Some similarities are traceable even farther, into northeast Siberia. Carvings that resemble Tsagaglalal have been dated about 3200 to 4500 cal. BP in British Columbia, but figures essentially identical to the Tsagaglalal at Wishram are limited to the Columbia River drainage (Hann 1989, Lundy 1976). It has been suggested that Tsagaglalal became prominent as a guardian spirit during the early period of Euroamerican

Fig. 3.17. Tsagaglalal, "she who watches," on an outcrop overlooking the Long Narrows of the Columbia (Kimberly Dunn photo).

contact, when smallpox, measles, whooping cough, dysentery, and other alien diseases raged throughout the Northwest. Thousands died from repeated epidemics along the lower reaches of the Columbia River between about 1775 and the early 1850s (Boyd 1998; Butler 1957; Keyser 1992; McClure 1984). Four sites with Tsagaglalal petroglyphs are known on the lower reaches of the Columbia, two overlooking known cemeteries. Also, nearly identical images carved in stone, bone, and antler have been found as offerings in cremation burial sites near The Dalles and elsewhere. Some of these were found along with trade items of copper and iron, and all are dated to about A.D.1700–1840

Portable Art of The Dalles Area. Jewelry made of cut shell disks, Dentalium shells, abalone pendants, and other materials is well represented in private collections from The Dalles, with imported glass beads of many kinds, and even copper tubes, metal buttons, and coins added during the contact-historic period (figs. 3.18, 3.19, 3.20). Small figures carved in stone, bone, antler, and wood are another notable art form characteristic of Plateau culture sites around The Dalles. In addition to anthropomorphic bone and antler carvings there are such items as stone fish effigies (fig. 3.21), full-figure human effigies shown in a distinctive "skeletonized" form, human faces and heads, stone mauls ornamented with carvings of anthropomorphic/zoomorphic heads, bird figures, and lizards. The arresting image on this book's cover is a carved stone vessel from the Purgatory site (35GM15), a small village occupied during the last ca. 1500 years in the John Day Reservoir area a few

Left, Fig. 3.18. Glass trade beads, dentalium, shell beads, and abalone pendant from The Dalles.
Right, Fig. 3.19. Historic period phoenix buttons, military uniform buttons, and Chinese coins from The Dalles area.

miles above The Dalles. A rich set of religious beliefs and spiritual beings is surely reflected by this diverse and striking iconography (Butler 1957; Strong 1943). Further, it is important to note that much of both the petroglyphic art and the portable stone art from The Dalles area shares close parallels with comparable specimens and motifs from the lower Fraser River region of British Columbia, and indicates a significant level of cultural linkage between these areas among the elite strata of society.

As previously mentioned, there were many large cemetery sites at The Dalles, offering further evidence of its importance as a population center over a long period, and increasingly after about 3,000 years ago. The Congdon, Indian Well, Leachman, and other sites on the Washington side of the Long Narrows included major cemeteries, while Grave Island and Upper Memaloose Island in the main channel were entirely dedicated to mortuary use. Farther upstream, Big Leap and the Stewart site near Celilo Falls were also major cemeteries, and farther still formal cemeteries were present at Wildcat Canyon, as will be further discussed below. Funeral arrangements took three common forms. Interments and cremations were both placed in cemetery areas at or near residential sites, while exposed bodies were allowed to decompose naturally inside wooden mortuary houses built on memaloose ("death") islands in the river. Interment and cremation were ancient practices, but the use of mortuary houses was a custom that arrived with the Chinookan-speakers from downstream. Wishram informants living at The Dalles in the early twentieth century told ethnographers they had never practiced cremation (Spier and Sapir 1930), which seems to affirm that the other grave types represent the Sahaptin-speaking peoples of the area.

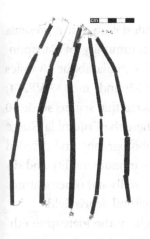

Left, Fig. 3.20. Historic period copper tube beads from the Middle Columbia area.

Above, Fig. 3.21. Fish effigy of ground stone from The Dalles.

The quite recent appearance of Chinookan speakers at The Dalles raises the question of exactly when they arrived there, and what forces may have encouraged their upriver movement. Minor and Walker (1993) suggest this movement occurred about A.D. 1650, noting that was the time when rectangular plank houses of Northwest Coast type replaced traditional Plateau-style circular semi-subterranean houses at the Cascades of the Columbia, not far below The Dalles. The massive Bonneville Landslide, which may have occurred as recently as ca. 300 years ago (O'Connor 2004; Pringle et al. 2002; Reynolds 2001), was large enough that it created a temporary earthen dam across the Columbia, briefly impounding its waters. This event is probably the origin of the Native American Bridge of the Gods legend, for which the place is now named. The river soon breached the landslide, but a legacy of the remaining rubble is the Cascades of the Columbia, which became an important fishing zone and in turn probably the magnetic force that drew the downriver Chinookans upstream in a move that ultimately reached The Dalles.

Minor and Walker (1993) also believe that mortality profiles studied at a late period cemetery near The Dalles (Hemphill 1990) reflect the catastrophic decline in Native American populations generally that is known to have been caused in early contact times by Euroamerican epidemic diseases (Campbell 1990; Dobyns 1966; Owsley 1992; Ramenofsky 1987). It therefore seems likely that Chinookan people had not long been established in the middle Columbia region when the epidemics struck. In this same vein, Endzweig (1994) has suggested that Euroamerican diseases afflicted Oregon Native populations not only along the Columbia, but up its tributary streams as well, as this may be among several reasons for a late period population decrease in Oregon's Plateau interior.

Mosier Mounds. A striking archaeological manifestation that represents the immediately pre-Chinookan and pre-epidemic community of Sahaptin-speaking peoples occurs on the south side of the Columbia about 10 miles below The Dalles (Connolly et al. 1997). The Mosier Mounds site (35WS274) is a great complex of walls, pits, troughs, trails, and cairns that sculpts some 30 acres of talus and rockslide debris on a steep slope where the Columbia Gorge cuts through the Cascade Range (fig. 3.22). Aerial photography and detailed computer-aided mapping at Mosier has made clear its monumentality and ritual significance by identifying over 3,000 feet of stone walls and other features organized along a winding path cleared through the natural debris field.

Rocky talus slopes were commonly used throughout the Plateau in ethnographic times for a variety of functions including burials, vision quests, spiritual training, and food storage (Spier and Sapir 1930; Murdock 1980). Smith (1910) reports terraced talus slope constructions very similar to those at Mosier from the Yakima Valley some 80 miles to the north. Teit (1928:127) describes burial areas established along the bases of talus slopes by Salish people farther up the Columbia, which over time came to form irregular terraces as burials were added higher and higher along the slope. No archaeological excavation has been carried out at the Mosier Mounds, but early reports of vandalized rock cairns, as well as scattered human bones and artifacts there, show that Mosier was certainly a cemetery, and an appropriate location for vision quest or other spiritual functions. Probably some of the talus slope features noted long ago by Smith (1910) and Teit (1928) on the Washington side of the river were functionally similar to the Mosier Mounds, and more

Fig. 3.22. Talus rock features at the Mosier Mounds.

recent research has identified additional sites of apparently of the same type.

Connolly et al. (1997: 290) observe that "The scale of the site and the tremendous labor required imply that its construction was orchestrated at a community level, even if built incrementally over a considerable period of time. Rock stacking on a grand scale at cemeteries, such as the Mosier site, was a public statement about the permanence of the community not only through time, but in a particular place." As a grand construction and continuing focus of community ceremonial observances, the Mosier Mounds would have been a prominent landmark known to all who passed along the Columbia River corridor. The authors conclude "It may be . . . that the Mosier site, with its dramatic exposure overlooking the Columbia River, served as an overt symbol to 'secure' the resident community's historic claim to local resources and territory and to 'legitimize' its place in the regional society" (Connolly et al. 1997: 298). At present the site's age is not precisely clear, but the practice of burying ancestors in stone graves on a hillside bespeaks mortuary customs very different from those of the historic period Chinookan peoples, who placed their dead in above-ground mortuary houses on islands in the Columbia. It is quite clear therefore that Mosier represents the traditions of long-time Plateau residents, which continued to be maintained even as more recent arrivals brought new concepts and customs to the area.

Social Complexity at The Dalles. The development of social status differentiation at The Dalles may have been reinforced with the arrival of Northwest Coast peoples from downriver, but it is important to note that strong evidence of wealth and high social status begins to appear much earlier. This is shown in the work of Schulting (1995), who reviews many poorly reported and unreported burial collections from The Dalles area, as well as the archival notes of amateur collectors. From these sources he describes a broad array of social status indicators in such large burial sites as Congdon, Indian Well, Big Leap, Maybe, Bead Patch, and others that fall between about 3,500 years ago and the contact-historic period. Cremation burials clearly entail more elaborate preparations and contain more and richer status items than talus slope or pit inhumation burials. Cremations commonly include shell and stone beads, stone pipes, stone carvings, clubs of stone and bone, and elaborate antler carvings. Status markers of comparable character are also found, however, in some non-cremation burial sites, notably at Big Leap, where burials containing the remains of multiple individuals were found to include a variety of carved stone pipes, zoomorphic sculptures, beads, pendants, pendants, and atlatl weights. It appears that cremation was commonly, though not invariably, the choice made by higher status people for burying their dead.

It is important to note that societal complexity had also been growing over many centuries in various other regional centers, with an aristocratic social tier like that seen at The Dalles similarly attested downriver on the Columbia, and especially in the lower Fraser River area of British Columbia. Close connections between these centers are indicated by striking similarities in the portable art of the lower Columbia and lower Fraser River areas, which no doubt grew out of long-range personal and trading relationships established through contacts at the great annual salmon-fishing rendezvous at The Dalles. The sharing of highly crafted, expensive status items of art and material culture suggests social exchanges among an aristocratic social tier that was regionally interconnected. Ames (2006) has likened the extended family societies and great communal houses of the lower Columbia, the lower Fraser, and other places to the "Houses" of the aristocratic lineages of Europe, a comparison that greatly illuminates our picture of the socioeconomic and sociopolitical processes that were ramping up through much of the late Holocene in northwestern America.

Salmon, Commodities, Manufactures, and Trade. For people whose home territory lay along the Columbia River, the rich and reliable annual salmon runs provided the opportunity not simply to obtain dependable winter stores, but also to accumulate wealth through catching and processing food surpluses for commercial trade. Centers of natural abundance and their substantial populations, not only at The Dalles but in other favored locations, made trade a major and defining characteristic of Plateau tradition. This commercial tradition also facilitated intensive interactions between Native Americans and the Euroamerican mariners, traders, and trappers who appeared on the horizon in the late 1700s (Anastasio 1972; Wood 1972).

As already noted above, the historic period Wasco and Wishram communities of The Dalles were upriver offshoots of a Chinookan-speaking nation on the lower Columbia and Pacific Coast that was famous for long-distance trade throughout the Northwest. From the Lower Chinook language spoken around the mouth of the Columbia there evolved a simplified trading language, the Chinook Jargon, which came to be used widely in the Plateau and up and down the Pacific coast from the Alaska Panhandle to northern California. Using a simplified Chinookan grammar, the jargon employed words from Chinook, Nootka, and a number of other native languages.

When Euroamerican mariners and overland traders arrived in the area, their adoption of Chinook Jargon added to it a great many French and English words as well.

During the annual congregation for fishing and trading at The Dalles, thousands of visitors bartered local products and manufactures from all over the Plateau and beyond (figure 3.23, table 3.1). When Lewis and Clark stopped at the Long Narrows on their way downriver in 1805, they remarked on the impressive stockpile of large 90-pound containers they saw there, filled with dried and pounded salmon ready for shipment (Moulton 2003). Their journals also comment on the foreign metal and glass items that had been brought to the mouth of the Columbia by Euroamerican mariners, but carried into the interior by native traders. At the same time, both manufactured items and bison hides were also reaching the Plateau from the east, brought over the Rockies by horse-mounted Plateau peoples who went to and from the northern Plains on annual bison hunts after obtaining imported Spanish horses in the 1700s from Indians farther south. Clearly, the sheer tonnage and variety of exotic articles seen in the flourishing trade of the 1800s were boosted by the heavy long-distance carrying capacities of foreign sailing ships and imported horses, but it would be wrong to think, as some historians and anthropologists once speculated, that the pervasive exchange network documented for the contact-historic Plateau came into being only with the arrival of alien merchants, trappers, and colonists.

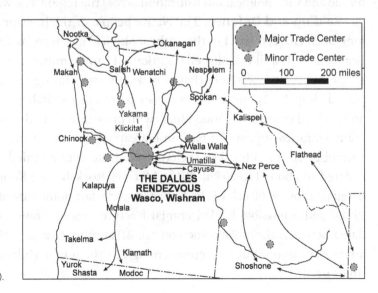

Fig. 3.23. Selected aspects of the Plateau trading system centered on The Dalles (modified from Wood 1972).

Upper Columbia and Western Plateau	Camas roots, hazel nuts, huckleberries, beargrass, fibers, basketry, tule mats, dried berries, hemp, stone artifacts, freshwater shell ornaments, hemp twine
Middle Columbia and Lower Snake	Salmon, camas, baskets, hats, freshwater shells
Northwest Coast	Marine shells, dried salmon, salmon oil, deerskins, wapato root
Great Basin	Edible roots, skin lodges, elk and buffalo meat
Klamath River	Wocas lily seeds, elk skins, beads, shells, bows
Great Plains	Catlinite toolstone and Catlinite pipes, buffalo skin tents, painted buffalo hide bags, pemmican, buffalo horn and robes, parfleches, dressed moose skins, buffalo bone beads, feather headdresses

Table 3.1. Items traded on the Plateau during the nineteenth century: Source areas and products (Anastasio 1972:120,136).

Another major aspect of this culminating period of cultural intensification, population growth, and flourishing trade on the middle Columbia is the growth in social stress and raiding that was part of Plateau Period socioeconomic and sociopolitical intensification across the region as a whole.

Raiding and Defense. The Native people of the Interior Plateau have long been characterized in the anthropological literature as fundamentally peaceful, with well-established traditions of intercommunity and intertribal cooperation, and certainly that was widely true during the ethnographic period (Ray 1932). Yet in all societies there are inevitably social stresses, and skeletal evidence of individuals with projectile wounds and blunt-force cranial injuries appears far back in Plateau prehistory. Chatters (2004) cites a number of examples. The skeleton of a male with a healed skull fracture is dated to about 11,600 cal. BP at Marmes Rockshelter; Kennewick Man, dated to about 9400 cal. BP, had a flaked stone dart point lodged in his pelvic girdle and a possible healed cranial fracture; healed cranial fractures are dated between about 7500 and 600 cal. BP at other sites as well. Such finds are not common, but numerous enough to show that violence did sometimes occur.

The growing population and social complexity of later times, however, generated a new and higher level of systemic stress within Plateau society. This is clearly seen in the crowding of many households into communities built in places obviously chosen for their defensibility. In the middle of the Columbia River about 15 miles above The Dalles, at least 200 house depressions are clustered on the upstream end of two-mile-long Miller Island, while a large cemetery occurs on its downstream end (Wilke et al. 1983). Another community where people obviously clustered together for defensive purposes is a large pithouse village on Strawberry Island, not far above Umatilla on the lower Snake River. Farther up the Columbia, more than 50 villages or redoubts are situated on highly inaccessible mesa tops or bluffs between Vantage and Spokane. These sites leave no doubt that intercommunity warfare became a serious problem in the Plateau period, as regional populations became larger, more socially complex, and more competitive (Chatters 2004; Schalk 1983).

The agglomeration of people into larger communities became pronounced about 2,500 years ago, coinciding with a time when the bow and arrow was replacing the atlatl and dart. Chatters (2004) suggests that the advent of the bow and arrow encouraged an increase in intercommunity raiding that ultimately drove previously scattered Plateau groups to coalesce into larger, more defensible settlements. He notes that an assailant armed with a bow and arrow can shoot from cover without exposing himself to missiles launched in return by his intended victims. He can also carry and launch more projectiles more rapidly than a man armed with the atlatl and dart, who moreover must stand in the open to launch his missile and thus expose himself to an enemy's return bolts. Thus, the newly arrived bow and arrow facilitated intergroup violence in a way that the older atlatl-dart technology did not.

Another factor that may have come into in play during the same period was competition for land and resources between Salish-speaking peoples moving into the Plateau from the Northwest Coast and the Nez Perce and Sahaptin-speaking peoples who had been in the Plateau for a long time. Linguistic evidence clearly shows that Salishan people who were established early on in the coastal zone of Washington and British Columbia later expanded their range up the Fraser River, across the Coast Mountains, and into the upper Columbia drainage. One view suggests that this movement began between about 5,700 and 4,500 years ago, but a later starting point has also been proposed, as has the possibility of a long period of Salishan expansion (Kinkade et al. 1998). The dating is not rigorously established, but it would seem that the agglomerated and fortified sites that begin to appear in the upper Columbia Basin about 2,500 years ago may be best explained as a reflection of conflict between Sahaptin and Salishan groups competing for territorial advantage.

As will be seen in the following accounts that take up the narrative of Plateau Period developments in Oregon east and south of The Dalles, the broader Plateau-wide rise of raiding and warfare, as well as the socioeconomic "draw" of large and prosperous communities along the Columbia, strongly affected Oregon natives south of the big river. The factors discussed above led them to shift away from their earlier pattern of many small dispersed settlements to one in which those who remained in the hinterland formed fewer but larger communities which afforded them greater defensibility and security against raiding.

Wildcat Canyon. About 30 miles upstream of The Dalles, the Wildcat Canyon site (35GM9), located on a high terrace of the Columbia, saw its most intensive occupation during the Wildcat Phase, about 2600–1000 cal. BP (Dumond and Minor 1983), which coincided with a time of great cultural growth at The Dalles. Six substantial pithouses, many living surfaces, fire hearths, earth ovens, rock clusters, pits, and 13 quite deep pits identified as wells pertain with little doubt to the Wildcat Phase, though not all dating ambiguities could be resolved.

Large corner-notched dart points were present early in the Wildcat phase, with smaller arrow points appearing later and ultimately becoming predominant (see fig. 3.12 on p. 167). Other artifacts include mortars and pestles, milling stones, mauls, flaked stone bifaces, knives, scrapers, choppers, drills, gravers, and net sinkers. Bone awls and toggling harpoon heads of both one-piece and composite types were also well represented (fig. 3.24). In all, the excavations revealed an impressive inventory of household tools for a variety of tasks. Many objects relate to obtaining and preparing food, and others to the probable manufacture of leather, wood, and textile items, which were not preserved in the moist deposits. Exotic and artistic items included beads of Dentalium shell brought most likely from a prominent source area near Vancouver Island, beads and pendants of bone and other marine shells, and ochre or other pigment stones.

People of the Wildcat Phase enjoyed a diverse diet. Fish bones give evidence of not only anadromous Chinook salmon and steelhead trout, but also year-round freshwater bridgelip sucker, largescale sucker, mountain sucker, chiselmouth, northern squawfish, and peamouth. Freshwater mussel was

Fig. 3.24. Wildcat Phase mauls and pestles from the Wildcat Canyon site.

collected as well. Deer and bighorn sheep were the best-represented larger animals, but elk, goat, and bison bone were also present. Jackrabbit predominated among the smaller forms, which also included a miscellany of small rodents and birds. Vegetal remains were not recovered, but many pestles and hopper mortars give evidence of root and seed processing.

The buried skeletons of 10 dogs were found at various places within the household area of the site. Metric analysis of the remains showed that they were very close in size to the sledge dogs of Siberia, and thus large enough to have served the Wildcat Canyon villagers as traction or pack animals. The finds offer an unusual glimpse of a human-animal working relationship that was probably more commonplace than is usually attested in archaeological records.

A cemetery area that contained the remains of perhaps 80 individuals was also used mainly during this time, confirming it as the era of most stable residence at Wildcat Canyon. Burial goods, found in many but not all graves, included various utilitarian items such as projectile points, knives, mauls, and pestles. More distinctive offerings included a set of 42 perforated elk teeth, presumably once strung or attached to a garment, a small stone effigy of an eel or fish, another small effigy of a dog or bear, and various fragmentary shaped and decorated bone objects.

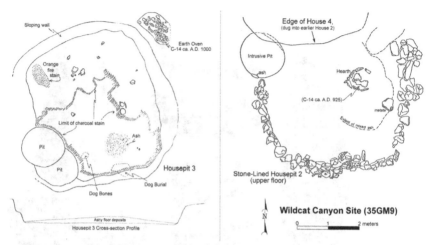

Fig. 3.25. Housepits 2 and 3 of the Wildcat Phase, Wildcat Canyon Site (from Dumond and Minor 1983)

People of the Wildcat Phase made substantial pithouses of the type that served as winter dwellings throughout the Plateau well into historic times (fig. 3.25). Their floors were made in shallow excavated pits, and posthole patterns suggest sturdy timbered superstructures covered with brush and earth. Typically the houses were roughly square in plan and measured 20 to 25 feet across. Two housepits had their wall bases lined with upright basalt slabs. Fire hearths were either encircled by stones or simply laid on the floor. There were also traces at the site of more lightly built tipi-like structures, probably mat-covered, like those historically used at Plateau fishing camps during the hot summer season. The fact that both house types were found together during the Wildcat Phase suggests that the site might have been occupied year-round. It is not clear how many households may have made up the settlement at any one time, because the entire site was not excavated. It is evident, however, that the community was long-lived, as overlapping floors and other features show that houses were built and rebuilt in the same places.

The Quinton Phase at Wildcat Canyon, dating from about 1000 cal. BP into historic times, presents quite a different picture. Its deposits are shallow and lack houses, suggesting the site saw only occasional use during this period. The very small pin-stem arrow points from these deposits are of types common on the lower Columbia and probably reflect the late upriver movement of Chinookan peoples that is attested at The Dalles. The paucity of late occupation at Wildcat Canyon reflects a widespread trend as people aggregated into fewer but larger communities during this period, especially in the favored region around The Dalles.

Umatilla Rapids. About 60 miles up the Columbia main stem from Wildcat Canyon, a major focal point of fishing and trade is dated at the Umatilla Rapids from about 4,000 years ago into historical times (Schalk 1980, Shiner 1961). Numerous archaeological sites lay along both sides of the Columbia here, clustering around the confluence where the Umatilla flows in from the south. Today most of this once well-populated but little-studied nexus lies beneath the waters of McNary Reservoir. Lewis and Clark visited a large Native community at Umatilla Rapids in 1805, and on their return up the Columbia in 1806 they estimated that about 700 people in some 50 lodges were encamped there awaiting the spring salmon run. Only very limited scientific excavations were made at Umatilla Rapids before the construction of McNary Dam flooded the area, but for years prior to that event many amateur collectors dug thousands of artifacts from cultural deposits reportedly 5 to 10 feet deep in places, and some of that evidence also contributes to our understanding of human occupation there.

Specimens found beneath a layer of Mount Mazama volcanic ash show that people were frequenting the Umatilla Rapids before about 7600 cal. BP, but the area's major occupation is placed by ^{14}C dates between about 4000 and 200 cal. BP. Most of these dates came from the Umatilla Townsite (35UM1, 35UM35), a deposit that revealed traces of over 30 pithouses, a figure which is thought to be only a small fraction of the total actually present at the site. The earliest structures were generally circular, with a deeply excavated floor and a raised bench encircling the base of the housepit wall. Fire hearths were present, and interior storage pits were common. Houses found stratigraphically above those of this type were also circular, but had floors less deeply excavated into the earth, without benches and storage pits. A small rectangular structure, ^{14}C dated at 2500 cal. BP, shows that this historically known Plateau house form also extended far back in time. A cemetery that held over 230 burials is dated by associated point types between about 2600 and 250 cal. BP, contemporary with the later village remains.

Animal bones from 35UM35 show that people drew their food from both the Columbia River and its hinterlands. Salmon vertebrae confirm a long history of fishing at Umatilla Rapids. Jackrabbit and cottontail bones suggest hunting in the near vicinity, while bones of deer, elk, bighorn sheep, and antelope indicate hunting in the uplands to the south. The archaeological evidence is illuminated by ethnographic period accounts relating that the Umatilla, Nez Perce, and Cayuse tribes of the area regularly hunted in the adjacent Blue Mountains, where elk, antelope, and deer were abundant (Ray 1936:150).

Lower Deschutes River. The cultural picture in the Plateau interior south of the big river is best approached by beginning with the Deschutes River drainage. The Deschutes enters the Columbia just a few miles upstream of The Dalles region, immediately above Celilo Falls. An inventory survey of the 100 river miles or so of the Deschutes from its Columbia confluence to Warm Springs Bridge located 135 prehistoric sites, among them pithouse villages, rock art panels, talus pits, quarry-workshop sites, rockshelters, and open surface scatters of artifacts (Hibbs et al. 1976). Concentrations of freshwater mussel shell were also found at a number of locations. Two villages showed about 30 housepit depressions each; 25 other villages contained from one to six definite depressions, and 10 more sites were identified as probable pithouse villages. Excavations and mapping at the Mack Canyon and Paquet Gulch sites introduce the interior village life of the Plateau Period.

Mack Canyon. The Mack Canyon site (35SH23) is an aggregation of large and small depressions situated on an extensive river terrace about six miles up the Deschutes River from where it joins the Columbia immediately east of Celilo Falls (fig. 3.26). Housepits 1 and 3 were excavated to expose the shallow floors of circular pithouses like those common along the Columbia. The floors were roughly 20 and 15 feet in diameter respectively, each with a more deeply dug central area encircled by a slightly higher bench (fig. 3.27). In the central area were fire hearths and such domestic tools as hopper mortars, pestles, milling stones, pounding stones, flaked stone cutting and scraping tools, and projectile points. Some artifacts were also found scattered on the upper benches. The artifact concentrations no doubt reflect use of the central portion of the floor as the main domestic activity area, while the raised bench around it would have served for sleeping and storage (Cole 1969).

The artifact inventory recovered from test excavations was quite large and varied, typifying the life of a settlement that functioned as a year-round base of operations. Hunting was represented by projectile points of notched and stemmed types that closely resemble those from the Wildcat Canyon Site at the mouth of the John Day. Scrapers, knives, drills, awls, gravers, bone beads, and a fragment of a composite harpoon reflect the making and maintenance of clothing and equipment, while hopper mortars, pestles, and milling slabs were used in food processing. From

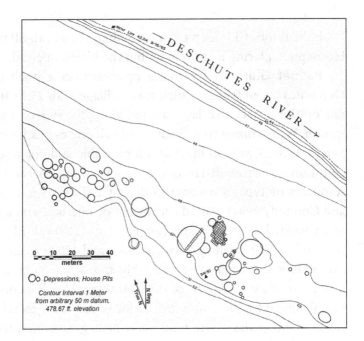

Fig. 3.26. Plan map of
the Mack Canyon Site
(from Cole 1969).

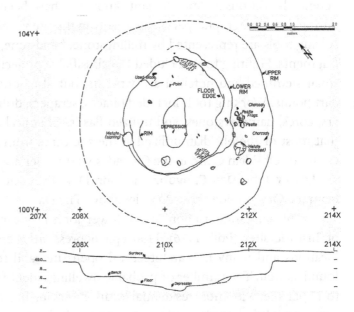

Fig. 3.27. Housepit 3
at Mack Canyon
(from Cole 1969).

about 1,000 pieces of bone were identified deer, elk, bighorn sheep, jackrabbit, cottontail, beaver, coyote, and bobcat. Fish bones and fragments
of freshwater mussel shell attest the availability of aquatic fauna as well.
The village is dated by one ^{14}C determination of 1900 cal. BP on charcoal

from the floor of Housepit 1 and another of 700 cal. BP from the floor of Housepit 3, placing it entirely within the Plateau Period.

Paquet Gulch. A few miles upstream on a small tributary of the Deschutes called Paquet Gulch was a village with 75 to 100 housepits visible on the surface that lay scattered along the side of a sheltered canyon mouth. With a major root ground and oak groves nearby, the Paquet Gulch Site (35WS123) was an ideal spot for a stable and populous winter village community, surrounded by a wide variety of seasonal and year-round food resources of types amenable to drying and over-winter storage (Jenkins and Connolly 1994). Partial excavation of one housepit and testing of another yielded seven ^{14}C dates ranging from 2300 cal. BP to modern, with most of the dates falling between 1600 and 1200 cal. BP. Bones from the house floor show that deer, elk, rabbits, rodents, birds, salmon and freshwater mussels were all part of the diet. Vegetal foods identified from pollen samples included lomatium roots, acorns, currants, gooseberries, elderberries, and the small seeds of wild buckwheat, grasses, and other seed-bearing perennials. Various additional plants known to have been important foods during the ethnographic period also grow in the site vicinity, and plant processing tools are represented by millingstone, handstone, pestle, and maul fragments. Hunting tools included 138 classifiable projectile points, mostly small stemmed and notched arrowpoints, but also some larger notched dart points. Working tools included bifaces, scrapers, drills, gravers, abraders, cores, hammerstones, and utilized flakes. Chemical analysis indicates that most of the obsidian utilized at the site came from either Newberry Crater or Obsidian Cliffs, in the Cascades west of Bend.

Lower John Day Canyon. The John Day River enters the Columbia from the Oregon side about 30 miles above The Dalles. A cultural resource survey of a 160-mile ribbon of the lower John Day canyon recorded 76 prehistoric sites (Polk 1976). Housepit depressions were recorded at 47 locations and many non-architectural open sites and rockshelters were found as well. The number of probable dwellings identified varied from 1 to 17 per site, with most residential locations having between three and six housepits visible on the surface; 230 housepit depressions were counted in all. The survey evidence indicates a growing number of people, once more broadly dispersed, who were moving closer together in favorable places near the Columbia during a period when the regional population as a whole was forming increasingly nucleated settlements along the big river. Associated non-residential locations included rock art panels, rock alignments, and a number of small pits and cairns found in talus slopes. It has been speculated that these talus pits and cairns represent burials, which seems probable for the cairns, but the pits were perhaps more likely storages left open after removal of their contents.

Pine Creek. A comparable pattern is seen on Pine Creek, a small tributary of the John Day that comes in some 80 miles above its confluence with the Columbia (Atherton and Houck 1976; Endzweig 1991, 1994). In 68 sites recorded along Pine Creek, housepits were commonly observed, as were activity locations that included rockshelters, talus pits, cairns, pictographs, tool stone quarries, lithic flake scatters, projectile points, and grinding stones. Excavated pithouse structures have provided evidence of living floors and fire hearths, and yielded ^{14}C dates between 2600 and 300 cal. BP. Indian Canyon 2 (35WH13), on a small tributary of Pine Creek, was a special plant-processing site. Excavations there in a culture-bearing deposit about three feet deep retrieved over 100 specimens and fragments of flat stones with battered surfaces that were probably hopper mortar bases and grinding slabs, and over 50 pestles and manos. In the deepest levels of the excavation, where a ^{14}C date of 1400 cal. BP was obtained, clusters of such plant-processing stones were the dominant feature. Higher up, in addition to more such stones, were many clusters of blackened and fire-cracked rocks and charcoal. These clusters are believed to represent earth ovens. They lay for the most part above a level from which a ^{14}C date of 1000 cal. BP was obtained, and continued to the top of the deposit, where another date of 400 cal. BP and the finding of a glass trade bead indicate late prehistoric and historic occupation. Plant food remains were not recovered from the excavations, but the extensive processing of root crops is clearly indicated by the hopper mortar bases and earth ovens that dominate the site. Other sites indicating a considerable population in the area were Pentecost Shelter (35WH2), Jones Canyon (35WH21), and Cove Creek (35WH7) (Endzweig 1991; Mazany 1980).

Mitchell Cave. Along the John Day above Pine Creek, where the Deschutes-Umatilla Plateau gives way to the Blue Mountains, pithouse settlements have not been found. As noted for the preceding period, it appears that the higher mountains remained a hinterland visited in seasonal hunting and harvesting forays by people whose main settlements were elsewhere. Mitchell Cave (35WH122), not far from Pine Creek, exemplifies the continuation of the earlier pattern into recent times, as indicated by ^{14}C dates of 1400, 1000, and 300 cal. BP. The principal artifacts were small arrow points, point fragments, and point preforms, along with flakes and informal tools, while the dominant activity was hunting and the processing of meat and hides (Connolly et al. 1993). For this period the best candidate for a regional base settlement is Big Summit Prairie, farther south.

Big Summit Prairie. South of the John Day River and Mitchell Cave is Big Summit Prairie, located about midway between the cities of John Day and Bend. It is a vast high meadow lying along the southern base of the rugged Ochoco Mountains, which comprise the western end of the Blue Mountains Province. Surface survey here identified extensive lithic scatters and mapped some 40 depressions believed to be housepit features; archaeological testing of two such depressions affirmed that identification. One housepit gave ^{14}C dates of about 2100 and 1300 cal. BP from lower and higher levels, while the other yielded a date of about 800 cal. BP (Zancanella 1998).

The Dudley Site (USFS671NA22), on U.S. Forest Service land along the timbered edge of the prairie at about 4,500 feet elevation, was selected for further study (Barber and Holzapple 1998). Four depressions about 18 to 24 feet in diameter were profiled by trenching them from rim to center. Depression 1 gave indications of two house floors, and a hearth from the uppermost one yielded a radiocarbon date of about 1500 cal. BP. Depression 2 had a well-marked floor and bench but no hearth was found and the unit was not dated. Depression 15 had evidence of a floor, but no hearth was found and the unit was not dated. The excavations yielded a substantial array of small bifaces, scrapers, utilized flakes and other specimens. Additional dating information is provided by a collection of about 75 projectile points and fragments of small triangular stemmed, triangular notched, and triangular stemless forms, which correspond to types known from the 1000 cal. BP–historic Quinton phase at Wildcat Canyon.

The rich and varied natural resources of Big Summit Prairie and vicinity obviously made it an attractive place for people to live, as it is well known both for its camas, lomatiums, wildflowers and berries and for the deer, elk, and antelope that herd there. Offsetting its rather high and seasonally cold elevation, which would seem to make it less attractive as an overwintering site, the extensive root grounds could provide a never-failing and eminently storable abundance of winter provender that was immediately at hand. Like Cottonwood Creek in an earlier period, Big Summit Prairie was well situated to serve as a stable logistic base from which to hunt and harvest the rugged higher elevations of the western Blue Mountains. An additional factor encouraging a large settlement there would have been the general rise of raiding and warfare noted above for the Plateau Period, which encouraged fewer but larger community aggregates for defensive purposes.

Coming of the Northern Paiute. An important culture-historical question in the late prehistory of Oregon's Plateau region is that of when Northern Paiute people, originally from the Great Basin, began to arrive there. We know from ethnography and historical documents that Paiutes were exerting pressure as horse-mounted raiders on southern Plateau Natives and Euroamerican immigrants alike during the early and middle 1800s (Ray et al. 1938). For the Upper Deschutes/John Day area, a decline in ^{14}C dated occupations about 200-300 cal. BP in the Pine Creek drainage suggests that Plateau peoples had by then withdrawn from the area. The earliest dates attributable to Northern Paiute in Oregon's adjacent Northern Great Basin area are about 500–300 cal. BP, so the circumstances suggest that Paiutes and perhaps their Shoshone-Bannock relatives were living along the Plateau's southern edge by the end of the 1700s, and may have flowed in with little resistance when catastrophic reduction of the local populations by epidemic Euroamerican disease opened up rich new hunting-fishing-gathering territory (Endzweig 1994a, 1994b; Jenkins and Connolly 1994).

From ethnohistoric and ethnographic data, Ray et al. (1938) map one Northern Paiute band in the upper Deschutes River drainage, two in the upper John Day drainage, and one in the Malheur River drainage, all tributary to the Columbia. Teit (1928) and Berreman (1937) suggested that predation by horse-mounted Northern Paiutes after about A.D. 1750 pushed Nez Perce and Sahaptin speakers out of the Deschutes and lower John Day areas, while Endzweig (1994a, 1994b) proposes that epidemic Euroamerican disease may have played an important role in the late abandonment of this area by Plateau peoples. It is important to note that the warfare and disease explanations could both apply, as Nez Perce-Sahaptin groups ravaged by epidemics would have had limited ability to resist Paiute incursions.

Archaeology of the Historic Period

Historic records can provide information on the timing of farming, logging, and mining developments, and their impact on the broader economy, but archaeology can often offer insights lacking in the written record, such as family-level economic realities on a remote homestead, or the structure of railroad logging systems and daily life in crew camps. Archaeology can also provide a historical presence to minority communities under-represented or misrepresented in existing histories. There exists enough information on the historic archaeology of Oregon to fill another book, but for reasons of space and proportion only a few illustrative cases are offered in the present text.

From Explorer's Camps to Colonial Infrastructure. Various perspectives on Oregon's immigrant newcomers are reflected in the traces of explorer's camps, toll roads, homesteads, placer mines, ranger stations, lumber camps, railways, ghost towns, and other features that are scattered throughout the woods and open lands of the Plateau region (Beckham 1998, Walker and Sprague 1998). In the earliest recorded Euroamerican venture into central Oregon, Peter Skene Ogden's trapping brigade of 1826 traveled east up the Columbia from the Hudson's Bay Company base at Fort Vancouver, and above The Dalles turned south up the Deschutes to its conjunction with the Crooked River near modern-day Madras. Ascending the latter, the brigade crossed the Blue Mountains and dropped down into the Malheur Lake basin near modern-day Burns. From there the party turned back toward the west, passing the two high lakes in the caldera of Newberry Volcano and striking south along the Little Deschutes River. One of Ogden's 1826 camps is known near East Lake in the Newberry Caldera, and another beyond the caldera at Suttle Lake in the eastern Cascades. In 1834 Nathaniel Wyeth's group camped in the same vicinity at Fly Lake, a site used again in 1843 by John C. Frémont's U.S. Army Topographic Engineers during a journey of exploration. In 1855 Lt. Abbot of the Williamson Survey, which was seeking a railroad route from the Sacramento Valley to the Columbia River, camped at Prairie Farm, the Metolius Ford, and a place called Whispering Pines. Along their route these surveyors explored Newberry Volcano, which is named after Dr. John Newberry, the expedition's geologist and botanist.

Roads were built into Central Oregon from the west beginning in the 1850s, especially following the 1861 discovery of gold in the Blue Mountains, as some of the 1840s Oregon Trail immigrants, who had originally bypassed the desert country for the wetter and greener Willamette Valley, began to seek their fortunes back across the Cascades. The Willamette Valley and Cascade Mountain Road, which partly followed the earlier Minto Trail from Sweet Home into the Sisters area (roughly the route of modern Highway 20), was completed in 1866 and became a key route of settler migration into eastern Oregon from west of the Cascades. Various traces of it are still to be seen, including the sites of the Cache Creek Toll Station near Black Butte and a way station, post office, and store at Camp Polk, an abandoned 1865 military garrison now engulfed by modern Sun River. Traces also persist of the Central Oregon Military Road over Willamette Pass (roughly modern Highway 58), which was built at about the same time. Another road completed in 1871 across McKenzie Pass between Eugene and Sisters, following the 1862 Scott Trail, also remains in use today (Beckham 1998; Walker and Sprague 1998).

The Kam Wah Chung Company. A rich site of distinctive character is that of the Kam Wah Chung Company (35GR2086) in the frontier mining town of John Day (Barlow and Richardson 1979; Schablitsky et al. 2007). A relic of northeast Oregon's mining boom during the 1860s, the Kam Wah Chung site represents an important aspect of late nineteenth- and early century immigration history in the southern Plateau. Gold and silver were discovered in 1861 along the upper John Day River, in a rich belt that ultimately produced some three-quarters of all the gold mined in Oregon (Orr et al. 1992). In the placer mining technique most commonly used, great gouts of water were sprayed under high pressure through nozzles called "giants" to wash down ancient river terraces, the gravel being then processed through sluice boxes to recover the gold dust and nuggets it contained. The cuts and gravel piles thus created are still prominent on the landscape, some in the immediate vicinity of the Kam Wah Chung Company in downtown John Day. Dams, ditches, ands flumes used to channel the water used in "placering" also left many traces on the local landscape.

The John Day strike, along with the somewhat earlier gold rush in the Rogue River country of southwest Oregon, brought the state into full participation in a great worldwide nineteenth-century mining boom that saw rushes in gold and other precious metals in California, Oregon, Idaho, Nevada, Utah, Colorado, Arizona, Mexico, Peru, Bolivia, Alaska, Canada, Russia, Australia, Africa, and India, among other places. Most of the labor that supported the mining boom around John Day and in the western United States generally was drawn from Guangzhou (old "Canton") Province in southwest China, whence the prospect of jobs drew thousands of immigrants who were suffering under catastrophic economic conditions at home. The 1879 Census enumerated 2,468 Chinese and 960 whites in the gold fields of eastern Oregon. The Chinese were virtually all men, who came to work and send money back home to their families. Although many ultimately stayed on in the United States, most were by original intention "sojourners," who came to work for a time and then return home to China.

Now a National Landmark and State Heritage Site, the Kam Wah Chung building in John Day was probably built in the late 1860s and was purchased in 1887 from its previous Chinese owner by two Chinese immigrants, Ing Hay and Lung On. "Doc" Hay was an herbal doctor of high repute throughout the region, and Lung On a successful businessman. The Kam Wah Chung ("Golden Flower of Prosperity") building was where they lived and worked into the 1940s, and they deeded it to pass upon their deaths to the City of John Day as a museum and monument to the Chinese community of eastern Oregon. The durable stone walled building (its fort-like steel-clad door and small windows a testament to hostility experienced by many Chinese) sat closed up with all its voluminous and fascinating contents for over 20 years until it was rehabilitated and opened to the public in the mid-1970s. In 2005 archaeologists studied the building's surroundings using ground-penetrating radar, trenches, and shovel probes to learn more about the historical and cultural context within which the Kam Wah Chung Company functioned. An interpretive center has since been built nearby to tell this story more fully.

In addition to being its owners' residence, the Kam Wah Chung building was a general store, doctor's office, medicinal herb shop, post office, labor-contracting office and temple for the regional Chinese community. One small room with wooden bunks provided sleeping quarters for a few miners or travelers. Heavily smoked walls, opium tins, and pipes show that it also hosted opium smokers at some point, while many unopened bottles of liquor found buried in sawdust under the floorboards hint that the Kam Wah Chung Company may also have been a source of illegal alcohol during the 1920–1933 Prohibition Era.

The Kam Wah Chung Company served a substantial Chinatown that surrounded it in the early days, which is gone now but has been partially traced by archaeological investigations. Nearly 1,200 bones excavated around the site show that chicken, turkey, duck, goose, and other birds, as well as pig, cow, and sheep, were all part of the community's diet. High proportions of broken-up pig and bird bones reveal food choices and a mode of butchery by chopping that are recognizable as distinctively Chinese. A melon seed and preserved remains of weedy plants suggest the location of a garden plot. Widely distributed in the neighborhood of the main building were fragments of fired clay opium pipe bowls and liquor bottles, glass medicine vials and gaming pieces, celadon jars, and porcelain dishes that illustrate the many different community activities centered there. There is high potential for future archaeological research here to illuminate the lives and contributions of the many Chinese workers who came and went during the early period of Euroamerican settlement. In addition to the placer mining attested around John Day and other such places, there was much labor-intensive construction of roads, railroads, canal systems, fences, and buildings done by Chinese workers throughout the western United States during the late nineteenth and early twentieth centuries.

Homesteads and Ghost Towns. During this same period, the growth of homesteading and stock raising—both sheep and cattle operations, their incompatibilities leading to a brief "range war" around 1915—left cabin and camping sites, cemeteries, and stock pens at various places around central Oregon. Excavations at the Crooked River Bridge southwest of Prineville produced a fascinating perspective on the life of an evidently prosperous homesteading family (Endzweig 2005). The archaeological inventory included stone house foundations, cut iron nails, broken window glass, iron stove and wagon parts, fragments of a child's writing slate and pencil lead, fragments of a porcelain doll's head, dinnerware fragments, glass jars, lamp chimneys, tin cans, clothing buttons, shoe fragments, combs, medicine bottles, whiskey and wine bottles, tobacco tins, horse shoe nails, a mower blade, rifle and pistol cartridge casings in .22, .32, .41, .44, and .50 calibers, and other items. The bones of domestic horse, cow, sheep, pig, and chicken, along with bones of native deer, jackrabbit, and fish, bespeak a household economy primarily based on stock raising but significantly augmented by hunting and fishing. The various traces at the site show that a family homestead existed there perhaps as early as 1870, when the nearby town of Prineville was newly founded, with a focus of activity between about 1890 and 1910. A photo taken in 1893 shows a single-family board and batten house with a gabled roof at the site locality.

Two ghost towns in the Sisters area, Grand View and Geneva, existed only briefly, but digging of the Pilot Butte Canal between 1902 and 1904 got irrigation agriculture underway in the foothills of the Cascades. Dams and canals still in use today were created around Tumalo, north of Bend, beginning in 1902, and by 1920 at Crane Prairie, 30 miles to the southwest. A broad stretch of the sagebrush-juniper Great Basin landscape traversed by modern Highway 20 east of Bend attracted many would-be farmers in a classic western land swindle between about 1913 and 1918, but they soon found rainfall-dependent agriculture in the desert a practical impossibility and abandoned the area, many for work in the timber industry then ramping up around Bend.

Lumber Mills and Railroads. Many historic archaeological sites inventoried in the Deschutes National Forest south and west of Bend illustrate the momentous forces that converged in that region as settlers flooded into the area during the later nineteenth and early twentieth centuries (Goddard et al. 1979; Nixon et al. 2000; Ross, Bowyer, and Speulda 1995; Sekora and Ross 1995; Tonsfeldt 1995). The birth of a major economic and social force there is represented in the Deschutes National Forest by scattered sites of very small and basic "pre-industrial" sawmills that produced only what was needed for local use. The Spoo mill near Sisters and the McKinley mill near Bend are two examples of this type. Each was powered by a small steam engine and used a single circular saw rig. The mills apparently did not have planers, and produced only rough lumber. Nor was evidence of kilns found at either site, implying that the lumber went to its buyers in green condition. The steam engines were fired with bark, sawdust, and milling waste; excess material was burned at one of the mills, while at the other it was dumped over an embankment.

Mill sites built for national-scale industrial production of lumber blossomed soon after the Oregon Trunk Railroad from The Dalles reached Bend in 1911. Well before then lumber tycoons from the Great Lakes region had taken note of the Bend area's vast pine forests and had begun acquiring timberland and designing huge mills with the latest high-volume technologies. The Shevlin-Hixon and Brooks-Scanlon mills, the two largest in Bend, both went on line in 1915. Each comprised an integrated system that included not only the mill proper, but also movable logging camps, railroads and other infrastructure necessary to feed it. The archaeological traces of the new industry, which still flourishes today, are everywhere to be seen throughout the region.

Typical sites of the Sisters area are the Shevlin-Hixon logging camp and railroad trestle, the Brooks-Scanlon water tanks, many grades built for spur railroads to haul logs to the mill and move logging camps, and the big Brooks Camp at Bull Springs, which included modular buildings and logger's quarters on skids that could be loaded on cars and shipped by rail to new locations once an area had been cut over. Railroads were built throughout the woods, to be later removed and re-laid to access new timberlands, and many of the forest roads in use around Bend today follow old railroad grades. An additional large class of sites related to the logging industry are U.S. Forest Service ranger stations, trails, watchtowers, and other installations that are still to be seen throughout the area, many created before 1915. The lumber companies had privately purchased much timberland in advance of the logging boom, but the national forests also made timber sales. It is interesting to note, too, that some of the Forest Service trails date back far beyond the logging era, being originally Native American trails that foresters encountered and used in the course of their routine management activities (Goddard 1979; McKinley et al. 2000).

Summary

As shown in the preceding pages, Oregon's Plateau region has a very long human history. Not far beyond the Plateau's southern edge, in the Paisley caves of Oregon's Northern Great Basin province, unmistakable human DNA and artifacts have been directly ^{14}C dated to about 14,500 cal. BP, currently the oldest rigorously established date for human presence in North America (Chapter 2). Scattered Clovis points found in Oregon's Plateau region suggest humans were present at least by 13,200–12,800 cal. BP, a time range established by radiocarbon dates for Clovis points in the Southwestern U.S. Numerous locally dated artifacts from the earliest occupations at The Dalles, Cooper's Ferry, and the Paulina Lake site show that people became well established across that area between about 13,000 and 9500 cal. BP. A well-built house defined by postholes and a fireplace, dated to about 9500 cal. BP at Paulina Lake, represents the oldest dwelling structure currently documented anywhere in the Interior Plateau.

After about 7600 cal. BP, the date of the Mt. Mazama volcanic eruption and ashfall, many sites are known from surface indications throughout Oregon's Plateau region. Excavations at some of them have yielded large stemmed, leaf-shaped, and notched points, grinding stones, animal bones, and seeds or other plant parts. The people of this time were foragers, taking a wide variety of small and large animals and plant foods, moving frequently as they harvested the resources of various productive localities, and rarely building shelters durable enough to be archaeologically preserved. Increasing site numbers indicate growing population density, while substantial pithouses show small groups staying longer at home bases in certain favorable spots. From these stable logistic bases people could range out on collecting forays and return to prepare and store some of their harvest for later winter consumption. In later times the scattered pithouse occupations grew into hamlets or villages, and as people became more numerous they increasingly organized themselves at levels beyond the immediate family and scheduled cooperative activities to improve the productivity of the community's labors.

By 3,000 years ago strong signs of growing social complexity were appearing in the densely settled area around The Dalles and at other places along the Columbia River. Finely crafted objects of art and trade, often embellished with images of distinctive character and symbolic significance, were increasingly made, and some of the same images appear as engraved rock art at ritually significant locations. All these phenomena give evidence of increasingly class-organized local societies, and broad-scale trade and exchange. Shared art motifs and finely crafted ritual objects suggest growing relationships among the dominant lineages that made up a regionally interconnected social elite stratum which was coming to power at The Dalles, along the lower Columbia, in the Lower Fraser River region of British Columbia, and elsewhere.

Evidence of increased competition, raiding, and warfare among neighboring regional communities soon appeared as well. Fortified sites and large sites in defensible locations appeared along the Columbia River, and increasingly drew people out of Oregon's Plateau interior. In the interior, the remaining communities became fewer but larger, and more defensible. The bow and arrow, which spread rapidly across all of North America between about 3,000 and 2,000 years ago, proved an effective weapon of war and surely facilitated the pattern of intercommunity raiding and conflict that was endemic in the Northwest when the first Euroamerican explorers came in the early nineteenth century.

When encountered by Euroamerican explorers in the early 1800s, the lower Columbia main stem supported a number of well-established towns dominated by "great houses," and the middle Columbia around The Dalles was similarly a dominant nexus of fishing, trading, and social interaction. It was occupied year round by several thousand people, and each summer's salmon runs made it a magnet drawing thousands more who came to fish, trade, reunite with friends and relatives, find marriage partners, and ultimately return to distant homes. Visitors made the trek annually from as far north as the Canadian border, from California to the south, and from as far east as the northern Plains and Wyoming Basin. Archaeology shows that this mature "Plateau Pattern" of life began to emerge about 3,000 years ago and flourished increasingly after that time. Spanish horses traded up from the south in the 1700s enhanced the mobility and prosperity of many Plateau people and led to large intertribal parties crossing the Rockies to hunt buffalo and trade on the High Plains. Many new elements of material and social culture appeared in the Plateau as the result of these recent contacts.

The contact-historic period started slowly, with rare appearances of European and American mariners along the Pacific coast after the mid-1500s. It may be said to have effectively begun for the Oregon Plateau with the 1805–1806 visit of Lewis and Clark, after which traders and trappers became a rapidly growing presence within far-reaching Native exchange networks that had been in existence for thousands of years. Even before Lewis and Clark, however, the tide of alien diseases brought to the New World by European immigrants had spread overland through the Native populations, ravaging them into the mid-century. Christian missionaries appeared on the Columbia system in the 1830s, and the white influx swelled so rapidly from the 1840s onward that by the mid-1850s Native Americans throughout Oregon were being forcibly dispossessed of their lands. In the Plateau, the John Day gold rush of the 1860s brought a fresh influx of immigrants, including not only Euroamericans but other people from as far away as southern China who came to work in the booming gold fields. Roads, homesteads, and logging camps grew rapidly in the 1860s, and Plateau Natives were increasingly forced onto reservations that occupied only a fraction of their ancestral lands.

The Plateau tribes of contact-historic and subsequent times are not systematically treated here but more can be read about them in the many ethnographic sources cited throughout the text. A massive and comprehensive sourcebook is the *Plateau* volume of the *Handbook of North American Indians* (Walker 1998), while a more compact source featuring many contemporary Native American authors is *The First Oregonians* (Berg 2007). As these books illustrate, despite being massively outnumbered and overrun by the nineteenth-century Euroamerican incursion, the Plateau's Native American tribes have survived and sustained their traditional values. In the twenty-first century they are again a strong cultural and social force throughout their traditional homeland, among other things producing a wealth of artistic works that embody traditional themes and playing a key role in environmental protection and cultural preservation matters as legislatively established equals with state and national government agencies.

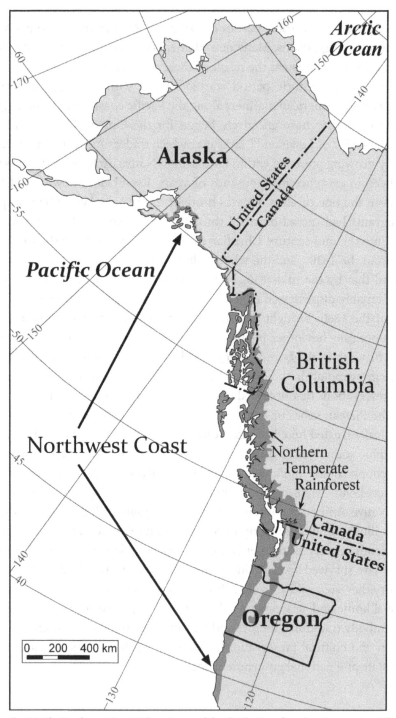

Fig. 4.1. The Northwest Coast Culture Area and the distribution of northern temperate rainforests.

Chapter 4
Lower Columbia and Oregon Coast

The Oregon Coast in Context

The coast of Oregon is part of the Pacific Northwest Coast Culture Area, which stretches from the vicinity of Yakutat Bay, Alaska to about Cape Mendocino in northern California (fig. 4.1). The "culture area" designation implies certain shared traits along this broad coastal zone, many of them due to common environmental features. Human populations on the Pacific Northwest Coast were packed along a thin, ribbon-like zone of enormous biotic richness at the continent's edge, where the terrestrial resources of the continent, the marine resources of the ocean, and those of the littoral zone (the intertidal shore) were concentrated. The region's robust biotic productivity has long made it one of relatively high population density and sedentary occupation, factors which have fostered the development of increasingly complex societies.

Elements of shared culture along the Northwest Coast can be seen in the technology of fishing and hunting and in the realms of art and religion. But there are many local variations as well—overall, the cultural diversity of this zone is considerable. In terms of language, for example, the Northwest Coast is the single most diverse region in all of North America. This fact suggests that cultural similarities throughout the Northwest Coast are a function of common adaptations to similar environments and to convergences resulting from widespread trade and social interaction, rather than deriving from a common cultural and genetic heritage.

The Pacific coast from Alaska to California is backed by rugged mountains that often drop steeply to the ocean, leaving a narrow strip of coastal plain, or none at all. Annual precipitation typically exceeds 100 inches/year, producing lush temperate rainforests and vigorous coastal rivers. Indeed, the Northwest

211

Coast "cultural area" corresponds closely to the distribution of the northern temperate rainforest. This zone produces one of the earth's highest biomass concentrations, including trees that grow to massive proportions such as Sitka spruce, western hemlock, western red cedar, and coast redwood.

Small mountain meadows are intermittently present, and provide a source of berries, nutritious roots, and game. The marine environment provides a great abundance of fish, birds, and sea mammals. The littoral zone is rich in shellfish, including mussels and barnacles along rocky shores and clams on sand beaches and mudflats. The shore zone is also where sea mammals and shore birds concentrate in great numbers for mating and rearing their young. Coastal estuaries, tidally influenced river outlets where freshwater and sea water commingle, are especially productive.

Oregon and the Northwest Coast Culture Area

The highly concentrated "ribbon of riches" represented by the coastal ecotone (fig. 4.2), combined with the geographic constraints on human settlement imposed by bordering ocean and rugged mountains, resulted in a population density along the North Pacific coast that was among the highest in all of pre-contact North America. And while economies were based on hunting, gathering, and fishing, Northwest Coast societies exhibited features commonly associated with agriculturalists, including permanent towns and villages, ownership of property rights, elaborate and complex material culture, stratified societies, and full-time specialists (see inset box).

In spite of recognized commonalities, there are many important differences along the Northwest Coast. To the north, including the Alaska Panhandle and portions of coastal British Columbia, the bordering mountains

Fig. 4.2. The coast provides a concentrated "ribbon of riches" from marine, terrestrial, and littoral environments: *a*, sea lions and cormorants; *b*, mussel colonies on tidal rocks; *c*, mussel colony detail.

Features common to the diverse cultural groups who lived along the North Pacific Coast

- Subsistence derived primarily from the sea and littoral (shore/headlands/ estuaries) environments, especially fish, shellfish, and sea mammals.
- The use of wood, especially cedar, as a primary material for the manufacture of material goods, including houses from split cedar planks, dugout canoes made from whole logs, storage containers such as bentwood boxes, carved dishes and cooking utensils, weapons and armor. Cedar was also an important source of fiber for cordage, basketry, clothing, and other necessities.
- Basketry and fiber were used extensively for storage containers, clothing, fishing nets and traps, matting and other household furnishings.
- Society was stratified, with social ranking based on inherited status, wealth, and resource holdings. Distinct classes were recognized, with ranking from nobles to commoners among the freeborn, and a slave class.
- Distinctive art traditions were developed; these differed from north to south, with the northern art being highly stylized and predominantly executed in two dimensions, and the southern being more representational and most commonly three-dimensional (sculptural).
- Permanent settlements were established, along with specialized methods of taking and preserving great quantities of periodically abundant foods (using nets, hook and line, harpoons, tidal traps); permanent houses served as both residential centers and food storage facilities.
- The region was noted for an intense degree of economic activity in the form of regular trade, and also economic links established among neighboring communities by the tradition of the potlatch.

---

are steep and high, with glacier-cut gorges and generally no coastal plain. The coastline is highly convoluted, with many offshore islands; as a result, marine waters are relatively protected and highly accessible to coastal dwellers, and access to terrestrial resources is relatively more limited. By contrast, the coasts of Washington, Oregon, and northern California are straight and unprotected, and pummeled by unimpeded ocean waves on one of the earth's most high-energy coastlines. Compared with those to the north, the coastal mountains are less imposing, with intermittent strips of narrow coastal plain.

In the north, a highly structured society was organized around the control of wealth (including the ownership of critical resources such as the most productive fisheries), coupled with the status and social influence necessary to organize a community for the harvesting and distribution of resources, and the ability to support the construction of massive plank houses, dugout canoes, and other necessities. Because of north-to-south environmental differences, people of the southern Northwest Coast (including the Oregon coast) may have had a relatively greater degree of subsistence flexibility than is reflected in other elements of culture. For example, while wealth was an important status indicator throughout the North Pacific coast, accumulated wealth could be as important as inherited wealth on the southern Northwest Coast, while to the north, ascribed status and inheritance were much stronger factors. The southern groups were also less complexly structured, being organized primarily as patrilocal family groups, rather than by totemic clans and moieties as was the case to the north.

Cultural patterns documented in ethnohistoric accounts of groups living along Oregon's coast reveal a bi-seasonal annual cycle of subsistence activities. Life centered on permanent settlements where substantial houses of split cedar planks were built. These structures also served a critical function as storehouses for foods that had been processed and preserved during times of ripening or high abundance. Houses were square to rectangular in form, with a gabled or shed roof (fig. 4.3). On the southern Oregon coast small single family homes were the rule, these homes being typically clustered into small towns. On the northern Oregon coast and along the lower Columbia River, larger multiple-family structures were common.

Villages consisted of groups of households occupied by related men and their wives and families. While village communities occupying a common river system shared a common language and collective identity, the village—rather than the larger language or tribal community—was the most

Fig. 4.3. Drawing of a plank house near the mouth of the Umpqua River, which originally appeared in *Frank Leslie's Illustrated Newspaper* in 1858.

meaningful social, political, and economic unit. People generally identified themselves as belonging to a particular village, rather than to the larger community (Tveskov 2000b, 2007).

A main settlement was sometimes referred to as the "winter village," because the entire community was present in that season. The village might never be completely empty, but small task parties or family groups traveled to other locations, especially from spring through fall, to harvest foods and materials to consume or trade.

A "village" might consist of one or many houses. Paul Schumacher (1877:31), working on Oregon's south coast for the Smithsonian Institution in the early 1870s, noted the remains of "50 depressions of former houses" at the abandoned Chetlessenten Village near the mouth of Pistol River. Nearer the Columbia River, houses could be very large, and subdivided into apartments for many individual families. Throughout the region, individual households served as the fundamental political and economic unit, but the nature of households could vary substantially.

A great variety of fish, including smelt, herring, flounder, perch, rock fishes, and salmon, was harvested throughout the year using traps, weirs, hook and line, and nets; community-maintained weirs were particularly important for providing reliable food throughout the year. Clams, mussels, crabs, and barnacles were collected from estuaries, tide pools, beaches, and rocky shores. Sea mammals were hunted, by club or harpoon, at haul-outs and rookeries, at both onshore and offshore rocks. It has generally been assumed (cf. Drucker 1937) that whale hunting was not pursued on the Oregon coast, as it was farther north, but recent archaeological evidence confirms that whale hunts were indeed conducted at least on the northern Oregon coast (Losey and Yang 2007). Chinook salmon migrated up coastal rivers in midsummer, followed by Coho and dog salmon in early fall. Steelhead ran in the late fall and through the winter months. Upriver fishing camps were established to harvest these fish as well as lampreys.

Due to the richness of the fishery resource, the Alsea (on Oregon's central coast) considered hunting "an adventuresome way of augmenting the fish diet" (Drucker 1939:83). When pursued, deer and elk were stalked along trails or in small forest clearings; pit traps were sometimes used, but the labor required to dig them limited their use. Sea birds and waterfowl were taken with traps, or bow and arrow. Upland meadows were also visited for the harvest of roots, greens, berries, fruits, seeds; camas was dug in great quantities from summer through fall, with the surplus being prepared for winter storage. Skunk cabbage and fern roots were harvested in the spring. Salmonberries, blackberries, huckleberries, strawberries, acorns, and hazelnuts were gathered when ripe.

The linguistic diversity of the north Pacific coast reflects the fact that in spite of a number of shared cultural traits, the region has a complex cultural and linguistic heritage. Suttles (1990) observes that there were 39 different languages spoken along the Pacific Northwest Coast, representing 11 different language families. Three different unrelated language families are represented on the Oregon coast (Penutian, Salish, Athapaskan), expressed in seven distinct languages and more than two dozen dialects (fig. 4.4).

Languages linked to the Penutian family are found throughout the West, from southeast Alaska to southern California; Oregon represents an approximate center of gravity for these dispersed languages, and it is thought that the Penutian languages may have the most ancient roots of all Oregon Native tongues. The Chinook languages and dialects found along the lower Columbia as far upstream as The Dalles (Clatsop, Cathlamet, Skilloot, Multnomah, Clackamas, Cascades, and Wasco) are all Penutian, as are those of the central Oregon coast (Yaquina, Alsea, Siuslaw, Kalawatset [lower Umpqua], Hanis [Coos], and Miluk [Coos]).

The northern Oregon coast, from Tillamook Head to Cape Foulweather, was home to speakers of Tillamook, represented by five dialect communities (Nehalem, Tillamook, Nestucca, Salmon River, and Siletz). Tillamook is in the large Salish language family, which is dominant in the Salish Sea (Puget Sound-Gulf of Georgia) region around the modern U.S.-Canada border, and on the interior Columbia-Fraser Plateau from central Washington to southern British Columbia. The Tillamook represent the southernmost outpost of the Salish languages.

The people of Oregon's south coast, from approximately Coquille Point into northern California, spoke dialects of Tututni, a language in the Athapaskan family. Athapaskan languages are found across subarctic Canada, and are believed to have spread across the northern tier of the continent from southeast Alaska. This language spread, thought to have occurred within the last 2,000 years, spawned migrations of Athapaskan-speakers to the south; among these migrant groups are ancestors of the Navajo and Apache in the American Southwest, and ancestors of the Pacific Coast Athaspaskans who came to occupy the southern Oregon (Tututni) and northern California

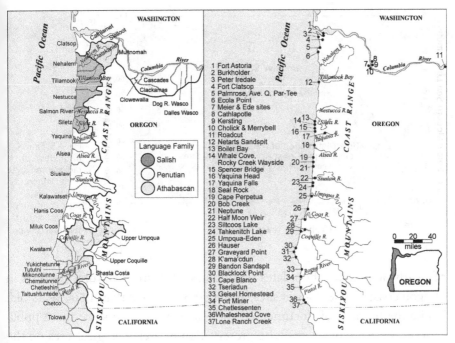

Fig. 4.4. Oregon coast language communities and archaeological sites.

(Tolowa) coasts. The Oregon Athapaskans may have traveled down the Pacific coast from a southeast Alaska homeland.

The distinctive cultural patterns associated with the Pacific Northwest Coast (rectangular plank houses, a focus on marine/littoral resources, social stratification, a distinctive art tradition, etc.) are documented by historians and ethnographers. Some archaeologists (e.g., Matson and Coupland 1994) have characterized the archaeology of the region as an inquiry into the age and origin of the "Developed Northwest Coast Pattern," recognizing that the cultural patterns of ancient times would have looked much different than historic ones. The following narrative traces the outline of Oregon coast cultural history, based on archaeological evidence.

Geologic History and the Archaeological Record

Moss and Erlandson (1995:14) remarked in 1986 that "there is little evidence for human occupation earlier than about 4,000 years ago" for the section of Pacific coast lying between the Canadian border and Monterey Bay, California, including the Oregon coast. Erlandson and Moss (1999) later reported that

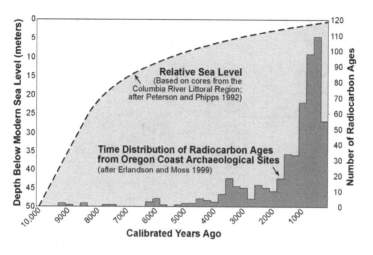

Fig. 4.5. Time distribution of radiocarbon ages from Oregon coast cultural sites, compared to a reconstructed sea level curve.

of nearly 300 radiocarbon dates on samples taken from cultural contexts in Oregon coast archaeological sites, about 90% were less than 1,500 years old. While the number of documented early sites has grown since these publications, there are problems with preservation of archaeological sites on the Oregon coast that are unmatched anywhere else in the state (fig. 4.5).

There are several reasons why early coastal sites are rare; the Oregon coast is constantly changing due to erosion and landslides, tectonic uplift and subsidence, and the impact of tides and high-energy waves (Komar 1998). Perhaps the most significant factor, however, has been a continually rising sea level over the past ca. 18,000 years (Dillon and Odale 1968; Peterson and Phipps 1992; Peterson et al. 1984). During the last ice age, much of the earth's

Fig. 4.6. Eroding cultural shell midden on the central Oregon coast.

water was locked in glacial ice—a mile or more thick in some places—across the earth's northern latitudes. As a result, global sea levels were far lower than they are today, by 100 meters or more. On the Oregon coast, this would have exposed vast stretches of the continental shelf, and the coastline itself would have been several miles west of its current position.

As sea level rose throughout the Holocene, rising water submerged former shorelines and drowned former river mouths. As vigorous coastal rivers met rising seawaters, they dropped their sediment loads, which ultimately formed broad, shallow embayments that buried former land surfaces beneath many meters of bay mud. Along the coast itself, the increasingly high water resulted in extensive erosion of sea cliffs and headlands, a process which continues today (fig. 4.6).

Tectonic activity has also likely affected the archaeological record. Just off the Pacific coast between southern British Columbia and northern California is the contact between two tectonic plates. The westerly (Juan de Fuca) plate is pushing beneath the continental plate along a contact known as the Cascadia Subduction Zone. The subduction process is one of gradual uplift of the coastal margin as strain between the plates builds, punctuated by sudden releases that result in abrupt subsidence and devastating tsunamis. This process of uplift and subsidence is somewhat rhythmic, occurring regularly every 300 to 600 years and contributing to the coast's ever-changing landscape.

One result of these geologic processes is a significant loss of archaeological sites to erosion, submergence, and burial. Not every ancient site has been lost, but the geologic history of this dynamic coast presents exceptional challenges to the documentation of local coastal cultural histories. One hopeful reality is that tectonic forces are not uniformly expressed along the coast. Along the central and northern Oregon coasts, rising sea levels throughout the Holocene have been responsible for a submerging coastline. On some segments of Oregon's south coast, however, tectonic uplift has been occurring at a rate that outpaces the rate of sea level rise, producing an emergent coast.

By Land or by Sea? The Coastal Migration Hypothesis

During the last ice age, when sea levels were much lower, Asia and North America were connected across the "Beringia" land bridge, the shallow land shelf now submerged below the Bering Sea. The traditional view of the populating of the Americas is that mobile hunters crossed the land bridge from northeast Asia during their familiar routine of following migrating game. This view has long been supported by the fact that the earliest well-documented cultural evidence from the Americas has predominantly revealed hunting folk in the continent's interior. According to this model, the earliest coastal residents would have slowly learned to take advantage of the productivity of coastal environments by adjusting away from a terrestrial hunting heritage. This point of view is clearly articulated in many writings on the early archaeology of the Oregon coast (Cressman 1977; Ross 1990).

In recent decades archaeologists have been more open to the possibility of migrations to the Americas by coastal travelers using boats (Fladmark 1979; Erlandson et al. 2007; Erlandson et al. 2008). The greatest impediment to serious examination of this possibility is the fact that critical archaeological evidence from Pleistocene shore lines may be submerged deep in offshore waters, but several compelling arguments remain. Australia appears to have been occupied by 60,000 years ago, and the Japan archipelago and other Pacific islands accessible only by watercraft were occupied some 30,000 to 40,000 years ago. It is clear that people capable of managing seaworthy craft were living on the Pacific coast of Asia prior to the colonization of the Americas.

Paleoenvironmental studies have also suggested that an "ice-free corridor" between the Cordilleran and Laurentide ice sheets may have been quite inhospitable at a time when ice-free refugia along the Pacific coast may have been biotically quite productive. More recently, scientists have pointed out that the rich marine environment provided by offshore kelp forests extends in a continuous chain between the Pacific coasts of Asia and the Americas, requiring no adjustment to unfamiliar environments along the route, as a land-based migration would have done (Erlandson 2002).

Evidence from the Oregon coast cannot presently contribute in a significant way to this discussion, but findings from sites elsewhere on North America's Pacific coast have clear implications for the cultural history of the Oregon coast (see Erlandson et al. 2008; Davis et al. 2008). Evidence from two of these sites is summarized here.

On-Your-Knees Cave (49PET408) is located at the northern tip of Prince of Wales Island, near the southern end of the Alaska Panhandle. Human remains from the cave have been directly dated to about 11,000 years ago, and a bone tool to about 12,000 years ago. Associated obsidian artifacts came from two different sources, Mount Edziza on the British Columbia mainland (about 200 miles distant) and Sumez Island in Southeast Alaska (about 65 miles distant), both of which could have only been reached by boat. Analysis of carbon isotopes in the human bone shows that the person had a diet dominated by foods from marine environments, such as marine fishes, sea mammals, and shellfish (Dixon et al. 1997).

California's Channel Islands have produced an impressive record of terminal Pleistocene human occupation, and among the most significant is Daisy Cave (CA-SMI-261). Even when sea levels were at their lowest during the Pleistocene, access to the island would have required watercraft. The lowest occupation levels of the cave, marked by ephemeral scatters of chipped stone artifacts, marine shells, and fish bone, date to about 12,000 years ago. Occupations intensify over the next several millennia, leaving a dietary record dominated by shellfish and the bones of marine fish. The tool assemblage includes fishing gorges and fragments of netting, and fish remains suggest regular access to offshore kelp beds. The record clearly indicates sophisticated knowledge of watercraft, and a diet focused on marine environments (Erlandson 2007; Erlandson et al. 1996; Erlandson et al. 2005; Rick et al. 2001).

Terminal Pleistocene/Early Holocene (ca. 13,000 to 7,500 Years Ago)

Recognizing that the Oregon coast has been significantly altered during the time of human presence there, especially since the terminal Pleistocene/early Holocene period, Loren Davis (2006) and his colleagues (Davis et al. 2004; Davis et al. 2008; Hall et al. 2003, 2005; Punke and Davis 2006) have conducted studies focused on identifying older landforms along the Oregon coast where archaeological sites may have survived. Their work has been aided by that of geologists studying the coast's landform history (Kelsey 1990; Peterson et al. 2002; Verdonck 1995).

Davis and his colleagues have taken note of the fact that nearly all known older sites on the Oregon coast occur on headlands or uplifted marine terraces, primarily on Oregon's southern coast. They identify several localities where ancient soils of terminal Pleistocene/early Holocene age have been preserved, and which also appear to have at least traces of associated cultural lithics (flakes and fire-cracked rock). None of these sites has produced an extensive early cultural record, and in most cases the presence of overlying cultural materials of much younger age raises questions about the origin of the deeper cultural materials (could they have been displaced downward into ancient strata from overlying cultural levels by rodents or other natural causes?). Nonetheless, the age of the old land surfaces is not in question, and we anticipate a fuller body of evidence from ongoing fieldwork.

At Indian Sands (35CU67), for example, Davis et al. (2008) found that people appear to have initially occupied a Pleistocene-age landform on which sediments were accumulating; during the Holocene the deposition process was reversed, with sediment being removed by wind erosion. The erosion left early cultural material behind on deflated surfaces; this removal of cultural artifacts from their original depositional context complicates the confirmation of their age. One cultural locality at this site has been reported by Moss and Erlandson (1995), who found a scatter of burned and broken mussel shell and chipped stone tool debris on a deflated surface. Three radiocarbon dates from different mussel shell fragments produced an average age of 8,600 years ago. Davis et al. (2004) have dated the stratum underlying this deflated surface to 12,300 years ago. Cultural flakes were also present in this layer, and appear to be associated with the radiocarbon age, but it is also possible that cultural lithics from the deflated surface had worked their way down into the older layers. If the association can be confirmed, this represents one of Oregon's oldest sites.

Davis et al. (2008) note the presence of buried soils at several other sites that have been exposed to erosion, as at Indian Sands, but then later buried by other sediment. These sites show a stratified sequence, but one from which some intervening time is missing. Examples include Neptune State Park (35LA3; Lyman 1991), Bandon Ocean Wayside (35CS9; Hall et al. 2005; Moss and Erlandson 1998; Moss et al. 2006; Davis et al. 2006), Tahkenitch Landing (35DO130; Minor and Toepel 1989), Cape Blanco (35CS82; Minor and Greenspan 1991; McDowell and Willson 1991), and Blacklock Point (35CU75; Minor 1993).

At the Neptune site, for example, a date of 9330 cal. BP (8310±110 rcybp) is reported from an ancient buried soil that produced "a few lithic flakes" (Lyman 1991:314), but which immediately underlies a shell midden that postdates 400 cal. BP (320±45 rcybp) (Zontek 1983). At 35CS9, Hall et al. (2005; also see Moss et al. 2006) report a few cultural flakes and fire-cracked rock from within a sediment layer that has produced a radiocarbon sample dating to 12,700 (calibrated) years ago, but this is immediately below a much more robust occupation of middle to late Holocene age (ca. 3,250–3,000 years old).

The Tahkenitch Landing site is on the central coast between the Siuslaw and Umpqua rivers. When occupied, Tahkenitch Lake was an estuary open to the ocean; about 3,000 years ago dune sand blocked the outlet and the freshwater lake that remains today was formed. The site's earliest stratum, dating between about 8,900 and 7,600 years ago, produced just a handful of stone tools, but is most notable for a diverse assemblage of marine fish, representing eleven different genera, and waterfowl (Minor and Toepel 1986). As at Neptune, this early occupation is capped by a later shell midden, in this case one of middle Holocene age.

It is likely that cultural materials at some, and maybe all, of these sites are truly ancient, but the close proximity of possibly ancient artifacts to demonstrably later cultural materials is cause for only tentative acceptance of great antiquity. Nonetheless, this important research has focused attention on surviving ancient landforms, and the ongoing work is recognizing a growing number of sites with apparent human occupations of truly ancient age. None of these sites presents entirely unassailable evidence for occupations of terminal Pleistocene age, but taken together they offer an increasingly compelling body of evidence.

The best documented early cultural tradition in the Americas is marked by distinctive lanceolate projectile points which feature channels or "flutes" struck from the base that run up the faces of the point. The channel allowed the point to be inserted into the end of a split dart shaft. Fluted points, in the Clovis or Folsom traditions (towns in New Mexico where such points were first found in the 1920s–1930s) occur throughout North America, and when found in well-dated contexts are consistently in the neighborhood of ca. 12,000 years old. A fluted point has been reported on the Oregon coast (fig. 4.7), found as an isolate on the shore of Siltcoos Lake (Minor 1985).

Several other coastal sites probably date from the early Holocene, based on the presence of artifacts that are stylistically like those from well-dated early sites elsewhere in the Pacific Northwest. Many early tool assemblages contain stemmed or leaf-shaped points, including the Roadcut site (35WS4) near The Dalles. This site is well known because it contained thousands of salmon bones in cultural layers dating between 10,000 and 7,000 years ago, suggesting that mass harvesting of this once-abundant resource has truly ancient roots (Butler 1993; Cressman et al. 1960).

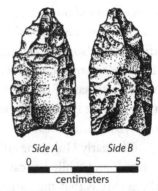

Side A   Side B
0   5
centimeters

Fig. 4.7. Fluted projectile point from Siltcoos Lake (from Minor 1985).

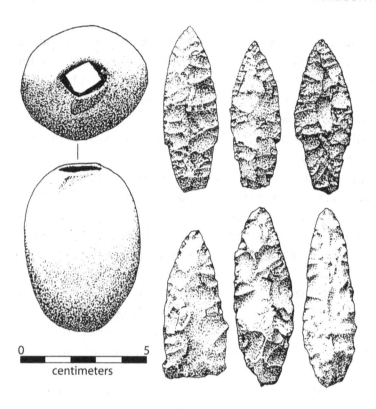

Fig. 4.8.
Early cultural
assemblage
representative of
the Youngs Bay
Complex (from
Minor 1984).

0   5

centimeters

Stemmed and leaf-shaped projectile points similar to those found at the
Roadcut site have been found at the Burkholder site (35CLT31) along the
eastern side of Youngs Bay, near Astoria (Minor 1884a) (fig. 4.8). Similar, and
presumably early, assemblages have been reported at several "bluff sites" on
the southern Oregon coast, at the Blacklock Point, Cape Blanco, and Indian
Sands sites (Minor 1993; Minor and Greenspan 1991) (fig. 4.9). Several of these
sites are found on high sea cliffs above beach gravels that contain high-quality
chert tool stone, and although several of these sites have early components,
they were also used throughout the Holocene as tool stone quarries (Minor
1993). Many of the tools recovered from these sites are from deflated surfaces
where artifacts of different ages are commingled, making it difficult to sort
truly ancient materials from the products of later tool stone quarrying based
on stylistic attributes.

The early Holocene cultural record for the Oregon coast remains impoverished, and while we can anticipate occasional new evidence of great age,
the reality is that the early record will never be robust, given the geological
history of the Oregon's Pacific coast. It is notable, however, that the earliest

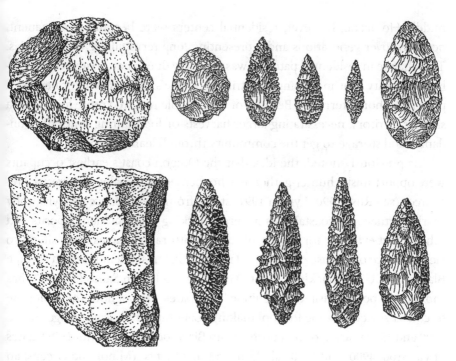

Fig. 4.9. Stylistically early tools and quarry debris from Indian Sands (from Minor and Greenspan 1991).

Oregon coast sites with direct dietary evidence indicate regular use of marine/littoral resources. Based on broader regional evidence, it is likely that the earliest coastal occupants were opportunistic and highly mobile hunters-fishers-gatherers who moved frequently from one productive harvest area to the next, but likely did not establish long-term residential bases.

The Middle Holocene (ca. 7,500 to 3,000 Years Ago)

Population density was probably quite low in the early Holocene, and people moved around large territories that were not seriously restricted by neighboring populations. They stayed at camps that were temporary, to which they may or may not have later returned. In the middle Holocene, we see the first substantial housepits in some parts of the Pacific Northwest. These imply longer-term residential stays, and possibly the beginnings of regular food storage, a practice requiring that the home also functioned as a food storage facility. At first, residences were moved regularly; a residence might be occupied for a period of weeks or even a year, but seldom longer. By the end of the middle Holocene, however, residential centers were becoming permanent, occupied over generations and representing long-term village communities. This change in residential patterns was probably due in part to growing population density that increasingly restricted people's free movement beyond a prescribed home territory. Because of this, people required more food from a smaller territory, necessitating larger harvests of food during times of abundance, and storage to get the community through lean seasons.

As previously noted, the idea that the Oregon coast's earliest occupants were opportunistic hunter-gatherers who focused principally on terrestrial resources (see Ross 1990; Lyman 1991) stems from the presence of stylistically "early" artifacts at coastal sites generally lacking shell midden deposits and other direct evidence for the use of marine/littoral resources (such sites also lack evidence of the use of terrestrial resources). Subsequent research at Cape Blanco (35CU82), Blacklock Point (35CU75), and Indian Sands (35CU67) has shown that people visited these lithic "bluff sites" throughout the Holocene to collect siliceous stone for tool making. Calibrated radiocarbon ages of ca. 8300 and 4970 years ago are reported from Blacklock Point (Minor 1993), dates of ca. 6100, 4900, and 1200 cal. BP from Cape Blanco (Minor and Greenspan 1991, 1998), and dates of 8600, 2400, 1700, and 1100 cal. BP from Indian Sands (Minor and Greenspan 1991; Moss and Erlandson 1994). The presence of large bifaces, hammerstones, and abundant tool-making debris indicates that these sites served primarily as specialized tool stone quarries—rather than food procurement and processing sites—throughout their long period of use.

The best information on middle Holocene lifeways on the Oregon coast comes from four sites: Tseriadun (35CU7), located on the southern margin of Garrison Lake (a former estuary) and at the foot of the Port Orford headland; Tahkenitch Landing (35DO130), between Florence and Reedsport; Boiler Bay (35LNC45), located on the Government Point headland near Depoe Bay; and Yaquina Head (35LNC62) near Newport.

Historically, Tseriadun was an Athapaskan town occupied until after the Rogue River War; shell midden deposits and housepit depressions from recent centuries are present. The modern soil has formed in dune sand that contains a deeply buried cultural surface dating to about 5,100 years ago (based on two radiocarbon tests). An apparent house floor and adjacent shell midden were exposed in an eroding bank profile on the 5,100-year-old surface. The probable house floor is a charcoal-rich organic lens at least three meters across. The adjacent thin shell midden contains mussel shell, sea urchin spines, sea

Modern soil developed in dune sand

5100 cal BP cultural soil

7700 cal BP cultural soil

Beach

Fig. 4.10. Site profile exposed by erosion at the Tseriadun site, with cultural dates (photo courtesy Scott Byram).

lion bones, and a variety of marine fish bones. Artifacts from this occupation include large side-notched and Coquille Series projectile points, types stylistically consistent with those found at other southwest Oregon sites of middle Holocene age. Although documented in profile, no systematic excavation of this feature was conducted due to the instability of the bank (fig. 4.10). The sand dune caps an alluvial surface that has been dated to ca. 7,700 years ago, and which also contained a small number of chert flakes and burned rock. Cultural materials from the earliest occupation are sparse, but sufficient to confirm the great antiquity of human use of the site (Byram 2005a, 2005b; Cohen and Tveskov 2008).

The Boiler Bay site (35LNC45), along with another site (35LNC44) located farther north at the end of the Government Point headland, is within Boiler Bay State Park immediately north of the small coastal town of Depoe Bay. Formal testing of the site in 1993 anticipated access modifications from U.S. Highway 101 (Tasa and Connolly 1995). The testing procedure involved the excavation of 50x50 centimeter test holes on a 10-meter grid, which

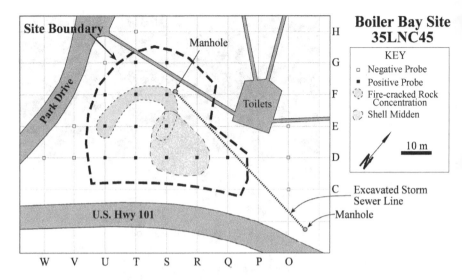

Fig. 4.11. Boiler Bay site map, showing the horseshoe-shaped footprint of a house and associated shell midden.

provided information on site boundaries, depth, and internal structure (fig. 4.11). The site includes a shell midden, bordered on the west by a ca. 25 meter diameter area containing an abundance of fire-cracked rock. Particularly high concentrations of fire-cracked rock occurred in a horseshoe shape that appears to define the perimeter of a living space excavated slightly below the contemporary ground surface. Four radiocarbon ages from top to bottom of the ca. 50-centimeter thick midden (of marine shell) were statistically identical, at ca. 4250 cal. years old. The base of the shell midden included bay clams (butter clams and Pacific gapers) and rock-dwelling species (giant acorn barnacles, California mussels, and black katy chitons), but the clams are almost completely absent in the upper levels. The majority of recovered vertebrate remains were identifiable as marine fish, followed closely in frequency by birds. Mammal remains include harbor seal, elk, and unidentified cetaceans (whales). Lithic debitage and formed artifacts were recovered from within the midden and probable house, and from an area extending for ca. 15 meters beyond these features. The cultural assemblage included projectile points (one made of obsidian traced to Obsidian Cliffs in the Oregon Cascades), a cobble tool used as both as an abrader and a hammer, two spire-lopped *Olivella* shell beads, and an incised point that has the appearance of ivory. This could be ivory of the Pacific walrus, which occupies primarily arctic water in the Bering Sea area, but sperm whale and orca teeth are a more likely source.

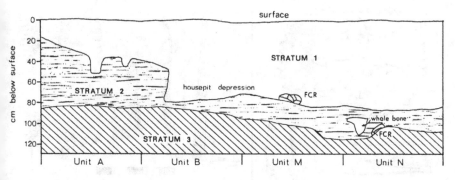

Fig. 4.12. House floor shown in profile at the Yaquina Head site (from Minor et al. 1987).

The occupation history at the Yaquina Head site (35LNC62) is fixed by 22 radiocarbon ages (Minor 1991b, 1995; Minor et al. 1987). The earliest set (ca. 7300–5800 calibrated years ago) came from a charcoal-rich stratum (perhaps from an old forest fire) below the cultural layers, and is not clearly associated with cultural materials (Minor 1995). The remaining dates suggest repeated, more or less continuous occupation between ca. 4,800 and 2,800 years ago. Botanical evidence from site sediment suggests the setting at the time of occupation was likely a conifer forest that would have provided protection from coastal winds. Fieldwork mainly focused on two discrete shell middens; the Area A midden was exposed along the headland's north face, while Area B is a small midden farther from the sea cliff edge south of Area A. The Area B shell midden appears to date between ca. 4,600 and 4,000 years ago. Exposed features included concentrations of fire-cracked rock, bone, and artifacts. No clear structural remains were noted, but Feature 12 was described as an apparent fire pit (ca. 50 centimeters diameter, 25 centimeters deep) that produced a calibrated age of ca. 4000 years ago, and an associated scatter of worked bone, sandstone abraders, a bird bone whistle fragment, and other artifacts. Fish bone (representing at least seven taxa) and terrestrial and marine mammals were also found with the feature (Minor 1991b). Excavations in Area A opened 42 square meters, of which 20 contiguous units exposed an extensive living surface (perhaps a house floor), possibly contemporary with or below the Area A midden deposits. This surface has associated dates of ca. 4650 and 3700 cal. BP.

Most of the radiocarbon dates from Area A suggest that a period of intensive occupation occurred between ca. 4,000 and 3,000 years ago. Minor (1991b: 176) suggests, based on current radiocarbon evidence, that intensive shellfish harvesting appears to have begun about 4,000 years ago. A housepit

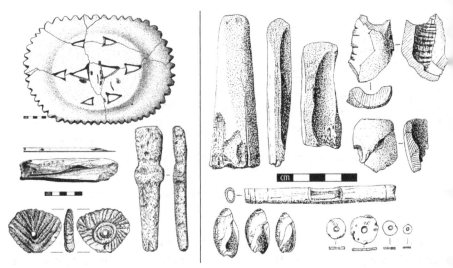

Left, Fig. 4.13. Carved bone artifacts from the Yaquina Head site (from Minor et al. 1987 and Minor 1991).
Right, Fig. 4.14. Artifacts from the Tahkenitch Landing site: *clockwise from top left*, bone splitting wedges, steatite and fired clay smoking pipe fragments, clam shell disc beads, Olivella shell beads, bird bone whistle (from Minor and Toepel 1986).

floor exposed in the profile of the eroding sea cliff (fig. 4.12), as well as two apparently associated burials, are from this time. One burial was that of an adult male (ca. 25 to 30 years of age at death); the other was that of an infant (possibly newborn), covered by a carved whalebone artifact with "scalloped edges and eight triangles cut into its flat face" (Minor et al. 1987:32). A portion of the artifact was dated to ca. 3670 cal. BP, and that date is thought to also apply to the complex of features associated with the house (fig. 4.13). Following this, at least intermittent occupation continued at the site; a date of ca. 2,300 years ago may represent the latter phases of residential use. It appears from the reports (Minor et al. 1987; Minor 1991b) that the "discrete" Area B midden may be slightly older than the more intensive Area A occupation. Throughout the occupations, molluscan remains are dominated by mussels; barnacles, cockles, and piddock clams are well represented. The vertebrate faunal assemblages include terrestrial mammals, and a great range of marine mammals, waterfowl, and especially fish. The latter reflect both nearshore and offshore environments, and include skate, herring, tomcod, surfperch, rockfish, greenling, lingcod, sculpin, cabezon, flounder, salmon, and hake. The relatively large quantities of hake, in particular, may indicate offshore fishing.

As noted above, the Tahkenitch Landing site (35DO130) may have been initially occupied more than 7,500 years ago (Minor and Toepel 1986).

However, dates from the most intensive occupations, associated with cultural shell midden deposits, range from ca. 5,900 to ca. 3,300 years ago (Minor and Toepel 1986:40; Minor et al. 1987:145). The site's earlier middle Holocene occupations (radiocarbon dated to 5900 and 4870 cal. BP) may reflect short-term residential use or temporary camp episodes, but they represent "the earliest evidence of the intensive exploitation of marine mollusks along this section of the Pacific coast" (Minor et al. 1987:143). Six of the eight radiocarbon dates from this middle Holocene set cluster at ca. 3,500–3,000 years ago, suggesting that the sustained residential use of the site (i.e., the Tahkenitch "village" component) dates from near the end of the middle Holocene. The shell midden from this time contained a majority of the recovered artifacts and vertebrate faunal remains, including all the whale bone and most of the other sea mammal bones. The site's molluscan remains are dominated by bay mussel, followed by a variety of clams (bent-nose clam, butter clam, horse clam, and cockle) indicative of a quiet-water (estuarine) environment. The vertebrate faunal assemblage is dominated by marine fishes (sculpins, tomcod, Pacific herring, surfperch, flounders, hake, and others). Waterfowl and shore birds are common; mammals, a minor constituent of the assemblage, are mostly sea mammals (whale, seals). It is clear from the variety of marine fish, shellfish, birds, and mammals recovered that the present freshwater lake was an estuary open to the ocean at the time of occupation. Utilitarian tools from the site include cobble hammers and chopping tools, lanceolate-shaped chipped stone projectile points and knives, sandstone abraders, and bone and antler wedges. Like the contemporary sites noted above, the artifact assemblage also includes items reflecting artistic, ornamental, leisure, or spiritual interests, including a bird-bone whistle, tubular bone beads, steatite and clay pipe fragments, clam shell disc beads, and *Olivella* spire-lopped beads (fig. 4.14). About 3,000 years ago the estuary mouth appears to have been dammed by dunes, transforming the estuary to the freshwater lake it is today and initiating the environmental changes that led to the site's abandonment (Minor and Toepel 1986).

The Raymond Dune Site (35CU62) is located a short distance north of the mouth of the Pistol River. A bulldozer cut made during construction work on the new Oregon Coast Highway in 1961 exposed an apparent house floor and disturbed associated shell midden and human remains representing at least four individuals. A charred wooden beam was found lying horizontally on the exposed floor. The beam returned a radiocarbon age of 3200 years old (3000±90 rcybp; Cressman 1977). Although it was not systematically exposed, the house appears to have lacked the plank superstructure typical of later houses, and may have been more similar to interior pithouses. Minor et al. (2001) suggest that this house, along with one of comparable antiquity reported at Yaquina Head (35LNC62; Minor et al. 1987; Minor 1991b), represents a house form associated with the earliest sedentary occupations of the coast. Sub-round pithouses reported from later times at the Umpqua-Eden site on the lower Umpqua River (35DO83), near Cape Creek at Cape Perpetua (35LNC57), and at the Par-tee site within modern Seaside may be later examples of this more ancient house form (Minor and Greenspan 1995).

The Bussman (35CS158) and Blue Barn (35CS61) sites are located along the Coquille River several miles upstream from its mouth. Both sites were intermittently used during at least the last 4,000 years, but the local environment changed markedly during that time. During the earliest occupations, before about 3,000 years ago, people were harvesting clams, cockles, crab, herring, salmon, perch, sculpin, flatfish, and seals and sea lions from a productive estuary. Over time, tectonic uplift raised the land, and the former estuary retreated to the narrow river channel that now passes some distance from the sites. Though people continued to camp at the sites, later occupants focused on the hunting of terrestrial game, though sea lion bones were also common (Tveskov and Cohen 2007).

In addition to those discussed above, other coastal sites have produced limited evidence for human presence in the middle Holocene age. The Palmrose site (35CLT47), located in the modern community of Seaside, was occupied as a permanent village between 2,700 and 1,600 years ago (see below), but two of the dates indicate an initial occupation of the gravel storm ridge underlying the site's main shell midden at about 4,000 years ago. Whale bone is associated with the site's earliest radiocarbon date (Connolly 1992:39).

The Neptune site (35LNC3) includes distinct middens, designated A and B, separated by about 100 meters. An early radiocarbon age of ca. 9300 cal. BP (8310 rcybp) is reported from an organic stratum below the Area B shell midden that is firmly dated to the late Holocene; the early date is generally considered to be non-cultural (Barner 1981; Lyman and Ross 1988; Zontek 1983; Moss and Erlandson 1998). In Area A, a hearth eroding from a sea cliff, 130 centimeters below the modern ground surface, was dated to 5550 cal. BP (4780±40 rcybp; Tasa and Connolly 2001; Connolly and Tasa 2008). In addition to charcoal, an obsidian microflake and starchy plant residue were found within the hearth.

Site 35LNC68, at the Rocky Creek Wayside, also contains a late occupation dating to ca. 600 years ago, based on a sample taken from the eroding sea cliff (Erlandson and Moss 1993). Test probes dug some 40–50 meters back from the cliff edge identified an older occupation, dated to ca. 4,100 years ago (Tasa and Connolly 2004; Connolly and Tasa 2008). Although only a few cultural flakes and a chert core were recovered, the dietary remains were diverse, including whale, harbor seal, and bird, and a variety of shellfish (California mussel, barnacle, chiton, piddock, crab, and others).

A site partially exposed by deflation on the sand split north of the Coquille River (Twin Dunes, 35CS120) produced a single radiocarbon age of ca. 5,900 years ago. The midden constituents included marine shell (primarily California mussel and barnacle, but also including chiton, butter clam, horse clam, razor clam, and dogwinkle), fire-cracked rock, mammal bone, and chipped stone flakes (Erlandson and Moss 1993:65).

Middle Holocene Cultural Patterns. The limited early Holocene cultural record for Oregon's coast is modestly improved for the middle Holocene, including at least a dozen sites. Several, notably Boiler Bay, Tahkenitch Landing, Yaquina Head, and Tseriadun, provide key evidence that—when placed in the context of broader Pacific Northwest cultural patterns—permits a consideration of changing land-use strategies.

Based on what we know of human lifeways throughout the Pacific Northwest region, the early Holocene can be characterized as a time when small bands of wide-ranging hunter/fisher/foragers moved broadly on land and shore. By the late Holocene, residential settlements of long duration were firmly established within defined community territories, sustained by a storage-based economy and complex social institutions that began to reflect the historic patterns documented along the Pacific Northwest Coast. The middle Holocene was a time of transition between these two states, marked by important changes in residential habits (increasingly sedentary), food procurement (larger harvests of seasonally abundant foods and the processing of food for long-term storage), and social institutions. It is clear, however, that these important economic and social shifts were not events; rather, they were long processes that spanned millennia and did not happen at the same speed everywhere. At one extreme, Cannon and Yang (2006) note that Namu, a site located on the central coast of British Columbia, was a residential center dependent on a storage-based economy at least 7,000 years ago. At the other, Matson and Coupland (1994) note that the generally smaller size of many archaeological houses suggests that full emergence of the historic Northwest Coast patterns significantly postdates 2000 BP in some areas.

Beyond the coast, similar trends are evident. The earliest pithouses appear on the southern Columbia Plateau of Oregon after about 7,000 years ago (Ames and Marshall 1980; Brauner 1976; Campbell 1985; Schalk et al. 1995). Sites of this time are commonly associated with a significant increase in milling stones and other evidence, including storage pits and larger food processing features, all of which suggest more intensive harvesting of abundant resources, particularly salmon and roots (Brauner 1976; Ames 1991; Chatters 1995; Jenkins 2004; Jenkins et al. 2004b; O'Neill et al. 2004). Even after the regular appearance of substantial houses and food processing and storage facilities, the character of residential stability changes in important ways. Pithouse sites on the southern Plateau dating before 3500 BP often occur in isolation and appear to be occupied for a limited period (possibly for a season?) before being abandoned as local resources became exhausted. Food preservation and storage were practiced, but were not central to subsistence (Chatters 1989).

This type of short-term residential use may be seen at both the Boiler Bay and Tseriadun sites. Boiler Bay, occupied about 4,400 years ago, produced statistically identical dates from the bottom to the top of the midden, suggesting a brief but intensive period of occupation. Midden constituent analysis chronicles the decrease in clam species and an increase in barnacle harvesting, possibly suggesting that harvesting pressure had begun to impact the availability of the preferred meatier species. The site was not revisited after it had been abandoned. At Tseriadun, a probable 5,200-year-old house floor is associated with a thin midden deposit, suggesting a relatively brief period of residence.

After about ca. 3500 BP, residential sites throughout Oregon's coastal region appear to be occupied on a more continuous basis, marking the beginning of the establishment of "permanent" villages; those occupied year after year, generation after generation. The Tahkenitch Landing site appears to have supported sustained residential use from about 3,500 to 3,000 years ago, contrasting with earlier dates from shell midden deposits (ca. 5,900 and 4,870 years ago) that may reflect more intermittent and short-term residential stays. In Area B at Yaquina Head a fire pit and associated scatter of bone and stone tools, fire-cracked rock, and bone (indicating a possible house, although architecture elements were not identified) dates between ca. 4,600 and 4,000 years ago. While requiring a little more speculation, this area may represent a temporary residence, while evidence for more sustained residential use (house floors, burials, a dense midden, and an elaborate artifact assemblage) is clearly present at Yaquina Head after ca. 4000 BP.

Food storage and larger-scale harvesting of seasonally abundant foods (especially salmon and roots) became increasingly important in the middle Holocene (Chatters 1989, 1995). Such a change did not require any real advancement in terms of storage technology; the principles of air drying, smoking, and freezing foods had been known from ancient times. Rather, the change was driven by need; demographic models suggest a significantly accelerated regional population growth ca. 4000–3000 BP. Population growth on a regional scale increasingly limited any one group's potential procurement range. A strategy of high mobility (moving when easily harvested local resources become depleted) became increasingly difficult—and dangerous— when new harvest areas were increasingly occupied by others. Storage ensured that adequate supplies of food were available to ever-growing populations relying on increasingly restricted home ranges (Ames 1991, 1995; Croes and Hackenberger 1988).

By 3,500 years ago, sustained residential occupations are evident at Tahkenitch Landing and Yaquina Head; by 3,000 years ago a plethora of other sites provide evidence that the first clearly "permanent" villages were being populated along much of the Oregon coast. An early house feature, with a date of ca. 3,200 years old from a structural timber, comes from the Raymond's Dune site near the mouth of the Pistol River (Minor et al. 2001). The Hauser site, a large, complex, and deep shell midden that probably represents a former village, dates between ca. 3,600 and 2,700 years old (Minor 1992b; Minor and Greenspan 1998). Occupation at the Umpqua-Eden site began by ca. 3,140 years ago; this and other residential sites will be discussed in greater detail below.

The Late Holocene (After 3,000 Years Ago)

In their review of Northwest Coast archaeology, Ames and Maschner (1999:95) suggest that by about 3,000 years ago Pacific coast cultures had taken on a form and structure that "differed little, if at all, from those observed and recorded by the first European visitors to the coast." The historic land-use system included permanent settlements surrounded by satellite resource camps that were occupied by a portion of a community during productive harvest times. Although the late Holocene was a turbulent period, marked by demographic shifts, ongoing landscape changes, and both peaceful and violent exchanges, elements of the "Developed Northwest Coast Pattern" described by Matson and Coupland (1994) become increasingly evident in the archaeological record.

Although preservation may be a factor, the earliest fish weirs dated on the Oregon coast are between 3,500 and 3,000 years old (Byram 2002). Such structures are maintainable over long periods, and historically were an important accompaniment to permanent settlements. Could such structures be a reliable correlate to the establishment of permanent settlements? It has been observed that middle Holocene residential sites, including Boiler Bay, Rocky Creek Wayside, and Yaquina Head, appear to have been set back from the edge of the coast and likely within sheltered forest environments. This pattern may stand out only because coastal erosion has likely destroyed sites nearer the coast. However, due to the increasing economic importance of building large and maintainable fishing structures (weirs), and a corresponding greater reliance on food storage that emerged toward the end of the middle Holocene (cf. Moss and Erlandson 1995), it is possible that proximity to critical resource features became a greater priority over time than shelter from the coastal winds.

What also became clear during the late Holocene was the emergence of distinctive regional cultural patterns. Again, some of the apparent regionalism may be simply a function of a more robust archaeological record, in which such patterns are more readily apparent, but the greater sedentism characteristic of this time, and the solidification of defined and defended home territories, certainly play a role. In addition, the historic distribution of Native languages indicates that historic Indian communities on Oregon's coast derive from multiple linguistic and cultural roots, rather than from common ancestors, and this is also a factor in the cultural variation observed archaeologically.

As noted in the introduction to this chapter, Native communities on Oregon's Pacific coast spoke languages that can be assigned to three unrelated families. People of the central coast spoke Penutian languages, whose presence in Oregon may be the most ancient. The Tillamook languages of the northern coast are historically linked with the Salish languages of the Puget Sound-Gulf of Georgia region around the modern U.S.-Canada border. The presence of Athapaskan-speakers on Oregon's lower Columbia River and south coast serves as evidence for a migration from a southeast Alaska homeland, from which Athapaskan-speakers dispersed within the last two millennia. The following discussion is organized to reflect these histories; the central coast, the Chinook-Salish area of the north coast and lower Columbia River, and the Gunther Pattern zone of the south coast.

The Central Coast. The Hauser site (35CS114) is a large and deep (ca. 1.5 meters) shell midden located in the dunes several miles north of Coos Bay. The size of the site and the quantity of shell suggest a substantial and sustained occupation, and (as at the Tahkenitch site to the north) the shellfish assemblage indicates proximity to an estuary that is no longer extant due to shifting sand. Radiocarbon dates fall into a relatively narrow range from 3,300 to 2,600 years ago. Like Tahkenitch, Hauser was probably a substantial residential site located adjacent to productive estuaries when it was occupied, but dune-building activity altered the setting and the site was abandoned (Minor 1992b; Minor and Greenspan 1998).

A site on the Umpqua River estuary, known as Umpqua-Eden (35DO83), was excavated by various parties over multiple years from the early 1970s to 1980 (Stenhouse 1974; Ross and Snyder 1979, 1986). Although limited by the quality of the excavation records and catalogs, Lyman (1991) reexamined the collected materials. The earliest stratum, which includes a shell midden deposit averaging 15 centimeters thick, has an associated age of ca. 3,100 years. Above this is a non-shell cultural lens dating to ca. 1,900 years ago. The best represented component, dating within the last ca. 800 years (based on five radiocarbon ages), includes the remains of at least three houses (fig. 4.15). Two of the houses are relatively small (one measuring 3x4 meters and the other 2.5x3 meters); both have excavated floors. One of the small houses,

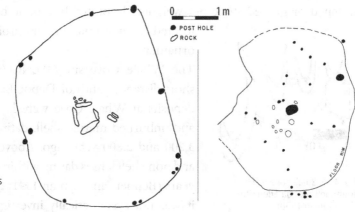

Fig. 4.15. House floor plan sketches (modified from Ross and Snyder 1979 and Lyman 1990).

dug by Stenhouse in the early 1970s, had postholes and grooves around the periphery of its clay floor, suggesting that planks were set on edge against vertical supports to form walls. A fire hearth outlined by vertically-set stones was placed near the center of the floor. The other small house exhibited a large pit in the center (which produced a radiocarbon age of ca. 600 years ago), and numerous smaller postholes placed irregularly around it, some distance from the walls. The posthole patterns seen in excavation do not readily suggest the nature of this unit's superstructure. It is possible that later activities at the site obliterated some of the house features. The third house appeared as a long trench (estimated to be ca. 8x30 meters in size), and was interpreted as a "large semi-subterranean plank structure" (Ross and Snyder 1986:86). Because the feature was dug through other dated occupation layers it was thought to represent the later residential use of the site, probably dating from the eighteenth and early nineteenth centuries.

The tool inventory from the Umpqua-Eden site is large and diverse, and includes projectile points, bifaces, scrapers, net weights, a bowl fragment, bone wedges, harpoons, and fishhooks (fig. 4.16). Ross and Snyder (1986) provide some observations regarding chronological patterns, but Lyman (1991:113–116) had difficulty replicating the tallies on which their chronology was based. Ross and Snyder (1986) suggest that large, unilaterally barbed, single-piece harpoons dominate in the earlier strata, while smaller and more delicate composite harpoons are more common in later deposits. Smoking pipes are also present; a sandstone pipe is associated with the pre-house occupation debris, but a number of baked clay pipes appear to be from strata dating within the last several hundred years (Nelson 2000). Artifacts associated only with the later occupations include carved bone J-shaped fishhooks, notched or girdled stone net weights, decorated bird bone beads, and per-

Fig. 4.16. Small bone fish hooks from the Umpqua-Eden site (from Lyman 1990)

forated sea-mammal incisors probably used for ornaments.

The Whale Cove site (35LNC60) is located a short distance south of Depoe Bay. The earliest deposits at Whale Cove were layers of burned and unburned marine shell, dating between ca. 3,200 and 2,800 years ago. Above this are shell and non-shell lenses dating within the last ca. 650 years (Bennett and Lyman 1991: 244). Although it was not systematically investigated, a trench

exposed following excavation revealed the apparent profile of a semisubterranean housepit floor associated with the later deposits. Like many coastal
middens, the site produced a relatively small assemblage of flaked and ground
stone artifacts but a robust collection of bone tools. Pointed bone implements, eyed needles, and awls were relatively numerous, suggesting that sewing and perhaps basket-making were important site activities. Wedges and
chisels of bone and antler, as well as beaver incisor scribing tools, indicate
woodworking activity. Other recovered artifacts include whistles and beads
of bone (some incised with ornamental markings), a carved bone spoon, and
several bone fishing lures.

Fish remains were recovered from Whale Cove, but not identified or
quantified. Some 20 species of shellfish were also identified, but their relative
proportions were not analyzed. Terrestrial and marine mammals were, however, studied in detail. The faunal assemblage from the early component was
dominated by elk and deer, with a variety of marine mammals represented
(harbor seal, northern fur seal, Steller sea lion, California sea lion, and sea
otter). In the later components the faunal assemblage was overwhelmingly
represented by harbor seals, with other species present in much lower frequencies (Bennett 1988; Bennett and Lyman 1991).

This change in sea mammal profiles is a pattern seen consistently along
the Oregon and California coasts in the late Holocene, possibly reflecting
population changes due to hunting pressure. Dominant males in sea lion
and fur seal populations defend rookery sites where harems of females give
birth and nurture pups for up to several months before dispersing on seasonal
migrations. Because of this behavior, these "migratory breeders" are potentially the easier prey. Harbor seals and sea otters are not migratory, and use
opportunistic rookeries that are not defended, choosing instead to flee from
threats. It is argued that hunting pressure from growing late Holocene human
populations depleted sea lion and fur seal rookeries, particularly at mainland
sites. In relatively rare coastal areas where offshore rocks provided greater
security for sea mammals, hunting of migratory breeders continued with sophisticated watercraft, but elsewhere people resorted to more labor-intensive
hunting of the more elusive resident harbor seals and sea otters (Hildebrandt
and Jones 1992; Jones and Hildebrandt 1995).

The Seal Rock site (35LNC14), located about four miles north of Alsea
Bay, is likely the remains of the Alsea village of *Ku-tau'-wa* (Berreman 1937:37;
Dorsey 1890:229). In modern times, developments in the small community

of Seal Rock and construction of U.S. Highway 101 have degraded the site. Extensive excavations (more than 130 cubic meters) were carried out in the early 1970s (Clark 1988, 1991).

Based on radiocarbon dating, the investigated areas of the site appear to have been occupied during the last ca. 500 years (Clark 1988, 1991; Moss and Erlandson 1995; Rambo 1978; Zontek 1983). Rambo (1978) reports the presence of a 4x4 meter plank house at the site, with an artifact assemblage indicating occupation in the mid-nineteenth century. Although no other architectural features were identified, the presence of human burials at the site, as well as the abundance of bone and antler chisels—commonly used to split planks for house construction—provide at least indirect evidence for the presence of houses (Clark 1991:213).

Stone tools from Seal Rock include stone projectile points (triangular, basal notched and barbed, concaved base, side-notched, and contracting stem varieties), scrapers, gravers, drills, adzes, hammerstones, pestles and other ground stone. Bone artifacts include wedges, points and awls, ornaments and pendants, bird-bone whistles, and whalebone clubs (Clark 1991). Also among the bone tools were many simple and composite fishhooks, and barbed and composite harpoon elements, which reflect the importance of fishing and sea-mammal hunting. This is supported by an abundance of fish and sea-mammal bone, the latter due to the site's proximity to a sea lion rookery. Sea-mammal remains included Steller and California sea lions, sea otter, northern fur seal, harbor porpoise, and whale. Fish remains included salmon, seaperch, surfperch, rockfish, greenling, lingcod, sculpin, cabezon, flounder, and sole (Zontek 1983). Shellfish, especially mussel, were also abundant, although neither bird nor shellfish remains were systematically identified or tabulated (Lyman 1991; Rambo 1978; Zontek 1983). Age profiles of animal remains indicate year-round occupation of the site; sea mammals suggest spring and summer visits, when they were migrating along the coast (Rambo 1978:82), while elk and deer remains indicate summer, fall, and mid-winter use (Lyman 1991).

Midden constituents were not quantified, but included bay mussel, bent-nose clam, butter clam, and cockle as dominant constituents. Present in lesser quantities were little neck clam, gaper clam, and horse clam. Lyman (1991:128) characterizes the collection of fish bones from the site as "huge," but it has not been systematically studied. Ross and Snyder (1986:95) report that flounder and other flat fish were common; also represented were salmon, sturgeon, rock fish, greenling, surfperch, herring, and buffalo sculpin. Birds were also well attested, and Ross and Snyder (1986:95) estimate that ducks represent up to 85% of all bird remains; many of the bird bones display butchering marks (Lyman 1991:128). The vertebrate faunal assemblage is varied (deer, elk, bear, raccoon, beaver, sea and river otter, seals and sea lions, and whales), but remains from the earlier components are dominated by harbor seal. Harbor seals remain important throughout the later occupation, but whalebone accounts for half of the bone assemblage (Ross and Snyder 1986; Lyman 1991).

The Siuslaw National Forest sponsored several archaeological investigations at fast-eroding sites within the Cape Perpetua Scenic Area on Oregon's central coast (Minor et al. 1985; Minor and Greenspan 1995). Radiocarbon dates from four sites (35LNC54, -55, - 56, and -57) confirm continuous use of the area during the last ca. 1,500 years. Although not sufficiently excavated to expose dimensions and architectural features, the remains of a small housepit were recorded at the Cape Creek site (35LNC57). The presence of numerous additional hearth and occupation surfaces suggests that several structures may have been present during the centuries the site was in use, but distinctive house features may have been masked by the disturbances of later residents. The presence of substantial shell middens and comparable artifact assemblages at the other Cape Perpetua sites suggests they may have also been residential sites, at least for some portion of the year.

Most of the artifacts from the Cape Perpetua sites are unspecialized bone, antler, flake, and cobble tools, including wedges, abraders, cutting tools, and hammerstones. Also present were *Olivella* shell beads, decorated clay pipe fragments, and harpoon point and valve components made of bone (fig. 4.17). Historic glass and brass trade beads were also recovered from the Cape Creek site; comparison with beads of known age from Fort Vancouver suggest a time from ca. 1820 to 1850. The beads confirm continued occupation of the site into the early nineteenth century fur trade period.

A number of sites extending south of Cape Perpetua to Neptune State Park have been investigated, including the Good Fortune Point site (35LNC55), the Good Fortune Cove site (35LNC56) and the Neptune site (35LA3) (Barner 1981; Clark 1991; Keyser 1991; Lyman 1991; Minor 1992a; Minor et al. 1985; Rambo 1978; Tasa and Connolly 2001; Zontek 1983).

Excavations at the Good Fortune Cove site (35LNC56) were also conducted in 1983 in response to threatened destruction by a proposed pedestrian

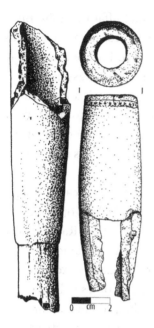

Fig. 4.17, Fired clay pipes from the Cape Creek site, Cape Perpetua (from Minor and Greenspan 1995).

underpass (Minor et al. 1985). Hammerstones, cobble choppers, and antler wedges indicate extensive woodworking activity, and a fired clay pipe was also recovered. Five hearths were exposed, ranging in age from ca. 1,300 to 400 years old. Molluscan remains recovered from the site were mostly mussel (>95% of analyzed sample), followed by relatively lower frequencies of barnacles and other species. Vertebrate faunal remains were overwhelmingly fish (72%, including rock fish, surfperch, sculpins, flatfish, etc.), followed by large terrestrial mammals (cf. elk, deer; 14%), birds (gulls and ducks, 10%), and sea mammals (seals, sea lion, sea otter, whale; 5%). The faunal assemblage indicates a primary subsistence focus on the rocky shore and marine offshore environments.

A possible housepit depression was identified at the nearby Good Fortune Point site (35LNC55). Faunal remains were mostly fish, including greenling, herring, and rockfish. Mammalian and avian remains included deer, pinnipeds, common loon, and common murre. Shellfish was primarily California mussel, with minor presence of Pacific razor clam, limpets, dogwinkles, barnacles, black katy chiton, common Pacific littleneck, flat-tipped piddock, horse clam, bent-nosed clam, heart rock dweller, and crab. Radiocarbon dates suggest that occupation of the site occurred initially around 1,400 years ago and lasted until about 100 years ago (Tasa and Connolly 2001; Keyser 1991).

As previously noted, the Neptune site (35LNC3) includes distinct middens, designated A and B, separated by about 100 meters. When the site was first recorded, Collins (1951) reported several housepits in an area later graded and paved for parking. Minor (1986:53) characterized the site as an "extensive village site complex." Radiocarbon dating indicates the settlement was occupied at least throughout the last 1,000 years. It is listed on the National Register of Historic Places.

Area B was investigated in 1973 by an archaeological field school led by Richard Ross of Oregon State University. A radiocarbon date of ca. 9350 cal. BP from charcoal-rich sediment may not be cultural (Lyman 1991:32,

1997:264; Minor 1995; Moss and Erlandson 1998). Cultural radiocarbon ages from the Area B midden fall within the last ca. 400 years, while dates from Area A are as early as ca. 1000 BP (Barner 1981; Zontek 1983; Erlandson and Moss 1993). The 1973 excavation has not been fully reported, but master's theses on some elements of the research have been produced, as noted below.

Area B was revisited in 1977 by Debra Barner (1981), for the purpose of collecting column samples through the midden for systematic analysis of shellfish remains. These columns penetrated cultural midden at least 120 centimeters thick (elsewhere the midden is reported to be up to 150 centimeters thick). Barner (1981:69) also tabulated other faunal remains from the site, and found that "[t]he orientation of the economy towards marine resources is shown by the heavy reliance on shellfish, sea mammals, and fish, as opposed to land mammals." A second thesis by Zontek (1983), examined fish remains from the site. The relatively late radiocarbon ages from this area of the site (postdating ca. A.D. 1650) are consistent with the discovery of an iron wedge at the bottom of the midden, possibly introduced to the area as drift iron on a wrecked ship.

The Bob Creek Site (35LA10) occupies Neptune State Park lands south of the creek and Siuslaw National Forest land to the north. When first recorded, the site was described as several large shell middens up to six feet deep, but damaged by shell mining (shell middens were frequently mined for road bed material; Byram 2009); housepit depressions were visible (Collins 1951, 1953). Two burials have also been reported at the site (Harrison 1978; Tasa et al. 2009), one in Area A and one in Area B, and apparent copper staining was noted on the bones of the latter individual (a 30–35 year old male). The presence of both housepits and burials indicate the site was a village.

Erlandson and Moss (1993) identified three areas of the site; Area A north of Bob Creek; Area B extending for ca. 140 meters south of the creek, and Area C south of a swale beyond the south end of Area B. Samples for radiocarbon dating were collected at visible midden exposures from all site areas. Formal testing of the site was conducted in several short trips from 2000 to 2002 (Tasa et al. 2009), and four additional radiocarbon samples were run. The seven radiocarbon dates reported from the site range from ca. 800 to 300 years ago.

Shellfish was dominated by rock-dwelling species; mussels were predominant but barnacles were also abundant and chitons were common. Sandy beach species, including razor, littleneck, and gaper clams, were present in small numbers. The vertebrate faunal assemblage suggests a heavy reliance on fishing, as fish account for 79% of identified specimens. Target species included herring, hake, greenling, sculpins, cabezon, lingcod, and a variety of rockfishes and surfperch. Remains of seals, sea lions, sea otters, deer and elk, and a small number of shore birds were also present.

The sites discussed to this point have been primarily located on the outer coast, but people also made regular use of river corridors and small mountain valleys. Writing about the Alsea, Zenk (1990a:568) reports that "it was inland, upriver, that the Alseans had their summer camps," where winter foods were harvested and processed for storage. The Alsea River was navigable by canoe upstream to Alsea Valley, and there the Alsea often met with Kalapuyans from the Willamette Valley (Santee and Warfield 1943:60; Zenk 1990a).

The Yaquina Falls Site (35LNC98) is situated in a small upriver meadow next to a small falls where the Yaquina River drops just a few feet over a shelf of bedrock. Fall Chinook salmon, Coho salmon, chum salmon, winter steelhead trout, and both sea-run and resident cutthroat trout ascend the Yaquina River as far as the falls, located a few miles above the head of tidewater. At the center of the site are two notable depressions that have the appearance of housepit features. A large quantity of fire-cracked rock and charcoal, typically indicators of fire-assisted food processing, are abundant throughout the cultural deposits but are most notably concentrated around the depressions. Analysis of the cultural charcoal led to the identification of a dozen different tree species used as fuel, dominated by Douglas-fir, pine, and western hazelnut. It was also noted that much of the charcoal had a highly vitrified appearance, which is commonly attributed to the burning of green wood, a feature that also—along with the abundance of fire-cracked rock—suggests the use of pit ovens or the fueling of smoky fires to process foods. A hearth feature near the base of the cultural deposit was dated to ca. 950 cal. BP. Woodworking tools include ground adze blades and a stone splitting wedge (Connolly 2005) (fig. 4.18).

Small calcined bone fragments were common in the soil samples, indicating that animals were butchered and processed at the site. Fragile fish bone was not preserved, but the site's location suggests that anadromous fish or lampreys were likely a primary focus of food collection and processing activities. A small number of historic artifacts, including a lead musket ball and glass bottle fragments from the ca. 1880s, indicate some late-nineteenth-century use. For many reservation Indians, starvation was averted only by a return to traditional fishing and hunting practices. In 1877 land speculator and developer Wallis Nash (1882:229) described a fishing camp on a Yaquina River tributary:

They had a salmon-camp . . . and there, in a wide pool, into which the river fell over the ridge of rocks, hardly to be called a fall, the Indians had their dam and traps. Just below the fall they had planted a row of willow and hazel stakes in a bed of the stream close together and tied with withes. In the center was an opening—a little lane of stakes leading into a pocket some six feet wide. The Indian women sat out on the rock by the side of the pocket with dip-nets and ladled out the salmon, which had been beguiled by their instinct of pushing always up the stream into entering the fatal inclosure. The Indian tyhees or shelters were on the bank close by . . . made of boughs, and some old boards they had carried up–hung round with . . . blankets to keep in the smoke. Poles were set across and across, and from these hung the sides and bellies of the salmon, while a little fire of damp wood and grass was kept constantly replenished in the middle of the floor.

The Yaquina Falls site was used for at least a thousand years, into the latter part of the nineteenth century. This historic fishing account, from post-reservation times, provides a clear picture of both the manner of fishing (with weirs, traps, and nets) and the processing procedures (salmon split and cured in smoke houses) that certainly reflect more ancient traditions (Connolly 2005).

Fig. 4.18. Stone wedge and schist adzes from the Yaquina Falls site.

The Lower Columbia and North Coast: Salish-Chinook Pattern. The lower Columbia River, from Celilo Falls near The Dalles through the Wapato Valley (the Portland Basin) to its mouth, was occupied historically by tribes of Chinookan-speaking peoples. They were closely linked with the Salishan Tillamook, sharing many cultural traits in spite of language differences. There were extensive economic and political ties among villages, maintained through constant trade and facilitated through alliances cemented by marriage. The explorers Lewis and Clark were struck by the intensity of river commerce along this stretch; Lewis recorded on January 11, 1806 (Thwaites 1905:3:338):

> The Cuthlâhmâhs [Cathlamet] left us this evening on their way to the C[l]atsops, to whom they purpose bartering their wappetoe for the blubber and oil of the whale, which the latter purchased for beads &c. from the Killamucks [Tillamook]; in this manner there is a trade continually carried on by the natives of the river each trading some article or other with their neighbours above and below them.

Because the Columbia carries a heavy sediment load, the lower course of the river and the outer coast adjacent to its mouth have changed significantly over time. The Clatsop Plains is a ridged landform made of stabilized dune sand stretching between the Columbia River and Tillamook Head. The sand derives primarily from Columbia River sediment that is returned to the outer coast due to high-energy waves. The dunes have formed entirely within the last ca. 5000 years, developing a ridged topography in a time progression from east to west. Initial attempts to date the dune sequence relied on peat deposits that formed in inter-dune areas (Rankin 1983; Reckendorf et al. 2001); archaeological evidence is contributing to a refinement of the dune chronology.

The Earl Dune site (35CLT66) was initially used about 1,350 years ago (Tasa and Connolly 2008). The initial occupation appears to have been on an open sandy beach on the ocean side of the dunes, where marine fishes (primarily hake and sculpin) were harvested, and razor clams were opportunistically collected. Subsequent short-term occupations were on a low developing dune. Marine fishing continued, but anadromous fish were also taken, along with small mammals including beaver, large quantities of razor clams, and occasional gaper clams. As the dune continued to accumulate sand, the occupations became increasingly ephemeral, consisting primarily of low-density scatters of razor clam shells and fire-cracked rock from cooking ovens. Use of the site had ended by about 1200 years ago.

The Palmrose site (35CLT47) is located at the southern end of the Clatsop Plains, near the Necanicum River in modern-day Seaside. This is one of the earliest clearly "permanent" communities on the Oregon coast. It is an enormously large and deep shell midden, roughly half a mile inland from the present shoreline. Although people frequented the site area by ca. 3,900 years ago, it was about 2,700 years ago that a large rectangular plank house—the earliest known large plank house on the southern Northwest Coast—was built (Phebus and Drucker 1979; Connolly 1992). The house may have been much like the wooden long houses seen by Lewis and Clark on the lower Columbia in 1805–1806. The excavators detected several phases of reconstruction during its millennium-long occupation, based on the presence of overlapping features, multiple floors, and clusters of radiocarbon ages at about 2600–2400 BP, 2200–2100 BP, and 1850–1650 BP. The overall length of the Palmrose plank house could not be determined because the eastern end was not excavated, but it was estimated to be over twenty feet [6 meters] wide and at least forty feet [12 meters] long (Phebus and Drucker 1979:13). The floor of the house was excavated two feet into the cobble beach ridge underlying the site, and a boxed hearth (or a series of hearths?) was identified along its central axis.

Analysis of mollusk shells from the Palmrose site shows that horse clam, butter clam, and littleneck clam were commonly harvested; these are all species that live in the sheltered waters of bays and estuaries, a habitat which is rare today in the Seaside vicinity. Their presence indicates that when the site was occupied, it likely bordered a Necanicum River estuary that was much larger than the modern one. It is likely that infilling of the former estuary accompanied the formation of the Clatsop Plains complex (Connolly 1995).

The Palmrose site vertebrate faunal assemblage is diverse, with 25 species of birds, 23 species of fishes, and 14 species of mammals. In order of abundance, the most common fishes were skates, greenlings, surfperches, hake, salmon, rockfish, flatfish, and sturgeons. The most abundant birds were murres, shearwaters, ducks, geese, and swans. Sea mammals included cetaceans (whales), sea otter, sea lions, and fur seals. The dominant land mammals were deer and elk. Apart from salmon, which may have been harvested from fresh water during spawning runs, the faunal remains indicate that sustenance overwhelmingly came from marine/littoral environments (Greenspan and Crockford 1992).

The tool assemblage included medium- to large-stemmed and notched projectile points, atlatl weights, stone mortars, hand mauls, antler digging-stick handles, abrading stones of pumice, antler splitting wedges, composite bone harpoon points, shark-tooth pendants, and many pieces of worked and decorated bone or antler. A number of carved bone and antler artifacts show motifs closely similar to those of contemporary Marpole Phase sites of the Lower Fraser River/Gulf of Georgia region in southern British Columbia (figs. 4.19 and 4.20). These similarities show clearly that close contacts were being maintained over great distances up and down the coast by about 2,700 years ago. These ancient connections may be a factor in the presence of Salish languages in Oregon, which otherwise dominate the Washington and southern British Columbia coasts to the north (Connolly 1992).

The Palmrose site may have been largely abandoned by about 1,600 years ago, about the time that two other nearby residential sites, the Avenue Q (35CLT13) and Par-Tee (35CLT20) sites, experienced a population surge. It is possible that this shift in village location is one consequence of population adjustments necessitated by a major subsidence earthquake that may have occurred at this time. The Avenue Q site, when first formally recorded in 1951, was described as a "huge" residential site (Collins 1953:61) that

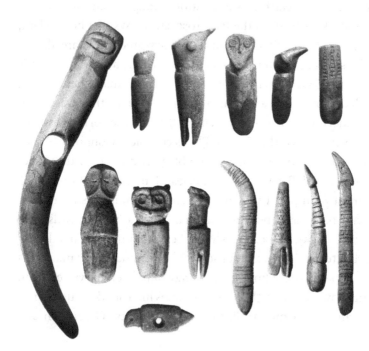

Fig. 4.19.
Decorated slotted
bone handles from
the Palmrose site.

contained a quantity of carved bone and stone artifacts, including a whale-bone club. Collins reported that exposures left by shell mining (for road beds and other uses) indicated a cultural midden nearly ten feet (2.8 meters) deep. Subsequent small-scale investigations (Phebus and Drucker 1979; Connolly 1992; Connolly and Tasa 2004) confirmed remaining cultural deposits up to 1.7 meters deep. Cultural radiocarbon ages from the site range from ca. 3,500 years ago to between ca. 700 and 1,000 years ago, with the most intensive occupations (as a continuously occupied residential site) dating from ca. 1,700 to 1,000 years ago, postdating the main occupation at the nearby Palmrose site. The site also has abundant and well-preserved dietary remains (especially bone and shell).

The excavations at Avenue Q have not been of sufficient scale to recognize larger features such as house remains. At Par-Tee, house features appear to be

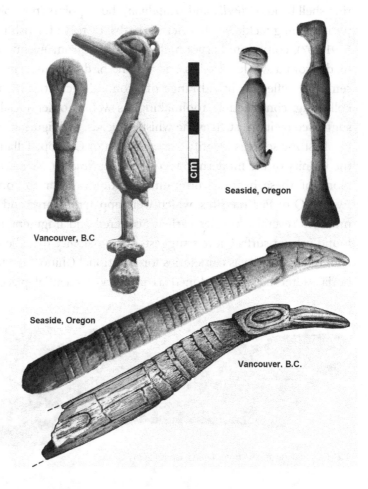

Seaside, Oregon

Vancouver, B.C

Seaside, Oregon

Vancouver, B.C.

Fig. 4.20. Stylistically similar bone sculptures from the Palmrose site (Oregon) and the Marpole site (British Columbia).

circular in outline, unlike the large Palmrose plank house. The faunal assemblage from Avenue Q indicates a subsistence focus on marine environments. Fish represented 67% of identifiable bone, and this class is clearly dominated by marine species (halibut, lingcod, cabezon, etc.). Pacific trouts and salmons, which can be taken from either marine or freshwater environments, are present but not abundant. Of the mammal bone, 73% represents marine species (sea otters, harbor seals, sea lions, and cetaceans [whales, dolphins, and porpoises]), while the balance (26%) represent terrestrial animals (elk and deer, dogs or coyotes, rabbit, and rodents). The littoral zone was clearly important to the residents of the Avenue Q site, but offshore marine environments were also critical.

Recovered artifacts include bone wedges, bird-bone whistles and needles, antler digging-stick handles, whale bone atlatls, barbed bone harpoons, marine shell beads (*Olivella* and *Dentalium*), bone points (possibly parts of composite fishing tackle, such as leister barbs, or teeth for fish rakes; cf. Lyman 1991:207), composite harpoon elements, and, from Avenue Q, a large bowl made from a whale vertebra and a stone bird figurine. The diverse tool assemblage reflects a broad range of economic activities (fishing, plant food collecting, construction, toolmaking) as well as other social considerations suggested by items such as the whistles, beads, and figurine.

Historic sources identify three Clatsop or Clatsop/Tillamook villages in the vicinity of the modern town of Seaside, *Neacoxy*, *Necanicum*, and *Necotat*. None of these historic communities would appear to correspond to the Avenue Q or Par-Tee sites, which were apparently large and populous communities several centuries earlier. Scattered and fragmentary human bone found in near-surface levels suggests the possibility that the old village sites continued to serve as cemeteries for traditional Chinook-style above-ground burials after being abandoned as primary residential places; at least one

4.21 Carved bone artifact from Netarts Sandspit (35TI1)

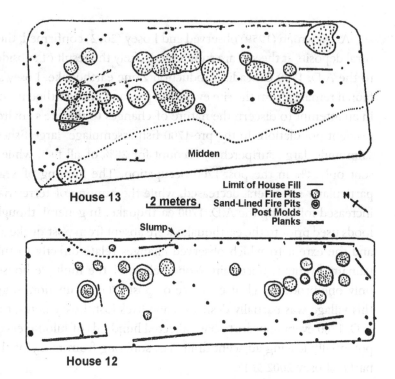

Fig. 4.22.
Housepits
at Netarts
Sandspit (35TI1)
(modified from
Newman 1951)

historic source appears to mention Par-Tee as being "covered with human bones, skulls and canoes in all stages of decay" in 1852 (Miller 1958).

Another important village was located about 35 miles south of Seaside, on the Netarts Bay sand spit. A series of excavations at the 35TI1 site (Newman 1959; Losey 2002, 2007) have documented a community of sizable rectangular plank houses arranged in two rows (figs. 4.21 and 4.22). Newman (1959) numbered 13 house depressions, and excavated in at least six. Partial excavation of pits 5 and 10 provided the best structural evidence. The ends of the Pit 5 house were excavated, revealing a structure 17.1 meters long and 4.6 meters wide, built in a pit excavated up to 1.5 meters deep. Pit 12 contained the remains of a 4.5 meters by 16 meters house, and House 13 measured 5x12 meters. Post and plank molds were present in all; in some cases rotted cedar was still present, representing planks up to 4.5 meters long. All the houses also contained multiple and sometimes overlapping floor hearths, showing that hearth positions may have changed over the course of long occupations. Several houses also had larger (ca.1x3 meters) hearth areas, bounded by planks, along the house centerline. Most radiocarbon dates indicate that the houses were in use for at least several hundred years, from ca. A.D. 1400 to 1800.

As Newman (1959) observed and Losey (2002) confirmed, the lowest cultural deposits at the site are submerged, likely the result of subsidence related to the A.D. 1700 Cascadia Subduction Zone earthquake. Losey's analysis of faunal remains from the site evaluated pre- and post-earthquake occupations, in an attempt to discern the nature of changes to the site's environment and resident population. In the pre-1700 fish assemblage, large fishes (flatfishes, salmonids, large surfperches) account for 28% of all fish, while they represent only 4% in the post-1700 occupation. The hunting of sea mammals, particularly sea otters, decreased, while the hunting of terrestrial mammals increased following the A.D. 1700 earthquake. In general, though, no major foods used prior to the earthquake were absent from post-quake assemblages, and the extent to which observed changes relate directly to subsidence or tsunami events is uncertain. Nonetheless, of the multiple houses at 35TI1, only one produced clear evidence of post-1700 occupation, suggesting that this village was partially destroyed and lives lost. Losey notes, too, that "the A.D. 1700 event appears to have affected hundreds of kilometers of coastline, potentially leaving adjacent drainages suffering from many of the same impacts" (Losey 2002:561).

House 13, the one occupied after the A.D. 1700 earthquake, contained fragments of Chinese porcelain, oxidized metal fragments, and a copper pendant. Some porcelain sherds had been chipped into projectile points (Beals and Steele 1981; Woodward 1986; Lally 2008). These are thought to have been salvaged from a ship that wrecked on the Oregon coast, near Nehalem Bay. The nature of the debris suggests the ship was a Spanish trading galleon lost on the Manila-Acapulco route. Because of the abundance of beeswax among the recovered artifacts, the wreck is commonly known as the "beeswax ship," and pollen from the beeswax identifies its source as the Philippines. Radiocarbon dating and the age of identifiable ceramics suggest a probable age in the latter 1600s to ca. 1700. The two most likely candidates for missing vessels from this time period, based on Spanish records, are the *Santo Christo de Burgos* (lost in 1693) or the *San Francisco Xavier* (lost in 1705). Based on age analysis of design elements on recovered porcelain fragments, Lally (2008) concluded that the *Santo Christo de Burgos* is the more likely candidate.

Numerous other villages were occupied along the north coast. A site on the north shore of Nehalem Bay (35TI76) contains the remains of at least two houses; one partially excavated house was estimated to be 8 meters wide by 17 meters long, and the second had estimated dimensions of 10 meters by 18 meters. Like 35TI1 at Netarts, the houses and adjacent middens contained Chinese porcelain, unglazed Asian stoneware, beeswax, glass trade beads, fragments of green bottle glass, and highly oxidized iron fragments, some identified as wrought-iron nails. One porcelain fragment had been made into a bifacially flaked projectile point, and three arrow points had been cut from sheet copper, glass trade beads, and fragments of green bottle glass. While some of these items certainly came from the "beeswax ship," others (particularly the trade beads) date from the later fur trade, as late as the mid-nineteenth century (Losey 2002; Woodward 1986).

Investigations were carried out at a site on Ecola Point (35CLT21) that had been damaged by landslides. Surface topography suggested the presence of four rectangular houses; based on the site map, the houses appear to be about six meters wide and nine to twelve meters long (Minor 1991a: figure 2-1). Radiocarbon ages span the last ca. 900 years, and metal fragments confirm that site use continued after contact. A Steller sea lion rookery is present today on the nearby offshore rocks, and the abundance of sea lion bones at the site confirms that this was a main attraction to the site residents throughout the last millennium. Seasonal indicators indicate that the main occupations occurred primarily during the summer months.

Roughly 25 miles up the Columbia from its mouth at Astoria, sites at Eddy Point (35CLT33) and Indian Point (also known as Ivy Station, 35CLT34) near the town of Knappa represent occupations spanning the last ca. 3,000 years. The Indian Point site also produced an abundance of historic porcelain, window glass, glass beads, metal buttons, nails, and other evidence to show that it was occupied well into the historic period. Both sites produced rich and essentially similar faunal inventories. Deer and elk were most abundant, and harbor seals were well represented. Fish (salmon, sucker, sturgeon, and marine fishes), waterfowl (duck, goose, and swan), and marine shellfish (gaper and butter clams) were present. Bone wedges and composite harpoon parts, chipped stone projectile points, and heavy stone mauls and net sinkers were found at both sites. The limited excavations revealed no clear evidence of house structures, though both were probably village settlements (Minor 1983:112–147; Minor et al. 2008).

The Lower Columbia Valley was an especially rich and densely occupied zone, and a central place in regional cultural spheres. In 1805, Lewis and Clark estimated that some 8,000 people lived along the Columbia between the mouth of the Willamette River at modern-day Portland and the mouth of the Cowlitz River near modern-day Longview (Washington), about 40 miles downstream. Some of the native villages were large enough to be called towns, and travelers on the river were never long out of sight of a settlement. One of the largest in the area was a town of about 900 (according to Lewis and Clark's 1806 estimate) on the Washington side of the Columbia. Identified by Lewis and Clark as a village of the "Quathlapotle Nation," it is now commonly identified as Cathlapotle (45CL1). This town contained 14 plank houses, the largest measuring ca. 60 meters long by 14 meters wide, enclosing approximately 9,000 square feet. Its population decimated by introduced diseases, the town was abandoned within a few decades of Lewis and Clark's visit (Ames et al. 1999; Sobel 2006).

The Meier site (35CO5) is on the Oregon side of the Columbia opposite Cathlapotle, on a tributary draining to the Columbia River's Multnomah Channel bordering the west side of Sauvie Island. Here the remains of a large Chinook-style plank longhouse, estimated to be about 35 meters long and almost 14 meters wide, have been partially uncovered (Ames et al. 1992; Smith 2006). Radiocarbon dates, and a few glass trade beads and pipe fragments, indicate that the structure was built some 700 years ago, and occupied continuously thereafter into historic times. The dwelling was repaired and rebuilt many times during its use-history, demonstrated by myriad cross-cutting and superimposed postholes and plank impressions. Clusters of overlapping postholes show that some main wall and roof support members had been shored up or replaced as many as eight to ten times over the life of the house. In one major reconstruction phase, the orientation of the entire structure was shifted by 15 degrees (Ames et al. 1992; Smith 2006).

Excavations revealed that a series of formal boxed hearths were built along the centerline of the house; each of these would have served numerous related families (fig. 4.23). Bordering both sides of the central hearth area were excavated corridors that served as storage cellars, probably covered by flooring planks. The continuous sets of overlapping storage pits had been dug, filled, and re-dug many times by generations of householders over several centuries of occupation. The pits yielded an abundance of fire-cracked rock and tens of thousands of bone fragments from elk, deer, salmon, sturgeon, and other animals, the remains of food that was stored, cooked, and eaten in the house. Aspects of the food quest were represented by bone points, barbs, and foreshafts (probably for harpoons), and perforated stones interpreted as net sinkers. Vegetal food processing is indicated by stone mortar fragments, heavy shaped and unshaped pestles, and a perforated deer antler tine identical to those used historically as digging stick handles.

Manufacturing activities are represented by splitting wedges of bone and antler, abrading stones of pumice and hard igneous rock, and flaked stone graving tools, all probably used in woodworking; hammerstones and antler tine flakers, probably used in making flaked stone artifacts; and pointed bone splinters that may have functioned as awls in the manufacture of leather and basketry items. Objects of artistic, ornamental, or ceremonial importance were well represented at the Meier Site. Aboriginal craft work and concepts are portrayed by incised clay tablets, clay figurines, simple stone and bone sculptures of birds and other creatures, beads and pendants of ground stone and shell, and a perforated shark's tooth pendant. Euroamerican trade goods, attributable to the very latest part of the occupation, included rolled copper tube beads, glass trade beads, and some unidentified metal fragments. There are indications of a status hierarchy within the structure as well; the most expensive (in terms of production time or effort) and exotic items are concentrated at the north end

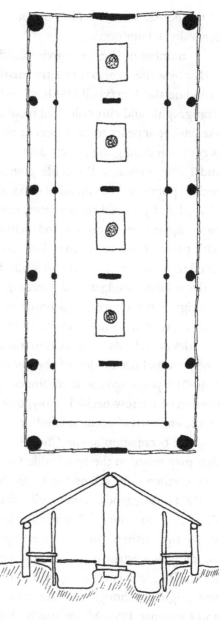

4.23 Idealized reconstruction of the Meier site house, showing the approximate arrangement of structural posts and planks, and hearth boxes for family living quarters; profile view shows below-floor storage cellars, and elevated sleeping lofts around the edge (modified from an image by Ken Ames).

of the house, an area within the household where food processing activities generally did not occur.

A number of sites on Sauvie Island were extensively dug in the 1970s and earlier by artifact collectors; later small-scale testing was conducted at several, including the Merrybell (35MU9) and Cholick (35MU1) sites, to establish a stratigraphic and chronological record (Pettigrew 1981). The Merrybell Site, like Meier, appears to have been a major village. Radiocarbon ages suggest occupation during the last ca. 3,000 years, with major use between ca. 2,500 and 1,750 years ago. Projectile points included both medium-sized, broad-necked points used to tip atlatl darts, and small, narrow-necked arrowpoints. Shaped and grooved stones interpreted as atlatl weights were also present. Net weights were common, and included notched or girdled stones, or stones with perforations to secure a line. Shaped and unshaped stone pestles indicated the processing of vegetal foods. Small tabular stone axe- or adze-heads, antler splitting wedges, and abrading stones made of pumice, sandstone, or hard igneous rock were apparently used for working wood, bone, and antler (Pettigrew 1981). Faunal remains were poorly preserved, but identified bone includes deer, birds, salmon, minnows, suckers, and sturgeon (Saleeby 1983). The principal occupation of the nearby Cholick Site followed Merrybell (ca. 1750–100 years ago), and continued into the historic period. A higher proportion of narrow-necked arrowpoints, and large cutting tools referred to as "mule-ear knives" occur at Cholick.

The occupation at the Cholick site is broken by a major flood episode that may relate to the Bonneville Landslide. The landslide created a temporary earthen dam across the Columbia (probably the origin of the Bridge of the Gods legend), temporarily impounding the waters of the Columbia River near the site of Bonneville Dam upstream from the Portland Basin. When the earthen dam was overtopped and breached, it caused catastrophic flooding downstream that almost certainly destroyed many Native settlements. There is conflicting evidence relating to the age of the landslide; it was originally thought to have occurred 700 or more years ago (Lawrence and Lawrence 1958; Minor 1984b), but recent research suggests it was more recent—possibly as recent as ca. 300 years ago, a time that coincides with the last great Cascadia Subduction Zone earthquake, which occurred in A.D. 1700 (O'Connor 2004; Pringle et al. 2002; Reynolds 2001).

The landslide debris created Cascade Rapids, which became an important center for Native fishing and commerce; Lewis and Clark recorded many Native settlements in the vicinity. Oregon missionaries Lee and Frost (1844:200) were reportedly told by Indians that "these falls are not ancient, and that their fathers voyaged [from the sea] without obstruction in their canoes as far as The Dalles." Most of the many archaeological sites in this area postdate the Bonneville landslide. Perhaps the best known is site 45SA11, the historic village known as Claclellah, located on the north side of the river. Lewis and Clark noted "four large houses" here in October 1805; archaeological investigations revealed seven plank houses arranged in two rows fronting on the Columbia. The site dates from the early and mid-eighteenth century. There is evidence, from deeper levels, of shallow oval housepits suggestive of the Plateau summer mat lodges that immediately predate the plank houses. It is possible that temporary fishing camps on the slide debris predate the permanent villages. Euroamerican trade goods were also common at the site (Dunnell and Beck 1979; Minor 1989; Minor et al. 1989; Warren 1959).

Lower Columbian and North Coast Social Complexity. The large plank houses in the lower Columbia River region, including the structures at the Meier and Palmrose sites and elsewhere throughout the region, are indicative of a social dynamic, widespread on the Northwest Coast, which extends beyond the household as a family dwelling. Ames (2006) argues that these structures represent "Houses," akin to the houses of European aristocratic families—corporate entities that control resources, have longer lives than the people who are their members, a membership that is not restricted to kinship, and a hierarchical organization.

The presence of such corporate structures on the lower Columbia and northern Oregon coast is in line with the social landscape that prevailed along much of the Pacific coast to the north. But their presence, and the iconographic great house buildings that represent them, can be seen as just one tier of a complex social structure. People of the region also made smaller semisubterranean dwellings and above-ground mat lodges like those of the Plateau. Excavations at the Ede Site (35CO34), on the Columbia just west of Portland, exposed a shallow, semisubterranean house with a saucer-shaped floor somewhat over 25 feet in diameter. Beneath this floor was found part of another. Radiocarbon dates provide ages of ca. 1,700 and 1,500 years ago for these successive occupations (Minor 1989). At the nearby Kersting site (45Cl21), circular semisubterranean houses were documented from the same level as a rectangular house that was dated by three radiocarbon determinations to about 2,000 years ago (Jermann et al. 1975). At the Par-tee (35CLT20) site in Seaside, numerous circular houses were present; the site is located near the Palmrose site, where a large plank house was built, but Par-tee was occupied at a later time than Palmrose. At sites near Skamania and Camas, farther upriver, excavations revealed circular housepits containing projectile points like those at the Merrybell site (2500–1750 BP). These structures are said to closely resemble the traditional pithouses of the interior Plateau region. A bit farther upstream, near the outlet of the Columbia Gorge, the Caples site (45SA5) revealed oval semisubterranean housepits (dating from ca. 800 to 200 years ago) that were also said to resemble Plateau winter houses.

Some of these differences may be chronological; large plank houses are generally later than circular pithouses in the region. But many smaller houses are clearly contemporary with or later than big plank houses, a fact which reinforces the reality of increasing social complexity, and the rise of some wealthy and influential lineages that achieved a level of regional economic prestige and power not shared by all.

Another element that marks the development of social stratification is the increased occurrence of artistically embellished artifacts. A well-developed representational art style, expressed in embellished objects of bone and stone, is notable at the Palmrose, Meier, and Netarts sites. Knife and club handles at the Palmrose, Netarts, and other sites are rendered in bone, and impressive basalt sculptures are found in the Portland Basin and in the Celilo Falls neighborhood. Many sculpted stone objects are known from undocumented contexts, primarily from the Portland Basin and The Dalles vicinity (Wingert 1952; Duff 1975; Carlson 1983). A series of sites bordering Lake River, on the Washington State side of the Columbia River west of Vancouver, have yielded fired clay figurines and other objects (Stenger 2009). The figurines typically taper from a broad end to a rounded tip, and lack appendages. Some are anthropomorphic, with faces represented by incised lines. Cut pieces of shell impressed into the clay before firing sometimes indicate hair or facial features. Other figurines, not of human form, exhibit punctated and incised decorative patterns. Occasional fired clay sherds, apparently representing vessel fragments, have also been found. These molded clay artifacts are known primarily from contexts dating less than ca. 700 years old.

Representational anthropomorphic and zoomorphic three-dimensional sculptures (sometimes as bowls or other functional forms) often have broad round faces, horizontal almond-shaped eyes, a continuous nose/brow ridge, and exposed ribs. Anthropomorphs may be shown with a headdress, or an apron or skirt. Animal figures are usually recognizable (owls, seals, etc.) and are also frequently depicted with a single nose/brow ridge and exposed ribs. Lewis and Clark recorded that the Chinook "are very fond of sculpture in wood of which they exhibit a variety of specemines about their houses." They particularly noted the common presence of carvings on principal structural supports: "I saw some of these which represented human figures setting and supporting the burthen on their sholders" (Thwaites 1905:4:198–199). These carved house timbers parallel the totem poles common along the Pacific coast to the north.

Another feature common throughout this larger region is the use of cranial reshaping (head flattening). Cranial reshaping was a privilege available only to the children of high status families; in a society where the practices of slave-holding and slave-raiding were commonplace, cranial reshaping was a sign of status that could never be removed (Ames and Maschner 1999).

In addition to sharing these elements of art and culture, the lower Columbia and adjacent northern Oregon and Washington coasts were active participants in an extensive southern Northwest Coast trading network that extended to the British Columbia coast. This is most easily marked archaeologically by the regular presence of Oregon obsidian at many sites in the Salish Sea region (Chapter 3). The set of closely shared cultural traits and art traditions was reinforced by the famous trade language known as Chinook Jargon (also Chinuk Wawa or Tenas Wawa). This trade language was built on a pre-contact substrate of Chinook, Salish, and Nootkan, reflecting both the importance of the lower Columbia and Vancouver Island/Gulf of Georgia trade centers in native commerce, and the ancient connectedness of these centers. Elements of English and French were later added (Hodge 1979; Harris 1994). The distribution of these traits confirms both a far-reaching economic sphere and a broadly shared social ethos across a privileged tier of Native society that crossed deep cultural, linguistic, and geographic boundaries.

The Southern Oregon Coast: Gunther Pattern. The most prominent feature of the late Holocene cultural record on the southern Oregon coast is known as the Gunther Pattern, named for the signature site on Gunther Island (now known as Indian Island or Duluwat Island) in Humboldt Bay, northern California. The site was the historic Wiyot village of Tuluwat.

Wiyot and the neighboring Yurok language are classified as an Algic language family, distantly related to Algonquian. Based on linguistic and archaeological evidence, Algic ancestors are thought to have arrived in northwestern

California about 1,700 years ago. These groups are surrounded by Athapaskan speakers, who probably arrived centuries later, and subsequently spread northward along the southern Oregon coast (Jacobs 1937; Connolly 1986). The better known sites of the archaeological Gunther Pattern were occupied continuously into the Historic period, and identified as villages of Algic or Athapaskan speakers.

The Gunther Pattern is recognizable along the Southern Oregon/ Northern California Coast (Heizer and Elsasser 1964; Fredrickson 1973, 1984; Connolly 1988) by traits that included nucleated villages with many small plank houses (in contrast to the large multi-family houses on the lower Columbia and north coast), finely chipped projectile points with exaggerated barbs (Gunther Barbed), concave-base projectile points, notched and grooved net sinkers, steatite dishes or lamps, stone and clay tubular pipes, bone and shell artifacts incised with geometric designs, stone adze handles, flanged mauls and pestles, and a wealth complex that included exotic obsidian blades, and beads and ornaments of *Olivella*, *Dentalium*, and *Haliotis* (abalone).

Social ranking was less pronounced on the southern Oregon Coast than on the lower Columbia, but it was definitely important, and was achieved and reinforced by the acquisition and display of wealth. As Hildebrandt (2007:84) notes, "wealthy families owned many . . . capital intensive technologies, as well as important resource areas such as acorn groves, river eddies for obtaining fish, and portions of offshore sea lion rookeries. Individual households possessing superior pools of labor could generate substantial food surpluses and other items of wealth, ultimately separating themselves from the less successful family units."

The Lone Ranch Creek archaeological site (35CU37), located a short distance north of the California border, represents the remains of a Chetco (Athapaskan) village known as *Nateneten* (Dorsey 1890:236; Schumacher 1874:360–361; Waterman 1925:542). The site includes a large midden on the south side of Lone Ranch Creek, while north of the creek Schumacher (1874) reported seeing "depressions marking the sites of former huts still plainly visible." Berreman (1944) excavated the site in 1936 and 1937, digging a five-foot-wide trench from north to south through the center of the midden, a perpendicular trench extending west from the center of the midden toward the beach, and other supplemental trenches and pits. Some of the excavation was done by hand, and some using a Fresno scraper.

Berreman's excavation was done long before radiocarbon dating, but later dating of shell exposures north of the creek returned ages of about 280 and 1,010 rcybp, consistent with an occupation during the last millennium (Moss and Erlandson 1994). The site produced no trade articles of non-Native manufacture, and may have been abandoned some time before contact, around 200 years ago. Portions of five houses were encountered by Berreman. Houses were rectangular and small; two for which dimensions could be determined measured about 3x3 and 3x5 meters in size. They had packed-clay floors and well-defined firepits, the floors having been excavated about two feet below the contemporary ground surface. Vertical cedar plank walls were set inside a horizontal base board that was secured by pegs driven in at about two-foot intervals along its outer side.

Thirty-two burials were excavated; the remains of at least 27 were later transferred to the University of Oregon where they were analyzed. Tasa (1997) examined a suite of metric and non-metric traits on the skeletal remains, and found greater variation among females than males. This is consistent with a patrilineal pattern, with related males seeking wives from outside the community. Tasa also found that, in general, the Oregon Athapaskans are physically distinct from other Oregon Indian populations, and most similar to Tlingit, far up the Northwest Coast. Tasa (1997:195–196) cautions that this does not mean the Oregon Athapaskans "derived from the Tlingit, but rather probably from a geographically proximate Athapaskan population in close relationship with the Tlingit." This is an observation that squares well with linguistic evidence for the Oregon Athapaskans' area of origin (Foster 1996).

Mussel accounted for more than 90% of the identified shell in the midden, along with a variety of clams and barnacles. In addition, Olivella and Dentalium shell beads, and ornaments of Haliotis (abalone) shell were present, most commonly in burials. Mammal bone included elk, deer, seal, sea lion, and whale. Bird remains included California condor. Fish bone was reported to be relatively scarce (possibly a product of the recovery procedures), and included salmon, surf fish, and small bone that may represent anchovy (Berreman 1944). Fishing and sea-mammal hunting is suggested by fishhooks, barbed and composite harpoon points, elements of two-piece V-shaped bone fishhooks, and notched and grooved net sinkers. Foliate and small barbed projectile points represent weaponry. Grinding slabs attested the milling of seeds or nuts.

Other artifacts of note include implements decorated with incised geometric patterns, made of pieces of flat bone or sea lion teeth, which are consistent with "head scratchers" used by women (Loud 1918). A couple of whale bone clubs were noted, as was a whale vertebra apparently used as a stool. Baked clay and tubular stone pipes, ground stone adze handles, bell-shaped mauls, and flanged pestles all exhibit stylistic elements consistent with the Gunther Pattern. A shallow stone dish is probably an oil lamp, of a type used on the northern Northwest Coast that hints at the northern (Alaskan?) heritage of the Oregon Athapaskans.

The Tututni Athapaskan village of *Chetlessenten*, also known as the Pistol River site (35CU61), sat on a bluff high above the ocean at the river's mouth. The site was visited in 1875, and was noted to contain "about fifty depressions of former houses, some of them obliterated by others of a subsequent occupation" (Schumacher 1877:31). The site was largely wiped out by construction of U.S. Highway 101 in the early 1960s, before the implementation of modern legislation that protects cultural sites. A modest recording effort was made by the University of Oregon (summarized several decades later by Erlandson et al. 1997), but most of what is now known of the site is due to the work of a determined amateur (Heflin 1966, 1981).

Heflin (1966) mapped 42 housepit depressions, of which 18 were at least partially excavated (fig. 4.24). One of the structures may have been a sweathouse, featuring a 4.6-meter long entrance tunnel. Houses were typically rectangular, averaging about 4x4.5 meters in size. Floors were excavated from half a meter up to 1.5 meters deep, covered with hard-packed clay. Walls were of vertical cedar planks backed by horizontal baseboards. A stone-lined hearth was typically located rearward of the floor's center. Radiocarbon ages on cedar planks from house structures, and on mussel and clamshell from the midden, indicate occupation during the last ca. 400 years (Erlandson et al. 1997).

Numerous burials were excavated at Chetlessenten; several by Schumacher (1877), from which at least three crania were sent to the Smithsonian; one by a private collector in the 1940s that was ultimately turned over to the University of Oregon; 20 removed by Heflin, the locations of which remain largely unknown; four burials and the partial remains of two others found within a single house, and seven from just outside the house, that were removed by UO excavations (Tasa 1997). Several of the burials in this house had associated historic trade goods (glass beads, metal buttons, and a Chinese coin). Erlandson et al. (1997:235) speculate that burials outside the house may have been part of a formal cemetery, while those inside may have been victims of one of the epidemics that decimated the Tututni in the early 1800s.

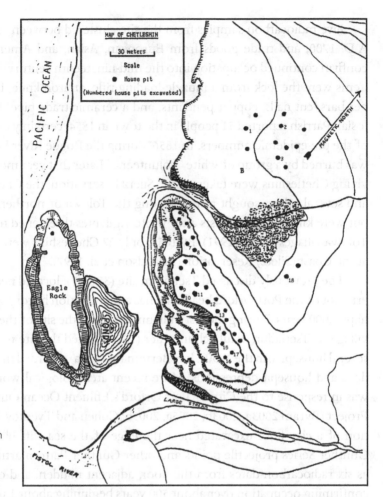

MAP OF CHETLESHIN

30 Meters

Scale

● House pit

(Numbered house pits excavated)

PACIFIC OCEAN

MAGNETIC NORTH

Eagle Rock

B

A

LARGE STREAM

PISTOL RIVER

4.24 Sketch of the Cheltlesenten Village showing house locations; modified from Heflin 1966).

A wide range of artifacts from the site attests diverse activities by its occupants. Flaked stone arrow points and knives, bone spearpoints, and harpoon foreshafts indicate hunting of terrestrial and marine species. Bone fishhooks, bipointed fish gorges, and an abundance of notched net sinkers made from river cobbles and pebbles give evidence of fishing. Plant food processing is indicated by ground stone pestles, hopper mortar bases, and bowls. Manufacturing activities are reflected by mauls, cobble chopping tools, adze handles, elk antler splitting wedges, flaked stone drills, scrapers, and gravers. Many of these tools exhibit strong stylistic parallels to those reported from Lone Ranch Creek and other Gunther Pattern sites, as well as artifacts such as bone head-scratchers, whalebone clubs, a stool and a bowl made from whale vertebrae, and numerous tubular pipes of fired clay.

Five radiocarbon samples from the site clustered between A.D. 1600 and A.D. 1700, and trade goods from European, Asian, and American sources confirm continued occupation into the mid-nineteenth century; among these items were the lock from a muzzle-loading rifle, an iron knife, iron and copper bars, cut nails, copper pendants, and a ceramic trade pipe. Indian Agent Josiah Parrish reported 51 people in the town in 1854, certainly only a fraction of the pre-epidemic numbers. In 1856, during the Rogue River War, the town was burned by a group of white "volunteers." Later that year most of the surviving Chetleshins were taken to the Siletz Reservation; the Chetleshin chief and several others sought refuge among the Tolowa of northern California, but were killed by their hosts after white vigilantes threatened to destroy the Tolowa villages (Chase 1991). By 1858, only 27 Chetleshins were enumerated at the Coast (Siletz) Reservation (Erlandson et al. 1997).

The previously discussed Tseriadun site (35CU7), located near the northern foot of the Port Orford headland, has an occupation history spanning perhaps 7,000 years. During the last millennium it was the site of the Athapaskan village of Tseriadun. Paul Schumacher (1877) visited the site in 1875, noting several housepits; in the 1930s, Joel Berreman (1935a) recorded thick shell middens and housepit depressions. More recent archaeological work at the site was in response to the City of Port Orford's Effluent Ocean Outfall Pipeline Project (Byram 2003a, 2003b, 2005a, 2005b; Cohen and Tveskov 2008). A portion of a clay floor excavated near the edge of the sea cliff bluff produced Gunther Series projectile points and other Gunther Pattern artifacts, as well as six radiocarbon dates from the floor, adjacent midden, and overlying fill, confirming occupation over about 500 years beginning about 1,000 years ago (Byram 2005a).

Analysis of faunal remains from Tseriadun compared probable meat weights extrapolated from bone and shell weights, using experimentally derived conversion ratios. Cohen and Tveskov (2008) found that shellfish (primarily California mussel) accounted for 80% of the meat represented by faunal remains, followed by mammals (14%, mostly California sea lion). Fish accounted from less than 5%, and birds less than 1%.

Cohen and Tveskov (2008) report that Tseriadun may have been abandoned as a permanent Native settlement before the 1850s, but was used by the U.S. Army as an internment camp to hold Natives during the Rogue River War before they were sent to the Coast Reservation in northern Oregon. They also note that in this area, "White settlement and the decimation of Oregon's

Native people occurred with alarming suddenness; the first White American pioneer landed in the vicinity of Tseriadun in 1851, and by 1856—a mere five years later—a majority of the Indian people of what is today Curry County had either been killed by war or disease or removed to a distant reservation."

Excavations at the Bandon Sandspit site (35CS5) were carried out in 1952 by a University of Oregon crew. Limited reporting of the initial fieldwork was published (Cressman 1953); more thorough reporting followed decades later. The site was actively eroding when visited in 1952, and now appears to be gone (Tveskov 2000a, 2000b).

Excavations revealed the remains of at least two small plank houses, each with multiple occupation floors. Complete architectural details were not preserved, but one structure appears to have been about 5 meters square, with three wood posts (probable ridge supports, 10–20 centimeters diameter) along the house centerline. A second house may have been partially burned; it had horizontal planks set on edge around the perimeter of the excavated floor, which braced tightly placed vertical plank walls. A fire pit was at one end.

The artifact assemblage included small barbed and triangular concave base arrow points, blue schist adze blades, stone pestles, a girdled stone net weight, a shallow steatite bowl (probably an oil lamp), unilaterally barbed bone harpoon heads, and bone points and toggles from composite harpoons (Connolly 1986:103). Faunal remains reflect a diverse diet, including sea birds, fish (herring, perches, sturgeon, halibut, cod, rockfish, and salmon), and both terrestrial and marine mammals (whale, seals and sea lions, otters, elk, deer, bear, and several fragments of domestic cow.

Radiocarbon dating and historic artifacts indicate that the site was occupied during the last millennium and into the latter half of the nineteenth century. Hundreds of blue and amber glass trade beads, a rolled copper bead, and two clay pipe stems (manufactured in Glasgow, Scotland and consistent with pipes found at Fort Vancouver), confirm occupation during the nineteenth-century fur-trade era.

The largest Native community complex on the lower Coquille River, K'ama'cdun Village, is located on the estuary about three miles above the mouth. Recorded as a complex of archaeological sites, including the Philpott site (35CS1), the Bullards Beach State Park sites (35CS2 and 35CS3), and the Osprey Weir site (35CS130), this is the most extensively studied archaeological complex in the original territory of the Coos and Coquille. Projects have included the excavation of three plank houses (Leatherman and Krieger 1940), the recovery of burials threatened by imminent river erosion (Harrison 1977; Ross 1976), the mapping of an extensive complex of wood-stake fish weirs on the tidal mud flats (Byram and Erlandson 1996; Byram and Witter 2000; Tveskov 2000b; Byram 2002), and other archaeological studies (Draper 1982, 1988; Roth and Hall 1995; Byram et al. 1997).

The village stretched along the north side of the Coquille River; a former landowner, Howard Bullard, recalled a dozen or more housepit depressions on the Bullard property (Hall 1995:110). Three houses were excavated in 1938; two fully excavated structures measured about 4x5 meters in size (fig. 4.25). Floors were excavated into the dune sand, and walls of horizontal cedar planks were partially preserved (Leatherman and Krieger 1940:21). Sites 35CS1, -2, and -3, recorded in 1951 (Collins 1951), included midden deposits, multiple housepit depressions, and wood posts "that suggest a fish weir." In 1974 Ross (1976) removed three human burials that had been exposed in eroding bank exposures. Ross reported two temporal components; an older shell midden radiocarbon dated to about 890 cal. BP, and an upper midden (with which the burials were associated) containing historic artifacts including some 1,200 glass trade beads thought to date from the early nineteenth century. An additional burial was removed in 1976 (Harrison 1977). Further test excavations

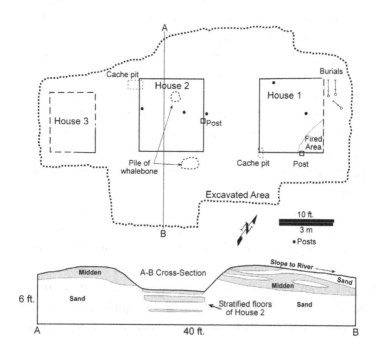

4.25 Pit houses at the Bullards Beach site (after Leatherman & Krieger 1940)

were done at the site in 1995 (Roth and Hall 1995). Detailed analysis of bulk samples recovered at this time indicate that California mussel and giant acorn barnacle were the dominant shellfish species present, while a large and diverse assemblage of fish bone was dominated by herring and salmon, with perch, greenlings, sculpins, rockfish, and flatfish well represented (Losey 1996; Roth and Hall 1995).

Stretching upstream from Bullards is a large complex of wood-stake alignments preserved in the mudflats and exposed during minus tides. At least 28 separate weir features (incorporating more than 3,000 stakes), and eleven pieces of open-twined fence panels representing fish trap components have been recorded (Tveskov 2000b; Byram 1998, 2002; Ivy and Byram 2001). Many of the alignments overlap, an indication that weirs were rebuilt multiple times. Most alignments at the west end of the complex are oriented northwesterly, and most at the east end are oriented northeasterly; these may be arms of large V-shaped weirs built at the mouth of a tidal tributary slough (Byram 2002). Several non-linear stake or post features may represent trap anchors or pilings used to tie up canoes. Seven radiocarbon ages taken from wood samples throughout the complex range from ca. 850 to less than 200 cal. BP, but four cluster in the 650–500 cal. BP time period.

Although it was originally thought that weirs were used for the seasonal mass harvest of salmon, the mesh size of the woven fence panels, a consideration of ethnographic sources, and analysis of fish bone in cultural middens indicate that weirs were used and maintained regularly throughout the year, and produced a continuous, predictable food supply consisting of a wide range of large and small fish species. Byram (1998:215) observes that the fine gauge (with openings averaging 9 mm wide) of the woven fences recovered from the Coquille estuary require considerably more effort to make than coarser structures would, suggesting that small fish were intentionally targeted.

At the upstream end of the weir complex is a large midden (the Philpott site, 35CS1) that may represent a fishing camp used opportunistically throughout the year. Analysis of bulk samples recovered from the site in 1997 indicate that fish (herring, salmon, sculpins, and a large quantity of unidentifiable small fish bone) contributed more than 86% of calculated meat weight; the balance is represented by a trace of shellfish, and mostly small and unidentifiable fragments of mammal bone (Losey 1996; Tveskov 2000b; Draper 1988). The 1997 research also provided information about the site history; the midden appears to have accumulated on a levee that began forming within the last 800 years. A wood-stake weir feature, radiocarbon dated to 800 cal. BP, had been previously built on a mudflat beneath the levee/midden deposits. The growth of this levee may be due to tectonic uplift, but Byram and Witter (2000) suggest that sediment accumulation causing gradual downstream migration of the estuary during the last millennium may be responsible for this localized change.

K'ama'cdun is noted numerous times in historic accounts, and its demise is also well documented. In the early 1850s, tensions were escalating between the Coquille Indians and the increasing number of white settlers and miners. In early 1854 a vigilante group (the "Coos County Volunteers") about 40 in number attacked several settlements without warning, including K'ama'cdun. Eighteen Indian men and women were killed, and their homes burned. Indian agent F. M. Smith characterized the attack as "out and out barbarous murder" [letter to Joel Palmer, Oregon Supt. of Indian Affairs]. Nonetheless, the rampage went unchecked, and at least six more Coquille Indians were found dead during the following week. Likely in retaliation for the ongoing murders, the bodies of two white men were found floating in the Coquille River. In response, several Indians were hanged for the killing of the white men. There were no consequences for the killings of nearly 30 Coquille Indians.

Late Holocene Cultural Patterns. The patterns that made the Northwest Coast a distinctive cultural area are clearly present within the last ca. 3,000 years; among these is the development of permanent settlements with substantial plank houses. Permanent settlements are concentrated about the mouths and lower courses of tidal streams, particularly in resource-rich tidal estuaries. More than 80 wood-stake weir sites have been recorded in Oregon coast estuaries, which confirm the central importance of these structures to native economies. Most weirs are simple or converging fences set to direct fish in tidal channels to traps, or designed to strand fish on mudflats behind the outgoing tide; nonetheless, their construction and maintenance implies proprietary interest by nearby communities, consistent with the concept of ownership and status tied to resource holdings such as productive fisheries. Anthropologists have historically focused on the importance of salmon fishing on the Northwest Coast, but oral testimony and archaeological evidence make clear that a great variety of large and small fish were harvested. Estuarine fishing that included the construction of fish weirs was regarded "as part of the day-to-day productive activities of individual households, and all members of a family (including children) would participate in their construction and use" (Tveskov and Erlandson 2003:1025; also Byram 1998, 2002).

The plank house was not just a family base, but the headquarters of an extended family "estate" that served as a central storage facility for foods harvested and processed throughout the year (Ames 1996). Many methods of taking and preserving great quantities of periodically abundant foods were employed: for marine fishes, for example, nets, hook and line, and harpoons, as well as weirs and tidal traps were used. Social stratification with social ranking based on inherited status, wealth, and resource holdings, as well as the emergence of distinctive art traditions, are also prominent features of the late Holocene, most visibly along the lower Columbia and north coast, and on Oregon's south coast. Particularly for the Chinook area of the lower Columbia, the presence of large-scale facilities for the production and storage of surplus food and goods—in the absence of traditional farming and domesticated livestock—challenges the traditional intellectual link between agriculture and social complexity (Ames et al. 2008).

Distinct cultural zones are apparent along the Oregon coast. These zones correspond broadly with the distribution of language families. On the lower Columbia and northern Oregon coast, within the Chinook (Penutian) and Salish language areas, village communities included one or more large multifamily plank houses. In this area, household size is seen to reflect the organized labor of large corporate kin groups, and to indicate relative household status and wealth (Ames and Maschner 1999). At the Palmrose site, a large plank house measures at least 6x12 meters; houses at the Netarts Sandspit site were of comparable size or larger (up to 1.8 meters long). The Meier site plank house was 35 meters long by nearly 14 meters wide, and a house at Cathlapotle, on the Washington side of the Columbia opposite the Meier site, was reportedly more than 60 meters long. A well-developed representational art style, expressed in embellished objects made of bone and stone, is also notably present, and links this area with closely parallel forms in the Puget Sound/Lower Fraser River/Gulf of Georgia region of northwest Washington and southern British Columbia.

Large multifamily houses are not found on the southern Oregon coast; rather, houses averaging about 4–5 meters a side were typical. Walls were built of vertically-set planks. A community might consist of just a few scattered houses, but Chetlessenten, a town at the mouth of the Pistol River, had nearly 50 homes (Heflin 1966; Erlandson et al. 1997). South of the Coquille River–Coos Bay area, and continuing into northern California within the Athapaskan language area, a consistent set of artifacts known as the archaeological Gunther Pattern is found. Gunther Pattern assemblages appear archaeologically within the last 1,700 years (and later as one proceeds north from the California border); they likely mark first an immigration of Athapaskan speakers from the far northern Northwest Coast to northern California, then their spreading influence in a northerly direction along the southern Oregon coast.

Archaeology of the Historic Period

The Lewis and Clark expedition was seminal in the history of western North America, and Fort Clatsop, where the party lived during the winter of 1805–06, remains an important symbol of their accomplishments. A series of investigations, beginning ca. 1857 and continuing through to recent years, has attempted to locate archaeological traces of the fort, using excavation and ground imaging techniques such as magnetometry (Caywood 1948; Garnett 1995; Stein et al. 2006). Numerous pits and amorphous fire features have been identified that may relate to the 1805–06 occupation, but later disturbances (land clearing, plowing, etc.) have been extensive and the origin and association of many of the features remains uncertain. A few probable period artifacts have been recovered, including a cast brass bead with a chemical composition typical of the 1793–1820 period, a small lead musket ball, and a faceted blue glass bead.

Evidence for contact between Indians and non-Natives has been noted at the Athapaskan towns of Chetlessenten and K'ama'cdun, and at the Bandon Sandspit and Netarts Sandspit sites. The presence of a Chinese coin at Chetlessenten suggests possible contact with immigrant Chinese gold miners in the early 1850s. An abundance of items of Asian origin, including fragments of Chinese and Japanese porcelain, teak artifacts, and large quantities of beeswax blocks (which analysis confirms contain pollen of Asian origin) have been found in the Tillamook area, principally about the mouth of Nehalem Bay. Analysis of the porcelain items suggests they were likely made between about 1650 and 1700 (with a mean ceramic date of 1686), (Beals and Steele 1981; Lally 2008). The "Nehalem beeswax ship," as the carrier of these items has come to be known, was probably a Spanish trade ship that wrecked, and historic records suggest the probable candidates all foundered near the turn of the seventeenth century (Erlandson et al. 2001; Williams 2008; the mostly likely is the *Santo Christo de Burgos,* lost in 1693 [Lally 2008]). The convergence of half a dozen radiocarbon dates on beeswax, a teak cane, and a wooden rigging block found in the Nehalem area, all items consistent with those used on seventeenth-century Spanish vessels, seem to suggest an earlier shipwreck in the Nehalem area about A.D. 1630–1640. But the earlier radiocarbon ages may reflect dating of artifacts made from the heartwood of trees that would have returned ages decades older than sapwood from the same trees, formed nearer the time the trees were actually cut.

For 250 years, from 1565 to 1815, Spanish galleons sailed the Pacific Ocean annually (and sometimes semi-annually) between Acapulco in Spanish America and Manila in the Philippines. Ships sailing from Manila generally crossed the Pacific around 40 degrees north latitude before turning south to follow the coast down to Mexico; Erlandson et al. (2001:51) observe that, of what was likely scores of galleons that passed along the Oregon coast, some "almost certainly made contact with Oregon coast tribes." This was clearly so for the Nehalem beeswax ship; memories of the ship have been recorded in at least one Native account, and the Tillamook Chief Kilchis was said to be descended from a survivor of the wreck (Erlandson et al. 2001).

As seen at Chetlessenten and K'ama'cdun, the appearance of sites in the historic record can significantly enhance the archaeological evidence. Tribal histories have also been important in contextualizing the cultural record of Oregon's coast. Byram (2008) has explored a series of violent conflicts that occurred in 1832 between Hudson's Bay Company fur trappers and the Alsea and Yaquina of the central Oregon coast, based on HBC correspondence and Native accounts. In the HBC record, the destruction of a Native village and the killing of six men were justified by the killing of two trappers. In the Native accounts, the trappers were killed by members of the Alsea tribe, but in retaliation an entire Yaquina village—including up to 400 men, women, and children—was destroyed. The inhabitants of the village, probably the largest Yaquina community at the time, may not even have been aware of the killings that triggered their demise.

A Native account also explains the archaeological record at Whaleshead Cove, located a few miles north of Lone Ranch Creek. Berreman (1944:11) explored the Whaleshead Cove site (35CU35) while working at Lone Ranch, and his reporting of the site is limited to finding "nothing markedly different from the Lone Ranch site," but he noted that much of the site may have been "partly covered up by slides from the high bluff behind it." Apart from Berreman's unreported work, no systematic excavations have been done at

Whaleshead Cove, but radiocarbon samples have been taken from middens visible in eroding sea cliffs (Connolly et al. 2008; Moss and Erlandson 1994). In one exposure, a cultural shell midden was observed deeply buried beneath a poorly sorted layer of cobbly loam, probably representing landslide debris. The midden returned a date of ca. A.D. 1480, suggesting that a landslide event occurred about A.D. 1500 or later. This event, confirmed archaeologically, was recalled by Coquelle Thompson to John P. Harrington (1942: Reel 26, frame 799): "There was a big Indian town there [at Chetco]. An old woman living there was pretty observing. One morning she said: I see no smoke come out of that ra[ncheria?] upcoast. Men went at once in canoes upcoast, and to their wonderment found that the village had been buried in the night by a slide. They said [there are no people]. The mountain had come down and an avalanche had buried the whole village . . . ."

The discovery of gold in southwest Oregon was a major catalyst in the Euroamerican settlement of the region; the town of Gold Beach takes its name from the discovery of gold in the local beach sands, and the community became a center for placer mining. These newcomers brought infectious diseases that decimated the Natives, and new towns and gold mining operations displaced them from their traditional gathering, fishing, and hunting areas. Euroamerican settlement of the Port Orford area began with a particularly inauspicious interaction between Natives and the new immigrants; on June 9, 1851, land speculator William Tichenor landed a party of nine men with the hopes of establishing a town near the natural harbor that would serve as a base to supply the mining camps in the interior. These men were to lay out a townsite and search for a trail into the mountains. With Tichenor promising to return with more men and supplies in two weeks time, the men settled on what is now known as Battle Rock, armed with a few rifles and a small cannon. The following morning, a group of curious Natives gathered at the rock; the outnumbered whites, thinking the worst, fired the cannon into the gathered Indians, killing about 30. The landing party held out on Battle Rock for fourteen days, killing one more man during that time. When Tichenor failed to return as expected, the nine men escaped Battle Rock at low tide and made their way north to Umpqua City (Beckham 1971; Peterson and Powers 1977).

Work at the new townsite progressed, and in August 1851 a party of men under William T'Vault left Port Orford to seek an overland route to the interior valleys. This mission failed due to the dense brush and rugged terrain, and several members of the party were killed by Indians on the lower Coquille

River. Upon learning of the T'Vault party deaths, the U.S. Army dispatched two companies of mounted soldiers to launch an offensive against the Indians of the Coquille River. Although the Indians had fled their estuary villages, the dragoons pursued them up the river where they met in a skirmish that killed about 15 Indians and two U.S. soldiers. The troops stayed on, and established Fort Orford on the headland near the nascent Port Orford community. From 1852 to 1855 the army maintained a small presence at this modest outpost. Growing hostility in southwest Oregon between the Indians and an ever-growing number of whites, many committed to extermination of the Natives (Wilkinson 2010), finally erupted into open conflict in 1855, and Fort Orford became a principal supply depot for military operations during the Rogue River War. At the close of hostilities, the fort served as an incarceration center for Indians bound for removal to the Coast Reservation.

Archaeological testing of the fort site was conducted in 1979 (Minor et al. 1980). It was found that urban development had destroyed much of the fort, but of fifteen structures documented on an 1855 map, remains of at least seven were identified. Remains of a large fireplace with a foundation of dry-stacked boulders were located, and thought to be associated with either a cookhouse or barracks. Recovered artifacts included cut nails, ironstone and stoneware ceramics, and glass fragments of liquor and medicine bottles, pane glass, and oil lamp chimneys. Personal items included ceramic pipe fragments, clothing buckles, and military shirt buttons of metal and glass. It was also discovered that the fort was partly built on a more ancient Native harvesting and food processing camp. A radiocarbon age of ca. 2000 cal. BP was recovered from the base of the cultural deposit. Food remains include shellfish (dominated by mussels, littleneck and gaper claims, and barnacles), sea lions, and some marine fishes (Minor et al. 1980).

The 1855–56 Rogue River War erupted when the Indians' efforts to maintain their homeland with diplomacy were frustrated. Following a series of violent conflicts and retaliations in 1853, treaty negotiations established the Table Rock Reservation, but the underlying resentments persisted. In October of 1855 an agitator for Indian extermination (and newly elected representative to the Territorial Legislature), James Lupton, led a group of vigilantes in an attack on a small band of Indians, resulting in an estimated 40 dead, mostly women, children, and old men (Schwartz 1997:85; Wilkinson 2010:199). Retaliation was swift; several bands of Indians swept downriver and along the Oregon-California road, killing and burning, leaving dozens dead (estimates range from about 30 to more than 100) over a period of several days. The final phase of the Rogue River War had begun.

War in the Rogue River basin brought anxiety along the adjacent coast. Some Gold Beach settlers, along with a group of local miners camped north of the river, built a fortification near the camp that came to be known as "Fort Miner," consisting of two log structures surrounded by a water-filled ditch and earthen rampart (Dodge 1898; Beckham 1971). Word of spreading hostilities reached Gold Beach in February 1956, and the community retreated to Fort Miner, where they stayed for a month. Several miles north of Gold Beach was the homestead of the John and Christina Geisel family. By 1856 they had built a new two-story, twelve-room home that served as a hotel, along with a large nearby building used as a store and three one-room "miner's cabins." During an attack by Indians on February 22, 1856, John and three sons were killed, and their home was burned with the bodies of all four inside. Christina was later interred at the site as well, following her tragic murder in 1899 (Dodge 1898; Tasa et al. 2004). This homestead and cemetery are recorded as archaeological site 35CU232.

Although the village of Tseriadun, near modern-day Port Orford, may have been abandoned prior to 1850, the site's proximity to the army's Fort Orford made it a convenient holding camp during the spring and summer of 1856 for Indian internees, prior to their removal to the Coast Reservation. Despite the presence of an estimated 1,500 Indians, the relatively short occupation left only a light, though discernable archaeological signature. Cohen and Tveskov (2008) identified a diffuse scatter of mid-nineteenth century artifacts, including glass beads, bottle glass, and a ceramic pipe of European manufacture. Food was mostly provided by the U.S. government, but small shell midden deposits indicate that internees also relied on traditional hunting, shellfish gathering, and inshore fishing practices.

While most southwest Oregon Indians were removed north to the Coast Reservation following the Rogue River War, some Native women escaped removal by virtue of marriages to white men. Others escaped the reservation to return to their homelands, where they lived in hiding among these relatives (Bensell 1959; Tveskov 2000b, 2007; Wasson 1994, 2001). The number of off-reservation Indians may have also grown following the close of the Alsea Subagency in 1876; rather than removing to the remnants of the Coast Reservation, they had "dropped off the edge of the earth [with respect to agency oversight] and had been left to shift for themselves as homeless indigents" (Schwartz 1991:257).

One off-reservation refuge was South Slough, a southern arm of Coos Bay. Among its advantages was isolation from populated places on other portions of Coos Bay; here, Indians who had managed to escape the reservation round-ups remained largely invisible to their non-Indian neighbors. Although marginally participating in the dominant economy as laborers, or by selling fish and hand-made baskets, for these people traditional subsistence practices remained vitally important. Tveskov (2000b) has documented the continuity of subsistence traditions from ancient times into the twentieth century by archaeological work at the Graveyard Point site (35CU142). Dating from at least 1,300 years ago, the upper levels of the site contain a robust assemblage of Euroamerican goods that indicate continued use into "the latter half of the nineteenth century and the first decades of the twentieth century—an occupation dating after the removal of most of the Coos and Coquille to the Coast Reservation in 1856" (Tveskov 2000b:478). The most common items were machine-cut nails, in common use before the turn of the twentieth century, and bottle glass of many types dating from as early as the 1840s to the early 1900s. Accompanying these materials were the remains of shellfish, fish, birds, and game that closely matched the earlier subsistence profile, and "point to the importance of traditional subsistence activities after 1856" (Tveskov 2000b:488). Tveskov observes that without the iron nails, bottle glass, ceramics, and other items, the later occupations would not be notably different from the pre-contact components.

The lower Siuslaw was another place of refuge for off-reservation Indians. When initially established by Executive Order in 1855, the Siletz (Coast) Reservation stretched from Cape Lookout on the north to Siltcoos Lake on the south, including the drainage of the Siuslaw River. The southern portion of the reservation (Alsea River to Siltcoos Lake) was administered from Fort Umpqua (Umpqua Subagency). Subagent Edwin P. Drew wrote, in July of 1857 (Drew 1859), that his charge included "the Siuslaw and Alsea bands located on the Siuslaw River, numbering about two hundred and forty." Many of the Coos and Umpqua were removed to the agency farm at the mouth of the Yachats River, but others simply moved to the Siuslaw, then within the reservation boundaries. In 1875 Congress opened lands of the Alsea Subagency for settlement, and Euroamerican settlers poured in. While many of the Natives in the Alsea district gave up their homes and fled to Siletz, many of the Coos, Lower Umpqua, and Siuslaw residing there reunited with their Siuslaw relatives.

In 1942 linguist and ethnographer John Peabody Harrington (affiliated with the Smithsonian Institution's Bureau of American Ethnology) recorded information on the language and culture of the Coos, Lower Umpqua, and Siuslaw while he resided at the home of informant Frank H. Drew near the mouth of the North Fork Siuslaw. Here he gathered information from Drew and other Native residents, including Cary Barrett, Jim Buchanon, Andrew Charles, and Spencer Scott. Andrew Charles told Harrington (1942[23]: 435) that "They [the Siuslaws] had about five or six villages and then each village had a head man, or chief." The most frequently mentioned village in the Harrington notes is located at the mouth of the North Fork. Associated with this community is a weir complex that was repeatedly described to Harrington. A typical account is that of Frank Drew (Harrington 1942[23]:480): "There is a mudflat in the Main River . . . [location omitted] . . . at which spot they used to catch fish and fish-traps—they had several fishtraps there.

Remains of several weirs can still be found in the Siuslaw estuary during extreme low tides. The largest, known as the Half Moon Weir (site 35LA1104), includes the remains of more than 1,500 vertical wood stakes (most of those examined have sharpened bases) and dozens of horizontal elements (Byram 1998, 2002; Erlandson and Moss 1993). Stakes are generally 2–5 centimeters in diameter, and include both "rounds" (whole small tree limbs) and split stakes (probably cedar). Overlapping runs of stakes indicate that the weir was maintained or rebuilt over some period of time (fig. 4.26). Three radiocarbon-dated stakes all indicate ages within the last ca. 300 years for some elements. Site 35LA1108, located about a half mile from 35LA1104, was built of splits from milled lumber. Both weirs were evidently in active use during the late nineteenth and early twentieth centuries.

Minor (1994) reported on a small late-nineteenth-century Native settlement (site 35CLT86) near the mouth of Neacoxie Creek at the Necanicum River estuary in modern Seaside. The site produced a great number of glass trade beads, as well as porcelain and metal buttons, glass bottle fragments, crockery, cut nails, pane glass, coins (one with a legible date of 1839) and a presidential campaign token from 1841. The range of artifacts, with both domestic items and structural remains, suggests residential use by a Native individual or family. A majority of the datable artifacts indicate a period of use during the second half of the nineteenth century, between ca. 1850 and 1890. Historic sources indicate that a group of Clatsop Indians lived near the mouth of the Necanicum River during this period; descendants of this group continue to reside in the area today (Minor 1994).

Fig. 4.26. View along one side of the remains of a V-shaped weir built in a tidal channel of the Siuslaw estuary.

Kathlamet Village (35CLT35), located on Aldrich Point about 30 miles above the mouth of the Columbia, was one of several settlements of a larger community also collectively known as the Kathlamet. Lewis and Clark noted that this Native town consisted of nine plank houses and estimated a population of 300. In subsequent decades, introduced diseases reduced the Kathlamet so precipitously that later ethnographers reported the village as abandoned by 1810 and considered the community either extinct or as an indistinct part of a broadly defined Lower Chinook population (e.g., Ray 1938). By contrast, archaeological work at the Aldrich Point village site indicates that a remnant Kathlamet community continued to live at the site well into the mid-nineteenth century. Evidence includes a robust collection of introduced trade goods, including lead musket balls, metal artifacts such as projectile points and bangles, thimbles, rolled copper beads, rings, and buttons. Items dating from the mid-nineteenth century or later include Phoenix buttons, thought to have been introduced to the region in the early 1830s, clay pipes imported from Glasgow after 1848, and pipes brought from France that may not have been available in the Pacific Northwest before ca. 1860. Some of the large collection of glass beads may not have been available on the lower Columbia before the middle of the nineteenth century (Minor 1983; Minor and Burgess 2009).

On the northern Oregon coast in Lincoln County, replacement of the Highway 101 bridge over Spencer Creek led to investigation of the Spencer

Creek Bridge site (35LNC95). The western portion of the site is exposed along an eroding sea cliff. The ancient sandstone that underlies the site tilts gradually upward from north to south; by contrast, the site deposits appear to be level, and the southern edge of the site terminates abruptly. From this, it appears that the surface had been intentionally formed by means of a modest excavation into the hill slope, probably to accommodate a small structure backed into the hill. A test pit excavated near the edge of the sea cliff produced cultural materials including charcoal, fire-cracked rock, calcined bone fragments (identifiable only as medium-sized mammal), and chert flakes, all consistent with a Native American food processing camp. A soil sample for flotation analysis was collected from the central area where the organic staining was most intense. Charcoal was the only botanical material recovered; that is, no charred seeds or processed edible tissues were identified. The charcoal was notably diverse, being dominated by pine and spruce, but also including western redcedar, Douglas-fir, and alder. Approximately 15% of the charcoal (by weight) was unidentifiable due to its vitrified (glassy) appearance. Vitrified charcoal is often the result of wood that was burned when it was green. In a cultural setting such as site 35LNC95, and particularly in association with a quantity of fire-cracked rock, the burning of green wood suggests intentional creation of the smoky fires used to process fish or meat for long-term storage (Bland et al. 2005; Connolly et al. 2008).

Also recovered from throughout the cultural levels were heavy ferrous pieces corroded beyond recognition. This combination of material suggests an occupation in the post-contact era, and could relate to an early reservation-era camp. Following the Rogue River War, southwest Oregon tribes were forcibly removed from their home territory and resettled at the Siletz Agency. Among those resettled were John Spencer and his family, members of the Chetco tribe who were relocated to the Siletz Agency from the southern Oregon coast. Although there are no clear records from the period for the decades immediately following establishment of the reservation, John Spencer was granted an allotment, in 1894, at the mouth of the creek that now bears his family name. John Spencer received a clear title to his allotment, which included the area of site 35LNC95, in 1907.

The Dawes Act, passed by the U.S. Congress in 1887, was purportedly aimed at creating responsible farmers in the Euroamerican tradition. This would be accomplished by assigning land parcel title to individual Indians. The corollary social impacts included a reduction in the influence of tribal communities and traditions, and the releasing of "surplus" (unallotted) tribal lands for settlement by non-Indians (within decades following the passage of the act, the vast majority of what had been tribal land in the West was in non-Indian hands). Although the stated goals of the Dawes Act included the establishment of individual farms, most lands allotted to coastal Indians in Oregon were not tillable land; of lands allotted on the Coast Reservation between 1887 and 1904, an estimated 12.6% was classed as tillable (Schwartz 2010). During this same period, the reservation was reduced from 225,000 acres to 3,600 acres, removing this land asset from Indian control. Elsewhere along the coast, Indians lost allotted lands and associated resources, sometimes in less than honest dealings with non-Indian businessmen (Ivy 2001). Since farming wasn't a viable option for most, many Indians continued traditional subsistence practices of hunting, gathering, and fishing. Based on the age of the Spencer Creek site, it may be associated with the Spencer family, and may represent the persistence of traditional subsistence practices in the late 1800s following establishment of the Coast Reservation.

Many ships have wrecked on the Oregon coast in addition to the beeswax ship noted previously (Woodward 1986). One of Oregon's best known is the *Peter Iredale*, a four-masted steel sailing ship built in 1890 that wrecked on Clatsop beach in 1906. Storm waves during the winter of 2007–08 exposed the remains of the *George L. Olson*, a 223-foot-long wood-hulled schooner that hauled lumber between coastal ports from 1917 to 1944, when it ran aground on Coos Bay's North Jetty. During that storm season two cannons were found near Arch Cape, south of Cannon Beach. These are thought to be from the *USS Shark*, a U.S. survey schooner that sank when trying to cross the Columbia bar in 1846. The community was named after an 1898 discovery of one of the cannons from this wreck. The Oregon Department of Parks and Recreation has since removed the cannons so that they can undergo restoration.

Another notable shipwreck is probably the *Great Republic*, a sidewheel steamboat lost in 1879. The wreck was discovered in 1986, and a team of underwater archaeologists tentatively identified it initially as the remains of the *Isabella*, a cargo ship lost in 1830 while carrying goods to Fort Vancouver for the Hudson Bay Company. The *Isabella* site was listed on the National Register of Historic Places, and investigation of the site resumed in 1996 and 2004. Shifting sands exposed much more of the vessel with each visit, revealing a number of features that brought the ship's identity into question. Finally, a sample of wood from the wreck was identified as southern yellow pine, suggesting an American-made ship rather than a British-made vessel built of northern European timber (Roberts 2008).

A review of recorded shipwrecks revealed the *Great Republic* as the most likely candidate. It grounded on Sand Island, near the mouth of the Columbia River, after leaving Portland with 1,000 passengers bound for San Francisco. Passengers were evacuated to Astoria while the crew unsuccessfully attempted to refloat the vessel. When it began to break up, the last 14 men abandoned ship, but their boat capsized, resulting in 11 deaths (Roberts 2008).

Oregon's natural resource wealth was a lure for rapid industrial development during the later nineteenth century. The state's salmon canning industry began in 1866, and by 1883 there were 39 canneries along the Columbia River. Their profitability was based on highly efficient fish wheels (water-powered nets that scooped migrating salmon into a holding bin) and cheap processing labor. The Warrendale cannery (site 35MU53) operated from 1876 to 1930, when fish wheels were outlawed in Oregon due to declining fish stocks. Chinese immigrants and sojourners provided the bulk of the labor force for the cannery; apart from census and business records, there is little documentary evidence on the lives of the Chinese workers. Archaeological investigations conducted at the cannery site revealed dense concentrations of Chinese ceramics and other domestic refuse east of the pilings on which the cannery sat, while American and English pottery dominated the area to the west, signaling ethnic segregation (Fagan 1993; Reese 1989).

An abundance of imported Chinese materials was present in the Chinese residence area, including brown stoneware shipping and storage jars, ceramic liquor jars, Chinese cups, bowls, sauce dishes, and teapots, opium tins, glass gaming pieces, and other artifacts. Historic photos and surviving concrete footings indicate that the Chinese bunkhouse was a two-story structure measuring about 8.5x15 meters. Archaeological study of on-site debris identified the location of the activity areas, kitchen and related disposal areas, garden, and rock-walled terraces that served as sites for ancillary structures (bathing and toilet areas, a pigpen, etc.). Evidence suggests that acculturation to American ways was superficial; while both Chinese and American alcoholic beverages were consumed, and buttons and other hardware indicate that American-made clothes and footwear were often used, the Chinese residence area was an enclave where the workers could live and work within a traditional Chinese community, maintaining their own culture and language. During off-hours they engaged in traditional games and relaxed with opium. Traditional foods were prepared in familiar ways, using traditional utensils and cooking techniques, and eaten from familiar dishes (Fagan 1993; Reese 1989).

Lumber was also an important industry throughout the Coast Range area, and many large and small operators emerged. In his *History of Benton County*, Fagan (1885:499) noted that the Alsea Valley "abounds in timber. Not far from the head of the valley, David Ruble has a flouring-mill and saw-mill as well, while, at the head of the South Fork of the Alsea River . . . are two more saw mills, the lumber of which is transported over the mountains and into the Willamette Valley." Ancient stumps with the scars of springboards, on which loggers stood while using big crosscut saws, are found throughout Oregon's coastal forests.

During the first decades of the twentieth century, the Coast Range was penetrated by short-line logging railroads. During archaeological study for a bridge replacement project near the small community of Mist in the Nehalem Valley, the remains of an early-twentieth-century logging railroad camp and associated grades were identified (35CO61). The camp and grades were built by the Kerry Timber and Logging Company between ca. 1917 and 1925. The grade west of the camp was from a branch leaving the main line of the Columbia & Nehalem River Railroad, better known as the Kerry Line (after company head Albert S. Kerry). Like other logging main lines, the Kerry Line was built to high engineering and construction standards, with heavy rail and hardware. Branch and spur lines that radiated out into the woods from the main line were considered temporary; they were built to more modest standards, with lighter rails, steeper gradients, and less robust earthwork.

The camp itself was built on stilts above the ground, as it bordered an elevated trestle approach at the Nehalem River crossing. The site's cultural assemblage was dominated by wire nails, institutional ceramic tableware ("hotel ware"), and glass. Nails were used for both the camp's elevated structures and the supporting scaffolding. Glass artifacts included an oil lamp chimney, a patent medicine bottle, and pane glass. The ceramic fragments include pieces of plates, bowls, cups, and other tableware that likely represents debris from a crew mess facility. Several pieces bore the stamp of the W. S. George Pottery Co., which produced wares under the W. S. George trade name from 1904 to the late 1950s (Lehner 1988). Railroad and logging gear was also recovered, including brake shoes, rails spikes, and bolts. Based on the size of bolts and rail spikes found east and west of the camp, it appears that the line to the camp was built with heavier rail than the line beyond the camp. In other words, it appears that the line to the camp, from the Kerry main line, was built to mid-range branch standards, while the multiple lines continuing east of the camp were built to a lower spur standard (Bland et al. 2009).

Summary

Rising sea levels and a dynamic, high-energy coast present significant challenges for Oregon coast archaeology. The surviving record is strongly biased to within the last ca. 1,500 years, and it is certain that scores of ancient occupation sites have disappeared due to erosion and rising sea levels. Human presence along the Oregon coast is confirmed by at least 8,000 years ago, but evidence from Pacific coasts to the north and south (and possible evidence from the Oregon coast itself) assure us that people were present thousands of years earlier. At present, too little is known about the earliest coastal residents, but general cultural patterns likely paralleled those of adjacent areas. Regionally, it appears that early populations were relatively low, and people were highly mobile, moving frequently from one resource patch to another without establishing permanent residential bases.

The earliest houses currently known appear in the middle Holocene, between 5,000 and 4,000 years ago, about the time that substantial shell midden accumulations begin to regularly appear. These features reflect an increasingly settled habit—a fundamental change in the way people relate to their environment and one involving both risks and rewards. The advantages of high mobility include relatively high reward and low risk, by maintaining the option to take best advantage of optimal resource bounty wherever it presents itself. Increasing population density was certainly a factor in the shift away from this way of life. Sedentism entails a commitment to a particular geography, and is generally accompanied by the need to extract more food efficiently from a smaller resource area. One strategy to accomplish this end is to harvest more at times of great abundance, and to process and store food for later use. This strategy requires a central place to maintain food stores; this function, perhaps even more than a requirement for shelter, is a critical factor behind the establishment of substantial, and at least semi-permanent, houses.

The elements of the distinctive Northwest Coast culture area (see the sidebar at the beginning of the chapter) emerged fully within the last ca. 3,000 years, including permanent settlements with substantial plank houses and associated structures such as community weirs. These sometimes impressive constructions establish both claims to specific geographies and exclusive rights of access.

The discovery of gold in southwest Oregon in 1851 brought miners by the thousands; many were openly hostile to the resident Indians, and their activities seriously damaged or destroyed age-old resources on which the Native population had long been reliant. These conflicts flared into the Rogue River War, which ultimately brought to an end the Indians' hold on their traditional homelands. The Coast (or Siletz) Reservation was established in 1855, with boundaries extending from Cape Lookout in the north to a point south of the Siuslaw River. These boundaries allowed many central and north coast groups (the Alsea, Yaquina, Siuslaw, and others) to retain residency in their traditional homelands for a time, but southwest Oregon tribes were forcibly removed from their home territory and resettled at the Siletz Agency following the Rogue River War. In 1865 President Andrew Johnson opened 200,000 acres of the reservation for white settlement. Another 700,000 acres of reservation lands were opened for settlement in 1875. With each reduction, the Indians were removed to the diminishing remainder of the Siletz Agency.

In 1954 the Siletz and other Oregon coast tribes were legally "terminated"; their remaining reservation lands, their status as sovereign tribal governments, and their tribal identity and treaty rights were all lost. The goal of termination was to complete the assimilation of Indians into mainstream society, but it was culturally, politically, and economically damaging to the affected tribes, in some cases devastatingly so. Termination affected Oregon tribes very disproportionately since more than half of the 109 tribes and bands terminated by this federal law had their ancestral homelands in Oregon. While much had been lost through Termination, tribal identity had not. Following decades of legal challenges the Confederated Tribes of the Siletz Reservation were restored in 1977, the Confederated Tribes of Coos, Lower Umpqua, and Siuslaw were restored in 1984, and the Coquille Tribe was restored in 1989.

Economic development of the lower Columbia and the coast region in the late nineteenth and early twentieth centuries took great advantage of the region's natural resources, including timber and fish. Archaeology is making contributions to our understanding of social and technical details of this growth that are not visible in existing written histories.

Chapter 5
The Willamette Valley

Physical Setting

A large portion of the modern Willamette Valley floor was formed near the end of the last ice age, between about 20,000 and 15,000 cal. BP, when glacial Lake Missoula, impounded by a lobe of the Cordilleran ice sheet, repeatedly breached its ice dam and sent floods of enormous scale down the Columbia River valley to the Pacific Ocean. The constricted river channel at Kalama Gap, below the Portland Basin, temporarily caused the flow to back-flood to the southern end of the Willamette Valley. The sediment that settled from these temporarily stilled floodwaters of the "Willamette Sound" formed an undulating plain with pothole lakes, marshes, and bogs. The modern Willamette River and its tributaries negotiated their courses across this new surface.

About 20 miles wide and 100 miles long, the Willamette Valley is flanked east and west by the coniferous forests of the Cascades and Coast ranges. Prior to twentieth century agricultural land clearing, gallery forests of deciduous and evergreen trees followed the watercourses, and most of the valley floor was open grassland with scattered groves of oak (Towle 1982; Boyd 1999). The earliest writings of the valley describe an idyllic scene; Robert Stuart, an employee of John Jacob Astor's Pacific Fur Company, reported in 1811 that the valley was "delightful beyond expression," one of "the most beautiful Landscapes in nature" (Rollins 1935:32). Modern botanists acknowledge that the Willamette Valley landscape described by early trappers and farmers was anthropogenic, created and maintained by Native people using judicious controlled burning (Boyd 1999; Johannessen et al. 1971; Lewis 1990; Towle 1979). In describing the Willamette prairie in 1845, James Clyman (1960:121) recorded that he "walked out over a fine rounded ridge covered with green grass now springing up Beautifully and haveing [sic] the appearance of wheat fields in the

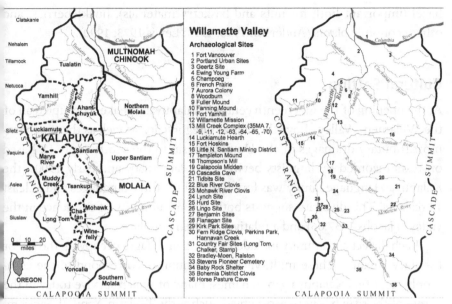

Willamette Valley
Archaeological Sites

1 Fort Vancouver
2 Portland Urban Sites
3 Geertz Site
4 Ewing Young Farm
5 Champoeg
6 French Prairie
7 Aurora Colony
8 Woodburn
9 Fuller Mound
10 Fanning Mound
11 Fort Yamhill
12 Willamette Mission
13 Mill Creek Complex (35MA 7, -9, -11, -12, -63, -64, -65, -70)
14 Luckiamute Hearth
15 Fort Hoskins
16 Little N. Santiam Mining District
17 Templeton Mound
18 Thompson's Mill
19 Calapooia Midden
20 Cascadia Cave
21 Tidbits Site
22 Blue River Clovis
23 Mohawk River Clovis
24 Lynch Site
25 Hurd Site
26 Lingo Site
27 Benjamin Sites
28 Flanagan Site
29 Kirk Park Sites
30 Fern Ridge Clovis, Perkins Park, Hannavan Creek
31 Country Fair Sites (Long Tom, Chalker, Stamp)
32 Bradley-Moen, Ralston
33 Stevens Pioneer Cemetery
34 Baby Rock Shelter
35 Bohemia District Clovis
36 Horse Pasture Cave

Fig. 5.1. Kalapuya language and dialect communities documented in the mid nineteenth century (*left*) and location of key archaeological sites (*right*).

states at this season of the year." While some early explorers complained that the extensive burning of the valley floor left them inadequate forage for their horses at some times of the year, others commented on the "wheat field"-like appearance of Oregon's western valleys (Applegate 1914:69; Riddle 1953:51; Church 1951:11); this is likely the product of intentional burning which fostered the growth of even-aged stands of seed-bearing annual plants. The bordering forests also bore the evidence of active maintenance; Charles Wilkes (1845:358) noted in 1841 that "This part of Willamette Valley is a prolonged level, of miles in extent circumscribed by the woods, which have the appearance of being attended to and kept free from undergrowth. This is difficult to account for, except for the agency of fire destroying the seeds. . . . That this is the case appears more probable from the fact that since the whites have had possession of the country [and discontinued the annual burning practiced by the Indians], the undergrowth is coming up rapidly in places."

Annual burning greatly enhanced food production in the valley; frequent burning favors the growth of certain plants over conifers and shrubs, including seed-bearing annuals and grasses, geophytes such as camas, and fire-tolerant species such as oaks—all staple foods for the Native Kalapuya. Fire was also used to manage some shrubby plants in multi-year burning cycles, such as hazel (important both for nuts and basketry materials), huckleberries, and other economic plants (Anderson 1990, 1993; Lewis 1973, 1990).

Cultural Setting

At the opening of the nineteenth century, Kalapuyan speakers occupied all of the Willamette Valley above the falls at Oregon City, as well as the northern-most tributary drainages of the Umpqua basin to the south (fig. 5.1). Based on texts recorded by linguists between the late 1880s and early 1900s, the Kalapuyan language family was found to include three languages and at least 13 dialects. This diversity suggests both "a long antiquity of residence in the valley" (Jacobs 1937:66) and a relatively settled populace.

Each dialect community included a group of villages occupying the major tributary streams. These multi-village communities correspond to the commonly identified Kalapuya group names, many of which survive today in the names of the river basins they occupied, such as the Tualatin, Yamhill, Santiam, Luckiamute, and others. Other group names are known from the 1851 Champoeg and 1855 Dayton treaties, including the Ahantchuyuk (Pudding River), Marys River, Muddy Creek, Tsankupi, Chelamela (Long Tom), Chafan, Mohawk, Winefelly, and Yoncalla (in the northern Umpqua Basin).

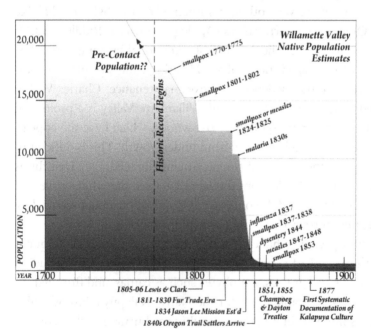

Fig. 5.2. Native population decline in the Willamette Valley due to introduced diseases.

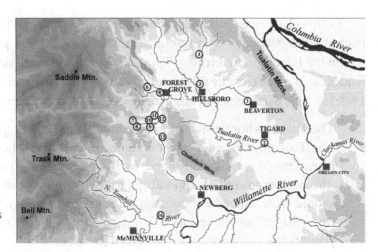

Fig. 5.3. Location of Tualatin villages (modified from Zenk 1994).

Only the barest outline of Kalapuya native culture is known; the valley's poor ethnohistoric record is a legacy of devastating epidemics that thoroughly disrupted pre-contact lifeways. The most reliable estimates put the Kalapuya population approaching 20,000 in 1770 (Boyd 1990b), but by the mid-1840s (when the "Oregon Trail" migrations of American settlers began) the total Kalapuya population was estimated at less than 600 (Wilkes 1926), representing a mortality rate of more than 95% in fewer than 70 years (fig. 5.2). We should bear in mind that observations and writings about the Kalapuya during this time reflect a period of catastrophic devastation, not conditions that can be construed as typical. The most valuable ethnographic records on the Kalapuya, generated by anthropologists beginning in the late 1870s directly from Native informants, include recollections from before the reservation period (Frachtenberg 1915, 1918; Jacobs et al. 1945; Swadesh 1965; Zenk 1976, 1990b, 1994), but even these memories do not predate the catastrophic population declines (Zenk 1994).

The Tualatin, for whom the historic record is most complete (Zenk 1994), were apparently dispersed in 15 to 20 distinct villages or hamlets (fig. 5.3). There are some half dozen named village groups recorded for both the Yamhill and Luckiamute (cf. Barry 1927; Berreman 1937; Hodge 1979), but it is possible that these numbers reflect consolidations of formerly independent village units. Only a few names have been recorded for the upper Willamette Valley (primarily from treaty documents), and it is frequently unclear if they apply to independent villages, larger multi-village communities, or some combination of these.

Each village was politically autonomous, but village clusters (dialect communities) shared certain resources in common, such as game animals, within the larger group territory. These territories were well defined and defended, as is made clear by this translation from Gatschet's text (Jacobs et al. 1945:187–188, parentheses in original; brackets added for clarity here):

> The Tualatins hunted half way in the mountains . . . Perhaps if they [the Tualatin] crossed to the Yamhill country a man who hunted (there) might get killed. (Beyond) half the mountain at *pa'naxDin* [the northernmost Tualatin village] if (the people of that village) should cross over (the mountain) to Clatskanie country, perhaps (the villager) would be killed. If a Clatskanie should cross over, possibly the Clatskanie would be killed (by a Tualatin).

The threat of death for trespass expressed in this quote may by exaggerated (Zenk 1976 footnote), but it is clear that group boundaries were recognized and defended. Within a group's territory, resources such as fields of edible seeds were controlled by specific villages, and plots within these allotments were, in turn, individually owned. Access to another's territory was not restricted for legitimate purposes, such as trade (which was conducted extensively throughout the region), as long as ownership rights were respected. The Gatschet texts make it clear that the Tualatin sometimes went to the Columbia River to hunt seals (probably in the territory of the Multnomah Chinook), but never to fish, and that they could collect lampreys at Willamette Falls—where they traded for salmon with the resident Clackamas Chinook—but did not fish with dip nets (Zenk 1976:49–50).

The warmer seasons of the year were times of major food-gathering activity. People camped in the open or used casual brush shelters. During the camas harvest, from early through late summer, bulbs were dug in great quantity from meadows. Camas bulbs were baked, transforming indigestible complex starches to more digestible simple sugars and greatly enhancing their food value. This process also changed the camas, in the words of Lewis and Clark (Thwaites 1959:5:128,131), from a "glutinous or somewhat slymey" bulb with little taste into a product "of a sweet agreeable flavor." Fires were built in large baking pits, to which stream cobbles were added. When the rocks were hot the fire was raked away, the pit filled with camas bulbs, and earth placed over the top. After baking for two or three days, the bulbs were removed and pounded into cakes for winter stores. A great variety of seeds, berries, and other plant foods were gathered throughout summer and early fall. Hunting was primarily a fall season pursuit, though deer, elk, waterfowl, and smaller animals were present—and taken to some extent—year-round. Throughout the productive season, foods were dried and stored for winter, which was not a time of major food-getting activity.

During the cool, wet months of the year families returned to their home village where substantial multifamily houses were maintained. One type of structure, described by a native of the Marys River area in the southwestern corner of the valley, was said to be up to 60 feet in length. It had a pole frame, bundles of grass tied to the frame to make up the walls, and a nearly flat roof shingled with bark slabs. Inside, the house was partitioned off to accommodate as many as ten families. The interior was furnished with mats of tule grass. Beds were laid along the walls, and from the rafters hung baskets and bags containing stored provisions. Another type of structure, only sketchily described, was a roughly conical shelter about 15 to 20 feet across which contained, among other things, drying racks for salmon and roots. This was apparently used during the summer season (Mackey 1974).

Terminal Pleistocene/Early Holocene (ca. 13,000–7,500 years ago)

The earliest cultural record is sparse in the Willamette Valley. Several Clovis projectile points, distinctive artifacts that consistently date to the ca. 12,000 B.P. time horizon throughout North America, have been found in the upper Willamette Valley. Clovis points are known from the Mohawk Valley (Allely 1975), the Cottage Grove vicinity (Minor 1985), Blue River Reservoir (Ozbun and Stueber 2001), and Fern Ridge Reservoir (fig. 5.4; Connolly 1994). All are from undated contexts; obsidian hydration dating of the Cottage Grove and Blue River points is imprecise, but confirms their considerable antiquity (Ozbun and Stueber 2001).

Evidence from other potentially early sites has been reported, but in most cases the evidence is more suggestive than solid. Two large lanceolate points were reportedly found with

Fig. 5.4. Two sides of the Fern Ridge Reservoir Clovis projectile point.

mammoth bones in the side wall of a drainage slough near the Calapooia River, but because these finds were made in 1895 and reported from memory half a century later, the association cannot be confirmed (Cressman and Laughlin 1941; Cressman 1947). Modest evidence of a human presence associated with terminal Pleistocene peat deposits has also been reported near Woodburn, formed in depressions on the Missoula Flood silt. Radiocarbon dates from the peat beds range from about 17,000 to 10,000 years ago, and clues from the latter end of this time range include animal bone fragments (primarily bison) that exhibit possible butchering marks, stone fragments that appear to be flaking debris from stone tools, and possibly human hair (Stenger 2000, 2002; Connolly 2003).

Relatively few Willamette Valley sites have produced radiocarbon dates of early Holocene age; among the most significant are Cascadia Cave, a rockshelter in the foothills of the western Cascades, and several sites in the Long Tom River basin on the valley floor, near the town of Veneta. The older cultural deposits in the upper Long Tom Basin are found at depths of five feet (ca. 1.5 meters) or more (fig. 5.5), and a long history of flooding throughout the Willamette Valley has certainly buried early archaeological sites to even greater depths in some areas, presenting a significant impediment to their discovery and study.

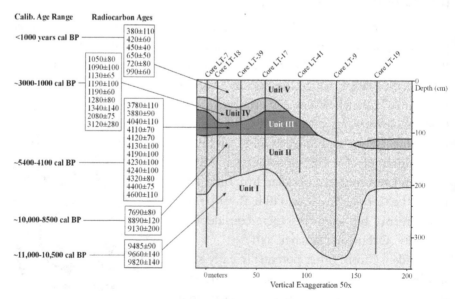

Fig. 5.5. Radiocarbon ages from Veneta-area archaeological sites shown in a schematic of their stratigraphic context (modified from Friedel et al. 1989).

A new alignment for a segment of Oregon Highway 126 west of Veneta, including the property that hosts the Oregon Country Fair, was developed in the late 1980s and generated an intensive archaeological study involving more than a dozen sites (O'Neill et al. 2004). The early Holocene is represented by small sites containing simple tool assemblages. At site 35LA861 a small lens of charcoal and fire-cracked rock dating to 10,500 cal. BP is associated with a few cultural flakes of chert and basalt; at the Stamp site (35LA658) a small lens of charcoal and burned earth dating to 10,900 cal. BP is associated with obsidian flakes and several charred hazelnut meats; a lens of charcoal and burned earth dating to ca. 8480 cal. BP is associated with an obsidian scraper at site 35LA860; a cluster of fire-cracked rock, charcoal, and burned earth associated with obsidian chips and a formed obsidian scraping tool dates to 9910 cal. BP at the Long Tom site (35LA439). These ephemeral camps confirm an early human presence in the valley, and suggest opportunistic hunting and gathering by a highly mobile population.

The Hannavan Creek site (35LA647) is a continuous scatter of lithic artifacts that extends for nearly half a mile along a small tributary of the Long Tom River, downstream from the Veneta sites. Located within the pool of Fern Ridge Reservoir, investigations at a number of sites, including Hannavan Creek, were supported by the Corps of Engineers in the mid-1980s (Cheatham 1988). The reservoir behind the Fern Ridge flood-control dam was formerly known as the Long Tom Marsh.

The Hannavan Creek Site was exposed and investigated during an annual winter drawdown of the reservoir. The fluctuating waters of Fern Ridge Lake have washed the Hannavan Creek Site over many years. Five major concentrations of artifacts were exposed in a broad zone along the stream, including many small clusters of fire-cracked rocks that mark former fire hearths and baking ovens. Excavation of one such rock cluster yielded some 350 camas bulbs that had been charred, an accident that insured their preservation (fig. 5.6). Two sets of charred camas bulbs were radiocarbon dated, returning ages of 8,500 and 7,650 years old. Though the dates are not fully consistent with one another, they nonetheless

Fig. 5.6. Charred bulbs from a Willamette Valley camas oven.

Fig. 5.7. Projectile points from Cascadia Cave; Cascade-style points in top two rows (courtesy Paul Baxter)

confirm the great antiquity of the baking pit, and provide the earliest clear example of a food-processing oven from the valley (Cheatham 1988). At the nearby Ralston site, a similar oven feature seen eroding from a stream bank dates to ca. 7,500 years old (Cheatham 1988). Camas was an important staple food in the valley during the middle and late Holocene, and these sites provide the earliest evidence for systematic camas processing on a significant scale.

Artifacts from Hannavan Creek include projectile points and other tools that are of styles used throughout the middle and late Holocene, showing that the area was used as a hunting and food processing camp for millennia. Chipped stone scrapers and knives used for butchering tasks were present, along with fragments of ground stone tools used to process plant foods. Hammerstones, anvils, cores, flaked stone debris, choppers, drills, spoke-shaves, and gravers indicate the working of stone, bone, and wood. This is a generalized tool kit that may have been used over thousands of years with little change, and it is likely that other areas of this large site were repeatedly visited long after the camas-baking oven was used.

Cascadia Cave (35LIN11) lies on the north bank of the South Santiam River about two miles upriver from the town of Cascadia. Excavations were conducted at the site in 1964 in advance of the proposed Cascadia dam and reservoir, a project which was later abandoned (Newman 1966). The site had been well known prior to this time; Cressman (1937) had described some of the cave's rock art panels, and Howard and Howard (1963) reported digging a pit 12 feet deep into cultural deposits. Other artifact collectors disturbed the site extensively, and Newman reported that disturbed fill, sometimes up to two meters in depth, was removed to reach intact deposits.

The site produced a large artifact collection that included more than a hundred projectile points of the Cascade type, willow-leaf shaped points made on large flakes, and often retaining a portion of the flake's original striking platform at the base of the point (fig. 5.7). Tools commonly associated include edge-ground cobbles, possibly used for hide-processing, and well-worked steep-bit endscrapers that were probably used in woodworking (Connolly and Baxter 1986). This set of features is associated with the Cascade Phase on the Columbia Plateau, which dates from ca. 9,000 to 5,000 years ago, consistent with a radiocarbon date on charcoal from just above the cave's bedrock floor that returned a calibrated age of ca. 8650 years ago (Newman 1966, 1967). However, cognate artifacts are also found at sites of middle and late Holocene age throughout western Washington and Oregon, making them poor temporal markers (Burtchard 1990; Connolly 1986; Connolly and Baxter 1986). Assemblages from throughout the region sharing these technological traits have been generally identified as belonging to the Old Cordilleran Tradition

Fig. 5.8. A small portion of the Cascadia Cave pictographs panel

(Butler 1961, 1962, 1965); a local expression of this tradition, known as the Glade Tradition is prominent in southwest Oregon (refer to Chapter 6).

Cascadia Cave was revisited in 1988, as part of an assessment for a nomination to the National Register of Historic Places, to which it was added in 1990 (Baxter 1989a). Within the scope of this project, the site was mapped and photographed, the petroglyph panels were extensively recorded (fig. 5.8), a 1x2 meter test pit was excavated, and a study of the sediment and stratigraphy was undertaken. The cultural deposit reached a depth of four meters (about 13 feet). This work produced two additional radiocarbon ages, 7230 cal. BP and 5650 cal. BP.

In addition to foliate points, Cascadia Cave produced scrapers, large ovate knives, drills, and ground stone tools, an assemblage that suggests that hide processing and woodworking were frequent tasks. The bones of deer were found in every level of the excavations, and elk, snowshoe rabbit, marmot, weasel, and grouse bones—but no fish—were also found. Hazelnuts found at one spot during the excavations, as well as a dozen or so hand grinding stones, or manos, show that vegetal foods such as nuts and seeds were crushed and milled at the site. Occupation in late summer and fall is suggested (Newman 1966; Baxter 1989). Newman (1966:18) speculated that an increase in the frequency of scrapers in the upper levels, accompanied by more abundant bone, indicated a shift in site use over time from more generalized hunting and foraging to the hunting and processing of game.

Several other sites are known in the uplands of the Western Cascades with tool assemblages comparable to that from Cascadia Cave. The Geertz (35CL1), Ripple (35CL55), Blitz (35LIN147), and possibly the Canyon Owl (35LIN336) sites also contained Cascade foliate projectile points, likely signaling early Holocene occupations in the Western Cascades (Minor and Toepel 1984b). At the Geertz site, located above a major tributary of the Clackamas River, foliate forms were the only projectile point type recovered, and no ground stone tools were noted. Based on these findings Woodward (1972) interpreted the site as a hunting and game processing camp, contemporary with the early Cascadia Cave occupations. The Ripple site, also in the Clackamas drainage, contained both foliate and broad-necked notched points, suggesting at least partial contemporaneity with Geertz, as well as possibly later occupations. The frequency of bifaces and biface fragments, and high densities of stone flaking debris, suggested use of the site as both a hunting camp and a lithic reduction station (Lebow 1985). The Canyon Owl site (35LIN336) is in the upper South Santiam River drainage; based on the presence of Cascade and later projectile points, and supported by obsidian hydration data, the site appears to have been intermittently occupied throughout most of the Holocene (Fagan et al. 1992). Analysis of blood proteins on projectile points indicates that mountain sheep, deer and/or elk, and upland game birds were hunted. The site also functioned as a lithic reduction station, processing cherts from nearby sources and obsidian from the more distant Obsidian Cliffs source.

The early component of Baby Rock Shelter (35LA53; Olsen 1975), which lies below a Mazama ash layer, also provides evidence of occupation of the Western Cascades at an early time; unfortunately, the early cultural assemblage is sparse, comprising only a single biface, a used flake, chipped stone debris, and fragments of deer bone. Notably, the site also had a red pictograph of what appeared to be a horse and rider, indicating use into the post-contact period as well.

The Middle Holocene (7,500 to 3,000 Years Ago)

The middle Holocene is well represented in the Willamette Valley, but is best known from excavations along Mill Creek in the central part of the valley and on the Long Tom River in the upper valley. Like the occupations along Hannavan Creek, many sites in the vicinity of the Long Tom Marsh (now Fern Ridge Reservoir) show evidence of repeated, short-term visits from the middle Holocene to recent times.

Mill Creek is a Willamette River tributary which cuts from south to north through the Salem Hills at Turner Gap, then turns northwest through Salem. The Mill Creek cultural record is based on work at ten sites located along the former channel segment of Mill Creek (which was re-routed when the I-5/Highway 20 interchange was built) originally known as Hager's Grove. The chronology is fixed with over 60 radiocarbon ages spanning the last ca. 6,000 years, nearly all from rock-lined pit ovens. All sites show also some evidence of having been occupied during the last ca. 1,500 years, and several of them (35MA9, 35MA64, 35MA69) were primarily used during this time, but more than half of the directly dated oven features are between 5,500 and 3,000 years old.

The physical history of the Mill Creek vicinity can be derived from the geologic record. Three distinct strata were documented at all sites. A gravelly stratum underlies the cultural levels. The gravels are widespread throughout the Mill Creek valley, and are generally much larger than a stream the current size of Mill Creek could have deposited, indicating that their source was terminal

Fig. 5.9. Camas ovens from the Mill Creek sites: *a*, Feature 20, site 35MA70, 5750 cal. BP; *b*, Feature 3, site 35MA9, 5600 cal. BP; *c*, Feature 4, site 35MA9, 5150 cal. BP; *d*, Feature 2, site 35MA9, 1300 cal. BP.

Pleistocene glacial outwash deposited by a much larger, higher velocity river. It is thought that the North Santiam River formerly flowed through Turner Gap, before taking its present course south of the Salem Hills (Hodges 1998; O'Connor et al. 2001). These gravel deposits have produced radiocarbon ages between 15,000 and 14,000 years ago (O'Connor et al. 2001:18). Overlying the gravels is a gravelly sandy clay that probably represents a lahar—a hot mud flow associated with a volcanic event. It may have been this event that plugged Turner Gap and diverted the North Santiam River to its present course. Mill Creek now occupies a relict channel abandoned by the North Santiam River, but because its channel is floored by gravels larger than it can effectively move, the Mill Creek channel has been relatively stable. Above the lahar deposit is a dark gray or brown clay loam, formed by Mill Creek flood deposits during the last ca. 6,000 years Connolly et al. 1997; Hodges 1998).

The middle Holocene evidence from Mill Creek consists primarily of food processing oven features that produced abundant evidence of charred camas bulbs, and occasional evidence of charred hazelnuts and acorns associated with amorphous charcoal and burned-earth stains (fig. 5.9). The evidence suggests that the baking of camas and the drying of nuts were important activities.

Chipped and ground stone tools are present, but in relatively low frequencies. Projectile points include fairly large, leaf-shaped specimens, and large stemmed and occasionally side-notched points, which were likely used to tip darts for use with atlatls (fig. 5.10). The sites appear to have been primarily used as seasonal food gathering and processing localities during the middle Holocene.

Fig. 5.10. Middle and late Holocene projectile points from site 35MA64.

The cultural record of the Veneta / Country Fair complex (Long Tom and Chalker Sites) echoes that of Mill Creek, with frequent camas ovens, typically containing charred camas bulbs and occasional charred hazelnut shells and acorn meats (fig. 5.11). Modest portable artifact sets are dominated by flaked cobble choppers, expedient flake tools, and dart-sized corner-notched projectile points (mostly made of cherts). A probable residential area at the Long Tom site (35LA439) produced shaped stone bowls, a hopper mortar base, pestles, and cobble-sized hammer stones (fig. 5.12).

The environmental history of the upper Long Tom drainage is also recorded in the natural stratigraphy (O'Neill et al. 2004; Freidel et al. 1988). The earliest cultural deposits (outlined above), were associated with the lowest two strata; a clayey paleosol found at depths of ca. 200–250 centimeters (dated between 11,000 and 10,500 years ago), and a silty clay loam to fine sandy loam found between ca. 150 to 250 centimeters deep (ca. 10,000 to 8,500 years old). Following these earliest deposits was a 3,000 year period of stability or

Fig. 5.11. Veneta-area camas ovens: a, Feature 6, Chalker site (35LA420), 4650 cal. BP; b, Feature 24, Long Tom site (35LA439), 4100 cal. BP.

Fig. 5.12. Stone bowls, a maul, and flaked cobble chopping tool from the Long Tom site (35LA439).

erosion that left no sediment record (and no cultural record). The sandy loam that overlies the early deposits is fixed by at least a dozen radiocarbon dates, ranging from 5,300 to 4,100 years ago. Most dates are from in-ground earth ovens, many of which produced carbonized camas bulbs and fragments of charred hazelnuts or acorns. The middle Holocene sandy loam from the upper Long Tom suggests frequent flooding and active deposition.

Notably, this active depositional environment has produced a robust cultural record (O'Neill et al. 2004; Freidel et al. 1988). It is clear from both the ethnographic and archaeological records that there is a very strong relationship between cultural sites and wetlands in the Willamette Valley. This wetlands focus of the native people was observed by early fur traders and explorers, including James Clyman (1960:153), who remarked in May 1845 that "the Calapooyas live exclusively on roots but whare [sic] hogs are introduced they soon destroy the cammerce [camas] fields . . . these extensive fields are always on wet land and in many places no other vegitable [sic] is found to intermix with it." Archaeological studies have repeatedly shown that the majority of cultural sites in the valley are on surfaces subject to seasonal flooding, or on the edges of landforms and terraces that border active floodplains. Cheatham (1988:159–176) found that most sites in the Fern Ridge Reservoir area of the upper Willamette Valley were on surfaces subject to seasonal inundation, a pattern he relates to camas habitat. He hypothesized that winter settlements were perched on levees and relatively higher ground around the annual floodplain, but that warm-season use and occupation was confined almost entirely to the adjacent active floodplain.

Gilsen (1989) reports a similar case based on a systematic survey of the Luckiamute River basin, one of the Willamette's major westside tributaries. He notes that 85% of recorded sites are located on the edge of landforms that abut seasonally inundated floodplains. More recently, Ellis (1996) examined soil associations of archaeological sites along a pipeline corridor through the Willamette Valley, and found that most sites were on soils that were saturated and probably not habitable during part of the year, or in settings that bordered such soils. He echoes Cheatham in saying that while winter occupations may have been limited to stable surfaces above the level of seasonal ponding, it is the seasonally wet surfaces that appear to have been the primary focus of land and resource use. This pattern was clearly established in the middle Holocene, and is reflected in the upper Long Tom archaeological record.

The Flanagan Site (35LA218) is located on an old stream meander channel that drains to the Long Tom below the Fern Ridge Reservoir area. The low-lying terrain around the site, saturated by the spring floods that were endemic to the valley before modern dams were built, no doubt supported camas lilies in great abundance. Like many Willamette Valley sites, intermittent occupations at Flanagan began in the middle Holocene, becoming more regular and continuous in recent millennia. Over a dozen radiocarbon dates on charcoal, from deposits up to three feet deep, cluster around 6500, 3500, 1700, 900, and 500 cal. BP (Toepel 1985; Beckham, Minor and Toepel 1981).

Preparation of vegetal foods was well attested at the Flanagan Site. Rock-lined pit-ovens up to two meters (six feet) across were found, as well as scatters of fire-cracked stream cobbles and charcoal fragments that had obviously been raked out of such roasting pits. The ovens produced charred bulbs tentatively identified as camas. A few charred acorn hulls, and some pits of wild cherry and Klamath plum, also represent foods probably gathered by the site's aboriginal occupants. The importance of hunting is also attested in the Flanagan artifact assemblage, which included projectile points along with butchering and hide-processing tools such as biface knives, scrapers, perforators, and use-modified flakes. Wood- and bone-working are suggested by hammerstones, choppers, drills, spokeshaves, and a grooved sandstone abrader that might have served to smooth down arrowshafts or comparable artifacts. Stone tool manufacture is suggested by many exhausted stone cores. The Flanagan Site was probably used by family groups who came in summer to gather plant foods and hunt game such as deer and elk in the woods along the stream where the site lay. The wide range of artifacts suggests that people stayed for perhaps several weeks or longer, carrying out various food-processing and tool-manufacturing chores while there.

Other representative middle Holocene sites, including the Lingo (35LA29) and Chalker (35LA420) sites, produced similar evidence. Processing of nuts (acorns and hazelnuts) and especially camas roots are dominant themes in middle Holocene sites; some camas ovens are more than two meters in diameter, suggesting the bulk processing of foods for deferred consumption or trade. Throughout the Pacific Northwest, it is during the middle Holocene that the first substantial winter residences and storage facilities appear; although storage pits have not yet been confirmed in Willamette Valley sites of middle Holocene age, the scale of food processing at this time is consistent with the broader regional patterns. All middle Holocene sites investigated in the valley suggest occupations of limited duration, indicating a relatively mobile population.

The Late Holocene (From 3,000 Years Ago to the Contact Era)

Many sites with a record of intermittent occupation during the middle Holocene—including the Benjamin (35LA41, -42), Lingo (35LA29), Lynch (35LIN36), Hurd (35LA44), Flanagan (35LA218), Chalker (35LA420), Calapooia Midden (35LIN468), Mill Creek (35MA7, -9, -64, 65), and other sites—appear to have seen continuous or near-continuous occupation during the last ca. 3,000 years, and particularly after about 2,000 years ago. These sites represent the growing number and density of established residential places in the Willamette Valley, reflecting an increasingly sedentary pattern that contrasts with the earlier practice of moving among numerous temporary task camps and base camps. This increasingly residential pattern is reflected in the many late Holocene mound sites that appear in the valley, representing the accumulation of debris from continuous residential use. In many cases, the village communities described in ethnographic records were diffuse collections of homesteads, occupied by related families, that lined segments of river corridors or bordered marshy expanses.

From the Western Cascades, there is also substantial evidence for continued use of higher elevation sites throughout the Holocene, and the intensity of upland use may have dramatically increased from middle to late Holocene times. Hunting was always a central activity in the uplands; the procurement and processing of tool stone, and the harvesting and processing of huckleberries and other vegetal resources, were consistent pursuits but more variable from site to site.

Although excavations have occurred at a few notable upland sites, small-scale sampling has been conducted at dozens of higher elevation sites on lands administered by the U.S. Forest Service. In most cases, this work has been done to identify site boundaries so that they can be protected from road building, timber sales, and other disturbances. Thus, while relatively few upland sites have studied extensively, many have received some level of investigative attention. As a result, studies of site geography that reflect patterns of human land use have been possible (Baxter 1986; Burtchard 1990; Snyder 1987, 1991; Kelly 2001). Most notable in these studies is a bimodal site distribution pattern by elevation, with lower elevation sites most commonly occurring below 2,000 feet, and upper elevation sites between 3,600 and 5,200 feet. The higher sites are most often associated with upland meadows and huckleberry patches, where hunting and berry harvesting were most productive.

The evidence for increasing sedentism in the Willamette Valley during the late Holocene is accompanied by indications that people were beginning to manage the local landscape more intensively in order to enhance the productivity of important plant foods. A sediment core extracted from a small oxbow lake near Corvallis produced a record of microscopic charcoal, which reflects the local fire history. The amount of charcoal increases beginning about 3,500 years ago, and the record suggests both higher fire frequency and lower fire intensity (Pearl 1999; Walsh et al. 2010). Importantly, the charcoal is identified as being primarily from grass and herbaceous plants, rather than wood charcoal. These factors suggest a pattern of regular low-intensity controlled burning of the prairies surrounding the lake, rather than infrequent, catastrophic natural fires, and most likely reflects the Kalapuya Indians' system of fire management of the landscape. It is likely that higher elevation meadows and huckleberry patches were also maintained and expanded by controlled burning.

The Perkins Park Site (35LA282) is located less than a mile from Hannavan Creek, on a peninsula that now juts into Fern Ridge Lake but would have once overlooked the vast Long Tom Marsh. Numerous scatters of fire-cracked rock and chipped stone tools occur along the course of an adjacent creek bed, and probably represent activity areas associated with what was probably a long-term settlement. Limited testing produced animal bone, too fragmentary to be identified beyond the fact that birds and mammals were both represented. Macrobotanical remains included charred camas bulbs, acorn and hazelnut hulls, and cherry seeds. Radiocarbon dates confirm occupation between ca. 1,300 and 1,000 years ago.

The Hurd Site (35LA44), near Coburg on the eastern edge of the valley, includes the remains of a semisubterranean house structure; its location on higher ground and its distinctive artifact assemblage further indicate that the site was a more permanent settlement (White 1975). The occupied area is on the forward edge of the Winkle geomorphic terrace, overlooking a lower flood plain through which the McKenzie River flows toward its confluence with the Willamette, several miles west of the site. Though the difference in relief between the two land surfaces is only a few feet, it was sufficient that the Hurd Site, on the higher Winkle surface, would be above the level of all but the most unusual flooding (Balster and Parsons 1968).

A ^{14}C assay on charcoal from a firehearth on the house floor gave a date of 2800 BP; a confirming date of 2820 BP came from a second hearth intruded into the housepit. The house was oval in plan, defined by the outlines of a large, shallow pit a few inches deep and about 16 by 23 feet across. In addition to the firehearth there were a number of small pits, probably post-holes that mark the locations of the house's support structure. These small pits did not add up to a complete pattern of wall and roof supports for the house; but if the superstructure were lightly built, some of its fainter traces may have been obliterated by the passage of time, or missed in excavation. The shallowness of the housepit, and the lack of evidence for really substantial support timbers, suggests that the structure may have resembled the semi-conical grass-thatched lodges of historic Willamette Valley peoples rather than their more substantial long, rectangular houses with sunken floors and bark-shingled roofs.

A cluster of eleven ^{14}C dates on charcoal from various fire hearths and earth ovens elsewhere in the Hurd site indicates a second major period of occupation extending from 1100 BP to late pre-contact times. No house structure was identified for the later occupation; instead, there were many large and small earth ovens and fire hearths. The lack of evidence for later house remains may reflect the limitations of the archaeological sample. However, house remains have been elusive in the valley, probably due to the fact that the evidence for light-framed structures does not preserve well in sites where intense and focused activities, including the excavation and re-excavation of hearths and ovens, were ongoing. The processing of vegetal foods is well attested by an abundance of earth ovens, and by charred camas bulbs, pestles, and mortar fragments. Based on historical accounts, Darby (2008) reports that Willamette Valley houses may have been most commonly made of grass-thatched walls over a pole frame, buttressed on the outside with a low earth bank, and roofed with bark slabs. The remains of such structures are very difficult to detect archaeologically.

Like many other residential sites used during the last 2,000 years, the Hurd site produced hundreds of projectile points. Bow and arrow technology was introduced to the area within the last ca. 2,000 years, and sites of this period exhibit arrow point frequencies that are *ten times* that found in comparable excavated volumes from middle Holocene sites (e.g., O'Neill et al. 1999; also see further discussion on this point below). Although some have suggested that the common occurrence of arrow points indicates the importance of hunting in the valley, it is likely that their sudden proliferation reflects more ominous social circumstances, and a heightened concern with defense, raiding, and boundary maintenance. This reality follows the late period evidence for increased violence noted on the Columbia Plateau (Chatters 2004) and in the Klamath Basin (Sampson 1985:515), and is consistent with the accounts of raiding noted frequently in ethnohistoric accounts. An example of these relationships in the Willamette Valley was recorded by Hudson's Bay Company brigade leader John Work (Scott 1923:264–265) in 1834 near the "River Lauries" (Marys River). He notes in his journal that the Marys River Kalapuya ("Lautaude") were on alert for a retaliatory raid from the Umpqua, in response to a prior raid by the Lautaude. He continues: "They [the Indians] . . . inform us that 4 men of Lautaude [Marys River?] Indians have been killed & 3 children taken slaves a short time since, as they suppose by a party of Faladin [Tualatin] or Yamhill Indians."

The Benjamin sites (35LA41-42), a number of low mounds, are scattered along old meanders of the Long Tom River several miles north of Fern Ridge Lake. Excavations of varying scope were carried out in several of the mounds, and major digging in two of them provided abundant evidence of human activity (Miller 1975). Each mound rose about three feet above the surrounding terrain. One was roughly circular and about 60 feet in diameter. The other was ellipsoidal, measuring about 50 by 100 feet. As is typical of many late, probably residential sites, no architectural remains were found in either mound.

The Benjamin mound cluster is typical of late Holocene mound groups found throughout the Willamette Valley, generally associated with sinuous stream courses or marshlands. Such mounds could have been occupied at the same time (as a small community), or sequentially by a resident group who occasionally shifted the focus of their primary residence (fig. 5.13). Based on interpretations derived from the ethnographic record, it is thought that small corporate groups (related families and associates), such as those who occupied these kinds of homestead sets, probably had exclusive rights over specific resource areas (Zenk 1976).

Plant food gathering and processing was certainly a major focus of attention at the Benjamin sites. The mounds contained much fire-cracked

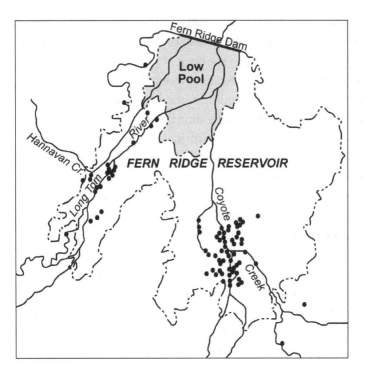

5.13
Archaeological site clusters along the Long Tom River and Coyote Creek in the Fern Ridge Reservoir area, Lane County (modified from Cheatham 1988).

rock, fire-reddened earth, and charcoal, related to many small fire hearths and large earth ovens. Some of the latter were as much as two feet deep and five feet across. Charred camas bulbs made it clear that they functioned as roasting pits. Additional clues come from mortar and pestle fragments, which probably served in the cracking and grinding of hard-shelled nuts such as the acorn and hazelnut. No nutshells were recovered from the archaeological deposits, but in prehistory the Benjamin sites were no doubt flanked by streamside gallery forests where oak and hazel are common, as is still the case today. Two ^{14}C dates on charred bulbs from the earth ovens were 2300 and 1600 BP, but projectile point styles suggest that human use began earlier and continued later than these dates indicate. The number of arrow points recovered—nearly 250—reflects the growing importance of bow and arrow technology to the latter occupants.

Excavations at a set of midden sites in Kirk Park, at the north end of Fern Ridge Reservoir on the Long Tom River not far upstream from the Benjamin sites, suggest a comparable homestead set (as opposed to a single homestead site). These sites (35LA565-568) were occupied during the last ca. 3,000 years, taking on a more settled and residential character over time. They are all essentially contemporaneous, but somewhat functionally distinct, and are thought to represent residential sites and seasonal task camps for a single small resident group.

Although many sites were in use earlier, all radiocarbon dates from the hundreds of mound sites found throughout the Willamette Valley fall within the last 3,000 years. The number of mound sites, as well as the presence of midden mounds themselves, attests to a large and increasingly sedentary population.

Excavators of the Chalker site (35LA420), located in the upper Long Tom River basin west of Veneta, report that during its earliest use (>4,000 years ago) the site served primarily as a food processing camp. The later occupations, most intense from ca. 1,300 to 900 years ago, appear to be more residential, but probably do not represent a permanent settlement. The partial outline of a small structure (possibly about 4x5 meters in size) was identified by the pattern of fire pits, post molds, and charcoal-stained earth. The site may have functioned as a seasonal hunting and harvesting base camp; although carbonized camas bulbs were recovered from the later occupation levels, no camas ovens were identified (an oven associated with the earlier occupation was dated to ca. 4,600 years ago), and no ground stone tools (mortars and pestles, typically associated with plant food processing) were recovered (O'Neill et al. 2004).

A portion of the former channel of Mill Creek, near southeast Salem, is now occupied by the Interstate Highway 5/Santiam Highway (OR 22) interchange. The Mill Creek or Hager's Grove set of sites along the former channel were investigated during interchange reconstruction and highway widening. As previously noted, features associated with the earlier radiocarbon ages (>3,500 years ago) are predominantly rock-lined earth ovens, including some very large ones exceeding two meters in diameter. A small number of features from this early set of radiocarbon ages were pits marked by burned-earth rims; the functions of these features may have varied, but at least some were probably camas ovens from which the rock had been scavenged. It is clear that camas processing was a focal activity at the Mill Creek sites prior to ca. 3,500 years ago.

Later radiocarbon ages are associated with a relatively more diverse feature assemblage, including rock-lined ovens, bisque (burned earth) stains, large and small bisque-filled pits (frequently associated with charred nut fragments), and "living floors," surfaces with relatively robust artifact concentrations. These surfaces suggest that the later occupations were less exclusively

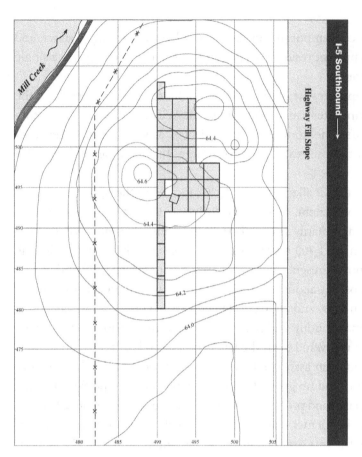

Fig. 5.14. Contour map showing the site 35MA64 adjacent to Mill Creek in Marion County.

focused on a narrow set of resource extraction activities (i.e., camas collection and processing), and were instead more residential in character, serving as operational bases for a broader range of functions. Sites 35MA9, 35MA64, and 35MA65 all had substantial midden accumulations dating within the last ca. 1,500 years, and the latter two could clearly be characterized as mounds (fig. 5.14). This interpretation is confirmed by tool assemblages; earlier components had sparse chipped stone tool assemblages in association with oven features, but tools associated with the later occupations were abundant and varied, including chipped stone artifacts (projectile points are particularly abundant), pestles and stone bowl fragments, hammerstones and mauls, and flaked cobble chopping tools (fig. 5.15).

Projectile points were made in relatively greater numbers in the late Holocene period, a pattern that has been noted previously in the Willamette Valley (e.g., Miller 1975; Pettigrew 1980b). O'Neill et al. (1999) observe that

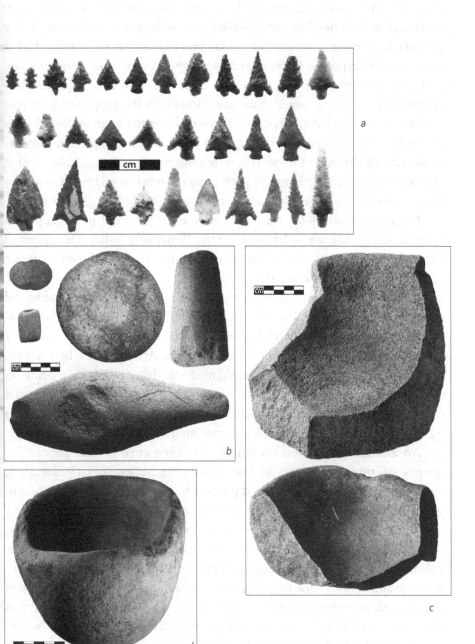

Fig. 5.15   Late Holocene artifacts from Mill Creek site 35MA64: *a*, arrow points; *b*, cobble tools (notched net weight, anvil stone with red pigment, hand maul, smoking pipe bowl, stone splitting wedge); *c and d*, stone bowl fragments.

extensive excavations in middle Holocene components (ca. 5,000–4,000 years ago) at the Long Tom and Chalker sites in the upper Willamette Valley produced extensive evidence for camas processing, but only about half a dozen projectile points. Excavation of a roughly comparable volume of late Holocene (<2,000 years ago) deposits at these sites produced approximately 60 projectile points. A similar dramatic increase in the frequency of arrow points is seen at the Salem sites; based on time estimates from obsidian hydration values, obsidian artifacts dating 2,000 years and older represent just 18% of tested artifacts, and of these 41% were projectile points (fig. 5.15a). Tested artifacts estimated to be less than 2,000 years old represent 82% of the assemblage, and of these projectile points represented 64% of the tested obsidian.

Pettigrew (1980:66–67) was the first to note that obsidian use appeared to increase significantly at later sites in the Willamette Valley. He suggested that the greater use of obsidian in later times may relate to the introduction of the bow and arrow, which took place within the last ca. 1,500–2,000 years. Larger dart points were typically reduced from even larger bifacial blanks and preforms. Since the obsidian available in the Willamette River gravels occurs primarily as pebble-sized nodules, obsidian would have been of relatively limited use for the production of stone dart tips. Arrow points, by contrast, are much smaller, and were frequently made on flakes rather than being reduced from larger bifacial preforms. With the introduction of bow and arrow technology, the small, locally available obsidian pebbles would have become a significantly more useful and valuable raw material.

An increasing emphasis on hunting has been cited for the greater frequency of projectile points in late Willamette Valley sites (Miller 1975; Pettigrew 1980); however, as noted previously, it is likely that the increase in weaponry also reflects a growing concern with defense and warfare. Sapir (1907:252, 272) notes that some western Oregon groups "were accustomed to make raids" on their neighbors "to procure supplies of food and other valuables," and that the "principal weapon of offensive warfare was of course the bow and arrow." One incentive for raiding in the Willamette Valley was to secure slaves, who were often taken to trading centers on the Columbia River (Jacobs et al. 1945:191, 193, 349; Jacobs et al. 1945:41). Zenk (1976:5–6) reports that the Tualatin brokered in slave trading, and "at least occasionally conducted slave-raiding expeditions in such areas as the southern Willamette Valley and the central Oregon coast." John Work's comment in his journal about raiding between Marys River and Umpqua people, and about Marys

River people being raided for slaves by more local neighbors, has already been mentioned (Work 1923:264). Whatever the motivation, the dramatic increase in projectile points within the last ca. 1,700 years is clear.

One of the valley's most carefully documented mound sites is the Calapooia Midden (35LIN468), found on the Calapooia River between Brownsville and Albany (Roulette et al. 1996), and one of at least 125 other mound sites known to exist on a sinuous 30-mile run of the river (fig. 5.16). Several functionally distinct areas were identified within the ca. 150-meter-long site. Area A appears to have been used for food, especially camas, processing. Area B, on a sandy

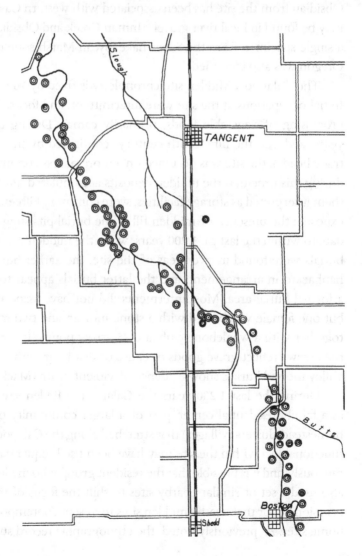

Fig. 5.16. A portion of a map of "Calapooia Prehistoric Mounds" produced ca. 1926, showing mound density along an approximately eight mile segment of the Calapooia River in Linn County (courtesy the University of Oregon Museum of Natural and Cultural History).

point bar adjacent to the river, was used partly as a disposal area. Area C was the focus of occupation at the site, containing midden deposits and the bulk of the tool and faunal assemblages. The Calapooia Midden's tool assemblage is diverse, and includes a broad range of chipped stone tools, stone bowl mortars and pestles, metates and manos (grinding slabs and handstones), and pipe stems and bowls made of baked clay and soapstone. The faunal assemblage (much of which had been burned) also reflects a broad range of prey species, including deer, elk, grizzly and black bear, dog or coyote, bobcat, beaver, raccoon, rabbit, gopher, squirrel, Canada goose, blue goose, and pintail duck. Obsidian from the site has been associated with western Cascade sources that may be found in local river gravels (Inman Creek and Obsidian Cliffs sources); a single specimen from the Silver Lake/Sycan Marsh source in south-central Oregon was also identified.

The Calapooia Midden site chronology is fixed by 16 radiocarbon dates. Initial occupations at the site were intermittent, and focused on the seasonal processing of vegetable foods, primarily camas. During the last ca. 1,200 years, and into the nineteenth century (confirmed by the presence of glass trade beads), the site was occupied on a more or less continual basis, and it is during this time that the midden deposits accumulated. Pit features, most of them interpreted as storage facilities, were common. Fifteen burials were also exposed; the presence of midden fill in the burial pits suggests that these all date to within the last ca. 1,200 years, when the midden deposits formed. The burials were found in two areas of the site; the earlier burials appear more haphazard in arrangement, and the latter burials appear to be organized in a formal burial area. Most interments did not have associated grave goods, but one female was buried with a stone mortar, and two males were buried together with a whalebone club and 25 arrow points. It is not clear whether the arrows reflect grave goods or cause of death, or both. Other Willamette Valley mound burials show evidence of violent death (Mackey 1974:53).

During the last 1,200 years the Calapooia Midden site probably served as a family residential center, part of a larger community of homesteads or homestead clusters (villages) that stretched along the Calapooia River. Various functional loci within the site may have been used sequentially or contemporaneously, and it is possible that the resident group who made their home here also used a set of similar nearby sites to shift the focus of primary residence occasionally, or that nearby midden sites represent contemporary neighboring home sites. As previously noted, the ethnographic record suggests that small corporate groups (related families and associates), such as those who resided at the Calapooia Midden, exercised exclusive rights over specific resource areas (Zenk 1976; Ames 2006), and the presence of an organized burial ground at the Calapooia Midden implies strong spiritual ties to the locality.

The Fuller and Fanning mounds, located on the Yamhill River near McMinnville at the northern end of the valley, also probably date (based on an assessment of artifacts) largely within the last millennium (excavations took place before the development of radiocarbon dating). Both sites were excavated in the early 1940s, mostly by a medical doctor (W. T. Edmundson) from nearby Newberg, whose interest in the sites was largely focused on human burials. The work appears to have lacked systematic excavation controls, and much of the documentation derives from correspondence with William Laughlin of Willamette University, and Laughlin's notes from his participation in part of the excavation (Laughlin 1943). Subsequent reports are based on reference to the early documents, and analysis of some of the other recovered materials (Collins 1951; Murdy and Wentz 1975; Woodward, Murdy, and Young 1975; Stepp 1994).

The Fuller and Fanning mounds were probably stable residential locations, and may have been larger villages than the homestead site represented by the Calapooia Midden. Although no evidence of house structures was recovered, as is typical of the late residential sites in the valley, both sites contained much evidence of fire hearths and fire-cracked rock, many human burials, and a wide variety of artifact types, including larger ground stone bowls and other items that are not highly portable.

Other recovered tools reflect a great range of domestic activities: flaked stone knives, scrapers, and an awl used in hunting and hide working; bone points and pieces that represent parts of composite harpoons or fish spears; grooved pebbles that served as sinkers for fishing nets; mortars and pestles that may have been used to mill wild seeds, acorns, hazelnuts, and other foods; large, heavy antler wedges for splitting planks and other wood working tasks; stone hammers for driving wedges, pounding stakes, and splitting tool stone.

Game animals identified in the bone assemblage include elk, deer, beaver, fox, various birds, and fish. A number of large perforated elk antler tines, used historically as handles for root-digging sticks, attest to the importance of camas and other roots; the collecting and processing of wild vegetable foods on a large scale is suggested by abundant fragments of fire-cracked rock, certainly from earth ovens.

Artistic and ceremonial aspects of life were well represented at the Fuller and Fanning sites by artifacts of both native and Euroamerican manufacture. Many such objects were owned by people of high status and wealth, recognizable by their Chinookan-style cranial reshaping, a privilege reserved for high-status families throughout the southern Northwest Coast region. A large, beautifully flaked double-ended obsidian knife is of a type considered to be a wealth blade used ceremonially by some Native groups in southern Oregon and northern California. Two large paddle-shaped "fish clubs," beautifully carved from whalebone, are of types best known from the southern Northwest Coast, including the lower Columbia River and Pacific coast from Oregon to British Columbia. Shell beads of *Olivella*, *Glycymeris* (a clam), and *Haliotis* (abalone), strung as necklaces or bracelets, represent marine species imported from the Pacific coast (fig. 5.17)

The richness of the artistic and ceremonial complex from the Fuller and Fanning sites is striking, and parallels the remarkable artifact inventory at the Gold Hill site in southwest Oregon. A clear implication is that the people of the Willamette Valley participated fully in the society and economy of the broader Pacific Northwest. While households (and larger kin-based communities) were the primary economic, political, and social unit throughout the region, they were also corporate entities. As Ames (2001, 2006) notes for the Pacific coast region, chiefs were first household chiefs, but they also represented the corporate household in regional networks of alliance, commerce, and competition.

Relatively few mound sites, and fewer burials, which might allow clearer documentation of these relationships, have been excavated in recent decades.

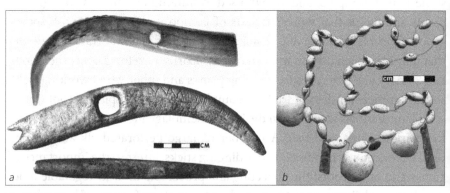

Fig. 5.17. Artifacts from Fuller and Fanning mounds: *a*, antler digging stick handles and bone pin; *b*, marine shell beads and brass pendants.

Laughlin (1941) reported excavation of a burial in a mound site near Harrisburg, in the upper Willamette Valley. The adult male had a flattened cranium, and was buried with *Dentalium* and copper beads, and possibly a bearskin robe. It is worth recalling that Kalapuya mounds were highly attractive to artifact hunters from at least the late 1800s. Based on undocumented excavations in the Willamette Valley mounds in the early 1900s, some early writers speculated that the "mound builders of Oregon" must have been related to the sophisticated Neolithic cultures of northeast Asia and Japan, owing to the variety and richness of the artifacts found within (Wright 1922:87; Horner 1919).

The Fuller and Fanning mounds produced hundreds of projectile points, a remarkably uniform collection of small triangular arrowpoints (either corner-notched or stemmed at the base) very similar to points from other late Willamette Valley sites. Again, this proliferation of arrowpoints suggests a heightened concern with defense and boundary maintenance, considerations of relevance to settled communities with lands and proprietary resources to defend.

The Contact Period

The artifact assemblages from the Fuller and Fanning mounds included historic trade goods such as brass buttons and rings, glass trade beads, and rolled copper bangles, indicating occupation of the sites into the nineteenth century. The richness reflected by these sites contrasts sharply with the Kalapuya communities encountered by the earliest Euroamerican visitors to the valley. Missionary Gustavus Hines (1851:118) recorded in 1840 his meeting with "the Callapooah chief [and] about sixty of his people . . . Many of them were sick, and they appeared wretched beyond description." Most early writers were not cognizant of the near total devastation that a greater than 95% epidemic mortality brought to the Kalapuya and their social institutions, caused by previously unknown Euroamerican diseases such as smallpox and malaria, which drove them from their traditional settlements where persistent contagion lurked. The most reliable estimates put the Kalapuya population at close to 20,000 in 1770, but by the mid-1840s the total Kalapuya population was estimated at less than 600. This small number represented a degraded, demoralized, and impoverished Native community that offers a poor measure of pre-contact Kalapuya lifeways, political organization, and social institutions. While fatal diseases affected all of North America, the Willamette Valley was probably among the most devastated areas of the continent in what one writer has called "the greatest demographic disaster in the history of the world" (Denevan 1976:7).

The reports of mid-nineteenth-century encounters with the Kalapuya differed so sharply from the evidence of a settled and culturally sophisticated people revealed in the valley's mound sites that early writers consistently attributed the archaeological findings to someone other than the Kalapuya. Anthropologist Joel Berreman (1937:20) commented that "So early and so complete was the extermination that [missionaries Jason] Lee and [Joseph] Frost, who spent ten years in Oregon (1834–1844) and were constantly at the Salem mission in the heart of the Willamette Valley, ridicule Samuel Parker (also a missionary who visited the Willamette Valley in the 1830s) for saying that there were many tribes and a numerous people. They state that there never was but one tribe, and that the valley is uninhabited save for a few families on the Yamhill River and a small remnant of Calapuya farther up the valley." Unfortunately, the image of nomads who wandered throughout the valley persisted with many later writers, belying the more accurate characterization of a populous valley with a highly managed landscape, dotted with many dozens of settled communities.

Fatal sickness remained a chronic reality throughout the contact period, and the devastation caused by the epidemics of the early 1830s is most grimly documented. Nathaniel Wyeth (1899:180) observed that "There appears much sickness amon[g] the people here . . . . the main disorder is an intermittent fever which has carried off all or nearly all the Indians . . . ." Father Pierre de Smet (1906:122–123) recorded that "The population of entire villages was cut off by this terrible pestilence." John Kirk Townsend (1978:223), who was at Fort Vancouver in 1834, observed that "Probably there does not now exist one, where, five years ago, there were a hundred Indians." Samuel Parker (1967:191–192) noted that the "great mortality" waned only "from want of subjects."

A formal record of "tribal" groups was made at the Champoeg treaty proceedings in 1851 and again at the Dayton proceedings in 1855, but the extent to which these groups reflect pre-epidemic social relationships is unknown. The most detailed ethnographic records—which represent only a few Kalapuya bands, however—were made by linguists who interviewed native speakers in 1877 and later decades, a generation or more after pre-reservation lifeways were discontinued (Gatschet 1877, 1899; Frachtenberg

1915, 1918; Jacobs et al. 1945). Most Kalapuya descendents are now affiliated with the Confederated Tribes of the Grand Ronde and the Confederated Tribes of Siletz reservations of Oregon.

Archaeology of the Historic Period

Before the Oregon Trail. One relatively little-known aspect of Oregon's contact period history involves French-Canadian and Metis (French-Canadian-Indian) fur trappers who worked for the British Hudson's Bay Company. By 1829 some of them had begun to retire and establish farms in that portion of the northern Willamette Valley now known as French Prairie—a decade before the great western migration of American settlers who followed the Oregon Trail in the 1840s and 1850s. Most of these trappers had local Indian wives and families. Archaeological study has identified more than a hundred of their homestead sites (Brauner 1989), and a sample of ceramic fragments has been systematically collected, primarily from the home sites of Etienne Lucier (35MA261), Joseph Despard (35MA262), Joseph Gervais (35MA248), and Michel Laframboise (35YA17). Analysis of this large ceramic collection has been reported by Chapman (1993); she notes that the economic dominance of the British Hudson's Bay Company can be seen in the household assemblages, at a time preceding the American influence that later overwhelmed the valley.

Fort Vancouver was the principal hub of Euroamerican activity in the Pacific Northwest prior to 1850. Established in 1824 and largely destroyed by about 1866, the fort is of course known from its managerial documents, but archaeology is an important source for key kinds of information on the site that was so central to nineteenth-century developments in the Pacific Northwest. The earliest excavations, carried out when the fort was designated a national monument in 1948, identified the location of many of its fortifications, buildings, and trash pits and produced an "almost unbelievable quantity of historical objects" (Caywood 1955:71). Dozens of archaeological studies have since been conducted, providing information about the fort's role in the region's nineteenth-century economy; the vast artifact collections are also important for research and comparative analyses (Langford n.d.; Wilson et al. 2003)

American Settlement of the Valley. Champoeg is now the name of a state park located on the south bank of the Willamette River north of Woodburn. The name probably derives from a Kalapuya word for an edible root that grew there, and may have also referred to an ancient Native community located in the area (Zenk 1976). As French Prairie was settled in the 1830s, Champoeg developed as an economic and social center, and was a budding town by the early 1840s. It served as a shipping point for agricultural produce, was the site for the Willamette Valley's first grist mill, built in 1835, and hosted the meeting that formed Oregon's first Provisional Government in 1843. In 1861 the town was destroyed by flooding; though partially rebuilt, its end came in 1892 following another devastating flood. Archaeological investigations of the Champoeg townsite (35MA186) were carried out during the 1970s and intermittently thereafter (Atherton 1975; Brauner 1987; Middleton 1975; Speulda 1988; Peterson 2008). This work has established the location of original streets and buildings, and provides insight into the community's economic life. Speulda (1988:124) notes that the influx of American settlers in the 1840s and 1850s shifted the principal source of supplies from British (through the Hudson's Bay Company) to American manufacturers. Peterson (2008) conducted a study of locally produced ceramics recovered from Champoeg, using Instrumental Neutron Activation Analysis to derive geochemical profiles of the constituent clays, and comparing these to samples from four known Oregon and Washington late-nineteenth-century pottery production sites. The study yielded only one match of a Champoeg vessel to a nineteenth-century Oregon potter. More research is clearly needed to trace the valley's many nineteenth-century craft potters who supplied such wares in the decades before manufactured products were readily available (see Schablitsky 2007).

Archaeological work has also been conducted at the nearby Robert Newell Farmstead site (35MA41). Newell occupied the site from 1843 to 1854, but archaeological data attest to prior occupants as well (Manion 2006). The first may have been John Ball, who had joined an expedition organized by Nathaniel Wyeth to travel overland to the Oregon Territory in 1832; upon reaching Fort Vancouver, Ball stayed on for a year as a teacher before turning to farming. He built a small cabin in the Champoeg area in 1833 which he occupied for less than a year. The following year, Nathaniel Wyeth may have taken advantage of Ball's abandoned homestead, installing caretakers at the site. Due to failing health, Wyeth abandoned his farming ventures in the Oregon Territory in 1836. William Johnson, who arrived in French Prairie in 1836 after retiring from the Hudson's Bay Company, then occupied the site with his Native wife, children and two Native slave boys (Wilkes 1974:104). He stayed until 1842. Newell's subsequent occupation lasted from 1843 until he built a new home on higher ground in 1854. It left the biggest archaeological imprint on the site, due to his large family, increasing access to manufactured products, and architectural upgrades to the original cabin (including adding a wood floor, replacing the wattle and daub chimney with a brick fire box, and installing glass-pane windows). Faunal analysis indicates that the meat consumed by Newell's family was from entirely domesticated stock, primarily sheep (or goat), pig and cattle. This homestead was effectively abandoned by 1854, when Newell rebuilt on higher ground after flooding in 1853. Manion (2006) correctly notes that this unusually early (1833–1853) homestead history would not have come to light in the absence of archaeology.

The Willamette Mission represented a clearly American presence in the Willamette Valley. Located just north of what would become the city of Salem, the mission was established in 1834 by the Methodist minister Jason Lee. Although the Mission converted few Indians and its operation was discontinued in 1843, some of the participating clergy were later active in the formation of Oregon's government. The actual location of the mission was lost until it was relocated by archaeological study in 1980 (Sanders and Weber 1980). The size of the complex and its internal integrity were assessed, and it subsequently became the centerpiece of the Willamette Mission State Park. Over 9,500 artifacts were recovered from 190 square meters of excavated area; analysis confirmed the pre-1850 age of the assemblage, and provides insight into activities and diet. Excavations also revealed information on the architecture and organization of the mission complex. For example, the small size of many recovered fragments indicates that the mission grounds were neatly maintained, while the lack of artifacts associated with the Hudson's Bay Company reflects the missionaries' strategy of keeping their dependence on Fort Vancouver to a minimum (Sanders et al. 1983).

Another early American presence in the Willamette Valley was Ewing Young, who made a name for himself in the West as a trapper, trader, and carpenter. In 1834 he set out for Oregon from California, and settled in the Chehalem Valley, a short distance northwest of the modern community of Newberg. He was a principal partner in the Willamette Cattle Company, formed in 1837 for the purpose of bringing cattle to the valley; they drove a herd across the Siskiyou Mountains from California, arriving in the Willamette Valley with 630 head. When he died a few years later, in 1841, he was perhaps the wealthiest person in the region; on his death he left a large estate that included livestock, a sawmill, a gristmill, and a house. But Young left no will or family, and no legal authority to determine the disposition of his holdings. Meetings of valley residents to discuss his estate included "nearly every male inhabitant south of the Columbia" (Hines 1851:415), and are seen as the catalyst for development of a provisional local government, which was formally established at Champoeg in 1843. In 1987 an archaeological investigation was made to determine the location of Young's homestead. Test probes and mapping of surface artifacts identified the location of a habitation structure built prior to 1841, and the artifacts themselves indicate a period of occupation between ca. 1835 and 1850 (Speulda et al. 1987). The site (35YA16) was found to have good archaeological integrity, and measures were taken to ensure its preservation.

By the early 1840s many American farmers and businessmen living east of the Mississippi River were taking a keen interest in the western "frontier," an interest fueled by economic depression in the east, promoters touting the endless opportunities available in the West, and politicians pointing to the fear of British domination of the Northwest. The first groups of Americans with serious intentions of settling in the West left the banks of the Missouri River in 1841. Over the next three decades an estimated half a million people followed the Oregon Trail west; perhaps a third of this number ended up in the Willamette Valley.

Due in large part to the devastation wrought by epidemic diseases on the Native population, American settlement of the Willamette Valley was largely uncontested. Nonetheless, as settlers increasingly impinged on Native homelands and critical resource areas throughout the West, tensions increased. In the Willamette Valley, Superintendent of Indian Affairs Anson Dart negotiated treaties with the Kalapuya, but they were not ratified by the U.S. government. Joel Palmer assumed the superintendency when Dart resigned in frustration, and he entered a situation where white settlers were anxious to claim title to lands on which Indian ownership had not been ceded. Palmer ultimately established the Coast (Siletz) and Grand Ronde reservations and ordered Native populations into them. Two military posts were established: Fort Hoskins to protect access to the Coast Reservation, and Fort Yamhill to guard Grand Ronde.

Second Lieutenant Philip Sheridan, who would later make his name as a Union general in the Civil War, served as commander at Fort Yamhill and sited Fort Hoskins in 1856. The posts' purpose was not just to monitor the recently displaced Indian population and protect the valley's white settlers, but also to protect the Indians from some of the immigrant whites who expressed hostility toward them. Archaeological investigations have explored Fort Hoskins (35BE15) and Fort Yamhill (35PO75); these efforts have not only identified the layout and internal structure of the posts (Adams and Garnett 1991; Brauner and Stricker 2006), but have provided important insights into the nature of daily life for the resident soldiers, including differences between officers' and enlisted men's diet and recreation habits (Bowyer 1992; Schablitsky 2006). Fort Yamhill is a property within the Oregon State Parks system, and Fort Hoskins is managed by Benton County; both serve as interpretive centers for this important slice of Oregon history. The archaeological studies continue to serve as guides as visitor facilities are developed, to make sure that the archaeological record of these posts is long preserved.

In early 2008, construction at a new hospital complex in Springfield, Oregon, exposed a set of human remains (Connolly et al. 2010). Further investigation showed this to be one of twelve burials in a long-forgotten late-nineteenth-century family cemetery (35LA1461). It was on the donation land claim of William M. and Hixey Stevens, who crossed the plains with ten children by wagon in 1847 and established their claim by October of that year. Their eleventh child, a daughter, was born in 1849, the only child of the family born in Oregon and likely the first child of European descent born in Lane County. Her death in 1854, just prior to her fifth birthday, was probably the first interment in the family plot. Later that same year their second youngest, a son, died shortly before his tenth birthday (fig. 5.18).

Over the next 25 years the cemetery received 12 burials. Probably the last addition to the cemetery was the family matriarch, in 1879. Following her

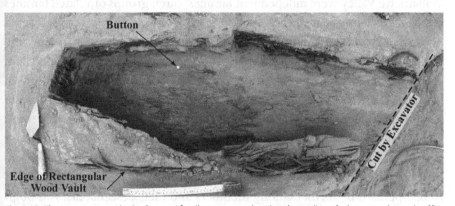

Fig. 5.18. The empty grave 4 in the Stevens' family cemetery, showing the outline of a hexagonal wood coffin.

death the family property was divided among the heirs, and Lane County title documents confirm that the parcel with the cemetery was sold outside the family within the following decade. By the turn of the century, survivors chose to remove family remains to another location; this initial move is likely the reason why memory of the family cemetery was forgotten, until the inadvertent rediscovery of four burials that had been left behind.

Although some of the graves were empty, their size and associated artifacts provided valuable information. The cemetery's population profile confirms the difficult realities of life in a frontier setting. Of the twelve burials, only five were adults. The children (58% of burials) included a probable teen, and six under the age of ten, including two infants. Hixey Stevens, the family matriarch, was the only one of twelve family members to survive to a senior age (72). The other adults died relatively young, ranging from their late 20s to age 55.

The earliest graves featured simple wood coffins, lacking ornamental hardware. Graves from the 1860s had coffin screws and lining tacks, but no elaborate hardware. Graves from the 1870s are distinguished by mass-produced ornamental coffin hardware, including coffin rests and caplifters (lid grips), and decorative casket handles. These burial trends are emblematic of the dramatic changes experienced in the Willamette Valley from ca. 1850 to 1880. The early graves, simple and dominated by children, are consistent with the realities of life in a remote frontier setting. By the time use of the cemetery was discontinued in 1879, the Willamette Valley was on the threshold of being linked to a national rail network, with access to the commercial products of a rapidly industrializing nation.

Many of the new settlers who claimed lands and built homesteads in the Willamette Valley were independent families; often groups of related families established claims near one another. One notable exception was the Utopian Society of Aurora, a communal settlement established by a charismatic religious leader, Dr. William Keil. In 1856 Keil purchased a donation land claim along the Pudding River, south of Oregon City, and established the town Aurora Mills. The colony of some 600 people prospered under Keil's austere leadership, building farms, shops, and mills on the 18,000 acres that were ultimately acquired with communal funds, and producing fruits and other agricultural produce, as well as lumber, clothing, and furniture. The colony dissolved shortly after Keil's death in 1877, but Aurora's businesses continued to be operated by former colony members and their descendents. Although much modified by later developments, many elements of the Aurora Colony have been preserved; Aurora was Oregon's first district to be placed on the National Register of Historic Places.

The Stauffer-Will Farm, located about two miles from Aurora, is one of the district's elements. In 1979 archaeological work at the farm was conducted in areas that were to be modified in order to develop it as a living history center (Minor et al. 1981). Much of the recovered artifact assemblage was architectural (bricks, nails, window glass), and the evolution of the farm was revealed in the sequence of building construction. Other artifacts reflect an ethic of austere self-sufficiency; for example, clothing buttons and fasteners were recovered, but jewelry and ornamental items were not. Nonetheless, the production of cash crops involved regular economic contact outside the community, a reality reflected in the origin of many manufactured goods (dishwares, glassware and medicine bottles, clothing fasteners) from the eastern United States (Minor et al. 1981).

Urbanization and Industry

While agriculture was the centerpiece of the emergent Willamette Valley economy, other industries—especially mining, lumbering, and brick-making—were also important. The need for grain milling in the valley grew quickly with the development of farms. In 1858 a flour mill was built on the Calapooia River, and the adjacent town of Boston was platted in 1861. In 1870 the town had 13 homes and a population of about 50, but it was largely gone within five years. The community's demise is linked with construction of the Oregon and California Railroad a mile to the west, where the new village of Shedd developed. Among those who stayed in Boston was the Simmons family, who operated the mill beginning in 1866. The mill was subsequently purchased by Martin Thompson; it remains a working mill and is now managed by Oregon State Parks as the Thompson's Mill State Heritage Site. Archaeological study of the Boston townsite (35LIN713) revealed few traces of the townsite as a whole, but remains of the Simmons home (35LIN712) were located. Among the interesting finds were sherds of redware pottery produced by local potter Barnett Ramsay (fig. 5.19). Ramsay is representative of numerous farmer-potters who settled in the Willamette Valley, supplementing their farming income with handmade wares. By about the 1880s, these craftsmen faded from the scene as improved transportation networks (especially railroads) effectively linked the valley with the industrial east (Schablitsky 2007).

Fig. 5.19. Fragments of Ramsay redware pottery recovered from excavation of the Simmons home at the Boston townsite; the insets show impressions of the potter's fingerprints preserved on the shards.

Activity in the Little North Santiam River mining district may have begun as early as the 1850s, following the discovery of gold in California and southwest Oregon, but remained on a relatively modest scale until the late 1890s. In 2005 an archaeological study (Connolly et al. 2006) was made of a small mining camp in the district (35MA266) within a claim named Dolores #10 (fig. 5.20). The identity and affiliation of the miners who used this small camp remain undetermined; the Dolores claims from which the site derives its name were registered decades after this camp fell into disuse. The remains of two structures, probably floors for tent cabins (one probably a cooking facility and the other living quarters) were identified and mapped along with associated debris scatters. The period of most consistent age overlap among items in the artifact assemblage is ca. 1900–1910, a time that corresponds with the period of most intensive mining activity in the Little North Fork district, when a great number of small, independent operators worked the area. Following this period, the history of the district is one of consolidation by a small number of larger enterprises (Connolly et al. 2006).

The development of urban centers followed the establishment of farming and other industries. In 1850 the area that would become Portland was little more than a stopping point between Fort Vancouver and Oregon City, the capital of the Oregon Territory. But Portland had the advantage of its location at the confluence of the Willamette and Columbia rivers and its ability to accommodate deep-draft vessels, and it quickly grew as the major port

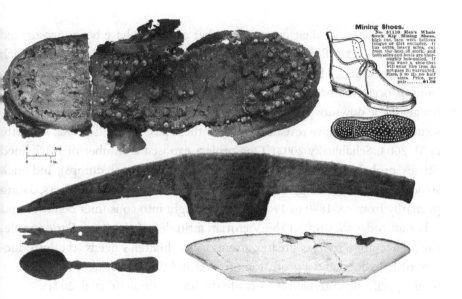

Mining Shoes.

No. 31110 Men's Whole Stock Kip Mining Shoes, high cut, lace with bellows tongue or dirt excluder. It has extra heavy soles, cut from the best of stock, and both soles and heels are thoroughly hob-nailed. If you want a shoe that will wear like iron do not pass it; warranted. Sizes, 6 to 11; no half sizes. Price, per pair.........$1.99

Fig. 5.20. Artifacts from the Dolores mining camp on the Little North Santiam River: sole of a hob-nailed mining boot, mining pick, and eating utensils.

of the Pacific Northwest. By the end of the century, Portland had become a city with a commercial downtown, a bustling waterfront, and active industry. Portland's rapid growth from frontier to city over the span of a few decades in the late nineteenth century is matched by transformations throughout the twentieth century that were equally dramatic, and new developments regularly expose the city's earlier remnants.

Archaeological studies conducted in the downtown area in the mid 1990s, prior to construction of a new federal courthouse, revealed a history of late-1880s occupation associated with a Chinese laundry and adjacent residential quarters that housed both Chinese and non-Chinese tenants (35MU169). The analysis suggested that the Chinese launderers were generally less well-off than their non-Chinese working-class neighbors, but that they were not consistently buying the least expensive goods and foodstuffs; it found rather that they were "frugal without being miserly" (Roulette et al. 1994:iii). The assemblage also provides clues to acculturation; for example, butchered animal remains reflect continued use of the traditional Chinese cleaver in food preparation, but food choices (increased use of beef, decreased use of fish) and other indicators show the adoption of more typically American eating patterns.

Privies, which often functioned as convenient disposal pits, have the potential to provide very informative profiles of the diet, economic position, and social values of their users. A number of privies have been investigated in Portland, each reflecting much about the different neighborhoods in which they were found. Historic maps reveal that the Portland State University campus occupies former residential neighborhoods which developed on the fringe of the downtown core in the late 1870s, and a number of campus construction projects have revealed traces of these past uses (Ellis 1982; Roulette et al. 2004; Schablitsky 2002). One project exposed a number of brick-lined privies, probable unlined privies, other pits (probable trash dumps), and brick structures that may have been plumbing features. Associated artifacts, dating primarily from ca. 1880 to 1900, provide insight into consumer behavior and other attitudes that reflect the Victorian attitudes of the time. For example, the archaeology reflects greater attention to children's needs (the introduction of baby food and a profusion of toys) and the increasing importance of items specifically intended to beautify the home (Roulette et al. 2004).

Another construction project exposed a residential privy (35MU120) dating to the mid-1890s (Schablitsky 2002). Research associated the feature with a prosperous middle-class family who resided at the address from ca. 1893 to 1896. The privy was used for occasional daily refuse disposal, but a large single dumping event may mark the family's 1896 departure. Although the bulk of the assemblage reflects a middle-class status, it also includes gilded imported porcelain tea cups and evidence of the occasional consumption of caviar and wine (Schablitsky 2002). In a more recent project, a wood-lined privy shaft (35MU129) was inadvertently discovered during the repair of a water main adjacent to the Naito Parkway, which traverses a formerly working-class neighborhood of boarding houses and single-family homes adjacent to the industrialized Willamette River waterfront. Ceramics, soda bottles, and local

Fig. 5.21. A patent medicine bottle and Ireland "Home Rule" pipe from a the Naito Parkway privy.

medicine bottles date the privy deposit to the mid- to late 1880s (fig. 5.21). The assemblage contained no definitive markers of a male presence in the associated household, but jewelry, shoes, and perfume bottles indicate the presence of one or more women, and a child's presence is confirmed by the presence of toys and a child's cup. Inexpensive table and serving wares, frugal meat cuts, and clay pipes are consistent with a working-class neighborhood demographic; a pipe with an Irish political slogan and a Chinese bowl are indicative of the neighborhood's multicultural profile (Rose et al. 2007).

These studies provide reminders that formation of the archaeological record is ongoing, and while the most recent portions of the archaeological record are much enhanced with associated historic documentation, an archaeological perspective serves to contextualize recent human endeavors into the much longer narrative of Oregon cultural history, and reveals that history on a human and personal level.

Summary

Cultural radiocarbon dates from the Willamette Valley approach an age of ca. 12,000 years, indicating an ancient and persistent human presence. However, the number of known sites in the valley older than about 6,000 years is very low. This is partly a function of the fact that early sites are more likely than recent ones to be deeply buried by sediment, or destroyed by migrating watercourses, on the valley's floodplain. Most early sites have small cultural assemblages, and provide a picture of family groups moving frequently from one hunting or foraging site to another through a sparsely populated landscape, leaving a relatively light footprint. Beyond the valley floor, Cascadia Cave presents a more substantial site, with a relatively robust cultural assemblage. This site appears to have been regularly used, especially during summer and fall months, as a base for hunting, gathering, woodworking, and food processing.

A few camas-processing ovens dating older than 7,000 years have been reported, but their numbers increase dramatically after about 6,000 years ago. Camas ovens are the most common and visible archaeological feature in the Willamette Valley, and their common occurrence in the period after 6000 BP marks the beginning of large-scale harvesting and food processing, and may signal the beginning of regular food storage that is correlated with a more settled residential strategy. Throughout the Columbia River basin and along the Pacific Northwest Coast we see construction of substantial houses, and the intensive harvest of certain abundant foods (such as salmon and camas) during the middle Holocene (Ames 1985, 1991; Ames and Marshall 1980, Chatters 1989, Jenkins 1994b; Moss and Erlandson 1995; Thoms 1989). In the Willamette Valley, where salmon were never sufficiently abundant to be a primary staple food, this change is reflected in the onset of intensive harvesting and processing of camas (Cheatham 1988; Thoms 1989; Connolly et al. 1997, O'Neill 1987).

The record for intensive fire management of the valley's biotic landscape, which intensifies ca. 3,500 years ago, coincides with the common appearance of midden mounds, which are found in abundance along major streams throughout the valley. Annual burning dramatically increased available foods by favoring the propagation of seed-bearing annuals over woody perennials; expanding the natural ranges of camas, huckleberries, and other food plants; and favoring fire-resistant acorn-bearing oak trees over non-food-bearing competitors. Active landscape management increased the amount of food available within a given area, an important development in an increasingly populated valley. In contrast to the characterizations of early ethnologists, who characterized the Kalapuya as nomadic foragers, the land management and food producing practices of the Willamette Valley Natives over the last several millennia appear to occupy a point on the economic spectrum that is much nearer to farming than to foraging (e.g., Deur 1998; Deur and Turner 2005; Hannon 1990; Suttles 1951; Thoms 1989).

Active landscape management also brought with it a concern with ownership and the establishment and maintenance of boundaries. A common feature of the valley's residential mound sites used during the last 2,000 years is a stunning abundance of small arrow points. The great increase in their numbers cannot be attributed to a suddenly increased interest in hunting, but suggest a more ominous social landscape, including heightened concern with defense, raiding, and boundary maintenance.

A number of late sites also provide evidence for a developed social hierarchy, reflected by cranial reshaping practiced by high-status individuals, who were often accompanied in death by exotic wealth items. These accoutrements of high status mark their owners as chiefly individuals—those who represented their household in dealings with other corporate entities on a regional scale.

The staggering and abrupt impact of introduced diseases in the Willamette Valley was a tragedy that ruined Native society so thoroughly that most early observers simply could not credit the bedraggled survivors they saw with the rich and sophisticated society reflected by their archaeological residue. And, as a result of the precipitous depopulation of the valley, early trappers, and later American farmers, miners and entrepreneurs, soon overwhelmed the diminishing Native population.

The Willamette Valley became the destination of choice for thousands of Americans who, beginning in the 1840s, braved the rigors of the Oregon Trail to carve their version of civilization out of what an America tied to the eastern seaboard saw as the Western frontier. Within a few decades the valley was transformed from a remote frontier of scattered farms to a well-populated and rapidly industrializing economic center.

Chapter 6
Southwestern Mountains and Valleys

Southwest Oregon shares with northwest California the massive and deeply dissected Klamath Mountains, which include the distinctive Siskiyou range that lies athwart the Oregon-California border. Some of Oregon's oldest rocks occur here; the Paleozoic shales, sandstones, reefs, and submarine pillow basalts of the Klamaths reveal that they began more than 250 million years ago as a series of island arcs developed on the eastward-moving Pacific plate. The great folding, distortion, and metamorphism seen in their stratigraphy reflects the pressure and heat of an inexorable slow-motion collision of these exotic terranes with the North American continent, when the accumulating mountains also absorbed huge magma intrusions from below as the oceanic plate carrying them dived beneath the continental edge (Orr et al. 1992). The volcanic Cascades that are so prominent today formed just east of the Klamaths much later, beginning only some 30 million years ago, and the two mountain systems now crowd one another so closely that the regional landscape is almost all steep and rocky. Interior valley systems are few and small, and their rivers penetrate to the Pacific through steep, narrow canyons. The Klamath Mountains are comparatively low, however, with few peaks above 7,000 feet and most interior valley floors around 1,000–1,500 feet above sea level. Corresponding to this altitudinal range, the high mountains are snowy in winter but the lower elevations have relatively mild winters and hot summers that are the driest in western Oregon. Archaeological sites that people occupied at different seasons for varied purposes are widely scattered in this complex landscape (fig. 6.1).

Its exceptionally rugged physiography makes remoteness and isolation a dominant characteristic of southwestern Oregon, and has strongly shaped its plant, animal, and human communities. The biota is varied and complex, including some species that exist only here, and others that have persisted in

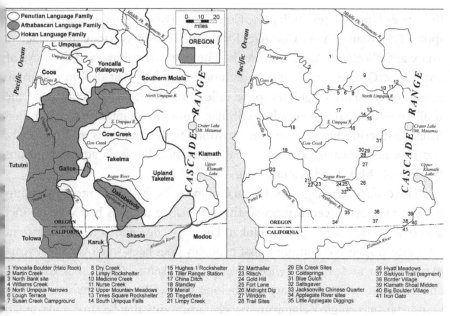

Fig. 6.1. Southwest Oregon ethnic group territories and site locations.

isolation after spreading into the region from neighboring wetter or dryer areas as climates fluctuated over time (Detling 1968; Todt 1990). Human societies were also affected by this cut-up landscape, as indicated by the high degree of linguistic and ethnic differentiation within its comparatively small geographic area.

The Cultural Context

The native people were separated by the deep dissection and ruggedness of their country into many scattered bands. The Shasta, a Hokan-speaking group, extended from the middle Rogue River southward to the Klamath River in California. Speakers of Penutian languages included the Lowland Takelma of the upper Illinois and middle Rogue River valleys, the Upland Takelma of the upper Rogue, and the Cow Creek Umpqua and Yoncalla of the Umpqua Basin. Speakers of Athapaskan languages occupied both sides of the Klamath Mountains, their range extending along the coast and upriver to include the Upper Umpqua and Upper Coquille valleys. Islands of Athapaskan speakers also lived in the Medford-Grants Pass area, surrounded by people using Penutian languages. Athapaskan groups included, from north to south, the Upper Umpqua (excluding the Cow Creek Band of Upper Umpqua, who spoke Takelman), Upper Coquille, Kwatami, Tututni, Shasta Costa, Chetco, Tolowa, Galice, and Applegate bands. The material culture and life ways of Southwest Oregon's various communities shared a great deal in common, even though many neighbors spoke different and unrelated languages—the similarities being due no doubt to similar economic adaptation to a hunting-fishing-gathering lifestyle, similar environmental conditions and materials, and routine intermarriage and social interaction between adjacent groups (Sapir 1907; Miller and Seaburg 1990).

The diverse languages spoken in Oregon's southwestern mountains during the nineteenth century reveal that the native peoples had very distinct ancestries. The Shasta speak a Hokan language, descended from an ancient far-western speech community that probably goes back well over 5,000 years in the region, and possibly twice as long. The Takelma, Cow Creek Umpqua, and Yoncalla, whose languages all belong to the Penutian phylum, are descended from a single Kalapuyan speech community that became widespread in western Oregon 5,000 or more years ago. A much later migration was that of the Athapaskans, who came from a far northern region in southeast Alaska, probably arriving between about 1,500 and 1,000 years ago (Foster 1996; Moratto 1984; Shipley 1978).

A surviving illustration of an Umpqua house from the 1850s shows a substantial rectangular plank building with a gabled roof, in its construction very similar to the plank houses known farther up the Northwest Coast, but much smaller than the multi-family lineage structures that were built there. Takelma, Shasta, and Athapaskan houses were of similar construction, some with plank covering, others sheathed with slabs of bark, and all generally scaled to accommodate an individual family. Lightly built temporary structures served for shelter during seasonal sojourns away from the main settlements.

The people of southwestern Oregon made their living from the wide variety of resources to be found along the big rivers, small interior valleys, narrow canyons, and upland zones they typically visited over the course of an annual round (Gray 1987; Hannon 1990; LaLande 1990). Many groups centered themselves in small lowland settlements of a few households each, where there was suitable water, while more populous villages were generally located in resource-rich settings on alluvial terraces of the larger salmon streams. Many lowland settlements occupied through the winter might be all but abandoned for much of the summer, as families scattered into small, temporary but annually re-occupied camps in the surrounding higher elevations to hunt, collect vegetal foods, obtain tool stone, and gather materials for weaving and other crafts.

Fishing was the focal event of summer and early fall, when salmon, steelhead, and eels abounded in the rivers leading up from the Pacific. Many households came together at these times for mass harvests, which were only obtainable in a relatively small number of favorable locations. The best spots were at falls or in places where brush weirs could be built in the river channel to guide the spawning fish through narrow gateways for spearing or catching in basketry traps.

Other major food sources included year-round populations of trout, suckers, crayfish, and freshwater mussels from the streams; deer, elk, bear, squirrels, rabbits, acorns, pine nuts, berries, and other items from the woodlands; and camas bulbs, acorns, sunflower seeds, tarweed seeds, and other plant foods from the grasslands. Camas roots were dug in early spring and summer, baked in earth ovens, and stored for the coming winter. Acorns were gathered in early fall as another eminently storable winter staple. To make them edible they were pulverized in a hopper mortar, and the resulting meal was then leached in water to remove its bitterness. Thus processed, it could be boiled as gruel or baked in leaf-wrapped cakes.

With winter approaching, households regrouped in their permanent settlements. They occupied themselves during the cold season with such food-getting efforts as were profitable, and with domestic chores. Hunting and fishing went on all year, but hunting was most important in fall and winter, after the plant gathering and salmon seasons had ended. Deer were stalked by hunters disguised with deer heads and skins, or driven by men with dogs, or caught in deep winter snow. Some hunters took deer and elk in deep pit traps dug in game trails. These pits contained upright sharpened stakes to impale and dispatch the unlucky creatures falling into them. Deer and elk were also taken with rope snares that were hung over game trails in appropriate spots.

The social landscape in southwestern Oregon during the ethnographic period included two levels of community organization: many scattered hamlets of a few related family households, and a much smaller number of large villages situated on the main salmon rivers or in other resource-rich localities that could support many households. Each community, large or small, was an autonomous unit, with the heads of prosperous and dominant families assuming leadership for the group as a whole. The larger villages, however, were places where greater disparities in wealth and power could grow between families of varying circumstances, and where social status differences could become pronounced. They were also focal points where the regional populace as a whole would gather seasonally for important events such as the salmon harvest. With these characteristics the large villages were also centers of ceremony, trade, the negotiation of marriages, and sociopolitical interactions of all kinds.

Like the socially complex societies farther up the Northwest Coast, southwestern Oregon communities observed important rank and status distinctions, but individual family households had more autonomy than was common in the north. Oregon leaders maintained their elevated status and influence by their intelligence, social skills, generosity, and charisma, rather than by the kind of more coercive institutionalized authority the chiefly class was allowed to exercise farther north.

A strong sense of identity and territoriality was shared among local communities, and skirmishes were sometimes fought over trespasses by people from outside the established networks. Raiding other communities for wives, goods and resources, and even slaves, who might be sold outside the local area, were also part of the regional social milieu, as was retaliatory counter-raiding. Sapir (1907:272) was told that the Upland Takelma "were accustomed to make raids to procure supplies of food and other valuables," and were also known to sell slaves taken in such raids to neighboring Klamath people, who in turn resold them at rendezvous at The Dalles on the Columbia River.

Acting to somewhat mitigate these stresses were occasions when large groups of neighbors got together for ritual observances, trade, and other social interactions at major fishing sites or other productive localities. Such gatherings in a positive atmosphere of thankfulness to the spirits of the fish and other animals who gave themselves for the sustenance of the people also offered individuals the chance to accommodate old grievances. They similarly helped people keep up good social relationships in general, through the gifting between families and friends of a wide variety of products such as acorns, camas, dried salmon, pine nuts, and baskets. Especially important in these social contexts was the rule of exogamy–which required women to marry out of their natal community–because it fostered ties of marriage and kinship that linked families and villages over a considerable area. Thus, women played a prominent role in all intersocietal arenas, both as the producers of most of the goods that were shared and as the social glue between their biological families and those they married into. Insightful discussions by Tveskov (2007) and Tveskov and Cohen (2006:14–20) detail the key roles that women played in shaping and stabilizing the social order and traditions of southwestern Oregon, even while men were the publicly acknowledged political leaders.

As outlined above, the ethnographically known lifeway of southwestern Oregon was built up out of a long, stable, and continuous aboriginal tradition of living with the land. This inherited knowledge, much of it still alive today or recorded in ethnographic sources, guides and enlivens our understanding of the archaeology and deep human past of the region, and most of this chapter is devoted to that historical narrative. First, however, it is important to detail more fully the natural landscape within which that history was played out.

The Natural Environment

The Coast Range and seaward side of the Klamath Mountains are generally covered by western hemlock and Douglas-fir forest. Sitka spruce grows in the coastal fog belt, western redcedar is common in moist settings, and ponderosa and sugar pine occur on drier sites. In the Cascades, the higher elevations are covered with forests of Pacific silver fir, Shasta red fir, and Grand fir. These montane evergreen forests ring a compact interior zone of mixed coniferous and broadleaf forest that covers the intermediate and lower elevations. This lower-elevation forest, with intermingled stands of Douglas-fir, broadleaf evergreen tan oak, and madrone, is similar to the dry Californian woodlands farther south. In the lowest-lying interior valleys around Roseburg, Medford, and Grants Pass, there occurs yet another kind of vegetational mosaic. This assemblage, adapted to the hot, dry summers of the area, includes varying mixtures of Douglas-fir, ponderosa pine, Oregon white oak, California black oak, and manzanita. Again, the greatest similarity is with Californian rather than Oregonian vegetation patterns (Franklin and Dyrness 1973).

The mammalian fauna of southwestern Oregon includes black bear, Roosevelt elk, mule deer, rabbits, squirrels, and many smaller mammals, to name only a few of the species known to have been important in the traditional diet. Characteristic birds included grouse, woodpecker, band-tailed pigeon, and a host of small passerine species. Salmon and steelhead ran in the Umpqua, Coquille, Rogue, Illinois, and Klamath rivers in great numbers and along with lamprey eels were a major and dependable food source for the people of southwest Oregon, as they were for Oregon's Plateau peoples. Trout, suckers, and other year-round freshwater fishes were important as well.

Temperature and moisture set the conditions of existence for each kind of plant, and the fact that southwestern Oregon is a transitional zone between moist coast and dry interior, warm south and cool north, is reflected in a highly varied vegetational cover. Salal, rhododendron, and evergreen huckleberry are primarily coastal species that are found in the southwestern Oregon interior as well. Sagebrush, antelope bitter brush, mountain mahogany, western juniper, and other species are plants common to the Great Basin that have found a foothold in southwestern Oregon. Plants of northern affinities are subalpine fir and Engelmann spruce, while plants of southern habitats include digger pine, buckbrush, manzanita, and three-leaf sumac. This present-day flora offers clues to the climatic history of the region, and makes it clear that the same postglacial fluctuations in warmth and moisture as mentioned in other chapters affected southwestern Oregon as well (Todt 1990).

The summer-dry "Californian" climate of southwestern Oregon was established in pre-human times. Drought-adapted species moved up from the south during warm intervals. Cooler and drier intervals allowed northern and Great Basin species to extend into the area. With mid-postglacial warming, species that flourish in warmer and drier conditions were able to expand their geographical range, giving prominence to the oak, manzanita, and buckbrush that characterize the valleys of southwestern Oregon today. At higher elevations, in steep and shaded valleys, and in other local microenvironments fostered by the rugged terrain, species originally of coastal, northern, or Great Basin origins were able to survive in patches of suitable habitat. This climatic and vegetational history has made Southwestern Oregon a mosaic of great biotic diversity, with one of the most varied floras in North America (Detling 1968; Todt 1990:71).

During the mid-postglacial period of increased warmth and dryness, beginning after about 7600 cal. BP, oak savannahs probably dominated the lower and middle elevations of the mountains, while grassland and brushy chaparral species occupied the valley floors and lower foothills. Coniferous species were forced upward to higher, cooler elevations. The last 5,000 years or so have brought somewhat cooler, moister conditions, and some e-expansion of coniferous woodlands downslope at the expense of oak and chaparral. Because grasslands veined with oak savannah along streams are rich in edible seeds and acorns, it is thought that the expansion of such vegetation during the warm mid-postglacial may have greatly benefited the native people.

It is well documented that recent southwest Oregon natives regularly set fires in order to make their landscape more productive. Jedediah Smith recorded Tututni Indians setting fires near the mouth of the Rogue River in 1828. In September 1841, members of the U.S. Exploring Expedition, who had been traveling through smoky and charred countryside for some days, watched an elderly Indian woman "busy setting fire to the prairie and mountain ravines" (LaLande and Pullen 1999: 255). George Riddle, an early 1850s settler in the Umpqua Valley, wrote of Takelma Indians burning off the grasslands every summer, and described how native women used fire to harvest the abundant tiny seeds of tarweed, which covered whole hillsides in some places. Fire applied to a stand of tarweed would quickly burn off the combustible sticky sap, but leave the plants standing. The gleaners would then pass through the stand with sticks, beating the tarweed stalks to knock "copious amounts" of seeds into their open-mouthed burden baskets.

Fire was also used to maintain open, park-like landscapes favorable to deer, elk, and other food animals, and to drive and harvest them in due course. In their systematic use of regular burning to manage their landscape and maintain it in a productive condition, the Indians of Southwestern Oregon were at one with native peoples all up and down the West Coast and indeed much farther afield, as well-documented by historical, anthropological and environmental research (Anderson 2005, Boyd 1999; Hannon and Olmo 1990; Lewis 1973, 1990; Whitlock and Larson 2001). As noted in Chapter 5, the radiocarbon dating of repeated charcoal influxes preserved in Willamette Valley bog sediments shows that fire management of western Oregon landscapes was well established by about 3,500 years ago.

Early Holocene/Pre-Mazama Era (13,200 to 7,600 Years Ago)

The earliest known occupation in Oregon's southwestern mountains is indicated by rare surface finds of Clovis fluted points, which are not radiocarbon-dated locally but have been closely dated in the southwestern U.S. between about 13,200 and 12,800 cal. BP (Waters and Stafford 2007). Clovis points

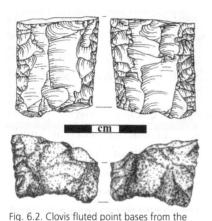

Fig. 6.2. Clovis fluted point bases from the Seneca site (upper, from Ozbun and Fagan 1996) and Hyatt Meadows (lower, from Tveskov and Cohen 2006).

have been found in the upper elevations of the Cascade Range within both the Rogue and Umpqua River drainages, one in the vicinity of upper Butte Creek, a tributary of the Rogue River (Dyck 1982; LaLande and Fagan 1982), and another at Hyatt Meadows, also in the Upper Rogue River drainage near the California border (Deich 1977; Tveskov and Cohen 2006). Another such point is reported from the Umpqua river area near Roseburg (Hanes 1978). These fluted points show that pioneering early people were present in southwest Oregon near the beginning of human times on the continent (fig. 6.2).

Upper Elevation pre-Mazama Occupations. Early Holocene and early middle Holocene occupation is attested by the occurrence of Broad Stem, Side-notched, and large foliate points in the Upper Rogue drainage at Hyatt Meadows and the nearby Cold Spring and Windom sites (Tveskov and Cohen 2006). The upper drainages of the Umpqua River system, particularly the North Umpqua, have also produced considerable evidence that is datable to the early Holocene by its stratigraphic context. With the massive eruption of Mt. Mazama that formed the Crater Lake caldera 7,600 years ago, the upper Umpqua drainage was initially blanketed with airfall volcanic ash, and subsequently by fluvially redeposited ash as well. Many archaeological sites of pre-Mazama age, buried deeply beneath this volcanic outfall, have been found during excavations carried out for hydropower projects, highway building, campground development, and other construction activity. Research at various locations down the drainage documents an important ecological and cultural gradient.

The Medicine Creek site (35DO161) is a rockshelter that contained early Holocene artifacts sealed beneath small stony or glassy airfall lapilli fragments from the Mt. Mazama eruption. A small assemblage thus buried included leaf-shaped and broad-stemmed obsidian points along with scrapers, used flakes, cobble choppers, and large andesite bifaces (Snyder 1981). Small-scale test excavations on a high riverside bench at the nearby Medicine Creek Bridge Site (35DO672) penetrated an approximately two-meter-thick deposit of redeposited volcanic ash and sand to discover a buried clay-loam paleosol that contained a dense deposit of waste flakes, a serrated foliate projectile point, a large utilized flake, and the distal fragment of a large andesite biface (O'Neill 1996). The debitage was dominated by flakes of local andesite, but exotic trans-Cascadian obsidian was also present.

At the Dry Creek site (35DO401), on a broad riverside bench where the creek joins the North Umpqua River, a dense concentration of debris was found in an ancient soil buried by Mazama ash. The eastern portion of the site was relatively rock-free, and appears to have been intentionally cleared. Within this area were three small hearths, one of which yielded a slightly aberrant radiocarbon age of 7400 cal. BP. Among the artifacts of this early Holocene component are foliate and broad-necked projectile points, bifaces (including large specimens made of coarse andesite), endscrapers, spoke-shaves, formed and unformed unifaces, flake knives and scrapers, cores, cobble choppers, hammerstones, grinding slabs, manos, edge faceted cobbles, and drilled stones (fig. 6.3). The debitage collected from the paleosol was dominated by exotic obsidian (Jenkins and Churchill 1989; O'Neill et al. 1999).

The Florence, or Nurse Creek site (35DO554) is located on a minor tributary of the North Umpqua River. Test probes excavated through Mazama ash and lapilli there encountered a buried clay loam paleosol from which two obsidian foliate projectile points, edge-modified flakes, and debitage were recovered. Nearly all of the tool stone recovered from Nurse Creek was obsidian (97%), the rest being chert or jasper cryptocrystalline silicates (CCS). (O'Neill and White 1994; O'Neill 2009, 2010). The Upper Mountain Meadows

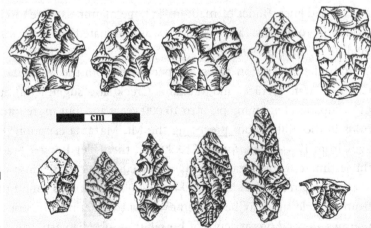

Fig. 6.3. Pre-Mazama broad-stemmed points from Dry Creek (from O'Neill et al. 1996).

site (35DO556) is situated on a broad, well-watered flat lying above Toketee Reservoir. Cultural materials were located there both above and below pockets of Mazama ash by test probes placed around a boggy mire near the head of one of the surrounding drainages. Limited excavation produced a broad-stemmed Windust-like projectile point, a large obsidian bifacial core, CCS biface fragments and end scrapers, and small fragments of bone (O'Neill and White 1994).

The Lough Terrace site (35DO641) was exposed in a roadcut through a volcanic ash-covered bench along the North Umpqua Highway. Test excavations focused on the post-Mazama deposits above the ash, but also confirmed a pre-Mazama component below it. The small sub-ash assemblage included CCS and obsidian waste flakes, a poorly formed biface, utilized flakes, and a hammerstone (O'Neill and White 1994). The Susan Creek Campground site (35DO383) occupies a series of terraces adjacent to the North Umpqua River. Much of the site's cultural record dates from the middle and late Holocene, but a pre-Mazama soil exposed in two small excavation units produced a small cultural assemblage that included andesite bifaces similar to those associated with the pre-Mazama component at Medicine Creek (Musil and O'Neill 1997).

The Umpqua National Forest's Tiller Ranger Station site (35DO37) is located at the confluence of Elk Creek and the South Umpqua River. Excavations there penetrated the Mazama ash to expose a buried soil containing a diverse cultural assemblage of leaf-shaped and wide-stem projectile points, bifaces, scrapers, used flakes, cores, cobble unifaces, milling slabs, manos, an abrader, and a fragment of a slate ornament having marginal grooves and incised lines. Bones of medium-to-large mammals were too fragmentary to identify to species. Lithic debitage was dominated by exotic obsidian (Bevill et al. 1994; Draper 1996).

Obsidian hydration dates on specimens from the Medicine Creek, Dry Creek, Lough Terrace, and Williams Creek sites suggest multiple episodes of occupation beginning prior to 10,000 years ago, but more intense occupations in the millennium preceding the Mt. Mazama eruption. Radiocarbon ages from Dry Creek, Susan Creek, and the Tiller Ranger Station support this estimate, concentrated in the ca. 8500–7400 cal. BP time range. These studies required great care, as O'Neill (2002, 2008) has found that obsidian from a single site may have been exposed to differing ambient temperature regimes, depending on depth of burial; thus, obsidian artifacts deeply buried by Mazama volcanic ash can hydrate much more slowly than shallowly buried post-Mazama artifacts.

The early Holocene assemblages documented in the above series of sites show close ties with the east side of the Cascades; obsidian from eastern sources is common in pre-Mazama site deposits, and represents the dominant lithic material in most. Obsidian from the Spodue Mountain and Silver Lake/ Sycan Marsh sources in the Klamath Lake and Silver Lake basins is most common, but western Cascades sites also include obsidian from Quartz Mountain, McKay Butte, the Big/Buried Obsidian Flow in and around Newberry Volcano, and from Obsidian Cliffs on the North Sister in the Central High Cascades farther north. Far from constituting a barrier between eastern and western Oregon, the Cascades are thus seen to be an important zone of interaction between the two regions, as discussed further below.

Varying Effects of Early Mid-Holocene Warming. A dramatic increase in human use of the western Cascades, beginning in the millennium preceding the Mt. Mazama eruption, corresponds to a notable environmental deterioration east of the high Cascades. As seen in chapter 2, growing warmth and dryness during the early mid-Holocene placed stress on local biotic environments in the Great Basin landscape of central Oregon for at least a millennium prior to the Mt. Mazama eruption (Bedwell 1973; Grayson 1979; Beck and Jones 1997). Bedwell (1973:157–59) perceived that in the Fort Rock Basin, just south of Newberry Volcano, a period of intense occupation about 9,800–9,500 years ago was followed by a slow decline, brought on by increasing aridity and consequent shrinkage in the favorable lake and marsh environment there. The desertification continued with growing intensity through and beyond the time of the Mt. Mazama eruption, causing a notable decrease in signs of human occupation. Connolly (1999) observed a parallel trend at Paulina Lake in the Newberry Caldera, where a substantial residential base camp dating to 9,500 years ago is followed by the more ephemeral camps of small, mobile hunting parties. For the Columbia Plateau to the north, Ames (1988) similarly found that increasing desiccation encouraged greater mobility and shortened periods of stable residence between Windust and early Cascade Phase times. The southwest Oregon evidence shows that another aspect of this human adjustment to changing climate was increased use of the western Cascades. Here, in an inherently moister, Pacific-facing environmental context, the same climatic warming created more favorable conditions for human populations by helping the biotically productive oak and hazel woodlands of the lower western valleys

expand into a broad band of higher-elevation terrain (Sea and Whitlock 1995
O'Neill 2004).

Lower Elevation pre-Mazama Occupations. Fewer sites of pre-Mazama
age are known from southwestern Oregon's lower-lying interior valleys, but
significant and related finds are known on both sides of the Oregon-California
border. Sites on the alluvial terraces of the Applegate River just north of the
Oregon-California border (Brauner 1981) belong to pre-Mazama time, as at
Applegate River site 35JA53, where squat, broad-stemmed lanceolates and
willow-leaf bipoints of medium size (fig. 6.4) have been compared to the early
Holocene Windust type of the Plateau by Brauner (1981). The same types also
appear widely in the early Holocene of northern California, where they are
identified as Borax Lake or Borax Lake Wide Stem points (Harrington 1948;

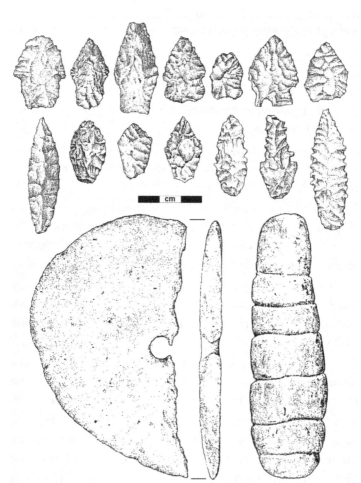

Fig. 6.4. Early
stemmed lanceolate
projectile points
and ground stone
artifacts from
35JA53, Rogue
Applegate Area
(from Brauner and
Nisbet 1983).

Fig. 6.5. Early stemmed and leaf-shaped projectile points from the Rogue-Applegate area.

Clewett and Sundahl 1983; Fredrickson 1984; Sundahl 1988; Fredrickson and White 1988: 82–83). As will be discussed further below, these wide-stem and willow-leaf point types have been identified by Connolly (1986, 1988) as early markers of a long-lived Glade Tradition in the Oregon-California borderlands.

Applegate site 35JA53 shows the character of such occupations. There, two 30-foot square excavations on a high river terrace recovered over 80 broad-stemmed Windust-like points (fig. 6.5), along with edge-faceted cobble tools, flaked stone scrapers, and cutting tools, all probably used in butchering and hideworking. Some peculiar circular discs, an inch or so across and flaked entirely around their edges, are enigmatic. Traces of crushed and decomposed bone were also found with the artifacts, supporting the idea that the site was a hunting and butchering station. No house remains were identified, but cleared camping and work spaces were observed amid the rocks of an upper river terrace. On the next lower terrace a number of serrated leaf-shaped points were found in association with stone bowl mortars, shaped pestles, hopper mortar bases, and mano and milling slab fragments. The grinding tools indicate the processing of such plant foods as camas roots, acorns, and grass seeds, while the projectile points give evidence of hunting.

Another good pre-Mazama example is the Marial site (fig. 6.6), on the Rogue River just above its plunge through the Oregon Coast Range, which has a similarly early stone tool assemblage and a radiocarbon date on its Stratum 2 of about 9600 cal. BP (Griffin 1983; Schreindorfer 1985). Marial is very well situated with regard to diverse food resources. It commands a good salmon and steelhead fishing locality, being embedded in a terrace that

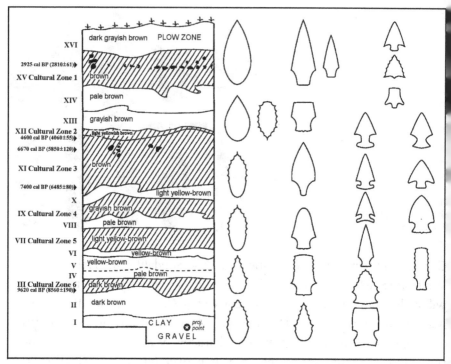

Fig. 6.6. Idealized stratigraphic sequence at Marial, showing depositional layers, occupation zones, radiocarbon dates, and point type distributions (Based on Ross 1987).

overlooks quiet water between major rapids above and below. Other species available to its occupants would have included freshwater mussels, otter, and beaver from the river, and deer, elk, bear, raccoon, rabbit, squirrel, acorns and seeds from the riverside oak-conifer woodlands. An exceptionally advantageous locality, the site was used into later times as well, with small stemmed and triangular arrowpoints appearing after about 3,000 years ago. Some 15 miles farther downstream, at the confluence of the Rogue and Illinois rivers near Agness, the historic period Shasta Costa Athapaskan site of Tlegetlinten (35CU59) has given evidence of early point types like those of Marial and probably was occupied equally far back in time (Tisdale 1986).

Middle Holocene and Early Late Holocene (7,600 to 1,700 Years Ago)

Technologically and stylistically, the cultural assemblages of southwestern Oregon show marked stability and persistence over long periods. During the middle Holocene and continuing into late Holocene times, stemmed and foliate projectile points showing formal continuities from earlier times remained common. Associated artifacts included broad-necked side-notched and stemmed projectile points, globular stone bowl mortars, hammer/anvil stones, edge-faceted cobbles, and thick-bit end scrapers. The most striking characteristic of assemblages sharing these artifacts is that they span most of the Holocene, marking a cultural/technological tradition of unusual conservatism and duration in southwest Oregon. This persistent technology, named the Glade Tradition, has confounded attempts to delineate discrete cultural periods in this region's long record of occupation, at least prior to ca. 1,700 years ago (Connolly and Baxter 1986; Connolly 1986, 1988).

Both stylistic and technological aspects of Glade Tradition assemblages suggest a relationship to the early Pacific Northwest Cascade Pattern (Nisbet 1981; Brauner and Nisbet 1983; Connolly 1986:124–143; Connolly and Baxter 1986). Indeed, a number of sites lacking radiocarbon dates have been assigned early Holocene ages because of the morphological similarity of their projectile points to the Windust and Cascade points of the Columbia Plateau. In local support of this chronological assignment, three radiocarbon dates from early components with similar artifacts at the Marial site fall between 5,500 and 9,000 years ago (Schreindorfer 1985), an expected range for Cascade Pattern and earlier assemblages in the Plateau. However, similar artifacts are also predominant in later-dated components from this and other sites throughout southwest Oregon. Indeed, radiocarbon dates from the Standley site, which range between 2,400 and 300 years ago (Connolly 1986:23), suggest that elements of the Glade Tradition persisted in some areas until protohistoric times. Comparable continuity has been noted in adjacent areas of northern California as well (Fredrickson 1984). The long duration of the Glade Tradition suggests at least a partial explanation for why the development of a refined typologically-based culture chronology for southwestern Oregon has been so elusive.

The Glade Tradition is seen as a regional continuation of the Old Cordilleran or Cascade Pattern, dated to early times throughout the Pacific Northwest (Connolly 1986, 1988; Connolly and Baxter 1986). Comparative statistical analysis of 47 artifact assemblages from the southwestern mountains of Oregon and adjacent California shows that this Glade Tradition began perhaps 9,000 years ago and persisted until quite late prehistoric times in the Umpqua and Coquille river basins (Connolly 1988). The deep, stratified Marial site just mentioned dates its emergence in pre-Mazama early Holocene times on the lower Rogue, while the Standley site documents continuance of the tradition in the upper Coquille/Umpqua region into the last millennium.

Winthrop (1993:253; cf. Chartkoff 1989) suggests that during this time highly mobile small groups moved frequently among scattered resource patches. As she notes, sites investigated in the upper Rogue River and Klamath River Canyon suggest sporadic, low-intensity hunting and food processing (Pettigrew and Lebow 1987; Chartkoff 1989; Nilsson and Kelly 1991; Mack 1991; Winthrop 1993; Connolly et al. 1994). In the Elk Creek drainage of the upper Rogue, Pettigrew and Lebow (1987) report evidence for seasonal hunting (notably deer), and hide and plant processing. For the Trail vicinity, Connolly et al. (1994) suggest short-term warm-season use as a hunting and gathering resource area. Mack (1991:77) reports that sites in the Klamath River Canyon contain generalized tool assemblages including projectile points, cores, and chipped stone gravers, knives, scrapers, and portable stone bowls, and she concludes that the "evidence points to generalized hunter/ gatherers who probably used the canyon seasonally."

North Umpqua Narrows. A key middle Holocene site type is seen a few miles northeast of Roseburg at the Narrows of the North Umpqua River, near where it exits the western Cascades. The authors of an 1855 cadastral survey report described the place as an important Indian fishery, and many artifacts and a series of radiocarbon dates, with the earliest falling about 7000 and 5800 cal. BP, show that people used it from early middle Holocene times on into the modern period (O'Neill 1989, 1990). Perishable food remains were extremely scarce in the archaeological deposits, but fishing, hunting, and plant-gathering activities are clearly implied by the location itself, and borne out by an array of flaked stone projectile points, biface and uniface cutting and scraping tools, cobble choppers, hammerstones, pounding tools, ground stone mortars and pestles, and thousands of cores and flakes.

Saltsgaver Site. A quite different aspect of economic life during the middle Holocene is portrayed by the Saltsgaver site in the Rogue Valley near Medford, where over a hundred roasting pits or earth ovens were exposed by the tilling of a field (Prouty 1989). Fires made in the pits had baked the surrounding earth red and brick-hard, rendering the pit rims clearly visible when agricultural work disturbed the surface soil. Archaeological excavation of several pits revealed charcoal and fire-cracked rocks, and from one pit charred nutshells were recovered. Though the identification is not certain, they were probably acorn hulls. A charred specimen from another pit is probably a camas bulb. Oak trees and camas lilies are now abundant in the general area of the site, and may have been more common before the area was converted to farmland. A ^{14}C date of about 6000 cal. BP from one of the pits shows use of the site beginning in the early middle Holocene, while obsidian hydration readings and associated artifacts of generally late Holocene age indicate the site's continued use into recent times.

The Standley Site. Site numbers increased during and after the late middle Holocene, as shown by evidence from the Standley Site in Camas Valley southwest of Roseburg (Connolly 1991), a number of sites in the Umpqua Basin (Beckham and Minor 1982), a series of sites in the Trail–Elk Creek area of the upper Rogue, and others in the Klamath River Canyon around the Oregon-California border (Brauner and Lebow 1983; Budy and Elston 1986; Connolly et al. 1994; Davis 1983; Nilsson and Kelly 1991; Pettigrew and Lebow 1987; Mack 1983, 1990). Typical hunting assemblages included medium and small foliate points, short, broad Coquille Series points with contracting stems, and a variety of corner- and side-notched dart points. Common plant-processing tools include bowl mortars, cobbles either end-battered or edge-worn as grinders, and flaked cobble choppers. Human evidence is widespread and sites are increasingly abundant, while the cultural patterns for this time remain largely consistent with earlier ones in terms of artifact forms and variety, still giving evidence of highly mobile hunter-gatherer-fisher folk who moved frequently from one short-term harvest or task camp to another.

The Standley site, near the headwaters of the Upper Coquille River, has become a key reference point for understanding the nature of long-term cultural continuity in the southwestern mountains. Standley was a long-used and substantial encampment overlooking the small Camas Valley flood plain (Connolly 1986, 1988, 1991). It yielded an artifact assemblage dominated by leaf-shaped bipoints, shouldered and contracting-stem Coquille Series points, broad-necked stemmed points, edge-faceted cobbles, and stone bowl mortars, all of which are hallmarks of the southwestern Oregon Glade Tradition (fig. 6.7). The Standley Site documents continuance of this tradition on the Coquille/Umpqua divide well into the most recent millennium.

Standley Site obsidian hydration dates indicate that the earliest occupation began there about 5,000 years ago, while 11 radiocarbon ages ranging between about 2350 and 300 cal. BP, along with some 40 obsidian hydration measurements, place its most intense and continuous occupation between about 3,000 years ago and late prehistoric times. Excavation revealed a number

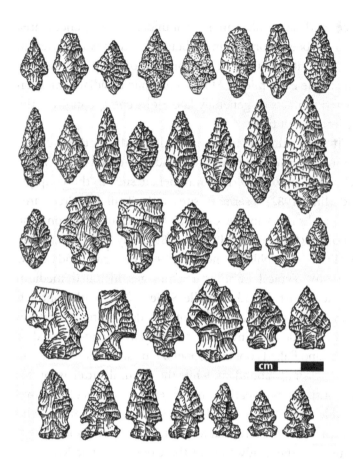

Fig. 6.7. Glade Tradition foliate and stemmed projectile points from the Standley site (from Connolly 1991).

of buried cultural features, mostly consisting of fire-broken stones, burned earth, and charcoal. Some of these features contained charred hazelnut hulls or camas bulbs, and were undoubtedly fireplaces or the remains of earth ovens. Concentrations of burned wood and bark suggested the presence of dwelling structures, but none could be defined with certainty. In any case, its cultural features, artifacts, and dense evidence of occupation suggest that the Standley site functioned as a major base of operations for its general area.

In addition to the key artifacts noted above, a diverse assemblage of hammers, anvils, cores, flakes, knives, scrapers, drills, gravers, abrading stones, distinctive end scrapers and gouges, pestles, clay figurines, and painted tablets gives evidence of toolmaking, woodworking, butchering, plant processing, and ceremonial activities. Obsidian, a surprisingly common tool stone at the Standley site despite the lack of geological sources in western Oregon, gives evidence of distant exchange relationships as well. Of 40 specimens studied by geochemical analysis, 70% came from the Northern Great Basin Silver Lake, Sycan Marsh, and Spodue Mountain sources nearly 150 miles east across the Cascades. Most of the rest came from California's Medicine Lake Highlands, which are even more distant.

It is clear from the above examples that certain favored locations within the southwestern mountains region became well established during late middle Holocene times as base camps from which hunting, plant gathering, and often fishing activities could all be conducted during extended stays. Such a pattern fits the forager model, where people occupy a locality and make broad use of all its resources before moving on, while the paucity of evidence for substantial structures indicates that group mobility remained high even as population continued to grow. At the same time, the strong evidence for technological continuity bespeaks populations that were well adapted and strongly attached to their region.

Late Holocene (1,700 to 200 Years Ago)

In dramatic contrast with earlier periods, for the late Holocene there is a substantial suite of radiocarbon ages from a number of sites that provide evidence of an increase in population density that started about 1,700 years ago and intensified after about 1,000 years ago. Also notable is the fact that many of the sites are winter villages or hamlets with semi-subterranean houses, in contrast to the pattern seen earlier where most sites were apparently temporary but intensively used resource harvesting camps (Davis 1983; Brauner and Lebow 1983; Pettigrew and Lebow 1987). A clear measure of the boom is the fact that nearly 90% of some 50 radiocarbon dates obtained at 40 pithouse villages, hamlets, and related sites in the Trail/Elk Creek area fall within the last 1,500 calendar years (Brauner and Lebow 1983, Davis 1983; Nilsson and Kelly 1991; Pettigrew and Lebow 1987). Mack (1991:75) similarly reports for the Klamath River Canyon that the Canyon 2 Subphase (1000–350 cal. BP) "clearly seems the most intensive period of occupation." The late Holocene also brought important changes in tool assemblages, most obviously the proliferation of small arrow points, including corner notched specimens with flaring bases generally identified as Rose Spring points, and base-notched points with sometimes exaggerated barbs known as Gunther Barbed.

An intermediate stage in the transition to this new pattern may be represented by site 35JA189 near Trail on the Upper Rogue River, which had been repeatedly visited in earlier times as a short term stopover, but by about 1700 BP was serving as a base camp occupied and used over an extended summer season for a great range of hunting, harvesting, and food processing tasks (Connolly et al. 1994). Manos and metates, hopper mortar bases, and boulder anvils with pecked surfaces indicate the processing of various plant foods, while flaked stone artifacts and bones bespeak the hunting and processing of game. The faunal assemblage demonstrates that both deer and rabbits were favored prey.

The Siskiyou Pattern. The above changes, marking the inception of the Siskiyou Pattern (Connolly 1986, 1988), opened a new chapter in southwestern Oregon cultural history. Additional new elements included the prominent use of metates and hopper mortars, the proliferation of small side-notched, corner-notched and basal-notched Rose Spring or Gunther Barbed projectile points (fig. 6.8), and a renewed florescence in long-distance trade that moved Klamath Basin and Medicine Lake Highlands obsidian westward and Pacific marine shells eastward. Connolly suggests that these major changes and interactions arose in part from in-migration or infiltration of new people from the direction of Klamath-Modoc country in the Northern Great Basin. The Siskiyou Pattern appeared by about 1,700 years ago, but did not entirely replace the long-established Glade Tradition in the Klamath, Rogue, and Umpqua river drainages. In the interrelated set of small interior valleys between the Cascades and Coast Range that links the Klamath, Rogue, Upper Coquille, South Umpqua and North Umpqua river systems, the Siskiyou Pattern is most recognizably linked with the ethnohistoric period cultures of the Klamath, Shasta, and Takelma peoples.

Obsidian sourcing studies (O'Neill 2004) confirm that the people of southwestern Oregon had long maintained contacts to the east, as most obsidian tool stone was imported from trans-Cascadian sources, primarily those of the Klamath Basin (Spodue Mountain and Silver Lake/Sycan Marsh), and surrounding areas. Further, work presented in Chapter 2 reveals indications of a population shift into the Klamath country

Fig. 6.8. Siskiyou Pattern projectile points from the Middle Klamath River area; *Top row,* Gunther Barbed and small basal notched point; *middle row, left,* Desert Side-notched, *right,* small stemmed points; *bottom row,* earlier stemmed and leaf-shaped forms.

from more easterly basins at this time, and the resultant pressure could have encouraged some established Klamath-Modoc area residents to push their own borders farther west into southwest Oregon/northwest California.

The Gunther Pattern. Another distinctive cultural manifestation appeared in Southwest Oregon at about the same time or perhaps slightly later, as discussed in chapter 4. The Gunther Pattern was initially recognized from a signature site on Gunther Island (also known as Indian or Duluwat Island) in northwestern California's Humboldt Bay, which was the location of the historic Wiyot village of Tolowot. The Gunther Pattern brought distinctive triangular concave-based points, bone harpoon points, shallow steatite oil lamps, large ceremonial obsidian blades, baked clay figurines, flanged pestles, bell-shaped mauls, zoomorphic stone clubs, and a variety of bone and shell ornaments (fig. 6.9; also see ch. 4). Because these new elements appear in the area occupied historically by Athapaskan peoples, whose language identifies them unmistakably as immigrants from

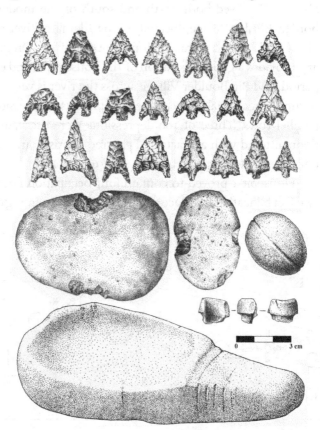

Fig. 6.9. Gunther Pattern diagnostic artifacts from the Limpy Creek site (from O'Neill and Tveskov 2008).

southeast Alaska, Connolly (1988) suggests that the sudden appearance of the Gunther Pattern marks the arrival of Athapaskans in the western California-Oregon borderlands. An estimate of about 1,500 to 1,300 years ago for this event fits well with the pertinent archaeological evidence previously discussed in chapter 4. As also noted there, these data suggest that Oregon's late Athapaskan immigrants landed first on the coast of Northern California, and thereafter spread northward up the Oregon coast and eastward into the southwestern valleys and mountains, establishing the range they occupied in ethnographic times.

Border Village. The Middle Klamath River Canyon saw an early human presence about 8500 cal. BP, as shown by a ^{14}C date from Klamath Shoal Midden. It did not become a major locus of occupation until the late Holocene, however (Mack 1983, 1990), with artifact assemblages typically of the Siskiyou Pattern. The area was shared in historic times by the Klamath, whose homeland was centered farther east and north in Oregon, and the Shasta, who lived both north and south of the modern California-Oregon border. Border Village, located on the Klamath River not far from Klamath Shoal Midden and a scant half-mile north of the Oregon/California boundary, provides a good illustration of the house types and economic focus of the period, and Big Boulder Village across the river is very similar. Border Village occupies an alluvial terrace where 18 pithouse depressions are present in two parallel rows. Three of the depressions were excavated, revealing pithouse floors littered with artifacts and charred debris from the probably accidental burning of their superstructures (figs. 6.10, 6.11).

Housepit 1 proved to contain four occupation floors, the deepest about two feet beneath the surface and the others representing episodes of rebuilding

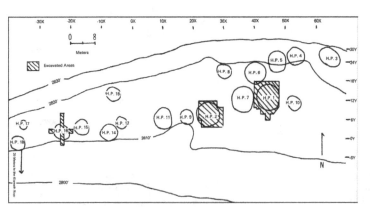

Fig. 6.10. Plan map of Border Village, Middle Klamath River (from Mack 1983)

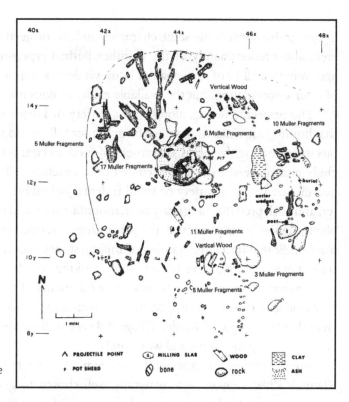

Fig. 6.11. Plan map of House 1 at Border Village (from Mack 1983).

or refurbishing the structure (fig. 6.11). The floor was circular, slightly over 21 feet in diameter. In the center was a large firepit, and lying on the floor were scattered artifacts, including many muller fragments and several milling slabs. Charred wooden posts and slabs lay on the floor, and the stubs of three roof support posts remained in vertical position near the center of the unit. Two vertically placed wooden planks, as well as the wood fragments lying on the floor, suggest that the superstructure of the dwelling had consisted of wooden planks leaned inward from the edges of the housepit to rest against the support posts near its center. The three upper floors had both a central firepit and a subsidiary fire area to one side nearer the house wall. Burned materials found on all four floors showed that each occupation had been terminated by fire, after which a new structure had been built over the same pit.

A ^{14}C determination made on a vertical post stub associated with the third occupation floor indicated an age of about 550 cal. BP. It seems that no great amount of time separated the four occupations represented within the housepit, because the same kinds of projectile points, predominantly Gunther Barbed, were found throughout. Excavations showed the other two houses to have much the same character, and the projectile points excavated were also predominantly of the Gunther Barbed type, suggesting a similar age. Whether all 19 of the apparent housepit depressions were the same age is of course speculation, but the available evidence does not suggest otherwise.

The projectile points, along with a variety of knives and scrapers, show that hunting activities were staged from Border Village. Bones from the house-pits indicate a highly varied assortment of food species; fish included salmon, chub, and suckers; mammals included deer, antelope, elk, mountain sheep, beaver, porcupine, a variety of small rodents, jackrabbit, cottontail, river otter, and such predators as grizzly bear, mountain lion, and red fox. Though no plant remains were preserved, the processing of seeds, nuts, berries, and the like is indicated by a large number of milling stones and manos or mullers, as well as over 400 fragments from pottery cooking vessels. Flaked stone cores, drills, gravers, knives, scrapers, and a few fragments of twined basketry also give evidence of toolmaking. Such numerous and varied specimens make it clear that the people of Border Village did very well harvesting both the river and its flanking meadows and woodlands.

Site distribution data show that settlement and activity locations in the Klamath River canyon were generally well chosen to give their occupants optimum access to the area's natural resources (Mack 1990: 15–17). Sites were typically located on the first or second terrace of the river, adjacent to wide stretches of shallow water, and near springs or places where small streams joined the main river. Such spots offered flat, well-drained ground on which to live, fresh water, good fishing, and immediate access to the varied flora and fauna of the riparian zone along the stream as well as the wooded mountains through which the river cut. In such places people could have maintained year-round settlements, making forays as needed to nearby hunting areas, root grounds, and acorn-gathering localities. The floral and faunal evidence just described from Border Village seems to exemplify precisely such a pattern.

Iron Gate. Farther down the Klamath River a few miles south of the Oregon border is the Iron Gate site, named for a constriction in the river course that made it an ideal spot for harvesting the spring and fall runs of Chinook and Coho salmon, and steelhead trout, before the Iron Gate dam was built (Leonhardy 1967). Excavations there provided radiocarbon dates of about 400 to 300 years ago and an archaeological assemblage characterized by a predominance of Gunther Barbed arrow points along with a few clay figurine fragments. Mapping conducted in advance of dam construction showed the

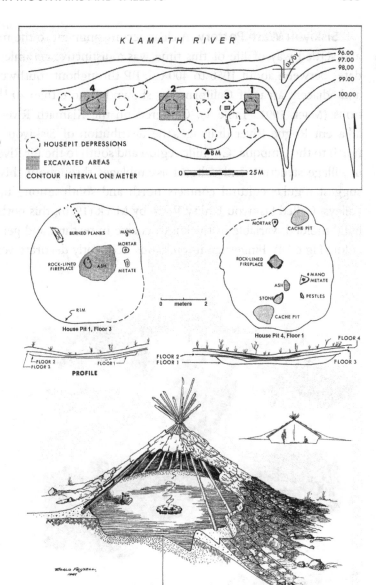

Fig. 6.12. Plan map of Iron Gate site showing pithouse depressions (from Leonhardy 1967).

Fig. 6.13. Floor plans and interpretive drawings based on Iron Gate pithouses (from Leonhardy 1967).

presence of 13 circular house depressions roughly 15 meters in diameter, of which three were excavated. The houses displayed 3 or 4 superimposed floor levels, indicating repeated occupations over a long use-life. Rock-lined fireplaces were centrally located, and manos, metates, mortars, and pestles had been left on the uppermost floor levels. A reconstruction drawing based on this evidence provides an excellent illustration of the regional house type (figs. 6.12, 6.13).

Siskiyou Ware Pottery. A clear accompaniment to the more populous and settled way of life of this time was a distinctive ceramic tradition that dates between about 1050 to 400 cal. BP throughout southwestern Oregon and adjacent areas of California, as shown by more than 20 ^{14}C determinations (Mack 1991: Table 1). Centered on the Klamath River Canyon and adjacent Rogue River drainage, the distribution of Siskiyou Ware extends north to the Umpqua/Coquille region and south to the Pit River. Similarities in village structure and cultural assemblages throughout this same region suggest regular cultural contacts north and south among upland interior valleys. Called Siskiyou Utility Ware by Mack (1990), this pottery is crudely hand-molded, variable in thickness, coarse in texture, and generally buff in color (Fig 6.14). Fingernail impressions frequently decorate vessel rims, and

Fig. 6.14.
Fragments of
Siskiyou Utility
Ware pottery
from the middle
Klamath River.

incised lines occur on body surfaces. Exterior surfaces are often exfoliated and rough, while interior surfaces are smooth. Wide-mouthed shallow bowls seem to have been the most common utilitarian form, but cups have also been identified, and fired clay smoking pipes. Small hand-molded animal and anthropomorphic figurines are also part of the tradition, as described further below (Mack 1987, 1989; Endzweig 1989).

Siskiyou Ware was manifestly a local tradition; Mack (1986) compares it to late prehistoric brown wares in the surrounding Sacramento/San Joaquin Valley, Columbia River drainage, and Great Basin, and shows that none of the other wares definitively link with Siskiyou Ware. It is likely, however, that the birth of the Siskiyou type was aided by the thriving interregional communication so evident during this period, and that its adoption was encouraged by increasingly stable residential habits.

Siskiyou Ware Clay Figurines. Small, simply made figurines are well attested in archaeological sites along the middle and upper reaches of the Pit, Klamath, and Rogue rivers, which are the historic territories of the Achomawi, Shasta, Takelma, and Athapaskan peoples (Deich 1982; Mack 1991). The figurines exhibit the same reddish brown color, coarse texture, hand modeling, and fingernail-impressed decoration seen on Siskiyou Utility Ware pottery, and generally occur together with such pottery in archaeological sites. Animal representations including deer, elk, fish, rodents, carnivores, owls, and possibly bears account for most of the figures; only about 10% appear to be human. Breasts or penises show the sex of some of the human figures, but for most specimens sex is not indicated. Most of the human figures exhibit no facial features, but animal's heads often show such details as eyes, ears, mouths, muzzles, and antlers, which allow different species to be identified. Most of the known figurines are broken or damaged, though complete objects have also been found. They may have symbolic significance, representing spiritual entities, or they could have served more casual purposes, perhaps as children's toys. Fired clay figurines are known from neighboring central California, some parts of the Great Basin, and the middle Columbia River, but the figurines of these areas lack the focus on animal representations and the realistic depictions of facial features and limbs that set apart those of the Oregon-California borderlands (Endzweig 1989). It is evident that the Siskiyou figurines comprise a distinct tradition, unique to that area. Notably, it is spread across a territory that in historic times was home to some very different tribal/linguistic groups, which ethnohistoric evidence shows to have nevertheless interacted intensively in trade, exchange of mates, and occasionally raiding and warfare.

Elk Creek Sites. In the intermediate elevations of the western Cascades southeast of Roseburg and west of Crater Lake, the evidence from Elk Creek is of particular interest because a major research project there has provided a rich database that describes the environmental setting and resources as well as the cultural remains (Budy and Elston 1986; Lyman 1987; Pettigrew and Lebow 1987). Low water often limits the late summer and fall salmon runs in Elk Creek, a tributary of the South Umpqua River, but spawning salmon are present from September to February, and steelhead peak there between December and May. People could have obtained exhausted, spawned-out fish from the shallow stream even without special equipment, simply by flipping them onto the bank with their hands. Elk Creek receives winter snowfall, but it normally melts off quickly, and the valley is a favored cold-season refuge for elk and deer. In modern times hard, snowy winters in the region have only increased the concentration of deer along Elk Creek, as they drive stragglers more thoroughly from the mountains to the east.

During spring, summer, and fall, people could take small animals and plants for food and artifact making from a series of local environments that were an easy day trip from their encampments. Environmental zones extended from thickets of alder, ash and cottonwood along the stream course, upward through buckbrush and mountain mahogany scrub into forests of oak, madrone, and

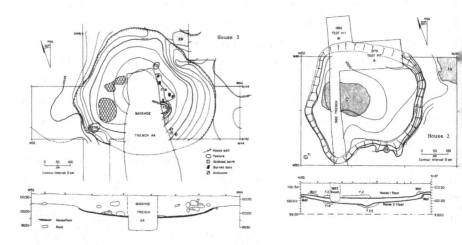

Fig. 6.15. Pithouse plans and profiles from Elk Creek sites (from Pettigrew and Lebow 1987).

Ponderosa pine. Especially important were oak groves at intermediate eleva-tion, where great quantities of acorns offered a readily storable winter staple. Higher up grew Douglas-fir, hemlock, white pine, and sugar pine. On more distant peaks above 5,000 feet, where snow lingered until July, were forests of red fir and white fir with abundant gooseberries, huckleberries, elderber-ries, and currants growing in the understory. One such place was Huckleberry Mountain, about 10 miles away. Archaeological evidence detailed below shows that the native people made very good use of this highly productive habitat.

Some three dozen archaeological sites were found by systematic survey along a seven-mile reach of Elk Creek. Only sparse flakes of worked stone ap-peared on the surface of some, but at others flaked stone was more abundant and a few also showed apparent housepit depressions. Six sites were excavated to a significant extent, revealing an archaeological record in Elk Creek Valley that began about 6,000 years ago with occasional short-term visits but only became quite settled within the last 1,500 years. Scattered dart points of broad-necked and willow leaf types indicate early visits to Elk Creek by mo-bile foragers, but most of the archaeological specimens date considerably later (Brauner and Lebow 1983; Budy and Elston 1986; McDowell and Benjamin 1987; Pettigrew and Lebow 1987).

At site 35JA100 four housepits were excavated, and 13 radiocarbon dates on debris found in them indicate several episodes of occupation and reoc-cupation between about 1,500 and 200 cal. BP (Pettigrew and Lebow 1987).

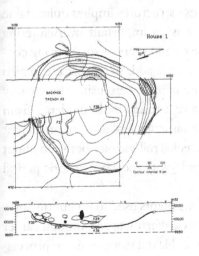

One housepit was roughly rectangular, measuring about 11 by 19 feet across and a foot deep. The others were roughly cir-cular, about 14 feet across and one or two feet deep. Typically they had the remains of wall posts around their edges, central fireplaces, and small pits dug into the floor, probably for storage; one structure had six such pits (fig. 6.15). Splotches of burned earth on the floors, along with charcoal and scattered patches of charred bark, suggest a fiery end to pole-and-bark house superstructures. One structure had been used after its abandonment for a cremation burial, as indicated by a fragmentary human skeleton found within a dense concentration of charcoal. Outside, between two of the houses, partial excavation revealed an apparent food-processing oven consisting of a pit about two feet deep and three feet in diameter, and containing numerous fire-cracked rocks; 27 acorns of the Oregon white oak were recovered near it.

A single housepit excavated at 35JA59 was roughly circular, about 16 feet in diameter. It had been dug into a hillslope so that the downhill edge of the level floor was at the ground surface, while the uphill edge lay at a depth of about two feet. A large irregular hearth near the floor's center yielded a ^{14}C age of about 700 cal. BP. As in the 35JA100 houses, red-fired earth and charred bark suggested burning of the pithouse superstructure. Six additional dates from the housepit's later fill imply that it continued in use as a refuse dump between about 550 cal. BP and historic times (Budy et al. 1986; Pettigrew and Lebow 1987).

Elk Creek site 35JA27A apparently once had housepits, but uncontrolled digging by looters prior to the archaeological study made this impossible to verify. Excavations there yielded a concentration of cobble tools, a cluster of cobbles, a cluster of fire-cracked rocks, and a small shallow pit with heavily fire-reddened walls. Also found were a few fragmentary human bones, evidently placed as a disarticulated burial in a small pit about a foot deep. The burial pit was lined with stream cobbles, and with seven milling stones, or metates. Seven radiocarbon dates showed episodes of occupation at this site between about 1500 cal. BP and historic times (Pettigrew and Lebow 1987).

The finding of many substantial pithouse structures implies quite stable occupation at Elk Creek, and suggests it was an important overwintering location for local populations during the past 1,500 years or so. A strong convergence of artifactual, faunal, and floral evidence adds to this picture, which shows clearly that during the late Holocene people were using the vicinity more intensively than ever before, and on a year-round basis. Evidence from 35JA189 and 35JA190, later excavated in the same general area, suggests that occupational intensity peaked in the Elk Creek-Trail vicinity between about 1,500 and 600 years ago, then tailed off rapidly into the early historic period (Connolly et al. 1994:169).

All the Elk Creek sites yielded flaked stone points used to tip hunting projectiles. These were mostly small, narrow-necked arrowheads, though earlier atlatl dart points were also found on occasion. Flaked stone tools for processing meat, hide, and bone included bifacial and unifacial knives and scrapers, drills, burins, and large cobble choppers. Numerous distinctive keeled end scrapers from Elk Creek 35JA107, which showed heavy use-wear and much resharpening, suggest that woodworking was particularly important at that site (Budy and Elston 1986). The fine-grained stone used in toolmaking was predominantly chert, locally available in stream gravels and rock outcrops, and local basalt was also used. But obsidian brought from remote sources was important as well, comprising 3% to 10% of the flaked tool stone at various Elk Creek sites. Obsidian does not occur locally, and the limited fragmentation of flaking debris, as well as the absence of weathered cortex on flake debitage, indicate that it was imported as already shaped and retouched tool preforms (Spencer 1987).

The Elk Creek occupants' more distant travels and connections are documented by chemical analysis of the obsidian tool stone found in their sites. The obsidian of some 200 lithic artifacts from Elk Creek was traced by geochemical "fingerprinting" to three distant source areas: Silver Lake/Sycan Marsh and Spodue Mountain, about 70 miles east over the Cascades in the Klamath Basin, and Grasshopper Flat, about 90 miles to the southeast in the Medicine Lake Highlands of northern California. The three sources were all strongly represented in the Elk Creek samples. There was somewhat less obsidian from Grasshopper Flat, as might be expected given its greater distance, but at the same time Grasshopper Flat obsidian reached its highest local proportions in those Elk Creek sites nearest that source (Hughes 1987; Nilsson and Kelly 1991; Zeier 1986). This obsidian may have been obtained through trading interactions with groups living across the mountains, although given the distances it would also have been quite possible for parties from Elk Creek to go there and collect it themselves if they had the right relationships with local residents.

The importance of hunting is further shown by substantial faunal evidence. Bones and bone fragments from the excavated sites numbered more than 26,000 specimens, of which 650 were complete enough to be identified to genus or species. Most of the identified bone represented deer; much less common were elk, beaver, pocket gopher, mountain lion, canids (dog, coyote, or wolf), fox, turtle, and salmon. The modern excellence of Elk Creek as a winter deer habitat is shown by these data to be of long standing. The dental age profiles also showed young and old animals in disproportionately great numbers, while prime adults were rarely taken. This implies individual hunting, because the very young and very old are most likely to fall prey to human (or other) stalkers, while alert, healthy adults are most likely to escape (Lyman 1987). Chemical analysis of projectile points and butchering knives confirmed the importance of deer hunting at Elk Creek, by identifying cervid (deer, elk) blood on most of the artifacts examined (Loy 1987). Finally, analysis of the stages of eruption and wear on deer teeth indicates that the animals in the sample were killed throughout the fall, winter, and spring, strong evidence that the area was an important overwintering location for the native people.

Ground stone tools included bowl-shaped mortars, hopper mortar bases, pestles, metates, manos, and edge-faceted cobbles. Battered hammer and anvil stones probably served various functions. Charcoal and charred seeds from firehearths and soil samples taken at the Elk Creek sites reflect a prehistoric vegetational mosaic comparable to that existing in the area today.

Cooking in pottery vessels is documented as well. Almost 600 sherds of Siskiyou Utility Ware pottery were found at Elk Creek 35JA100 and 35JA27A. A broken but reconstructable shallow bowl, eight inches in diameter and about four inches deep, was found on a housepit floor at 35JA100. It was thick and hand-modeled, as shown by numerous finger impressions. The inside of the bowl rim had been decorated with fingernail incisions, and the inner surface was incised in an irregular crosshatch pattern. The bowl exterior was rough, the surface having largely exfoliated or eroded away. Baking in an open fire had given the vessel an uneven reddish brown color. Found with the pottery were a few fired clay figurines—small and very simply made items of household art—these included a deer's head, a human torso, a fish tail, and some nondescript flattened and conical broken pieces (Endzweig 1989; Mack 1983, 1987).

It is reasonable to suggest that the development of year-round settlements would not have occurred in the higher elevation Trail-Elk Creek vicinity without some considerable incentive. Sapir (1907:252) noted that the Latgawa, or Upland Takelma, occupied "the poorer land of the Upper Rogue, east, say, of Table Rock toward the Cascades." He further states that the "Upland Takelma were much more warlike than their western neighbors, and were accustomed to make raids on the latter in order to procure supplies of food and other valuables. The slaves they captured they often sold to the Klamath of the Lakes, directly to the east" (Sapir 1907:252). It is not known whether the development of villages and hamlets on the upper Rogue or in the Klamath River Canyon relates to growing population pressure in more favorable downstream localities, or to other economic reasons such as establishing a favorable trading position with trans-Cascade groups such as the Klamath, or to some combination of these. However, it is clear from the ethnographic literature of the region that both trading and raiding were firmly established economic traditions (Sapir 1907; Gray 1987; Sampson 1985).

Gold Hill Village and Cemetery. In the broad central valley of the Rogue River, south and west of the higher elevation Elk Creek sites and contemporary with their later occupations, the Gold Hill Site gives evidence of a quite intensive and socially elaborated way of life during the last thousand years or so. Gold Hill, on a terrace of the Rogue River at a small town of the same name, was the first major site to be archaeologically studied in southwestern Oregon. A landowner who was leveling a knoll in a cultivated field discovered the site as he was plowing deeply to break up the soil, then dragging the loosened earth with a horse-drawn scraper to an adjacent low place. When the knoll had been reduced in this way by some three feet, the plow began to bring up human remains and artifacts. Dr. L. S. Cressman, a University of Oregon professor trained in sociology, was called in and subsequently directed the first archaeological excavation of his career at the site in 1930, 1931, and 1932 (Cressman 1933a, 1933b).

The area investigated at Gold Hill measured about 120 feet across, and in places excavations reached a depth of seven feet. Approximately 30 areas of concentrated occupation were recorded, mostly in the northern part of the mound, and 39 human burials were uncovered, mostly in the southern part of the mound. The human remains had all been placed in a flexed position, in small pits. The areas of concentrated occupation were circular or ovate in plan, and up to 15–20 feet across. They contained fire hearths and associated fire-cracked stones, ash, and charcoal, along with stone artifacts and fragments of bone and antler. These features are consistent in size with housepits subsequently identified at other sites of comparable age. No house floors or housepits were clearly recognized at Gold Hill, but this is not surprising as Cressman, with no previous archaeological training or experience, had adopted the landowner's plow-and-scraper method of excavation for his own work. Given the extent of the site and the abundance and variety of artifacts and human remains found there, however, it was unquestionably a large and stable settlement. The predominant occurrence of occupational debris at the north end of the site, and burials at the south end, indicates that Gold Hill was a major residential village with an associated cemetery.

The Gold Hill site has not been radiocarbon dated, as the fieldwork took place 20 years before the method was developed. Nevertheless, the many small and finely made Gunther Barbed points found there, now dated at other archaeological sites, show that it was principally occupied during the last 1,000 years (fig. 6.16). The site also contained large ceremonial blades of obsidian and other finely made artifacts that were still made and used during the nineteenth century. The artifact assemblage clearly identifies Gold Hill as a representative

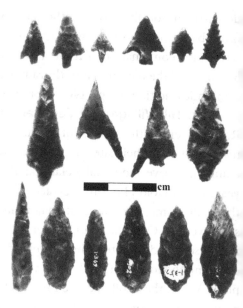

Fig. 6.16. Projectile points from the Gold Hill Site.

of the Gunther Pattern, but the site also contained small leaf-shaped points that reflect cultural continuity from earlier Glade Tradition times.

The economy of the Gold Hill settlement is indicated by abundant projectile points, associated with hunting, and many ground stone pestles, stones, and hopper mortar bases that represent the processing of vegetal foods such as camas roots and acorns (fig. 6.17). Some of the pestles were very finely made and ground with raised bosses on either side of the handgrip area. In addition, a long-time local resident and collector (Moore 1977; fig. 169) illustrates two highly distinctive two-horned mullers from the site that are of the well-known historical Klamath type. The occurrence of these highly diagnostic horned mullers well outside Klamath territory is striking, but not surprising given the extensive interregional connections shown by other items from the Gold Hill assemblage. Manufacturing tools reported from the site are limited,

Fig. 6.17. Stone bowl from the Gold Hill Site.

Fig. 6.18. Obsidian blade from the Gold Hill Site.

but included numerous flaked stone scrapers and pounding/rubbing stones, as well as many well-made flaked stone drills.

The most sociologically informative finds at the Gold Hill site were the human graves and their contents. A number of the 39 buried individuals were accompanied by grave goods, including exquisitely shaped blades 8 to 12 inches long, evenly flaked over both surfaces, and slightly constricted at the midpoint (fig. 6.18). These were mostly of obsidian, though some were of ground schist. In total some 22 such blades have been reported. They occurred singly or in pairs in most of the graves that possessed them, but one interment held five obsidian blades and one comparable specimen made of slate. Another grave held a quantity of beads made from seeds of the digger pine, several hundred beads of the marine *Olivella* shell, and several pieces of *Glycymeris* (cockle) and abalone shell. Yet another burial yielded seven tubular smoking pipes of serpentine or greenstone schist, finely shaped and smoothed, and varying between four and eight inches in length (fig. 6.19).

Fig. 6.19. Tubular steatite pipes from the Gold Hill Site.

The large obsidian blades from Gold Hill are of a type still used in eth-nohistoric times by the Hupa, Karuk, Wiyot, and Yurok people of northern California in their ceremonial White Deerskin Dance, and their appearance at Gold Hill shows that ancient Oregon groups belonged to the same far-reaching intertribal ceremonial network. The White Deerskin Dance was an important ritual in which highly valued family treasures and heirlooms were displayed. In addition to being important ceremonies that expressed the people's spiritual convictions and the elevated social status of community leaders, these dances brought together friends and partners from different communities and different tribes, and constituted major occasions for trade and sociopolitical interaction over a broad area. The White Deerskin Dance unquestionably has prehistoric roots, as was first shown by the finding of large obsidian "dance blades" in archaeological context at Gunther Island, near Eureka on the northern California coast (Loud 1918; Hughes 1978), and subsequently by the Gold Hill artifacts. A large blade of the same form has also been found at Fuller Mound in the northern Willamette Valley, not far from Portland.

Geochemical analysis of the large obsidian blades from Gold Hill has matched their trace element composition to that of distant obsidian flows east of the Cascades (Hughes 1990). Six different sources are represented, with 11 of the 20 studied Gold Hill blades made of obsidian from the Silver Lake/Sycan Marsh and Spodue Mountain sources in the Klamath Basin, about 100 miles east of Gold Hill. One blade was of obsidian from Glass Buttes in east-central Oregon, some 175 miles from Gold Hill, and two others were of Horse Mountain and Quartz Mountain obsidian from the same general area. Six specimens were made of Buck Mountain obsidian from extreme north-eastern California, nearly as far from Gold Hill as Glass Buttes. Not only the large size and exquisite workmanship of these obsidian blades made them precious, but also the distant places from which they came, and the far-flung social alliances and travels that they imply.

Beautifully made serpentine smoking pipes from Gold Hill also have their closest comparisons among specimens from northern California. These blades and pipes were extraordinarily precious and valuable objects, and clearly demonstrate a high degree of sociocultural interaction and emulation among the most influential elite persons of the Oregon-California borderlands. The wealth and number of elite personages buried at Gold Hill suggest it was a pre-eminent sociopolitical center of its time in Oregon's southwestern mountains.

Limpy Creek Camp. The Limpy Creek site, about 30 miles down the Rogue River from Gold Hill and shown by artifact types and radiocarbon dates to overlap with it in age, offers a snapshot of lowland economic pursuits during late Holocene and early historic times, as native people continued their traditional way of life into the time when Euroamerican trappers, traders, miners, settlers, and soldiers began to penetrate the region (O'Neill and Tveskov 2008). People were surely attracted to the spot for its excellent salmon fishing, as they still are today. Many small arrow points of predominantly Rogue River Barbed and Triangular Concave Base types, along with animal bones and the analysis of blood residues found on stone tools, show they also hunted deer and bear, and in the ethnohistoric era, after the arrival of Euroamerican settlers, perhaps cattle as well. Postholes and a slab-lined hearth excavated into a bedrock shelf identified a prepared camp site, apparently a shed-roofed shelter set against the hillside and open to the southeast, overlooking the confluence of Limpy Creek with the Rogue River. Nearby were deposits of fire-cracked rock and other occupation residues. Typical artifacts included cores and flakes, hammerstones, drills, knives, end scrapers, gravers, and other items, including a set of notched stone net weights, neatly arrayed as if originally attached to a now-decayed fishing net. This extensive toolkit bespeaks the daily economic and household activities of the little encampment. It may well have served as a seasonal hunting and fishing outpost of the nearby Ritsch and Marthaller sites, situated a short distance upstream where Applegate Creek flows into the Rogue. Both of these were housepit villages, shown by small Gunther Barbed and concave-base points as well as radiocarbon dates to be contemporaneous with Limpy Creek Camp during the period about 1500–500 years ago.

In the residential area of Limpy Creek Camp was found a distinctively carved soapstone bowl that tested positive for bear antiserum, clearly showing it had served as a lamp in which bear grease was burned. It is a fascinating "signature" item, coming as it does from a site within the ethnographic range of the Athapaskan-speaking *Dakubetede*, whose language identifies them as immigrants from Alaska/Canada, where such oil lamps are common. Also found were drilled soapstone pendants, pipe fragments, and other evidence for the making and use of items not strictly utilitarian. The nineteenth century Euroamerican presence is indicated by glass trade beads, buttons, buckles, a piece of copper, a musket ball fragment, and an 1838 half-dime. Soon after that date the site was abandoned, perhaps in 1856 when Native people were removed by the U.S. Army from all of Southwestern Oregon following the Rogue River War.

There must certainly have been other seasonally utilized harvesting camps like Limpy Creek in the area, and in fact throughout the southwestern mountains as a whole. Some well-situated sites which had previously been visited over thousands of years, and which persisted into the time of year-round late Holocene pithouse village settlements, may have become even more important as the human population expanded. Marial and Saltsgaver, located farther downstream on the Rogue River, for example, and the Standley site in the Lower Umpqua River area, are prominent places of this type that continued to serve people at least seasonally throughout the late Holocene (O'Neill 1990).

High Altitude Seasonal Camps in the Upper Rogue River Drainage. From the higher Cascades slopes to the east, Tveskov and Cohen (2006) report a series of sites in the winter snow zone near Crater Lake that offer evidence of warm-season visitation, which began in the late Pleistocene/early Holocene and persisted over time. As previously noted, early human use of Hyatt Meadows is attested by the finding there of a Clovis fluted point base, while it and the nearby Blue Gulch, Cold Springs, Windom, and Midnight Dig sites all give much evidence of subsequent visitation, with small arrowpoints of the last 1,500 years or so showing the late Holocene as the most intensive period of human use. Manifestly, people who wintered at stable pithouse villages in the lower elevations came to the higher western Cascades each summer to hunt deer, elk, and other game, and to gather the many plant foods available there. Hunting is attested at their camps by projectile points and other tools, and by a great deal of highly fragmented animal bone, most likely of deer and elk. The processing of vegetal foods is shown by manos, pestles, hopper mortar bases, and stone bowl fragments. The working of bone, hide, and wood is suggested by flaked stone knives and scrapers as well as edge-ground cobbles, hammerstones, anvils, abraders and polishers. These sites also contained an abundance of debitage from the manufacture and repair of lithic tools. Most of the tool stone was local chert, but there were also significant percentages of obsidian, geochemically identified as coming from known trans-Cascadian sources in southern Oregon and northern California.

As Tveskov and Cohen (2006: 203–204) have emphasized, the people represented by this archaeological evidence were family groups, with the work of both men and women well attested. Such seasonal sites are often termed "hunting camps," for the activities of the males there; however, as the authors point out, the economic contributions of women to the life of these communities probably loomed larger. The sites are typically situated on ecotones where a wooded terrace overlooks a meadow and open oak prairie. Ethnohistorically such biotic settings were kept free of brush and excess trees by annual burning, mainly carried out by women, in order to maintain productive habitats for the acorn-bearing oak trees, tarweed, ipos, camas, and other geophytes they harvested, as well as for the deer, elk, and other game obtained by men. Thus women not only brought in a reliably larger harvest of essential and highly storable plant food, they also saw to maintaining the productivity of the family's summer range, in addition to managing the household itself. As discussed further below, the strong sense of individual family solidarity and independence that was built up and passed down through the generations by annually recurring summer sojourns at "their" place in the uplands no doubt became a powerful factor in sustaining the traditional family autonomy that was so strongly marked in ethnohistoric times.

Upper Umpqua Drainage Interregional Aggregation Sites. A number of summertime aggregation sites are known in the uppermost reaches of the North Umpqua River that drew people from settlements on both sides of the Cascades during nineteenth- and early-twentieth-century ethnohistoric times. Illahee Flat was an area that each summer drew Yoncalla, Cow Creek, and Upper Umpqua groups from the southwestern mountains and valleys, while Molala, Klamath, and Modoc groups came from the lower western and eastern Cascades foothills, and Paiutes from the adjacent Great Basin country farther east (O'Neill 1991). Farther south along the Cascades, Huckleberry Mountain near Crater Lake was another major summer gathering place of the Klamath, Molala, and Takelmans. That this ethnographic pattern of "international" summertime gatherings in the uplands was widespread and extends as far back as early Holocene times is strongly suggested by archaeological traces seen at these same places, as well as other Cascades sites mentioned in the Plateau and Northern Great Basin chapters.

South Umpqua Falls. The South Umpqua Falls, Hughes 1, and Times Square rockshelters comprise a complex of base camp and hunting sites situated within several miles of one another deep in the western Cascades west of Crater Lake. The falls of the South Umpqua River seasonally concentrated salmon and steelhead trout, as well as lamprey eels, on their fall runs to upstream spawning grounds. In addition to these anadromous species the river is inhabited year-round by rainbow and cutthroat trout, suckers, chubs, sticklebacks, and squawfish. The vicinity is further important as an overwintering area for deer and elk, lying as it does somewhat below the elevation of persistent winter snowpack. The South Umpqua Falls area is a traditional camping and fishing location of the Cow Creek Band of Umpqua Indians who still use the area today (Minor 1987).

Two small rockshelters overlook the South Umpqua Falls, and excavation revealed that both were occupied prehistorically. Similar projectile points and other artifacts from the two shelters suggest that both span approximately the same time range, and three glass trade beads from the lower shelter indicate that its occupation continued into historic times. A radiocarbon determination of about 600 cal. BP dates occupation in the lower shelter, while another places the earliest upper shelter occupation at about 3400 cal. BP. People encamped in the rockshelters left behind flaked stone projectile points, knives, scrapers, drills, and other tools. They also left cores of tool stone and thousands of flakes of chipped stone debitage. Cobble tools included hammerstones, anvils, and grinding stones. Bone or antler artifacts included wedges, stone-flaking tools, awls, and sharpened bone splinters. Also found were shell disk beads, *Olivella* shell beads, and a number of bear claws perforated at one end for suspension. The inventory represents various hunting, food processing, and manufacturing tasks, suggesting that people spent a considerable amount of time at this location, probably on repeated visits. The remains of five human burials found in the upper shelter may imply its use as a last resting place by people dwelling nearby at a yet unknown residential site.

Animal bone from the South Umpqua Falls rockshelters included more than 46,000 items, mostly fragmentary. Some 4,300 identifiable specimens represented predominantly mammals (55%) and fish (36%). There were also small or trace amounts of land snails, freshwater clams, birds, reptiles, and crustaceans. Deer were by far the most common species among the identified mammals, and most of the unidentified skeletal fragments were also of the size and thickness of deer bone. Other mammal species included cave dwellers as small as shrews, voles, and wood rats, and as large as mountain lion. The fish bones were not tabulated quantitatively by species, but included salmon, sucker, squawfish, sucker, chub, and lamprey eel.

Seeds and nuts from the same excavations included predominantly pine nuts, hazelnuts, Douglas-fir seeds, and seeds of the rose family. Some hazelnut shells and rose seeds were charred, suggesting that they had been roasted or toasted. The bulk of the seeds and nuts, however, could not be certainly identified with human agency. Although people may have brought them into the sites it seems highly possible that rodents brought them in or that they reflect the natural "seed rain." At the least, all are known historically to have been used as food, and their occurrence in the rockshelters shows that they were available in the near vicinity should the human occupants have chosen to seek them out.

Hughes 1 Rockshelter. Much less abundant and diverse evidence of occupation was found at Hughes I Rockshelter, high on a densely forested slope about a mile from South Umpqua Falls. Projectile points, knives, and scrapers dominated the small artifact assemblage, and a grinding slab and handstone were also found. A date of about 950 cal. BP on charcoal from an ash lens dates the deposit. Over 1,700 whole and fragmentary bone specimens were recovered from the small test excavations, most of them so broken up as to be unidentifiable. Of the bones that could be identified, 96% were of deer. Most of the other fragments are also believed to represent deer, based on their size and thickness. Clearly this was a periodically used hunter's camp where deer were brought for processing.

Times Square Rockshelter. This site, about three miles above South Umpqua Falls, contained substantial evidence of upland hunting. It lies in an area of considerable biotic diversity, within the Mixed Conifer zone but close to the boundaries of the Subalpine Mountain Hemlock and Interior Valley vegetation zones; plant associations characteristic of all these zones occur in the vicinity of the site (Minor 1987; Spencer 1989: fig. 4). Growing in the immediate vicinity of the rockshelter are salal, blackberry, Oregon grape, gooseberry, strawberry, thistle, wild buckwheat, ferns, manzanita, chinquapin, madrone, ponderosa and sugar pine, white oak, and hazel, all of which yield edible berries, seeds, roots, or nuts. Most of these plants ripen during August and September. The fish and mammalian species available near the site are essentially the same as those named for the South Umpqua Falls rockshelters.

Animal bones were recovered in abundance from the dry Times Square deposits, consistent with artifactual indications (below) that it served as a hunting camp. Although the bones were heavily fragmented, specimens of 14 mammalian species were identified, in addition to remains of unidentified fishes, birds, reptiles, and amphibians (Schmitt 1989). Hundreds of rodent and rabbit-sized bones were partially digested, making it clear that carnivores and possibly raptors had delivered them into the cave in fecal pellets. Woodrats also commonly collect bones in their nests, and woodrat bones show that these creatures did live there. On the other hand, many flakes of heavier bone, bones with butchering marks, and bones showing evidence of burning give ample evidence of human processing as well. Deer and elk bones most commonly exhibited these traces, and a great amount of highly fragmented deer and elk bone shows that in addition to being butchered for meat, skeletons were pounded and broken to extract their marrow.

Radiocarbon dates of about 3500, 2800, 1400, 1300, and 800 cal. BP were obtained on charcoal from Times Square Rockshelter, but most of the archaeological specimens came from the uppermost strata and are referable to about the last 1,500 years. Two small white glass trade beads, a piece of wrought iron, and a fragment of tinware bring the evidence of human occupation into early historic times. Remnants of a recent pole-supported shelter attest contemporary usage of the site.

A flaked stone assemblage readily identified with hunting, butchering, and tool-maintenance activities included a number of fragmentary projectile points, many cutting and scraping tools made on flakes, cores, and nearly 10,000 flakes of working debris from artifact manufacture. The high percentage of broken projectile points, as well as the abundant lithic manufacturing debris, indicates that broken points were replaced at Times Square Rockshelter in the process of refurbishing damaged arrows. Some plant food processing also went on at the site, as attested by two pestles and three hopper mortar bases, one ground into a bedrock ledge. Most of the tool stone was chert, with a small but significant percentage of obsidian also present. A few obsidian artifacts from the site, their chemical compositions identified by the X-ray fluorescence method, were traced to Klamath Basin sources at Silver Lake, Sycan Marsh, and Spodue Mountain, while a single specimen was traced to Newberry Crater. These obsidian flows lie some 70 to 80 miles away, up the Umpqua drainage and across the Cascades.

A number of artifacts made of normally perishable plant materials were preserved in the dryness of Times Square Rockshelter (Fowler 1989). Such specimens are especially important because they are so rarely found in the humid lands west of the Cascades. Five fragments of twined basketry have been described, and some 70 fragments of cordage. Many of the latter were knotted, suggesting that they may be fragments of light nets, fish line, or snares. Several small packets, or envelopes, were made by folding madrone leaves together and tying them with strips of fiber or grass. Miscellaneous plant stems and fibers of maidenhair fern, bear grass, dogbane, rushes, and cedar bark represent materials known to have been used in weaving by many historic native groups. Their presence, along with the formed specimens, strongly suggests that basketry and cordage were not only used at the site, but manufactured there as well. Wooden artifacts included a bow stave fragment, two arrow shafts, two projectile foreshafts, three wooden points, several awls and eyeless needles, and a firedrill hearth, along with less readily identifiable specimens. As in the case of the fiber specimens, manufacturing activities are suggested at the site itself by many wood chips and sticks that have been peeled, cut, and broken.

Hunting camps are often thought of as representing male-only activity locations. Men typically manufactured and repaired the lithic tools used in hunting and butchering, and in most sites lacking exceptional preservation the lithic artifacts and perhaps the bones of the hunter's quarry are all that is preserved for later analysis. The recovered evidence thus tends to suggest male-only occupations. At Times Square Rockshelter, however, where dryness favored the preservation of wood and fiber artifacts, typically female activities like weaving and cordage-making are also well represented among the recovered specimens. Thus with better archaeological preservation a significantly fuller picture emerges. Instead of relatively brief and single-minded all-male hunting forays into the uplands we see more sustained occupations that were familial in character, with women manufacturing needed items, obtaining and processing storable plant resources, and surely attending to children as well (Fowler 1989).

North Umpqua Narrows. A third major focus of occupation in the southwestern mountains region is the North Umpqua River Basin. A location visited over millennia is the Narrows site (35DO153) on the North Umpqua River near the community of Idleyld, where the stream churns through a tight chute and over a falls about 10 to 15 feet high. The place was described as a prominent Indian fishing camp in an 1855 cadastral survey report, and salmon, steelhead trout, and other species are still taken there in considerable abundance. Not far below the falls the river emerges from its deep canyon into a broad, open flood plain, the locality comprising an ecotone where the woodland species of the Cascades and the grassland species of the Umpqua Valley intergrade. People camping there would have had ready access not only to fish from the river, but also to the varied range of plants and animals characteristic of two quite different natural habitat zones. O'Neill (1989:

Table 5) tabulates 31 plant species identified from the vicinity, virtually all of which have some nutritive, medicinal, or industrial use.

Archaeological excavations have revealed a long history of fishing, hunting, and plant food gathering at the Narrows. Occupations going back to Glade Tradition times are represented by ^{14}C dates of about 7100 and 5850 cal. BP, and heavy use over the last thousand years is indicated by ^{14}C dates of about 950, 500, 400, 350, and 140 cal. BP (O'Neill 1989, 1990). There is evidence throughout this time span for flaked stone projectile points, biface and uniface cutting and scraping tools, cobble choppers, hammerstones and pounding tools, and ground stone mortars and pestles. Many cores and thousands of flakes of chert, basalt, and obsidian show that stone tools were manufactured on the spot throughout the history of the site. Bone was rarely found in the excavations, and plant remains other than charcoal not at all, owing to poor conditions for preservation. Nevertheless, its location and the tools found there clearly imply that fishing, hunting, and gathering activities were all staged from the site. Traces of a pithouse, ^{14}C dated on hearth charcoal to about 950 cal. BP, suggest more stable residence at that time, and probably other such evidence remains to be discovered.

Martin Creek. About 40 miles downstream from the Narrows site, below the confluence of the North and South Umpqua rivers and close to where the main stream enters on its meandering passage through the Coast Range, another productive contemporary fishery around the Martin Creek confluence gives similar evidence of aboriginal use (O'Neill 1989). The Martin Creek site (35DO147) occupation is placed in time by three radiocarbon dates from excavations in two protected rockshelters overlooking the river, which fall between about 400 and 435 cal. BP. The artifact assemblage included 31 whole and fragmentary arrowpoints, representing both Gunther Pattern barbed types and straight-stemmed triangular Siskiyou Pattern specimens. In addition there were bifaces, unifaces, choppers, cores, cobbles, and hammerstones, several pestle fragments, an abrading tool, and a number of split and worked pieces of bone and antler.

Bones and shells from the two shelters attest salmon, freshwater suckers, and freshwater mussels from the Umpqua, while charred hazelnut and myrtle nut hulls and the bones of deer, hare, and squirrel represent products of the adjacent woodlands. The faunal assemblage was dominated by highly fragmented large mammal bone, most probably of deer. Fish bone was much less abundant, but it is suspected this paucity of material may be due to fish having been processed mainly outside the rockshelters. The site's location would have made it a highly favorable fishing station in the past, as it is at present, and the botanical and faunal evidence clearly suggests that people were there in late summer and early fall, a period of strong salmon runs.

Limpy Rock Shelter. Back upstream above the Umpqua Narrows, Limpy Rock Shelter (35DO389) is one of numerous sites deep in the rugged North Umpqua River headwaters that have been identified as seasonal upland hunting camps (Baxter 1989b: table 1, fig. 2). The site is a large overhang filled with rocky rubble. Limited excavations recovered some 200 flaked stone tools, including projectile points, knives, scrapers, and other items. More than 4,000 pieces of flaked stone debitage and a few spent cores indicate that toolmaking was one of the activities carried out at the site. All the flaked stone tools, especially the projectile points, can be associated with hunting tasks; a few grinding slab fragments and a hopper mortar base indicate the processing of plant foods as well. The centrality of hunting at Limpy Rock Shelter is confirmed by the recovery of nearly 3,300 bones of mammals, birds, and fishes, most of the identifiable specimens being of deer or other medium-to-large mammals. As with many such finds, it is not wholly clear to what extent the bones may reflect the activities of other predators besides human hunters. The faunal inventory is certainly congruent, however, with a tool assemblage unmistakably suited to hunting and butchering tasks. No occupation floors or distinct cultural features were found at Limpy Rock Shelter. Scattered charcoal suggests that campfires were made there, but no definite hearths were discovered. A ^{14}C determination of about 450 cal. BP on charcoal gathered from the excavated deposits dates the occupation to the late prehistoric period.

North Bank Site. Located east of Roseburg on the North Umpqua River just above Whistler's Bend State Park, the North Bank site (35DO61) saw intermittent occupation beginning about 3,000 years ago, as attested by a sparse and generalized tool assemblage, but 23 of the site's 25 radiocarbon ages are from the last ca. 800 years, an age congruent with the prevalence at the site of small basally notched and stemmed arrowpoints (fig. 6.20). Components I and II included the floor and fill of a housepit, and Components III and IV represent the upper and lower portions of an associated midden. The midden accumulation indicates sustained occupation, at least for some periods during the past 800 years; clusters of radiocarbon ages at ca. 600–500 years ago and at 350–300 years ago indicate more intense occupation periods. The lower midden contained three well-formed cobble-lined ovens probably used for food processing.

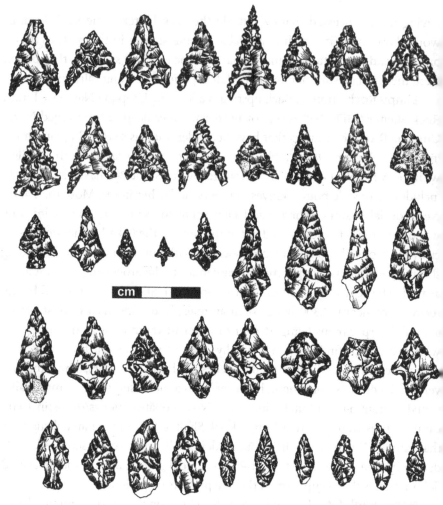

Fig. 6.20. Small basally notched and stemmed arrowpoints from the North Bank Site (35DO61; from Gray 2001).

The housepit (fig. 6.21) had a shallowly excavated floor with a concave profile, about 25 centimeters lower in the center than around its perimeter. Although the edges were not all exposed, the structure was estimated to be 4 meters wide and at least 7 meters long. A hearth positioned on the central axis of the house floor, about a third of the distance from the north end, produced a date indicating use within the last 200 years, A piece of ferrous metal and fragments of two glass trade beads indicate occupation into the early eighteenth century. Although some fragments of wood were found that could have been part of the house superstructure, no clear architectural

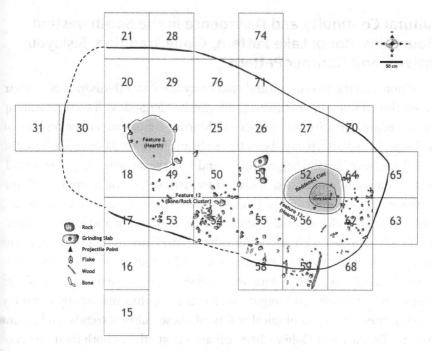

Fig. 6.21. Plan of pithouse from the North Bank site (35DO61; from Musil 2005).

features, such as postholes, were identified. The house feature clearly dates from near the end of the site's use history, but the presence of a substantial midden suggests earlier houses as well, the presence of which may have been masked by preparations for construction of the last house.

Halo Rock. Native rock art from the southwestern mountains and valleys is documented in a series of drawings and brief descriptions by Loring and Loring (1983:1–15). The most striking manifestation is Halo Rock, named for a respected traditional chief of the Yoncalla Kalapuyan tribal territory in which it lies, which spans the North Umpqua and southern Willamette valleys. A large stone about four by six feet across, it is incised with many short, deep grooves generally arranged as sets of parallel lines or inverted v-shapes. Much longer grooves form bands enclosing these sets of lines in broad and narrow panels. The overall effect is strikingly geometric and the heavily engraved surface makes a powerful impression. This great stone is of a type long shaped by aboriginal Californian and neighboring peoples for use in rain and other ceremonies, and some deeply weathered examples studied scientifically are estimated to be as much as 7,000 to 9,000 years old (Parkman 1993). Clearly Halo Rock marks a traditional place of great spiritual and ceremonial importance.

Cultural Continuity and Divergence in the Southwestern Mountains: Borax Lake Pattern, Glade Tradition, Siskiyou Pattern, and Gunther Pattern

A few notes on the strong cultural continuity seen over thousands of years in the southwest Oregon-northwest California borderlands will serve to sum up the preceding narrative. In northern California, significant characteristics of the Borax Lake Pattern have been traced from about 9,000 years ago into the final "Emergent" period beginning around 1,500 years ago (Fredrickson 1973, 1984). As already mentioned above, in southwest Oregon a similar cultural continuity has been recognized in the Glade Tradition, a "conservative and stable cultural/technological tradition of great antiquity and long duration" that finally blended with newly introduced Siskiyou and Gunther patterns between about 2,000 and 1,000 years ago (Connolly 1986:118; 1988, 1991; Connolly and Baxter 1986). Statistical analysis of projectile point assemblages from nearly 50 Southwest Oregon and Northern California sites by Connolly demonstrates the archaeological reality of these cultural trends, and recent work by Tveskov and Cohen (2006) expands cogently on both their archaeological basis and their ecological interpretation.

The cultural stability in evidence throughout the region derives from both ecological and social factors. The rugged terrain enclosing many small and isolated valleys created a mosaic of productive and highly varied habitats that offered both great resource redundancy and reliability, and made possible the persistence of ancient lifeways. Within the social realm, Tveskov and Cohen (2006: 27) suggest that the social dynamics underlying the long-term continuity of the Glade Tradition are modeled in the ethnographic peoples' strong emphasis on family household autonomy and mobility. That such cultural values might well be retained from ancient times seems very plausible in view of the obvious economic utility of a highly mobile and self-sufficient way of life to people who made their living from southwestern Oregon's markedly diversified biogeography. Support for the interpretation can also be found in Winthrop's (1993) analysis of southwestern Oregon settlement patterns. She studied 92 archaeological site assemblages, grouping them into "task specific," "seasonal camp," and "village" categories. These were then ordered according to Pettigrew and Lebow's (1987) typologically based chronology for the area, the results indicating that ancient patterns of small-group mobility and autonomy continued to dominate even as semi-permanent villages began to appear on the main rivers of the region after about 4,000 years ago and became more numerous as population grew. Although the Pettigrew/Lebow comparative chronology has been rightly criticized as poorly supported by locally available radiocarbon dates, it has nevertheless proven to be heuristically useful and broadly congruent with the radiocarbon-dated progression of similar projectile point types from many sites across the Pacific Northwest.

A key finding of Winthrop's analysis is that small task-specific and seasonal camp sites, readily equated with those used by individual households in ethnographic times, were extremely numerous in every period and continued to represent the great majority (73%) of archaeological components identified even in the latest time period. Thus the implication is clear that the family household autonomy and mobility so strongly valued during the ethnographic period was a tradition that had been maintained since early times in the region and continued strongly into the latest period of growing population and societal complexity.

Considering the data from another point of view yields essentially the same result. Tveskov and Cohen (2006) note that 90% of the Glade Tradition sites identifiable in Winthrop's sample are classified as "seasonal camps" or "task-specific" locations, and only 10% as "villages." In the case of the Siskiyou and Gunther Pattern sites that appeared within the last ca. 1,700 years, 37% are identified in her analysis as "village" locations, reflecting a major growth of population and the appearance of sizeable communities during that period, but 63% of all sites are still classified as "seasonal camps" or "task-specific" locations. Thus the land-use pattern shows that family household autonomy and mobility, being so well suited to the enduring ecological realities of the region, persisted in significant degree from earliest Glade Tradition times into the ethnographic period of more settled communities.

Archaeology of the Historic Period

The southwestern mountains and valleys, as other parts of Oregon, contain many archaeological traces marking the activities of immigrant outsiders and their interactions with the native people. European and Euroamerican mariners, traders and trappers began to arrive in the early 1800s, followed by the great influx of newcomers that began with a trickle of settlers coming up from California in the 1830s and became a flood of "overlanders" from the Midwest during the 1840s. They were followed in turn by the "boomers" of the great Rogue River gold rush of the 1850s. The U.S. Army came too, seeking to facilitate the influx and keep order in the conflicts that arose between native people and immigrants. Not all the new arrivals were Europeans and Euroamericans, either; they also included Hawaiians, Chinese, and other participants in a growing international economy, who came for the remunerative work and entrepreneurial opportunities available on the new frontier. Some evidence of initial encounters between southwest Oregon Natives and the new arrivals has already been noted for the Limpy Creek and South Umpqua Falls sites. The following pages describe how archaeological research on the Siskiyou Trail, Old Fort Lane, Rogue River gold mining sites, and the town of Gold Hill brings to life some iconic local manifestations of the dominant themes and social processes of this time of great change.

The Siskiyou Trail. In the late 1820s a rugged Native track across the Siskiyou Mountains of the Oregon-California borderlands became the key passage of a long north-south route later known as the Oregon-California Trail, which linked a growing population of British Hudson's Bay Company and independent American trappers around the Columbia-Willamette confluence with the substantial community already flourishing around the port of San Francisco in Mexican California (Tveskov et al. 2008). In the winter of 1826–27 a Hudson's Bay Company brigade of trappers and camp followers captained by Peter Skene Ogden was led by Shasta Indian guides over the Siskiyou Summit, as they turned at the far end of a long loop east of the Cascades from the Columbia to the Klamath River and headed back to their base at Fort Vancouver. Thereafter Hudson's Bay Company traders used the route regularly, and in the 1830s the American settler Ewing Young turned from trapping to driving horses and cattle up from California for sale to the growing Willamette Valley population.

In 1834 Young's men fired on and killed a number of Indians who tried to take meat from a drying scaffold. This and other atrocities committed by an ever-growing number of travelers soon led to a situation in which parties of Whites passing through the region were regularly ambushed by the resident "Rogue" Indians, who had a long-established tradition of repaying violence with violence. Incidents continued to occur as gold rushes in California and the Rogue River country turned the flow of travelers into a flood, and as the western Oregon valleys were increasingly occupied by homesteaders who came to stay. The Lupton Massacre of October 8, 1855, when a group of "volunteers" led by James Lupton slaughtered at least two dozen (and possibly many dozens) Indian men, women, and children at Little Butte Creek, finally precipitated the all-out Rogue River War that ended with virtually all of the Native population being removed by the U.S. Army to a reservation on Oregon's north coast.

Thereafter the trail across the Siskiyou Summit was increasingly developed as a key link in the emerging capitalist landscape of the Far West. It was established as a toll road in 1860, a telegraph line was strung along it in 1864, and what began as the Oregon and California Railroad was completed in 1887 (after the failure of the original company) as the Southern Pacific Railroad. Gangs of Chinese laborers worked prodigiously with dynamite, picks, shovels, horse-drawn scrapers, and wagons to create the many tunnels, cuts, and fills needed to snake a track for the Iron Horse over an almost impossible hard-rock landscape.

Today Interstate Highway 5 follows essentially the same course as the old Siskiyou Trail, but over time the original track has become obscured as the route was engineered and re-engineered to accommodate different modes of transportation. An archeological survey by Southern Oregon University archaeologists in 2002 worked ingeniously with metal detectors to trace out and map an early historic segment of the Siskiyou Trail (Tveskov et al. 2001). They found a surprising amount of detailed evidence marking out an old course of travel. It included 190 metal artifacts, among them wagon parts, horse, ox, and mule shoes, nails that attached such shoes to the animals' hooves, a buckle and ring used in harness rigging, a wheel hub, a whiffle-and-hook rigging assembly, pieces of telegraph wire, and other items. These were all plotted using global positioning instruments (GPS) and found to track closely an old segment of a route shown on pre-1860s maps. An artifact assemblage more evocative of everyday life on the trail—and the nature of the traffic it carried—can hardly be imagined.

Fort Lane. This frontier army post memorializes the most conflict-laden aspects of the Euroamerican taking of Indian lands in southwestern Oregon. In response to the great influx of settlers and gold miners who were displacing the native people and interfering with their normal way of life, Fort Lane and the Table Rock Reservation were established near Ashland to enforce Federal Indian policy and keep the peace. The fort, built in 1853, was central to a maelstrom of conflicting interests involving settlers, miners, frontier "militias," Indian groups, federal policy, and the U.S. Army. After a "volunteer militia" destroyed an Indian village and killed many of its men, women, and children in the Lupton Massacre of 1855, the situation exploded. Some

Natives gathered at Fort Lane under U.S. Army protection, but other massacres followed, and Indian raiding parties retaliated by burning out or killing White settlers along the river. The worst skirmishes of this Rogue River War took place through the fall of 1855 and the spring of 1856, pitting volunteer "militias " (or vigilante groups) of Euroamerican miners and settlers against the native Takelma, Shasta, and Athapaskan people of the region, while the U.S. Army strove with both sides to maintain federal policy (Tveskov and Cohen 2008).

As a result of this outbreak the Territorial Government, Department of Indian Affairs, and the U.S. Army, under heavy pressure from the considerable number of immigrant settlers by then established in Oregon, determined to round up the Indians of southwestern Oregon and remove them to the Coast Reservation on Oregon's then-wild north coast. Fort Lane and Fort Orford on the nearby coast became military camps where native people were kept under guard until they began to be marched or sent on steamships to the Coast Reservation in January of 1856. Most of the region's Takelma, Latgawa, Athapaskan, Coos, Coquille, and Umpqua people were removed by that fall, and Fort Lane and the Table Rock Reservation were then abandoned.

Fort Lane slowly decomposed thereafter. The Daughters of the American Revolution erected a stone monument there in 1929, and Jackson County surveyors mapped the traces still visible on the surface in the 1970s and 1980s. In 1987 Jackson County acquired the site, and in 1988 it was placed on the National Register of Historic Places, based on documentation assembled by local historian Kay Atwood. Since then archaeologists from Southern Oregon University, working with students and volunteers from the Southern Oregon Historical Society, have mapped and excavated at the fort, locating the original buildings and finding various building features and artifacts of the period. An 1855 sketch of Fort Lane (fig. 6.22) shows officers' and enlisted men's quarters, a storehouse, a guardhouse, a hospital, and a blacksmith's shop.

Excavations have revealed the foundations of fireplaces in the post hospital and officers' kitchen, a midden of food debris, and a number of artifacts (figs. 6.23 and 6.24). Notable artifacts recovered include underwear buttons, a .69 caliber musket ball, an iron arrowhead, buckles from horse gear, and a cavalryman's spur made from an 1854 U.S. silver quarter that had been cut with a hot iron. Unexpectedly, excavations also revealed the remains of a pioneer cabin that had been burned by Indians in 1853, before the fort was constructed in the same locality. It is known from historical documents to have been the

Fig 6.22. Sketch of Ft. Lane drawn in 1855 by post commander Captain Andrew Jackson Smith (National Archives and Records Administration).

Fig. 6.23. Chimney footing for the Ft. Lane infirmary (photo courtesy Mark Tveskov).

home of Albert B. Jennison and his family, and its artifacts and architectural traces give a rare glimpse of early Euroamerican family life on the Rogue River frontier. The research establishes Fort Lane, now an Oregon State Park maintained for historical and educational purposes, as an iconic place where the lives of soldiers, Indians, settlers, and gold miners intersected and clashed in the context of a "manifest destiny" that to many White Americans justified the violent purging of Indian families and the importation of their own "new

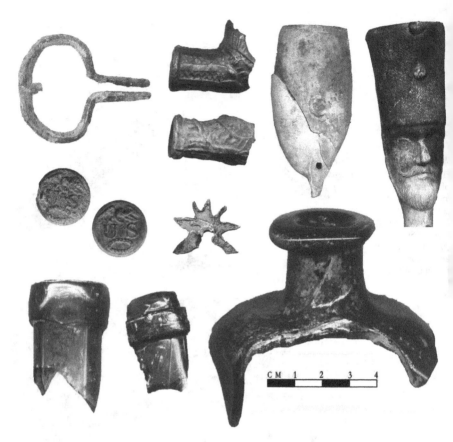

Fig. 6.24. Artifacts from Fort Lane: *clockwise from upper left*, mouth harp, clay pipes, gin bottle neck, wine or champagne bottle necks, military coat buttons, spur cut from 1854 quarter dollar (from Tveskov and Cohen 2008).

and better way of life" throughout the continent-wide "wilderness" of the American frontier.

Ditches, Placer Mines, and Tailings. Archaeological traces of the extensive gold mining that precipitated the Rogue River War and led to the Native American removal are prominent in the landscape of southwestern Oregon still today, widespread reminders of that turbulent time and the diverse players caught up in it. The human stampede along the Rogue River began as a northern extension of the California Gold Rush, and the miners who then flowed north into Oregon were a polyglot array of Euroamericans, Europeans, Mexicans, and Chinese, among others. LaLande (1981) gives an engrossing account of the major role played by Chinese miners and laborers in the Rogue Valley over several decades, from the time of the first strike at acksonville in 1851 until 1882, when the U.S. Chinese Exclusion Act, among ther factors, led to a rapid decline in the region's Chinese population. By 857 there were already between 1,000 and 2,000 Chinese men working in the mines or living in and around the Jacksonville Chinese Quarter, and the local government had enacted a Foreign Miners Tax to draw municipal revenue rom their meager earnings.

Prominent local landmarks created by Chinese workers during their sojourn in the Jacksonville area are the China Ditch, the Palmer Creek Ditch, the Grand Applegate Ditch, the Squaw Creek Ditch, and the Sterling Creek Ditch. These are some of the most impressive among hundreds of miles of canals dug to carry water to the high-pressure hydraulic nozzles that were used to wash down gravel terraces at placer mines along the Applegate River, Little Applegate River, Squaw Creek, Palmer Creek, and other places. The ditches, flumes, gravel tailings, settling ponds, mining camps, and trash dumps left by the Rogue River mining boom remain as archaeological sites to be seen throughout the region. White American enterprises controlled the largest mining efforts, hiring Chinese laborers, but small companies of Chinese miners also operated placer mines of their own. They typically bought and reworked small claims that had been abandoned by the big companies due to diminishing profitability, and made them pay through sheer tenacity and hard work.

Another "China Ditch" that was dug well north of the Rogue River country, near Myrtle Creek in Douglas County, reflects the common history of immigrant Chinese laborers who did so much heavy mining, construction, and agricultural work all across the western frontier in the late nineteenth and early twentieth centuries. This particular China Ditch was dug to carry water for some 33 miles from the headwaters of the East Umpqua River to the North Myrtle Creek area, in order to boost the hydraulic mining and profitability of gold-bearing gravel deposits found there. Work began in 1891 with up to 200 Chinese laborers on the job at a reported 25 cents day, and the ditch was still not completed when the Myrtle Creek Consolidated Hydraulic Gold Mining and Manufacturing Company went bankrupt after the 1893 revelation that the gold "clean-up" at the placer mines for which the new waters were being so laboriously garnered was shockingly less than backers had been led to expect. Today this China Ditch, on the National Register of Historic Places, epitomizes not only the heavy labor, but also some of the risks and frauds of the frontier (http://www.blm.gov/or/districts/roseburg/recreation/chinaditch/history.php).

Chinese Sojourners and Immigrants. A highly successful Chinese miner—vastly more prosperous than any of his countrymen in the region— was Gin Lin of Jacksonville, one of whose mining camps at the "Little Applegate Diggings" has been studied by LaLande (1981). No buildings are visible today, but two dense clusters of artifacts and associated house remains indicate the former presence of living quarters and evoke the everyday lives of Gin Lin's Chinese miners, who made their homes there. The items include machine-cut square nails, windowpane glass, a broken kerosene lamp chimney, many fragments of porcelain and stoneware dishes and containers, and much broken bottle glass. The sojourners were adaptable men who readily took to Euroamerican clothing and mining equipment, but at the same time tenaciously preserved their Chinese cultural and dietary habits. Effectively 100% of the abundant ceramic fragments found there were of Chinese origin, showing that even in remote southwest Oregon the miners were cooking their pork and vegetables in the Chinese style, flavoring their meals with soy sauce, salted cabbage, pickled lemon, shrimp sauce, and other condiments, and drinking "Tiger Whiskey," all imported from China. The broken containers document in the most matter of fact way the global scope of the social and economic processes then being acted out in southwestern Oregon.

Another residential complex, associated with construction of the Klippel Ditch around 1880, was the Squaw Creek Chinese Camp (LaLande 1981).

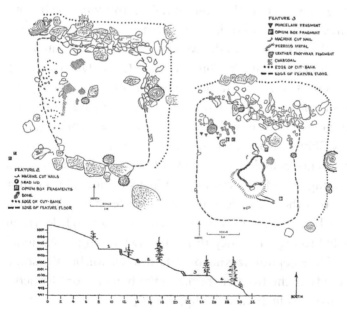

Fig. 6.25. Chinese mining camp in the Applegate Valley, showing home sites cut into terraced hill slope (from LaLande 1981)

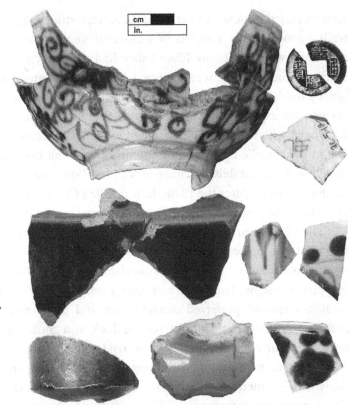

Fig. 6.26. Artifacts from the Jacksonville Chinese Quarter: *clockwise from upper left,* bowl with Double Happiness pattern, Ch'ing era coins, ceramic fragment with Chinese character, three bowl fragments with bamboo pattern, celadon (Chinese ceramic) bowl fragment, stoneware opium bowl fragment, stoneware food jar fragment (from Schablitsky and Ruiz 2009).

There, a series of rectilinear tent or hut platforms about 16 feet square were cut into a steeply sloping hillside, their downslope edges buttressed by stacked rock retaining walls (fig. 6.25). Artifacts found in and around the platforms included square nails, brass opium boxes, a porcelain rice bowl decorated with the "Double Happiness" character, fragments of bottle glass, ferrous metal artifacts, a brown-glazed stoneware soy sauce jug, a food jar, possible eating utensils, and a wire bucket handle (fig. 6.26). The Chinese workers who lived at the camp may have been employed to dig mining ditches during the late 1860s–early 1870s, or were perhaps those who worked Squaw Creek Dam in the 1880s.

The main corridor through the City of Jacksonville (Highway 238/ California Street) was rebuilt in 2004, and elements of the city's nineteenth-century history were revealed during the associated construction work, including evidence of Oregon's first Chinatown. Archaeological excavations carried out for the City of Jacksonville (Ruiz and O'Grady 2008, Schablitsky and Ruiz

2009) revealed evidence of early drains, gutters, stone walkways, cisterns, and wells surrounded by a matrix of nineteenth century artifacts. A set of rails associated with the Rogue River Valley Railroad, which operated from 1891 to approximately 1900, was identified. Nineteenth century street refuse from nearby residences and businesses was abundant. The most significant discovery was the exposure of a dense layer of Chinese and Euroamerican artifacts associated with Jacksonville's Chinese Quarter. The Chinese had begun to arrive in Jacksonville by 1851, working on isolated mining claims, and by 1860 there was a well-established cluster of Chinese businesses and residences along California Street. After the 1880s, Jacksonville's Chinese community declined, and it had disappeared as a coherent entity by the turn of the twentieth century.

The Chinese artifact assemblage from Jacksonville and vicinity contains fragments of brown stoneware bottles and jars; redware and stoneware opium bowls and tins; and coarse porcelains in celadon, Bamboo, and Double Happiness designs. The faunal assemblage reflects Chinese culinary practices, both in terms of preferred dietary items and preparation methods. Pork and poultry (including chicken, turkey, duck, and goose) are common, with beef, domestic cat, fish, shellfish, and wild game much less frequent. Bones are sawn, cut with a knife, or chopped with a cleaver, the latter a distinctively Chinese method of butchery. A third of the artifacts from the Chinese Quarter were manufactured in China, attesting to the strong link that Chinese sojourners maintained with their homeland. The mixture of Euroamerican material goods in association with Chinese artifacts reflects the degree to which Chinese immigrants necessarily had to integrate into the dominant economy to secure the essentials of life. Unlike large Chinese enclaves in urban centers such as San Francisco and Sacramento, where a wide variety of Chinese goods would have been available, in-filling with Euroamerican goods would have been necessary in the southern Oregon frontier, even if Chinese goods were preferred (Ruiz and O'Grady 2008; Schablitsky and Ruiz 2009).

Archaeological Depiction of a Small Town's Growth: Roads, Railroads, and Commerce. Research in conjunction with a repaving project along the main street of Gold Hill, not far from Jacksonville, gives an interesting perspective on the community's history (Ruiz and Connolly 2005). The town is named for a gold discovery on the adjacent Rogue River and is very near the Gold Hill archaeological site mentioned above. Euroamerican miners and farmers lived in the area from the 1850s onward, but Gold Hill was not formally platted as a town until 1884, when it was chosen as the site for a depot of the Oregon and California Railroad then being built between Portland and San Francisco by gangs of Chinese laborers.

The archaeological record consists of items dropped and buried along the often deeply muddy road that came to comprise the town's main street. Artifacts of all kinds accumulated in the roadbed from the 1880s until about 1930, when it was first paved as a section of the Pacific Highway—now known as Oregon Highway 99. The hundreds of collected items illustrate major changes over these 50 years in domestic life, personal hygiene, social activity, community infrastructure, transportation, and the expanding national economy.

Evolving transportation systems are represented by iron shoes for large draft horses, smaller riding horses, and mules, along with rings from bridle rigging, a snaffle bit, railroad spikes, the rims, spokes, and seats of bicycles, spark plugs, a windshield wiper blade, part of a gas tank, and a kerosene headlamp for a Model T Ford. The community's electrification is documented by ceramic and glass insulators, copper wire, and lead fuses, while community sanitation improvements appear in the form of ceramic sewer pipe.

Personal hygiene and health concerns are represented by a wide range of bottles for cold cream, lotions, medicines, elixirs, and home remedies, including Bromo-Seltzer. Socializing is well attested by beer, wine, whiskey, and soda water bottles, as well as a gilded teacup. Differences in family prosperity are attested by dinner dishes ranging from the plainest of thick, white wares to celadons and blue-and-white painted china. The amusements of children are reflected in a porcelain doll's arm and a glass marble. Collectively, the recovered items reflect the growing economic role of Gold Hill as a service center for a larger regional community as it evolved over a period of about 50 years, becoming an important transportation nexus for moving goods and people and tying the region into the growing national economy.

Summary

Archaeological research in Oregon's southwestern mountains has progressed remarkably in recent years, and an increasingly detailed picture of the regional prehistory is emerging. Fluted spearpoints of the Clovis type show that people were in the region by about 13,000 years ago. Early Holocene sites at Medicine Creek, Dry Creek, and the Tiller Ranger Station have been found buried under the volcanic ash laid down the by the 7600 cal. BP eruption of nearby Mount Mazama, and the earliest evidence from the deep long-occupied Marial site on the Rogue River has been radiocarbon dated to pre-Mazama times as well. Archaeological data remain limited overall, but a lifeway with an economic base of broad-spectrum foraging by seasonally mobile people is clearly indicated. The beginnings of a notable long-term culture-historical continuity in the southwestern mountains are marked by the emergence of the persistent Glade Tradition later in this period, linked to the Borax Lake Pattern of northern California and the Old Cordilleran or Cascade tradition widespread in northern Oregon and Washington.

During the early middle Holocene about 7,600–4,500 years ago, the evidence shows people using an expanded range of site settings, but population densities remained quite low. The Saltsgaver Site gives evidence of camas roasting in earth ovens by about 5,300 years ago, for which there is comparable and even earlier evidence in the Willamette Valley to the north. Faunal assemblages are dominated by deer, but camas ovens and the appearance of the mortar and pestle show plant foods to be of increasing importance.

For late middle Holocene times, about 4,500–1,500 years ago, a considerably larger number of occupations are known. A marked intensification of human activity occurred as time went on. A variety of projectile point types and meat-processing tools are known, and faunal remains indicate an emphasis on taking deer, but at the same time there is also a notable range of plant-processing tools in use, including metates, manos, hopper mortar bases, and boulder anvils with pecked surfaces. Specialized bone tools used in fishing appear in Klamath River sites during this time as well, though earlier site locations along rivers suggest fishing had long been important.

During late Holocene times, about 1,500–200 years ago, there was a proliferation of housepit village sites throughout Oregon's southwestern mountains and valleys. The trend is most graphically illustrated by extensive research in the Trail/Elk Creek area, where nearly 90% of the 53 obtained ^{14}C dates fall within the last 1,500 years. The earlier Glade Tradition continues into this time in the Coquille and Umpqua basins, but elsewhere expanding Siskiyou and Gunther Patterns are marked by small Corner-notched, Side notched, and Gunther Barbed arrowpoints that suggest increasing interactions with the Klamath Basin and northern California.

Increased site numbers in remote canyons and upland valleys suggest growing populations. Formalized interregional trade in marine shell beads from the Pacific Coast and obsidian from the Klamath Basin and Medicine Lake

Highlands expanded markedly at the same time. Intergroup competition and conflict is also seen during this time of growing interaction, particularly at the Nightfire Island Site on Lower Klamath Lake, which provides unmistakable evidence of raiding and violent death in the regional borderlands (Sampson 1985). On the other hand there was obviously peaceable community interaction in the ceremonial sphere during the same period, as particularly attested by the large blades made of trans-Cascadian obsidian that were used into ethnohistoric times as part of the White Deerskin Dance. Centers of such activity are revealed by the many blades of this type found at Gunther Island in northern California and Gold Hill in southern Oregon, though they are known from other places as well. It is thus clear that organizational complexity, economic interchange, and individual social status differentiation grew in the region during this era and continued on into contact-historic times.

It is noteworthy how people of very different ethnic origins and languages came to share a common way of life in Oregon's southwestern mountains and adjacent northwest California. The distinctively rigorous natural environment of the Klamath Mountains encouraged common economic, demographic, and residential patterns, even as individuals and groups continued to preserve their different ancestral identities. Speakers of Hokan, Penutian, Athapaskan, and Algonquian languages interacted closely in ethnohistoric times, and marriage partners of different ethnolinguistic identity were common. Important socio-ceremonial observances also united diverse groups, as seen in the White Deerskin Dance, which archaeology suggests had a broad distribution and long history in both northern California and southwestern Oregon. On a more homely level, the making of Siskiyou pottery has a similar distribution, while other commonalities in the archaeological record also indicate close interaction among communities.

Finally, research in historical archaeology adds an on-the-ground perspective on the cultural dynamics of the last 200 years or so in southwestern Oregon. It has been an era of great change, in which the Native people were crowded in on and brutally displaced by Euroamericans and other foreign immigrants, while the natural and cultural landscape was forever altered by the growth of farming, mining, transportation, and other activities that have increasingly linked the region into a worldwide socio-economic system.

Chapter Seven

Oregon Native American Cultural Diversity and Integration

with an Epilogue on Cultural Resource Management Archaeology in Oregon

The Oregon of today, a rectangular area about 200 miles north to south by 400 miles east to west, adjoins or overlaps with parts of the Northwest Coast, Interior Plateau, Great Basin, and Californian regions of western North America (see fig. 1.1). Thus, Oregon Native Americans all had close cultural and linguistic relatives hundreds of miles away in one or another direction, while their more physically proximate neighbors might well have been people of different language and beliefs. The foregoing chapters parallel these broader environmental and cultural divisions, but it is important to stress in this summarizing discussion that aboriginal Oregon's regionally distinctive communities, despite their far-flung connections, were far from being strangers to one another. They all shared in the same broad developmental trends throughout their parallel histories, due to factors inherent in hunter-gatherer logistics, environmental change, population growth, and social and spiritual life. Motivated by these forces, people of adjacent regions regularly hunted, gathered, traded, married, and sometimes raided across their customary borders in a far-reaching "internationalism." The densely populated area of The Dalles, particularly in later times, might reasonably be called a multi-ethnic community, where several different tribes of Sahaptin and Chinookan-speaking people lived in proximate "neighborhoods" and probably interacted on a daily basis.

Oregon-wide Parallels in Environmental and Cultural History

A number of the same themes were played out over time in each of Oregon's cultural regions. In all areas, the first people arrived near the end of Pleistocene times, when a warming global climate was bringing a retreat of mountain glaciers in the interior and rising sea levels along the coast. The climatic changes improved biotic productivity in many different settings, and thus led to a greater availability of food and other resources for the initially thin human population that began to appear about 14,500 years ago. Archaeological traces from earliest times are scarce and widely scattered, showing that human groups were then few, small, and highly mobile. They moved encampments often in the course of seeking out and harvesting available food resource patches. Not only motivated by the food quest, groups had routinely to maintain relations with other bands across considerable distances in order to obtain non-kin marriage partners for their young adults and keep up intercommunity relationships and friendships that could be mutually relied on in times of need.

Over thousands of years the human population grew slowly as the climate continued to warm. People living throughout Oregon from the time of earliest occupation until roughly 7,500 years ago formed very small communities of foragers who sheltered themselves in light, quickly built structures and moved often from one productive place on the landscape to another. Specific plant and animal resources varied, of course, according to the prevalence of desert, montane, riverine, and coastal landscapes in the different parts of Oregon, but the basic socioeconomic, technological, and mobility patterns were much the same everywhere. In the earliest millennia of the region's human history, the movement of people was structured by a food quest that was minimally restricted by social competition in a vast, varied, and abundant landscape.

By about 3,000 years ago, all Oregon regions had adjusted to a very different set of social and environmental influences which fostered larger nucleated communities within more compact territories, and where people built more permanent houses and practiced food storage to a significant degree. Overall population growth was an important factor in these developments. Trade in shell beads, obsidian tool stone, and other commodities became increasingly common, while social class distinctions and intergroup cooperation and competition also grew.

By the nineteenth-century contact-historic period, the middle and lower Columbia River valley was a densely populated zone of considerable societal complexity, with the less densely populated sectors of the broader region forming comparable but somewhat less elaborated patterns. In coastal Oregon, the early record of cultural development seen elsewhere is largely missing before about 5,000 years ago, because continued melting of northern glacial ice raised the sea level and flooded earlier coastlines and estuaries for some thousands of years after the end of the Pleistocene. Early Holocene sites found on high bluffs and headlands show that people were living in the coastal zone as early as anywhere else in Oregon, but the archaeological record of those times is limited. Flooding, erosion, and redeposition dispersed or buried archaeological traces left by early people in low-lying areas, but the evidence that does survive from higher ground suggests an early cultural trajectory for the coast that is comparable to developments seen in other parts of Oregon, and that trajectory is continued by substantial evidence for the period after the sea level stabilized.

Language History in Aboriginal Oregon: Old Settlers and Later Arrivals

Pertinent to all the preceding chapters is the length of time that Oregon's various aboriginal languages have been spoken here, and the directions from which they came. Oregon's high level of linguistic diversity is a microcosm of the broad picture for North America as a whole, where an estimated 400 distinct languages belonging to 61 families were spoken at the time of the Euroamerican incursion (Goddard 1996). This tremendous linguistic differentiation reflects millennia of preceding human history and change, because each family of languages is ultimately descended from a single speech community that existed long ago, with repeated divergences among sister languages over time fostering the branching growth of whole "family trees." Such ramification comes about because spoken languages are continuously changing, not only with regard to popular expressions and words, but also in phonology and grammar. Such changes are gradual, but over time they become substantial. When a community speaking a single language spreads out far enough, or sends out an offshoot into new territory, the originally shared speech of people no longer in close communication will diverge slowly into different dialects and with more time into distinct "sister languages."

Many languages were spoken in aboriginal Oregon; authorities offer conflicting counts because there is a lack of consensus about where to draw the line between languages and dialects, but the number was unquestionably large. Beyond the divergence that occurs within language families, resulting in distinct but related languages (such as, for example, the recognizably common Indo-European heritage of English, German, and Italian), Oregon is home to six distinct language families with no discernable relationship to one another. Figure 7.1 shows Oregon's major language families, while Table 7.1 shows

Native Languages and Language Families

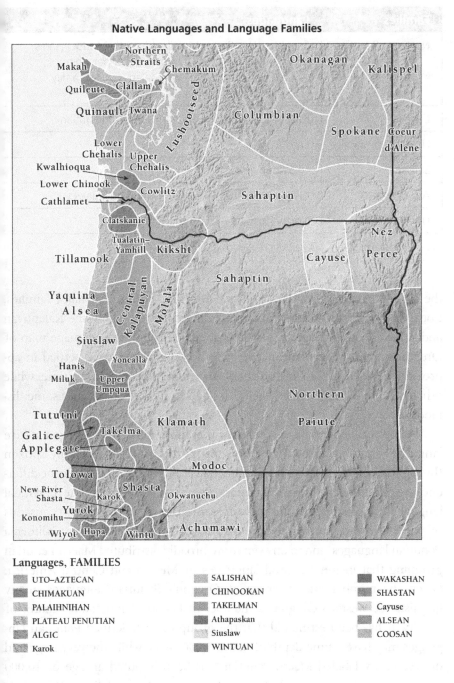

Languages, FAMILIES

- UTO–AZTECAN
- CHIMAKUAN
- PALAIHNIHAN
- PLATEAU PENUTIAN
- ALGIC
- Karok

- SALISHAN
- CHINOOKAN
- TAKELMAN
- Athapaskan
- Siuslaw
- WINTUAN

- WAKASHAN
- SHASTAN
- Cayuse
- ALSEAN
- COOSAN

Fig. 7.1. Map of Oregon Native Languages (based on Goddard 1996).
(*Reproduced in color on inside front cover*)

Families	Languages
Northern Penutian	Sahaptin, Nez Perce, Molalla, Klamath-Modoc, Hanis Coos, Miluk Coos, Lower Chinook, Upper Chinook, Alsea, Siuslaw, Takelma, and Kalapuyan subfamily (Tualatin-Yamhill, Santiam, Yoncalla)
Cayuse	Cayuse (anciently linked with Northern Penutian?)
Hokan superfamily	Shasta
Salishan	Tillamook
Athapaskan	Clatskanie, Tututni, Tolowa (with many dialects)
Uto-Aztecan	Northern Paiute, Shoshone-Bannock

Table 7.1 Aboriginal Language Families of Oregon (Foster 1996, Zenk 1990b).

the sister languages that separated out over time within the major families. Local dialect variants present additional differentiation within the Kalapuyan and Athapaskan languages. As will be discussed below, the language map of Oregon suggests that many native speech communities were settled in approximately their contact-historic period territories for a very long time, while others moved in relatively few centuries ago from previous homes some distance away.

Possibly the oldest and certainly the most numerous Oregon native languages are a set linked together as the Northern Penutian family, spoken throughout the northern and western parts of the state. Significant differences in phonology and grammar mark deep divisions between the individual languages, suggesting that they have co-existed in Oregon for many thousands of years. More distantly, they are also related to the numerous California Penutian languages, and to an even more broadly distributed Macro-Penutian grouping that includes several languages of Mexico and Central America. Given the number and diversity of Oregon's Penutian languages, many linguists see western Oregon as the ancient Penutian homeland's center of gravity. It has been estimated that the group of well-defined Penutian languages may have a time depth of about 5,000 years, while the very large and diverse entity labeled Macro-Penutian has been imputed an age of 10,000 years or more by some analysts, based on an amalgam of linguistic and archaeological evidence (Foster 1996; Sapir 1929).

An example of local "sister language" formation in Northern Penutian is afforded by the Kalapuya and Takelma peoples of the Willamette and northern Upper Umpqua valleys, who all speak Penutian languages. They are linked in chain relationships which suggest that long ago a community speaking a single ancestral Penutian language spread out across the Willamette, Upper Umpqua, and Rogue valleys, and as time went on speech differences accumulated between different localities that were semi-isolated from one another. Local dialects diverged and eventually became so different as to form sets of separate daughter languages, each with numerous dialects. The languages of the Northern Penutian group occupy quite compact territories, especially in western Oregon. The Takelman language of southwest Oregon, Kalapuyan's closest relative, represents a more ancient split between these sister languages. It is likely that this linguistic pattern developed because of the biotic richness of the coast-interior valley zone, where local communities could support themselves within comparatively small territories. While the different communities certainly interacted with one another, their contacts were not intense enough to maintain fully shared speech patterns and their languages gradually diverged from one another.

Also thought to represent an ancient presence is the language of the Shasta, a mostly northern California people whose ethnographic range extended into the Rogue Valley of southwestern Oregon. Shasta is a member of the far-flung and ambiguously defined Hokan superfamily that includes languages scattered the length of California and on into Arizona and northwestern Mexico. Like Macro-Penutian, Hokan is a highly diverse grouping with major differences between some of its individual languages, showing that they have been separated from one another for thousands of years. In historic-period California, Hokan languages were seen to be scattered in the Sierra and Coast ranges while Penutian speakers occupied the central valley. This geographical distribution suggests that Hokan speakers, dominant in California in ancient times, were crowded back into the mountains by Penutian speakers intruding southward from Oregon into the central valley perhaps 5,000 years ago. Thus Shasta, as a clearly ancient Hokan language, was arguably spoken in southern Oregon even before the time of the southward Penutian intrusion (Foster 1996; Sapir 1929).

The Tillamook language, spoken on Oregon's northwestern coast, obviously appeared rather late within a landscape populated by Penutian speakers whose homeland centered on western Oregon. Tillamook belongs to the widespread Salishan family of northwest Washington, British Columbia, Eastern Washington, Idaho, and Montana. Deep differences among Coast Salish languages spoken along the inland waterway between Puget Sound and the Fraser Delta mark that as the Salishan family's ancient homeland and original center of diversification. Some members of this early speech community began moving up the Fraser River an estimated 5,000 years ago. They subsequently crossed the mountains into interior British Columbia and spread south and east, perhaps displacing Northern Penutians in some parts of eastern Washington. In the Plateau and Rockies these more recent immigrants are known as the Interior Salish. The Oregon Tillamook language belongs to the older Coast Salish division and is most closely linked to the Puget Sound area. Whether it represents an expansion of Salish speakers into previously Penutian territory, or perhaps the adoption of Salish speech by northwest Oregon Penutian speakers for social and political reasons, is an intriguing question worthy of further research.

Oregon's languages of the Athapaskan family, which have their closest relatives in southeast Alaska, clearly arrived later than any of the above. Ancestral Clatskanie speakers moved in along the Lower Columbia, while Tututni speakers established themselves down the south coast and up its river valleys. The related Tolowa occupied the Oregon-California borderland and extended some distance south along the California coast. All three of these Pacific Athapaskan groups moved into established Penutian and/or Shasta territory, and by ethnohistoric times their descendants were extensively intermarried with people speaking the languages of their linguistic predecessors. The statistical analysis of basic vocabulary suggests that the original Athapaskan language family in its northern homeland began to expand and diversify about 2,400 years ago, while archaeological evidence from the northern California/southern Oregon coast and adjacent interior suggests that Pacific Coast Athapaskans appeared there about 1500 to 1300 years ago (refer to ch. 6 of this volume).

East of the Cascades the Northern Paiute language was spoken throughout central and southern Oregon in ethnohistoric times. Northern Paiute belongs to the Uto-Aztecan family, a far-flung set of many languages that historically dominated the arid interior lands between the Rockies and Sierra-Cascades from northern Idaho south to Mexico City and slightly beyond (Miller 1986). The Shoshone-Bannock of Idaho and Nevada were close relatives of the Paiute speakers who also ranged into eastern Oregon during the contact-historic period and perhaps earlier. Scenarios presented in the Great Basin and Plateau chapters suggest that Northern Paiute may have spread into Oregon only several centuries ago, though other evidence implies an early and widespread presence of Uto-Aztecan speakers in the Great Basin as a whole (Aikens and Witherspoon 1986; Aikens 1994).

Intellectual, Economic, and Spiritual Connections to the Land

Hunting, fishing, and gathering people, which all Native Oregonians were, necessarily develop a deep knowledge of the landscape they live in. They must know well the behavioral and seasonal habits of their quarry if they are to succeed in catching, trapping, surrounding, shooting, picking, or digging what they need to feed their communities, and in scheduling such activities around the annual calendar in the most productive ways. They must have such knowledge for a great number of different species, so they will always have alternatives to fall back on when afflicted by the recurring dry spells, cold spells, and fluctuations in availability that periodically affect all natural populations. Beyond food, people must know the properties and locations of a great array of medicinal plants that help them cope with various kinds of illness and injury. They must also have significant knowledge of the properties and locations of tool stone sources, natural fibers, kinds of wood, and other materials needed for the manufacturing of tools, shelters, clothing, and so on.

Thus, the list of what aboriginal people must know about their homeland is very long, and every community maintains a great body of inherited practical knowledge that is continuously renewed by use and passed down through the generations. People typically gain this knowledge through the teaching and example of their elders, becoming equipped to make a living in their natal land as they are growing up. They also become the de facto owners of that land through generations of family use and residence, and naturally tend to remain over generations in areas that belong to them by inheritance and to which they are adapted by their acquired body of knowledge.

In addition to practical considerations, there is also a strong emotional component to peoples' geographical connections. Many contemporary Oregon Native Americans still follow a long tradition of keeping up personal and spiritual relationships with the land and its creatures beyond their human relatives. As just noted, these relationships stem from long experience and are kept alive as traditional values continue to be passed down by parents and grandparents to each new generation. Living close to the land generates deep emotional ties to a place, and in the Native experience those ties go back to a time beyond memory. Ancestral lands are the places where count-less generations of family were laid to rest, and where spiritually they still reside.

The spiritual pantheon is also linked very closely to the land. This is seen clearly in traditional ceremonies that are still practiced in Oregon and the Northwest to welcome back the salmon each spring and thank them for giv-ing themselves to feed the people. Spiritual observances of this sort do not pertain only to salmon but to many living beings, and even to geographical features, because in Native tradition the entire world is animated by spirits to whom respect is due. Natural landmarks associated with important past events are recalled in oral tradition, and over the span of many generations may have become associated with traditional legends and spirits. Thus, natu-ral places of distinction such as waterfalls, ponds, groves, cliffs, and moun-taintops may have spirits of their own. In aboriginal Northwest tradition individuals may seek various kinds of spirit helpers for guidance and support in life. Because of this practice many places bear evidence of continuing human communication with the spirit world—stone cairns, small offerings, or symbols and pictures made on rock faces, for example. The resting places and bones of the dead also command respect because people's spirits still abide in them.

Traditional beliefs and obligations continue to inform and motivate many Native American individuals and groups today, and are accorded re-spect alongside contemporary educational, scientific, and environmental concerns in the modern federal, state, and tribal heritage resource protection laws that govern the practices of all Oregon land-management agencies and institutions. There is more detail about these and related considerations in the epilogue to this chapter.

Cultural Diversity and Social Interaction Among Regional Groups in Native Oregon

Native North America was home to many different cultural communities, and socioeconomic diversity among them was fostered by regional differences in natural environment and material culture. In central Mexico, the Southwest, he Eastern Woodlands, and parts of the Great Plains, farming economies developed that in later times supported ceremonial centers, towns, and cities. In the far west, in biotically rich littoral settings like the Northwest Coast, Fraser Delta, Puget Sound, lower and middle Columbia River, San Francisco Bay, and Santa Barbara Channel, populous, prosperous, and socially complex communities grew impressively from an economic base of fishing, hunting, and collecting.

Ecologically based cultural variation is particularly evident within Oregon because the modern state boundaries lie across the junctures of broad environmental zones that contrast greatly in geographical character. In the well-watered but mutually isolated mountain-valley and estuary-bay-shore landscapes of western Oregon's coastal zone, many local communities could obtain what they needed within a relatively small area. Some practiced "commuter economies," harvesting resources generally at no great distance from their permanent main settlements, and frequently within daily walking range (Byram 2002). In the drier interior Columbia, Willamette, and Rogue river drainages, residentially stable communities that had to reach farther for needed resources regularly sent parties of younger members afield to fish, gather, and hunt during the warm season, when such task groups based themselves in various short-stay camps on the rivers, adjacent plains and highlands, perhaps returning between times to their stable year-round settlements. In the still drier Northern Great Basin, highly mobile and relatively small foraging bands made annual warm-season "marches" that took effectively the entire community on a circular tour of harvesting and hunting camps across a vast landscape of mountain ranges and desert basins, returning them in the fall to fixed winter-time settlements more or less permanently established in especially favorable areas such as Malheur Lake, the Klamath Basin, and Fort Rock Valley.

In the context of all these kinds of economically motivated mobility, individual groups from different localities naturally met and interacted with one another in productive resource settings. Thus, the diverse geographical and economic circumstances of Oregon's different Native American communities gave each one a distinctive pattern of life, and at the same time fostered social interactions among regionally neighboring communities that were renewed regularly over generations.

Aboriginal Trade and Travel Networks

Every region had its characteristic natural and craft products, and trade and travel to procure necessary materials and objects were facts of everyday life throughout Oregon. Ethnohistoric documents from the 1800s describe widespread exchange relationships, and archaeological evidence shows that long-distance trade continued over thousands of years. As noted in the Plateau chapter, a great trading center at The Dalles of the Columbia River drew people from throughout the Northwest, and the trading that went on there was fed by and in turn fed into down-the-line exchange networks extending all the way across the Rockies into the northern Plains, northward into British Columbia, and southward into California. Chinookan peoples from the lower Columbia and the Nootka of British Columbia's Salish Sea were famed as waterborne traders, and were the original developers of the famed "Chinook Jargon" trading language that was widely used throughout the Northwest (Wood 1972; Anastasio 1972; Galm 1994; Stern 1998a). Californians of the Santa Barbara Channel region collected seashells and made them into perforated beads that were traded into communities all across the far west, from Arizona-New Mexico to Oregon (Ericson and Baugh 1993; Baugh and Ericson 1994; Ford 1983; Hughes and Bennyhoff 1986; Bennyhoff and Hughes 1987).

Hundreds of marine shell beads of various types from Pacific waters have been found east of the Cascades, excavated from sites in the Fort Rock Basin, the Klamath Basin, and the Columbia River corridor (Jenkins and Erlandson 1996; Jenkins et al. 2004; Largaespada 2006; Sampson 1985; Schulting 1995). The earliest date from at least 9,000 years ago and the trade continued into historic times. These shells were mainly of *Olivella biplicata,* a small sea snail that occurs all along the Pacific shore. Central Oregon Natives could have procured this snail directly by traversing the Cascades and Coast Range over a distance of 170 miles or so, but strong evidence points to the arrival of *Olivella* shells mainly by trade from the south over much longer distances.

Tiny shells of *Olivella dama,* a sea snail that lives only far down the Pacific Coast and is a dominant species in the Sea of Cortez, reached the Fort Rock Basin over a distance of at least 800 miles. Some very distinctive *Olivella* Grooved Rectangle beads that were quite definitely manufactured in the Santa Barbara Channel region of southern California reached eastern Oregon over a distance of some 600 miles. The Santa Barbara Channel region was long a major center for the making of *Olivella* shell beads, as is known from many workshop sites there, and specimens from that source reached sites throughout the Southwest and Great Basin over millennia. An impressive number of different bead types were made by selecting shells of different sizes and by cutting, punching, and grinding them in different ways (Bennyhoff and Hughes 1987; Hughes and Bennyhoff 1986). Thirteen different *Olivella* bead types have been found at the Fort Rock sites, matching the types made for thousands of years in the Santa Barbara region and constituting strong evidence that the Fort Rock beads stemmed from the same source.

In addition to *Olivella*, the shells of various other marine species are known from Fort Rock Sites. Three beads made from long, slender *Dentalium* shells, one of which was dated to about 5000 cal. BP, probably came from southern Vancouver Island. This would be the nearest main source of these shells, which were widely traded throughout the Plateau region. Other shell types found in the Fort Rock Basin were *Alia carinata, Haliotis cracherodi, Haliotis rufescens, Saxidomus, Astysis gausapata, Pododesmus macrochisma, Fissurella Volcano,* and *Lacuna vincta.* Their specific sources are not identified, but they could have come from various places along the Pacific coast, adding to the picture of long-distance contact and exchange. Some 19 *Haliotis* fragments date between about 4000 and 6000 cal. BP, and 57 *Alia* shells fall in the same time range.

In Native society beads might be strung as necklaces or armbands, worn as earrings, pendants, and hair ornaments, and sewn on headbands or clothing. People wore them not only to improve their personal appearance but also to communicate their social position to others. Beads were not merely ornaments but also a form of wealth. As such they might be used to pay an Indian doctor for treatments, as obligatory gifts to the family of a new bride, or in other situations where some form of compensation or act of generosity was called for. The long-established aboriginal bead trade guaranteed a waiting market for Euroamerican entrepreneurs in ethnohistoric times. Starting in the late 1700s, glass beads of various types manufactured in Europe and eastern North America were introduced into the aboriginal networks and quickly became extremely popular. The tradition continues today as a vibrant contemporary Native American art form.

Obsidian, a volcanic glass that is readily worked into projectile points, knives, and other tools, is abundant in eastern Oregon. Volcanic activity in the Cascades and pervasive deep extensional faulting in the Basin and Range province to the east has allowed obsidian-producing rhyolitic magma to reach the surface in many places. Because obsidians from different geological sources contain distinctive sets of trace elements, geochemical analysis enables archaeologists to

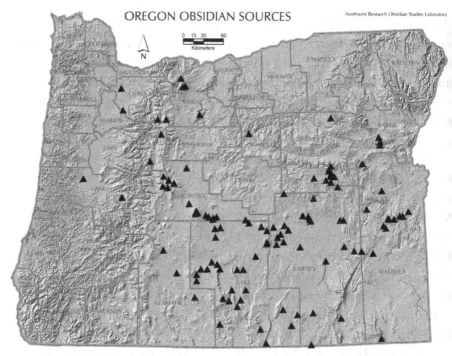

Fig. 7.2 Map of Obsidian sources in Oregon (Northwest Obsidian Research Laboratories).

identify the original sources of the obsidian artifacts found in old occupation sites. Using this information they can learn much about the regular travels of Native American groups over long distances. A great deal of obsidian research has been done in Oregon, and figure 7.2 maps many sources that have been geochemically characterized as an aid in ongoing archaeological research.

A study of more than 1,600 obsidian artifacts found in Fort Rock Basin sites over many years of investigation has identified specimens made of tool stone from 46 different geological sources (Hughes 1986; Oetting 2004; Skinner and Winkler 1994). These include three predominant nearby sources, many central Oregon sources at considerably greater distances, and a few very distant sources in northern California, northern Nevada, and eastern Oregon. Discussion of these and related matters in Chapter 2 showed how Northern Great Basin foragers typically obtained obsidian tool stone from many different sources in the course of their annual hunting and gathering circuits over a great reach of eastern Oregon during a period of more than 11,000 years.

Another distinctive sphere of tool stone circulation was that of obsidian from Newberry Volcano in Oregon's Plateau area south of Bend, which was also used over thousands of years, from well before the 7600 cal. BP eruption of Mt. Mazama on into historic times. Newberry obsidian was widely used as a tool stone among the people of Oregon's Plateau area, along with material from Obsidian Cliffs near Sisters and other sources in the Blue Mountains, but also came to have an important function as a commodity item in long-distance trade. As noted in the Plateau chapter, Newberry Obsidian, along with Obsidian Cliffs tool stone from a source on the North Sister volcano in the High Cascades, occurs on archaeological sites all the way down the Deschutes River drainage to The Dalles on the Columbia River. From there it crossed the big river in considerable quantity, having been identified at archaeological sites along the flanks of the eastern Cascades in Washington, in the Puget Sound area west of the Cascades, and in coastal southwestern British Columbia. Some of it also came into the northern Willamette Valley. Obsidian from these sources obviously circulated within the vast trading network centered on The Dalles, going north in the baggage of summertime fishing/trading parties as they returned to homes in obsidian-poor northern Washington and British Columbia and perhaps being traded farther down the line from there.

Other trading pathways led west across the Cascades from Newberry Volcano and Obsidian Cliffs, and from a set of Oregon and Californian sources that stretched south as far as the Medicine Lake Highlands. An early date for trans-Cascadian obsidian transport is indicated by a Clovis fluted point found in the western Cascades that was made of Buck Mountain obsidian from northeastern California, and a light trickle of obsidian tool stone from Californian and Oregon sources continued to reach the southwestern mountains and Oregon coastal regions for thousands of years thereafter. Closer to the main sources, in sites on the Upper Umpqua River at the Tiller Ranger Station, Susan Creek Campground, Medicine Creek, and Dry Creek, obsidian from various trans-Cascadian flows is well attested in levels buried by volcanic ash from the 7600 cal. BP eruption of Mount Mazama (O'Neill 2004). A more modest local obsidian source used by Native people west of the Cascades was first identified in the gravels of Inman Creek, in the Willamette Valley not far from Eugene, but now known to be more widely present in Willamette River gravels. This obsidian apparently erupted from Cascades volcanoes far back in geological time and was transported by *lahars*, or volcanic debris flows, into drainages tributary to the Willamette Valley. Obsidian of the Inman Creek type occurs typically as very small water-borne nodules or pebbles, which restricted its use, but it nevertheless circulated in limited quantity up and down the Willamette Valley (Skinner and Winkler 1994; Skinner and Winkler 2010).

Footpaths facilitating all the above kinds of trade, as well as the daily and seasonal movements of people going about all the other ordinary business of making a living, created a web of trails throughout every community's habitual range. These naturally linked with those of their neighbors on all sides, adding up to a far-reaching continental network that was sustained over thousands of years (Ericson and Baugh 1993; Baugh and Ericson 1994; Aikens 2009). The *Olivella* shell bead trade mentioned earlier, which began in the Sea of Cortez and Santa Barbara channel regions of northern Mexico/southern California, operated on trail systems that stretched north toward Oregon on both sides of the Sierra Nevada range (Hughes and Bennyhoff 1986; Bennyhoff and Hughes 1987). The *Dentalium* shell trade involved analogous movements southward, flanking the Cascades, from Vancouver Island to The Dalles on the Columbia River and on up the Deschutes valley—probably by the same routes that returned Oregon obsidian in the opposite direction. On-the-ground identification of the ancient trail systems that facilitated these pervasive and persistent Native travels is a work in progress that will not soon be completed, but major segments already known show its extensive and ramifying character.

Extensive documentation of aboriginal trail systems in Oregon is provided by old General Land Office (GLO) maps and current National Forest and Bureau of Land Management cultural resource management reports. Many of these record aboriginal trails that were discovered, adopted, and maintained for management use by government agencies over the past 150 years or so. Old administrative records report that many of the trails used by early Deschutes National Forest employees around Bend were originally Indian trails (Goddard et al. 1979), and similar information is available from other National Forest districts in the Cascades as well.

A well-documented Indian travel route along the eastern slope of the Cascades between the Klamath Basin and the great regional fishing and trading center at The Dalles came to be known as the Klamath Trail. Although Stern (1966:22) suggests that Klamath use of this route (and its identification as the "Klamath" Trail) may be partly a product of post-contact circumstances, archaeological evidence shows that the route is an ancient one (Connolly et al. 2008). A branch of the Klamath Trail turned west across Santiam Pass and joined the Molala Trail, which crossed through Molala territory along the North Fork Santiam River (approximating the route of Highway 22) and continued on to the vicinity of Willamette Falls at Oregon City, east of Portland. This area was, like The Dalles, a major fishing and trading center. In the Mount Hood National Forest a trail segment identified on early GLO maps as the Molala Trail was maintained from an early date by the forest service as the South Fork Trail. Recent research shows that it is part of an aboriginal system extending from the Molala River to the Clackamas, a tributary of the Willamette, and several pre-contact lithic sites identified along the route confirm the antiquity of its aboriginal use. An aboriginal route crossing the Cascades in the same general area was the historic Abbot Road, which follows a well-defined ridge-line trail system from the Warm Springs Reservation east of the Cascades to Estacada on the west, and is well marked by lithic scatters, peeled cedar trees, and other indicators of its aboriginal origin (McClure 2008).

Unnamed ancient trails that surely served to facilitate the mining and transport of tool stone from Obsidian Cliffs and other long-used Cascades sources have also been identified (Churchill and Jenkins 1991; Lindberg-Muir 1984; Winthrop and Gray 1985). East of Salem, a number of old lithic scatters are known to exist along currently maintained ridgeline trails, including the historic-period Table Rock Trail that is documented on the National Register of Historic Places and was a major Cascades crossing for Native Americans long before it was used by White settlers (Philipek and Edwards 1988). Finally, the Molala Trail also branched southward to connect the Northern and Southern Molala territories, the latter bordering the Klamath homeland to its east as far down the Cascades as Crater Lake. The trail's precise course is not well documented, but it is known to have run through the western Cascades, crossing the upper Willamette, Umpqua, and Rogue River drainages. A well-beaten pathway that exhibits pre-contact archaeological traces and was probably one of its segments was the Calapooya Trail, which crossed the high Calapooya Divide between the Upper Willamette and North Fork Umpqua River watersheds along a system of intersecting ridgelines that links the two (Kramer 2008).

In far northeastern Oregon is documented the beginning of the Nez Perce National Historic Trail, along which the U.S. Army pursued dissident "non-treaty" Nez Perce bands led by Chief Joseph for nearly 1,200 miles between June 15 and October 5, 1877 as they attempted an escape into Canada. The Oregon segment of this trail was a regular route for Nez Perce bands moving from summer camps in the Wallowa Mountains to winter settlements along the Imnaha River. It linked up in turn with other aboriginal trail segments which the fleeing Nez Perce followed east across the Snake River at Dug Bar over the Rockies at Lolo Pass, down the front of the Bitterroot mountains to Yellowstone Park, and thence north until Chief Joseph's battle-ravaged group was finally surrounded by U.S. soldiers and forced to surrender near Bear Paw Mountain, Montana, a heartbreaking 40 miles short of the Canadian border. The route of this epic running battle dramatically illustrates the great reach of aboriginal Native American trail systems, and according to historical research many Nez Perce Trail segments have become the roads and highways of today (Nez Perce Trail Study Report 1982).

Operating across these same trail systems, seasonal gatherings of native communities that probably took place annually in traditional localities constituted a pivotal "international" aspect of traditional Oregon Native American life. Many summertime rendezvous or aggregation sites are known where communities of different tribes and languages often came together for fishing, hunting, or other harvesting of natural resources seasonally available in mass quantities. The great annual salmon fishery at The Dalles (Chapter 3) hosted the grandest gathering of them all and the one that inarguably drew the largest numbers of people from the farthest distances, but many smaller aggregation sites are known ethnohistorically and more surely await archaeological discovery. South of The Dalles, Sherar's Bridge on the Deschutes River is a much smaller but long-established fishery that is still important today, now predominantly used by members of the Confederated Tribes of Warm Springs. Archaeological knowledge of the place is limited, but rock art and other traces suggest early occupation. Another major fishery approaching the scale of The Dalles was Willamette Falls near Oregon City, just a few miles up the Willamette River from its confluence with the Columbia (Chapter 5). Like The Dalles, it was an "international" venue where people of several different nations and languages gathered to fish and interact. In the ethnohistoric period Willamette Falls was presided over by the local Clackamas, who maintained proprietary control of the fishery but permitted visitor access to other resources. The Tualatin Kalapuya sometimes went to the Columbia River to hunt seals, and to collect lampreys at Willamette Falls in the territory of the Multnomah or Clackamas Chinook, but never went to fish; instead, they traded for salmon—a proprietary Clackamas Chinook commodity (Zenk 1976:49–50). The fur trader Alexander Henry (1992:658) reported his 1814 encounter with a party of Yamhill Kalapuyans enroute to the falls carrying "bags of raw Cammoss," and their return three days later, "this time loaded with dried salmon." Archaeological evidence from the falls and surrounding area suggests that the place has a long history of human visitation, probably extending over thousands of years. Along the lower Columbia there were two primary sets of villages within the larger Chinookan-speaking Clatsop community, one cluster bordering the Columbia River estuary and another in the area of modern Seaside. Historic sources suggest that the Columbia River villages had their highest population during the spring and summer salmon runs, when their numbers were supplemented by Clatsop relatives from the Seaside villages. Wilkes (1845[5]: 116) observed at Astoria in 1841 that spring "was the season of the fishery . . . and the Kilamukes [Tillamook], Clatsops, and Chinooks were collected in the neighborhood." In fall the population swelled at the nearby Seaside villages, when salmon ran in the Necanicum and its tributaries (Lee and Frost 1844:275). Similar bounty available for mass harvesting by periodic community aggregations also existed at bays and river mouths all down the Oregon coast (Chapter 4).

In Oregon's southwestern mountains and valleys, the North Umpqua Narrows near modern Roseburg was of major importance. An 1855 cadastral survey report describes the area as an extensive Indian fishery, while archaeological evidence shows it was visited over a long period going back to about 7100 cal. BP (Chapter 6). In the North Umpqua Valley toward the Cascades crest, Illahee Flat was central to an area that each summer drew tribes from both sides of the mountains—Yoncalla, Cow Creek, Upper Umpqua, Molala, Klamath, Modoc, and Paiute. Huckleberry Mountain, 15 miles south of Crater Lake, was a major summer gathering place of the Klamath, Molala, Takelma, and Cow Creek. Other such high-mountain summer rendezvous are known from the ethnohistoric period, while archaeological sites including Medicine Creek, Dry Creek, Upper Mountain Meadows, and Crescent Lake show that people have come together there, too, since early Holocene times. In the Klamath Basin, Journalist Samuel Clarke (who was in the Klamath Basin to report on the Modoc War in the early 1870s) learned from Native informants that in the Sprague River valley below Yainax Butte, "the surrounding tribes met semi-occasionally and held seasons of trade and of festival. Here they exchanged their products, sold horses, and traded generally; . . .Yainax was the central spot most conveniently located for the getting together of Klamaths, Summer Lake Snakes, Modocs, Shastas, and Warm Springs."

In the drier country east of the Cascades, the vast root grounds of Stinkingwater Pass, east and north of Burns, were a magnet that drew not only the local Harney Basin Northern Paiute, but other Great Basin and Plateau peoples from as far away as western Idaho, southeastern Washington and northern Nevada in the ethnohistoric period. Archaeological sites scattered over this large area yield evidence of camps that were repeatedly visited throughout middle and later Holocene times (Chapter 2). Still farther east, the Ladd Canyon/Stockhoff/Pilcher Creek complex in the eastern Blue Mountains was a seasonally attractive locality that drew people from a wide area (Chapter 3). In the ethnohistoric period it was a zone shared between Paiute and Bannock peoples to the south and Nez Perce and Cayuse to the north. Archaeological traces in this area show it as closely linked to the Plateau region from early Holocene times onward, while projectile points of Great Basin types indicate that visitors also entered from the south in middle and later Holocene times.

Aggregation sites like those enumerated above facilitated seasonal harvesting by many communities in especially productive localities throughout Native Oregon. Very importantly, they were of great sociological as well as economic significance. As already mentioned, they regularly constituted "international" conclaves where neighboring peoples, often of different tribes and languages, came together for a few weeks each summer to work, socialize, and know each other. In the ethnohistoric period, and no doubt earlier, gambling, dancing, athletic contests, and get-togethers with relatives and friends enlivened such gatherings. They provided also special opportunities for trade, for the sharing of information, and for young adults to find marriage partners.

A distinctive kind of socially important site common in Oregon is discussed in a fascinating study by Griffin (1986), who addresses the use that aboriginal people throughout the Northwest made of the region's abundant geothermal springs. His account shows geothermal springs to have often been important multifunctional sites that drew aboriginal individuals and groups as places for medicinal sweat bathing and mud bathing, for ritual purification, and for important rites associated with puberty and childbirth. Geothermal springs might also be used by shamans as places connected by their miraculous waters to the underworld, where they could seek spiritual contacts for healing and other purposes. Finally, the vicinity of a geothermal spring might be a good place for siting a more stable settlement as well, as game and plant foods also tended to be available in such settings. Oregon has dozens and dozens of known and mapped geothermal springs, and archaeological traces commonly found around them show that many were visited repeatedly over thousands of years.

Ecological and Sociopolitical Roles of Women

Studies by Tveskov and Cohen (2006; Tveskov 2007; Tveskov et al. 2001) in southwestern Oregon have explored the important functions of women in defining traditional usages of the natural landscape and managing intergroup social relations, and these authors' observations have clear implications for aboriginal Oregon generally. Deliberate burning of selected landscapes to clear brush and improve the natural yield of food plants and animals was widely observed in western Oregon during the nineteenth century, and has been traced back to about 3,500 years ago by pollen and geological studies in the Willamette Valley. It is well-documented from ethnohistoric times that women were the principal harvesters of tarweed, acorns, and other plant food staples that flourished in the meadows and prairies of western Oregon, and it is equally clear that women were pre-eminently the ones who kept those meadows and prairies free of brush and dense forest by setting and tending seasonal fires. Their work also enhanced the productivity of male hunters, who typically pursued the deer, elk, and other game animals that were drawn into such habitats. Thus women played a central role in managing the communal landscape and maintaining the productivity of traditional community labors over millennia.

Women played other crucial sociopolitical roles as well. Tveskov and Cohen (2006) point out that in the small communities of Southwestern Oregon it was by custom the daughters of a family who left their natal villages to find non-kin marriage partners, while the sons remained at home. Women were therefore important links connecting the various community groups of a region, key actors in facilitating cooperation through their family ties. Many women necessarily acquired another language when they married into neighboring groups speaking a different tongue—commonplace in linguistically diverse Oregon—and this made them important cross-cultural communicators. The intercommunity linkages constituted by women who married "out" were a crucial form of social security insurance, giving their families whole sets of additional relatives from whom they might gain support if they suffered drought or blight, or with whom such women could reason effectively in intercommunity conflict situations.

Conflict

While trade, periodic community aggregations, and marriage ties all linked individual communities to one another and smoothed connections, interactions were not always amicable. Earlier chapters have mentioned a general regionwide increase in the level of conflict that began about the time bow and arrow technology spread widely in the Northwest, leading to some adjustments in overall settlement patterns. Those elevated stresses notwithstanding, people did not cease to range widely in the conduct of their normal and necessary pursuits, but it has to be noted that in addition to peaceful meetings at common root-digging grounds in the Blue Mountains, conflicts between the ethnographic Northern Paiute and their Sahaptin neighbors to the north are also documented (Elliot 1909; Murdock 1938, 1980; Ray 1939; Spier 1930; Stewart 1939; Sutton 1986; Teit 1928:98). Farther south, Sampson (1985:515) observes that in the Nightfire Island site on Lower Klamath Lake, when trade appears to accelerate in the Klamath Basin around 2,200–1,500 years ago (indicated by the increased presence of exotic marine shell ornaments, for example), there is also increased evidence of violent death. As previously noted, Samuel Clarke reported that the Sprague River Valley below Yainax Butte was the central spot most conveniently located for the getting together of Klamaths, Summer Lake Snakes, Modocs, Shasta, and Warm Springs. At the same time, "Yainax was . . . the great slave mart of the interior basin. The Modocs warred on and captured the Pitt Rivers; the Klamaths raided on the wigwams of the Rogue Rivers, across the Cascade range; the Warm Springs made war on the Snakes beyond Goose Lake . . . " (Clarke 1873). Slavery was another aspect of aboriginal Oregon society known ethnographically to have been routinely practiced in some quarters.

The Euroamerican Taking of Oregon Native Lands: Trade, Disease, Settlers, War, and Treaties

Oregon Indians and their cultural traditions were dealt a staggering blow by the arrival of Euroamericans, beginning with the previously unknown epidemic diseases they caught from early explorers and traders, one part of an epic mortality that swept the globe during the Age of Discovery. From 1565 until 1815 the trading galleons of the Spanish empire sailed annually across the Pacific between west Mexico and the Philippines, on round trips that brought ships sailing east from Manila close to the Oregon coast. Sir Francis Drake, carrying the flag of England around the world for the first time, may have landed at several places on the Oregon coast in 1579 to measure his longitude (a major surveying task), repair his ships, and take on fresh water (Bawlf 2004, Gitzen 2008). No Oregon landfalls are historically recorded for the Manila galleons, but many ships failed to complete the trip (see chapter 4) and there were very likely some instances of contact between shipwrecked Spanish mariners and Native Americans. Blue-and-white trade porcelains of the Chinese Ming and Qing dynasties (1573–1722), found in archaeological sites at Nehalem and Tillamook, surely came from the cargo of a wrecked Spanish galleon that fetched up somewhere nearby. Blocks of exotic beeswax found in the same area have been traced to the Philippines by their embedded pollen.

Seaborne contacts, all of them potential vectors of European disease, occurred with increasing regularity over time. The Vizcaino/Aguilar expedition of 1602 had named Cape Blanco in southern Oregon on a voyage that also established a boundary claim for Mexican California at about 42 degrees North latitude, a juncture that marked the U.S./Mexico border until 1845. A Russian trading presence began spreading down from the Bering Sea region in the 1730s, reaching Fort Ross in Northern California by 1812. In 1792 Robert Gray, a Boston ship's captain, crossed the Columbia River bar on a trading expedition, and that same year Captain George Vancouver of Britain's Royal Navy sent a small boat 100 miles up the river during his 1792/93 exploring and mapping expedition to the Northwest Coast. Lewis and Clark wintered near the mouth of the Columbia in 1805/1806, having arrived there overland from St. Louis via the Missouri and Columbia River systems in an exploration of the United States' vast new Louisiana Purchase. Fort Astoria was established at the mouth of the Columbia in 1810, and Fort Vancouver at the Columbia/Willamette River confluence in 1824. A common feature of American historical narrative is the characterization of early Euroamericans in the region as explorers and discoverers. Regrettably, the disastrous unintended effects of previously unknown epidemic diseases that these explorers brought with them were left out of this narrative—indeed were unknown to most early narrators—and only recognized and acknowledged decades later.

Carried along by this rapidly expanding alien presence, repeated epidemics of smallpox, measles, malaria, influenza, and dysentery—common European and American diseases previously unknown to Native America—reduced Oregon's indigenous population by 80% or more (fig. 7.3). Native Americans had no established immune responses to the new foreign diseases, nor any experience of how to treat them medically. On the lower Columbia and in western Oregon, where native populations were dense and epidemics spread rapidly, mortality in some places exceeded 95% between about 1770 and 1840 (Boyd 1998). When Lewis and Clark floated down the lower Columbia River in 1805, their party encountered empty Indian villages and signs of smallpox. By the time "overlanders" from the Midwestern states flooded into Oregon during the 1840s, the natives had been reduced by epidemic disease to a fraction of their former numbers, as discussed in Chapter 4. It is estimated for the Lower Willamette/Lower Columbia region that a population numbering about 20,000 people around 1800 had been reduced to a few hundred by 1830 (Boyd 1998).

White incursions met with little initial resistance in a contact situation where the Native people had already been catastrophically devastated by epidemic disease, and early interactions were peaceable. Soon, however, the continuing influx of alien settlers brought increasing conflict as the newcomers pressed for more and more land. During the Cayuse and Yakima wars of 1847–1856, a number of battles erupted between Indians and settlers along the middle Columbia River. In the Rogue River Wars of southwest Oregon, dozens of battles were fought between 1851 and 1856, many of them outright massacres of Indian people by "volunteer militias" made up of gold miners and settlers. In central and southeast Oregon the Snake Wars of 1854–1866 and the Bannock War of 1878 were brought on by Native resentment of the settlers' having taken over the best-watered and most productive parts of their otherwise arid homelands—the areas most critical to their own sustenance. The U.S. army became involved in these later wars, seeking to "pacify" the Indians, and it played a major role in the Modoc War of 1872–1873 that was fought in the Oregon-California lava lands. As already mentioned above in another connection, the running Nez Perce War of 1877 was initiated on the Oregon-Idaho border, where a group of Nez Perce bands began their attempted flight to Canada.

During the period 1851–1865, U.S. Indian Agents negotiated 19 treaties with different Oregon groups. The natives, heavily outnumbered and outgunned, had no realistic choice but to acquiesce. Under great duress, Indian leaders endorsed documents ceding the greater part of Oregon to the U.S. Government. The Indians were to receive certain payments for their land, and certain areas would be reserved for their use and residence, where they

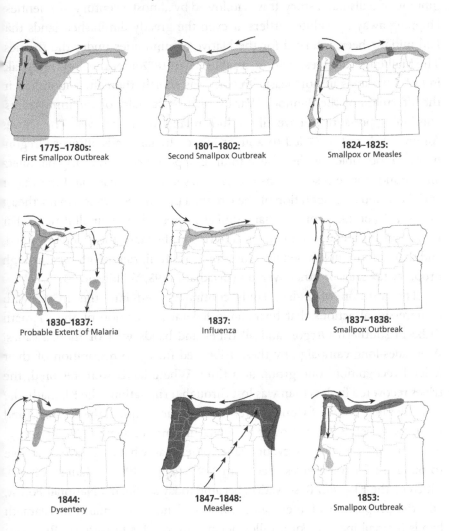

Epidemic Disease in Oregon

1775–1780s:
First Smallpox Outbreak

1801–1802:
Second Smallpox Outbreak

1824–1825:
Smallpox or Measles

1830–1837:
Probable Extent of Malaria

1837:
Influenza

1837–1838:
Smallpox Outbreak

1844:
Dysentery

1847–1848:
Measles

1853:
Smallpox Outbreak

Fig. 7.3. Epidemic Disease in Oregon 1775-1853 (based on *Atlas of Oregon* 2001 pp. 16-17).

would continue to exercise their sovereign rights as independent nations. Many of these treaties were never ratified by the U.S. Congress. Neither the Oregon coast nor most of southeast Oregon was ever ceded by any ratified treaty, but immigrant Whites took the Indian lands anyway. Such recompense as Oregon's Native Americans actually received was paltry at best.

The taking of Indian lands by the treaties of 1851–1865 was just the beginning of a dismal history. It was followed by almost a century of relentless chipping away by White settlers at even the greatly diminished lands that had initially been reserved for the Native communities under the treaties. The Malheur Indian reservation, established in 1872 after the non-treaty taking of vast areas in northeast Oregon, was shortly thereafter abolished in the aftermath of the Bannock War of 1878—a casualty of the immigrants' continuing pressure to have all the Indian land for themselves. The Dawes Allotment Act of 1887 led to a great loss of Indian lands all over Oregon. It was responsible for the nearly total disappearance of the original Siletz and Grand Ronde reservations on Oregon's northern coast, and the major shrinkage and fragmentation of the Umatilla Indian Reservation in northeast Oregon. To be sure, some Indian families prospered on their allotments. Far more, however, could not eke out a living on the lands they were assigned, and their allotments passed into the hands of immigrant neighbors through property tax sales or other avenues (Beckham 1998; Wilkinson 2010).

The attrition of Indian lands continued even into the 1950s, with Congressional actions that terminated federal recognition of the Klamath Tribe in southern Oregon and all tribes and bands west of the Cascades. A decades-long campaign by these tribes led finally to restoration of their federal recognition, one group at a time. Where lands were restored, the tribes recovered far less than was lost through termination. The Klamath, the Confederated Tribes of Coos, Lower Umpqua, and Siuslaw, the Coquille, and the Cow Creek Band of Lower Umpqua Indians are again federally recognized, but do not have reservation lands other than what they have been able to purchase for themselves (Beckham 1991; Pepper 1991; Wilkinson 2010). Much of the Klamath Reservation became today's Winema National Forest, and the proportion of their ancestral homeland that remains in Klamath hands is small indeed. For a fuller perspective on this history see Beckham (1986, 1998); Clemmer and Stewart (1986); Walker and Sprague (1998).

Today there remain only two reservations of substantial size in Oregon, the Confederated Tribes of the Umatilla Indian Reservation and the Confederated Tribes of the Warm Springs Indian Reservation. Beyond those two, the land holdings of Oregon's many other tribes are very small, and some communities are not officially recognized by the U.S. government and have no reservations at all. Most of Oregon's Native American people today do not live on reservations, but in towns, cities, and rural areas throughout the state.

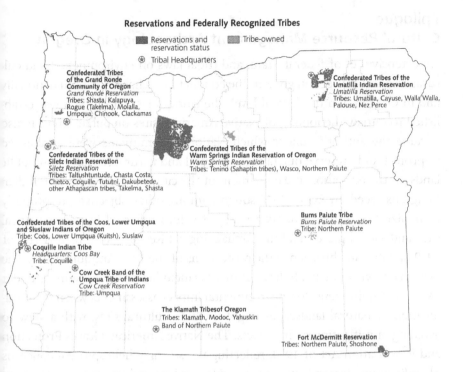

Reservations and Federally Recognized Tribes

Reservations and reservation status
Tribe-owned
⊛ Tribal Headquarters

Confederated Tribes of the Grand Ronde Community of Oregon
Grand Ronde Reservation
Tribes: Shasta, Kalapuya, Rogue (Takelma), Molalla, Umpqua, Chinook, Clackamas

Confederated Tribes of the Umatilla Indian Reservation
Umatilla Reservation
Tribes: Umatilla, Cayuse, Walla Walla, Palouse, Nez Perce

Confederated Tribes of the Siletz Indian Reservation
Siletz Reservation
Tribes: Taltushtuntude, Chasta Costa, Chetco, Coquille, Tututni, Dakubetede, other Athapascan tribes, Takelma, Shasta

Confederated Tribes of the Warm Springs Indian Reservation of Oregon
Warm Springs Reservation
Tribes: Tenino (Sahaptin tribes), Wasco, Northern Paiute

Confederated Tribes of the Coos, Lower Umpqua and Siuslaw Indians of Oregon
Tribe: Coos, Lower Umpqua (Kuitsh), Siuslaw

Coquille Indian Tribe
Headquarters: Coos Bay
Tribe: Coquille

Cow Creek Band of the Umpqua Tribe of Indians
Cow Creek Reservation
Tribe: Umpqua

Burns Paiute Tribe
Burns Paiute Reservation
Tribe: Northern Paiute

The Klamath Tribes of Oregon
Tribes: Klamath, Modoc, Yahuskin
Band of Northern Paiute

Fort McDermitt Reservation
Tribes: Northern Paiute, Shoshone

Fig. 7.4 Reservations and Federally recognized tribes of Oregon (based on *Atlas of Oregon* 2001 p. 17). *(Reproduced in color on inside back cover)*

Despite all that has happened, however, Oregon's Native American community is now in the midst of a strong cultural resurgence. The U.S. Census for the year 2000 lists 45,000 people of Native American descent living in Oregon, and there are nine Federally recognized tribal governments managing Native American affairs and interests all over the state. Figure 7.4 shows the locations of Oregon's current Indian reservations and federally recognized tribes, and also lists the names of many smaller groups that were originally independent. The English term "tribe" is a colonial period concept that at best only roughly approximates the character of original Native sociopolitical groupings. Today's federally recognized tribes are mostly confederations made up of originally distinct groups that were brought together by U.S. government administrators for management purposes. For more about the recent history and current status of Oregon's Native American communities a collected volume by Berg (2007) is highly recommended.

Epilogue:
Cultural Resource Management Archaeology in Oregon

An extensive set of federal, state, and tribal laws on environmental and cul tural resource protection governs the conduct of archaeology both nationally and in Oregon. On the federal level, the Antiquities Act of 1906 was estab lished to outlaw the looting of Native American sites on public lands. It also became the authority under which National Monuments were established to protect and preserve outstanding cultural and natural resources on public lands for the education and enjoyment of the citizenry. The American Indian Religious Freedom Act of 1978 sought, among other objectives, to properly recognize the Native American spiritual values reflected in archaeological sites and sacred places, and the Archaeological Resources Protection Act of 1979 updated and broadened the protections of the 1906 Antiquities Act. The National Environmental Policy Act of 1969 included cultural resources under its broad requirements for environmental impact assessments when the mod- ification of natural landscapes might threaten cultural sites, with a view to avoiding or mitigating such impacts. The Native American Graves Protection and Repatriation Act of 1990, reflecting the strongly held spiritual concerns of indigenous descendants, created rules and procedures for the return to culturally affiliated groups of human remains, associated burial goods, and objects of cultural patrimony found in newly excavated archaeological sites or held in museums and other repositories. These are key pieces of federal legislation among a much larger array of laws and administrative procedures that today regulate activities which may affect cultural and natural resource sites on public lands in Oregon.

On the state level, Oregon legislation mandating the protection of Indian burials and improving the archaeological permitting process (ORS. 97.740 and ORS 273.705) was promulgated in 1977 with strong input from the Oregon Archaeological Society, a predominantly Portland-based citizen group. The burial law was augmented and strengthened in 1979 by legislation sponsored by the Cow Creek Band of Lower Umpqua Indians, an event marking the beginning of much increased tribal involvement in cultural heritage legisla- tive and management issues. The Commission on Indian Services, which had been established by the State Legislature in 1975 to deal with Indian health and education issues, was also concerned with cultural heritage matters on an ongoing basis. It published a cultural resources handbook (Gorospe 1985) and between 1986 and 1989 convened a series of annual two-day workshops for professional archaeologists, cultural resource managers, and Native American community leaders that showed the way to the collaborative interagency relationships which characterize cultural resource management decisions and actions in Oregon today.

Today, an extensive set of federal, state, and tribal laws, regulations, and procedures guides the policies of land-management agencies that include tribal governments, the U.S. Forest Service, Bureau of Land Management, U.S. Army Corps of Engineers, U.S. Fish and Wildlife Service, Oregon Department of Transportation, and other parties. The Oregon State Historic Preservation Office provides centralized coordination and manages the archaeological permitting process through consultations among the concerned federal, state, and tribal agencies. Based on their original connection to the land and their tribal sovereignty as reserved under treaties going back to the 1850s, Oregon's nine federally recognized tribes interact with both federal and state institutions on a government-to-government basis and play a pivotal role in the conduct of all activities that affect cultural resource sites throughout the state (Griffin 2009).

The fundamental principle guiding all this legislation is that cultural sites are valued and respected as part of the national patrimony, representing our collective cultural heritage and history. It has further become clear that in addition to specific archaeological and historical sites there exist traditional cultural properties and landscapes of broader scope that are also part of this patrimony. At the same time it is recognized that society as a whole necessarily continues to depend on the land for its livelihood and well being, so cultural resource managers must routinely seek accommodations that will respect significant sites while not unduly restricting ongoing human use of the land that everyone shares. Highways must be built and improved, harbors must be dredged, buildings must be constructed, forests must be managed, and so on. In response to these realities there has developed in the United States a broad discipline of public agency oversight and management, scientific research, preservation, and education commonly referred to as Cultural Resource Management (CRM).

Preservation is a primary goal of CRM, and site preservation by avoidance is the most common outcome of the cultural resource management surveys and evaluations that are carried out in advance of ground-disturbing projects. However, in cases where an important cultural site cannot reasonably be avoided, a project may be allowed to proceed after careful scientific investigation of the site involved has been completed. The site is "preserved", in effect, by preserving the historical and scientific information that can be derived from the cultural features and specimens it contained. The specimens, maps, photos and other records obtained in an investigation are permanently preserved in museums and other appropriate repositories, and the scientific and historical conclusions of the work are made available to the public through reports, books, libraries, museum exhibitions, and other media.

The items and records thus recovered have continuing potential to yield new information through scientific analysis, because new investigative techniques are always being developed. In addition, new questions often arise that can be investigated by further analysis of evidence that is already in hand. For these reasons, site collections and records are by law kept in permanent repositories where they will always be protected and available for further study. The University of Oregon Museum of Natural and Cultural History (identified in state statutes as the Oregon State Museum of Anthropology) is Oregon's official repository for state-owned anthropological and archaeological collections, carrying a mandate established by the Oregon Legislature in 1935. It cares for collections from all over Oregon and participates in certifying the facilities and qualifications of other State institutions that also take on such responsibilities, as at Oregon State University and Southern Oregon University.

The historical and cultural knowledge obtained through archaeological research reaches the public through museum exhibitions, public lectures, online catalogs, media presentations, magazine articles, and books such as the present one. In its exhibits hall, the University of Oregon Museum of Natural and Cultural History surveys the state's Native American cultural areas, and other museums around the state that offer rich topical presentations include the Oregon Historical Society Museum, Columbia Gorge Discovery Center, Wasco County Historical Museum, Tamastslikt Cultural Institute, Museum at Warm Springs, High Desert Museum, Douglas County Museum of Natural and Cultural History, and Umpqua Discovery Center, among others. With 14,500 years or more of human history known to be represented in Oregon there is always more to be learned, and the research policies and processes described above continuously enlarge our knowledge.

References

Adams, W.H., and K. Garnett 1991. The Historical Geography of Fort Yamhill. Pp. 35–58 in *Fort Yamhill: Preliminary Historical Archaeological Research Concerning the 1856–1866 Military Post*. W. H. Adams, ed. Oregon State University. Corvallis.

Aikens, C. Melvin 1982. Archaeology of the Northern Great Basin: An Overview. Pp. 139–155 in *Man and Environment in the Great Basin*. Society for American Archaeology Papers No. 2, David B. Madsen and James F. O'Connell, eds. Washington, D.C.

———— 1984. Archaeology of Oregon. USDI BLM, Oregon State Office.

———— 1985. The Nightfire Island Lakeshore Adaptation in the Broader Context of Desert West Prehistory. Pp. 519–528 in *Nightfire Island: Later Holocene Lakemarsh Adaptation on the Western Edge of the Great Basin* by C. Garth Sampson. University of Oregon Anthropological Papers No. 33. Eugene.

———— 1993. Archaeology of Oregon, 2nd edition. USDI BLM, Oregon State Office.

———— 1994. Adaptive Strategies and Environmental Change in the Great Basin and its Peripheries as Determinants in the Migrations of Numic-Speaking Peoples. Pp. 35–43 in *Across the West: Human Population Movement and the Expansion of the Numa*. David B. Madsen and David Rhode, eds. University of Utah Press.

———— 2006. Paleoindian: West. Pp. 194–204 in *Environment, Origins, and Population, Vol. 3, Handbook of North American Indians*. Douglas H. Ubelaker, ed. Smithsonian Institution.

———— 2009. Walking and Running in the Sierra Tarahumara: A Reflection on Pedestrian Mobility and the "Known World" in Desert West Culture History. Pp. 32–48 in *Past, Present, and Future Issues in Great Basin Archaeology: Papers in Honor of Don D. Fowler*, Bryan Hockett, ed. USDI Bureau of Land Management, Nevada, Cultural Resource Series No. 20.

Aikens, C. Melvin, David Cole, and Robert Stuckenrath 1977. *Excavations at Dirty Shame Rockshelter, Southeastern Oregon*. Tebiwa Miscellaneous Papers of the Idaho State University Museum of Natural History No. 4. Pocatello.

Aikens, C. Melvin, Donald K. Grayson, and Peter J. Mehringer, Jr. 1982. *Final Report to the National Science Foundation on the Steens Mountain Prehistory Project, Part III, Technical Description of Project and Results*. University of Oregon. Eugene.

Aikens, C. Melvin, and Ruth L. Greenspan. 1988. Ancient Lakeside Culture in the Northern Great Basin: Malheur Lake, Oregon. *Journal of California and Great Basin Anthropology* 10:32–61.

Aikens, C. Melvin and Dennis L. Jenkins, eds. 1994a. *Archaeological Researches in the Northern Great Basin: Fort Rock Archaeology Since Cressman.* University of Oregon Anthropological Papers 50. Eugene.

———— 1994b. Environment, Climate, Subsistence, and Settlement: 11,000 Years of Change in the Fort Rock Basin, Oregon. Pp. 1–19 in *Archaeological Researches in the Northern Great Basin: Fort Rock Archaeology Since Cressman.* C. Melvin Aikens and Dennis L. Jenkins, eds. University of Oregon Anthropological Papers No. 50. Eugene.

Aikens, C. Melvin and David B. Madsen 1986. Prehistory of the Eastern Area. Pp. 149–60 in *Handbook of North American Indians, Volume 11: Great Basin.* Warren L. d'Azevedo, ed. Smithsonian Institution, Washington, D. C.

Aikens, C. Melvin and Rick Minor 1978. *Obsidian Hydration Dates for Klamath Prehistory.* Tebiwa Miscellaneous Papers of the Idaho State University Museum of Natural History No. 11. Pocatello.

Aikens, C. Melvin and Younger T. Witherspoon 1986. Great Basin Numic Prehistory: Linguistics, Archaeology, and Environment. Pp. 7–20 in *Anthropology of the Desert West: Essays in Honor of Jesse D. Jennings,* Carol J. Condie and Don D. Fowler, eds. University of Utah Press, Salt Lake City.

Aikens, C. Melvin, Irina S. Zhushchikhovskaya, and Song Nai Rhee 2009. Environment, Adaptation, and Interaction in Japan, Korea, and the Russian Far East: The Millennial History of a Japan Sea Oikumene. *Asian Perspectives* 48(2):207–248.

Aikens, C. Melvin and Irina Zhushchikhovskaya 2010. Late Pleistocene and Early Holocene Cultural Connections between Asia and America. Pp. 17–46 in *Maritime Adaptation and Seaside Settlement in the North Pacific during the Pleistocene-Holocene Boundary,* Jim Cassidy, Robert Ackerman, and Irina Ponkratova, eds. North Pacific Prehistory Vol. 3. The University Book, Madrid.

Allely, Steven 1975. A Clovis Point from the Mohawk River Valley, Western Oregon. Pp. 549–552 in *Archaeological Studies in the Willamette Valley, Oregon.* C. Melvin Aikens, ed. University of Oregon Anthropological Papers No. 8. Eugene.

Allison, John 1994. The Cultural Landscape of the Klamath, Modoc, and Yahooskin Peoples. Spirit, Nature, History. On file at the Oregon State Historic Preservation Office, Salem.

Ames, Kenneth M. 1985. Hierarchies, Stress and Logistical Strategies among Hunter-Gatherers in Northwestern North America. Pp. 155–180 in *Prehistoric Hunter-Gatherers, the Emergence of Cultural Complexity,* C. Douglas Price and James A. Brown, eds. Academic Press, Orlando.

———— 1988. Early Holocene Mobility Strategies on the Southern Columbia Plateau. Pp. 325–360 in *Early Human Occupation in Far Western North America: The Clovis-Archaic Interface.* Judith A. Willig, C. Melvin Aikens, and John L. Fagan, eds. Nevada State Museum Anthropological Papers 21. Carson City.

———— 1991. Sedentism, A Temporal Shift or a Transitional Change in Hunter-Gatherer Mobility Strategies. Pp. 103–133 in *Between Bands and States.* Susan Greg, ed. Center for Archaeological Investigations Occasional Paper No. 9. Southern Illinois University Press. Carbondale.

———— 1995. Chiefly Power and Household Production on the Northwest Coast. Pp. 155–187 in *Foundations of Inequality.* T. D. Price and G. M. Feinman, eds. Plenum Press, New York.

—— 1996. Life in the Big House, Household Labor and Dwelling Size on the Northwest Coast. Pp. 178–200 in *People who Lived in Large Houses, Archaeological Perspectives on Large Domestic Structures*, Cary Coupland and E. B. Banning, eds. Prehistory Press, Madison.

—— 2001. Slaves, Chiefs and Labour on the Northern Northwest Coast. *World Archaeology* 33(1):1–17.

—— 2006. Thinking about Household Archaeology on the Northwest Coast and Elsewhere, Pp. 16–36 in *Household Archaeology on the Northwest Coast*, Elizabeth A. Sobel, D. Ann Trieu Garr & Kenneth M. Ames, eds. International Monographs in Prehistory, Ann Arbor.

Ames, Kenneth M., Don E. Dumond, Jerry R. Galm, and Rick Minor 1998. Prehistory of the Southern Plateau. Pp. 103–119 in *Handbook of North American Indians. Vol. 12: Plateau*. Deward E. Walker, Jr., ed. Smithsonian Institution. Washington, D.C.

Ames, Kenneth M. and A. G. Marshall 1980. Villages, Demography and Subsistence Intensification on the Southern Columbia Plateau. *North American Archaeologist* 2(1):25–52.

Ames, Kenneth M. and Herbert D. G. Maschner 1999. *Peoples of the Northwest Coast: Their Archaeology and Prehistory*. Thames & Hudson, London.

Ames, Kenneth M., Doria F. Raetz, Stephen Hamilton, and Christine McAfee 1992. Household Archaeology of a Southern Northwest Coast Plank House. *Journal of Field Archaeology* 19(3):275–290.

Ames, Kenneth M., Cameron McP. Smith, and Alexander Bourdeau 2008. Large Domestic Pits on the Northwest Coast of North America. *Journal of Field Archaeology* 33(1):3–18.

Ames, Kenneth M., Cameron M. Smith, William L. Cornett, Elizabeth A. Sobel, Stephen C. Hamilton, John Wolf, and Doria Raetz 1999. Archaeological Investigations at 45CL1 Cathlapotle (1991–1996), Ridgefield National Wildlife Refuge, Clark County, Washington: A Preliminary Report. *Wapato Valley Archaeology Project Report #7*. Ms. on file at Portland State University.

Ames, Kenneth M., James P. Green, and Margaret Pfoertner 1981. *Hatwai (10NP143) Interim Report*. Archaeological Reports No. 9, Boise State University, Boise, Idaho.

Anastasio, Angelo 1972. The Southern Plateau: An Ecological Analysis of Intergroup Relations. *Northwest Anthropological Research Notes* 6:109–229.

Anderson, M. Kat 2005. *Tending the Wild: Native American Knowledge and the Management of California's Natural Resources*. University of California Press. Berkeley.

—— 1990. California Indian Horticulture. *Fremontia* 18(2):7–14.

—— 1993. Native Californians as Ancient and Contemporary Cultivators. Pp. 151–174 in *Before the Wilderness: Environmental Management by Native Californians*, Thomas C. Blackburn and Kat Anderson, eds. Ballena Press, Menlo Park.

Andrefsky, William, Jr. 2008. Projectile Point Provisioning Strategies and Human Land-Use. Pp. 195–214 in *Lithic Technology: Measures of Production, Use and Curation*. William Andrefsky, Jr., ed. Cambridge University Press, Cambridge.

Andrefsky, William, Jr., Lisa Centola, Jason Cowan, and Erin Wallace 2003. *An Introduction to the Birch Creek Site (35ML181): Six Seasons of WSU Archaeological Field Study 1998–2003*. Contributions in Cultural Resource Management No. 69. Center for Northwest Anthropology and Department of Anthropology, Washington State University. Pullman.

Andrefsky, William, Jr., Sarah Van Galder, and Kira Presler 1999. *Archaeological Investigations at Birch Creek (35ML181): 1998 Season Interim Report*. Contributions in Cultural Resource Management No. 64. Center for Northwest Anthropology, Washington State University. Pullman.

Andrefsky, William, Jr., and Kira Presler 2000. *Archaeological Investigations at Birch Creek (35ML181): 1998–1999 Interim Report*. Contributions in Cultural Resource Management No. 66. Center for Northwest Anthropology, Washington State University. Pullman.

Aoki, Haruo 1963. On Sahaptin-Klamath Linguistic Affiliations. *International Journal of American Linguistics* 29(20):107–112.

Applegate, Jesse 1914. *Recollections of My Boyhood*. Review Publishing. Roseburg.

Armitage, Charles L. 1995. *An Archaeological Analysis of Central Oregon Upland Prehistory*. PhD Dissertation, University of Oregon Department of Anthropology. Eugene.

Atherton, John H. 1975. Archaeological Investigations at Champoeg, Oregon, 1973. Pp. 103–120 in *Pacific Northwest Historical Archaeological Research*. Lester A. Ross, ed. Northwest Anthropological Research Notes Special Issue No. 9(1). Moscow, Idaho.

Atherton, John A., and Michael C. Houck 1976. *An Introduction to the Natural History of Camp Hancock and the Clarno Basin, North-Central Oregon*. Oregon Museum of Science and Industry. Portland, Oregon.

Bailey, Vernon 1936. *The Mammals and Life Zones of Oregon*. USDA Bureau of Biological Survey, North American Fauna No. 55. U.S. Government Printing Office, Washington, D.C.

Balster, Clifford A., and R. B. Parsons 1968. *Geomorphology and Soils, Willamette Valley, Oregon*. Oregon Agriculture Experiment Station, Oregon State University, in cooperation with the USDA Soil Conservation Service, Special Report No. 265. Corvallis.

Barber, Richard L., and Terry L. Holtzapple 1998. *Dudley House Pit Excavations at Big Summit Prairie, Ochoco Mountains*. Archaeological Society of Central Oregon Report No. 1. Manuscript on file at Deschutes and Ochoco National Forests, Bend.

Barker, M. A. R. 1963. *Klamath Texts*. University of California Publications in Linguistics 30, Berkeley and Los Angeles.

Barlow, Jeffrey, and Christine Richardson 1979. *China Doctor of John Day*. Binford & Mort, Portland.

Barner, Debra C. 1981. *Shell and Archaeology: An Analysis of Shellfish Procurement and Utilization on the Central Oregon Coast*. M.A. Thesis, Department of Anthropology, Oregon State University. Corvallis.

———— 1993. Determination of Eligibility and Data Recovery Plan for the Tiller Site, 35DO37. On file, Umpqua National Forest. Roseburg.

Barrett, Samuel A. 1910. The Material Culture of the Klamath Lake and Modoc Indians of Northeastern California and Southern Oregon. *University of California Publications in American Archaeology and Ethnology* 5(4):239–292.

Barry, J. Neilson 1927. The Indians of Oregon—Geographic Distribution of Linguistic Families. *Oregon Historical Quarterly* 28(1):49–61.

Barton, C. Michael, Steven Schmich, and Steven R. James 2004. The Ecology of Human Colonization in Pristine Landscapes. Pp. 138–161 in *The Settlement of the American Continents: A Multidisciplinary Approach to Human Biogeography*. C. Michael Barton, Geoffrey A. Clark, David R. Yesner, and Georges A. Pearson, eds. University of Arizona Press. Tucson.

Basgall, Mark E., and William R. Hildebrandt 1989. *Prehistory of the Sacramento River Canyon, Shasta County, California*. Center for Archaeological Research at Davis, Publication No. 9.

Baugh, Timothy G., and Jonathon Ericson, eds. 1994. *Prehistoric Exchange Systems in North America*. Plenum Press. New York and London.

Bawlf, Samuel 2003. *The Secret Voyage of Sir Francis Drake 1577–1580*. Penguin Books. London.

Baxter, Paul W. 1986. *Archaic Upland Adaptations in the Central Oregon Cascades*. PhD Dissertation, Department of Anthropology. University of Oregon. Eugene.

———— 1989a. *A Preliminary Report of Investigations at Cascadia Cave, Linn County, Oregon*. Heritage Research Associates Report. On file at the State Historic Preservation Office. Salem.

———— 1989b. Limpy Rock Shelter: An Upland Hunting Camp in the North Umpqua Valley. Pp. 55–75 in *Contributions to the Archaeology of Oregon 1987–88*. Rick Minor, ed. Association of Oregon Archaeologists Occasional Papers No 4. Eugene.

Baxter, Paul W., Richard D. Cheatham, Thomas J. Connolly, and Judith A. Willig 1983. *Rigdon's Horse Pasture Cave: An Upland Hunting Camp in the Western Cascades*. University of Oregon Anthropological Papers 28, Eugene.

Baxter, Paul W., and Thomas J. Connolly 1985. Vine Rockshelter: A Report of Excavations at an Intermittent Hunting Camp in the Western Cascades. Document on file at the Willamette National Forest, Eugene.

Beals, Herbert K., and Harvey Steele 1981. *Chinese Porcelains from Site 35TI1, Netarts Sand Spit, Tillamook County, Oregon*. University of Oregon Anthropological Papers No. 23. Eugene.

Beaton, John M. 1991. Paleoindian Occupation Greater than 11,000 yr B.P. at Tule Lake, Northern California. *Current Research in the Pleistocene* 8:5–7.

Beck, Charlotte 1984. *Steens Mountain Surface Archaeology: The Sites*. PhD Dissertation, Department of Anthropology, University of Washington. Seattle.

Beck, Charlotte, and George T. Jones 1997. The Terminal Pleistocene/Early Holocene Archaeology of the Great Basin. *Journal of World Prehistory* 11:161–236.

———— 2009. Artifact Analysis. Pp. 77–228 in *The Archaeology of the Eastern Nevada Paleoarchaic, Part I: The Sunshine Locality*. University of Utah Anthropological Papers No. 126. Salt Lake City.

———— 2010. Clovis and Western Stemmed: Population Migration and the Meeting of Two Technologies in the Intermountain West. *American Antiquity* 75(1):81–116.

Beck, Charlotte, George T. Jones, Dennis L. Jenkins, Craig E. Skinner, and Jennifer J. Thatcher 2004. Fluted or Basally Thinned? Re-examination of a Lanceolate Point from the Connley Caves in the Fort Rock Basin. Pp. 281–294 in *Early and Middle Holocene Archaeology of the Northern Great Basin*. Dennis L. Jenkins, Thomas J. Connolly, and C. Melvin Aikens, eds. University of Oregon Anthropological Papers No. 62. Eugene.

Beckham, Stephen Dow 1971. *Requiem for a People.* Oregon State University Press, Corvallis, Oregon.

———— 1986. *Land of the Umpqua: A History of Douglas County, Oregon.* Douglas County Commissioners, Roseburg, Oregon.

———— 1991. Federal-Indian Relations. Pp. 39–54 in *The First Oregonians.* Carolyn M. Buan and Richard Lewis, eds. Oregon Council for the Humanities. Portland, Oregon

———— 1998. History Since 1846. Pp. 499–514 in *Handbook of North American Indians, Vol. 12: Plateau.* Deward E. Walker, Jr., ed. Smithsonian Institution, Washington, D.C.

Beckham, Stephen Dow, Rick Minor, and Kathryn A. Toepel 1981. *Prehistory and History of BLM Lands in West-Central Oregon: A Cultural Resource Overview.* University of Oregon Anthropological Papers No. 25. Eugene.

Beckham, Stephen Dow, and Rick Minor 1982. *Cultural Resource Overview of the Umpqua National Forest, Southwestern Oregon.* Heritage Research Associates Report No. 125. Eugene.

Beckham, Stephen Dow, Rick Minor, Kathryn Anne Toepel, and Jo Reese 1988. *Prehistory and History of the Columbia River Gorge National Scenic Area, Oregon and Washington.* Heritage Research Associates Reports No. 75. Eugene. On file at the USDA Forest Service, Columbia River Gorge National Scenic Area, Hood River, Oregon.

Bedwell, Stephen F. 1970. *Prehistory and Environment of the Pluvial Fort Rock Lake Area of Southcentral Oregon.* PhD Dissertation, Department of Anthropology, University of Oregon. Eugene.

———— 1973. *Fort Rock Basin Prehistory and Environment.* University of Oregon Books. Eugene.

Bedwell, Stephen F., and Luther S. Cressman 1971. Fort Rock Report: Prehistory and Environment of the Pluvial Fort Rock Lake Area of South-Central Oregon. Pp. 1–25 in Great Basin Anthropological Conference 1970: Selected Papers. *University of Oregon Anthropological Papers 1.* Eugene.

Benito, G., and J. E. O' Connor 2003. Number and Size of Last-glacial Missoula Floods in the Columbia River Valley Between the Pasco Basin, Washington, and Portland, Oregon. *Geological Society of America Bulletin* 115:624–638.

Bennett, Ann C. 1988. *Whale Cove (35LNC60): An Archaeological Investigation on the Central Oregon Coast.* M.A. Thesis, Oregon State University, Corvallis, Oregon.

Bennett, Ann C., and R. Lee Lyman 1991. Archaeology of Whale Cove (35LNC60). Pp. 241–277 in *Prehistory of the Oregon Coast: The Effects of Excavation Strategies and Assemblage Size on Archaeological Inquiry,* by R. Lee Lyman. Academic Press, New York.

Bennyhoff, James A., and Richard E. Hughes 1987. Shell Bead and Ornament Exchange Networks between California and the Western Great Basin. Pp. 79–175 in *Anthropological Papers of the American Museum of Natural History* No. 64(2).

Bensell, Royal A. 1959. *All Quiet on the Yamhill: The Civil War in Oregon.* The Journal of Corporal Royal A. Bensell, Company D, Fourth California Infantry, Gunter Barth, ed. University of Oregon, Eugene.

Berg, Laura, ed. 2007. *The First Oregonians, Second Edition.* Oregon Council for the Humanities. Portland, Oregon.

Berreman, Joel V. 1935a. A Preliminary Survey of Shell Mounds and Other Occupied Sites of the Coast of Southern Oregon and Northern California. Ms. on file at the Oregon State Museum of Anthropology. Eugene.

—— 1935b. Field notes, summer 1935. Ms. on file at the Oregon State Museum of Anthropology. Eugene.

—— 1937. Tribal Distribution in Oregon. Memoirs of the American Anthropological Association 47. Supplement to American Anthropologist 39[3] Part 2. Menasha.

—— 1944. Chetco Archaeology: A Report of the Lone Ranch Creek Shell Mound on the Coast of Southern Oregon. American Anthropological Association General Series in Anthropology. Menasha.

Bettinger, Robert L. 1999. Faces in Prehistory: Great Basin Wetlands Skeletal Populations. Pp. 321–332 in Prehistoric *Lifeways in the Great Basin Wetlands: Bioarchaeological Reconstruction and Interpretation.* Brian E. Hemphill and Clark S. Larsen, eds. University of Utah Press. Salt Lake City.

Bevill, Russell, Michael S. Kelly, and Elena Nilsson 1994. *Archaeological Data Recovery at 35 DO 37, A Pre-Mazama Site on the South Umpqua River, Douglas County, Southwest Oregon.* Mountain Anthropological Research. Submitted to Umpqua National Forest, Roseburg, Oregon. On file at the Oregon State Historic Preservation Office, Salem.

Bland, Richard L., Thomas J. Connolly, Jaime L. Dexter, and Elizabeth A. Kallenbach 2005. Archaeological Evaluation of Site 35LNC95, Spencer Creek Bridge Replacement, Oregon Coast Highway (US 101), Lincoln County. *University of Oregon Museum of Natural & Cultural History Report No. 2005-116.* Eugene.

Bland, Richard L., Thomas J. Connolly, and Ward Tonsfeldt 2009. *Archaeological Subsurface Reconnaissance and Testing of Sites 35CO60 and 35CO61 at the Nehalem River (Banzer) Bridge (#03140A) on Oregon Highway 202, Columbia County.* University of Oregon Museum of Natural & Cultural History Report 2009-034, on file at the Oregon State Historic Preservation Office, Salem.

Blyth, Beatrice 1938. The Northern Paiute Bands in Oregon. *American Anthropologist* 40:402–405.

Boldurian, Anthony T., and John L. Cotter 1999. *Clovis Revisited. New Perspectives on Paleoindian Adaptations from Blackwater Draw, New Mexico.* The University Museum, University of Pennsylvania. Philadelphia.

Bonstead, Leah 2000. *The Nials Site: An Early Holocene Occupation in the Harney Basin, Oregon.* Master's Thesis, Department of Anthropology, University of Nevada, Reno.

Bottman, Tobin C. 2006. *Stable Isotope Analysis to Determine Geographic Provenience of Olivella Biplicata Shell Beads Excavated from Archaeological Sites in the Northern Great Basin: Implications for Reconstructing Prehistoric Exchange.* Master's Thesis, Department of Anthropology, University of Oregon. Eugene.

Bowyer, Gary 1992. *Archaeological Symbols of Status and Authority: Fort Hoskins, Oregon 1856–1865.* Masters Thesis, Department of Anthropology, Oregon State University. Corvallis.

Boyd, Robert T. 1990a. Demographic History 1774–1874. Pp. 135–148 in *Handbook of North American Indians, Volume 7: Northwest Coast.* Wayne Suttles, ed. Smithsonian Institution. Washington, D.C.

———— 1990b. *The Coming of the Spirit of Pestilence: Introduced Infectious Diseases and Population Decline among Northwest Coast Indians, 1774–1874.* University of Washington Press. Seattle.

———— 1998. Demographic History Until 1990. Pp. 467–483 in *Handbook of North American Indians, Volume 12: Plateau.* Deward E. Walker, Jr., ed. Smithsonian Institution. Washington, D.C.

———— 1999. Strategies of Indian Burning in the Willamette Valley. Pp. 94–38 in *Indians, Fire and the Land in the Pacific Northwest.* Robert Boyd, ed. Oregon State University Press. Corvallis.

Branigan, Alyce 2000. *Preliminary Report of Test Excavations at the Biting Fly Site (35HA1260), Harney County, Oregon.* Report on file at the Burns District Bureau of Land Management, Hines, Oregon.

Brashear, M. Ann 1994. Assemblage Variation, Site Types, and Subsistence Activities in the Boulder Village Uplands, Fort Rock Basin, Oregon. Pp. 385–430 in *Archaeological Researches in the Northern Great Basin: Fort Rock Archaeology Since Cressman.* C. Melvin Aikens and Dennis L. Jenkins, eds. University of Oregon Anthropological Papers No. 50. Eugene.

Brauner, David R. 1976. *Alpowai: The Culture History of the Alpowa Locality Vol. I, Vol. II.* Washington State University, Pullman.

———— 1981. *The Archaeological Recovery of Sites 35JA52 and 35JA53 in the Applegate Lake Project Area, Jackson County, Oregon.* Report submitted to the U.S. Army Corps of Engineers, Portland District. Department of Anthropology, Oregon State University. Corvallis.

———— 1985. *Early Human Occupation in the Uplands of the Southern Plateau: Archaeological Excavations at the Pilcher Creek Site (35UN147), Union County, Oregon.* Report submitted to USDA Soil Conservation Service and the National Geographic Society. Department of Anthropology, Oregon State University. Corvallis.

———— 1987. *Archaeological Evaluation of Site ORMA72: The Hudson's Bay Company Granary Site, Champoeg State Park, Marion County, Oregon.* Report on file at the Oregon State Historic Preservation Office, Salem. Department of Anthropology, Oregon State University. Corvallis

———— 1989. *The French-Canadian Archaeological Project, Willamette Valley, Oregon: Site Inventory and Settlement Pattern.* Report of the to the National Park Service, on file at the Oregon State Historic Preservation Office. Salem. Department of Anthropology, Oregon State University. Corvallis.

Brauner, David R., and Clayton G. Lebow 1983. *A Re-evaluation of Cultural Resources within the Proposed Elk Creek Lake Project Area, Jackson County, Oregon. Phase II: Site Evaluation.* Submitted to the U.S. Army Corps of Engineers, Portland District. Department of Anthropology, Oregon State University. Corvallis.

Brauner, David R., and Robert Nisbet, Jr. 1983. *The Re-evaluation of Cultural Resources within the Proposed Elk Creek Lake Project Area, Jackson County, Oregon. Phase III: Archaeological Salvage of sites 35JA52 and 35JA53.* Submitted to the U.S. Army Corps of Engineers, Portland District. Department of Anthropology, Oregon State University. Corvallis.

Brauner, David R., and Nahani A. Stricker 2006. *Fort Hoskins Illustrated: An Archaeologist Reflects.* Benton County Historical Society and Museum. Philomath, Oregon.

Brogan, Phil F. 1977. *East of the Cascades,* 4th Edition. Binford & Mort. Portland, Oregon.

Budy, Elizabeth E., Michael P. Drews, and Robert G. Elston 1986. *Test Excavations at Site 35JA59, Elk Creek Lake Project, Jackson County, Oregon.* Submitted to the U.S. Army Corps of Engineers, Portland District. Intermountain Research. Silver City, Nevada.

Budy, Elizabeth E., and Robert G. Elston 1986. *Data Recovery at Sites 35JA102 and 35JA107, Elk Creek Lake Project, Jackson County, Oregon.* Submitted to the U.S. Army Corps of Engineers, Portland District. Intermountain Research. Silver City, Nevada.

Burtchard, Greg C. 1990. The Posy Archaeological Project, Upland Use of the Central Cascades; Mt Hood National Forest, Oregon. Cultural Resource Investigation Series Number 3. Report completed under Contract to the USDA Forest Service, Mt Hood National Forest, Gresham, Oregon.

Burtchard, Greg C., and Robert W. Keeler 1991. Mt Hood Cultural Resource Revaluation Project. A consideration of Prehistoric and Historic Land-Use and Cultural Resource Survey Design and Reevaluation Mt Hood National Forest, Oregon. Report completed Under Contract to the USDA Forest Service, Mt Hood National Forest, and Gresham, Oregon.

Butler, B. Robert 1957. The Art of the Lower Columbia Valley. *Archaeology* 10(3):58–65.

―――― 1959. Lower Columbia Valley Archaeology: A Survey and Appraisal of Some Major Archaeological Resources. *Tebiwa* 2(2):6–24.

―――― 1961. *The Old Cordilleran Culture in the Pacific Northwest.* Occasional Papers of the Idaho State College Museum, No. 5, Pocatello.

―――― 1962. Contributions to the Prehistory of the Columbia Plateau: A Report on Excavations in the Palouse and Craig Mountain Sections. Occasional Papers of the Idaho State College Museum, No. 9, Pocatello.

―――― 1963. Further Notes on the Burials and the Physical Stratigraphy at the Congdon site, a Multi-component Middle Period site at The Dalles on the Lower Columbia River. *Tebiwa* 6(2):16–32.

―――― 1965. The Structure and Function of the Old Cordilleran Culture Concept. *American Anthropologist* 67(5:1):1120–1131.

Butler, Virginia L. 1993. Natural Versus Cultural Salmonid Remains: Origin of The Dalles Roadcut Bones, Columbia River, Oregon, U.S.A. *Journal of Archaeological Science* 20(1):1–24.

Butler, Virginia L. 2007. Relic Hunting, Archaeology, and Loss of Native American Heritage at The Dalles. *Oregon Historical Quarterly* 108(4):624–643.

Byram, R. Scott 1994. Holocene Settlement Change in the Boulder Village Uplands. Pp. 369–384 in *Archaeological Researches in the Northern Great Basin: Fort Rock Archaeology Since Cressman,* C. Melvin Aikens and Dennis L. Jenkins, eds. University of Oregon Anthropological Papers No. 50. Eugene.

―――― 1998. Fishing Weirs in Oregon Coast Estuaries. Pp. 199–219 in *Hidden Dimensions: The Cultural Significance of Wetland Archaeology,* Kathryn Bernick, ed. University of British Columbia Laboratory of Archaeology Papers No. 1. University of British Columbia Press, Vancouver.

―――― 2002. *Brush Fences and Basket Traps: The Archaeology and Ethnohistory of Tidewater Weir Fishing on the Oregon Coast.* PhD Dissertation, Department of Anthropology, University of Oregon. Eugene.

———— 2003a. Archaeological Survey for the City of Port Orford Effluent Disposal Project, Curry County, Oregon. Prepared for SHN Consulting Engineers and Geologists, Inc., Coos Bay. On file at the Oregon State Historic Preservation Office. Salem.

———— 2003b. *Archaeological Evaluation of Site 35-CU-7, for the City of Port Orford Effluent Ocean Outfall Project.* Prepared for USDA Rural Development and the City of Port Orford. On file at the Oregon State Historic Preservation Office. Salem.

———— 2005a. *Archaeological Data Recovery at Site 35CU7, Tseriadun.* Prepared for the Ocean Outfall Phase of the Port Orford Effluent Disposal System Project. On file at the Oregon State Historic Preservation Office. Salem.

———— 2005b. Archaeological Excavations at Tseriadun, 35CU7, for Garrison Lake Outlet Modification, Port Orford, Oregon. On file at the Oregon State Historic Preservation Office. Salem.

———— 2009. Shell Mounds and Shell Roads: The Destruction of Oregon Coast Middens for Early Road Surfacing. *Current Archaeological Happenings in Oregon* 34(1):6–14.

Byram, Scott, and Jon Erlandson 1996. *Fishing Technologies at a Coquille River Wet Site: The 1994–95 Osprey Site Archaeological Project.* Ms. on file at the Oregon State Historic Preservation Office, Salem.

Byram, Scott, and Robert Witter 2000. Wetland Landscapes and Archaeological Sites in the Coquille Estuary, Middle Holocene to Recent Times. Pp. 60–81 in *Changing Landscapes: Proceedings of the 3rd Annual Coquille Cultural Preservation Conference, 1999,* Robert J. Losey, ed. The Coquille Indian Tribe. North Bend, Oregon.

Byram, Scott, Mark Tveskov, Jon Erlandson, Charles Hodges, and Robert Witter 1997. *Research in Response to Erosion at the Philpott Site, Coquille Estuary.* Report to the Coquille Indian Tribe Cultural Resources Program, on file at the Oregon State Historic Preservation Office, Salem.

Campbell, Sarah K. 1985. Synthesis. Pp. 481–514 in *Summary of Results, Chief Joseph Dam Cultural Resources Project, Washington,* S. K. Campbell, ed. University of Washington, Office of Public Archaeology, Seattle.

———— 1990. *Post Columbian Culture History in the Northern Columbia Plateau: A.D. 1500–1900.* Garland Publishing, New York.

———— n.d. *Untitled Report on Field Work at the Headquarters Site (Draft).* Manuscript on file, Malheur National Wildlife Refuge Headquarters, Princeton, Oregon.

Cannon, Michael D., and David J. Meltzer 2004. Early Paleoindian Foraging: Examining the Faunal Evidence for Large Mammal Specialization and Regional Variability in Prey Choice. *Quaternary Science Reviews* 23(18/19):1955–1987.

Cannon, William J., C. Cliff Creger, Don D. Fowler, Eugene M. Hattori, and Mary F. Ricks 1990. A Wetlands and Uplands Settlement-Subsistence Model for Warner Valley, Oregon. Pp. 173–182 in *Wetland Adaptations in the Great Basin.* Joel C. Janetski and David B. Madsen, eds. Brigham Young University Museum of Peoples and Cultures Occasional Papers No. 1. Provo, Utah.

Cannon, William J., and Mary F. Ricks 1986. The Lake County Rock Art Inventory: Implications for Prehistoric Settlement and Land Use Patterns. Pp. 1–23 in *Contributions to the Archaeology of Oregon 1983–1986.* Kenneth M. Ames, ed. Association of Oregon Archaeologists Occasional Papers No. 3. Eugene.

Cannon, A., and D. Y. Yang 2006. Early Storage and Sedentism on the Pacific Northwest Coast: Ancient DNA Analysis of Salmon Remains from Namu, British Columbia. *American Antiquity* 71:123–140.

Carlson, Roy 1983. *Indian Art Traditions of the Northwest Coast.* Simon Fraser University. Burnaby, British Columbia.

———— 1994. Trade and Exchange in Prehistoric British Columbia. Pp. 307–361 in *Prehistoric Exchange Systems in North America,* T. G. Baugh and J. E. Ericson, eds. Plenum Press, New York.

Carter, J., and D. Dugas 1994. *Holocene Occupation at Sodhouse Spring: Results of the 1993 Field Season.* Paper presented at the 24th Great Basin Anthropological Conference. Elko, Nevada.

Caywood, Louis R. 1948. The Exploratory Excavation of Fort Clatsop. *Oregon Historical Quarterly* 49(3):205–210.

———— 1955. *Final Report: Fort Vancouver Excavations.* National Park Service. San Francisco.

Centola, Lisa 2004. *Deconstructing Lithic Technology: A Study from the Birch Creek Site (35ML181), South Eastern Oregon.* Master of Arts Thesis, Department of Anthropology, Washington State University. Pullman.

Chapman, Judith Sanders 1993. *French Prairie Ceramics: The Harriet D. Munnick Archaeological Collection, Circa 1830–1860.* Anthropology Northwest No. 8, Department of Anthropology, Oregon State University. Corvallis.

Chartkoff, Joseph L. 1989. Exchange, Subsistence, and Sedentism along the Middle Klamath River. Pp. 285–303 in *Research in Economic Anthropology, Vol. 11,* Barry L. Isaac, ed. JAI Press, Greenwich, CT.

Chase, Alexander 1991. Shell Mounds of Lat 42 02', 43 05', & 42 15', Coast of Oregon; Description of Stone and Other Implements Found in Them, with Some Notes on Existing Tribes of That Section of the Coast (1873 ms., notated by R. Lee Lyman). *Northwest Anthropological Research Notes* 25(2):185–222.

Chatters, James C. 1989. Resource Intensification and Sedentism on the Southern Plateau. *Archaeology in Washington* 1:3–19.

Chatters, James C. 1991. Paleoecology and Paleoclimates of the Columbia Basin, Northwest America. PNL-SA-18715 Richland, Washington: Pacific Northwest Laboratory.

———— 1995. Population Growth, Climatic Cooling, and the Development of Collector Strategies on the Southern Plateau, Western North America. *Journal of World Prehistory* 9(3):341–400.

———— 1998. Environment. Pp. 29–48 in *Handbook of North American Indians, Vol. 12: Plateau.* Deward E. Walker, Jr., ed. Smithsonian Institution. Washington, D.C.

———— 2004. Safety in Numbers: The influence of the Bow and Arrow on Village Formation on the Columbia Plateau. Pp. 67–83 in *Complex Hunters-Gatherers: Evolution and Organization of Prehistoric Communities on the Plateau of Northwestern North America.* William C. Prentiss and Ian Kuijt, eds. University of Utah Press. Salt Lake City.

Chatters, James C., and David L. Pokotylo 1998. Prehistory: Introduction. Pp. 73–80 in *Handbook of North American Indians. Vol. 12: Plateau.* Deward E. Walker, Jr., ed. Smithsonian Institution. Washington, D.C.

Cheatham, Richard D. 1988. *Late Archaic Settlement Pattern in the Long Tom Sub-Basin, Upper Willamette Valley, Oregon.* University of Oregon Anthropological Papers No. 29. Eugene.

Cheatham, Richard D., Mark Robinson, Thomas J. Connolly, Guy L. Tasa, Vivien J. Singer, Dorothy E. Freidel, Melissa Cole Darby, Nancy A. Stenholm, and Cheryl Allen 1995. *Archaeological Investigations at the Bezuksewas Village Site (35KL778), Klamath County, Oregon.* State Museum of Anthropology Report 95-5. University of Oregon. Eugene.

Church, Eliza 1951. History of Local Names. Pp. 11–12 in *Old Days in Camas Valley.* Wilfred H. Brown, ed. The Camas Press. North Hollywood.

Churchill, Thomas E., and Paul C. Jenkins 1991. *Archaeological Evaluation of the Short Saddle Site.* Report prepared for the Detroit Ranger District, Willamette National Forest, Coastal Magnetic Search and Survey Report No. 53, July 28, 1991.

Clark, Linda A. 1988. *Archaeological Investigations at the Seal Rock Site, 35LNC14: A Late Prehistoric Shell Midden Located on the Central Oregon Coast.* M.A. Thesis, Department of Anthropology, Oregon State University. Corvallis.

———— 1991. Archaeology of Seal Rock (35LNC14). Pp. 175–240 in *Prehistory of the Oregon Coast: The Effects of Excavation Strategies and Assemblage Size on Archaeological Inquiry,* by R. Lee Lyman. Academic Press. New York.

Clarke, Samuel A. 1873. Early Modoc History. *The New York Times,* July 5, 1873. New York.

———— 1960. *The Samuel A. Clarke Papers (ca. 1873).* Klamath County Museum Research Papers No. 2. B. K. Swartz, Jr., ed. Klamath Falls, Oregon.

Clemmer, Richard O., and Omer C. Stewart 1986. Treaties, Reservations, and Claims. Pp. 525–557 in *Handbook of North American Indians, Volume 11: Great Basin.* Warren L. d'Azevedo, ed. Smithsonian Institution. Washington, D.C.

Clewett, S.E., and Elaine Sundahl 1983. *Archaeological Excavations at Squaw Creek, Shasta County, California.* Report on file, Shasta-Trinity National Forest, Redding, California.

Clyman, James 1960. *James Clyman, American Frontiersman, 1792–1881.* Charles L. Camp, ed. Champoeg Press. Portland, Oregon.

Cohen, Amie, and Mark Tveskov 2008. *The Tseriadun Site: Prehistoric and Historic Period Archaeology on the Southern Oregon Coast.* Southern Oregon University Laboratory of Anthropology Research Report No. 2008-3. Ashland.

Cole, Clint R. 2001. *Raw Material Sources and the Prehistoric Chipped-Stone Assemblage of the Birch Creek Site (35ML181), Southeast Oregon.* M.A. Thesis, Department of Anthropology, Washington State University. Pullman.

Cole, David L. 1967. *Archaeological Research of Site 35SH23, The Mack Canyon Site.* Report to the Bureau of Land Management. Museum of Natural History, University of Oregon. Eugene.

———— 1968. *Archaeological Excavations in Area 6 of Site 35GM9, the Wildcat Canyon Site.* Report to the National Park Service. Museum of Natural History, University of Oregon. Eugene.

———— 1969. *1967 and 1968 Archaeological Excavations of the Mack Canyon Site.* Report of the Museum of Natural History, University of Oregon to the USDI Bureau of Land Management.

Collins, Lloyd R. 1951. *The Cultural Position of the Kalapuya in the Pacific Northwest.* Master's Thesis, Department of Anthropology, University of Oregon. Eugene.

———— 1953. *Archaeological Survey of the Oregon Coast from June 1951–December 1952: Final Report.* Ms. on file at the State Museum of Anthropology, University of Oregon, Eugene.

Connolly, Thomas J. 1986. *Cultural Stability and Change in the Prehistory of Southwest Oregon and Northern California.* PhD Dissertation, Department of Anthropology, University of Oregon. Eugene.

———— 1988. A Culture-Historical Model for the Klamath Mountain Region of Southwest Oregon and Northern California. *Journal of California and Great Basin Anthropology* 10(2):246–260.

———— 1991. *The Standley Site (35Do182): Investigations Into the Prehistory of Camas Valley, Southwest Oregon.* University of Oregon Anthropological Papers No. 43. Eugene.

———— 1992. Human Responses to Change in Coastal Geomorphology and Fauna on the Southern Northwest Coast: Archaeological Investigations at Seaside, Oregon. *University of Oregon Anthropological Papers 45.* Eugene.

———— 1994. Paleo Point Occurrences in the Willamette Valley, Oregon. Pp. 81–88 in *Contributions to the Archaeology of Oregon, 1990–1994.* P. Baxter, ed. Association of Oregon Archaeologists Occasional Papers No. 5. Eugene.

———— 1995. Archaeological Evidence for a Former Bay at Seaside, Oregon. *Quaternary Research* 43:362–369.

———— 1999 *Newberry Crater: A Ten-Thousand-Year Record of Human Occupation and Environmental Change in the Basin-Plateau Borderlands.* University of Utah Anthropological Papers No. 121. University of Utah Press. Salt Lake City.

———— 2003. Human Hair from Terminal Pleistocene Peat Deposits in The Willamette Valley. *Current Archaeological Happenings in Oregon* 28(3/4):9–15.

———— 2005. Archaeological Evaluation of the Yaquina Falls Site (35LNC98), Pioneer Mountain-Eddyville Highway Realignment Project, Lincoln County. *University of Oregon Museum of Natural and Cultural History & State Museum of Anthropology Report No. 2005-001.* Eugene.

———— 2006. Implications of New Radiocarbon Ages on Coiled Basketry from the Northern Great Basin. Paper presented at the Great Basin Anthropological Conference, Las Vegas.

Connolly, Thomas J., and Pat Barker 2004. Basketry Chronology of the Early Holocene in the Northern Great Basin. Pp. 241–250 in *Early and Middle Holocene Archaeology of the Northern Great Basin.* Dennis L. Jenkins, Thomas J. Connolly, and C. Melvin Aikens, eds. University of Oregon Anthropological Papers No. 62. Eugene.

———— 2008. Great Basin Sandals. Pp. 69–74 in *The Great Basin: People and Place in Ancient Times,* Catherine S. Fowler and Don D. Fowler, eds. SAR Press, Santa Fe, New Mexico.

Connolly, Thomas J., and Paul W. Baxter 1986. New Evidence on a "Traditional" Topic in Pacific Northwest Prehistory. Pp. 129–146 in *Contributions to the Archaeology of Oregon 1983–1986.* Kenneth M. Ames, ed. Association of Oregon Archaeologists Occasional Papers No. 3. Eugene.

Connolly Thomas J., Paul W. Baxter and Dennis L. Jenkins 2008. *Suttle Lake and the Oregon Obsidian Trade: Archaeological Investigation at the Suttle Lake/Lake Creek Site*

Complex (35JE278 and 35JE355), Jefferson County. On file at the Oregon State Historic Preservation Office. Salem. University of Oregon Museum of Natural and Cultural History & State Museum of Anthropology Report No. 2008-010. Eugene.

Connolly, Thomas J., Jane E. Benjamin, Brian L. O'Neill, and Dennis L. Jenkins 1994. Archaeological Investigations at Two Sites on the Upper Rogue River (35JA189 and 35JA190), Southwest Oregon. *University of Oregon Anthropological Papers 48.* Eugene.

Connolly, Thomas J., and R. Scott Byram 2001. *The Bon Site: Middle to Late Holocene Land Use in the Upper Deschutes River Basin, Central Oregon.* State Museum of Anthropology, University of Oregon, Report No. 2001-3. Eugene.

Connolly, Thomas J., R. Scott Byram, and Robert Kentta 2008. Archaeology Illuminated by History, History Illuminated by Archaeology. Pp. 95–105 in *Dunes, Headlands, Estuaries, and Rivers: Current Archaeological Research on the Oregon Coast,* Guy L. Tasa and Brian L. O'Neill, eds. Association of Oregon Archaeologists Occasional Papers No. 8. Eugene.

Connolly, Thomas J., Pamela E. Endzweig, Patrick O'Grady, Christopher L. Ruiz, and Ward Tonsfeldt 2006. *Archaeology of the Caldera Springs Property.* Report to Caldera Springs Real Estate LLP, Sunriver, Oregon. Museum of Natural and Cultural History and State Museum of Anthropology Report 2006-16. Eugene.

Connolly, Thomas J., Dennis L. Jenkins, and Jane Benjamin 1993. *Archaeology of Mitchell Cave (35WH122): A Late Period Hunting Camp in the Ochoco Mountains, Wheeler County, Oregon.* University of Oregon Anthropological Papers No. 46. Eugene.

Connolly, Thomas J., and Dennis L. Jenkins 1996. *Mid-Holocene Occupations at the Heath Cliffs Site, Warm Springs Reservation, Oregon.* University of Oregon Anthropological Papers 53. Eugene.

———— 1997. Population Dynamics on the Northwestern Great Basin Periphery: Clues from Obsidian Geochemistry. *Journal of California and Great Basin Anthropology* 19:241–250.

———— 1999. The Paulina Lake Site (35DS34). Pp. 86–127 in *Newberry Crater: A Ten-Thousand-Year Record of Human Occupation and Environmental Change in the Basin-Plateau Borderlands,* by Thomas J. Connolly. University of Utah Anthropological Papers No. 121. Salt Lake City.

Connolly, Thomas J., and Elena Nilsson 1995. *Beyond the Border: An Assessment of Regional Cultural Patterns for Northwest California and Southwest Oregon.* Paper Presented at the Society for California Archaeology Symposium on "Modern Borders and Cultural Realities."

Connolly, Thomas J., Christopher L. Ruiz, and Patrick O'Grady 2006. *Archaeological Investigation of a Mining Camp on the Little North Santiam River: The Dolores #10 Site.* University of Oregon Museum of Natural & Cultural History Report No. 2006-048. Eugene.

Connolly, Thomas J., Christopher L. Ruiz, Jeanne McLaughlin, Guy L. Tasa, and Elizabeth Kallenbach 2010. The Archaeology of a Pioneer Family Cemetery in Western Oregon, 1854–1879. *Historical Archaeology* 44(4):28–45.

Connolly, Thomas J., and Guy L. Tasa 2004. *Archaeological Evaluation of the Avenue Q Site (35CLT13), Oregon Coast Highway (U.S. Highway 101), Clatsop County, Oregon.* University of Oregon Museum of Natural and Cultural History Report No. 2004-006, Eugene.

————— 2008. The Middle Holocene Cultural Record on the Oregon Coast: New Perspectives from Recent Work along the Central Oregon Coast. Pp. 73–81 in *Dunes, Headlands, Estuaries, and Rivers: Current Archaeological Research on the Oregon Coast*, Guy L. Tasa and Brian L. O'Neill, eds. Association of Oregon Archaeologists Occasional Papers No. 8. Eugene.

Connolly, Thomas J., Mark A. Tveskov, Howard A. Gard, and David Cutting 1997. Mapping the Mosier Mounds: The Significance of Rock Feature Complexes on the Southern Columbia Plateau. *Journal of Archaeological Science* 24(4):289–300.

Couture, Marilyn, Mary F. Ricks, and Lucile Housley 1986. Foraging Behavior of a Contemporary Northern Great Basin Population. *Journal of California and Great Basin Anthropology* 8(2):150–160.

Cowles, John 1960. *Cougar Mountain Cave in South Central Oregon.* Daily News Press. Rainier, Oregon.

Cressman, Luther S. 1933a. Aboriginal Burials in Southwestern Oregon. *American Anthropologist* 35:116–30.

————— 1933b. *Contributions to the Archaeology of Oregon: Final Report on the Gold Hill Burial Site.* University of Oregon Studies in Anthropology No. 1(1). Eugene.

————— 1937. *Petroglyphs of Oregon.* University of Oregon Monographs, Studies in Anthropology No. 2. Eugene.

————— 1940a. Studies on Early Man in South Central Oregon. *Carnegie Institution of Washington Year Book* 39:300–306. Washington D.C.

————— 1940b. Early Man in the Northern Part of the Great Basin of South-Central Oregon. *Proceedings of the Sixth Pacific Science Congress* 4:169–175. University of California. Berkeley.

————— 1947. Further Information on Projectile Points from Oregon. *American Antiquity* 13(2):177–179.

————— 1948. Odell Lake Site, a New Paleo-Indian Camp Site in Oregon. *American Antiquity* 14(1):57–58.

————— 1951. Western Prehistory in the Light of Carbon-14 Dating. *Southwestern Journal of Anthropology* 7(3):289–313.

————— 1953. Oregon Coast Prehistory: Problems and Progress. *Oregon Historical Quarterly* 54:291–300.

————— 1956. *Klamath Prehistory.* American Philosophical Society Transactions Vol. 46, Part 4. Philadelphia.

————— 1966. *The Sandal and the Cave: The Indians of Oregon.* Beaver Books. Portland, Oregon.

————— 1977. *Prehistory of the Far West: Homes of Vanished Peoples.* University of Utah Press. Salt Lake City.

————— 1986. Prehistory of the Northern Area. Pp. 120–126 in *Handbook of North American Indians Volume 11: Great Basin.* Warren L. D'Azevedo, ed. Smithsonian Institution. Washington, D.C.

Cressman, Luther S., with Frank C. Baker, Paul S. Conger, Henry P. Hansen, and Robert F. Heizer 1942. Archaeological Researches in the Northern Great Basin. *Carnegie Institution of Washington Publication 538.* Washington DC.

Cressman, Luther S., David L. Cole, Wilbur A. Davis, Thomas M. Newman, and Daniel J. Scheans 1960. *Cultural Sequences at The Dalles, Oregon*. American Philosophical Society Transactions, New Series 50(10). Philadelphia.

Cressman, Luther S., and W. S. Laughlin 1941. A Probable Association of Mammoth and Artifacts in the Willamette Valley, Oregon. *American Antiquity* 6(4):339–342.

Cressman, Luther S., and Howel Williams 1940. Early Man in Southcentral Oregon: Evidence from Stratified Sites. Pp. 53–78 in *Early Man in Oregon: Archaeological Studies in the Northern Great Basin*. University of Oregon Monographs, Studies in Anthropology No. 3. Eugene.

Cressman, Luther S., Howel Williams, and Alex D. Krieger 1940. *Early Man in Oregon: Archaeological Studies in the Northern Great Basin*. University of Oregon Monographs, Studies in Anthropology 3. Eugene.

Croes, Dale R., and Steven Hackenberger 1988. Hoko River Archaeological Complex: Modeling Prehistoric Northwest Coast Economic Evolution. Pp. 19–85 in *Prehistoric Economies of the Pacific Northwest Coast*, B. L. Isaac, ed. Research In Economic Anthropology, Special Supplement 3, JAI Press, Greenwich, Connecticut.

Darby, Melissa 2008. Native American Houses of the Kalapuya. Ms. on file at the Washington County Museum, Portland, Oregon.

Davis, Wilbur A. 1983. *Lost Creek Archaeology, Jackson County, Oregon, Contract CX 8099-2-0016, and 1974 Elk Creek Archaeology, Jackson County, Oregon, Contract CX 8099-2-0017*. Department of Anthropology, Oregon State University. Submitted to Interagency Archeological Services Division, Western Region, National Park Service.

Davis, Loren G. 2006. Geoarchaeological Insights from Indian Sands, a Late Pleistocene Site on the Southern Northwest Coast, USA. *Geoarchaeology: An International Journal* 21(4):351–361.

Davis, Loren G., Roberta L. Hall, Matthew Fillmore, Michele L. Punke, and Nicholas Debenham 2008. Some Natural Formation Processes Affecting Early Coastal Headland Sites on the Southern Oregon Coast. Pp. 119–115 in *Dunes, Headlands, Estuaries, and Rivers: Current Archaeological Research on the Oregon Coast*, Guy L. Tasa and Brian L. O'Neill, eds.. Association of Oregon Archaeologists Occasional Papers No. 8, Eugene.

Davis, Loren G., Roberta A. Hall, Samuel C. Willis 2006. Response to Moss et al. "An Early Holocene/Late Pleistocene Archaeological Site on the Oregon Coast? Comments on Hall et al. (2005)." *Radiocarbon*, 45(3):469–472.

Davis, Loren G., Michele L. Punke, Roberta L. Hall, Matthew Fillmore, and Samuel C. Willis 2004. A Late Pleistocene Occupation on the Southern Coast of Oregon. *Journal of Field Archaeology* 29(1):7–16. 2004.

Davis, Loren G., and Charles E. Schweger 2004. Geoarchaeological context of late Pleistocene and early Holocene occupation at the Cooper's Ferry site, western Idaho, USA. *Geoarchaeology: An International Journal* 19(7):685–704.

Davis, Carl M., and Sara A. Scott 1991. The Lava Butte Site Revisited. *Journal of California and Great Basin Anthropology* 13(1):40–59.

Davis, Owen K., and Charles H. Miksicek 1987. Plant Remains from Archaeological Sites in the Elk Creek Drainage, Southern Oregon. In *Data Recovery at Sites 35JA27, 35JA59, and 35JA100, Elk Creek Lake Project, Jackson County, Oregon, Volume 2, Appendices*.

Pp. B.1–B.11 in Infotec Research Incorporated, Report No. PNW87-7, Richard M. Pettigrew and Clayton G. Lebow, eds. Eugene.

d'Azevedo, Warren L., ed. 1986. *Handbook of North American Indians, Volume 11: Great Basin*. Smithsonian Institution. Washington, D.C.

Dean, Emily 1994. Faunal Remains from Structure 3 at the Big M Site, Fort Rock Basin, Oregon. Pp. 505–530 in *Archaeological Researches in the Northern Great Basin: Fort Rock Archaeology Since Cressman*. C. Melvin Aikens and Dennis L. Jenkins, eds. University of Oregon Anthropological Papers No. 50. Eugene.

Deich, Lyman 1977. Fluted Point Base from Western Oregon. *Current Archaeological Happenings in Oregon* 2(1).

———— 1982. *Aboriginal Clay Figurines from the Upper Rogue Valley in Southwestern Oregon*. Master's Thesis, Department of Anthropology, Portland State University. Portland, Oregon.

Denevan, William 1976. *The Native Population of the Americas in 1492*. University of Wisconsin, Madison.

De Smet, Father P. J. 1906. Oregon Missions and Travels Over the Rocky Mountains in 1845–46. Pp. 101–424 in Vol. 29 of *Early Western Travels 1748–1846*. Reuben Gold Thwaites, ed. The Arthur H. Clark Co. Cleveland.

Detling, Leroy E. 1968. *Historical Background of the Flora of the Pacific Northwest*. University of Oregon Museum of Natural History Bulletin 13. Eugene.

Deur, Douglas 1998. *Wetland Cultivation on the Northwest Coast of North America*. Master's Thesis, Department of Anthropology, Louisiana State University, Baton Rouge.

Deur, Douglas, and Nancy J. Turner, eds. 2005. *Keeping it Living: Traditions of Plant Use and Cultivation on the Northwest Coast of North America*. University of Washington Press, Seattle and University of British Columbia Press, Vancouver.

Dillon, William P., and Robert N. Odale 1968. Late Quaternary Sea-Level Curve: Reinterpretation Based on Glaciotectonic Influence. *Geology* 6:56–60.

Dixon, E. James 1999. *Bones, Boats, and Bison: Archeology and the First Colonization of Western North America*. University of New Mexico Press. Albuquerque.

Dixon, E. James, T. H. Heaton, T. E. Fifield, T. D. Hamilton, D. E. Putnam and F. Grady 1997. Late Quaternary Regional Geoarchaeology of Southeast Alaska Karst: A Progress Report. *Geoarchaeology: An International Journal* 12(6):689–712.

Dobyns, Henry 1966. Estimating Aboriginal American Population, I: An Appraisal of Techniques with a New Hemispheric Estimate. *Current Anthropology* 7(4):395–416.

Dodge, Orvil 1898. *Pioneer History of Coos and Curry Counties, Or.: Heroic Deeds and Thrilling Adventures of the Early Settlers*. Capital Printing, Salem, Oregon (republished 1969 by the Coos-Curry County Pioneer and Historical Association, Bandon, Oregon).

Dorsey, J. Owen 1889. Indians of Siletz Reservation, Oregon. *American Anthropologist* (old series) 2.55–61.

———— 1890. The Gentile System of the Siletz Tribes. *Journal of American Folklore* 3: 227–237.

Draper, John A. 1982. An Analysis of Lithic Tools and Debitage from 35CS1: A Prehistoric Site on the Southern Oregon Coast. *Tebiwa* 19:47–79.

——— 1988. *A Proposed Model of Late Prehistoric Settlement Systems on the Southern Northwest Coast, Coos and Curry Counties, Oregon.* PhD Dissertation, Department of Anthropology, Washington State University, Pullman.

——— 1996. *Archaeology of the Tiller Site: Pre-Mazama Occupation in the South Umpqua River Basin.* Report to the Umpqua National Forest by 4D-CRM, Darrington, Washington. On file at the Oregon State Historic Preservation Office, Salem.

Draper, John, and Kenneth Reid 1989. *Archaeology of Chokecherry Cave, 35 GR500, Grant County, Oregon.* Center for Northwest Anthropology, Washington State University, Pullman.

Drew, Edwin P. 1859. *Letter to Superintendent of Indian Affairs J.W. Nesmith, Salem, Oregon Territory, from Indian Sub-Agent E. P. Drew, Umpqua Indian Sub-Agency, July 1, 1857.* Report of the Commissioner of Indian Affairs, Accompanying the Annual Report of the Secretary of the Interior for the Year 1859, p. 359. William A. Harris, Printer, Washington, D.C.

Droz, Michael S. 1997. *Geomorphic and Climatic History of Holocene Channel, Playas, and Lunettes in the Fort Rock Basin, Lake County, Oregon.* M.A. Thesis, Department of Geography, University of Oregon. Eugene.

Drucker, Philip 1937. The Tolowa and their Southwest Oregon Kin. *University of California Publications in American Archaeology and Ethnology* 36:221–300.

——— 1939. Contributions to Alsea Ethnography. *University of California Publications in American Archaeology and Ethnology* 35:81–101.

——— 1943. Archaeological Survey on the Northern Northwest Coast. *Anthropological Papers 20, Bureau of American Ethnology Bulletin 133.* Washington.

Du Bois, Cora A. 1932. Tolowa Notes. *American Anthropologist* 34:248–262.

Duff, Wilson 1975. *Images Stone B.C.: Thirty Centuries of Northwest Coast Indian Sculpture.* Hancock House Publishers. Saanichton, British Columbia.

Dugas, Daniel P. 1996. *Formation Processes and Chronology of Dune Islands at Malheur National Wildlife Refuge, Harney County, Oregon.* Cultural Resource Series No. 12, U.S. Department of the Interior Fish and Wildlife Service, Region 1. Portland, Oregon.

Dugas, Daniel P., and Margaret Bullock 1994. *Headquarters Site: An Archaeological and Stratigraphic Assessment of HA403.* Cultural Resource Series No. 10, U.S. Department of the Interior Fish and Wildlife Service, Region 1. Portland, Oregon.

Dugas, Daniel P., Robert G. Elston, James A. Carter, Kathryn Ataman, and Margaret Bullock 1995. *An Archaeological and Stratigraphic Assessment of the Stubblefield Lookout Tower Site (35Ha53) Malheur National Wildlife Refuge.* Cultural Resource Series No. 11, U.S. Department of the Interior Fish and Wildlife Service, Region 1. Portland, Oregon.

Dumond, Don D., and Rick Minor 1983. *Archaeology in the John Day Reservoir: The Wildcat Canyon Site, 35-GM-9.* University of Oregon Anthropological Papers No. 30. Eugene.

Dunnell, R. C., and Charlotte Beck 1979. *The Caples Site, 45SA5, Skamania County, Washington.* Reports in Archaeology 6, Department of Anthropology, University of Washington, Seattle.

Dyck, John 1982. A Clovis Point From Southwestern Oregon. *Ohio Archaeologist* 32(2):32.

Eiselt, B. Sunday 1997. *Defining Ethnicity in Warner Valley: An Analysis of House and Home.* University of Nevada-Reno Department of Anthropology Technical Report 97-2. Reno.

―――― 1998. *Household Activity and Marsh Utilization in the Archaeological Record of Warner Valley: The Peninsula Site.* University of Nevada-Reno, Department of Anthropology Technical Report 98-2. Reno.

Elliott, T. C., ed. 1909. Journal of John Work, April 30th to May 31st, 1830. *Oregon Historical Quarterly* 10(3):296–313.

Ellis, David V. 1982. *The Rockwell Site: Historical Archaeology in Portland.* Department of Anthropology, Portland State University. Portland, Oregon.

―――― 1996. *Locational Analysis for the Willamette Valley Sites.* Pp. 12-1 to 12-72 in Northwest Pipeline Corporation System Expansion Phase I: Phase 3, Data Recovery and Site Treatment Reports for Oregon Segments, Volume V, Part 2, Willamette Valley, by Bill Roulette, Douglas C. Wilson, David V. Ellis, and Judy S. Chapman. Archaeological Investigations Northwest Report No. 50. On file at the Oregon State Historic Preservation Office. Salem.

Elston, Robert G., and Daniel P. Dugas 1993. *Dune Islands and the Archaeological Record in Malheur Lake.* Cultural Resource Series No. 7, U.S. Department of the Interior Fish and Wildlife Service, Region 1. Portland, Oregon.

Endzweig, Pamela E. 1989. Of Pots, Pipes, and People: Prehistoric Ceramics of Oregon. Pp. 157–177 in *Contributions to the Archaeology of Oregon 1987–88.* Rick Minor, ed. Association of Oregon Archaeologists Occasional Papers No. 4. Eugene.

―――― 1991. Current Archaeological Investigations in the Pine Creek Basin, North Central Oregon. *Current Archaeological Happenings in Oregon* 16(1):4–8.

―――― 1994a. Housepits on the John Day and Deschutes Rivers: A Summary of the Evidence. Pp. 45–63 in *Contributions to the Archaeology of Oregon 1989–1994.* Paul W. Baxter, ed. Association of Oregon Archaeologists Occasional Papers No. 5. Eugene.

―――― 1994b. *Late Archaic Variability and Change on the Southern Columbia Plateau: Investigations in the Pine Creek Drainage of the Middle John Day River, Wheeler County, Oregon.* PhD Dissertation, Department of Anthropology, University of Oregon. Eugene.

―――― 2001. Archaeological Investigations at the Cottonwood Creek Site (35GR1507): Middle and Late Holocene Occupations in the Upper John Day Valley, Oregon. State Museum of Anthropology, University of Oregon, Report No. 2001-1. Eugene.

―――― 2004. Archaeological Survey of the U.S. Highway 97 at South Century Drive (Sun River) Highway Construction and Improvement Project, Deschutes County, Oregon. Report of the State Museum of Anthropology, University of Oregon, to the Oregon Department of Transportation. On file at the Oregon State Historic Preservation Office. Salem.

―――― 2005. Archaeological Evaluation of a Historic Homestead Site (35CR1225) in Prineville, Crook County, Oregon. Museum of Natural and Cultural History and State Museum of Anthropology, University of Oregon Report No. 2005-165. Eugene.

Epstein, Ethan A. 2007. *Distant Cores: Lithic Technology, Group Mobility and Late Archaic Economic Adaptation at the Mortar Riddle Site, Steens Mountain, Oregon (35HA2627).* Master of Science Thesis, Department of Anthropology, University of Wisconsin. Milwaukee.

Ericson, Jonathon E., and Timothy G. Baugh, eds. 1993. *The American Southwest and Mesoamerica: Systems of Prehistoric Exchange.* Plenum Press, New York.

Erlandson, Jon M. 2002. Anatomically Modern Humans, Maritime Voyaging, and the Pleistocene Colonization of the Americas. Pp. 27:59–92 in *The First Americans: The Pleistocene Colonization of the New World.* N. G. Jablonski, ed. Memoirs of the California Academy of Sciences. San Francisco.

——— 2007. Sea Change: The Paleocoastal Occupations of Daisy Cave. Pp. 135–143 in *Seeking Our Past: An Introduction to North American Archaeology.* S. W. Neusius and G. T. Gross, eds. Oxford University Press. Oxford.

Erlandson, Jon M., Todd J. Braje, Torben C. Rick, and Jenna Peterson 2005. Beads, Bifaces, and Boats: An Early Maritime Adaptation on the South Coast of San Miguel Island, California. *American Anthropologist* 107(4):677–683.

Erlandson, Jon M., Michael H. Graham, Bruce J. Bourque, Debra Corbett, James A. Estes, and Robert S. Steneck 2007. The Kelp Highway Hypothesis: Marine Ecology, the Coastal Migration Theory, and the Peopling of the Americas. *Journal of Island & Coastal Archaeology* 2:161–174.

Erlandson, Jon M., Douglas J. Kennett, Lynn Ingram, Daniel A. Guthrie, Don P. Morris, Mark A. Tveskov, G. James West, and Phillip L. Walker 1996. An Archaeological and Paleontological Chronology for Daisy Cave (CA-SMI-261), San Miguel Island, California. *Radiocarbon* 38(2):355–373.

Erlandson, Jon M., M. Tveskov, D. Kennett, and L. Ingram 1996. Further Evidence for a Terminal Pleistocene Occupation of Daisy Cave, San Miguel Island, California. *Current Research in the Pleistocene* 13:13–15.

Erlandson, Jon M., Robert Losey, and Neil Peterson 2001. Early Maritime Contact on the Northern Oregon Coast: Some Notes on the 17th Century Nehalem Beeswax Ship. Pp. 45–53 in *Changing Landscapes: Telling Our Stories.* Proceedings of the Fourth Annual Coquille Cultural Preservation Conference, 2000. Jason Younker, Mark A. Tveskov, and David G. Lewis, eds. Coquille Indian Tribe. North Bend, Oregon.

Erlandson, Jon M., and Madonna L. Moss 1993. An Evaluation, Survey, and Dating Program for the Archaeological Sites on State Lands on the Central Oregon Coast. Report on file at the State Historic Preservation Office, Salem, Oregon.

Erlandson, Jon M., and Madonna L. Moss 1998. Early Holocene Adaptations on the Southern Northwest Coast. *Journal of California and Great Basin Anthropology* 20(1):13–25.

——— 1999. The Systematic Use of Radiocarbon Dating in Archaeological Surveys in Coastal and Other Erosional Environments. *American Antiquity* 64:431–443.

Erlandson, Jon M., Madonna L. Moss and Matthew Des Lauriers 2008. Life On the Edge: Early Maritime Cultures of the Pacific Coast of North America. *Quaternary Science Reviews* 27:2232–2245.

Erlandson, Jon M., Mark A. Tveskov, and Madonna L. Moss 1997. Return to Chetlessenten: The Antiquity and Architecture of an Athapascan Village on the Southern Northwest Coast. *Journal of California and Great Basin Anthropology* 19(2):226–240.

Fagan, Brian 2001. *People of the Earth: An Introduction to World Prehistory.* Prentice-Hall. Upper Saddle River.

Fagan, David D. 1885. *History of Benton County, Oregon, Including Its Geology, Topography, Soil and Productions.* A. G. Walling, Portland, Oregon.

Fagan, John L. 1988. Clovis and Western Pluvial Lakes Tradition Lithic Technologies at the Dietz Site in South-Central Oregon. Pp. 389–416 in *Early Human Occupation in Far Western North America: The Clovis-Archaic Interface.* Judith A. Willig, C. Melvin Aikens, and John L. Fagan, eds. Nevada State Museum Anthropological Papers No. 21. Carson City.

———— 1993. The Chinese Cannery Workers of Warrendale, Oregon, 1876–1930. Pp. 215–228 in *Hidden Heritage: Historical Archaeology of the Overseas Chinese*, Priscilla Wegars, ed. Baywood Publishing, Amityville, New York.

Fagan, John L., David V. Ellis, F. Paul Rushmore, and Douglas C. Wilson 1992. Archaeological Data Recovery Investigations at the Canyon Owl Site (35LIN336), Linn County, Oregon. Archaeological Investigations Northwest Report No. 20, on file at the Willamette National Forest, Eugene.

Fagan, John L., and Garry L. Sage 1974. New Windust Sites in Oregon. *Tebiwa* 16(2):68–71.

Fladmark, Knut R. 1979. Routes: Alternative Migration Corridors for Early Man in North America. *American Antiquity* 44:55–69.

Ford, Richard I. 1983. Inter-Indian Exchange in the Southwest. Pp. 711–722 in *Handbook of North American Indians, Volume 10: Southwest.* Alfonso Ortiz, ed. Smithsonian Institution. Washington.

Foster, Michael K. 1996. Language and the Culture History of North America. Pp. 64–110 in *Handbook of North American Indians, Vol. 17, Languages.* Ives Goddard, ed. Smithsonian Institution. Washington, D.C.

Fowler, Catherine S. 1989. Perishables. Pp. 397–443 in *Times Square Rockshelter: A Stratified Dry Rockshelter in the Western Cascades, Douglas County, Oregon*, by Lee F. Spencer. Lee Spencer Archaeology Paper No. 1989-4. On file Umpqua National Forest, Roseburg, Oregon.

———— 1992. *In the Shadow of Fox Peak: An Ethnography of the Cattail-Eater Northern Paiute People of Stillwater Marsh.* Cultural Resource Series No. 5, U.S. Department of the Interior Fish and Wildlife Service, Region 1. U.S. Government Printing Office. Washington, D.C.

Fowler, Catherine S., and Sven Liljeblad 1986. Northern Paiute. Pp. 435–465 in *Handbook of North American Indians, Vol. 11: Great Basin.* Warren L. d'Azevedo, ed. Smithsonian Institution, Washington D.C.

Fowler, Catherine S., and David Rhode 2006. Great Basin Plants. Pp. 331–350 in Environment, Origins, and Population, *Handbook of North American Indians, Vol. 3*, Douglas H. Ubelaker, ed. Smithsonian Institution, Washington D.C.

Fowler, Don D., Eugene M. Hattori, and C. Cliff Creger 1989. *Summary Report of Archaeological Investigations in Warner Valley, Lake County Oregon 1987–1988.* University of Nevada-Reno Department of Anthropology Technical Report 89-1. Reno.

Frachtenberg, Leo 1914. *Lower Umpqua Texts.* Columbia University Press, New York.

———— 1915. Ethnological Research Among the Kalapuya Indians. *Smithsonian Miscellaneous Collections* 65(6):85–89. Washington, D.C.

———— 1917. Myths of the Alsea Indians of Northwestern Oregon. *International Journal of American Linguistics* 1:64–75.

———— 1918. Comparative Studies in Takelman, Kalapuyan, Chinookan Lexicography: A Preliminary Paper. *International Journal of American Linguistics* 1(2):175–182.

———— 1920. *Alsea Texts and Myths*. Bureau of American Ethnology Bulletin 67, Washington, D. C.

Franklin, Jerry, and C. T. Dyrness 1973. *Natural Vegetation of Oregon and Washington*. Oregon State University Press. Corvallis.

Fredrickson, David A. 1973. *Early Cultures of the North Coast Ranges, California*. PhD Dissertation, Department of Anthropology, University of California. Davis.

———— 1984. The North Coastal Region. Pp. 471–527 in *California Archaeology*, by Michael J. Moratto. Academic Press. Orlando.

Fredrickson, David A., and Gregory G. White 1988. The Clear Lake Basin and Early Complexes in California's North Coast Ranges. Pp. 75–86 In *Early Human Occupations in Far Western North America: The Clovis-Archaic Interface*, Judith A. Willig, C. Melvin Aikens, and John L. Fagan, eds. Nevada State Museum Anthropological Papers, Carson City.

Freidel, Dorothy E. 1993. *Chronology and Climatic Controls of Late Quaternary Lake-level Fluctuations in Chewaucan, Fort Rock, and Alkali Basins, South-central Oregon*. PhD Dissertation, Department of Geography, University of Oregon. Eugene.

———— 1994. Paleolake Shorelines and Lake Level Chronology of the Fort Rock Basin, Oregon. Pp. 21–40 in *Archaeological Researches in the Northern Great Basin: Fort Rock Archaeology Since Cressman*. C. Melvin Aikens and Dennis L. Jenkins, eds. University of Oregon Anthropological Papers No. 50. Eugene.

———— 2001. Pleistocene Lake Chewaucan: Two Short Pieces on Hydrological Connections and Lake-level Oscillations. Pp. DF.1–DF.3 in *Quaternary Studies near Summer Lake, Oregon: Friends of the Pleistocene Ninth Annual Pacific Northwest Cell Field Trip September 28–30, 2001*. Rob Negrini, Silvio Pezzopane, and Tom Badger, eds.

Freidel, Dorothy E., Lynn Peterson, Patricia F. McDowell, and Thomas J. Connolly 1988. *Alluvial Stratigraphy and Human Prehistory of the Veneta Area, Long Tom River Valley, Oregon: The Final Report of the Country Fair/Veneta Archaeological Project*. Report of the Oregon State Museum of Anthropology and Department of Geography, University of Oregon. On file at the Oregon State Historic Preservation Office. Salem.

Galm, Jerry R. 1994. Prehistoric Trade and Exchange in the Interior Plateau of Western North America, pp. 275–305 in *Prehistoric Exchange Systems in North America*. Timothy G. Baugh and Jonathon Ericson, eds. Plenum Press. New York and London.

Garner, James C. 1963. An Analysis of Cranial material from the Congdon Site. *Tebiwa* 6(2):33–37.

Garnett, Keith 1995. *Summary Report of the Field and Cartographic Work at Fort Clatsop Astoria, Oregon*. Report to the Regional Archaeologist, National Park Service, Seattle, Washington. Electronic document also available http://www.nps.gov/lewi/historyculture/arch5758-overview.htm

Gatschet, Albert S. 1877. *Miscellaneous linguistic manuscripts*. On file at the National Anthropological Archives, Smithsonian Institution, Washington, D.C.

———— 1890. The Klamath Indians of Southwestern Oregon. *Contributions to North American Ethnology, Vol. 2, U.S. Geographical and Geological survey of the Rocky Mountain Region*. U.S. Government Printing Office. Washington, D.C.

——— 1899. Various Ethnographic Notes. The Kalapuya People. *Journal of American Folklore* 12:208–214.

Gehr, K. D. 1980. *Late Pleistocene and Recent Archaeology and Geomorphology of the South Shore of Harney Lake, Oregon.* M.A. Thesis, Department of Anthropology, Portland State University. Portland, Oregon.

Gilbert, M. Thomas, Dennis L. Jenkins, Anders Götherstrom, Nuria Naveran, Juan J. Sanchez, Michael Hofreiter, Philip Francis Thomsen, Jonas Binladen, Thomas F. G. Higham, Robert M. Yohe II, Robert Parr, Linda Scott Cummings, and Eske Willerslev 2008. DNA from Pre-Clovis Human Coprolites in Oregon, North America. *Science* 320:786–789.

Gilsen, Leland 1989. *Luckiamute Basin Survey: Phase I Survey.* On file at the Oregon State Historic Preservation Office. Salem.

Gitzen, Garry D. 2008. Francis Drake in Nehalem Bay, 1579: Setting the Historical Record Straight. Isnik Publishing, Wheeler, Oregon.

Goddard, Ives 1996. Native Languages and Language Families of North America, compiled by Ives Goddard. In *Handbook of North American Indians, Vol. 17, Languages.* Ives Goddard, ed. Map in pocket at end of volume. Smithsonian Institution. Washington, D.C.

Goddard, Linda, Richard Bryant, and John Nelson 1979. *Cultural Resources Overview: Deschutes National Forest, Oregon. Volume I.* Professional Analysts, Inc.

Goebel, Ted 2004. The Search for a Clovis Progenitor in Subarctic Siberia. Pp. 311–356 in *Entering America: Northeast Asia and Beringia Before the Last Glacial Maximum.* D. B. Madsen, ed. University of Utah Press. Salt Lake City.

Gorospe, Kathy 1985. *American Indian Cultural Resources: A Handbook.* Commission on Indian Services, Salem, OR.

Gramly, Richard Michael 1993. *The Richey Clovis Cache: Earliest Americans Along the Columbia River.* Persimmon Press. Buffalo.

Gray, Dennis J. 1987. *The Takelma and Their Athapascan Neighbors: A New Ethnographic Synthesis for the Upper Rogue River Area of Southwestern Oregon.* University of Oregon Anthropological Papers No. 37. Eugene.

——— 2000. *Preliminary Investigations at the North Bank Site, 35DO61, Douglas County, Oregon, 1997–1998.* Cascade Research report, Ashland, Oregon, to the USDI Bureau of Land Management, Roseburg District. On file at the Oregon State Historic Preservation Office, Salem.

——— 2001. *North Bank 2000: Further Investigations at Site 35DO61, Douglas County, Oregon.* Cascade Research report, Ashland, Oregon, to the USDI Bureau of Land Management, Roseburg District. On file at the Oregon State Historic Preservation Office, Salem.

Grayson, Donald K. 1979. Mount Mazama, Climatic Change, and Fort Rock Basin Archaeofaunas. Pp. 427–458 in *Volcanic Activity and Human Ecology.* Payson D. Sheets and Donald K. Grayson, eds. Academic Press. Orlando.

Green, Thomas J. 1982. House Form and Variability at Givens Hot Springs, Southwest Idaho. *Idaho Archaeologist* 6(1–2):33–44.

Green, Thomas J., Bruce Cochran, Todd Fenton, James C. Woods, Gene Titmus, Larry Tiezen, Mary Anne Davis, and Susanne Miller 1998. The Buhl Burial: A Paleoindian Burial from Southern Idaho. *American Antiquity* 63(3):437–456.

Greenspan, Ruth L. 1990. Prehistoric Fishing in the Northern Great Basin. Pp. 207–232 in *Wetlands Adaptations in the Great Basin*, Joel Janetski and David B. Madsen, eds. Museum of Peoples and Cultures Occasional Papers No. 1. Provo.

———— 1991. The Vertebrate Faunal Assemblage. Pp. 143–162 in *Archaeology of the McCoy Creek Site (35HA1263), Harney County, Oregon*, by Robert R. Musil. Heritage Research Associates Report 105. Eugene.

———— 1994. Archaeological Fish Remains in the Fort Rock Basin. Pp. 485–504 in *Archaeological Researches in the Northern Great Basin: Fort Rock Archaeology Since Cressman*. C. Melvin Aikens and Dennis L. Jenkins, eds. University of Oregon Anthropological Papers No. 50. Eugene.

Greenspan, Ruth L., and Susan Crockford 1992. Vertebrate Faunal Remains from the Palmrose and Avenue Q Sites. In *Human Responses to Change in Coastal Geomorphology and Fauna on the Southern Northwest Coast: Archaeological Investigations at Seaside, Oregon*, by Thomas J. Connolly, pp. 123–165. University of Oregon Anthropological Papers 45, Eugene.

Griffin, Dennis 1983. *Archaeological Investigation at the Marial Site, Rogue River Ranch, 35CU84*. Oregon State University, Richard E. Ross, Principal Investigator. Submitted to the Bureau of Land Management, Medford District, Oregon.

———— 1986. Prehistoric Utilization of Geothermal Springs in the Pacific Northwest. Pp. 62–79 in *Contributions to the Archaeology of Oregon, 1983–1986*, Kenneth M. Ames, ed. Association of Oregon Archaeologists Occasional Papers No. 3. Eugene.

———— 2009. The Evolution of Oregon's Cultural Resource Laws and Regulations. *Journal of Northwest Anthropology* 43(1):87–116.

Hall, Roberta L., ed. 1995. *People of the Coquille Estuary*. Words and Pictures Unlimited, Corvallis, Oregon.

Hall, Roberta L., Loren G. Davis, and Michele L. Punke 2003. A late Pleistocene site on Oregon's southern coast. *The Midden* 35(1):5–8.

Hall, Roberta, Loren Davis, and Samuel Willis, and Matthew Fillmore 2005. Radiocarbon, Soil, and Artifact Chronologies for an Early Southern Oregon Coastal Site. *Radiocarbon* 47:383–394.

Hammatt, Hallett H. 1977. *Late Quaternary Stratigraphy and Archaeological Chronology in the Lower Granite Reservoir Area, Lower Snake River*. PhD Dissertation, Department of Anthropology, Washington State University. Pullman.

Hanes, Richard C. 1978. *Archaeological Survey of the Upper Umpqua Region—1978*. On file, Bureau of Land Management Roseburg District, Oregon. Roseburg.

———— 1988. *Lithic Assemblages of Dirty Shame Rockshelter: Changing Traditions in the Northern Intermontane*. University of Oregon Anthropological Papers No. 40. Eugene.

Hann, Don 1989. *The Tsagaglalal Petroglyph of the Columbia River Gorge*. Special Problems Research Paper, Department of Anthropology, University of Oregon. Eugene.

Hannon, Nan 1990. *Hand to Mouth: Plant Food Resources and Prehistoric People in Southwest Oregon's Bear Creek Valley*. M.S. Thesis, Department of Social Science, Southern Oregon State College.

Hannon, Nan, and Richard K. Olmo, eds. 1990. *Living with the Land: The Indians of Southwest Oregon*. Southern Oregon Historical Society. Medford.

Harrington, John Peabody 1942. *The Papers of John Peabody Harrington in the Smithsonian Institution, 1907–1957. Alaska/Northwest Coast (microfilm).* Kraus International Publications, Millwood, New York.

Harrington, Mark R. 1948. *An Ancient Site at Borax Lake, California.* Southwest Museum Papers 16. Los Angeles.

Harris, Barbara P. 1994. Chinook Jargon: Arguments for a Pre-Contact Origin. *Pacific Coast Philology* 29(1):28–36.

Harrison, Brian F. 1977. A Unique Burial from the Lower Coquille River (Abstract). *Annals of the Oregon Academy of Science* 13:18.

———— 1978. Report of a Burial Excavation at Bob Creek (35LA10), Lane County, Oregon. Ms. on file at the Department of Anthropology, Oregon State University, Corvallis.

Hayden, B., and R. Schulting 1997. The Plateau Interaction Sphere and late prehistoric cultural complexity. *American Antiquity* 62:51–85.

Haynes, C. Vance, Jr. 1992. C-14 Dating of the Peopling of the New World. Pp. 503–518 in *Radiocarbon After Four Decades: An Interdisciplinary Perspective.* R. E. Taylor, Austin Long, and R. Kra, eds. Springer Verlag. New York.

Haynes, C. Vance, Jr., and Bruce B. Huckell 2007. *Murray Springs: A Clovis Site with Multiple Activity Areas in the San Pedro Valley, Arizona.* Anthropological Papers of the University of Arizona 71.

Haynes, Gary 2002. *The Early Settlement of North America: The Clovis Era.* Cambridge University Press. Cambridge and New York.

Heflin, Eugene 1966. *The Pistol River Site of Southwest Oregon.* Reports of the University of California Archaeological Survey No. 67.

———— 1981. The Bone Work of the Chetlessenten Indians of the South Coast of Oregon. *Central States Archaeological Journal* 28(2):66–71.

Heizer, Robert F., ed. 1978. *Handbook of North American Indians, Volume 8: California.* Smithsonian Institution. Washington, D.C.

Heizer, Robert F., and Martin A. Baumhoff 1962. *Prehistoric Rock Art of Nevada and Eastern California.* University of California Press. Berkeley.

———— 1970. Big Game Hunters in the Great Basin: A Critical Review of the Evidence. Pp. 1–12 in *Papers on the Anthropology of the Western Great Basin.* University of California Archaeological Research Facility Contributions No. 7. Berkeley.

Heizer, Robert F., and Albert B. Elsasser 1964. Archaeology of Hum-67, the Gunther Island Site in Humboldt Bay, California. *University of California Archaeological Survey Reports* 62:5–122. Berkeley.

Helzer, Margaret M. 2001. *Paleoethnobotany and Household Archaeology at the Bergen Site: A Middle Holocene Occupation in the Fort Rock Basin, Oregon.* PhD Dissertation, Department of Anthropology, University of Oregon. Eugene.

———— 2004. Archaeological Investigations at the Bergen Site: Middle Holocene Lakeside Occupations near Fort Rock, Oregon. Pp. 77–94 in *Early and Middle Holocene Archaeology of the Northern Great Basin,* Dennis L. Jenkins, Thomas J. Connolly, and C. Melvin Aikens, eds. University of Oregon Anthropological Papers No. 62. Eugene.

Hemphill, Brian E. 1990. *An Analysis of the Human Remains from the Crate's Point site (35WS228, Wasco County, Oregon).* Paper presented at the 43rd annual Northwest Anthropological Conference, Eugene, Oregon.

————— 1999. Wear and Tear: Osteoarthritis as an Indicator of Mobility among Great Basin Hunter-Gatherers. Pp. 241–289 in *Prehistoric Lifeways in the Great Basin Wetlands: Bioarchaeological Reconstruction and Interpretation*, Brian E. Hemphill and Clark S. Larsen, eds. University of Utah Press, Salt Lake City.

Hemphill, Brian E., and Clark S. Larsen 1999. *Prehistoric Lifeways in the Great Basin Wetlands: Bioarchaeological Reconstruction and Interpretation*. University of Utah Press. Salt Lake City.

Henrikson, L. Suzann 2003. Bison Freezers and Hunter-Gatherer Mobility: Archaeological Analysis of Cold Lava Tube Caves on Idaho's Snake River Plain. *Plains Anthropologist* 48(187):263–285. Lincoln.

Henry, Alexander 1992. *The Journal of Henry the Younger, 1799–181. Volume II: The Saskatchewan and Columbia Papers*. Barry M. Gough, ed. The Champlain Society. Toronto.

Hibbs, Charles H., Brian L. Gannon, and Cynthia H. Willard 1976. *Lower Deschutes River Cultural Resources Survey: Warm Springs Bridge to Mack Canyon, Sherman, Wasco, and Jefferson Counties*. USDI BLM Prineville District, Oregon.

Hicks, Brent A., ed. 2004. *Marmes Rockshelter: A Final Report on 11,000 Years of Cultural Use*. Washington State University Press. Pullman.

Hildebrandt, William R. 2007. Northwest California: Ancient Lifeways among Forested Mountains, Flowing Rivers, and Rocky Ocean Shores. Pp. 83–97 in *California Prehistory: Colonization, Culture, and Complexity*. Terry L. Jones and Kathryn A. Klar, eds. Alta Mira Press. Lanham, MD.

Hildebrandt, William R., and Terry L. Jones 1992. Evolution of Marine Mammal Hunting: A View from the California and Oregon Coasts. *Journal of California and Great Basin Anthropology* 2:165–174.

Hines, Gustavus 1851. *Life on the Plains of the Pacific*. George H. Derby and Co. Buffalo.

Hodge, Frederick Webb 1979. *Handbook of American Indians North of Mexico*, Parts 1 and 2. Reprint edition, Rowman and Littlefield. Totowa, New Jersey. [Originally published 1907–1910 as Bureau of American Ethnology Bulletin 30. Smithsonian Institution. Washington, D.C.]

Hodges, Charles M. 1998. Site Structure. In *Archaeological Investigations at the Mill Creek Site Complex: I-5/North Santiam Highway Interchange, Marion County, Oregon*. Draft ms. in possession of the authors. Oregon State Museum of Anthropology, University of Oregon. Eugene.

Holmes, Charles E. 1998. New Data Pertaining to Swan Point, the Oldest Microblade site known in Alaska. *Current Research in the Pleistocene 15:21–22.*

Holmes, Charles E., Richard Vander Hoek, and Thomas E. Dilley 2001. Swan Point. Pp. 319–23 in *American Beginnings: The Prehistory and Ecology of Beringia*. F. H. West, ed. University of Chicago Press. Chicago.

Horner, J. B. 1919. *Oregon: Her History, Her Great Men, Her Literature*. Gazette Times Press. Corvallis.

Housley, Lucile 1994. It's in the Roots: Prehistoric Plants and Plant Use in the Fort Rock Basin. Pp. 561–572 in *Archaeological Researches in the Northern Great Basin: Fort Rock Archaeology Since Cressman*. C. Melvin Aikens and Dennis L. Jenkins, eds., pp. 561–571. University of Oregon Anthropological Papers No. 50. Eugene.

Howard, Bob, and Virginia Howard 1963. Cascadia Cave and the Amateur. *Screenings* 12(5).

Howe, Carrol B. 1968. *Ancient Tribes of the Klamath Country*. Binford & Mort, Portland.

Hughes, Richard E. 1978. Aspects of Prehistoric Wiyot Exchange and Social Ranking. *Journal of California Anthropology* 5(1):53–66.

——— 1982. Age and Exploitation of Obsidian from the Medicine Lake Highland, California. *Journal of Archaeological Science* 9(2):173–185.

——— 1985. Obsidian Sources. Pp. 245–267 in *Nightfire Island: Later Holocene Lakemarsh Adaptation on the Western Edge of the Great Basin*, by C. Garth Sampson. University of Oregon Anthropological Papers No. 33. Eugene.

——— 1986. *Diachronic Variability in Obsidian Procurement Patterns in Northeastern California and Southcentral Oregon*. University of California Publications in Anthropology No. 17. Berkeley.

——— 1987. Obsidian Sourcing. Pp. E.1–E.16 in *Data Recovery at Sites 35JA27, 35JA59, and 35JA100, Elk Creek Lake Project, Jackson County, Oregon, Volume 2, Appendices*. Richard M. Pettigrew and Clayton G. Lebow, eds. Infotec Research Incorporated, Report No. PNW87-7. Eugene.

——— 1990. The Gold Hill Site: Evidence for a Prehistoric Socioceremonial System in Southwestern Oregon. Pp. 45–48 in *Living With the Land: The Indians of Southwest Oregon*. Nan Hannon and Richard K. Olmo, eds. Southern Oregon Historical Society. Medford.

Hughes, Richard E., and James A. Bennyhoff 1986. Early Trade. Pp. 238–255 in *Handbook of North American Indians, Volume 11: Great Basin*. Warren L. d'Azevedo, ed. Smithsonian Institution. Washington, D.C.

Hunn, Eugene, S., with James Selam and Family 1990. *Nch'i Wana (The Big River): Mid-Columbia River People and Their Land*. University of Washington Press. Seattle and London.

Ikawa-Smith, Fumiko 2004. Humans Along the Pacific Margin of Northeast Asia Before the Last Glacial Maximum: Evidence for Their Presence and Adaptations. Pp. 285–309 in *Entering America: Northeast Asia and Beringia Before the Last Glacial Maximum*. University of Utah Press. Salt Lake City.

Irwin, Ann M., and Ula L. Moody 1978. *The Lind Coulee Site (45GR97)*. Washington State University, Washington Archaeological Research Center. Project Report No. 56. Pullman.

Ivy, Donald B. 2001. "A Complicated and Messy Affair." Pp. 69–76. in *Changing Landscapes: Telling Our Stories*. Proceedings of the Fourth Annual Coquille Cultural Preservation Conference, 2000. Jason Younker, Mark A. Tveskov, and David G. Lewis, eds. Coquille Indian Tribe, North Bend, Oregon.

Ivy, Donald B., and Scott Byram 2001. Coquille Cultural Heritage and Wetland Archaeology. Pp. 120–131 in *Enduring Records, the Environmental and Cultural Heritage of Wetlands*. Barbara Purdy, ed. Oxbow Books, Oxford, England.

Jacobs, Melville 1937. Historic Perspectives in Indian Languages of Oregon and Washington. *Pacific Northwest Quarterly* 28:55–74.

——— 1939. *Coos Narrative and Ethnologic Texts*. University of Washington Publications in Anthropology, Seattle.

——— 1959. *Clackamas Chinook Texts*. University of Indiana, Bloomington.

Jacobs, Melville, Albert S. Gatschet, and Leo J. Frachtenberg 1945 *Kalapuya Texts (Pt. 1: Santiam Kalapuya Ethnologic Texts, by M. Jacobs; Pt. 2: Santiam Kalapuya Myth Texts, by M. Jacobs; Pt. 3: Kalapuya Texts, by A. S. Gatschet, L. J. Frachtenberg, and M. Jacobs)*. University of Washington Publications in Anthropology No. 11. Seattle.

Jaehnig, Manfred E.W. 1993. *The Odell Lake Project: Test Excavations at the Odell Lake Site, 35KL231, Sunset Cover Site, 35KL884 and Shelter Cover Site, 35KL482, Klamath County, Oregon.* Report on file, Deschutes National Forest, Bend.

Jenkins, Dennis L. 1994a. Archaeological Investigations at Three Wetlands Sites in the Silver Lake Area of the Fort Rock Basin. Pp. 213–258 in *Archaeological Researches in the Northern Great Basin: Fort Rock Archaeology Since Cressman.* C. Melvin Aikens and Dennis L. Jenkins, eds. University of Oregon Anthropological Papers No. 50. Eugene.

———— 1994b. Settlement-Subsistence Patterns in the Fort Rock Basin: A Cultural-Ecological Perspective on Human Responses to Fluctuating Wetlands Resources of the Last 5000 Years. Pp. 599–628 in *Archaeological Researches in the Northern Great Basin: Fort Rock Archaeology Since Cressman.* C. Melvin Aikens and Dennis L. Jenkins, eds. University of Oregon Anthropological Papers No. 50. Eugene.

———— 2000. Early to Middle Holocene Cultural Transitions in the Northern Great Basin of Oregon: The View From Fort Rock. Pp. 69–109 in *Archaeological Passages: A Volume in Honor of Claude Nelson Warren.* Joan S. Schneider, Robert M. Yohe II, and Jill Gardner, eds. Publications in Archaeology Volume 1. Western Center for Archaeology and Paleontology. Hemet, California.

———— 2002. *Obsidian Source Characterization and Hydration Analysis at the Connley Caves (35LK50) in South-Central Oregon.* Paper presented at the 55th Northwest Anthropological Conference. Boise.

———— 2004. The Grasshopper and the Ant: Middle Holocene Occupations and Storage Behavior at the Bowling Dune Site in the Fort Rock Basin, Oregon. Pp. 123–155 in *Early and Middle Holocene Archaeology of the Northern Great Basin.* Dennis L. Jenkins, Thomas J. Connolly, and C. Melvin Aikens, eds. University of Oregon Anthropological Papers No. 62. Eugene.

———— 2007. Distribution and Dating of Cultural and Paleontological Remains at the Paisley 5 Mile Point Caves (35LK3400) in the Northern Great Basin: An Early Assessment. In *Paleoindian or Paleoarchaic? Great Basin Human Ecology at the Pleistocene-Holocene Transition,* Kelly Graf and David Schmitt, eds., pp. 57–81. University of Utah Press, Salt Lake City.

Jenkins, Dennis L., C. Melvin Aikens, and William Cannon 1989. *University of Oregon Archaeological Field School, Fort Rock Basin Prehistory Project Research Design.* Department of Anthropology, University of Oregon. Eugene.

———— 1999. *University of Oregon Archaeological Field School, Northern Great Basin Prehistory Project Research Design.* Department of Anthropology and Museum of Natural History, University of Oregon. Eugene.

Jenkins, Dennis L., and Ann Brashear 1994. Excavations at Four Habitation Sites in the Boulder Village Uplands: A Preliminary Report. Pp. 431–484 in *Archaeological Researches in the Northern Great Basin: Fort Rock Archaeology Since Cressman.* C. Melvin Aikens and Dennis L. Jenkins, eds. University of Oregon Anthropological Papers No. 50. Eugene.

enkins, Dennis L., and Thomas J. Connolly 1990. *Archaeology of Indian Grade Spring: A Special Function Site on Stinkingwater Mountain, Harney County, Oregon.* University of Oregon Anthropological Papers No. 42. Eugene.

——— 1994. *Archaeological Investigations at the Paquet Gulch Bridge Site: A Pithouse Village in the Deschutes River Basin, Southwestern Columbia Plateau, Oregon.* University of Oregon Anthropological Papers No. 49. Eugene.

——— 1996. *Mid-Holocene Excavations at the Heath Cliffs Site, Warm Springs Reservation, Oregon.* University of Oregon Anthropological Papers No. 53. Eugene.

——— 2000. Project Summary and Conclusions. Pp. 335–376 in *Human Adaptations in Drews Valley: A Mid-Elevation Setting on the Northern Great Basin Periphery, South-Central Oregon.* Dennis L. Jenkins, ed. Report No. 2000-3, State Museum of Anthropology. University of Oregon. Eugene.

——— 2001. *Archaeological Testing of the Malheur Terrace (35ML984) and Malheur Terrace 2 (35ML1026) Sites, Malheur County, Oregon.* State Museum of Anthropology Report No. 2001-002, University of Oregon. Eugene.

——— 2010. *Central Oregon Bridges Archaeology: Data Recovery and Site Testing along the Malheur River, Malheur County, Oregon.* Museum Report No. 2009-023, University of Oregon. Eugene.

enkins, Dennis L., Thomas J. Connolly, and C. Melvin Aikens, eds. 2004a. *Early and Middle Holocene Archaeology of the Northern Great Basin.* University of Oregon Anthropological Papers No. 62. Eugene.

——— 2004b. Early and Middle Holocene Archaeology in the Northern Great Basin: Dynamic Natural and Cultural Ecologies. Pp. 1–20 in *Early and Middle Holocene Archaeology of the Northern Great Basin,* Dennis L. Jenkins, Thomas J. Connolly, and C. Melvin Aikens, eds. University of Oregon Anthropological Papers No. 62. Eugene.

enkins, Dennis L., Thomas J. Connolly, and Paul W. Baxter 2010. *Riverine Resource Use on the Oregon-Idaho Border: Archaeological Investigations at 35ML1328 and 35ML1379, North Ontario, Malheur County.* University of Oregon Anthropological Papers No. 69. Eugene.

enkins, Dennis L., Michael S. Droz, and Thomas J. Connolly 2004. Geoarchaeology of Wetland Settings in the Fort Rock Basin, South-Central Oregon. Pp. 31–52 in *Early and Middle Holocene Archaeology of the Northern Great Basin,* Dennis L. Jenkins, Thomas J. Connolly, and C. Melvin Aikens, eds. University of Oregon Anthropological Papers No. 62. Eugene.

enkins, Dennis L., and Jon M. Erlandson 1996. *Olivella* Grooved Rectangle Beads from a Middle Holocene Site in the Fort Rock Valley, Northern Great Basin. *Journal of California and Great Basin Anthropology* 18(2):296–302.

enkins, Dennis L., Leah L. Largaespada, Tony D. Largaespada, and Mercy A. McDonald 2004. Early and Middle Holocene Ornament Exchange Systems in the Fort Rock Basin of Oregon. Pp. 251–270 in *Early and Middle Holocene Archaeology of the Northern Great Basin.* Dennis L. Jenkins, Thomas J. Connolly, and C. Melvin Aikens, eds. University of Oregon Anthropological Papers No. 62. Eugene.

enkins, Dennis L., and Susan E. Norris 2000a. The Drews Creek Site. Pp. 61–88 in *Human Adaptations in Drews Valley: A Mid-Elevation Setting on the Northern Great Basin Periphery, South-Central Oregon.* Dennis L. Jenkins, ed. Report No. 2000-3, State Museum of Anthropology. University of Oregon. Eugene.

———— 2000b. The La Sere Site (35LK2101). Pp. 151–180 in *Human Adaptations in Drews Valley: A Mid-Elevation Setting on the Northern Great Basin Periphery, South-Central Oregon*. Dennis L. Jenkins, ed. Report No. 2000-3, State Museum of Anthropology, University of Oregon. Eugene.

———— 2000c. The Hay Creek Site (35LK2102). Pp. 95–126 in *Human Adaptations in Drews Valley: A Mid-Elevation Setting on the Northern Great Basin Periphery, South-Centra Oregon*. Dennis L. Jenkins, ed. Report No. 2000-3, State Museum of Anthropology, University of Oregon. Eugene.

Jenkins, Dennis L., Craig E. Skinner, Jennifer J. Thatcher, and Keenan Hoar 1999. *Obsidian Characterization and Hydration Results of the Fort Rock Basin Prehistory Project*. Paper presented at the 52nd Northwest Anthropological Conference. Newport, Oregon.

Jenkins, Paul C., and Thomas E. Churchill 1989. *Archaeological Investigations of the Dry Creek Site, 35DO401. Report to the Umpqua National Forest by Coastal Magnetic Search & Survey, Salem, Oregon*. On file at the Oregon State Historic Preservation Office, Salem.

Jennings, Jesse D. 1986. Prehistory: Introduction. Pp. 113–119 in *Handbook of North American Indians, Vol. 11: Great Basin*. W. L. d'Azevedo, ed. Smithsonian Institution. Washington, D.C.

Jermann, Jerry V., D. L. Lewarch, and S. K. Campbell 1975. *Salvage Excavations at the Kersting Site (35CL21): A Preliminary Report*. University of Washington, Office of Public Archaeology, Reports in Highway Archaeology 2. Seattle.

Johannessen, Carl L., William A. Davenport, Artimus Millett, and Steven McWilliams 1971. The Vegetation of the Willamette Valley. *Annals of the Association of American Geographers* 61(2):286–302.

Jones, George T. 1984. *Prehistoric Land Use in the Steens Mountain Area, Southeastern Oregon*. PhD Dissertation, University of Washington. Seattle.

Jones, Terry L., and William R. Hildebrand 1995. Reasserting a Prehistoric Tragedy of the Commons: Reply to Lyman. *Journal of Anthropological Archaeology* 14:78–98.

Jones, Terry L., and Kathryn A. Klar 2007. *California Prehistory: Colonization, Culture, and Complexity*. Alta Mira Press. Lanham, MD.

Kelly, Cara McCulley 2001. *Prehistoric Land-Use Patterns in the North Santiam Sub-basin on the Western Slopes of the Oregon Cascade Range*. Master's Thesis in Interdisciplinary Studies, Oregon State University, Corvallis.

Kelly, Isabel T. 1932. Ethnography of the Surprise Valley Paiute. *University of California Publications in American Archaeology and Ethnology* 31(1):67–210. Berkeley.

Kelsey, H. M. 1990. Late Quaternary Deformation of Marine Terraces on the Cascadia Subduction Zone Near Cape Blanco. *Tectonics* 9(5):983–1014.

Keyser, James D. 1991. The Cape Perpetua Shell Middens: An Evaluation of Four Sites at the Cape Perpetua Scenic Area, Siuslaw National Forest. Pp. 1–17 in *Shell Midden Excavation on the Siuslaw National Forest*. Billee W. Hoornbeek, ed. Studies in Cultural Resource Management No. 11. USDA Forest Service, Pacific Northwest Region.

———— 1992. *Indian Rock Art of the Columbia Plateau*. University of Washington Press. Seattle.

Kiigemagi, Peter 1989. Testing the Root-Processing Hypothesis through Use-Wear Analysis of Basalt Flakes from Indian Grade Spring, East-Central Oregon. Pp.

145–156 in *Contributions to the Archaeology of Oregon, 1987–1988*. Rick Minor, ed. Association of Oregon Archaeologists Occasional Papers No. 4. Eugene.

Komar, Paul D. 1998. *The Pacific Northwest Coast: Living With the Shores of Oregon and Washington*. Duke University Press, Durham, North Carolina.

Kramer, Steve 2008. Personal communication, Indian trails and sites in the Umpqua BLM district, Oregon.

Kinkade, M. Dale, William W. Elmendorf, Bruce Rigsby, and Haruo Aoki 1998. Languages. Pp. 49–72 in *Handbook of North American Indians, Vol. 12: Plateau*. Deward E. Walker, Jr., ed. Smithsonian Institution. Washington, D.C.

Krieger, Alex D. 1944. Review of Archaeological Researches in the Northern Great Basin, by L. S. Cressman, Frank C. Baker, Paul S. Conger, Henry P. Hanson, and Robert F. Heizer. *American Antiquity* 9:351–359.

Kroeber, Alfred L. 1925. *Handbook of the Indians of California*. Bureau of American Ethnology Bulletin No. 78. Washington, D.C.

——— 1939. *Cultural and Natural Areas of Native North America*. University of California Publications in American Archaeology and Ethnology 38. Berkeley.

LaLande, Jeffrey M. 1981. *Sojourners in the Oregon Siskiyous: Adaptation and Acculturation of the Chinese Miners in the Applegate Valley Ca. 1855–1900*. Master of Interdisciplinary Studies Thesis, Oregon State University. Corvallis.

——— 1990. The Indians of Southwestern Oregon: An Ethnohistorical Review. Pp. 95–119 in *Living With the Land: The Indians of Southwest Oregon*. Nan Hannon and Richard K. Olmo, eds. Southern Oregon Historical Society. Medford.

LaLande, Jeffrey M., and John L. Fagan 1982. Clovis Point: Possible Clovis Point Find— Butte Falls. *Current Archaeological Happenings in Oregon* 7(1):10.

LaLande, Jeffrey M., and Reg Pullen 1999. Burning for a "Fine and Beautiful Open Country:" Native Uses of Fire in Southwestern Oregon. Pp. 255–276 in *Indians, Fire, and the Land in the Pacific Northwest*. Robert Boyd, ed. Oregon State University Press. Corvallis.

Lally, Jessica 2008, *Analysis of the Chinese Porcelain Associated with the "Beeswax Wreck," Nehalem, Oregon*. M.S. Thesis, Central Washington University, Ellensburg.

Langford, Theresa n.d. *Research Guide: Fort Vancouver Archaeological Collection*. Electronic document: http://www.nps.gov/fova/historyculture/upload/Research%20Guide.pdf

Largaespada, Leah L. 2006. From Sand and Sea: Marine Shell Artifacts from Archaeological Sites in the Fort Rock Basin, Northern Great Basin. Pp. 1–68 in *Beads, Points, and Pit Houses: A Northern Great Basin Miscellany*. Brian L. O'Neill, ed. University of Oregon Anthropological Papers No. 66. Eugene.

Laughlin, William S. 1941. Excavations in the Calapuya Mounds of the Willamette Valley, Oregon. *American Antiquity* 7(2):137–155.

——— 1943. Notes on the Archaeology of the Yamhill River, Willamette Valley, Oregon. *American Antiquity* 9:220–229.

Lawrence, D. B., and E. G. Lawrence 1958. The Bridge of the Gods Legend, Its Origin, History, and Dating. *Mazama* 40(13):33–41.

Layton, Thomas N. 1972. Lithic Chronology in the Fort Rock Valley, Oregon: An Obsidian Hydration Study from Cougar Mountain Cave. *Tebiwa* 15:1–21.

Leatherman, Kenneth E., and Alex D. Krieger 1940. Contributions to Oregon Coast Prehistory. *American Antiquity* 6(1):19–28.

Lee, Daniel and Joseph H. Frost 1844. *Ten Years in Oregon.* J. Collard. New York.

Lebow, Clayton G. 1985. *Archaeological Investigations at the Ripple Site (35CL55) in the Mt. Hood National Forest, Clackamas County, Oregon.* Anthropology Northwest, Volume 2, Oregon State University. Corvallis.

Lebow, Clayton G., Richard M. Pettigrew, Jon M. Silvermoon, David H. Chance, Robert Boyd, Yvonne Hadja, and Henry Zenk 1990. *A Cultural Resource Overview for the 1990's, BLM Prineville District, Oregon.* USDI BLM Oregon State Office, Cultural Resource Series No. 5. Portland.

Lehner, Lois 1988. *Lehner's Encyclopedia of U.S. Marks on Pottery, Porcelain & Clay.* Collector Books, Paducah, Kentucky.

Leonhardy, Frank C. 1967. *The Archaeology of a Late Prehistoric Village in Northwestern California.* Museum of Natural History, University of Oregon, Bulletin No. 4. Eugene.

Leonhardy, Frank C., and David G. Rice 1970. A Proposed Culture Typology for the Lower Snake River Region, Southeastern Washington. *Northwest Anthropological Research Notes* 4(1):1–29.

———— 1980. *Lower Snake River Typology: Revision and Evaluation.* Paper presented at the 33rd Annual Northwest Anthropological Conference, Bellingham, Washington.

Lewis, David G. 2001. *Southwest Oregon Research Project: Inventory to the Archival Collection.* Coll. 268, Division of Special Collections and University Archives, Knight Library, University of Oregon. Eugene.

Lewis, Henry T. 1973. *Patterns of Indian Burning in California: Ecology and Ethnohistory.* Ballena Press, Ramona, California.

———— 1990. Reconstructing Patterns of Indian Burning in Southwestern Oregon. Pp. 80–84 in *Living with the Land: The Indians of Southwest Oregon.* Nan Hannon and Richard K. Olmo, eds. Southern Oregon Historical Society. Medford.

Lindberg-Muir, Catherine 1984. *Archeological Test and Evaluation of the Moose-Molalla One Site.* Report prepared for the Sweet Home Ranger District, Willamette National Forest, November 1984.

Loring, J. Malcolm, and Louise Loring 1982. *Pictographs and Petroglyphs of the Oregon Country, Part I: Columbia River and Northern Oregon.* Institute of Archaeology, University of California, Los Angeles, Monograph No. 21. Los Angeles.

———— 1983. *Pictographs and Petroglyphs of the Oregon Country, Part II: Southern Oregon.* Institute of Archaeology, University of California, Los Angeles, Monograph No. 22. Los Angeles.

Losey, Robert J. 1996. *Fishing on the Lower Coquille River: A Zooarchaeological Perspective.* M.A. Thesis, Department of Anthropology, University of Oregon.

———— 2002. *Communities and Catastrophe: Tillamook Response to the AD 1700 Earthquake and Tsunami, Northern Oregon Coast.* PhD Dissertation, Department of Anthropology, University of Oregon. Eugene.

———— 2005. House Remains at the Netarts Sandspit Village, Oregon. *Journal of Field Archaeology* 30(4):401–417.

———— 2007. Native American Vulnerability and Resiliency to Great Cascadia Earthquakes along the Oregon Coast. *Oregon Historical Quarterly* 108(2):201–214.

Losey, Robert J., and Dongya Y. Yang 2007. Opportunistic Whale Hunting on the Southern Northwest Coast: Ancient DNA, Artifact, and Ethnographic Evidence. *American Antiquity* 72(4):657–676.

Loud, Llewellyn L. 1918. *Ethnogeography and Archaeology of the Wiyot Territory.* University of California Publications in American Archaeology and Ethnology 14(3):221–436.

Loy, Thomas H. 1987. Elk Creek Lake Project: Residue Analysis of 50 Artifacts from Three Sites. Pp. I.1–I.8. in *Data Recovery at Sites 35JA27, 35JA59, and 35JA100, Elk Creek Lake Project, Jackson County, Oregon, Volume 2, Appendices.* Richard M. Pettigrew and Clayton G. Lebow, eds. Infotec Research Incorporated, Report No. PNW87-7. Eugene.

Loy, William G., et al., eds. 2001. *Atlas of Oregon, Second Edition.* University of Oregon Press. Eugene.

Lundy, Doris 1982. Styles of Coastal Rock Art. Pp. 89–97 in *Indian Art Traditions of the Northwest Coast.* Roy L. Carlson, ed. Simon Fraser University Press. Burnaby.

Lyman, R. Lee 1987. Elk Creek Zooarchaeology. Pp. D.1–D.38 in *Data Recovery at Sites 35JA27, 35JA59, and 35JA100, Elk Creek Lake Project, Jackson County, Oregon, Volume 2, Appendices.* Richard M. Pettigrew and Clayton G. Lebow, eds. Infotec Research Incorporated, Report No. PNW87-7. Eugene.

―――― 1991 *Prehistory of the Oregon Coast: The Effects of Examination Strategies and Assemblage Size on Archaeological Inquiry.* Academic Press, San Diego.

―――― 1997. Assessing a Reassessment of Early "Pre-Littoral" Radiocarbon Dates from the Oregon Coast. *Journal of California and Great Basin Anthropology* 19:260–269.

Lyman, R. Lee, and Richard E. Ross 1988. Oregon Coast Archaeology: A Critical History and Model. *Northwest Anthropological Research Notes* 22(1):67–119.

Lynch, Thomas F. 1999. The Earliest South American Lifeways. Pp. 188–263 in *The Cambridge History of the Native Peoples of the Americas, Vol. III, Part 1 South America,* F. Salomon and S. B. Schwartz, eds. Cambridge University Press. Cambridge.

Lyons, William H. 2001. *Where the Lost was Found: Geologic Sources of Artifact Raw Materials from Lost Dune (35HA792), Harney Basin, Southeastern Oregon.* PhD. Dissertation, Washington State University. Pullman.

Lyons, William H., and Peter J. Mehringer, Jr. 1998. *Archaeology of the Lost Dune Site (35HA792), Blitzen Valley, Harney County, Oregon: A Report of Excavations by the 1995 WSU Field School.* Submitted to U.S. Bureau of Land Management, Burns District, Oregon.

Mack, Joanne M. 1983. *Archaeological Investigations in the Salt Cave Locality: Subsistence Uniformity and Cultural Diversity on the Klamath River, Oregon.* University of Oregon Anthropological Papers No. 29. Eugene.

―――― 1986. Siskiyou Utility Ware and the Distribution of Fired Clay in South-Central Oregon. Pp. 63–70 in *Pottery of the Great Basin and Adjacent Areas.* Susanne Griset, ed. University of Utah Anthropological Papers No. 111. Salt Lake City.

―――― 1987. Elk Creek Ceramics. Pp. J.1–J.25 in *Data Recovery at Sites 35JA27, 35JA59, and 35JA100, Elk Creek Lake Project, Jackson County, Oregon, Volume 2, Appendices.* Richard M. Pettigrew and Clayton G. Lebow, eds. Infotec Research Incorporated, Report No. PNW87-7. Eugene.

———— 1989. Pottery and Figurines from Elk Creek, Southwestern Oregon. Pp. 37–53 in *Contributions to the Archaeology of Oregon 1987–88*. Rick Minor ed. Association of Oregon Archaeologists Occasional Papers 4. Eugene.

———— 1990. Archaeology of the Upper Klamath River. Pp. 10–25 in *Living With the Land: The Indians of Southwest Oregon*, Nan Hannon and Richard K. Olmo, eds. Southern Oregon Historical Society. Medford.

———— 1991. Ceramic Figurines of the Western Cascades of Southern Oregon and Northern California. Pp. 99–110 in *The New World Figurine Project, Volume 1*. Terry Stocker, ed. Research Press. Provo.

Mackey, Harold 1974. *The Kalapuyans: A Sourcebook on the Indians of the Willamette Valley*. Mission Mill Museum Association. Salem.

Madsen, David B., ed. 2004. *Entering America: Northeast Asia and Beringia Before the Last Glacial Maximum*. University of Utah Press. Salt Lake City.

Madsen, David B., and David Rhode, eds. 1994. *Across the West: Human Population Movement and the Expansion of the Numa*. University of Utah Press. Salt Lake City.

Manion, Mollie 2006. *A Settlement Model at the Robert Newell Farmstead (35MA41), French Prairie, Oregon*. Masters Thesis in Interdisciplinary Studies, Oregon State University. Corvallis.

Maschner, Herbert D. G., and Christopher Chippindale, eds. 2005. *Handbook of Archaeological Methods*. Alta Mira Press. Lanham, MD.

Masten, Ruth 1985. A Cultural Resources Survey and Site Testing of the Bonneville Power Administration's Malin-Warner 230 KV Transmission Line, Klamath County, Oregon, and Modoc County, California, Michael J. Rodeffer and Jerry R. Galm, editors. Eastern Washington University Reports in Archaeology and History 100-36, Archaeological and Historical Services, Cheney, Washington.

Matson, R.G., and Gary Coupland 1995. *The Prehistory of the Northwest Coast*. Academic Press, San Diego.

Mazany, Terry 1980. *Contributions to Oregon Archaeology*. Oregon Museum of Science and Industry. On file, University of Oregon Museum of Natural and Cultural History. Eugene.

McClure, Richard H., Jr. 1984. *Rock Art of The Dalles-Deschutes Region: A Chronological Perspective*. Master's Thesis, Department of Anthropology, Washington State University. Pullman.

———— 2008. Personal communication, Indian trails and sites in the Mt. Hood National Forest, Oregon.

McDowell, Patricia F. 1987. Soil Chemistry at Sites 35JA100, 35JA59, 35JA27A, and 35JA27B: Pedogenic and Cultural Influences. Pp. A.35–A.52 in *Data Recovery at Sites 35JA27, 35JA59, and 35JA100, Elk Creek Lake Project, Jackson County, Oregon, Volume 2, Appendices*. Richard M. Pettigrew and Clayton G. Lebow, eds. Infotec Research Incorporated, Report No. PNW87-7. Eugene.

McDowell, Patricia F., and Jane Benjamin 1987. Geomorphic Setting and Stratigraphy of Sites 35JA100, 35JA59, 35JA27A, and 35JA27B, Elk Creek Lake Archaeological Project, Jackson County, Oregon. Pp. A.1–A.34 in *Data Recovery at Sites 35JA27, 35JA59, and 35JA100, Elk Creek Lake Project, Jackson County, Oregon, Volume 2, Appendices*. Richard M. Pettigrew and Clayton G. Lebow, eds. Infotec Research Incorporated, Report No. PNW87-7. Eugene.

McDowell, Patricia F., and Lynn Wilson 1991. Geomorphic Setting, Stratigraphy, and Soil Chemistry of Lithic Sites along the Southern Oregon Coast. Pp. 5–13 in *Archaeological Testing at the Indian Sands and Cape Blanco Lithic Sites, Southern Oregon Coast*, by Rick Minor and Ruth L. Greenspan. Ms. on file at the Oregon State Historic Preservation Office, Salem.

McPherson, Penny, David Hall, Vince McGlone, and Nancy Nachtwey 1981. *Archaeological Excavations in the Blue Mountains: Mitigation of Sites 35UN52, 35UN74, and 35UN95 in the Vicinity of Ladd Canyon, Union County, Oregon. Volume II: Site Specific Analysis and Intersite Comparisons.* Western Cultural Resource Management, Inc. Boulder.

Mehringer, Peter J. Jr. 1985. Late-Quaternary Pollen Records from the Interior Pacific Northwest and Northern Great Basin of the United States. In *Pollen Records of Late-Quaternary North American Sediments*, V.A. Bryant and R.G. Holloway, eds., pp. 167–189. American Association of Stratigraphic Palynologists.

———— 1986. Prehistoric Environments. Pp. 31–50 in *Handbook of North American Indians, Vol. 11: Great Basin*. Warren L. d'Azevedo, ed. Smithsonian Institution. Washington, D.C.

———— 1988. Clovis Cache Found: Weapons of Ancient Americans. *National Geographic* 174(4):500–503.

Mehringer, Peter J., Jr., and William J. Cannon 1994. Volcaniclastic Dunes of the Fort Rock Valley, Oregon: Stratigraphy, Chronology, and Archaeology. Pp. 283–328 in *Archaeological Researches in the Northern Great Basin: Fort Rock Archaeology Since Cressman*. C. Melvin Aikens and Dennis L. Jenkins, eds. University of Oregon Anthropological Papers No. 50. Eugene.

Mehringer, Peter J. Jr., and Franklin F. Foit 1990. Volcanic Ash Dating of the Clovis Cache at East Wenatchee, Washington. *National Geographic Research* 6(4):495–503.

Mehringer, Peter J., Jr., and Peter E. Wigand 1986. Holocene history of Skull Creek dunes, Catlow Valley, southeastern Oregon, USA. *Journal of Arid Environments* 11:117–138.

———— 1990. Comparison of Late Holocene Environments from Woodrat Middens and Pollen: Diamond Craters, Oregon. Pp. 295–325 in *Packrat Middens: The Last 40,000 Years of Biotic Change*, Julio Betancourt, Thomas R. Van Devender, and Paul S. Martin, eds. University of Arizona Press. Tucson.

Meltzer, David Jr. 2009. *First Peoples in a New World: Colonizing Ice Age America*. University of California Press. Berkeley, Los Angeles, and London.

Meltzer, D. J., D. K. Grayson, G. Ardila, A. W. Barker, D. F. Dincauze, C. V. Haynes, Jr., F. Mena, L. Nuñez, and D. J. Stanford 1997. On the Pleistocene Antiquity of Monte Verde, Southern Chile. *American Antiquity* 62(4)659–663.

Menefee, L.C. and Lowell Tiller 1976. Cutoff Fever. *Oregon Historical Quarterly*, 68(4):309–340.

Middleton, Janice 1975. *Champoeg Historical Townsite, Oregon Historical Summary and Brief Artifact Analysis*. Report of the Oregon State University Department of Anthropology, on file at the Oregon State Historic Preservation Office. Salem.

Miller, Emma Gene 1958. *Clatsop County, Oregon: A History* Binford & Mort, Portland, Oregon.

Miller, Floyd E. 1975. The Benjamin Sites (35LA41, 42). Pp. 309–347 in *Archaeological Studies in the Willamette Valley, Oregon*. C. Melvin Aikens, ed. University of Oregon Anthropological Papers No. 8. Eugene.

Miller, Wick R. 1983. Uto-Aztecan Languages. Pp. 113–124 in *Handbook of North American Indians, Volume 10: Southwest*. Alfonso Ortiz, ed. Smithsonian Institution. Washington D.C.

_____1986. Numic Languages. Pp. 98–106 *in Handbook of North American Indians, Volume 11: Great Basin*. Warren L. d'Azevedo, ed. Smithsonian Institution. Washington, D.C.

Miller, Jay, and William R. Seaburg 1990. Athapaskans of Southwestern Oregon. Pp. 580–588 in *Handbook of North American Indians, Volume 7: Northwest Coast*. W. Suttles, ed. Smithsonian Institution. Washington, D.C.

Minor, Rick 1983. *Aboriginal Settlement and Subsistence at the Mouth of the Columbia River*. PhD Dissertation, Department of Anthropology, University of Oregon, Eugene.

——— 1984a. An Early Complex at the Mouth of the Columbia River. *Northwest Anthropological Research Notes* 18(1):1–22.

——— 1984b. *Dating the Bonneville Landslide in the Columbia River Gorge*. Heritage Research Associates (Eugene, OR) Report 31. On file with the U.S. Army Corps of Engineers, Portland, Oregon.

——— 1985. Paleo-Indians in Western Oregon: A Description of two Fluted Projectile Points. *Northwest Anthropological Research Notes* 19(1):33–40.

——— 1986. *An Evaluation of Archaeological Sites on State Park Lands along the Oregon Coast*. Heritage Research Associates, Report No. 44. On file at the Oregon State Historic Preservation Office, Salem.

——— 1987. *Archaeology of the South Umpqua Falls Rockshelters, Douglas County, Oregon*. Heritage Research Associates Report 64. Eugene.

——— 1989. The Ede Site and Its Importance in Lower Columbia Valley Prehistory. Pp. 113–144 in *Contributions to the Archaeology of Oregon, 1987–1989*, Rick Minor, ed. Association of Oregon Archaeologists Occasional Papers 4. Eugene.

——— 1991a. *Archaeological Investigations at the Ecola Point Site, Northern Oregon Coast*. Report of the Coastal Prehistory Program, State Museum of Anthropology, University of Oregon, to the Siuslaw National Forest. On file at the Oregon State Historic Preservation Office. Salem.

——— 1991b. Yaquina Head: A Middle Archaic Settlement on the North-Central Oregon Coast. USDI BLM Oregon State Office Cultural Resource Series No. 6. Portland, Oregon.

——— 1992a. Archaeology of the Cape Creek Shell Midden, Cape Perpetua Scenic Area, Central Oregon Coast: Interim Report of the 1991 Investigations. Coastal Prehistory Program, Oregon State Museum of Anthropology, University of Oregon. Report to the Siuslaw National Forest. Corvallis.

——— 1992b. *The 1991 Archaeological Testing Program at the Hauser Site*. Report of the Coastal Prehistory Program, State Museum of Anthropology, University of Oregon to the Siuslaw National Forest, on file at the Oregon State Historic Preservation Office. Salem.

————— 1993. *USDI/NPS National Register of Historic Places Registration Form for Blacklock Point Lithic Site (35CU75), Curry County, Oregon.* On file, Oregon State Museum of Anthropology, University of Oregon. Eugene.

————— 1994. An Assessment of Archaeological Resources within the Proposed Sahalie Condominiums Project Area, Seaside, Clatsop County, Oregon. Heritage Research Associates Report 167. On file at the Oregon State Historic Preservation Office, Salem.

————— 1995. A Reassessment of Early "Pre-Littoral" Radiocarbon Dates from the Southern Northwest Coast. *Journal of California and Great Basin Anthropology* 17(2):267–273.

————— 1997. Pre-Littoral or Early Archaic? Conceptualizing Early Adaptations on the Southern Northwest Coast. *Journal of California and Great Basin Anthropology* 19(2):269–280.

Minor, Rick, Stephen Dow Beckham, and Ruth L. Greenspan 1980. Archeology and History of the Fort Orford Locality: Investigations at the Blundon Site (35CU106) and Historic Fort Orford. Report of the Department of Anthropology, University of Oregon. On file at the Oregon State Historic Preservation Office, Salem.

Minor, Rick, Stephen D. Beckham, and Kathryn A. Toepel 1979. *Cultural Resource Overview of the BLM Lakeview District, South-Central Oregon: Archaeology, Ethnography, History.* University of Oregon Anthropological Papers No. 16. Eugene.

Minor, Rick, and Laurie E. Burgess 2009. Chinookan Survival and Persistence on the Lower Columbia: The View from the Kathlamet Village. *Historical Archaeology* 43(4):97–114.

Minor, Rick, and Ruth L. Greenspan 1991. *Archaeological Testing at the Indian Sands and Cape Blanco Lithic Sites, Southern Oregon Coast.* Report of the Museum of Anthropology, University of Oregon. On file at the Oregon State Historic Preservation Office, Salem.

————— 1995. *Archaeology of the Cape Creek Shell Midden, Cape Perpetua Scenic Area, Central Oregon Coast.* Coastal Prehistory Program, Oregon State Museum of Anthropology, University of Oregon, Eugene.

————— 1998. *The Hauser Site: Archaeological Evidence of a Paleo-Estuary in the Oregon Dunes, South-Central Oregon Coast.* On file at the Oregon State Historic Preservation Office, Salem.

Minor, Rick, Ruth L. Greenspan, and Debra C. Barner 2008. Chinookan Resource Exploitation in the Columbia River Estuary: The View from Indian Point. Pp. 37–55 in *Dunes, Headlands, Estuaries, and Rivers: Current Archaeological Research on the Oregon Coast.* Guy L. Tasa and Brian L. O'Neill, eds. Association of Oregon Archaeologists Occasional Papers No. 8. Eugene.

Minor, Rick, Ruth L. Greenspan, and Guy L. Tasa 2000. The Siuslaw Dune Site: Archaeology and Environmental Change in the Oregon Dunes. Pp. 82–102 in *Changing Landscapes: Proceedings of the Third Annual Coquille Cultural Preservation Conference, 1999,* Robert J. Losey, ed. Coquille Indian Tribe, North Bend, Oregon.

Minor, Rick, Linda K. Jacobs, and Theresa M. Tilton 1981. *The Stauffer-Will Farmstead: Historical Archaeology at an Aurora Colony Farm.* University of Oregon Anthropological Papers No. 24. Eugene.

Minor, Rick, and Lee Spencer 1977. *Site of a Probable Camelid Kill at Fossil Lake, Oregon: An Archaeological Evaluation*. Report of the Department of Anthropology, University of Oregon, Eugene, to the Bureau of Land Management, Lakeview District. Lakeview, Oregon.

Minor, Rick, Guy L. Tasa, and George B. Wasson, Jr. 2001. The Raymond's Dune Site and Its Place in the History of Southern Northwest Coast Archaeology. *Journal of California and Great Basin Anthropology* 21(1):77–92.

Minor, Rick, and Kathryn Anne Toepel 1984a. *Lava Island Rockshelter: An Early Hunting Camp in Central Oregon*. Idaho Museum of Natural History Occasional Papers No. 34. Pocatello.

———— 1984b. The Blitz Site: An Early-Middle Archaic Campsite in the Cascades of Western Oregon. Heritage Research Associates Report No. 34. On file at the Willamette National Forest, Eugene.

———— 1986. The Archaeology of the Tahkenitch Landing Site: Early Prehistoric Occupation on the Oregon Coast. Heritage Research Associates Report 46. Eugene.

———— 1989. Exchange Items or Hunter's Tools? Another Look at Lanceolate Biface Caches in Central Oregon. *Journal of California and Great Basin Anthropology* 11(1):99–107.

Minor, Rick, Kathryn Anne Toepel, and Ruth L. Greenspan 1987. *Archaeological Investigations at Yaquina Head, Central Oregon Coast*. USDI BLM Oregon State Office Cultural Resource Series 1. Portland, Oregon.

Minor, Rick, Kathryn Anne Toepel, Ruth L. Greenspan, and Debra C. Barner 1985. *Archaeological Investigations in the Cape Perpetua Scenic Area, Central Oregon Coast*. Heritage Research Associates Report No. 40. Eugene. On file at the Oregon State Historic Preservation Office. Salem.

Minor, Rick, Kathryn Anne Toepel, and Stephen Dow Beckham 1989. *An overview of Investigations at 45SA11: Archaeology in the Columbia River Gorge (revised)*. Heritage Research Associates (Eugene, OR) Report No. 39. Eugene.

Minor, Rick, and Lynda L. Walker 1993. *Late Prehistoric Cultural Dynamics in the Columbia River Gorge, Oregon and Washington*. Paper presented at the 58th Annual Meeting of the Society for American Archaeology. St. Louis.

Moessner, Jean 2004. DJ Ranch: A Mid- to Late-Holocene Occupation Site in the Fort Rock Valley, South-Central Oregon. Pp. 95–122 in *Early and Middle Holocene Archaeology of the Northern Great Basin*. Dennis L. Jenkins, Thomas J. Connolly, and C. Melvin Aikens, eds. University of Oregon Anthropological Papers No. 62. Eugene.

Moss, Madonna L., and Jon M. Erlandson 1994. *An Evaluation, Survey, and Dating Program for Archaeological Sites on State Lands of the Southern Oregon Coast*. Ms. on file at the Oregon State Historic Preservation Office, Salem.

———— 1995. Reflections on North American Pacific Coast Prehistory. *Journal of World Prehistory* 9:1–45.

———— 1998. Early Holocene Adaptations of the Southern Northwest Coast. *Journal of California and Great Basin Anthropology* 20:13–25.

Moss, Madonna L., Thomas J. Connolly, Jon M. Erlandson, and Guy L. Tasa 2006. Terminal Pleistocene or Early Holocene Occupation of the Oregon Coast? A Comment on Hall, et al. *Radiocarbon* 48:237–240

Moore, Earl 1977. *Silent Arrows: Indian Lore and Artifact Hunting*. Paul Tremaine Publishing. Klamath Falls.

Moratto, Michael J. 1984. *California Archaeology*. Academic Press. Orlando.

Moulton, Gary E., ed. 2003. *The Lewis and Clark Journals: An American Epic of Discovery. The Abridgment of the Definitive Nebraska Edition*. University of Nebraska Press. Lincoln and London.

Mueller, Emily J. 2007. *Multitasking on the Mountain: An Analysis of a Great Basin Zooarchaeological Assemblage, Mortar Riddle Site (35HA2627), Steens Mountain, Oregon*. Master of Science Thesis, Department of Anthropology, University of Wisconsin. Milwaukee.

Mulligan, Daniel M. 1997. *Crescent Lake: Archaeological Journeys into Central Oregon's Cascade Range*. MAIS Thesis, Oregon State University. Corvallis.

Murdock, George Peter 1938. Notes on the Tenino, Molala, and Paiute of Oregon. *American Anthropologist* 40:395–402.

———— 1980. The Tenino Indians. *Ethnology* 19(2):129–149.

Murdy, Carson N., and Walter J. Wentz 1975. Artifacts from Fanning Mound, Willamette Valley, Oregon. Pp. 349–374 in *Archaeological Studies in the Willamette Valley, Oregon*, C. Melvin Aikens, ed. University of Oregon Anthropological Papers No. 8. Eugene.

Musil, Robert R. 1987. *Archaeological Investigations at the Beatty Curve Site*. Oregon State Museum of Anthropology Report No. 87-5. On file at the Oregon State Historic Preservation Office. Salem.

———— 1990. *Archaeological Investigations at the Dunn Site (35HA1261), Harney County, Oregon*. Heritage Research Associates Report 95, Eugene. On file at the Oregon State Historic Preservation Office. Salem.

———— 1991. *Archaeological Investigations at the McCoy Creek Site (35HA1263), Harney County, Oregon*. Heritage Research Associates Report 105, Eugene. On file at the Oregon State Historic Preservation Office. Salem.

———— 1992. *Testing and Evaluation of the Susan Creek Campground Site, Douglas County, Oregon*. Report to the Roseburg District Bureau of Land Management by Heritage Research Associates, Eugene, Oregon.

———— 1995. *Adaptive Transitions and Environmental Change in the Northern Great Basin: A View from Diamond Swamp*. University of Oregon Anthropological Papers No. 51. Eugene.

———— 2002. *Archaeological Testing and Stratigraphic Assessment in the Southeast Area of the Headquarters Site (35HA403), Malheur National Wildlife Refuge, Harney County, Oregon*. Heritage Research Associates Report 250. Eugene.

———— 2004. If it Ain't Fluted Don't Fix It: Form and Context in the Classification of Early Projectile Points in the Far West. Pp. 271–280 in *Early and Middle Holocene Archaeology of the Northern Great Basin*. Dennis L. Jenkins, Thomas J. Connolly, and C. Melvin Aikens, eds. University of Oregon Anthropological Papers No. 62. Eugene.

Musil, Robert R., and Brian L. O'Neill 1997. Source and Distribution of Archaeological Obsidian in the Umpqua River Basin of Southwest Oregon. Pp. 123–162 in *Contributions to the Archaeology of Oregon, 1995–1997*, A. C. Oetting, ed. Association of Oregon Archaeologists Occasional Papers No. 6.

Nash, Wallis 1882. *Two Years in Oregon*. D. Appleton and Company, New York.

Nelson, Nancy J. 2000. *The Umpqua Eden Site: The People, Their Smoking Pipes and Tobacco Cultivation*. Master's Thesis, Oregon State University, Corvallis.

Nelson, Russell, Noriko Seguchi, and C. Loring Brace 2006. Craniometric Affinities and Early Skeletal Evidence for Origins. Pp. 679–684 in *Handbook of North American Indians, Volume 3: Environment, Origins, and Population*. Douglas Ubelaker, ed. Smithsonian Institution. Washington, D.C.

Newman, Thomas M. 1959. *Tillamook Prehistory and Its Relation to the Northwest Coast Culture Area*. PhD Dissertation, Department of Anthropology, University of Oregon. Eugene.

———— 1966. *Cascadia Cave*. Occasional Papers of the Idaho State University Museum No. 18. Pocatello.

Newman, Thomas M., R. Bogue, C. D. Carley, R. D. McGilvra, and D. Moretty 1974. *Archaeological Reconnaissance of the Malheur National Wildlife Refuge, Harney County, Oregon: 1974*. On file at the Oregon State Historic Preservation Office. Salem.

Nez Perce Trail Study Report 1982. U.S. Forest Service Northern Region, in Conjunction with the National Park Service. Missoula. Nez Perce Trail Study Report Online at www.fs.fed.us/npnht

Nilsson, Elena 1991. *Coming of Age: Archaeological Research within Shasta Valley, Siskiyou County, California*. Paper Presented at the 25th Annual Meeting of the Society for California Archaeology. Sacramento.

Nilsson, Elena, and Michael S. Kelly 1991. *Prehistory of the Upper Rogue River Region: Archaeological Inventory and Evaluation Within the Elk Creek Lake and Lost Creek Lake Project Areas, Jackson County, Southwest Oregon*. Mountain Anthropological Research, Chico, California. Submitted to the U.S. Army Corps of Engineers, Portland District. Portland, Oregon.

Nisbet, Robert A., Jr. 1981. *The Lanceolate Projectile Point in Southwestern Oregon: A Perspective from the Applegate River*. Master's Paper, Interdisciplinary Studies Program, Oregon State University. Corvallis.

Nixon, Joseph M., Ward Tonsfeldt, and Colleen Hamilton 2000. *Investigation of Three Sawmill Sites in Deschutes County, Oregon, for the Crown Pacific and Deschutes National Forest Land Exchange Project*. Applied Earthworks, Inc. Hemet, California. Submitted to Deschutes National Forest. Bend, Oregon.

Norris, Susan E., and Dennis L. Jenkins 2000a. Non-Significant and Non-Impact Site Descriptions and Test Excavations. Pp. 33–60 in *Human Adaptations in Drews Valley: A Mid-Elevation Setting on the Northern Great Basin Periphery, South-Central Oregon*. Dennis L. Jenkins, ed. Report 2000-3, State Museum of Anthropology. University of Oregon. Eugene.

———— 2000b. Eastern Spring Site (35LK2103). Pp. 127–150 in *Human Adaptations in Drews Valley: A Mid-Elevation Setting on the Northern Great Basin Periphery, South-Central Oregon*. Dennis L. Jenkins, ed. Report 2000-3, State Museum of Anthropology. University of Oregon. Eugene.

O'Connor, Jim E. 2004. The Evolving Landscape of the Columbia River Gorge: Lewis and Clark and Cataclysms on the Columbia. *Oregon Historical Quarterly* 105(3):390–421.Electronic document accessed December 28,2009: http://www. historycooperative.org/journals/ohq/105.3/oconnor.html.

O'Connor, Jim E., Andrei Sarna-Wojcicki, K. C. Wozniak, D. J. Polette, and R. J. Fleck
2001. *Origin, Extent, and Thickness of Quaternary Geologic Units in the Willamette Valley, Oregon.* U. S. Geological Survey Professional Paper No. 1620.

Oetting, Albert C. 1987. *Archaeological Testing at Five Sites in the Stinkingwater Mountains, Harney County, Oregon.* Oregon State Museum of Anthropology Report No. 87-4. University of Oregon. Eugene.

————— 1988. *Archaeological Investigations on the East Shore of Lake Abert, Lake County, Oregon, Volume 2.* Oregon State Museum of Anthropology Report No. 88-6. University of Oregon. Eugene.

————— 1989. *Villages and Wetlands Adaptations in the Northern Great Basin: Chronology and Land Use in the Lake Abert-Chewaucan Marsh Basin-Lake County, Oregon.* University of Oregon Anthropological Papers 41. Eugene.

————— 1990a. *The Malheur Lake Survey: Lacustrine Archaeology in the Harney Basin, Central Oregon.* Heritage Research Associates Report 96. Eugene. On file at the Oregon State Historic Preservation Office. Salem.

————— 1990b. *An Archaeological Survey on the Recently Flooded Shores of Malheur Lake, Harney County, Oregon.* Heritage Research Associates Report 97. Eugene. On file at the Oregon State Historic Preservation Office. Salem.

————— 1991. Recent Archaeological Surveys Around Malheur Lake, Harney County, Oregon. *Current Archaeological Happenings in Oregon* 16(1):9–13.

————— 1992. Lake and Marsh-Edge Settlements on Malheur Lake, Harney County, Oregon. *Journal of California and Great Basin Anthropology* 14(1):110–129.

————— 1993. *The Archaeology of Buffalo Flat: Cultural Resources Investigations for the CONUS OTH-B Buffalo Flat Radar Transmitter Site, Christmas Lake Valley, Oregon.* Heritage Research Associates Report No. 151. Eugene.

————— 1994a. Early Holocene Rabbit Drives and Prehistoric Land Use Patterns on Buffalo Flat, Christmas Lake Valley, Oregon. Pp. 155–170 in *Archaeological Researches in the Northern Great Basin: Fort Rock Archaeology Since Cressman.* C. Melvin Aikens and Dennis L. Jenkins, eds. University of Oregon Anthropological Papers No. 50. Eugene.

————— 1994b. Chronology and Time Markers in the Northwestern Great Basin: The Chewaucan Basin Cultural Chronology. Pp. 41–62 in *Archaeological Researches in the Northern Great Basin: Fort Rock Archaeology Since Cressman.* C. Melvin Aikens and Dennis L. Jenkins, eds. University of Oregon Anthropological Papers No. 50. Eugene.

————— 1999. An Examination of Wetland Adaptive Strategies in Harney Basin: Comparing Ethnographic Paradigms and the Archaeological Record. Pp. 203–218 in *Prehistoric Lifeways in the Great Basin Wetlands: Bioarchaeological Reconstruction and Interpretation.* Brian E. Hemphill and Clark S. Larsen, eds. University of Utah Press. Salt Lake City.

————— 2004. Obsidian Use on Buffalo Flat, Christmas Lake Valley, Oregon. Pp. 233–240 in *Early and Middle Holocene Archaeology of the Northern Great Basin,* Dennis L. Jenkins, Dennis L., Thomas J. Connolly, and C. Melvin Aikens, eds. University of Oregon Anthropological Papers 62, Eugene, Oregon.

O'Grady, Patrick W. 1999. *Human Occupation Patterns in the Uplands: An Analysis of Sourced Obsidian Projectile Points from Playa Villages in the Fort Rock Uplands, Lake*

County, Oregon. M.S. Thesis, Department of Anthropology, University of Oregon. Eugene.

———— 2004. Zooarchaeological Analysis of Cultural Features from Four Early to Middle Holocene Sites in the Fort Rock Basin. Pp. 187–208 in *Early and Middle Holocene Archaeology of the Northern Great Basin.* Dennis L. Jenkins, Thomas J. Connolly, and C. Melvin Aikens, eds. University of Oregon Anthropological Papers No. 62. Eugene.

———— 2006. *Before Winter Comes: Archaeological Investigations of Settlement and Subsistence in Harney Valley, Harney County, Oregon.* PhD Dissertation, Department of Anthropology, University of Oregon. Eugene.

O'Grady, Patrick W., and Scott Thomas 2008. Tally of Clovis Point Finds on the Harney BLM District. Personal communication.

O'Grady, Patrick W., Scott P. Thomas, and Michael F. Rondeau 2009. Recent Fluted-Point Finds in Eastern Oregon. *Current Research in the Pleistocene* 26:100–102.

Olsen, Thomas 1975. Baby Rock Shelter. Pp. 469–494 in *Archaeological Studies in the Willamette Valley, Oregon,* C. Melvin Aikens, ed. University of Oregon Anthropological Papers No. 8, Eugene.

O'Neill, Brian L. 1987. Archaeological Reconnaissance and Testing in the Noti-Veneta Section of the Florence-Eugene Highway, Lane County, Oregon. Oregon State Museum of Anthropology Report 87-6, University of Oregon, Eugene.

———— 1989. *Archaeological Investigations at the Narrows and Martin Creek Sites, Douglas County, Oregon.* USDI BLM Oregon State Office Cultural Resource Series 4. Portland, Oregon.

———— 1990. Toward a Definition of Middle and Late Archaic Phases in the Umpqua Basin of Southwest Oregon. Pp. 26–36 in *Living With the Land: The Indians of Southwest Oregon.* Nan Hannon and Richard K. Olmo, eds. Southern Oregon Historical Society. Medford.

———— 1996. *The Medicine Bridge Site (35DO672): Archaeological Investigations for PP&L's Soda Springs Sediment Placement Feasibility Study, North Umpqua Hydroelectric Project, Douglas County, Oregon.* State Museum of Anthropology Report 96-1. University of Oregon, Eugene.

———— 2002. Multiple hydration Rates on Pre-Mazama Obsidian Artifacts in the Umpqua Drainage, Southwest Oregon. *Current Archaeological Happenings in Oregon* 27(1/2):6–13.

———— 2004. Evidence for Early Holocene Interaction Between the Upper Umpqua River Drainage and the Northern Great Basin. Pp. 209–220 in *Early and Middle Holocene Archaeology of the Northern Great Basin.* Dennis L. Jenkins, Thomas J. Connolly, and C. Melvin Aikens, eds. University of Oregon Anthropological Papers No. 62. Eugene.

———— 2008. *Evaluation of the Williams Creek Site (35DO848), A Multicomponent Pre-Mazama Occupation on the North Umpqua River, Douglas County, Oregon.* State Museum of Anthropology Report 2008-032, Museum of Natural and Cultural History, University of Oregon. Eugene, Oregon.

———— 2009. *Evaluation of the Florence Site (35DO554), A Pre-Mazama Occupation on the Upper North Umpqua River, Douglas County, Oregon.* State Museum of Anthropology

Report 2009-058, Museum of Natural and Cultural History. University of Oregon, Eugene.

——— 2010. The Florence Site (35DO554) Investigations: A Small Pre-Mazama Hunting Camp in the Upper North Umpqua River Drainage. *Current Archaeological Happenings in Oregon* 35(1):7–12

O'Neill, Brian L., Thomas J. Connolly, and Dorothy E. Freidel 1996. *Streamside Occupations in the North Umpqua River Drainage Before and After the Eruption of Mount Mazama: A Report on the Archaeological Data Recovery Excavations in the Steamboat Creek to Boulder Flat Section, North Umpqua Highway, Douglas County, Oregon*. State Museum of Anthropology Report 96-2, University of Oregon, Eugene.

——— 2004. *A Holocene Geoarchaeological Record for the Upper Willamette Valley, Oregon: The Long Tom and Chalker Sites*. University of Oregon Anthropological Papers No. 61. Eugene.

O'Neill, Brian L., Vivien Singer, Melissa Cole-Darby, and Laura C. White 1999. Archaeology of the Dry Creek Site 35DO401). Pp. 217–333 in *Streamside Occupations in the North Umpqua River Drainage Before and After the Eruption of Mount Mazama*, by Brian L. O'Neill, Thomas J. Connolly, and Dorothy E. Freidel, Oregon State Museum of Anthropology Report 96-2. University of Oregon, Eugene.

O'Neill, Brian L., and Mark A. Tveskov 2008. *The Limpy Creek Site (35JO39): A Contact Period Fishing Camp on the Rogue River, Southwest Oregon*. University of Oregon Anthropological Papers 67. Eugene.

O'Neill, Brian L., and Laura C. White 1994. *Cultural Resource Inventory of the North Umpqua Hydroelectric Project, Douglas County, Oregon*. State Museum of Anthropology Report 94-2. University of Oregon, Eugene.

Orr, Elizabeth L., William N. Orr, and Ewart M. Baldwin 1992. *Geology of Oregon, Fourth Edition*. Kendall/Hunt Publishing Company. Dubuque.

Owsley, Douglas W. 1992. Demography of Prehistoric and Early Historic Northern Plains Populations. Pp. 75–86 in *Disease and Demography in the Americas*. J.W. Verano and D.H. Ubelaker, eds. Smithsonian Institution Press. Washington, D.C.

Ozbun, Terry, and Dan Stueber 2001. Obsidian Clovis Points in Western Oregon. *Current Archaeological Happenings in Oregon* 26(2):21–26.

Parker, Samuel 1967. *Journal of an Exploring Tour Beyond the Rocky Mountains under the Direction of the A.B.C.F.M., Performed in the Years 1835, '36, and '37; Containing a Description of the Geography, Geology, Climate, and Productions; and the Number, Manners, and Customs of the Natives, with a Map of the Oregon Territory*. Ross and Haines. Minneapolis. Originally published 1838.

Parkman, E. Breck 1993. Creating Thunder: The Western Rain-Making Process. *Journal of California and Great Basin Anthropology* 15(1):90–110.

Parks, Helen, ed. 1989. *Portraits: Fort Rock Valley Homestead Years*. Fort Rock Valley Historical Society. Maverick Press.

Paul-Mann, Teri 1994. Far View Butte: An Archaic Hunting, Gathering, and Vision Quest Site in the Silver Lake Valley, Oregon. Pp. 329–348 in *Archaeological Researches in the Northern Great Basin: Fort Rock Archaeology Since Cressman*. C. Melvin Aikens and Dennis L. Jenkins, eds. University of Oregon Anthropological Papers No. 50. Eugene.

Pavesic, Max G. 1979. *Public Archaeology in Weiser Basin and Vicinity: A Narrative Report.* Boise State University. Boise.

——— 1985. Cache Blades and Turkey Tails: Piecing Together the Western Idaho Archaic Burial Complex. Pp. 55–89 in *Stone Tool Analysis: Essays in Honor of Don E. Crabtree.* Mark G. Plew, James C. Woods, and Max G. Pavesic, eds. University of New Mexico Press. Albuquerque.

——— 1992. Death and Dying in the Western Idaho Archaic. Pp. 289–293 in *Ancient Images, Ancient Thought: The Archaeology of Ideology.* A. Sean Goldsmith, Sandra Garvie and David Selin, eds. Department of Archaeology, University of Calgary. Calgary.

Pendleton, Lorann S. 1979. *Lithic Technology in Early Nevada Assemblages.* Master of Arts Thesis, Department of Anthropology, California State University, Long Beach. Long Beach.

Pepper, Floy C. 1991. Oregon Indians Today. Pp. 59–66 in *The First Oregonians.* Carolyn M. Buan and Richard Lewis, eds. Oregon Council for the Humanities. Portland, Oregon.

Peters, Walter, and George Devoe 1946. *Raising Livestock.* McGraw-Hill. New York.

Peterson, Curt D., J. Baham, D. Beckstrand, C. Clough, C. Cloyd, J. Erlandson, G. Grathoff, R. Hart, H. Jol, D. Percy, F. Reckendorf, C. Rosenfeld, T. Smith, Phyllis Steeves, and E. Stock 2002. Field Guide to the Pleistocene and Holocene Dunal Landscapes of the Central Oregon Coast: Newport to Florence, Oregon. *Geological Society of America Field Trips Guide, Cordillera Meeting.* Corvallis, Oregon.

Peterson, Curt D., and J. B. Phipps 1992. Holocene Sedimentary Framework of Grays Harbor Basin, Washington, USA. Pp. 273–285 in *Quaternary Coasts of the United States: Marine and Lacustrine Systems,* C. H. Fletcher and J. F. Wehmiller, eds. SEPM Special Publication No. 48, Tulsa.

Peterson, C.D., K. F. Scheidegger, and H. J. Schrader 1984. Holocene Depositional Evolution of a Small Active-Margin Estuary of the Northwestern United States. *Marine Geology* 59:51–83.

Peterson, Ella M. 2008. *Recognizing Individual Potters in Historic Oregon Sites: A Visual and Chemical Analysis of Early Oregon Redware.* Master's Thesis in Interdisciplinary Studies, Oregon State University. Corvallis.

Peterson, Emil R., and Alfred Powers 1977. *A Century of Coos and Curry: History of Southwest Oregon.* Coos-Curry Pioneer and Historical Association, Coquille, Oregon.

Pettigrew, Richard M. 1979. *Archaeological Exploration of the Proposed Improvement to the Pike's Ranch-Valley Falls Section, North Unit, of the Burns-Lakeview Highway, Lake County, Oregon.* Report on file at the Oregon State Museum of Anthropology, University of Oregon. Eugene.

——— 1980a. The Ancient Chewaucanians: More on the Prehistoric Lake Dwellers of Lake Abert, Southwestern Oregon. Pp. 49–67 in *Proceedings of the First Annual Symposium of the Association of Oregon Archaeologists.* Martin Rosenson, ed. Association of Oregon Archaeologists Occasional Papers. Eugene.

——— 1980b. *Archaeological Investigations at Hager's Grove, Salem, Oregon.* University of Oregon Anthropological Papers No. 19. Eugene.

——— 1981. *A Prehistoric Culture Sequence in the Portland Basin of the Lower Columbia Valley.* University of Oregon Anthropological Papers 22, Eugene.

———— 1984. Prehistoric Human Land-use Patterns in the Alvord Basin, Southeastern Oregon. *Journal of California and Great Basin Anthropology* 6(1):61–90.

———— 1985. *Archaeological Investigations on the East Shore of Lake Abert, Lake County, Oregon, Volume 1.* University of Oregon Anthropological Papers No. 32. Eugene.

———— 1990. Prehistory of the Lower Columbia and Willamette Valley. Pp. 518–529 in *Handbook of North American Indians: Volume 7 Northwest Coast,* Wayne Suttles, ed. Smithsonian Institution, Washington, D.C.

Pettigrew, Richard M., and Charles M. Hodges 1995. *Site 35-JE-51B (The Johnson Site).* Pp. 8-1 to 8-87 in Volume IIB, Book 1, Archaeological Investigations PGT-PG&E Pipeline Expansion Project Idaho, Washington, Oregon, and California. Submitted to Pacific Gas Transmission Company. Michael J. Moratto, General Editor. INFOTEC Research, Inc. Fresno, California.

Pettigrew, Richard M., and Clayton G. Lebow 1987. *Data Recovery at Sites 35JA27, 35JA59, and 35JA100, Elk Creek Lake Project, Jackson County, Oregon.* Infotec Research Inc., Fresno, Report No. PNW87-7. Eugene. Submitted to US Army Corps of Engineers, Portland District. Portland, Oregon.

———— 1989. *An Archaeological Survey of the Trout Creek-Oregon Canyon Uplands, Harney and Malheur Counties, Oregon.* USDI BLM Oregon State Office Cultural Resource Series 2. Portland, Oregon.

Phebus, George E., and Robert M. Drucker 1979. *Archaeological Investigations at Seaside, Oregon.* Seaside Museum and Historical Society, Seaside, Oregon.

Philipek, Francis M., and Peter J. Edwards 1988. *Site 35CL34, The Table Rock Trail, Site 35CL25, and Site 35CL41: Evaluation of National Register Eligibility.* USDI Bureau of Land Management, Salem District.

Pinson, Ariane Oberling 1999. *Foraging in Uncertain Times: The Effects of Risk on Subsistence Behavior During the Pleistocene-Holocene Transition in the Oregon Great Basin.* PhD Dissertation, Department of Anthropology, University of New Mexico. Albuquerque.

———— 2004. Of Lakeshores and Dry Basin Floors: A Regional Perspective on the Early Holocene Record of Environmental Change and Human Adaptation at the Tucker Site. Pp. 53–76 in *Early and Middle Holocene Archaeology of the Northern Great Basin.* Dennis L. Jenkins, Thomas J. Connolly, and C. Melvin Aikens, eds. University of Oregon Anthropological Papers No. 62. Eugene.

Polk, Michael R. 1976. *Cultural Resource Inventory of the John Day River Canyon.* USDI BLM, Prineville District, Oregon.

Powers, Stephen 1877. Tribes of California. *Contributions to North American Ethnology 3.* U.S. Geographical and Geological Survey of the Rocky Mountain Region. Washington.

Prentiss, William C., and Ian Kuijt, eds. 2004. *Complex Hunter-Gatherers: Evolution and Organization of Prehistoric Communities on the Plateau of Northwestern North America.* University of Utah Press. Salt Lake City.

Pringle, Patrick T., Jim E. O'Connor, Robert L. Schuster, Nathaniel D. Reynolds, and Alex C. Bourdeau 2002. *Tree-Ring Analysis of Subfossil Trees from the Bonneville Landslide Deposit and the "Submerged Forest of the Columbia River Gorge" Described by Lewis and Clark.* Paper presented at the 98th Annual Meeting of the Geological Society of America. Corvallis, Oregon.

Prouty, Guy L. 1989. Ancient Earth Ovens at the Saltsgaver Site, Southwestern Oregon. Pp. 1–37 in *Contributions to the Archaeology of Oregon 1987–88*. Rick Minor, ed. Association of Oregon Archaeologists Occasional Papers 4. Eugene.

———— 1994. Root Crop Exploitation and the Development of Upland Habitation Sites: A Prospectus for Paleoethnobotanical and Archaeological Research into the Distribution and Use of Economic Plants in the Fort Rock Basin. Pp. 573–598 in *Archaeological Researches in the Northern Great Basin: Fort Rock Archaeology since Cressman*. C. Melvin Aikens and Dennis L. Jenkins, eds. University of Oregon Anthropological Papers No. 50. Eugene.

———— 2004. Plants and Prehistory: Paleoethnobotanical Investigations in the Fort Rock Basin Lowlands. Pp. 157–167 in *Early and Middle Holocene Archaeology of the Northern Great Basin*. Dennis L. Jenkins, Thomas J. Connolly, and C. Melvin Aikens, eds. University of Oregon Anthropological Papers No. 62. Eugene.

Pullen, Reg 1990. Stone Sculptures of Southwest Oregon: Mythological and Ceremonial Associations. Pp. 120–124 in *Living With the Land: The Indians of Southwest Oregon*. Nan Hannon and Richard K. Olmo, eds. Southern Oregon Historical Society. Medford.

Punke, Michele L., and Loren G. Davis 2003. Finding Late Pleistocene Sites in Coastal River Valleys: Geoarchaeological Insights from the Southern Oregon Coast. *Current Research in the Pleistocene* 20(1).

Punke, Michele L., and Loren G. Davis 2006. Problems and Prospects in the Preservation of Late Pleistocene Cultural Sites in Southern Oregon Coastal River Valleys: Implications for Evaluating Coastal Migration Routes. *Geoarchaeology: An International Journal* 21(4):333–350.

Rambo, Sandra 1978. *An Osteo-Archaeological Investigation of Penniped Remains at Seal Rock, Oregon (35LNC14)*. Master's Thesis, Oregon State University, Corvallis.

Ramenofsky, Ann F. 1987. *Vectors of Death: The Archaeology of European Contact*. University of New Mexico Press. Albuquerque.

Rankin, David K. 1983. *Holocene Geologic History of the Clatsop Plains Foredune Ridge Complex*. Master's Thesis, Department of Geology, Portland State University, Portland, Oregon.

Rasmussen, Morten, Linda Scott Cummings, M. Thomas P. Gilbert, Vaughn Bryant, Colin Smith, Dennis L. Jenkins, and Eske Willerslev 2009. Response to Comment by Goldberg et al. on "DNA from Pre-Clovis Human Coprolites in Oregon, North America." *Science* 325:148d.

Ray, Verne F. 1932. *The Sanpoil and Nespelem*. University of Washington Publications in Anthropology 5:1–235. Seattle.

———— 1936. Native Villages and Groupings of the Columbia Basin. *Pacific Northwest Quarterly* 27:99–152.

———— 1938. *Lower Chinook Ethnographic Notes*. University of Washington Publications in Anthropology 7(2), Seattle.

———— 1939. *Cultural Relations in the Plateau of Northwestern America*. Publications of the Frederick Webb Hodge Anniversary Publication Fund 3. The Southwest Museum. Los Angeles.

———— 1963. *Primitive Pragmatists: The Modoc Indians of Northern California*. University of Washington Press. Seattle.

Ray, Verne F., G. P. Murdock, Beatrice Blyth, Omer C. Stewart, J. Harris, E. Adamson Hoebel, and D. B. Shimkin 1938. Tribal Distribution in Eastern Oregon and Adjacent Regions. *American Anthropologist*, New Series 40(3):384–415.

Raymond, Anan W. 1994. *The Surface Archaeology of Harney Dune (35HA718), Malheur National Wildlife Refuge, Oregon*. Cultural Resource Series No. 9, U.S. Department of the Interior Fish and Wildlife Service, Region 1. Portland, Oregon.

Reckendorf, Frank, Curt Peterson, and David Percy 2001. *The Dune Ridges of Clatsop County*. Oregon Department of Geology and Mineral Industries, Open File Report O-01-07. Portland, Oregon.

Reese, Jo 1989. Microarchaeological Analysis of the Chinese Workers' Area at the Warrendale Cannery Site, Oregon. Pp. 197–221 in *Contributions to the Archaeology of Oregon 1987–1988*, Rick Minor, ed. Association of Oregon Archaeologists Occasional Papers No. 4, Eugene.

Reid, Kenneth C. 1988. *Downey Gulch Archaeology: Excavations at Two Seasonal Camps on the Joseph Upland, Wallowa County, Oregon*. Washington State University Center for Northwest Anthropology, Contributions in Cultural Resource Management No. 22. Pullman.

Reid, Kenneth C., and James C. Chatters 1997. *Kirkwood Bar: Passports in Time Excavations in the Hells Canyon National Recreation Area, Wallowa-Whitman National Forest*. Rain Shadow Research Project Report No. 28 and Applied Paleoscience Project Report No. F-6. Pullman.

Reid, Kenneth C., John A. Draper, and Peter E. Wigand 1989. *Prehistory and Paleoenvironments of the Silvies Plateau, Harney Basin, Southeastern Oregon*. Washington State University Center for Northwest Anthropology Project Report No 8. Pullman.

Reitz, Eowyn 1995. *Paiute Wadatika Ma-Ni-Pu-Neen: The History and Culture of the Burns Paiute Tribe*. Burns Paiute Tribe. Burns, Oregon.

Reynolds, Nathaniel D. 2001. Dating the Bonneville Landslide with Lichenometry. *Washington Geology* 29(3/4):11–16. Electronic document accessed December 28,2009 http://www.dnr.wa.gov/Publications/ger_washington_geology_2001_v29_no3-4. pdf

Rick, Torben C., Jon M. Erlandson and René L. Vellanoweth 2001. Paleocoastal Marine Fishing on the Pacific Coast of the Americas: Perspectives from Daisy Cave, California. *American Antiquity* 66(4):595–614.

Rick, Torben C., Jon M. Erlandson, René Vellanoweth, and Todd J. Braje 2005. From Pleistocene Mariners to Complex Hunter-Gatherers: The Archaeology of the California Channel Islands. *Journal of World Prehistory* 19:169–228.

Ricks, Mary F. 1995. *A Survey and Analysis of Prehistoric Rock Art of the Warner Valley Region, Lake County Oregon*. PhD Dissertation in Systems Science: Anthropology. Portland State University. Portland.

———— 1996. *A Survey and Analysis of Prehistoric Rock Art of the Warner Valley Region, Lake County, Oregon*. University of Nevada-Reno, Department of Anthropology Technical Report 96-1. Reno.

Ricks, Mary F., and William J. Cannon 1989. *Rock Art and Human Aggregation in the Warner Valley Region, Southern Oregon*. Paper presented to the Northwest Anthropological Conference. Spokane.

Riddle, George W. 1953. *Early Days in Oregon: A History of the Riddle Valley*. Myrtle Creek Mail. Myrtle Creek, Oregon.

Roberts, Andrew P. 2008. *Great Republic: A Historical and Archaeological Analysis of a Pacific Mail Steamship*. M.A. Thesis, Texas A&M University, College Station, Texas.

Rollins, Philip Ashton, ed. 1935. *The Discovery of the Oregon Trail: Robert Stuart's Narratives of His Overland Trip Eastward from Astoria in 1812–13*. Charles Scribner's Sons. New York.

Rondeau, Michael F. 2007a. *Results from the Study of Three Fluted Points from Lake County, Oregon*. CalFLUTED Research Paper No. 38. Rondeau Archaeological, Sacramento.

———— 2007b. *Fluted Bifaces from the Sage Hen Gap Site (35HA3548), Harney County, Oregon* CalFLUTED Research Paper No. 42. Rondeau Archaeological, Sacramento.

Rose, Chelsea, Christopher L. Ruiz, Tom Connolly, and Julie Schablitsky 2007. *Portrait from a Privy: A 19th Century Working Class Household, Naito Parkway Privy, Portland Oregon*. University of Oregon Museum of Natural and Cultural History Report No. 2007-049. Eugene.

Ross, Lester A., Gary C. Bowyer, and Lou Ann Speulda 1999. *Historical Demographic Patterns*. Pp 11-1/108 in Archaeological Investigations PGT-PG&E Pipeline Expansion Project Idaho, Washington, Oregon, and California, Vol. 4, Synthesis of Findings, Randall F. Schalk, Volume Editor. INFOTECH Research, Inc. On file at the Oregon State Historic Preservation Office. Salem.

Ross, Richard E. 1976. *Excavations on the Lower Coquille River, Coos County, Oregon*. Report of the Department of Anthropology, Oregon State University. On file at the Oregon State Historic Preservation Office, Salem.

———— 1987. *Marial*. Oregon State University Research Proposal Submitted to the Bureau of Land Management, Medford District. Corvallis.

———— 1990. Prehistory of the Oregon Coast. Pp. 554–559 in *Northwest Coast: Handbook of North American Indians, Volume 7*, Wayne Suttles, ed. Smithsonian Institution, Washington, D.C.

Ross, Richard E., and Sandra L. Snyder 1979. Excavations at Umpqua/Eden. Pp. 99–104 in *Umpqua River Basin Cultural History, Phase I Research*, T. Hogg, ed. Oregon State University, Corvallis.

———— 1986. The Umpqua/Eden Site (35DO83): Exploitation of Marine Resources on the Central Oregon Coast. Pp. 80–101 in *Contributions to the Archaeology of Oregon*, K. M. Ames, ed. Association for Oregon Archaeology Occasional Papers No. 3, Salem, Oregon.

Roth, Barbara, and Roberta Hall 1995. *Archaeological Testing at Site 35CS3*. Report to the Coquille Indian Tribe. On file, Department of Anthropology, Oregon State University. Corvallis.

Roulette, Bill R., David V. Ellis, and Maureen Newman 1994. *Data Recovery at OR-MU-57, the U.S. Courthouse Site, Portland, Oregon*. Archaeological Investigations Northwest Inc., Report No. 42. On file, Oregon State Historic Preservation Office. Salem.

Roulette, Bill R., William White, and Megan Harris 2004. *Nineteenth Century Stumptown, A Glimpse at the Historical Archaeology of Block 196: The Results of Archaeological Monitoring and Salvage Excavations at Site 35MU115 at the Native American Student and Community Center, Portland State University Campus, Southwest Portland, Oregon*.

Applied Archaeological Research Report No. 332. On file at the Oregon State Historic Preservation Office. Salem.

Roulette, Bill R., Douglas C. Wilson, David V. Ellis, and Judy S. Chapman 1996. *Northwest Pipeline Corporation System Expansion Phase I: Phase 3 – Data Recovery and Site Treatment Reports for Oregon Segments, Volume V, Part 2: Willamette Valley.* Archaeological Investigations Northwest Report No. 50. On file, Oregon State Historic Preservation Office. Salem.

Ruiz, Christopher L., and Thomas J. Connolly 2005. *Archaeological Monitoring of the Gold Hill Downtown Reconstruction Project, Oregon Highways 99 and 234, Jackson County.* University of Oregon Museum of Natural and Cultural History Report 2005-191. Eugene.

Ruiz, Christopher L., and Patrick O'Grady 2008. *Jacksonville Site A: Archaeological Test Excavations at the Main Street Warehouse and Chinese Quarter (35JA737).* University of Oregon Museum of Natural and Cultural History Report 2008-052.

Saleeby, Becky M. 1983. *Prehistoric Settlement Patterns in the Portland Basin of the Lower Columbia River: Ethnohistoric, Archaeological, and Biogeographic Perspectives.* PhD Dissertation, Department of Anthropology, University of Oregon, Eugene.

Sampson, C. Garth 1985. *Nightfire Island: Later Holocene Lake-Marsh Adaptation on the Western Edge of the Great Basin.* University of Oregon Anthropological Papers No. 33. Eugene.

Sanders, Judith A., and Mary K. Weber 1980. *Willamette Mission Project: Phase II, Preliminary Site Assessment.* Ms. on file at the Department of Anthropology, Oregon State University. Corvallis.

Sanders, Judith A., Mary K. Weber, and David R. Brauner 1983. *Willamette Mission Archaeological Project: Phase III Assessment.* Anthropology Northwest No. 1. Department of Anthropology, Oregon State University. Corvallis.

Sanford, Patricia Ruth 1983. *An Analysis of Megascopic Plant Remains and Pollen from Dirty Shame Rockshelter, Southeastern Oregon.* PhD Dissertation, Department of Anthropology, University of Oregon. Eugene.

Santee, J. F., and F. B. Warfield 1943. Accounts of Early Pioneering in the Alsea Valley. *Oregon Historical Quarterly* 44(1):56–60.

Sapir, Edward 1907. Notes on the Takelma Indians of Southwestern Oregon. *American Anthropologist* 9(2):251–275.

——— 1909a. Takelma Texts. *University of Pennsylvania, University Museum, Anthropological Publications 2(1):1–267.*

——— 1909b. *Wishram Texts.* American Ethnological Society.

——— 1929. Central and North American Indian Languages. Pp. 138–141 in *Encyclopedia Britannica* Vol. 5, 14th edition. New York. Reprinted 1949 in *Selected Writings of Edward Sapir in Language, Culture, and Personality*, David G. Mandelbaum, ed. University of California Press. Berkeley and Los Angeles.

Schablitsky, Julie M. 2002. *Profile of a Prominent Portland Family: The John D. Coleman Family, ca. 1895.* Report to Portland State University. On file at the Oregon State Historic Preservation Office. Salem.

——— 2006. *Duty and Vice: The Daily Life of a Fort Hoskins Soldier.* Master's Thesis in Applied Anthropology, Oregon State University. Corvallis.

———— 2007. *A Redware Jar on Every Table: The Archaeology of the Simmons House and Boston Town, Thompson Mills State Heritage Site, Linn County, Oregon.* University of Oregon Museum of Natural and Cultural History Report No. 2007-003. Eugene.

Schablitsky, Julie, Tom Connolly, and Chris Ruiz 2007. *Archaeological Testing (2006) at the Kam Wah Chung Site, Oregon.* University of Oregon Museum of Natural and Cultural History (State Museum of Anthropology) Museum Report 2007-047. Eugene.

Schablitsky, Julie, and Chris Ruiz 2009. Archaeological Monitoring and Investigations Along Oregon State Highway 238 Jacksonville, Oregon. University of Oregon Museum of Natural & Cultural History Report 209-061.

Schalk, Randall F. 1980. *Cultural Resource Investigations for the Second Powerhouse Project at McNary Dam, Near Umatilla, Oregon* Washington State University Laboratory of Archaeology and History Project Report 1. Pullman.

———— 1983. *The 1978 and 1979 Excavations at Strawberry Island in the McNary Reservoir.* Washington State University Laboratory of Archaeology and History Project Report 19. Pullman.

———— 1987. *Archaeology of the Morris Site (35GM9) on the John Day River, Gilliam County, Oregon.* Prepared by the Office of Public Archaeology, University of Washington, for the U.S. Army Corps of Engineers, Portland District. Portland, Oregon.

Schalk, Randall F., Ricky G. Atwell, William R. Hildebrandt, Clayton G. Lebow, Pat Mikkelsen and Richard M. Pettigrew 1995. Mobility and Intensification. In *Synthesis of Findings*, M. J. Moratto, ed. Archaeological Investigations PGT-PG&E Expansion Project Idaho, Washington, Oregon, and California. vol. IV. INFOTEC Research, Inc., Fresno. On file at the Oregon State Historic Preservation Office, Salem.

Schmitt, Dave N. 1989. The Zooarchaeology of Times Square Shelter: Faunal Accumulations and Human Subsistence. Pp. 447–476 in *Times Square Rockshelter: A Stratified Dry Rockshelter in the Western Cascades, Douglas County, Oregon,* by Lee F. Spencer. Lee Spencer Archaeology Paper 1989-4. Submitted to Umpqua National Forest, Roseburg.

Schreindorfer, Crystal 1985. *Marial 1984: Archaeological Investigations at 35CU84.* Oregon State University, Richard E. Ross, Principal Investigator. Submitted to the Bureau of Land Management, Medford District.

Schulting, Rick J. 1995. *Mortuary Variability and Status Differentiation on the Columbia-Fraser Plateau.* Archaeology Press, Simon Fraser University. Burnaby.

Schumacher, Paul 1874. Remarks on the Kjökkenmöddings on the Northwest Coast of America. Pp. 354–362 in *Annual Report, Smithsonian Institution for 1873.* Washington, D. C.

———— 1877. Researches into the Kjökkenmöddings and Graves of a Former Population of the Coast of Oregon. *Bulletin of the United States Geological and Geographical Survey of the Territories* 3(1):27–35.

Schurr, Theodore G. 2004. Molecular Genetic Diversity in Siberians and Native Americans Suggests an Early Colonization of the New World. Pp. 187–238 in *Entering America: Northeast Asia and Beringia Before the Last Glacial Maximum.* D. B. Madsen, ed. University of Utah Press. Salt Lake City.

Schwartz, E. A. 1991. Sick Hearts: Indian Removal on the Oregon Coast, 1875–1881. *Oregon Historical Quarterly* 92(3):228–264.

———— 1997. *The Rogue River Indian War and Its Aftermath, 1850–1980*. University of Oklahoma Press.

———— 2010. *Allotment Data. Native American Documents Project*. Electronic document accessed July 2010: http://www2.csusm.edu/nadp/index.html.

Scott, Leslie, ed. 1923. John Work's Journey from Fort Vancouver to Umpqua River, and Return, in 1834. *Oregon Historical Quarterly* 24:238–268.

Scott, Sara, Carl Davis, and J. Jeffrey Flenniken 1986. The Pahoehoe Site: A Lanceolate Biface Cache in Central Oregon. *Journal of California and Great Basin Anthropology* 8(1):7–23.

Sea, D. S., and Cathy Whitlock 1995. Postglacial Vegetation and Climate of the Cascade Range, Central Oregon. *Quaternary Research* 43:370–381.

Sekora, Linda J., and Lester A. Ross 1995. Historic Land-use Systems. Pp. 10–85 *in Archaeological Investigations PGT-PG&E Pipeline Expansion Project Idaho, Washington, Oregon, and California, Vol. 4, Synthesis of Findings*. Randall F. Schalk, Volume Editor. INFOTEC Research, Inc. On file at the Oregon State Historic Preservation Office. Salem.

Shiner, Joel 1961. The McNary Reservoir: A Study in Plateau Archaeology. *Bureau of American Ethnology, Bulletin 179; River Basin Surveys Paper 23*. Washington, D.C.

Shipley, William 1978. Native Languages of California. Pp. 80–90 in *Handbook of North American Indians, Volume 8, California*. Robert F. Heizer, ed. Smithsonian Institution. Washington, D.C.

Silvermoon, Jon M. 1994. *Archaeological Investigations at the Peninsula Site, 35KL87, South-Central Oregon*. Cultural Resource Series 11. U.S. Department of the Interior, Bureau of Land Management. Portland, Oregon.

Singer, Vivien J. 2004. Faunal Assemblages of Four Early to Mid-Holocene Marsh-side Sites in the Fort Rock Valley, South Central Oregon. Pp. 167–186 in *Early and Middle Holocene Archaeology of the Northern Great Basin*. Dennis L. Jenkins, Thomas J. Connolly, and C. Melvin Aikens, eds. University of Oregon Anthropological Papers No. 62. Eugene.

Skinner, Craig E., and Carol J. Winkler 1994. Prehistoric Trans-Cascade Procurement of Obsidian in Western Oregon: A Preliminary Look at the Geochemical Evidence. Pp. 29–44 in *Contributions to the Archaeology of Oregon 1989–1994*. P. W. Baxter, ed. Association of Oregon Archaeologists Papers No. 5. Eugene.

———— 2010. Online document: www.obsidianlab.com 2010.

Smith, Cameron McPherson 2006. Formation Processes of a Lower Columbia River Plankhouse Site. Pp. 233–269 in *Household Archaeology on the Northwest Coast*, Elizabeth A. Sobel, D. Ann Trieu Garr, and Kenneth M. Ames, eds. International Monographs in Prehistory, Archaeological Series 16. Ann Arbor.

Smith, Harlan I. 1910. *The Archaeology of the Yakima Valley*. American Museum of Natural History Anthropological Papers 6:1–171. New York.

Snyder, Sandra Lee 1978. *An Osteo-Archaeological Investigation of Pinniped Remains at Seal Rock, Oregon (35LNC14)*. Master's Thesis, Department of Anthropology, Oregon State University.

———— 1981. Medicine Creek: Pre- and Post-Mazama Occupation in the Cascades. *Tebiwa* 23:1–13.

———— 1987. *Prehistoric Land Use Patterns in the Central Oregon Cascade Range*. PhD Dissertation, Department of Anthropology, University of Oregon. Eugene.

———— 1991. Site Location Analysis in the Central Oregon Cascade Range. *Northwest Anthropological Research Notes* 25(1):117–137.

Sobel, Elizabeth A. 2006. Household Prestige and Exchange in Northwest Coast Societies: A Case Study from the Lower Columbia River Valley. Pp. 159–199 in *Household Archaeology on the Northwest Coast*, Elizabeth A. Sobel, D. Ann Trieu Garr, and Kenneth M. Ames, eds. International Monographs in Prehistory, Archaeological Series 16, Ann Arbor.

Sobel, Elizabeth, and Gordon Bettles 2000. Winter Hunger, Winter Myths: Subsistence Risk and Mythology among the Klamath and Modoc. *Journal of Anthropological Archaeology* 19:276–313.

Spencer, Lee F. 1987. *Archaeological Testing of the Horseshoe #6 Site (35D0400), a Middle Archaic Glade Tradition Site on the Steamboat District of the Umpqua National Forest*. Lee Spencer Archaeology Paper 1987-4. Submitted to Umpqua National Forest. Roseburg.

———— 1989. *Times Square Rockshelter: A Stratified Dry Rockshelter in the Western Cascades, Douglas County, Oregon*. Lee Spencer Archaeology Paper 1989-4. Submitted to Umpqua National Forest, Roseburg.

Spier, Leslie 1930. Klamath Ethnography. *University of California Publications in American Archaeology and Ethnology* No. 30. Berkeley.

Spier, Leslie, and Edward Sapir 1930. Wishram Ethnography. *University of Washington Publications in Anthropology* 3(3):151–300. Seattle.

Speulda, Lou Ann 1988. *Champoeg: A Frontier Community in Oregon, 1830–1861*. Anthropology Northwest No. 3. Department of Anthropology, Oregon State University. Corvallis.

Speulda, Lou Ann, Clayton G. Lebow, and Richard M. Pettigrew 1987. *Archaeological Investigations at the Ewing Young/Sidney Smith Cabin Site (OR-YA-1), Yamhill County, Oregon*. Infotec Research Inc. Report No. PNW87-9. On file at the Oregon State Historic Preservation Office. Salem.

Stein, Julie K., Roger Kiers, Jennie Deo, Kate Gallagher, Chris Lockwood, and Scotty Moore 2006. *A Geoarchaeological Analysis of Fort Clatsop, Lewis and Clark National Historic Park*. Report of the University of Washington Department of Anthropology to Lewis Clark National Historic Park, Astoria, Oregon. Electronic document available: http://www.nps.gov/lewi/historyculture/histcult-places-focl.htm

Stenger, Alison T. 2000. *Woodburn Paleoarchaeological Project, Interim Report: Fieldwork 1999*. Report to the City of Woodburn from the Institute for Archaeological Studies. Portland, Oregon.

———— 2002. Temporal Association of Paleontological and Archaeological Resources in Woodburn, ca. 12,000 BP: A Preliminary Report. *Current Archaeological Happenings in Oregon* 27(3/4):12–17.

———— 2009. *A Vanished People: The Lake River Ceramic Makers*. Institute for Archaeological Studies. Portland, Oregon.

Stenholm, Nancy A. 1990. The Botanical Assemblage. Pp. 81–86 in *Archaeological Investigations at the Dunn Site (35HA1261), Harney County, Oregon*, by Robert R.

Musil. Heritage Research Associates Report 95. On file at the Oregon State Historic Preservation Office. Salem.

———— 1991. The Botanical Assemblage. Pp. 132–142 in *Archaeological Investigations at the McCoy Creek Site (35HA1263), Harney County, Oregon*, by Robert R. Musil. Heritage Research Associates Report 105. On file at the Oregon State Historic Preservation Office. Salem.

———— 1994. Paleoethnobotanical Analysis of Archaeological Samples Recovered in the Fort Rock Basin. Pp. 531–559 in *Archaeological Research in the Fort Rock Basin: Fort Rock Archaeology since Cressman*. C. Melvin Aikens and Dennis L. Jenkins, eds. University of Oregon Anthropological Papers No. 50. Eugene.

Stenhouse, Peter J. 1974. *Progress Report on the Umpqua/Eden Archaeological Rescue Dig, 1974 (1st Phase)*. Oregon Coastal Archaeological Society.

Stepp, David 1994. *Descriptive Analysis of Human Remains from the Fuller and Fanning Mounds, Yamhill River, Willamette Valley, Oregon*. Master's Thesis in Interdisciplinary Studies, Oregon State University. Corvallis.

Stern, Theodore 1966. *The Klamath Tribe: A People and their Reservation*. American Ethnological Society Monograph No. 41. University of Washington. Seattle.

———— 1993. *Chiefs and Chief Traders: Indian Relations at Fort Nez Perces, 1818–1855*. Oregon State University Press. Corvallis.

———— 1996. *Chiefs and Change in the Oregon Country: Indian Relations at Fort Nez Perces, 1818–1855*. Oregon State University Press. Corvallis.

———— 1998a. Cayuse, Umatilla, and Walla Walla. Pp. 395–419 in *Handbook of North American Indians, Volume 12: Plateau*. Deward E. Walker. Jr., ed. Smithsonian Institution. Washington, D.C.

———— 1998b. Klamath and Modoc. Pp. 446–466 in *Handbook of North American Indians, Volume 12: Plateau*. Deward E. Walker, Jr., ed. Smithsonian Institution. Washington, D.C.

Steward, Julian H. 1938. *Basin-Plateau Aboriginal Sociopolitical Groups*. Smithsonian Institution Bureau of American Ethnology, Bulletin 120. Washington, D.C.

Stewart, John L. 1999. *Fremont's Greatest Western Exploration. Volume 1: The Dalles to Pyramid Lake*. SET, Inc., Publisher. Vancouver, Washington.

Stewart, Omer C. 1939. The Northern Paiute Bands. *University of California Anthropological Records* 2(3):127–149.

Stuemke, Scott 1989. *The Archaeology of the Peninsula I Site, 35-JE-53, a Central Oregon Rock Shelter*. Master's Paper, Department of Anthropology, University of Oregon. Eugene.

Strong, Emory 1959a. *Stone Age on the Columbia River*. Binford & Mort, Portland, Oregon.

———— 1959b. *Wakemap Mound and Nearby Sites on the Long Narrows of the Columbia River*. Oregon Archaeological Society Publication No. 1. Portland, Oregon.

Strong, William Duncan 1943. The Occurrence and Wider Implications of a "Ghost Cult" on the Columbia River, Suggested by Carvings on Wood, Bone, and Stone. *American Anthropologist* 47:244–261.

Sundahl, Elaine 1988. *Cox Bar (CA-Tri-1008): A Borax Lake Pattern Site on the Trinity River, Trinity County, California*. Shasta College Archaeology Lab. Redding, California.

Suttles, Wayne 1951. The Early Diffusion of the Potato among the Coast Salish. *Southwestern Journal of Anthropology* 7(3):272–288.

Suttles, Wayne, ed. 1990. *Handbook of North American Indians, Volume 7, Northwest Coast.* Smithsonian Institution. Washington, D.C.

Sutton, Mark Q. 1986. Warfare and Expansion: An Ethnohistoric Perspective on the Numic Spread. *Journal of California and Great Basin Anthropology* 8(1):65–82.

Swadesh, Morris 1965. Kalapuya and Takelma. *International Journal of American Linguistics* 31(43):237–240.

Swartz, B. K., Jr. 1963. Klamath Basin Petroglyphs. *Archives of Archaeology*, No. 21. Society of American Archaeology, Madison, Wisconsin.

Swift, Mark 1990. *Lithic Caches of Central Oregon: A Descriptive Comparison.* Paper presented at the 43rd Annual Northwest Anthropological Conference. Eugene.

Tasa, Guy L. 1997. *Skeletal and Dental Variation of Pacific Coast Athapaskans: Implications for Oregon Prehistory and Peopling of the New World.* PhD Dissertation, Department of Anthropology, University of Oregon, Eugene.

Tasa, Guy L., and Thomas J. Connolly 1995. *Archaeological Evaluation of the Boiler Bay Site (35LNC45), in the Boiler Bay State Park Section of the Oregon Coast Highway (US Highway 101), Lincoln County, Oregon.* State Museum of Anthropology, Report 95-2. University of Oregon. Eugene.

——— 2001. *Archaeological Investigations at Cook's Chasm Bridge, the Good Fortune Point Site (35LNC55), and the Neptune Site (35LA3).* University of Oregon Museum of Natural and Cultural History, Report 2001-4. On file at the Oregon State Historic Preservation Office. Salem.

——— 2004. *Archaeological Investigations of Three Sites within the Whale Cove-Otter Crest Loop Section of the Oregon Coast Highway (US 101), Lincoln County Oregon.* University of Oregon, State Museum of Anthropology, Report 2004-3 to the Oregon Department of Transportation. On file at the Oregon State Historic Preservation Office. Salem.

——— 2008. Archaeological Investigations at the Early Dune Site (35CLT66): Native Land Use Patterns and Dune Chronology on the Clatsop Plains. Pp. 57–64 in *Dunes, Headlands, Estuaries, and Rivers: Current Archaeological Research on the Oregon Coast*, Guy L. Tasa and Brian L. O'Neill, eds. Association of Oregon Archaeologists Occasional Papers No. 8. Eugene.

Tasa, Guy L., Julia A. Knowles, and Thomas J. Connolly 2009. *Archaeological Evaluation of the Bob Creek Site (35LA10): Oregon Coast Highway (U.S. Highway 101), Lane County.* University of Oregon, Museum of Natural & Cultural History Report No. 2004-066, Eugene.

Tasa, Guy L., Julia A. Knowles, and Jenna Peterson 2004. *Archaeological Resource Evaluation of Area 1 and Area 4, Oregon State Parks, 2003/2004 Surveys: Volume 1-Park Surveys.* University of Oregon, Museum of Natural & Cultural History Report No. 2004-007. Eugene.

Taylor, R. E., and Martin J. Aitken, eds. 1997. *Chronometric Dating in Archaeology.* Plenum Press. New York.

Taylor, R.E., C. Vance Haynes, Jr., and M. Stuiver 1996. Clovis and Folsom Age Estimates: Stratigraphic Context and Radiocarbon Calibration. *Antiquity* 70:515–525.

Teit, James A. 1928. The Middle Columbia Salish. *University of Washington Publications in Anthropology* 2(4). Seattle.

Thomas, David H. 1981. How to Classify the Projectile Points from Monitor Valley, Nevada. *Journal of California and Great Basin Anthropology* 3(1):7–43.

Thomas, Scott, Jon Loring, and Andrew Goheen 1983. An Aboriginal Pottery Site in Southeastern Oregon. Pp. 82–98 in *Contributions to the Archaeology of Oregon 1981–1982.* Don E. Dumond, ed. Association of Oregon Archaeologists Occasional Papers No. 2. Eugene.

Thoms, Alston V. 1989. *The Northern Roots of Hunter-Gatherer Intensification: Camas and the Pacific Northwest.* PhD dissertation, Department of Anthropology, Washington State University, Pullman.

Thwaites, Reuben Gold, ed. 1959. *Original Journals of the Lewis and Clark Expedition.* Republication of 1905 edition by Antiquarian Press. New York.

Tipps, Julie A. 1998. *High, Middle, and Low: An Analysis of Resource Zone Relationships in Warner Valley, Oregon.* University of Nevada-Reno Department of Anthropology Technical Report 98-1. Reno.

Tisdale, Lucille 1986. *The Tlegetlinten Site (35CU59) and its Place in Southwest Oregon Prehistory.* Master's Thesis in Interdisciplinary Studies, Oregon State University. Corvallis.

Todt, Donn L. 1990. Clues to Past Environments: Relict and Disjunct Plant Distributions along the California-Oregon Border. Pp. 71–79 in *Living With the Land: Indians of Southwest Oregon.* Nan Hannon and Richard K. Olmo, eds. Southern Oregon Historical Society. Medford.

Toepel, Kathryn A. 1985. *The Flanagan Site: 6000 years of Occupation in the Upper Willamette Valley, Oregon.* PhD Dissertation, Department of Anthropology, University of Oregon. Eugene.

Toepel, Kathryn A., William F. Willingham, and Rick Minor 1980. *Cultural Resource Overview of BLM Lands in North Central Oregon: Ethnography, Archaeology, History.* University of Oregon Anthropological Papers No. 17. Eugene.

Tonsfeldt, Ward 1995. Reconnaissance and Evaluation of Historic Railroad Systems: Chiloquin and Chemult Ranger Districts, Winema National Forest. Report on file at the Oregon State Historic Preservation Office. Salem.

Towle, Jerry C. 1979. Settlement and Subsistence in the Willamette Valley: Some Additional Considerations. *Northwest Anthropological Research Notes* 13:12–21.

—— 1982 Changing Geography of the Willamette Valley Woodlands. *Oregon Historical Quarterly* Vol. 83(1):66–87.

Townsend, John Kirk 1978. *Narrative of a Journey Across the Rocky Mountains to the Columbia River.* University of Nebraska Press. Lincoln.

Turner, Christy G. II 2002. Teeth, Needles, Dogs, and Siberia: Bioarchaeological Evidence for the Colonization of the New World. Pp. 123–158 in *The First Americans: The Pleistocene Colonization of the New World,* Nina G. Jablonski, ed. Memoirs of the California Academy of Sciences No. 27. San Francisco.

Tveskov, Mark A. 2000a. The Bandon Sandspit Site: The Archaeology of A Proto-Historic Coquille Indian Village. Pp. 43–59 in *Changing Landscapes: Proceedings of the 3rd Annual Coquille Cultural Preservation Conference, 1999.* Robert J. Losey, ed. The Coquille Indian Tribe. North Bend, Oregon.

—— 2000b. *The Coos and Coquille: A Northwest Coast Historical Anthropology.* PhD Dissertation, Department of Anthropology, University of Oregon. Eugene.

————— 2007. Social Identity and Culture Change on the Southern Northwest Coast. *American Anthropologist* 109(3):431–441.

Tveskov, Mark A., and Amie Cohen 2006. *The Archaeology of the Western Cascades of Southwest Oregon.* Southern Oregon University Laboratory of Anthropology. Ashland.

————— 2007. *Ni-Les'Tun Archaeology: The Bussman, Blue Barn, and Old Town Bandon Sites.* Southern Oregon University Laboratory of Anthropology Report 2007-1. On file at the Oregon State Historic Preservation Office. Salem.

————— 2008. *The Fort Lane Archaeology Project.* SOULA Research Report 2008-1. Southern Oregon University Laboratory of Anthropology. Ashland.

Tveskov, Mark A., and Jon M. Erlandson 2003. The Haynes Inlet Weirs: Estuarine Fishing and Archaeological Site Visibility on the Southern Oregon Coast. *Journal of Archaeological Science* 30:1023–1035.

Tveskov, Mark A., Kelly Derr, Nicole Norris, and Richard Silva 2001. *Archaeological Investigations of the Siskiyou Trail: Cascade-Siskiyou National Monument, Jackson County, Oregon.* SOULA Research Report 2001-1. Southern Oregon University Laboratory of Anthropology. Ashland.

Ubelaker, Douglas H., ed. 2006. *Handbook of North American Indians, Volume 3: Environment, Origins, and Population.* Smithsonian Institution. Washington, D.C.

USDA Forest Service 2003. *History. Deschutes and Ochoco National Forests and Crooked River National Grassland.* Electronic document accessed 7/7/03: website, http://www.fs.fed.us/r6/ centraloregon/about/history-1800.shtml.

Verdonck, D. 1995. Three-Dimensional Model of Vertical Deformation at the Southern Cascadia Subduction Zone, Western United States, *Geology* 23:261–264.

Voegelin, Erminie W. 1942. Culture Element Distributions: XX Northeast California. *University of California Anthropological Records* 7(2).

Waitt, Richard B., Jr. 1985. Case for Periodic, Colossal Jökulhlaups from Pleistocene Glacial Lake Missoula. *Geological Society of America Bulletin* 96:1271–1286.

————— 1994. *Scores of Gigantic, Successively Smaller Lake Missoula Floods through Channeled Scabland and Columbia Valley.* Chapter K in Swanson, D.A. and Haugerud, R.A., Geologic Field Trips in the Pacific Northwest (Geological Society of America Annual Meeting). Department of Geological Sciences, University of Washington. Seattle.

Waitt, Richard B., Jr., and Robert M. Thorson 1983. The Cordilleran Ice Sheet in Washington, Idaho, and Montana. Pp. 53–70 in *Late-Quaternary Environments of the United States, Volume 1: The Late Pleistocene.* Stephen C. Porter, ed. University of Minnesota Press. Minneapolis.

Walker, Deward E., Jr., ed. 1998. *Handbook of North American Indians, Volume 12: Plateau.* Smithsonian Institution. Washington, D.C.

Walker, Deward E., Jr., and Roderick Sprague 1998. History Until 1846. Pp. 484–498 in *Handbook of North American Indians, Volume 12: Plateau.* Deward E. Walker, Jr., ed. Smithsonian Institution. Washington, D.C.

Walsh, Megan K., Christopher A. Pearl, Cathy Whitlock, Patrick J. Bartlein, and Marc Worona 2010. An 11,000-Year-Long Record of Fire and Vegetation History at Beaver Lake, Oregon, Central Willamette Valley. *Quaternary Science Reviews* 29:1093–1106.

Warren, Claude N. 1959. A Re-Evaluation of Southwestern Washington Archaeology. *Tebiwa* 2(1):9–26.

Warren, Claude N., and Robert H. Crabtree 1986. Prehistory of the Southwestern Area. Pp. 183–193 in *Handbook of North American Indians, Volume 11: Great Basin*. Warren L. d'Azevedo, ed. Smithsonian Institution. Washington, D. C.

Wasson, George B. 1994. *The Coquille Indians and the Cultural, "Black Hole" of the Southwest Oregon Coast*. Master's Thesis, Department of Anthropology, University of Oregon, Eugene.

——— 2001. *Growing Up Indian: An Emic Perspective*. PhD Dissertation, Department of Anthropology, University of Oregon, Eugene.

Waterman, T. T. 1925. The Village Sites in Tolowa and Neighboring Areas in Northwestern California. *American Anthropologist* 27:528–543.

Waters, Michael R., and Thomas W. Stafford, Jr. 2007. Redefining the Age of Clovis: Implications for the Peopling of the Americas. *Science* 315(5815):1122–1126.

Weide, Margaret M. (Lyneis) 1968. *Cultural Ecology of Lakeside Adaptation in the Western Great Basin*. PhD Dissertation, Department of Anthropology, University of California. Los Angeles.

——— 1974. North Warner Subsistence Network: A Prehistoric Band Territory. *Nevada Archaeological Survey Research Papers* 5:62–79.

White, John R. 1975. The Hurd Site. Pp. 17–140 in *Archaeological Studies in the Willamette Valley, Oregon*, C. Melvin Aikens, ed. University of Oregon Anthropological Papers 8, Eugene.

Whiting, Beatrice Blyth 1950. *Paiute Sorcery*. Viking Fund Publications in Anthropology 15. New York.

Whitlock, Cathy, and Chris Larsen 2001. Charcoal as a Fire Proxy. Pp. 1–23 in *Tracking Environmental Change Using Lake Sediments Volume 3: Terrestrial, Algal, and Siliceous Indicators*. J.P. Smol, H. J. B. Birks and W. M. Last, eds. Kluwer Academic Publishers, Dordrecht, The Netherlands.

Wigand, Peter E. 1987. Diamond Pond, Harney County, Oregon: Vegetation History and Water Table in the Eastern Oregon Desert. *Great Basin Naturalist* 47:3:427–458

Wilde, James D. 1985. *Prehistoric Settlements in the Northern Great Basin: Excavations and Collections Analysis in the Steens Mountain Area, Southeastern Oregon*. PhD Dissertation, Department of Anthropology, University of Oregon. Eugene.

Wilde, James D., Rinita Dalan, Steve Wilke, Ralph Keuler, and John Foss 1983. *Cultural Resource Survey and Evaluations of Select Parcels in the John Day Reservoir, Oregon*. Geo-Recon International Report Submitted to the U.S. Army Corps of Engineers, Portland District. Portland, Oregon.

Wilke, Steve, James Wilde, Rinita Dalan, Karen James, Robert Weaver and David Harvey 1983. *Cultural Resource Overview and Survey of Selected Parcels in The Dalles Reservoir, Oregon and Washington*. Geo-Recon International report to Portland Corps of Engineers, Portland

Wilkes, Charles 1845. *Narrative of the United States Exploring Expedition During the Years 1838, 1839, 1840, 1841, 1842*. Lea and Blanchard. Philadelphia.

——— 1926. Diary of Wilkes in the Northwest. *Washington Historical Quarterly* 16(4):290–301, and 17(1):43–65.

——— 1974. *Life in Oregon Country Before the Emigration*. Oregon Book Society, Ashland.

Wilkinson, Charles 2010. *The People are Dancing Again: The History of the Siletz Tribe of Western Oregon*. University of Washington Press, Seattle and London.

Williams, Howel, and Gordon G. Goles 1968. Volume of the Mazama Ash-fall and the Origin of Crater Lake Caldera. In Hollis M. Dole, ed., Andesite Conference Guidebook, International Science Project, Science Report 16-S. *Oregon Department of Geology and Mineral Industries Bulletin* 62:37–41. Portland, Oregon.

Williams, Scott S. 2008. *Report on 2007 Fieldwork of the Beeswax Wreck Project, Nehalem Bay, Tillamook County, Oregon.* On file at the Oregon State Historic Preservation Office. Salem.

Williams, Shirley B., and John L. Fagan 1999. Blood Residue Analysis. Pp. 213–217 in *Newberry Crater: A Ten-Thousand-Year Record of Human Occupation and Environmental Change in the Basin-Plateau Borderlands*, by Thomas J. Connolly. University of Utah Anthropological Papers 121. Salt Lake City.

Willig, Judith A. 1982. *Pole and Thatch Structures in the Great Basin: Evidence from the Last 5,000 Years.* Master's Paper, Department of Anthropology, University of Oregon. Eugene.

——— 1988. Paleo-Archaic Adaptations and Lakeside Settlement Patterns in the Northern Alkali Basin. Pp. 417–482 in *Early Human Occupation in Far Western North America: The Clovis-Archaic Interface.* Judith A. Willig, C. Melvin Aikens and John L. Fagan, eds. Nevada State Museum Anthropological Papers 21. Carson City.

——— 1989. *Paleo-Archaic Broad Spectrum Adaptations at the Pleistocene-Holocene Boundary in Far Western North America.* PhD Dissertation, Department of Anthropology, University of Oregon. Eugene.

Willig, Judith A., and C. Melvin Aikens 1988. The Clovis-Archaic Interface in Far Western North America. Pp. 1–40 in *Early Human Occupation in Far Western North America: The Clovis-Archaic Interface.* Judith A. Willig, C. Melvin Aikens, and John L. Fagan, eds. Nevada State Museum Anthropological Papers 21. Carson City.

Willig, Judith A., C. Melvin Aikens, and John L. Fagan, eds. 1988. *Early Human Occupation in Far Western North America: The Clovis-Archaic Interface.* Nevada State Museum Anthropological Papers 21. Carson City.

Wilson, Douglas C., Robert Cromwell, Danielle Gembala, Theresa Langford, and Debra Semrau 2003. *Archaeology Lab Manual.* Ms. National Park Service, Fort Vancouver National Historic Site, Vancouver National Historic Reserve. Vancouver, Washington.

Wingard, George F. 2001. *Carlon Village: Land, Water, Subsistence, and Sedentism in the Northern Great Basin.* University of Oregon Anthropological Papers 57. Eugene.

Wingert, Paul S. 1952. *Prehistoric Stone Sculpture of the Pacific Northwest.* Exhibition Catalog. Portland Art Museum. Portland, Oregon.

Winthrop, Kathryn 1993. *Prehistoric Settlement Patterns in Southwest Oregon.* PhD Dissertation, Department of Anthropology, University of Oregon. Eugene.

Winthrop, Kathryn, and Dennis Gray 1985. *Moose Molalla One Data Recovery Evacuation (35 LIN 139).* Report prepared for Sweet Home Ranger District, Willamette National Forest, December 30, 1985.

Womack, Bruce 1977. *An Archaeological Investigation and Technological Analysis of the Stockhoff Basalt Quarry, Northeastern Oregon.* Master's Thesis, Department of Anthropology, Washington State University. Pullman.

Wood, W. Raymond 1972. Contrastive Features of Native North American Trade Systems. Pp. 153–169 in *For the Chief: Essays in Honor of Luther S. Cressman.* Fred W.

Voget and Robert L. Stephenson, eds. University of Oregon Anthropological Papers No. 4. Eugene.

Woodward, John A. 1972. The Geertz Site: An Early Campsite in Western Oregon. *Tebiwa* 15:55–62.

——— 1986. Prehistoric Shipwrecks on the Oregon Coast? Archaeological Evidence. Pp. 219–264 in *Contributions to the Archaeology of Oregon, 1983–1986*. Kenneth M. Ames, ed. Association of Oregon Archaeologists Occasional Papers No. 3. Eugene.

Woodward, John A., Carson N. Murdy and Franklin Young 1975. Artifacts from Fuller Mound, Willamette Valley, Oregon. Pp. 375–402 in *Archaeological Studies in the Willamette Valley, Oregon*. C. Melvin Aikens, ed. University of Oregon Anthropological Papers No. 8. Eugene.

Work, John 1923. *See* Scott, Leslie, 1923.

Wright, George William 1922. The Origin of the Prehistoric Mounds of Oregon. *Oregon Historical Quarterly* 23:87–94.

Wriston, Teresa A. 2003. *The Weed Lake Ditch Site: An Early Holocene Occupation on the Shore of Pluvial Lake Malheur, Harney Basin, Oregon*. Master's Thesis, Department of Anthropology, University of Nevada-Reno. Reno.

Wyeth, Nathaniel J. 1899. *The Correspondence and Journals of Captain Nathaniel J. Wyeth, 1831-6*. F.G. Young, ed. University Press, Eugene, Oregon.

Yohe, Robert M. II and James C. Woods 2002. *The First Idahoans: A Paleoindian Context for Idaho*. State Historic Preservation Office & Idaho State Historical Society. Boise.

Young, Craig D., Jr. 2000. *Late Holocene Landscapes and Prehistoric Land Use in Warner Valley, Oregon*. Sundance Archaeological Research Fund Technical Paper No. 7. Department of Anthropology, University of Nevada-Reno. Reno.

Zancanella, John 1998. New Data on Upland Occupation in the Ochoco Mountains of Central Oregon: A Preliminary Report. Paper presented at the 49th Annual Northwest Anthropological Conference, University of Idaho, Moscow, Idaho, 1998.

Zeier, Charles D. 1986. Obsidian Studies. Pp. 371–394 in *Data Recovery at Sites 36JA102 and 35JA107, Elk Creek Lake Project, Jackson County, Oregon*, by Elizabeth E. Budy and Robert G. Elston. Intermountain Research, Silver City, Nevada. Submitted to the U.S. Army Corps of Engineers, Portland District. Portland, Oregon.

Zenk, Henry B. 1976. *Contributions to Tualatin Ethnography: Subsistence and Ethnobiology*. Master's Thesis, Department of Anthropology, Portland State University. Portland, Oregon.

——— 1990a. Alseans. Pp. 568–571 in *Handbook of North American Indians: Volume 7 Northwest Coast*, Wayne Suttles, ed. Smithsonian Institution. Washington, D.C.

——— 1990b. Kalapuyans. Pp. 547–553 in *Handbook of North American Indians: Volume 7 Northwest Coast*, Wayne Suttles, ed. Smithsonian Institution. Washington, D.C.

——— 1994. Tualatin Kalapuyan Villages: The Ethnographic Record. Pp. 147–166 in *Contributions to the Archaeology of Oregon, 1989–1994*. Paul W. Baxter, ed. Association of Oregon Archaeologists Occasional Papers No. 5. Eugene.

Zontek, Terry 1983. *Aboriginal Fishing at Seal Rock (35LNC14) and Neptune (35LA3): Late Prehistoric Archaeological Sites on the Central Oregon Coast*. Master's Thesis, Oregon State University. Corvallis.

Index